KINABALU
SUMMIT OF BORNEO

A Revised and Expanded Edition

The immensity and sheer rawness of Kinabalu can be sensed even from afar.
(Photo: W.M. Poon)

KINABALU
SUMMIT OF BORNEO

A Revised and Expanded Edition

Edited by

K.M. Wong and A. Phillipps

THE SABAH SOCIETY
in association with

SABAH PARKS
Kota Kinabalu, Malaysia

1996

Published by

THE SABAH SOCIETY,
P.O. Box 10547,
88806 Kota Kinabalu, Sabah, Malaysia

in association with

SABAH PARKS,
P.O. Box 10626,
88806 Kota Kinabalu, Sabah, Malaysia.

Text copyright © The Sabah Society.

Copyright for photographs and line illustrations as credited.

All rights reserved. No part of this publication may be reproduced, stored in a retrieval system, or transmitted in any form or by any means, electronic, mechanical, photocopying, recording, or otherwise, without the prior permission of the copyright owner.

First published 1996.

The Sabah Society and its office-bearers, and the editors of this edition cannot be held responsible in any way for opinions expressed by individual authors, or for misinterpretations inadvertently represented as this account has been compiled and edited in good faith to provide an updated monograph on Kinabalu's most important aspects.

Perpustakaan Negara Malaysia   Cataloguing-in-Publication Data

Kinabalu : summit of Borneo / edited K.M. Wong and
    A. Phillipps. – A revised and expanded edition.
    ISBN 967-99947-4-0
    1. Mount Kinabalu National Park (Sabah). 2. Natural
    history—Borneo—Mount Kinabalu National Park (Sabah).
    3. Botany—Research—Mount Kinabalu National Park (Sabah).
    4. Zoology—Research—Mount Kinabalu National Park
    (Sabah). I. Wong, K.M.. II. Phillipps, A.
    915.9521

Printed in Malaysia
by Print & Co. Sdn. Bhd., Kuala Lumpur.

Kinabalu

here it stands, seemingly unshakeable, a mighty mountain. One hour it is there, the next nowhere—lost in the cloud world. Then there it is, safely back again at the first streak of day: that wonder lost twelve hours before, as the wet cold night clamped down across the moss forest. It is back, that incredible backdrop of teeth and fangs, gulley, precipice, cliff, plateau, gorge, peak, projectile, point—you name it, Kinabalu has it, up there above you, black and tense looking as if forged in iron and dropped into place as a vast casting. Surely this is the most complete statement of "I am a Mountain" made anywhere on this earth.

Tom Harrisson

CONTENTS

	Page
FOREWORD	xi

Datuk Tham Nyip Shen

PREFACE xiii
Tengku D.Z. Adlin

AN INTRODUCTION TO THE MONOGRAPH xv
Dr Ti Teow Chuan

ACKNOWLEDGEMENTS xvi

PART ONE — THE MOUNTAIN, ITS EXPLORATION AND FOLKLORE

KINABALU, THE WONDERFUL MOUNTAIN OF CHANGE 1
Tom Harrisson

GEOLOGY OF KINABALU 19
David Lee Tain Choi

THE PEOPLE AND FOLKLORE OF KINABALU 31
Patricia Regis

THE FIRST HUNDRED YEARS 41
A short account of the expeditions to Mt. Kinabalu 1851–1950
D.V. Jenkins

CLIMBING MOUNT KINABALU 69
Robert New

PART TWO — THE FLORA OF KINABALU

EVOLUTION AND PHYTOGEOGRAPHY OF THE KINABALU FLORA 95
John H. Beaman

THE PLANT LIFE OF KINABALU—AN INTRODUCTION 101
E.J.H. Corner, with minor revisions by John H. Beaman

FERNS 151
R.E. Holttum, revised by B.S. Parris

NOTES ON THE TREE FLORA OF KINABALU 167
Willem Meijer

THE RHODODENDRON AND BLUEBERRY FAMILY 181
George Argent

THE RAFFLESIA FAMILY 203
Kamarudin Mat Salleh

ORCHIDS 211
A. Lamb

GINGERS 245
Rosemary M. Smith

BAMBOOS 259
K.M. Wong & Soejatmi Dransfield

PALMS 269
John Dransfield

PART THREE — THE FAUNA OF KINABALU

LAND SNAILS 279
J.J. Vermeulen

BUTTERFLIES AND MOTHS 291
J.D. Holloway

BEETLES 315
C.L. Chan, Akira Ueda & Fatimah Abang

FRESH-WATER FISHES OF KINABALU AND SURROUNDING AREAS 333
Chin Phui Kong

FROGS AND TOADS 353
Robert F. Inger, Robert B. Stuebing & Tan Fui Lian

SOME INTERESTING BIRDS OF KINABALU PARK 369
B.E. Smythies

AN ANNOTATED CHECKLIST OF THE BIRDS OF KINABALU PARK 397
D.V. Jenkins & G.S. de Silva, revised by D.R. Wells & A. Phillipps

MAMMALS 439
Junaidi Payne

PART FOUR — PARK FUNCTIONS & LOCALITIES

KINABALU PARK: PAST, PRESENT AND FUTURE 455
Francis S.P. Liew

KINABALU PARK: RESEARCH AND CONSERVATION 475
Ghazally Ismail & Lamri Ali

THE KINABALU NATIONAL MEMORIAL, KUNDASANG 483
J.C. Robinson

KINABALU PLACE NAMES IN DUSUN AND THEIR MEANING 489
John H. Beaman, Rajibi Haji Aman, Jamili Nais, Gabriel Sinit & Alim Biun

NOTES ON CONTRIBUTORS 511

INDEX TO SCIENTIFIC NAMES 518

Photo: S. Pinfield

FOREWORD

Kinabalu, that beacon of biodiversity that looms over Borneo, continues to amaze. Whereas its recorded history began with Low's climb in 1851, nearly one and a half centuries ago, the mountain and its life are the product of nature's forces through millions of years. It is quite comprehensible, thus, that this highest peak between the Himalayas and the highlands of Irian Jaya continues to hold the interest of botanists, zoologists and experts of other disciplines, for its diversity of life and wonderful formations continues to reward study and observation.

The cumulative knowledge on Kinabalu is now far greater than when the Sabah Society published its first monograph of the mountain in 1978. We now know more that 4000 species of plants exist on the mountain, a haven for botanists for even generations to come, and a mine of treasure in terms of conserved genetic diversity. The insect life is one of the most enthralling ever known and continues to perplex the most experienced of scientists. The mountain harbours more than half of all Sabah's bird species, another subject of fascination since the last century, and an immensely rich variety of many other animal forms. Naturalists and tourists alike cannot but feel dwarfed, in different senses, by Kinabalu.

This new monograph, organised by the Sabah Society, brings together the most comprehensive commentaries available of the geology, biota, history, folklore, conservation and adventure of Kinabalu. It is a very special record of Sabah's most spectacular natural monument, and no doubt it shall inspire further insights into the wonder of Kinabalu.

Tham Nyip Shen
Minister of Tourism and
Environmental Development,
Sabah
1995

Photo: Robert New

PREFACE

A special mountain deserves a special monograph. The present work embodies a spirit of sharing by the many contributors who have, past and present, worked on Kinabalu in their own disciplines and who have generously distilled their understanding of the mountain for the benefit of a clearer picture of this awe-inspiring landmark. The authorship of the various chapters displays how much of an international impact Kinabalu has, and how important it is that we must continue to cooperate, between individuals, between disciplines and even countries to understand the fascination and complexities of nature.

Seldom has it been possible that so many facets have been addressed for any one site in Borneo or, for that matter, anywhere at all. This underscores both the interest in, and basic importance of studying Kinabalu. At the same time it reflects how worthwhile it has been for specialists in such a broad range of fields to continue to build on their understanding in a place that offers so much of nature and which remains securely conserved. Kinabalu has become not just a natural wonder to the people of Malaysia and of the world, but has also clearly emerged as an indispensable part of our scientific heritage. The Kinabalu Park which was established in 1964 is charged with protecting the mountain and managing and encouraging these very aspects and, we are proud to note, has been most successful in promoting the scientific, educational and recreational interest in the mountain.

It is our hope that even more will become known of this mountain and that the present edition of this monograph, will spur the interest to greater heights.

Tengku D.Z. Adlin
President,
The Sabah Society

Photo: Robert New

AN INTRODUCTION TO THE MONOGRAPH

This monograph is a revised and enlarged version of the edition published by the Sabah Society in 1978. The earlier documentation edited by M. Luping, Chin Wen and E.R. Dingley was inspired by the substantial interest generated by the results of two Royal Society expeditions to Kinabalu: in May–August 1961 which explored the eastern ridge of the summit and January–May 1964 which concentrated on the Pinosuk Plateau. The 1978 edition, however, went out of print in 1982. Requests for the publication continued to be received and, coupled with an increasing knowledge of the mountain, the Sabah Society decided in 1987 to undertake a revision and update. It was also recognised that this documentation will be another contribution to the promotion of this premier touristic asset of Sabah.

A number of salient changes have been made in this revised edition. There are 27 chapters in four parts, namely, the Mountain, its Exploration and Folklore; the Flora; the Fauna; and Park Functions and Locations. This increase from ten chapters in the 1978 edition comprises not only the inclusion of new chapters but also replacement as well as revision of some chapters. At the same time certain chapters have been retained in their original form. Most of the additions are in the part on the flora where there has been a significant accumulation of new knowledge. The fourth part consists of entirely new materials that cover aspects of exploration, park management research and items of general historical interest.

The monograph is a contribution of the Sabah Society to record the natural history of Sabah. The latter is one of the prime objectives of the Society and in this instance it is focussing on a centerpiece of the State's natural assets. Publication of this monograph has been one of the major projects undertaken by the Sabah Society.

Finally, on behalf of the Sabah Society, I will like to thank the authors for their voluntary contributions, and the editors, Dr K.M. Wong and Ms A. Phillipps for an excellent job. Grateful acknowledgement is also made to those who have helped in the publication, particularly Mr C.L. Chan whose input during the entire production process facilitated the completion of the publication within the targeted timeframe.

Dr Ti Teow Chuan
President,
The Sabah Society
1992–1993

ACKNOWLEDGEMENTS

The preparation of both the original edition and the present revised, expanded edition of this book has entailed discussion and consultation with a great many persons, and also received much encouragement and assistance from a number of individuals and institutions. We are much indebted to members and office-bearers of the Sabah Society, the Sabah Foundation, Sabah Parks, the Sabah Forestry Department's Forest Research Centre, the Sabah Museum, the Institute for Development Studies (IDS) in Sabah, and the Ministry of Tourism and Environmental Development in Sabah for their interest and support. The Sabah Society is truly indebted to Datuk Chin Kui Bee, Permanent Secretary to the Ministry of Tourism and Environmental Development, and Datuk Lamri Ali, Director of Sabah Parks, for their enthusiasm and help in arranging for funding for this project; it is especially noteworthy they wanted the production of this monograph to reflect the enormous efforts already put into its compilation. Likewise, a generous donation by Sabah Society honorary member John Tan Jiew Hoe towards the publication costs of this monograph deserves very special mention.

We record our special appreciation of Haji Awang Tengah bin Awang Amin (Director of Forestry in Sabah), Lee Ying Fah, Robert C. Ong and Anuar Mohammad (respectively past and present Heads of the Forest Research Centre in Sandakan), Datuk Wilfred Lingham, Patricia Regis (former Director of the Sabah Museum) and Tengku D.Z. Adlin (Deputy Director of the Sabah Foundation from the initiation of the project to its completion) for their sanction of this project and the allocation of facilities and specialists to assist with our work. The Tun Fuad Research Library of the Sabah Foundation and Zahra Yaacob have given immense support to the preparation of this book. John Beaman's research for the chapter on phytogeography and evolution was supported by US National Science Foundation Grant BSR-8507843.

D.V. Jenkins' revised chapter on 'The First Hundred Years' was compiled with assistance from Datuk Hywel George, Julia White and Betty Molesworth Allen; also acknowledged for this chapter are K.S. Lambert, formerly of the British Council in Kota Kinabalu (for providing much of the literature), Rev. Father Joseph Dapoz (for translating the Italian texts of Giacome and Bove), Masao Honma, the former Japanese Consul in Sabah (for providing details of the climbs by Japanese forces during the war), Datuk Stephen Lee, formerly Curator in the Sabah Museum (for access to the State Archives), and the late R.E. Holttum (for his personal reminiscences and valuable notes on the botanical and other expeditions to Kinabalu). Francis Liew, Deputy Director of Sabah Parks, kindly helped with information for Robert New's chapter and also provided valuable comments on various aspects. J.J. Wood, of the Royal Botanic Gardens, Kew, assisted in matters pertaining to orchid taxonomy in A. Lamb's account of the orchids of Kinabalu. Dato' Abdul Latiff Mohamed kindly commented on Kamarudin Mat Salleh's chapter on *Rafflesia*. John Sugau, of the Forest Research Centre, Sandakan, confirmed various local names of bamboos in the account by K.M. Wong and S. Dransfield.

Chin Phui Kong's manuscript was prepared with help from Winnie Chin. Fred Sheldon, Charles Francis, Ben King, Dennis Yong, S. Dingley, S. Jacobson, G.C. Johnson, S.C. Ng, C. Phillipps, Q. Phillipps and R. Yamie all gave valuable assistance and information in revising the annotated checklist of the birds of Kinabalu Park, and details of the bird collection at the Kinabalu Park Headquarters were provided by Jamili Nais and Tan Fui Lian. The authors of the annotated bird checklist acknowledge also K.S. Lambert for providing literature, as well as T.S. Bober (Smithsonian Institution, Washington, D.C.), D.W. Snow of the British Museum (Natural History), T.S. Kemp (University Museum, Oxford), E.A. Alfred (National Museum, Singapore), S.H. Chuang (University of Singapore), E.J.H. Berwick, C.M.G., and the Curator of the Sarawak Museum for providing particular references and information on collections. Clive Marsh kindly commented on the chapter on research and conservation. Richard Brewis and Rita Lasimbang reviewed the chapter on place names.

During the compilation stage, Stella Mojinkil of the Sabah Foundation was greatly involved in the production of typescripts, and we are grateful to have had her services. Gregory Silak also gave much assistance in the production stage. The patience and skill of Yap Soo Ching in type-setting is specially acknowledged. For proofreading, we had the help of Grace Tsang (Vermeulen's chapter on land snails), C.L. Chan, Reuben Nilus, Joan Pereira, John Sugau, Joseph Tangah, Lee Su Win, and Susan Phillipps.

The illustrations for this book have come from several sources, and we are happy to acknowledge the skills of these illustrators, especially Liew Fui Ling, Dixon Wong and Jamal Hassim of Natural History Publications Sdn. Bhd. Maureen Warwick provided the drawings in the chapter on the rhododendron and blueberry family by George Argent. Alvin Ki was responsible for a number of the fish drawings in Datuk Chin Phui Kong's chapter, which mostly used the late Chong Yun Fatt's drawings taken from Inger and Chin's 'The Fresh-water Fishes of North Borneo'. The maps used in the chapter on geology were prepared by Augustine Lambuk.

C.L. Chan, W.M. Poon, Robert New, Albert Teo, Doug Weschler and VIREO have all kindly rallied to our request for photographic materials by providing a large number for selection. Betty Molesworth Allen generously donated some photographs by Vivian Ryves for our use. Permission to reproduce artwork and photographs was kindly given by the Borneo Publishing Co. (the line-drawing of a Rafflesia flower used in the chapter on the Rafflesia family) and Joachim Gunsalam (the photograph of his grandfather, Gunting Lagadan, used in the chapter by Jenkins).

In the final stages of the production, the special skills required in layout and publishing fell upon C.L. Chan, Vice President of the Sabah Society, to shoulder. Chan was also, throughout the project, a catalyst for the completion of this project. Not least at all is acknowledged the sustaining interest shown by The Minister of Tourism and Environmental Development for Sabah, Datuk Tham Nyip Shen, the Director of Sabah Parks, Datuk Lamri Ali, and past and present Presidents of the Sabah Society, Ti Teow Chuan and Tengku D.Z. Adlin, respectively.

Photo: Robert New

PART 1

THE MOUNTAIN, ITS EXPLORATION AND FOLKLORE

Fig.1. Kinabalu from Kampung Lingkubong, Melankap. (*Photo: W.M. Poon*)

KINABALU, THE WONDERFUL MOUNTAIN OF CHANGE

Tom Harrisson

Kinabalu is one of the most wonderful mountains of the world. The outstanding mountains in the Andes and the Himalayas, in Europe and in Africa, have their separate, numerous splendours, but none exceed Kinabalu in what I can best term sheer strength and stark simplicity. The secret of this strength, this wonder, which stays with you from the very first sight through a lifetime, is the way the mountain is set; near the equator, rising darkly straight out of the tropical forest, one continuous, clean, black, bare rock mass, to the summit. Because of its breathtaking isolation Kinabalu has its own climate, a constant flux of cloud and wind, rain and cold, and the warmth from the forests below. So it is seldom in any sense a static mountain, one may be looking at it one moment, and the next it has disappeared.

Physically Kinabalu, at 4101 m (13,455 ft), the highest mountain between the peaks of the Himalayas and Wilhelmena in Irian Jaya (New Guinea), dominates most of Sabah. Small wonder that the first outside chronicler, captain Alexander Dalrymple, over 200 years ago, saw with awe and exclaimed: *"Though perhaps not the highest mountain in the world, it is of immense height"* (Dalrymple, 1769).

Nearly two centuries later, in World War II, the American airplanes flying over Sabah to assault the Japanese naval bases and camps, couldn't believe that Kinabalu could only be less than 14,000 ft: *"Say, that Goddamned thing cannot be 13,000. Why that's nothing. It must be near as high as Mount Everest. These Borneo maps are all to hell anyway."* (Harrisson, 1959).

Sure enough, by the end of that year, all maps used in General McArthur's theatre of war promoted Kinabalu with a large black over-stamp, elevating the highest pinnacle to 5800 m (19,000 ft)! However often you see it, it is hardly possible to believe that it is not a lot more that 4101 m (13,455 ft). The more one looks, the harder it becomes to analyse precisely why, precisely where, the magic lies. That magnificent assemblage of separate peaks rising from the sheer rock on top is something almost alone in the mountain world. It is scooped and twisted into weird fingers, grotesque pinnacles, soaring crests which seem tormented, each seemingly separate, yet all linked and surrounding some of the highest sheer cliffs in the world.

No other mountain achieves this dramatic effect of imposing its height so that the viewer in a very strange way identifies with it as if it were growing. It stands, a seemingly impregnable fortress in the skies which spiritually one cannot overcome.

Fig.2. Victoria Peak. *(Photo: Albert Teo)*

Fig.3. Low's Gully, from the summit plateau at 4000 m (13,000 ft). *(Photo: K.M. Wong)*

It is not easy to capture the meaning of Kinabalu, or share its excitements: the dramatic times, the hidden hours, the wreathing cloud world engulfing the dark jewel of rock. It is easier for the photographer or artist to represent it as something tremendous, beautiful and quiet. Sometimes, of course, it is quiet. There are long moments, even days of placidity when the peace of the mountain grows almost overwhelming. And although the mountain can be difficult and tough, wild and fierce, it is seldom savage, rarely dangerous. Yet it is worthy of respect, as Professor John Corner (1965), an eminent Cambridge scientist who has come to know the mountain very well, wrote of one part of it, it can be *"abominably draughty, cold and boggy."* Dr. Willem Meijer (1965), a botanist and forester who has contributed considerably to our knowledge of the plant life, summed it up for himself by saying that: *"Kinabalu is in general a mountain of mist and rain."* Foresters and botanists tend to look at the view in a slightly dampened way, I often think. Certainly, there is this cloud and mist and rain which the Kinabalu-lover learns to live with and even tries to enjoy. It was well put, more than half a century ago, by Oscar Cook (1924), who lived four years in Sabah *"Unconsciously the mountain wove itself into my life and thoughts; unconsciously when difficulties or perplexities beset me, I sought its might and solidity."*

So far we have looked at the finest mountain in South-east Asia from a rather outside viewpoint that is to some extent inevitable when writing and reading in English. Until recently, most of the native languages of Borneo have not been expressed in writing; so there is little comparable literature. Let us, first, bridge the gap between western literature and eastern mood, quoting again from the first reporter of the Sabah scene in English,

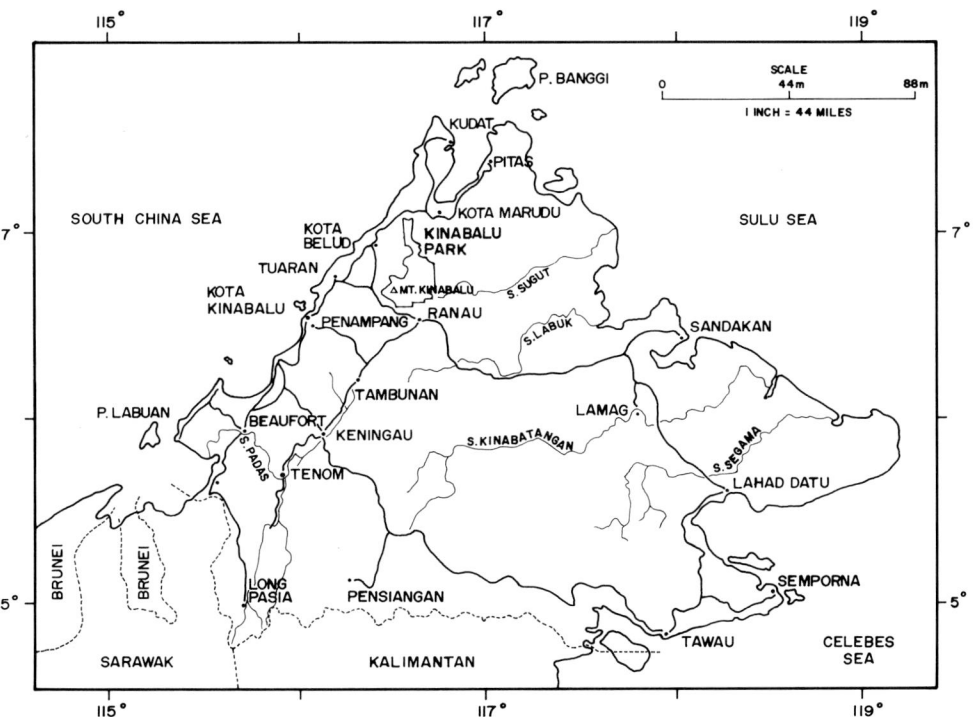

Fig.4. State of Sabah.

Alexander Dalrymple: *"The Idaan have very many whimsical religious tenets; paradise is generally supposed to be atop of Keeney-Balloo ... guarded by a fiery dog who is a formidable opponent to the female sex; for, whenever any virgins come, he seizes them as his legal prize; but whatever women have been cohabited with in this world he considers as unworthy of his embrace and lets them pass."*

Since Captain Dalrymple was famously lacking in any sense of humour, we cannot suppose, two centuries later, that he is being whimsical as well. He is only the first of very many who report (with varying degrees of superficiality), the view of the peoples who have lived for many centuries around Kinabalu. Those he calls Idaan are the same as those subsequently called Dusun; these Idaan-Dusun are nowadays called Kadazan. In their Idaan past, the great population of the north had a devout and somewhat fearful respect for the higher levels of the mountain. This is less apparent among their Kadazan descendants of today, but remains a strong and genuine feeling: how, indeed, can anyone approach this mountain let alone live on its foothills, without a feeling of awe, which only increases with time. Nowadays, we do not hear so much of the wilder old beliefs. They were still going strong when Owen Rutter wrote his book "British North Borneo" in 1922; he observed: *"Mount Kinabalu is undoubtedly the most striking physical feature of North Borneo ... a landmark from afar; it rises sheer and wonderful above a thousand hills ... it is no wonder the natives hold it in veneration as the resting place of departed spirits and a dragon's home."*

That the native peoples of Borneo long regarded the summit of Kinabalu with awe is sure, but we must remember, too, that in some ways they were very familiar with the mountain as a whole. They lived (and still do) in permanent villages as high as 1500 m (5000 ft), cultivating and hunting well above that. Only the bare summit area was awesome; why not? This was something entirely different from anything else in tropical island experience. In fact, there is nothing like it anywhere else in South-east Asia, and perhaps in the world. It is moreover, frequently exceedingly cold; and therefore very unlike tropical lowlands below. This and its beauty give immense visual impact, the black contrast with the unflinching green below impresses every mind and must always have done so. A few hundred years ago a similar landscape in the west would have been regarded as unworldly; thus a place for spirits, monsters, death and after-life. The extent to which the Idaan-Dusun-Kadazan peoples came to terms with the mountain and conquered nearly all of it, is far more remarkable than the way in which they left the top 1200 m (4000 ft) for the spirits, a place to which even the dead could not go easily, even the invisible were controlled—they had to qualify by death to climb. Further south, other Borneo people had no such landscape for the eye or mind. Their afterworlds and heavens are much vaguer places, generally under the ground. The Kinabalu view is much nearer, in essence, to the western concept of a heavenly heaven.

The first outside people to come to northern Borneo in a big way for trade and business were the Chinese. The Chinese delved deeper into the fantastic to explain to themselves, the astonishing sight which they beheld after crossing the South China Sea. The early Chinese literature of exploration and discovery in these seas is obscured by difficulties in the textual identification of place names; none of those mentioned in the early accounts can be pinpointed with any certainty today north of Brunei. But by the early Ming dynasty, Sabah was known to the early trading vessels of China and was probably visited by some of the ships from the great Armadas sent out under the Emperor Yung Lo, the third Ming ruler, who was on the throne from 1403 to 1424 A.D. His great admiral was the Moslem eunuch Cheng Ho, who mounted a series of expeditions in search of *"fine luxuries such as precious stones, fragrant woods, spices."* Cheng Ho is almost certainly related to a rather less substantial Chinese figure in Borneo mythology, called Ong Sum Ping, who appears in the sultanate of Brunei shortly after 1400 A.D. and subsequently married into the Royal family to establish Moslem blood in the household. The Brunei Royal Annals have it that he came to Borneo on the orders of the Emperor, in search of the great pearl believed to be held by a dragon on top of Mt. Kinabalu. Other forms of that Chinese belief recur in local lore (Harrisson & Harrisson, 1971).

At the beginning of the Ming period, if not today, the Chinese were every bit as superstitious as any Idaan ever met by Captain Dalrymple. The wildest extravagances and the most desperate legends were accepted back in Canton or Peking, as geographical realities from the *"barbaric south lands."* Some of those ideas must have spilled back, also, into local folklore, so that in prehistoric times there grew up a sort of melange of ideas about what happened up on the mountain top, and what marvellous qualities were to be obtained by those who climbed there. Owen Rutter wrote a sort of novelette about 1925 called "The Dragon of Kinabalu." It tells how the Emperor of China had three sons, and wished to test them to see who would best succeed him on the throne. He had heard, as

Fig.5. "One hour it is there, the next nowhere—lost in the cloud world." *(Photo: Tengku D.Z. Adlin)*

everybody had, of a great pink pearl, *"large as a peacock's egg"*, guarded by a huge dragon on the top of Kinabalu, where it *"made its home in a great lake upon the very summit"*. Each son is sent off in turn to get the pearl. The first is driven off the cliffs with many of his men killed. So is the second. Both are ashamed to return to their father, and settle in the lowlands, growing rice. Finally, after a long time, the youngest son, who is named Kong Wang, arrives, in quest not only of the jewel but of his missing brothers. He has filled a ship to everybody's amazement, with a load of iron cauldrons. He piles these up until they reach, as steps, to the very summit of Kinabalu. He peeps over the top and sees a moss-green dragon sitting beside the famous lake, *"playing with a carbuncle as red as the sunset and as large as a peacock's egg."* After a terrific battle with the beast, he gets away with the jewel. He then joins his brothers, who treat him with treachery and trickery. One of them, Sun Wang, arrives in Brunei and in the Chinese view, establishes a new dynasty there. Eventually, young Kong Wang returns to China and becomes the Emperor.

In the Sabah Society monograph, "The Prehistory of Sabah", Barbara Harrisson and I suggested that this whole Chinese symbolism of jewel and dragon on Kinabalu may be taken to signify the wealth of the trade across the China Sea, and of the power, strength and independence of the Sabah people, who resisted nearly every encroachment from the outside world. We also drew attention, there, to the way in which pearls stand for wealth, beauty and supernatural power, in much of Asian metaphor. Chinese and Indians alike saw

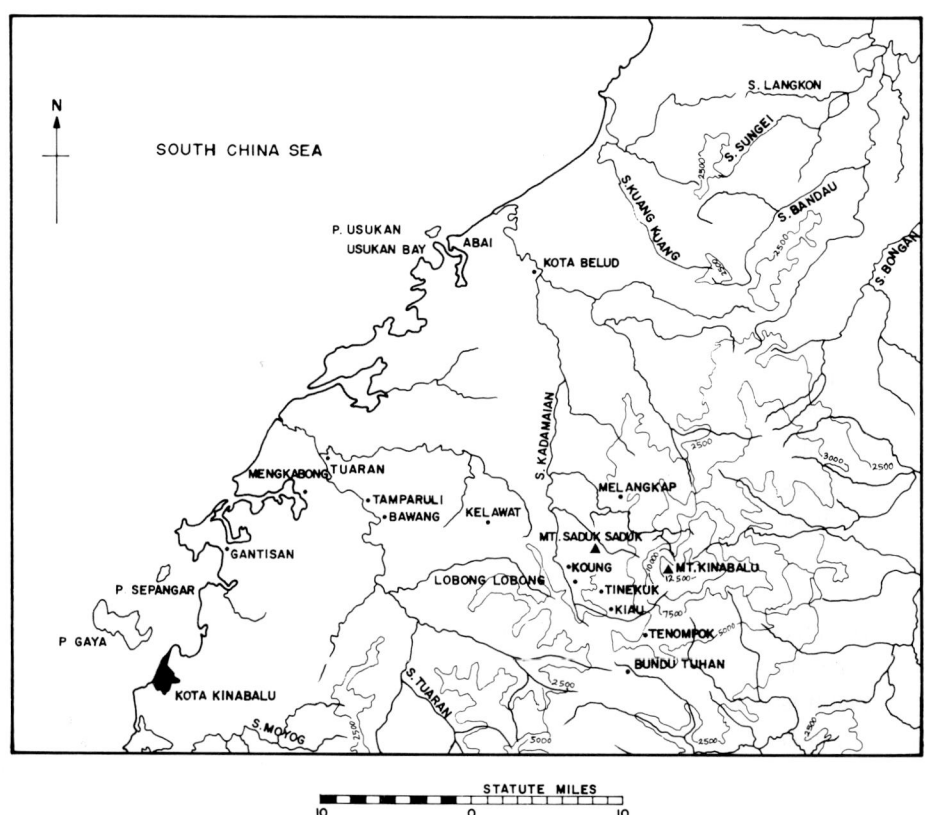

Fig.6. West coast of Sabah.

Mountain of Change

Fig.7. Solid and jagged, rising above the clouds, Kinabalu's stark yet mysterious summit presents a challenging frontier. *(Photo: Tengku D.Z. Adlin)*

a special affinity between the pearl and the moon; and in China pearls were the congealed *yin,* female essence, matter, one of the two absolute essentials in life (Harrisson & Harrisson, 1971).

Mention has already been made of the lake beside which the fearsome dragon dwelt. In Kinabalu today, any such belief might seem absurd in the mountain context. Yet lake stories continued until much later and more sophisticated times, not only in Chinese, but in local and in European belief. Thus Dalrymple writing in 1769 takes it for granted that everybody knows about it, believes in it and that it actually exists. The dragon might be a little doubtful; but the lake was there all right. As he puts it: *" ... the lake of Kenney-balloo. It is said that this lake lies on the south side of the mountain, and is so large that the land is not visible across it; in the middle are many islands ... almost all of the considerable rivers in Borneo, about 100 in number, flow from this lake"* (Dalrymple, 1769). Nearly a century later, Spenser St. John on his first ascent of the mountain, mentions that it is taken for granted the fact that: *"All Bajaus and Borneans are convinced that there is a lake on the very summit of this mountain"* (St. John, 1862).

Today, we know that there is no lake upon the summit. (There is a tiny pool in which ice sometimes forms.) Presumably, there never was a dragon either. But this dragon can easily be seen signifying the terrific power, the aggression, the ferocity of the mountain, the

Fig.8. An uncanny greyish blue as the morning progresses, Kinabalu's rocky summit makes a sheer drop into the depths of a silent Low's Gully. *(Photo: Albert Teo)*

storm and cloud, the majesty of the whole scene, which made an even greater impression in the old days than now. It may well be that the epic of the three Chinese brothers is really a folkmemory account of an actual assault and eventually successful ascent of the mountain centuries ago, from intrepid outside explorers who long preceded Low and St. John in the second half of the 19th century. More probably, the dragon is a metaphor for even fiercer times in the not so distant geological past. Kinabalu is one of the youngest, if not the youngest, great mountain on earth. It has certainly been classed by T. Kasma *et al.* as *"the youngest granite intrusion in the world today"* (Jenkins, 1971). The whole structure has emerged as granite through sandstone, in little more than a million years—mere child's play in geological time.

Much more important however, from the human point of view is the fact that a massive glacier formation overlay the mountain top until much more recent times. It did not finish melting until approximately 3000 years ago, well inside Chinese written history. At that time, there were large numbers of Idaan/Kadazan people living in the foothills and lowlands of Borneo. What tremendous changes and upheavals they and their ancestors must have experienced in what seems now a rather equitable equatorial atmosphere.

The great rocks and boulders all around the foot of Kinabalu spilling impressively into the plain of Ranau, are the debris of this glacial decay and of a lake left by the melting of the glacier higher up. It is these recent gigantic changes in the landscape of Kinabalu itself, that, rolling back into prehistory, folklore, myth and dream, have created the fantastic background we have been looking at so far; and which add to the wonder of what we see today.

From the wonder of the great young mountain to a study of its name, may seem mundane but there have been many arguments from whence the name was derived. The same sort of arguments rage about words like Sabah, Sarawak, even Borneo. There are two main arguments about the name Kinabalu which are feasible. One of these, over most of historical time the more popular view, is that *'Kina'* stands for China and therefore Chinese; and that *'Balu'* represents a widespread native dialect term for 'widow'. The Chinese influence is linked of course to the dragon and pearl stories which we have already heard.

The other main argument makes *'Balu'* mean 'solitary', which is also in conformity with some local languages. It then makes, with much more strain, *'Kina'* equal *'Aki'*, dropping the *'na'* and putting an extra *'a'* in front, as Owen Rutter devised it. *'Aki'* similarly, means father in many local languages, often respected father or ancestor. So in Rutter's view, Kinabalu means 'Solitary Father' (Rutter, 1922).

The reader will have noticed also that Dalrymple, in common with other early writers, never spelt it Kinabalu at all and made quite different phonetic sounds with two words. The Chinese call it Son San—God's mountain. Under the circumstances, it would probably be better to take the name, beautiful in itself, as signifying all we need to know.

So far, we have talked about the mountain itself but, if you discount the method of using metal cauldrons in the manner of the Chinese Emperors, not about climbing the mountain. To climb Kinabalu is one of the most interesting experiences that anybody in Sabah can have. Now, of course, it is very much easier than it was years ago. The achievement, however, remains important. It is also important to remember that the first authenticated climb of the mountain only occurred as recently as 1924, Oscar Cook could write that he was only the eighteenth person to have reached the top.

The first proven ascent of Kinabalu was that undertaken by Hugh, later Sir Hugh, Low in 1851. Low is a real hero of Kinabalu. For not only did he climb it first, but he did it twice more within a few years, each time with enormous difficulties. The worst difficulties in those days were not so much finding the way to the top as finding the way to the bottom, where the peoples were at war and the situation very difficult. The best account of these grievous times in Sabah history, when law and order were at a low ebb, is contained in the account by Spenser, later Sir Spenser, St. John, who accompanied Low on his second and third expeditions in 1858, himself a tremendous figure in the exploration of Sabah and Sarawak.

Anyone who is seriously interested in Kinabalu should read St. John's account in his wonderful book, "Life in the Forests of the Far East" (1862). In the short space available here, it would be impertinent to try and summarise, what was then a great achievement, a journey which remained by no means easy, even as late and as peaceful as 1958. I have

Fig.9. Silhouetted against the dawn, swept by mist and cloud, wind and sun, the mountain declares yet another day. Kinabalu as seen from Menggatal. *(Photo: W.M. Poon)*

mentioned that Oscar Cook, in 1924, reckoned he was only the eighteenth person to climb the mountain; there was no great rush after Low and St. John. In "Borneo, Stealer of Hearts", Cook comments: *"How strange it is that with this mountain at their very door so few people living in Borneo ever climbed it. Two only that I know of have scaled its peaks, and even their ascents were under government orders."*

Another explorer, John Whitehead, was a young professional collector of natural history specimens, who spent nearly two years on Kinabalu, three decades after St. John and Low. He explored, from the scientific point of view, the whole landscape of Kinabalu more thoroughly than anybody before. He wrote in his superbly illustrated and presented volume, "The Exploration of Kina Balu, North Borneo", *"for the zoologist it was yet a virgin field."* Some botanists had worked there before, but very little was known about the animal life. Through Whitehead's diligence, many of the large living things especially associated with Kinabalu and likely to be of interest to the visitor today, notably among the birds and mammals, were first collected and described by him.

For the following half century many of the species described from Kinabalu were thought to be peculiar there, and found nowhere else. Just as new geological research has changed our understanding of the mountain structure, so new and expanding zoological and botanical research has changed the scope of our knowledge of life on the mountain. It does not dim Kinabalu's lustre but increases its interest, that with more study, more exploration of other mountains, and also more excavations in the lowlands to find extinct forms there, the impact of mountain life is changing. Nothing will change the richness of life on Kinabalu, however, and no other mountain in Borneo, or anywhere else in South-east Asia, of comparable magnitude, offers anything like the opportunities for observing animal and plant life in the same way. Although specialists will deal with the various forms of life separately in following chapters, for a full appreciation of Kinabalu, it is useful to draw attention here to some of the wider aspects which cut across disciplines and indeed raise problems of fundamental interest.

Two of the commonest upper-level birds, the effusive Chestnut-capped Laughing Thrush *(Garrulax mitratus)* and the ebullient Malaysian Treepie *(Dendrocitta occipitalis)* have been found common and nesting almost at sea level down in the Trusan river behind Brunei Bay in recent years. The Pale-faced Bulbul *(Pycnonotus flavescens),* a rather inconspicuous bird which comes as high as Paka cave on Kinabalu, we found to be a resident in the mouth of the Niah caves, Sarawak, at sea level; while the lovely Sunda Whistling Thrush *(Myiophoneus glaucinus)* similarly nests in the Bau caves close to Sarawak's capital, Kuching, and again high up on Kinabalu.

Two birds thought to be absolutely exclusive not just to Borneo but to the top levels of Kinabalu, lost that high status in the 1950's when the Cambridge University Expedition to Mt. Trus Madi, far south of Kinabalu, collected there both the Mountain Blackeye *(Chlorocharis emiliae)* which must have been what St. John saw in 1858, long before it was known to science, when he described at the summit *"some small twittering birds, which looked like canaries"*, and the Kinabalu Friendly Warbler *(Bradypterus accentor).* The handsome little Blue Shortwing *(Brachypteryx montana)*—the female is mostly chestnut brown—long known only from Kinabalu, Mt. Trus Madi and Sarawak's highest peak, Mulu, has also appeared on the Plain of Bario in Sarawak's Kelabit Highlands down south, even coming out into the rice fields.

Birds, of course, can fly—though you will seldom see a Friendly Warbler do so if it can get away with hopping instead. This is not so with the nondescript looking small earth snake, whose only name is the scientific one *Oreocalamus hanitschi,* named after a naturalist who studied on Kinabalu at the end of the last century. Not only the species but the genus was long believed to be completely peculiar to the slopes of Kinabalu. This half-metre long creature was indeed only known by two examples, one of which is in the Smithsonian Institution at Washington, and the other in the National Museum at Singapore. A few years ago I broke this reptilian exclusivity by (to my amazement), collecting a specimen from the Kelabit highlands near Bario, well under 1200 m (4000 ft). Later Dr. Lim Boo-Liat (1970) of the Institute for Medical Research at Kuala Lumpur had the temerity to discover the same snake, identical, a thousand miles or so away, in the Cameron Highlands and more recently it has been recorded from the montane oak-forest on Mt. Lumarku in southern Sabah.

Almost as extraordinary is the mammalian case of the Lesser Gymnure *(Hylomys suillus)*, a fat, sluggish, largely nocturnal beast only known in Borneo in modern times from Kinabalu, Trus Madi, Mulu and the Kelabit Highlands. One night in February 1952 I had two of them at once in my sleeping bag at Paka cave. Yet in West Malaysia, on the mainland, it is common in the lowlands and in the mountains as well (Lim & Heynemann, 1968). Perhaps that was once true for Borneo too, as in our Niah cave excavations, down on the Sarawak coast, we have found *Hylomys* bones deep in the stone-age food deposits. More remarkable is the occurrence, in those deposits, at a level representing approximately 20,000 years ago, the exceedingly rare Ferret-badger *(Melogale personata),* only known alive in Borneo from the higher reaches of Mt. Kinabalu though it also occurs in other parts of South-east Asia. For that matter, the most obvious of the summit birds at Kinabalu, the cheerful Mountain Blackbird *(Turdus poliocephalus),* which usually does not occur below about 2750 m (9000 ft) is only a local race of the same species which occurs throughout the small islands of the western Pacific.

There are several theories put forward by biologists to explain these and other extraordinary phenomena, which are now becoming increasingly known to us—and as they become more known, have tended somewhat to confuse the previous theories. Indeed, it is probable that a good deal of what we see high up on Kinabalu is, so to speak, a 'living fossil' of something that was once much more widely distributed over all this part of South-east Asia, but has only survived the changes and upheavals of recent mill.ennia in a few places such as this. The strangest case of all is that of a plant, a tiny primitive liverwort *(Takakia)* which grows below the rhododendrons in the icy water of the Paka cave pool. In a recent study by Japanese botanists, what was once believed to be so exclusive is now known in Kinabalu, Japan and Alaska! (Meijer, 1971).

Liverworts are static, but birds fly, and can move if the pressure is too much. The Mountain Blackbird is one of those which does not seem to have lost the tameness under increasing human pressure for which all high-altitude Kinabalu birds were famous. Professor John Corner, writing of the Royal Society camp at 2950 m (9700 ft), described one as *"tame and ignorant of man, as all visitors to the mountain have noticed, that it sits like a giant robin with plum-coloured vest almost within arm's reach."* He thought it mistook him *"for a rhinoceros."* However, rhinoceroses now are probably extinct in the Kinabalu area, and probably soon for the whole of Borneo as well. Now that men begin to swarm on the mountains, there are signs that the wildlife of the park is shedding some of its pristine innocence. The Blue Shortwing which I found common near the highest levels in 1952, has seldom been reported up there in recent years. Has it been driven down? In the 1970 Park Warden's annual report there is a sad note. The Kinabalu Friendly Warbler which Whitehead had to shoo away from him before he could get far enough from one to collect it without blowing it up, and which was still touchingly friendly in 1952, was reported by the Park Warden in his 1970 annual report as: *"Not seen as often as in the past. A great number of climbers now walking the mountain trail have probably driven the birds to quieter areas."*

There are plenty of quieter areas within the Park, but it will be a great loss if those accessible to man suffer further withdrawal of the non-human forms. The balance between short-term human delight and the long-term responsibility to life as a whole is an intricate one, but no right on earth has given modern man the freedom to usurp and simply to take over nature from all its other constituents. Until little more than a century ago, the summit of Mt. Kinabalu belonged to the *"canary-like birds"* and associates. If we fail to understand that, we fail to understand the mountain in its deep and subtle moods.

Fig.10. "Surely the most complete statement of ... I am a mountain." A view of Mt. Kinabalu from Tuaran. *(Photo: Loi Pui King)*

The casual visitor who is not a trained naturalist will find that much of the animal life on Kinabalu is not very conspicuous. The birds, though beautiful and often colourful when seen closely, are small and not easy to pick out in the dense undergrowth. There are very few large mammals; and most of the small ones keep in the dense bushes or are nocturnal. Some butterflies are nearly as large as birds—the birdwings for instance; but perhaps the most interesting of them from an entomological point of view is the Green Hairstreak *(Austrozephyrus borneanus)*, still believed to be exclusive to Kinabalu, quite a small, easily overlooked little beauty.

There is another danger, once one starts disturbing the balance of nature in a wild sanctuary like this. The effect of man can be fairly easily measured and—with proper intelligence—corrected. There are a lot of secondary and not at all obvious follow-ups however, to the human explosion on Kinabalu. Let me give only one example, so that the reader can realise that these problems, though they may seem remote, in the long run can add up to serious damage for the future.

There are recent disturbing signs that some of the lowland rats have been following the roads and tracks and visitors up above the 1500 m (5000 ft) mark and higher. Previously the high levels of Kinabalu had their own rat population, including the Summit Rat *(Rattus baluensis)* which incidentally has retained its inquisitiveness and taken to visiting visitors at camps and hostels. The heavy voracious Muller's Rat, *(Sundamys muelleri)*, a pest to padi lower down, has now been trapped higher up. This sort of interloper, fighting with new conditions, and without local competition, can easily get out of hand and do irreparable damage, for instance to birds nesting, and to the resident smaller mammals (Lim & Heynemann, 1968).

One could write volumes about the fascinating wildlife of Kinabalu, just as one could go on for a long time about the history of exploration and discovery. Concluding this introduction, I want to go into the very recent history of the mountain and how this led to the founding of the National Park. The primary credit for recent developments on Kinabalu quite clearly goes to the Sabah Government. The changing pattern which paved the way for the new development however, is interesting, and it is only fair to give credit where credit is due.

The credit for widening and stirring interest in Kinabalu almost unwittingly belongs in the first place to the Japanese Army. After the Japanese defeat of the British and Australian forces in South-east Asia and their occupation of Borneo, in 1941, the tempo of the island drifted into another gear. The new broom attempted to sweep in new directions. The results were not altogether happy. In some respects they were altogether unhappy. The sweeping was very much conducted under the shadow and influence of Mt. Kinabalu.

Thus Albert Kwok's Kinabalu Guerilla Defence Force (as he termed it) staged an uprising against the occupiers which took them completely by surprise in October 1943. Kwok's Force occupied Kota Kinabalu, Tuaran, Kota Belud, and killed some 60 Japanese soldiers in the first surprise. The whole thing was premature and was put down with great savagery by the Japanese once they had recovered from the shock. At the same time, it made them profoundly uneasy; when before they had been very sure of themselves.

Mountain of Change

One side result of this was the infamous Sandakan–Ranau Death March, in which the Japanese moved some 2400 Australian and British prisoners of war 240 km from the north-eastern coast town to the principal large village—as it then was—in the Kinabalu foothills. Nowadays, you can do it by road in about six hours with a little thumping and concentration. In those days, it was a terrible journey through some of the most difficult terrain in South-east Asia. It took the column from September 1944 to August 1945 to go through the whole, horrible trauma. In the end, there were only six survivors, to look up with dying hope at the beautiful mountain glowing in the dawn (Carter, 1958).

The organisation called the Services Reconnaissance Department, a branch of British "cloak-and-dagger", was set up to initiate behind the lines a guerilla operation against the Japanese at this period. One of its principal objectives was to obtain information about surviving prisoners of war and if possible, rescue them. Major (Toby) Carter, D.S.O., and myself, among others, were dropped into the highlands of Borneo by parachute to found units of guerilla warfare and intelligence against the Japanese at this time. In Sabah, there was little left to do, the unfortunate prisoners were already dead.

Carter, himself a New Zealander, was profoundly affected by this experience. When the war was over he dedicated himself to memorialising the Death March disaster. Through his energetic interest, the Kinabalu Memorial Committee was formed with Tan Sri

Fig.11. The mountain protects, and is protected. *(Photo: A. Phillipps)*

Mohamed Fuad (Donald Stephens) actively interested, later Chairman of the Committee, and subsequently the first Chief Minister of Sabah. Mr. E.J.H. Berwick, C.B.E., then Director of Agriculture also took a major part in pushing forward this scheme. The Memorial, first dreamed up by Toby Carter, was the nucleus of the whole concept for preserving Kinabalu itself as an entity, a monument for the decency of man and a facility for the enjoyment of all in Sabah.

The emotional basis from which this began, out of natural feeling about the Death March, developed a more positive and objective aspect when Professor John Corner of Cambridge, one of the world's great botanists, who had himself experienced the Japanese occupation in Singapore, interested himself in Kinabalu from the ecological and systematic point of view. Corner organised and led two expeditions for the Royal Society of London, the strongest organisation of its kind in the world, which explored hitherto little known sections of the mountain, and in particular its flora, more systematically than ever before. Corner, as a keen conservationist, made his most important local contribution in 1961, a report to His Excellency the Governor of what was then the Crown Colony of North Borneo, entitled "The Proposed National Park of Kinabalu." He was influential in crystalising out British governmental thinking, before independence in Malaysia. The result was the National Park Ordinance of 1962. This in turn led to the formation of the actual Kinabalu Park, in 1964, with 753 sq. km (291 sq. miles)—an area the size of the whole of the Republic of Singapore.

Kinabalu is a mountain of unceasing change, fluctuation, movement, life, new problems. Over 130 years ago Spenser St. John reported in his 1858 diary as follows—*"We noticed the great change that had taken place in the ways and tastes of these people. When Mr. Low was here in 1851 beads and brassware were very much sought after. When we came last April (1858) the people cared nothing for beads; their hearts were set on brassware ... we now found that even brassware was despised and cloth eagerly desired. Chawats (loincloths) were decreasing and trousers coming in."*

A ghostly St. John, under Low's Peak today would meet with changes undreamed of then; a towering television aerial lifted above 2150 m (7000 ft) by helicopter; a modern resthouse with electricity and piped hot and cold water, and a restaurant at 3280 m (10,760 ft), plastic raincoats, bottles of coke, thermos flasks and much else to lessen the threshold of the supernatural and unknown above the cloud-line. Basically, though, the men (local Dusun or tourist Korean), like the mountain itself, remain unchanged. The world becomes in some ways more comfortable and easier for the more fortunate men. Kinabalu reminds all of us, however silently, that ease is not enough. Life's comforts do not satisfy the loftier needs of the soul. Not even the helicopter can wholly diminish the power of the high, wild place, giving deep rough comfort to the spirit of Man.

Meanwhile, Kinabalu, this splendid mountain, stands head and shoulders crowned in cloudland and misted dream-world, above human aspirations, political principles or polite decencies, as an inspiration not only to conservationists, climbers and naturalists but equally to all men and women of goodwill, up there to admire, enjoy and even (if you will) worship.

REFERENCES

Carter, G.S. 1958. A Tragedy of Borneo, 1941–1945. Privately printed. Brunei.

Cook, O. 1924. Borneo: Stealer of Hearts. Hurst & Blackett, London.

Corner, E.J.H. 1965. Mount Kinabalu East. *Sabah Society Journal* 2(4): 170–187.

Dalrymple, A. 1769. A Plan for extending the Commerce of this Kingdom and of the East India Company. London.

Harrisson, T. 1959. World Within. Cresset Press, London.

Harrisson, T. & Harrisson, B. 1971. The Prehistory of Sabah. The Sabah Society, Kota Kinabalu.

Jenkins, D.V. 1971. The first ascent of Mt. Kinabalu. *Malayan Nature Journal* 24(3): 190–191.

Lim, B.L. 1970. A genus of snakes *(Oreocalamus)* new to Malaya. *Sarawak Museum Journal* 18: 410–411.

Lim, B.L. & Heynemann, D. 1968. A collection of small mammals from Tuaran and the southwest face of Mt. Kinabalu, Sabah. *Sarawak Museum Journal* 16: 257–276.

Meijer, W. 1965. A Botanical Guide to the Flora of Mt. Kinabalu. In: Symposium on Ecological research on Humid Tropics Vegetation. Goverment of Sarawak and UNESCO.

Meijer, W. 1971. Plant Life in Kinabalu National Park. *Malayan Nature Journal* 24: 184–189.

Rutter, O. 1922. British North Borneo. Constable, London.

St. John, S. 1862. Life in the Forests of the Far East. 2 vols. Smith Elder & Co., London.

Whitehead, J. 1893. The Exploration of Kina Balu, North Borneo. Gurney & Jackson, London.

Fig.1. Low's Gully, cold and mysterious, the most daunting chasm in Kinabalu, is a U-shaped valley that once contained the main valley glacier which flowed northwards. *(Photo: Robert New)*

GEOLOGY OF KINABALU

David Lee Tain Choi

The wonderful mountain of Kinabalu was formed over a period of several million years. As a molten mass of magma pushed upwards, the intrusion brought with it from deep inside the earth's crust, rocks as old as 180 million years. In the process, this magma intrusion lifted up and pierced through a thick layer of ocean crust material and the overlying marine sediments that had been accumulating for 40 million years. As soon as these sediments were pushed up above sea level by a complex process of crustal movement some four to ten million years ago, nature went to work, carving the rocks into the features that we now see as Mt. Kinabalu and the adjacent mountain ranges.

ROCKS OF THE KINABALU AREA

The general geology of the Kinabalu area is shown in Map 1. The oval-shaped Kinabalu granite massif with a total area of 150 sq. km was emplaced into folded and faulted Tertiary sedimentary rocks and ultramafic (ultrabasic) rocks. Lenses of old metamorphic rocks were also brought up with the intrusion.

Metamorphic rocks
The oldest rocks in the Kinabalu area are the metamorphic rocks of schist and gneiss. They are found in pockets in the upper reaches of the Bambangan and Penataran rivers. These rocks were formed under great heat and pressure several kilometres beneath the surface of the earth, and their original characteristics have become completely changed. Similar schists and gneisses were also found extensively in the Segama area in eastern Sabah, where they came up in large chunks and are called the Crystalline Basement. These metamorphic rocks can be distinguished by their well-banded structure.

Ultramafic rocks
The next oldest rocks are the ultramafic rocks which occur along the southern and western parts of the Kinabalu massif. These are dark grey rocks which can be seen just below the Paka cave, that weather into yellow and dark brown with patches of oxidised iron, producing orange or red soils. The climb from the Telecoms Station at Kamborangoh at 2250 m to the Paka cave at *c.* 3100 m passes through about half a mile of these rocks, starting at about 2750 m. The rocks are normally sheared and fractured, and often have smooth, shiny, slick surfaces. The flaky, milky-green and grey-blue ultramafic rocks found in some areas are called serpentine or serpentinite. Ultramafic rocks such as those seen here are commonly found on the ocean floor and those found in the Kinabalu area are believed to be about 40 million years old.

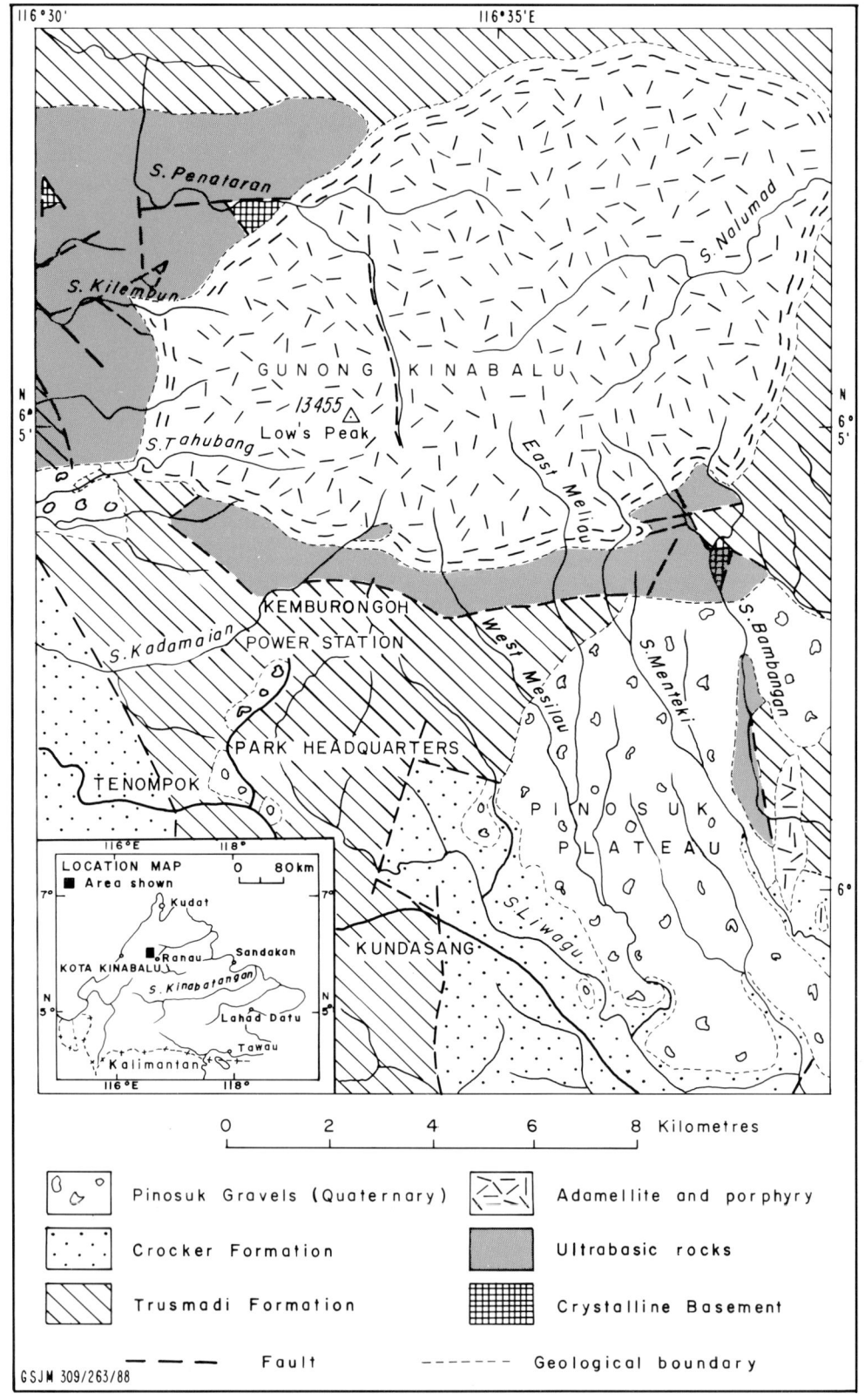

Fig.2. Geology of the Mt. Kinabalu area.

Fig.3. A sea of exfoliated granite on the smooth western slopes of Mt. Kinabalu, the result of alternate high and low temperatures acting on a surface glaciated by a westward flowing glacier. *(Photo: Albert Teo)*

Fig.4. The so-called "Sacrifice Pool". The tops of some of the minor peaks at the summit have been abraded and smoothened by ice-flow, suggesting that the ice-cap covering these peaks was very thick. *(Photo: Albert Teo)*

Fig.5. Like strange, white bands marked irregularly over the rocks, the aplite dykes intruding the exposed summit granite are easily seen at about 4000 m (13,000 ft). *(Photo: K.M. Wong)*

Sedimentary rocks

A thick sequence of sedimentary rocks surrounds the ultramafic rocks and the Kinabalu granite mass. These sedimentary rocks can be distinguished from other rocks by the typical layered sequences of sandstone and shale. They were originally deposited in a marine basin some 40 million years ago. In the Kinabalu area two distinct formations of these sedimentary rocks occur. One of these, the Trusmadi Formation is so called because these sequences are found mostly in the Trus Madi Range, and are typically of shale, slate, siltstone and thin sandstone beds. The other formation, the Crocker Formation, consists of sequences of thick sandstone and shale beds. These rocks form the whole of the Crocker Range.

Both formations are folded and faulted, and these movements have resulted in a stacking of the rock sequence, giving a false impression of the actual thickness. Usually faulting and thrusting occurs in thin straight zones, and the rocks appear broken. From the summit of Kinabalu one can see the long straight ridges and valleys built up by the Trusmadi and Crocker Formations to the south.

Fig.6. The final stretch up to Low's peak, 4101 m (13,455 ft), Kinabalu's highest point. Ice-plugging is evident from the broken rugged surface. *(Photo: Albert Teo)*

Kinabalu Granite

Mt. Kinabalu is formed entirely of an oval-shaped granitic batholith. The surface extent of the granite is 150 sq. km. The exposed parts of the batholith are much higher than the surrounding sedimentary rocks. The southern edge of the granite body starts from the Paka cave while its northern edge is in the headwaters of the Wariu and Kinapasan rivers, tributaries of the Sugut river. There are two varieties of granite on the mountain. One type called hornblende adamellite forms the main body while the other type, adamellite porphyry, forms the outer shell of the batholith. Both varieties look similar and can be distinguished from other rock types by their light grey colour, and coarse crystalline structure, with distinct elongate black hornblende crystals, often aligned in one direction, and large grey feldspars, some up to 5 cm across. Around the edges of the granite flow, exfoliation has developed. These features indicate that the granite was forcibly pushed up along a north–south axis, forming a dome. Major north–south and east–west faults developed at this time. One that runs along Low's Gully is especially prominent.

Several radiometric age determinations on the Kinabalu rocks indicate that cooling of the magma forming the Kinabalu granite took place from nine to four million years ago. A large molten mass usually takes millions of years to cool when it is deep inside the earth. The outer shell would cool first and the centre last.

Numerous slender bands or dykes of a different rock type, hundreds of metre long, which appear on the summit surface like road markings, represent the last phase of the granitic intrusion. These dykes have pierced through the granite along fractures. Two types can be seen. One is lighter in colour than the surrounding granite and is called aplite; the other type which is darker, is called a mafic dyke.

Pinosuk Gravels

Pinosuk gravels occupy the southern foothills of the mountain, mainly on the Pinosuk Plateau. These are poorly consolidated tilloid deposits formed 30,000 to 40,000 years ago. The deposits consist of stones up to boulder size, in a stiff clay matrix. The stones are usually angular and can be as much as 2 m across. Some of the boulders on the embankments along the Kundasang–Ranau road are part of the Pinosuk gravels. The stones are mostly granite that has been brought down from the summit. Some are sandstone blocks from the older sedimentary formations.

Radiocarbon dating of a wood sample from an upper unit of the tilloid deposit gave an age 34,300 years, and a sample from a lower unit gave an age of more than 40,000 years. These dates give the time of the formation of the Pinosuk gravels.

EVOLUTION OF MOUNT KINABALU

The birth of Mt. Kinabalu was the culmination of geological processes in western Sabah which began about 40 million years ago. At that time Sabah was part of an elongate sea basin in which marine sediments were accumulating rapidly. The sedimentary basin was situated between three crustal or tectonic plates—the South China Sea Plate to the north,

Fig.7. Exposed when the cloud and mist blow away periodically, the jagged peaks and steep walls that surround a cirque at the Donkey's Ears are an awesome sight. *(Photo: Robert New)*

Fig.8. Donkey's Ears, the landmark that contains the remnants of a U-shaped hanging valley. *(Photo: Robert New).*

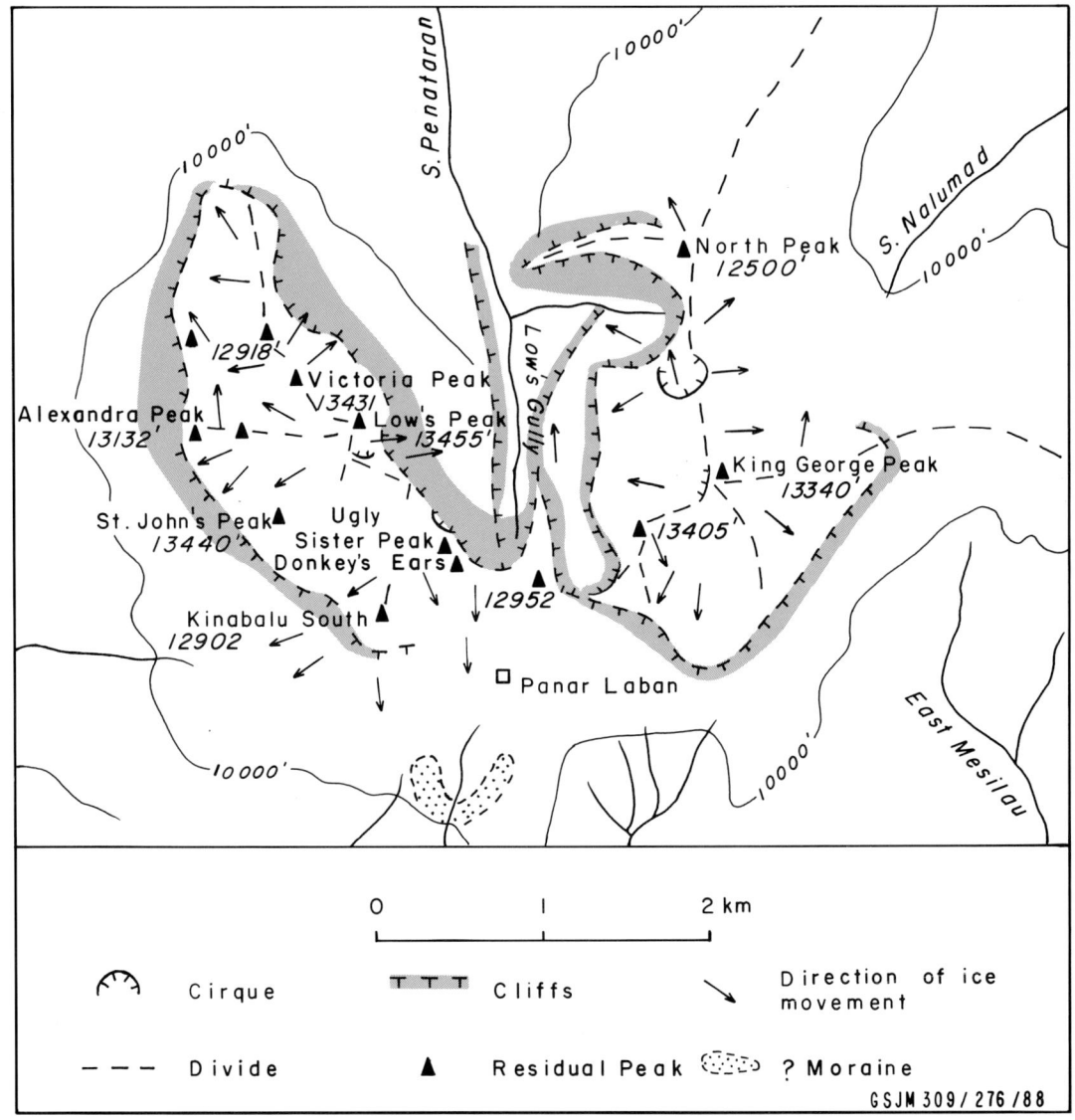

Fig.9. Glacial sketch map of Mt. Kinabalu.

the Sulu Sea Plate to the east and the main Eurasian Plate to the west. The collision of these plates moving and spreading resulted in one plate sliding over or under another. Tremendous heat along the plane of sliding was generated and this caused the melting of rocks which turned into magma. The magma was pushed up along weak zones or major fracture zones and later cooled and solidified to form the Kinabalu batholith. During the collision process, fragments of old rocks were also thrust up along the major fracture zones. Some of the large fragments that came up together with the granitic magma were of ocean crust material itself—these are the ultramafic rocks as well as some old metamorphic rocks. These old rocks together with the large body of granitic magma had not reached the surface when the major crustal plate movements slowed down around 10 million years ago. By this time the whole of the Crocker–Trus Madi area had been pushed up into mountain ranges. The sedimentary strata were squeezed, folded and tilted, and along certain zones the strata were torn apart and faulted. Erosion, of which the chief agents were rain-water and gravity, started to sculpt the uplifted masses of rocks. The highest part was around Mt. Kinabalu where it was cold enough to support a permanent ice-cap which became the chief agent of erosion at the summit. Over the years the sedimentary cover over Mt. Kinabalu was eroded by the ice action and exposed the granitic mass that we see today, which is said to be still pushing up at a rate of 5 mm a year.

GEOMORPHOLOGY

The most distinctive geomorphological feature of Kinabalu is the barren summit zone with jagged peaks sticking out above the smooth rock surface. Deep ravines dissect the 10-sq. km summit area, and the steep slopes on all sides; and the 1800 m-deep Low's Gully to the north practically splits the mountain into two halves—the Eastern Plateau, and the slightly higher, western Summit Plateau. The next most striking features are the smaller Pinosuk Plateau on the lower southern part of the mountain, and the herring-bone ridges of the foothills.

These features started to develop when this part of Sabah rose from the sea several million years ago. The rate of uplift appeared to be greatest around Mt. Kinabalu and this was

Fig.10. Signs of colder times: crescentic gouges indicate past glacier flow. *(Photo: David Lee)*

probably due to the overlying, enveloping ultramafic rocks which acted as a lubricant on the rising granite mass, so the rate of erosion here was greater than that of the surrounding areas. A circular drainage pattern developed on the uplifted granite massif. By the Pleistocene period, about 100,000 years ago, much of the sedimentary cover had already been eroded. At that time Mt. Kinabalu must have reached a greater height, probably one or two thousand feet more than the present height, allowing an ice-cap to form, and the seasonal changes resulted in alternate freezing and melting, causing vigorous erosion on the summit. Large chunks of sedimentary cover were torn off and washed down the steep slopes. Then the covering rocks were completely ripped off by the ice, exposing the granitic massif itself, which, in turn, was subject to the same ice action, reducing the height even further.

About 5.5 sq. km of the summit area has been subjected to this glacial action (Map 2). The northern and north-western slopes of the mountain are more deeply incised because these parts receive less sunlight compared to the southern and eastern slopes. Therefore more ice was accumulated on the western half and with the increased weight the erosion was more severe. Thus the Eastern Plateau, with a thinner layer of ice, now has a rougher, more rugged appearance than the western Summit Plateau.

At the summit one can almost see where the ice passed, from the features on the rocks. For instance, the open inclined passage between St. John's Peak and South Peak looks like a dried-up valley, through which much ice flowed. The east-west linear features on the rock surface point in the direction of the downflow slope. A deep chasm at least 1000 m in depth developed along Low's Gully from a valley glacier which scoured the already faulted zone.

SMALL-SCALE MORPHOLOGICAL FEATURES ON THE SUMMIT

Those who have climbed Mt. Kinabalu will most likely have noticed a number of features along the Summit Trail not found on rock formations at low altitudes. These features have been identified as being of glacial origin.

The most striking feature is the broad smooth surface of the western Summit Plateau which appears to have been polished. The gentle slopes west of the Donkey's Ears Peaks, and the steeper southern slope that can be seen from the Laban Rata Resthouse at 3280 m appear to have been bulldozed. The normal process of weathering by water could not have caused these broad, smooth, even surfaces, which were produced by the ice sheets slowly moving over the rock surface. There are also a number of other minor features which indicate that the summit of Mt. Kinabalu was once capped by ice. This ice-cap was the source of glaciers flowing west, south, east and north carving out the 'U'-shaped gullies and valleys found on the Summit Plateau and its slopes. The eastern branch of Low's Gully is 'U'-shaped with a smooth, broad valley floor and steep smooth walls. A pile of rock debris at the lower end strongly indicates that the gully was formed by a glacier, and the rock debris represents a terminal moraine, marking the furthest extent of the glacier (Koopmans & Stauffer, 1967). Another example of morainic material can be seen behind and above the Paka cave. A 'U'-shaped gully has also developed between St. Andrew's Peak and Oyayubi Iwu Peak.

Small-scale glacial features on the smooth rock surface include crescentic cracks aligned in the direction of the downflow, scratches, and ice-abraded surfaces. These features can be seen along the Summit Trail from the lower slopes of St. John's Peak and Sayat-Sayat hut at 3670 m onwards. Deep parallel grooves seen on a rock surface about 100 m above the Laban Rata Resthouse are also probably of glacial origin. A cirque, caused by the headward erosion of a glacier, which is like a tilted amphitheatre, can be seen between North Peak and King George Peak on the Eastern Plateau, from the western side. Four others can be identified along the cliffs between King George Peak and Low's Peak but they are not well-developed (Jacobson, 1970).

Most of the peaks stand out precipitously about 50–100 m above the general smooth surface. These peaks have rugged surfaces, some, like Low's Peak, resembling blockfields. These peaks appear to have been plucked by the ice-action, but no smoothing has taken place. The back of South Peak (the north slope) which is much lower than the other peaks is, however, polished by ice action.

The ice-cap on the Summit Plateau disappeared about 3000 years ago. Since then exfoliation of the smooth surface has taken place as a result of temperature changes and frost action. Loose slabs of granite are commonly seen on the slopes and summit. Small gullies have also developed on the smooth surface and pits 3–4 cm across have developed along these gullies as a result of frost action. A 5-m long, shallow depression caused by uneven scouring from the ice is located at the foot of Low's Peak. It is permanently filled with water and sometimes ice and has become a 'wishing pool' for climbers before they make the final assault on the peak.

REFERENCES

Jacobson, G. 1970. Gunung Kinabalu area, Sabah, Malaysia. Geological Survey Malaysia, Report 8 (Sarawak & Sabah Series).

Koopmans, B.N. & Stauffer, P.H. 1967. Glacial Phenomena on Mount Kinabalu, Sabah. Geological Survey Borneo Region, Malaysia. Bulletin 8.

Fig.1. A legend even in his own time, Gunting Lagadan was Mt. Kinabalu's first official guide. In his honour Sabah Parks named the mountain hut at 3200 m (10,500 feet) after him.

THE PEOPLE AND FOLKLORE OF KINABALU

Patricia Regis

"Onkowiyahai pinipi
Undu-undu'ii winorun
Om hilo Kinabalu
Om hilo Kinorungoi"

[Make a heart for the earth
Ho and behold here is Kinabalu
Ho and behold here is Kinorungoi] (from the Lotud genesis)

This stanza of a *rinait* or ritual verse is taken from the Lotud *Mamampang* or genesis. It describes how Mount Kinabalu was created. The Lotud, a Dusun/Kadazan tribe living on the Tuaran coastal plains have, and still observe, an elaborate ritual system which has a correspondingly rich oral tradition. Their creation epic describes how their supreme deities, Kinohoringan and his wife, Umunsumundu created the universe. Umunsumundu created the earth while Kinohoringan, the sky, cloud and all above the earth. The eagle, Kondiu, was sent to inspect all that they had created. Alas, the report was that the cloud was too small in relation to the earth. Kinohoringan, according to the *Mamampang rinait* about a conversation between Umunsumundu and him, was ashamed that he had created a cloud too small and wanted to create a new one. This was a blow to his pride. Umunsumundu understood his feelings and decided to reshape the earth instead, to make it equal in breadth to the cloud. She decided to create a mountain which she called Kinabalu or Kinorungoi. This mountain was to be the heart of the world.

Pongoluan is also a Lotud synonym for Kinabalu when reference is made of the resting place of the good spirits of their *dead* in their *rinait*. The Lotud and other Dusun/Kadazan kindred tribes all share a traditional belief based on the two supreme deities, a pantheon of good spirits, and evil spirits called *rogon*, which they have to continually propitiate to evoke assistance or to drive away depending on the occasion or need. The Lotud, in particular, perform elaborate rituals, through their ritual specialists called *tantagas* for these ceremonies. Kinabalu is mentioned or alluded to in nearly all their *rinait*, for the mountain towers not only as a massive backdrop to the scenic padi fields of the Tuaran plains but also commands a position that is visible on all sides from the west, north, and the east coast.

The early explorers and naturalists who reached the summit reported being able to see the west coast from Kimanis Bay to Marudu Bay and Ambong Bay, and even the head of

Fig.2. Mt. Kinabalu provides an imposing backdrop for Kampung Gundohon, Bundu Tuhan, where *babalian*, ritual specialists, were recruited in the past for the ascent. *(Photo: P. Regis)*

Fig.3. An interesting rock outcrop resembling Mt. Kinabalu located at Kg. Lobong-Lobong at the foot of Mt. Kinabalu is called *anak Kinabalu*, or "child of Kinabalu", by local people. *(Photo: P. Regis)*

Sandakan Bay (Bunbury, 1910) and Tambunan Plains (Hurrel, 1933). Even the early mariners who sailed the South China Sea used Mt Kinabalu as a navigational reference for the route between China, Borneo and the Philippines.

The mountain was clearly visible on many sides, but jungle cover and headhunting tribes living on its slopes kept it mysteriously distant for centuries. The quartz crystals (St. John, 1862) and waterfalls on the granite massif sometimes caught the sun and glistened like jewels. This phenomenon probably gave birth to the many legends concerning diamonds and pearls and the dragon guarding these jewels on the mountain. This, together with Kinabalu's dominating stature and local animistic beliefs gave rise to a rich local folklore. Like the Lotud, nearly all Dusun/Kadazan tribes living within sight of Kinabalu, particularly those living on its slopes, traditionally respect the mountain as the resting place of their dead.

Fig.4. In those days climbers were often accompanied by a large retinue of porters and carriers. These Bajau men were recruited to carry provisions and kit in back-carrying receptacles called *bongon*, for the seven-mile march to Kota Belud before starting the journey for a three-month trip to Mt. Kinabalu, in 1939. These receptacles are still in use today. *(Photo: V.W. Ryves)*

KINABALU—Summit of Borneo

ORIGINS OF THE NAME "KINABALU"

There have been many explanations based on local legend (Moulton, 1913) as to the origins of the name Kinabalu. One is that it refers to Chinese Widows, i.e., *kina balu*, because Chinese soldiers were killed trying to obtain the treasure guarded by a dragon on the summit (see also Harrisson, this volume). Many Chinese ladies became widows as a result of this quest. Another is *kina bahru* or New China, a corruption of the "r" due to the inability of the Chinese to pronounce this letter. This referred to some former colony of Chinese settlers in the region. Another early explanation is that *nabalu* in Dusun means "resting place of the dead". However, in recent interviews (conducted by Rajibi Hj. Aman

Fig.5. The *babalian*, a ritual specialist, was often an indispensable member of the climbing party. Tonggal, a *babalian*, poses with his religious paraphernalia of a chicken and a bunch of ritual objects before carrying out the first of the sacrificial rites to propitiate the spirits of the mountain, in 1939. *(Photo: V.W. Ryves)*

and Jamili Nais) with village elders from Kampung Kiau and Bundu Tuhan on the slopes of Kinabalu, the word *nabalu* in classical Dusun means "any big boulder" associated with spirits (see also Beaman *et al.*, this volume). *Ki* means the occurrence of boulders. Since the mountain consists of many boulders it is called Kinabalu. In the old days it was believed that big rocks were usually inhabited by spirits. Any big rock which is not associated with a spirit is called *pampang*. However, it seems that not all Dusun/Kadazan believe their dead go to Kinabalu. According to Tingoh bin Simpot of Kampung Kiau (Jenkins, 1971) the people of Kiau believed their dead went to Sadok-Sadok, a hill further down the Kedamaian valley on the slopes of Kinabalu.

ORIGINS OF THE SACRIFICIAL RITES

Since Hugh Low's recorded ascent in 1851, expeditions to Mt. Kinabalu went via the Tempasuk or Tuaran plains up Melangkap, Kaung, Lobong Lobong and Kiau. The Kiau Dusuns with villagers of Teung Tuhan who had land rights on the spurs of Kinabalu controlled the only pass to the summit (Whitehead, 1893). The guides for the ascent were traditionally obtained from Kiau, the highest village (1006 m or 3300 ft high) on the western slope of Kinabalu, as the track to the summit began from this kampung. An essential part of the early ascents was the fulfilment (Enriquez, 1927 & Anon., 1959) of sacrifices for which ritual specialists, who also served as guides, had to be employed. The rites were specified in the contract. The offerings, which were paid for by the visitor, consisted of seven eggs and seven white fowls (see also Jenkins, this volume). This was observed according to a precedence set by the seven original climbers recorded in a Kiau legend (Enriquez, 1927). In the story seven men from Kampung Kiau hunting for deer went up the mountain. At Sayat-Sayat "pearls" fell from the sky. After they had collected the pearls, they lost their way to Paka Cave. Realising that this was the effect of the pearls, all of them except one discarded the pearls. The seventh hunter hid one pearl in his loincloth. The other six men found their way to the cave, but the seventh with the pearl could not find his way and had to be led back. He fell ill and had to be carried to his village. When they removed his loincloth, the pearl fell out and he immediately recovered. As the pearl was found to have magical and healing powers, the seven men were sent up the mountain to find more. This time they took with them seven white cockerels and seven eggs for sacrifice to the spirits that lived on the mountain. At Panar Laban, the "place of sacrifice", they slaughtered the cockerels, placed the eggs on the ground and later brought the cockerels to Paka Cave where these were eaten. Pearls fell on the mountain but these were smaller and had no magical or medicinal effects. The original pearl was kept by the man who brought it down and it disappeared on his death.

CLIMBING RITUALS

These rites became a tradition which was observed, though not always assiduously, for many years by climbers. In some of the early ascents, these rites were accompanied by a volley of gunshots (Enriquez, 1927); two at the start of the final ascent at Panar Laban and two at the summit. These gun shots may have had their origin in the early collecting expeditions on the mountain, especially by zoologists, who may have had to resort to the use of firearms for the collection of animals (see also Jenkins, this volume). Spenser St. John and Hugh Low in 1858 also fired their guns to prove their superiority to the natives when they refused to concede to the latter's unreasonable demands. This could have also contributed to that tradition.

The offerings also included betel leaves and betel nut, but the rites generally varied according to the requirements of the guide-cum-priest leading the climbing party. From earlier accounts, there have been several versions of these offerings and rites. Not always were seven or white chickens used. For John Whitehead's ascent in 1888, his guide, Kuro, brought one cockerel for the sacrifice. During his incantations near the summit, he jerked out feathers from the cockerel's tail and planted them upright in a row in a small crevice in the rock at his feet.

Climbers also had to observe local taboos (Enriquez, 1927). They had to avoid making unnecessary noise, mentioning the names of streams on the mountain and had to refer to Kinabalu as Agayoh Ngaran or "Big Name". Not all of the climbers, however, conceded to the employment of these ritual specialists or *babalian* in the earlier ascents. In one descriptive and amusing episode (Clemens, 1932), a visitor claimed to be a famous spirit pacifier to avoid paying the additional expense and managed to decline the priestly service. In another account (Enriquez, 1927), a retired army chaplain told the people that he himself was a priest and "that he could very well manage for himself, although he belonged to a different creed".

THE FEES

By present standards, climbing Kinabalu in those days was an extremely expensive affair. Up to the 1950's climbing the mountain was a major expedition involving at least a 10-day trek on foot, on buffalo or pony via the Tuaran or Tempasuk plains or from the Interior. From the accounts of the early expeditions in the last century, the European climbers were accompanied by a large retinue of porters, carriers, collectors and servants, in addition to being well stocked with goods for exchange with hostile natives for guides and access to the mountain and its summit. The trail up to the summit encroached on the land rights of these people who had to be induced by goods to allow passage. Headhunting was practised and villagers seldom ventured very far outside their territory, except to barter at nearby *tamus* (markets). The goods that these Europeans brought were naturally a novelty and cloth which was scarce was in great demand. The natives could not afford the cloth used and sold by the Bajau and Illanun (Iranun) on the plains to the Dusun/Kadazan living there. Consequently, these European explorers noted, the higher up the mountain the fewer clothes these people had and wore. With the subsequent supply of cloth from the European climbers, native men began wearing the warmer home-made trousers in place of the traditional loincloth.

The 19th-century expeditions saw lengthy and tedious (to the Europeans) negotiations with the natives from Kaung to Kiau on the terms of the barter. The natives were equally determined to relieve the Europeans of their stock of goods as the latter attempted to gain the best possible bargain of the barter. Agreement was not always reached as in the case of Thomas Lobb (St. John, 1862), the naturalist who refused to concede to the demands of the people and was turned back in 1856.

By the end of the century as the North Borneo Chartered Company gained greater control over its territory through treaties with the people (Little, 1887), scarce goods became more common and the people sought more useful items such as soaps, matches and kerosene oil. With the treaties, headhunting also became outlawed. The macabre relics of this practice are stored in small shelters and can still be seen at Bundu Tuhan and Kiau.

With improvement of the route via the Tenompok Pass where the Kinabalu Park headquarters is located, better road connections and accommodation on the mountain, the ascent to and descent from the summit can be achieved in a matter of hours. The sacrificial practices for each climb, however, have since lapsed, becoming impractical as carrying of livestock up the mountain is somewhat cumbersome, due to the sheer numbers of ascents taking place each year. The gun salute has been dispensed with for many years. However, the reports of an occasional loss of a climber or an accident on the mountain has prompted the local *babalian* from Bundu Tuhan and Kiau, taking turns, to make the annual pilgrimage up the mountain to perform the propitiatory rites called *monolob*, albeit in an abbreviated form. Sometimes, depending on circumstances, two instead of the required seven white fowls, preferably the home-grown and not the commercially mass-produced variety, are employed for this purpose. The belief that Kinabalu is sacred and inhabited by spirits is still observed by animistic Dusun/Kadazan while their counterparts of other creeds residing in the villages around Kinabalu maintain a healthy respect for their tradition. As these male *babalian* are elderly and become fewer in number this traditional propitiation is likely to disappear.

GUIDES

With the opening of the new route via Tenompok Pass some 60 years ago, Bundu Tuhan became another source for the recruitment of guides and ritual specialists. Today, there are a total of some 60 registered guides, all males between the ages of 20 and 60 years coming from Bundu Tuhan and Kiau. Their employment and registration are regulated by their association whose membership includes Kinabalu Park officials so that standards are maintained to ensure maximum safety for climbers.

The 19th-century records offer a number of amusing accounts of the European explorers' difficulties in recruiting local guides. In many expeditions, these guides were the village chiefs themselves who occasionally doubled up as ritual specialists for the ascent. The negotiations usually tested the wits of both parties. However, St. John and Low appeared more than generous in parting with their goods in their farewell and were remembered for this. Several names have been recorded but among the more colourful characters of their ranks were the two chiefs, Limoung and Lemaing, of Kiau, who had accompanied St. John in 1851 and 1858 respectively. Whitehead also had memorable encounters with Kabong

Fig.6. Female Kadazan porters have now joined the ranks of their male counterparts for the ascent of Mt. Kinabalu. Note the back-carriers called *wakid*. This picture was taken at Panar Laban, 11,000 feet. *(Photo: K.M. Wong)*

and Kuro, two chiefs who guided him to the summit in 1887. The sons sometimes continued the tradition, like Umpoh, the son of Kabong, who became a guide for later expeditions.

The most famous of them all was perhaps Gunting Lagadan of Bundu Tuhan, who has been immortalised by the Sabah Parks. The mountain hut at 3200 m (10,500 ft) has been named after him. A somewhat legendary figure, Gunting was native chief of Bundu Tuhan and worked also as a guide. He became also the first registered Park guide with the gazetting of the Kinabalu Park in 1964. Apart from this, Gunting was believed (Pfeiffer,

1977) to have reached the summit long before Low's recorded conquest. Gunting was said to be endowed with extraordinary powers or *kabal*, as all climbers who had him as guide were guaranteed safety. Gunting died in 1966, a very old man said to have been 144 years old. The stories of his exploits continue to grow. The legends go on.

Among traditionally non-literate people like the Dusun/Kadazans and such people elsewhere, it is difficult to separate people from their legends. The two are often inextricably linked. To understand their worldview and to learn about their origins and history, it is necessary to know their folklore and appreciate their oral traditions which endorse their very existence. When a man's life ends, a new legend sometimes begins, especially if his life had been in some way unusual or remarkable. The folklore of Mt. Kinabalu is not only about fascinating stories about a mountain, but also a reflection of the character of the indigenous people that live on its slopes and within sight of it.

REFERENCES

Anon. 1959. Short Guide to Mt. Kinabalu, North Borneo. Department of Information and Broadcasting, North Borneo.

Bunbury, H.W.L. 1910. *British North Borneo Herald*, September 1, 1910.

Clemens, Joseph. 1932. *British North Borneo Herald*, April 16, 1932.

Enriquez, C.M. 1927. Kinabalu, The Haunted Mountain of Borneo. H.F. & G. Witherby, London.

Hurrel, B.W. 1933. *British North Borneo Herald*, March 1, 1933.

Jenkins, D.V. 1971. The First Ascent of Kinabalu. *Malayan Nature Journal* 24: 190–191.

Little, R.M. 1887. *British North Borneo Herald*, July 1, 1887.

Moulton, J.C. 1913. A Collecting Expedition to Mt Kinabalu. *Sarawak Gazette*, November 1, 1913.

Pfeiffer, Pat P. 1977. Guides to Adventures. *Asia Magazine*, June 1977.

St. John, Spenser 1862. Life in the Forests of the Far East. Oxford in Asia Historical Reprints, 1974.

Whitehead, John 1893. The Exploration of Mount Kina Balu. Gurney & Jackson, London.

Fig.1. Hugh Low.

THE FIRST HUNDRED YEARS
A short account of the expeditions to Mt. Kinabalu 1851–1950

D.V. Jenkins

The name of Hugh Low will always be associated with that of Mount Kinabalu for it was he, who on the 11th March, 1851 first reached the summit region of the mountain, gazed down into the vast depths of the abyss now known as Low's Gully and recorded the scene for posterity. His name is also remembered on the mountain with the highest point, Low's Peak (4101 m; 13,455 ft); with that most elegant of pitcher plants *Nepenthes lowii*, the Kinabalu Buttercup *Ranunculus lowii* and several other plants and animals.

Low was not content with his first climb, and made two more excursions to the mountain with his friend Spenser St. John and eventually on the third attempt reached the summit plateau.

THE EXPEDITIONS

It is remarkable that, in the one hundred years following Low's first ascent, only 53 recorded visits were made to Kinabalu. It is also remarkable, and a tribute to the perseverence and diligence of those few early scientists and collectors who made the journey, that so many of Kinabalu's natural wonders were revealed, described and documented. All is yet to be revealed, however, for even today, scientists are finding new species of plants and animals on the mountain with surprising regularity.

To write a detailed account of each expedition would take up the whole of this book. We have been obliged to limit ourselves to an annotated chronological listing of each expedition and to indicate to interested readers source material for further information and study. Maps 3 and 4 should be referred to.

1. **1851 : Hugh Low**
    Low left Labuan on the 21st February, 1851 in a native boat and reached the Tuaran river on the 26th. After spending several days in the area, he set out for Kinabalu from Kampung Bawang on the 4th March. His party consisted of forty two persons ... *"The Orang Kaya of Kimanis was director-in-chief of the caravan, under him were the Datu Pengiran of Menkabong, a celebrated old pirate, formerly a scourge of the neighbourhood of Singapore, but now retired from his enterprising profession, and the Datu Maharaja Denda, the Dusun chief of Tamparuli, a pretty village below Bawang, and a man of great influence along the river. The motley following was composed of Bajows, Borneans and Dusuns, and here and there a stray China and*

Manila Man" (Low, 1852). This large party, many of whom came along out of curosity, reached Kampung Kiau in the evening of the 6th March having spent the nights of the 4th and 5th at Kampung Kelawat and Kampung Bungol.

At Kiau, Low was relieved to find that although he was an object of some curosity—being the first white man most of the people had seen—the people's attention was diverted to the Chinese servant whose long pigtail attracted amazing curiosity. On the morning of the 7th, Low set off for the mountain leaving most of the men at Kiau. Lemaing, one of the Kiau villagers agreed to guide him and his party to the highest point known to his people. The first night was spent in a hut at a farm at the base of the mountain, the second night under an overhanging rock. On the third day, Paka cave was reached, and the following day spent resting and collecting specimens.

Fig.2. Kampong Kiau in February 1939. The Dusun residents of Kiau Village then were rarely seen without their carrying receptacles or *bongon*. *(Photo: V.W. Ryves)*

Paka cave was, as Low put it, " ... *the highest point the Dyaks* (sic) *had ever reached—all beyond was perfectly unknown"* (Low, 1852).

On the morning of the 11th March, Low pushed on for the summit and eventually reached the bare rock which he found *"very toilsome."* He climbed on till he arrived at the base of one of the peaks in the region of the present site of Sayat-Sayat. He then proceeded to climb the gap between two of the peaks, and was surprised to find himself on a narrow 15-cm (6-in) ridge. *"On placing my breast against it and looking over the ridge, I gazed into a circular amphitheatre about 80 yards broad, the bottom of which from its great depth and my position overhanging it, was undiscernable, though I imagine I could see down two thousand feet"* Rapidly lifting cloud caused Low to begin his descent but not before *"finishing an excellent bottle of madeira to Her Majesty's health and that of my far distant friends."* A note was placed in the bottle and left among the rocks. Low was rapidly overtaken by a *"Scotch mist"* and had to wait for two hours before going down. He descended to Kiau on the 12th March with his specimens, one of which was the remarkable *Nepenthes lowii.*

2. **1856 : Thomas Lobb**
Thomas Lobb was a plant collector for the firm of Veitch of Chelsea during the years 1843–1860. He tried to climb Kinabalu in 1856 to collect pitcher-plants for introduction to English gardens, but was prevented from doing so by the people of Kiau, apparently due to the fact that there had been a poor harvest following Low's visit and because he would not agree to pay what he regarded as the extortionate demands of the villagers. He did however manage to reach the top of Mt. Sadok-Sadok, 1673 m (5492 ft).

Lobb had met Low before his visit to the mountain, and Low, believing that potatoes might flourish around Kiau (how right he was), had sent some by Lobb for the villagers to plant. Lobb was surprised to find, the morning after presenting the potato seed, the village boys playing marbles with them (St. John, 1862; Veitch, 1897). No more is known of Lobb's expedition.

3. **1858 (April) : Hugh Low and Spenser St. John**
On Low's second expedition to Kinabalu he was accompanied by his friend Spenser St. John who was the British Consul in Brunei. Low and St. John left Labuan on the 15th April, 1858, reaching Abai on the 17th. They then proceeded to the Tempasuk river (probably in the region of the modern Kota Belud) where they remained for two or three days arranging guides and porters. They then set out for the mountain, and arrived at Kampung Kaung on the 25th. The next day they reached Kiau having managed to overcome some difficulties at Kampung Labang.

On the 28th they started the climb, but Low was by this time experiencing great difficulty in walking as his feet were suppurating. He had in fact walked all the way in bare feet, as a supply of shoes had not reached Labuan in time for their departure! Low remained in a bamboo hut in a padi farm at the foot of the mountain and St. John set out alone.

In two days he reached the Paka cave and the next day, May 1st, climbed to the summit. He found Low's bottle above Sayat-Sayat and named the place Low's Gully. The Low's Gully named by St. John is not the Low's Gully known today. The spot named by St. John, is that perpendicular cleft between the Donkey's Ears Peak and Tunku Abdul Rahman's Peak, and the ravine leading to it from the south. St. John proceeded to the west, reached the plateau, and climbed the South Peak, 3933 m (12,902 ft). This peak, so he was informed by his guides was *"the mother of the mountain"* (St. John, 1862), but St. John was chagrined to find that to the north were higher peaks. He concluded that the sons must have outgrown the mother! Rising cloud and wind forced St. John to return to Paka cave; the following day he returned to Kiau to find Low still unable to walk. Low made the greater part of the return to the coast by litter, and by raft down the Tempasuk.

4. **1858 (July) : Hugh Low and Spenser St. John**
    Low and St. John were not satisfied with the result of their previous expedition although a quantity of interesting plant specimens had been obtained, and resolved to return to the mountain. This they did in July, 1858. Leaving Labuan early in the month, they proceeded via Gantissan and Kampung Menkabong to Tuaran and then to Tamparuli, Low having decided that his original route was easier than the one along the Tempasuk valley. They then proceeded to Kiau via the villages of Bawang, Sinilau, Kelawat and Kaung. On arrival at Kiau, they spent several days on the Marai Parai spur collecting botanical specimens and there discovered several new species of *Nepenthes*, including the giant *Nepenthes rajah*. On their return to Kiau, they set off for the mountain, reaching Paka cave in three days. They then made for the summit and had no difficulty in reaching its western plateau. While Low collected plants and attended to his scientific instruments, St. John attempted to climb one of the north-western peaks, and almost succeeded, failing by only 12 m (40 ft). This peak is now known as St. John's Peak, 4097 m (13,440 ft). The highest peak, now known as Low's Peak seems to have escaped their notice possibly because the plateau slopes easily up to it and is not as Dramatic as the others, and the Driving sleet and hail that they suffered for two hours while on the summit obscured it. They eventually returned to Kiau and made quickly for the coast with their large collection of plants (St. John, 1862).

5. **1873 : Felice Giordano and party**
    Giordano, who was a well-known Italian geologist, visited the north coast of Borneo on the Italian warship 'Govornolo'. Accompanied by Giocome Bove, a naval officer; Dr Bocca, the ship's doctor; two soldiers named Gelmi and Vauzacchi; Ramasamy, an Indian interpreter and 30 Bajau porters, Giordano set out for Kinabalu from Mengkabong on the 12th April 1873. The objectives of the expedition were to see something of the local people, a study of the vegetation and geology, climb Kinabalu, and to see the legendary lake believed to be south-east of the mountain.

    Their route was through the villages of Tamparuli, Bawang, Sinilau, Kelawat, Bongol, Kaung and Labang to Kiau, which they reached on the 18th April. Two days were lost at Kiau in obtaining guides, but eventually three guides were found for a payment of 110 m (120 yards) of cloth. The party set out for the summit on the 20th April, leaving 15 of the porters at Kiau. A night was spent at a cave, which the altimeter showed to be 2700 m (*c.* 8800 ft). The following day dawned with a thunderstorm which reduced visibility to nil. Progress was impossible and as food was getting short, coupled with the delay at Kiau and the fact that the ship was awaiting their return, they decided to abandon the attempt to reach the summit. They descended to Kiau with great difficulty as the path was slippery and obstructed by fallen boulders and trees. The whole party reached Kiau about midnight, having left the cave at about 8.30 a.m. The return to Mengkabong was fraught with problems, as the Kadamaian river was in full flood and had to be crossed several times, and smallpox had struck the kampungs. Mengkabong was reached on the 27th April (Bove, 1875; Giordano, 1874).

Fig.3. The Ryves expedition in 1939, on the bridle path between Kampong Kaung and Kiau. Sulamain, expedition foreman, leading the porters and Baba, with gun on shoulder, bringing up the rear. *(Photo: V.W. Ryves)*

6. **1877 : F.W. Burbidge and P.C.M. Veitch**
Accompanied by two bird hunters and twenty six men, Burbidge (who, like Thomas Lobb, was a plant collector for Veitch), accompanied by Peter Veitch left Labuan on the 29th November, 1877. They reached Gantissan the next day. They then made for Kiau via Mengkabong, Tamparuli, Bawang, Sinilau, Kelawat, Bungol and Kaung, reaching Kiau on the 6th December. After a day at Kiau, they commenced their ascent accompanied by eight Dusuns and sixteen of their own men.

Rain hampered their climb and the first night was spent beneath a large overhanging rock. The next day they continued upwards to around 2750 m (9000 ft) where a camp was made in a cave. This was not the Paka cave used by previous climbers. The main object of the expedition was to collect plants, and they did not ascend *"beyond the top of the great ridge which leads to the foot of the granite cap"* (Burbidge, 1880). Three days were spent at the cave collecting plants and birds before they returned to Kiau, and then by the same route to Gantissan and Labuan.

7. **1878 : F.W. Burbidge, Mr. Smith and Mr. Boosie**
Burbidge made a second expedition to Kinabalu in August, 1878. He was accompanied by a Mr. Smith who was lent to him by the manager of the Labuan coal mine, and a Mr. Boosie. They started their journey to Kinabalu from Labuan on the 31st July and reached the Tempasuk river on the 6th August. They then made for Kiau, on buffaloes, which they reached in seven days. Delays were caused by the poor path, and heavy water on the river. From Kiau they climbed to the cave that Burbidge had used on his previous expedition, which they reached in two days. This was the 15th August. The 16th and 17th were spent in collecting plants, and on the 18th, they returned to Kiau. The highest point reached was about 3260 m (10,700 ft). Burbidge remarks, *"it must be pointed out, our object was to collect all the plants and seeds we could and not to reach the summit, if our object had been to ascend, nothing would have prevented us doing so"* (Burbidge, 1880). They left Kiau on the 19th, and followed the river down to the coast, which they reached in five days. They then sailed for Labuan reaching the island on August 30th.

8. **1879 : J. Peltzer**
Very little is known of his expedition but it is stated in several publications that this traveller climbed the Marai Parai Peak of the Kinabalu massif (probably Mt. Sadok-Sadok) (Peltzer, 1881).

9. **1887 : John Whitehead**
Whitehead had attempted to visit Kinabalu in 1885 and 1886 but unrest among the people of the district had prevented him from doing so. However on his third attempt he reached the mountain, but did not climb to the summit.

He left Labuan on January 1887 and proceeded towards Kinabalu by buffalo, following the river. At the junction of the Tempasuk and Penataran rivers he continued on foot following the Penataran as far as Kampung Melangkap. He was informed at the kampung that if he followed the river he would be able to ascend to the summit. After a few days he was convinced of the impossibility of this, and a hut was built for him in the forest, where he spent a month collecting. He then returned to Melangkap where a further three weeks were spent in collecting specimens, mainly birds. Some 300 birds were obtained, eighteen of which were new to science, as well as a number of mammals, reptiles and butterflies. He reached Labuan again on the 16th April (Whitehead, 1893).

10. **1887 : R.M. Little**
Little was an Assistant Resident in the service of the British North Borneo Company and his object in visiting the Kinabalu area was to obtain the submission of the district chiefs to the Government, and to establish peace between the coast and hill Dusuns. He had originally planned to accompany Whitehead but circumstances prevented this. His route to Kinabalu from Gaya island was via Menkabong, Tuaran, Sinilau, Bungol, Lobong-Lobong and Kiau. Treaty stones, signifying friendship between the coast and hill Dusuns were planted at Lobong-Lobong and Kiau. Little left Kiau for the mountain on the 9th March. Following the river, he then climbed to Paka cave via Kamborangoh which he reached on the 12th. The following day he and his followers—twelve in all—started for the summit. Little states that he reached the gap between Victoria Peak, and an adjacent peak which the Kiau men climbed. The next peak to the west he described as being St. John's Peak. Whitehead who made the ascent a year later, states that Little only reached Low's Gully and that Little had mistaken this for the summit. This is in all probability true, for Little states that he advanced to the southern rim of the abyss to look into the depths. If he had been on the Summit Plateau, then he would have advanced to the western rim of the abyss. He also states, that the side of Victoria Peak facing the east was at a moderate angle. In fact, the eastern face of Victoria Peak plunges into the abyss (now called Low's Gully). He reached Kiau three days later and there found that one of the guides had brought down Low and St. John's papers, the former in a bottle and the latter in a tin. He was annoyed about this, but does not confess to having arranged for their return, or give details of their disposal (Little, 1887; Whitehead, 1893).

11. **1888 : J. Whitehead**
Whitehead left Labuan for his second visit to Kinabalu in December 1887. He immediately went to Melangkap where he spent two weeks collecting and then on to Kiau. On January the 25th he started for the mountain, spending five days collecting at about 1460 m (4800 ft). On the 31st he moved to Kamborangoh where he stayed until the 3rd March collecting his zoological specimens. He made one excursion to the summit during his stay on the mountain. Leaving Kamborangoh on the 10th February, and sleeping the night at Paka cave, he and four Dusuns and two Kadayans made for the summit the following morning. They reached the spot where Low had left his bottle and then made to the west and onto the Summit Plateau, and up South Peak. From this point, he noted a large pile of loose rocks to his right, which appeared much higher. This he and his party reached, and climbed to the top. This was Low's Peak, which his anaeroid made to be 4122 m (13,525 ft). It is appropriate,

that it was John Whitehead, whose work on Kinabalu and his extensive exploration of the area first showed the mountain's zoological treasures to the world, was the first man recorded to have stood on the highest point of the mountain.

He returned to Kiau on the 5th March and then went to Melangkap where he collected for a further five days. He then returned to Kiau and then spent five weeks in the Pinokok valley. Not content with this, he returned to Melangkap for a further six weeks. He left Melangkap on the 23rd May for the coast, then by boat to Labuan via Gaya island where he arrived on the 30th May, an absence of nearly six months (Whitehead, 1893). His expedition to Kinabalu was described by contemporaries as one of the most successful scientific expeditions of modern times.

12. **1892 : Dr G.D. Haviland and Dr H.A. Haviland**
Dr G.D. Haviland who was Curator of the Sarawak Museum visited Kinabalu in March 1892 accompanied by his cousin Dr H.A. Haviland who was the medical officer in Kuching. The object of the expedition was to collect botanical specimens for the Sarawak Museum and the Kew herbarium. The expedition was successful, for among the plant species collected, 197 were new to science.

The Havilands left Kuching on the 1st March, and arrived at Tuaran on the 11th, having spent five days on Gaya island. They then proceeded towards the mountain reaching Kiau in five days via Bungol and Kaung. They spent five days at the Lobang cave before making for Kamborangoh where they spent the night, and then to Paka cave the following day—the 27th March. On the 28th, they made for the summit, and climbed to the Summit Plateau, reaching *"the top of the sharp northern ridge about its middle, (overlooking) a lofty precipice"* (Stapf, 1894). This was probably Low's Peak. Two hours were spent collecting and they then returned to Kamborangoh. They stayed on the mountain until the 10th April, and returned to Kiau in two days. A further 12 days were spent in the region of the mountain before returning to the coast.

13. **1892 : F.S. Bourns and D.C. Worcester**
Bourns and Worcester are famed for their explorations in the Philippines, but little is known of their visit to Kinabalu which took place during March and April 1892. No published record of their visit had been located by the author. However, bird skins at the Smithsonian Institution in Washington show that they were collected by Bourns and Worcester on Kinabalu in 1892 (Smythies, 1960). The earliest skin is dated the 15th March and the last, the 7th April. The Mountain Blackbird *(Turdus poliocephalus)* and Mountain Blackeye *(Chlorocharis emiliae)* being collected indicates that they did go towards the summit.

14. **1894 : J. Waterstradt**
John Waterstradt was Danish and a professional insect collector who was active in the Malayan region from 1888 to 1912. No written record of his ascent of the mountain has been found but a bottle recording his ascent in 1899 was discovered on

Fig.4. The Kabayu halting bungalow, on a hill side some distance above the Tempasuk River, used on the first stage of the Ryves expedition in 1939, from Kota Belud to Mt. Kinabalu. *(Photo: V.W. Ryves)*

Fig.5. The Kiau halting hut used in 1939 by the Ryves expedition. *(Photo: V.W. Ryves)*

one of the summit peaks in 1910 (Maxwell, 1910). Moulton (1915) was able to find out from the Kiau people, that Waterstradt made three lengthy visits to the mountain, the first about 1894, the second in 1899 when he went to the summit for the first time, and lastly, about 1908. Some birds were also obtained during the 1899 visit and were reported on by Blasius who remarks that they were obtained by Waterstradt on Kinabalu between November 1899 and January 1900.

15. **1899 : R. Hanitsch and P.M. de Fontaine**
Dr Hanitsch was Director of the Raffles Museum in Singapore and visited Kinabalu accompanied by his assistant P.M. de Fontaine for the purpose of obtaining specimens for the museum. They left Singapore on the 4th March 1899, reaching Gaya island on the 11th March. They then headed for the mountain the following day via Tuaran, Bandeian, Kapa, Kelawat, Bungol and Kaung, arriving at Kiau on the 18th March. On the 21st, a start was made on the ascent of Kinabalu, spending the first night under a slanting rock. The following night the Lobang cave was reached. Due to lack of time, it was decided to remain at the cave and collect on the spot instead of attempting a hurried climb of the mountain without any time for collecting. They left Kiau on the 25th March reaching Gaya island on the 9th April, and Singapore on the 14th. A considerable number of zoological specimens were obtained, of which six were new to science (Hanitsch, 1900).

16. **1899 : H.T. Burls**
Mr. Burls was a geologist, who visited North Borneo in order to prospect for oil. His visit to Kinabalu was for geological observations, and he was to have joined the Hanitsch expedition, but an injured knee prevented him doing so. Burls did not reach the Summit Plateau, failing by about 120 m (400 ft). He remarked, that the rock was so steep that it was impossible to walk on it with boots and *"being unprovided with any substitutes, was obliged to give in"* (Burls, 1899). His Chinese servant and four Dusun porters completed the ascent, taking with them the traditional bottle with a note recording the ascent as the 13th April.

17. **1899 : J. Waterstradt**
See No. 14

18. **1904 : G.H. Goss and D. Dodge**
Little is known of the visit of Goss and Dodge to Kinabalu except that they collected birds for the Smithsonian Institution, Washington D.C., who have 47 of the skins, recorded as being obtained on Mt. Kinabalu in "early 1904". A bottle was also found on the summit in 1910 containing the following note (Bunbury, 1910; Moulton, 1915):—

> "Oh what a crime, what a heinous sin,
> To leave you this empty bottle of gin
> But should we e'er meet in New York town
> We'll fill you with fizzy from your heel
> to your crown".

>   Compliments from George H. Goss
>   Manhattan Hotel
>   New York
>   and
>   Douglas Dodge
>   Sinisbury
>   Connecticut.

19. **1908: J. Waterstradt**
See No. 14

20. **1910 (February): Miss L. Gibbs and D. R. Maxwell**
Miss Lilian Gibbs was a botanist from the British Museum who visited Kinabalu for the purpose of collecting botanical specimens. Her visit was very successful for about 1000 plants in all were collected, of which 87 proved new to science. She added 129 species to the Kinabalu list produced by Stapf from the Haviland collections of 1892 (Gibbs, 1914).

Miss Gibbs was not only the first woman recorded to have reached the summit of Mt. Kinabalu but broke new ground in approaching the mountain from the east. She left Jesselton by train for Tenom, and then by bridle path to Keningau, Tambunan, Patau-Patau, Mensanggau, Renogong, Bundu Tuhan, and Kiau. At Kiau, she met Mr. D. R. Maxwell, Assistant District Officer, Kota Belud who had come to meet her, with Mr. Bunbury, the District Officer. Bunbury left the following morning, leaving Maxwell to organise the climb.

Several days were spent collecting on the Gurulau (Kiau) spur and the Marai Parai spur before a start was made on the ascent. Miss Gibbs states that the ascent started on the 22nd February, whereas a bottle containing a record of the ascent found by Moulton in 1913 records the summit being reached on the 20th February. The usual route to the summit was followed via Lobang, Kamborangoh and Paka cave. Low's Peak was reached, and the usual bottle and note left on the summit. The return journey to the coast was made by the Tempasuk route to Kota Belud and then via Tuaran to Jesselton.

21. **1910 (March) : F.W. Foxworthy**
Foxworthy's trip to Kinabalu was, as he put it, *"purely a vacation ramble"* (Foxworthy, 1911). He was therefore Kinabalu's first tourist! Foxworthy visited Sabah from Manila via Palawan and Kudat to Jesselton, thence to Usukan bay and Kota Belud. He then followed the path along the Tempasuk to Kiau accompanied by D. R. Maxwell, who organised the ascent for him at Kiau. The ascent started on the 10th March, and nights were spent at Lobang, Kamborangoh and Paka cave. The summit was reached on the 19th and the usual record placed alongside Miss Gibbs' bottle on Low's Peak. Kiau was reached on the 21st, and Kota Belud on the 24th March.

22. **1910 (June) : Capt. F.C. Learmonth, Lt. Harvey, R.W. Clarke, H.W.L. Bunbury and J. Scott Brown**
    This expedition was undertaken at the request of the British North Borneo Company and its objective was the survey of Mt. Kinabalu by Capt. Learmonth and Lt. Harvey—two naval officers of the Royal Navy survey ship HMS 'Merlin'. The other members of the party were Clarke of the British Borneo Exploration Company, H.W. L. Bunbury, District Officer Tuaran and Scott Brown of the Hepworth Cinematograph Company who made a film recording of the expedition. It is also reported that a bullterrier named Wigson accompanied the expedition, but it is not recorded whether he in fact reached the summit, but he probably did, and therefore has the honour of being the first, and probably the last dog to do so (Bunbury, 1910).

    The party set out from Kota Belud on the 12th June, reaching Kiau on the 15th, Lobang cave was reached on the 16th, and Paka the following day. On the 18th, Learmonth, Harvey and Brown went to the summit to reconnoitre for a new camp, and on the 19th all with the exception of Clarke moved to Sayat-Sayat where a camp was made. The whole party reached the summit on the 20th. Clarke returned to Kiau the following day having suffered from mountain sickness, but the rest remained at Sayat-Sayat for the next five days while the survey was completed. Lt. Harvey, however, spent one night at 3960 m (13,000 ft), just below Low's Peak.

    It was this expedition that fixed the height of Low's Peak at 13,455 ft, and named it so. The plan prepared following the survey, also named the other peaks and gave their heights. Mr. Clarke later wrote an amusing article on the expedition under the pen name of Insaf (1910).

23. **1910 (July) : R. Piltz**
    Dr Piltz was consulting geologist to the British Borneo Exploration Company, but unfortunately left no written account of his expedition to Kinabalu. All that is known is that a bottle containing a note of his name and the date, 27th July, 1910, was found on the summit of Low's Peak (Moulton, 1915).

24. **1911 : Albert Grauber**
    Nothing is known of this man or his expedition. Like that of Piltz, the only record is a note found in a bottle on Low's Peak containing his name, the fact that he came from Munich and the date, June 29th, 1911 (Moulton, 1915).

25. **1913 : J.C. Moulton and P. Skene Keith**
    J.C. Moulton was Curator of the Sarawak Museum and spent six weeks on the mountain collecting specimens of all kinds for the museum. His route was the usual one from Usukan bay and Kota Belud along the Tempasuk valley to Kiau. At Usukan, he was joined by Keith, the Assistant District Officer, Kota Belud who had been deputized to accompany him. Kiau was reached on the 20th August, Paka cave on the 24th and the summit of Low's Peak on the 25th. Keith descended on the 26th leaving Moulton and his collectors on and around the mountain for six weeks.

Several new species of insects and plants were collected (Moulton, 1913a; Moulton, 1913b).

26. **1915 : Joseph and Mary Strong Clemens and D. Le Roy Topping**
Joseph Clemens was a chaplain in the U.S. Army and was stationed in the Philippines from 1905. Mrs. Clemens began to collect botanical specimens in Mindanao in 1905 and gradually acquired considerable botanical knowledge. They both liked living in the wild, and made many travels to collect specimens. D. Le Roy Topping was an American government official in the Philippines, interested especially in ferns. On the 1915 visit, Topping and Mrs. Clemens collected ferns and Joseph Clemens collected orchids.

Several scientific papers were published on the collections describing several new species of ferns and the 155 species of orchids collected, of which 100 were new to science. Unfortunately, no details of travel are given, but it is known that the expedition took place during October–November 1915. Oscar Cook (1924) gives an amusing account of the Clemens' arrival in Tuaran after their visit to the mountain, but no mention is made of Topping.

27. **1916 : Oscar Cook and The Rev. and Mrs. C.E. Swinnerton**
Cook and his friends followed the usual valley route from Kota Belud to Kiau. Leaving Kota Belud on the 13th March, they reached Kiau on the 15th. They then spent nights at Lobang and Paka caves before the ascent was made to the summit on the 18th March, but Cook had to give in some distance above the cave as he was struck down with mountain sickness. The Rev. and Mrs. Swinnerton however made it to the top and deposited the usual bottle with the others on Low's Peak (Cook, 1924).

28. **1916 : George A. Greville Haslam**
Haslam visited Kinabalu in August 1914, having come to North Borneo from the Philippines for the purpose of collecting moths, butterflies and plants. Most of the plant specimens collected were deposited in the herbarium at Manila and were destroyed in 1945. Some others are in Singapore. One orchid collected was named *Dendrochilum haslamii* after him (Holttum, pers. comm. 1975). Haslam journeyed to the mountain from Kota Belud, and was accompanied by Oscar Cook as far as Kiau. No more is known of the visit.

29. **1921 : Rev. J. Strugnell, Dr C.H. Yeager and Barnet**
Little is known of this visit except that it took place in December 1921. Also of interest is the fact that carrier pigeons were taken up the mountain and released at intervals giving details of the whereabouts of the party. The record for a flight between the mountain and police headquarters was two hours (Anon., 1948).

Fig.7. Members of the 1939 Ryves expedition fording the Kadamaian in flood, between Kaung and Kiau. *(Photo: V.W. Ryves)*

climbed to Tenompok and followed the new route cut in 1923 to Paka, and then to the summit. The round trip from Kota Belud took ten days (Boden-Kloss, 1931).

36. **1929 : H.M. Pendlebury and F.N. Chasen**
    Pendlebury was Systematic Entomologist, Federated Malay States Museums, and Chasen was Curator of the Raffles Museum, Straits Settlements. They visited the mountain mainly for the purpose of collecting invertebrate animals, of which little was known. They arrived in Kiau on the 18th March, and then climbed via the new route to the summit which they reached on the 21st. They remained on and around the mountain until the 13th May when they started their return to Kota Belud. Many papers were published on the collections made, and a large number of new species of insects, etc. were described (Pendlebury & Chasen, 1932).

37. **1931 : Rev. Joseph Clemens and Mary Strong Clemens**
    Joseph Clemens retired from his chaplaincy in the U.S. Army around 1925 whereupon he and his wife became professional plant collectors. They had visited Kinabalu previously—in 1915—and returned in 1931 under the sponsorship of the British Museum to whom they gave the first set of specimens collected.

The Clemens spent most of 1931–1933 around Kinabalu with one visit to Bogor, Java in 1932. In 1931 they built themselves a house at Tenompok out of local timber, or rather it was built for them by Walter Gill, a nephew of Mr. Clemens who had been a lumberman in America. The Clemens' visit had stirred some interest in North Borneo, and the Rev. Joseph Clemens reported regularly on their travels in the British North Borneo Herald in 1932 and 1933.

The Clemens and Gill climbed Kinabalu in January 1932 reaching the summit in three days from Tenompok. Joseph Clemens, although over 70 years of age, was an accomplished rock climber and as well as climbing Low's Peak, also scaled Victoria and St. John's Peaks. A night was also spent on the summit. The remarkable plant collection of thousands of specimens made by the Clemens, are still being studied to this day.

38. **1931 : R.E. Holttum and Rev. Joseph Clemens**
R.E. Holttum, who later became Director of the Singapore Botanic Gardens, and an authority on Malaysian botany, visited Kinabalu between the 4th and 25th November 1931, with the object of studying the ferns of the mountain. During his stay, he climbed to the summit with Joseph Clemens by the Tenompok route, and also stayed with the Clemens for a few days in their log cabin (Holttum, pers. comm. 1975). A large number of new species of ferns were collected and later described by Holttum.

39. **1932 : Rev. Joseph and Mrs. Clemens, Rev. J.W. Rowland and Master N.W. Rowland**
The Rev. Rowland and his son Niels aged 12 years, visited the Clemens at Tenompok in May 1932. On the 30th May, accompanied by the Clemens, they made for the summit via Kamborangoh and Paka cave. The summit was reached on the 1st July. The Rowlands then came down the mountain, leaving the Clemens on the Summit Plateau where they spent the night (Clemens, 1932c).

40. **1932 : G.W. A. Bullock and G. Farelly**
Nothing futher is known of this climb which was made in October, (Anon., 1933c).

41. **1933 : His Excellency Mr. A.F. Richards, R.F. Evans, D. Round-Turner and B.W. Hurrell**
His Excellency A.F. Richards, the Governor of North Borneo, reached Bundu Tuhan on the 28th January having completed a tour of the Interior. There, he was met by Evans, Round-Turner and Hurrell. On the 30th January, they left for the mountain and reached the summit on the 1st February having stayed the nights at Kamborangoh and Paka cave. On the summit a bottle of champagne was broached, and the bottle put to good use as the receptacle for the traditional notes (Anon., 1933a). This was Evans' third climb of the mountain, having first climbed it in 1924.

42. **1933 : C.E. Carr**
Carr spent the months of March to August 1933 on Kinabalu collecting orchids for the Botanic Gardens, Singapore. In the six months spent on the mountain, Carr collected flowering specimens of approximately 700 species. It is not known whether Carr made the ascent to the summit, but his paper on the species shows that collections were made as high as Paka cave (Carr, 1935).

Fig.8. Cedric E. Carr *(Photo: R.E. Holttum)*

43. **1937 : John A. Griswold**
John Griswold was a member of the Asiatic Primate Expedition which visited Thailand and Borneo in 1937. Griswold was a research associate of the Museum of Comparative Zoology at Harvard and spent the period June 7th to August 20th 1937 collecting birds and mammals on Mt. Kinabalu. He set up collecting camps at Bundu Tuhan, Lumu-Lumu, Paka cave and Sayat-Sayat. He also made one ascent to the summit of Low's Peak (Griswold, 1939). Some 93 different bird species were collected and later described.

44. **1937 : E. Wenk**
Wenk was a geologist with the British Borneo Geological Survey Department and visited Kinabalu sometime in 1937 (Jacobson, 1970).

45. **1939 : Vivian W. Ryves**
Ryves, who was a retired rubber planter from Malaya, spent six weeks in Kiau during February and March 1939 collecting birds' eggs. During this period he climbed to the summit, spending four days at Paka cave. The collection was presented to the Raffles Museum, Singapore and later described by Gibson-Hill (1950) and Ryves (1957).

WAR YEARS: JAPANESE VISITS

46. **1942 : Lt. Ryuichi Yamaguchi**
In early May 1942, fifteen Japanese soldiers stationed in Jesselton led by Lt. Yamaguchi climbed the mountain. Their route was via Kota Belud to Ranau along the Tempasuk valley. They then returned to Bundu Tuhan and climbed to the summit with the assistance of ten porters. The round trip from Bundu Tuhan took five days (Honma, pers. comm.).

47. **1942 : Tokayuki Kobashi**
In June 1942, three soldiers led by Sergeant Kobashi of the Beaufort Defence Force climbed to the summit from Bundu Tuhan. Their route to the mountain was from Beaufort to Melalap by train, thence by car to Keningau. At Keningau eight ponies were hired and they proceeded to Ranau via Apin-Apin, Kitau, Tambunan and Patau. From Ranau they made for Bundu Tuhan having visited the hot springs at Poring. Five porters assisted in the climb which was accomplished in five days. They returned to Beaufort by the same route in seven days (Honma, pers. comm.).

48. **1943 : Lt. Kaoru Kobashi and party**
In June, 1943, the publicity team of Japanese Forces 37th Headquarters at Kuching climbed the mountain for the purpose of making a documentary film and to undertake some research work. The team was as follows: Lt. Kobashi, leader; Mr. Miyamura, botanist; Dr Nakamura, surgeon; Dr Yuihuchi, physiologist; Mr. Kurosawa, mineralogist; Mr. Ichikawa, zoologist; Mr. Ogasahara, meteorologist; Mr. Saito, photographer; Mr. Fujinami and Mr. Tsuneyoshi, film directors; a wireless operator, an interpreter and ten soldiers. A guide, Lapun, and a number of porters were recruited.

The route was along the usual path from Kota Belud to Kiau and thence to Bundu Tuhan. They then climbed to Kamborangoh where they stayed the night, and then to Paka cave for the next night. The following day, the 24th June, they climbed to the summit and returned to the cave. As the weather was fine, they moved camp to Sayat-Sayat where they stayed until the 2nd July. During the stay at Sayat-Sayat, Victoria Peak, AlexanDra Peak, St. John's Peak, King Edward's Peak and Gully Peak were climbed.

They then proceeded to Ranau and Poring Hot Springs and returned to Jesselton along the same route via Kota Belud. A 35-mm 8-reel black-and-white documentary film of one and a half hours' duration was produced during the visit and appropriately entitled "Mount Kinabalu". The film is presently housed at the film library of the National Modern Museum in Tokyo (Honma, pers. comm.).

POST-WAR VISITS

Post war ascents were mainly of an adventurous holiday nature and were all by the Tenompok route. They are of no great significance except that they indicate the increasing interest in Kinabalu as a recreational area. The visits will not be described in detail.

49. **Pre-1948 : Major Sparks**
    Major "Sparks" is probably a misprint for Major Marks, a Gurkha Officer known to have had an interest in Kinabalu. Details not known—see next expedition.

50. **1948 : Capt. J.W. Walne, B. Arrowsmith and R. McLean**
    Capt. Walne was Adjutant of the North Borneo Armed Constabulary, Arrowsmith was at the Jesselton Treasury, and McLean was District Officer, Kota Belud. Walne and Arrowsmith left Tamparuli on the 8th March, and were joined by McLean at Bundu Tuhan. The ascent to the summit started on the 9th, and they returned to Tamparuli on the 12th. They claimed the record for the trip as being five days, 12 hours and 27 minutes! This, so it was claimed, beat the previous record set by Major Sparks of the 4/2 Gurkha Rifles of nine days (Anon., 1948a).

51. **1948 : Beresford Pierce, D.S.H. Reddish and Ujin**
    The climb was undertaken in October 1948. No great details of the climb were given in the newspaper report of November, 1948 (Anon., 1948b). Ujin was the Native Chief of Tuaran where Beresford Pierce was District Officer.

52. **1950 (March): Dicky Wyile and Dorothy Lane**
    Dicky Wyile was married to a medical officer in Jesselton (Kota Kinabalu) and Dorothy Lane was a secretary working there. No further details are known except that a bottle containing their names was found on the summit in 1950 (Anon., 1950; George, pers. comm.).

53. **1950 : Messrs. Lawes, Balantine and Tuxford**
    This party consisted of three planters from Beaufort. A newspaper article of May 1950 reports their climb as "recent". They also recorded a Japanese record and the note left by Wyile and Lane. There is also mention of traces of other expeditions with paint marks on the summit rocks (Anon., 1950; George, pers. comm.).

LOGISTICS

The greatest problem that the early expeditions experienced in visiting Kinabalu was not the actual climb to the summit, but in the logistics involved in getting the expedition plus baggage to the foot of the mountain. The recruitment of a sufficient number of porters was always difficult as porters only contracted to carry the baggage for a certain stage of the journey. Obtaining an equal number for the next stage was a daunting experience and much bargaining took place with each group recruited.

The journey was also hazardous in the early days, as a bridle path from the coast to Kampung Kiau had not been cut. The route followed indistinct paths from village to village which crossed the swift flowing Tempasuk river at least 40 times—not a pleasant experience if the river was at all high. Guides had also to be recruited for each stage, with no guarantee that they actually knew the way!

The amount of baggage taken by each expedition added to the problems, for the amounts were phenomenal. Low on his first visit required at least 42 porters. On his second visit with St. John, only 30 could be recruited at first, and some baggage had to be sent for later. Eventually, 50 porters were employed. Whitehead—who it must be admitted did spend a considerable time on the mountain—hired 22 buffaloes on one occasion.

The prize however goes to the Learmonth expedition of 1910, who left Kota Belud for Kiau with over one hunDred porters. At Kiau, fifteen of these were sent ahead to Paka cave on the day before the ascent with advance stores, to be followed the next day by the party and ninety more porters! This is an enormous number of men considering that the official party only number five plus a dog and only ten days were spent on the mountain. On the other hand, the number is not surprising when it is learnt that all modern comforts in the way of beds, mattresses, chairs, etc. were carried up the mountain!

Eventually, the bridle path was opened, and small government rest houses were built in villages along the Tempasuk. The District Officer could also be relied upon to organise buffaloes, and pack horses and ponies for the visitors.

CEREMONIES

Over the years that climbs of Kinabalu have been made, various authors have described the religious ceremonies that have been performed by the guide involved. These ceremonies became more complex as the years went on.

Low, on his first visit makes no mention of religious ceremonies except that the guide was armed with a bundle of charms consisting of curious knots of wood, pieces of crystal, human and other teeth, etc., in all weighing about 3 Kampung St. John also records the bundle of charms and the duty that fell upon the guide " ... *of praying or repeating some forms"*. He attempted to find out what it was all about as he heard his name repeated several times and gathered that the spirit of the mountain was being solicited to favour the visit.

Little was the first to record that the guide brought up a white fowl and *"... a few paltry brass goods intended as propitiatory offerings to the spirits on Kinabalu"*. He notes no ceremony except that before the ascent was started the fowl was hurriedly sacrificed and the brass-ware left on the summit of South Peak.

By Whitehead's second visit to the mountain in 1888 a ceremony had been evolved, which has apparently not been repeated since. Whitehead relates that the guide brought a chicken with him to Paka cave, *"... the bird seems half dead with cold. As yet I do not understand his reason for doing this. Tonight (10th February) he has had a religious fit, and has remained in a kneeling position muttering Dusun prayers to the spirits and Dragons of the mountain. I hear my name mentioned occasionally, and my men who understand a little Dusun say that he is telling these mythical worthies that we have come only to see their home, and do not intend doing any harm. I am in bed, or rather lying at the further end of the cave on green boughs; presently a few Drops of cold water fall on my face; I imagine that it is Dripping from the roof of the rock above but after another and yet another dose, I discover that the water comes from the direction of the prayer-muttering Kuro (guide) who is baptising us indiscriminately."*

No other ceremony is described until the descent, when at about Sayat-Sayat, all are asked to sit by the guide. He stands upright with the *"miserable cockerel under his left arm, the bird's tail to the front"*. Then he prays, and "Tuan Burong"—Whitehead's Malay name, is mentioned several times and at about half-minute intervals feathers are jerked out of the cockerel's tail which are planted upright in a small crevice in the rock. They then descend to Paka cave where Whitehead was offered the cockerel to eat. He declined, so the guide killed it and it was eaten by the rest of the party.

By the time Maxwell and Miss Gibbs' visited Kinabalu in 1910, seven eggs had been introduced into the performance at Paka cave—these were left for the spirits, the usual prayers said, the fowl sacrificed and eaten by the party. It was also necessary on the ascent to fire a shot and pray at Sayat-Sayat and then fire two more shots—*"To announce that Tuan is coming up"*. On the descent, there were more prayers, and a final shot.

Moulton (1913) only records the prayers and shots at about Panar Laban, but Evans & Sarel (1924) record that seven fowl and seven eggs were sacrificed—the fowls were eaten—and that prayers were said at Lumu-Lumu, Paka, Sayat-Sayat and at the pool on the summit; shots were fired twice at Sayat-Sayat, three times on the summit and once before the final descent. The same basic format was witnessed by Pendlebury and Chasen.

Griswold in 1937 recalls a ceremony at Kamborangoh which he missed and another at the summit pool. At the pool, bundles of flowers were arranged and the men stood around in a circle, two eggs were placed on the rock with some tobacco, rice and betel nut. The priest then started a chant after arranging an enormous bundle of charms—which, from its description, is the same one described by Low over 80 years previously.

In post-war years, the sacrifice of fowls and offering of eggs continued for some time. Eventually the exclusive use of white fowls for the sacrifice was not a necessity—no doubt the increasing number of visitors in the late 1950's and 60's proved to be too great a strain on local stocks. The offering of eggs and prayers continued until 1966 when the chief guide Gunting bin Lagadan B.E.M. of Bundu Tuhan died. Modern guides still carry out a sacrificial ceremony once a year.

Why then the need for ceremonies? The Dusuns-Kadazans of the early years of the exploration of Kinabalu were pagans, and offerings had to be made to the spirits of the mountain, for most objects had a spirit or *'hantu'*. It is of course well known that most pagan Dusuns regarded Kinabalu as the resting place of the spirits of their ancestors, and the author believes that there is no way in which Dusuns who believed so, could have been enticed to such an awesome place.

Nevertheless, the Dusuns of Kampung Kiau and Kampung Bundu Tuhan climbed the mountain quite willingly, provided they were paid the rate for the job. The author was fortunate some years ago to meet Tingoh bin Sompot aged about 90 years—who was in fact one of the guides on the Maxwell/Gibbs expedition. On being asked whether he and his people were afraid to climb Kinabalu because of the spirits that rested there he replied with an emphatic "NO" because as he explained, the spirits of the dead of Kampung Kiau rested on the summit of Mt. Sadok-Sadok and not on Kinabalu.

Therein perhaps lies the answer. More than one writer remarks that the porters took no notice whatsoever of the ceremonies and just stood around talking while the guide did the necessary. The fowls and the eggs of course had to be paid for by the expedition, with the fowls being conveniently eaten by the guides and porters. As the Dusuns of Kiau and Bundu Tuhan existed by trading their produce with the people of the lowlands—and indeed still do, it is conceivable, that with the realisation that visitors to Kinabalu were gullible enough to pay for their produce while they retained the right to eat it, that the ceremonies became more complex and more fowls were required as the years went on. The Dusun guides were perhaps exhibiting their excellent qualities as enterpreneurs? The eggs of course were necessary to appease the spirit of the mountain, and not the 'spirits' that dwelt thereon.

REFERENCES

Anon. 1892a. Newspaper report on the Haviland expedition. *British North Borneo Herald* 10(4): 112, 1st April, 1892.

Anon. 1892b. Newspaper report on the Haviland expedition. *British North Borneo Herald* 10(7): 216, 1st July 1892.

Anon. 1899. A Trip to Mount Kinabalu: *British North Borneo Herald:* 225–226, 5th July 1899.

Anon. 1932a. An ascent of Mt. Kinabalu by Mr. and Mr.s. Joseph Clemens. *British North Borneo Herald* 50(4): 40.

Anon. 1932b. Mount Kinabalu: a lecture by Rev. Joseph Clemens. *British North Borneo Herald* 50(8): 77.

Anon. 1933a. H.E. the Governor's Ascent of Mount Kinabalu. *British North Borneo Herald* 51(5): 46.

Anon. 1933b. Mount Kinabalu—list of ascents. *British North Borneo Herald* 51(6): 52.

Anon. 1933c. Mount Kinabalu. *British North Borneo Herald* 51(18): 158.

Anon. 1948a. Newspaper report. *North Borneo News* 1(5): 7, 1st May 1948.

Anon. 1948b. Newspaper report. *North Borneo News* 1(18): 14 and 16, 16th Nov. 1948.

Anon. 1950. Newspaper report. *North Borneo News* 3(6): 18, 16th May 1950.

Blasius, W. 1901. *Vogel vom Kina-Balu (British Nord Borneo). Journal für Ornithologie* 1901: 68–69.

Boden-Kloss, C. 1931. Mount Kinabalu: A note. *Journal of the Federated Malay States Museum* 16: 286.

Bove, F. 1875. *Note di un Viaggio a Borneo. Cosmos di Guido Cora* 3: 41–54 ; 267–272; 291–297.

Bunbury, H.W.L. 1910. The ascent of Mount Kinabalu. *British North Borneo Herald*: 157–158, 1st September 1910.

Burbidge, F.W. 1880. The Gardens of the Sun. John Murray, London.

Burls, N.T. 1899. Observations on Mount Kinabalu. *Geological Journal* 14: 207–208.

Carr, C.E. 1935. Two collections of orchids from British North Borneo. Part. 1. *Gardens' Bulletin, Straits Settlements* 13(3): 165–240.

Christensen, C. & Holttum, R.E. 1934. The Ferns of Mt. Kinabalu. *Gardens Bulletin Straits Settlements* 8(3): 191–324.

Clemens, J. 1932a. Dallas News. *British North Borneo Herald* 50(1): 3–4.

Clemens, J. 1932b. Kinabalu News. *British North Borneo Herald* 50(10): 100–101.

Clemens, J. 1932c. The cleft mountain. *British North Borneo Herald* 50(14): 143–144.

Clemens, J. 1933a. Mount Kinabalu: a naturalist's description. *British North Borneo Herald* 51(1): 7.

Clemens, J. 1933b. Kinabalu notes. *British North Borneo Herald* 51(5): 48–49.

Clemens, J. 1933c. Kinabalu notes. *British North Borneo Herald* 51(13): 119.

Clemens, J. 1933d. Mount Kinabalu News. *British North Borneo Herald* 51(20): 186.

Clemens, J. 1933e. Mount Kinabalu: The roaring falls of Pinokok. *British North Borneo Herald* 51(23).

Cook, O. 1924. Borneo: The Stealer of Hearts. Hurst & Blackett, London.

Coolidge, H.J. 1940. Mammals and Birds collection of the Asiatic Primate Expedition—Introduction. *Bulletin Museum Comparative Zoology, Harvard.* 87: 121–130.

Evans, R.F. & Sarel, C.R. 1924. Mount Kinabalu. Ascent by Mr. Evans and Mr. Sarel in April. *British North Borneo Herald:* 179–180, 16th October 1924.

Enriquez, C.M. 1927. Kinabalu, The Haunted Mountain of Borneo. H.F. & G. Witherby, London.

Foxworthy, F.W. 1911. A vacation trip to Mount Kinabalu in British North Borneo. *Sierra Club Bulletin* 8 (1): 18–24.

Giordano, G. 1874. *Un esplorazione in Borneo. Bolletino della Societa Geographica Italiana.*

Gibbs, L.S. 1914. A Contribution to the Flora and Plant Formations of Mount Kinabalu and the Highlands of British North Borneo. *Journal of the Linnean Society, London, Botany* 42: 1–240.

Gibson-Hill. 1950. A Collection of Birds' Eggs from North Borneo. *Bulletin of the Raffles Museum, Singapore* 21: 106–115.

Griswold, J.A. 1939. Up Mount Kinabalu. *Scientific Monthly* 116: 401–414; 504–518, New York.

Hanitsch, R. 1900. An expedition to Mount Kinabalu, British North Borneo. *Journal of the Straits Branch Royal Asiatic Society* 34: 49–88.

Holttum, R.E. 1933. Ascent of Mount Kinabalu. *British North Borneo Herald* 50(1): 3.

Insaf. 1910. An unofficial account of an ascent of Kinabalu. *British North Borneo Herald:* 146–148, August 16th.

Jacobson, G. 1970. Gunong Kinabalu area, Sabah, Malaysia. Geological Survey Malaysia, Report 8 (Sarawak & Sabah series).

Jenkins, D.V. 1971. The first ascent of Mount Kinabalu. *Malayan Nature Journal* 24(3): 190–191.

Little, R.M. 1887. Report on a Journey from Tuaran to Kiau and an ascent of Kinabalu Mountain. *British North Borneo Herald* 5(7): 149–159, 1st July 1887.

Low, H. 1852. Notes of an ascent of the mountain Kina-Balow. *Journal of the Indian Archipelago* 6: 1–17.

Maxwell, D.R. 1910. Ascent of Mount Kinabalu. *British North Borneo Herald:* 65–67, April 1st, 1910.

Moulton, J.C. 1913a. A collecting expedition to Mt. Kinabalu. *The Sarawak Gazette.* November 1st, 1913: 248–250.

Moulton, J.C. 1913b : A collecting expedition to Mt. Kinabalu. *The Sarawak Gazette.* November 17th, 1913: 262–264.

Moulton, J.C. 1915. An account of the various expeditions to Mt. Kinabalu. *Sarawak Museum Journal* 6: 137–176.

Peltzer, J. 1881. 'Borneo'. *Bulletin de la Societe Belge de Geographic.*

Pendlebury, H.M. & Chasen, B.E. 1932. A zoological expedition to Mt. Kinabalu, British North Borneo (1929). *Journal of the Federated Malay States Museum* 17: 1–38.

Rutter, O. 1923. The Dragon of Kinabalu. Clement Ingleby, London.

Ryves, V. 1957. Nesting of Kinabalu Blackbird 1. *Sarawak Museum Journal* 8: 10 (25, old series): 250.

Ryves, V. 1958. Kinabalu, the sacred mountain of British North Borneo. Unpublished manuscript.

Smythies, B.E. 1960. The Birds of Borneo. Oliver and Boyd, Edinburgh.

Stapf, O. 1894. On the Flora of Mount Kinabalu in North Borneo. *Transactions of the Linnean Society, London, Botany* 4: 69–263.

St. John, Spenser. 1862. Life in the Forests of the Far East. Vol. 1. Smith Elder & Co., London.

Veitch, Harry J. 1897. Nepenthes. *Journal of the Royal Horticultural Society* 21(2).

Whitehead, J. 1893. The Exploration of Kina Balu, North Borneo. Gurney & Jackson, London.

Fig.1. View towards Low's Peak looking into Commando Cauldron from the bottom of Easy Valley. *(Photo: Robert New)*

CLIMBING MOUNT KINABALU

Robert New

Mount Kinabalu, being so much higher than surrounding terrain, and the highest mountain between the Himalayas and the Snow Mountains of Irian Jaya, has always attracted much interest. References to it can be found in the earliest of writings and in folk lore. The rigours of traditional life around the mountain precluded exploration above the natural hunting areas by local people. It was only by way of great endeavour and personal risk by individuals, or by organised expeditions, that the mountain became more fully explored.

The early accounts of exploration of the mountain have largely been confined to conquering the summit by the easiest available route; itself no mean feat at the time. During the post-war years, with improved road access to the base of the mountain, the numbers of attempted ascents have increased unabated every year since 1945. Reliable statistics are only available since the setting up of the Kinabalu Park but the following table illustrates the point:

Year	No. of Climbers	Year	No. of Climbers
1965	700	1980	4193
1966	959	1981	6045
1967	1298	1982	10,378
1968	1623	1983	12,492
1969	1581	1984	10,932
1970	1962	1985	14,485
1971	2074	1986	15,842
1972	1379	1987	18,444
1973	1728	1988	14,344
1974	2026	1989	16,548
1975	2126	1990	21,328
1976	2339	1991	24,209
1977	2459	1992	24,303
1978	3231	1993	28,134
1979	3065	1994	29,574

By far the majority of these climbers are local residents, motivated mainly by pride in Kinabalu as an outstanding local landmark and the personal desire to make the conquest. Accordingly, these visitors use the easiest available route and only a handful of special-interest parties; botanists, geologists, photographers or fully fledged mountaineers, attempt any alternative routes on the mountain.

KINABALU—*Summit of Borneo*

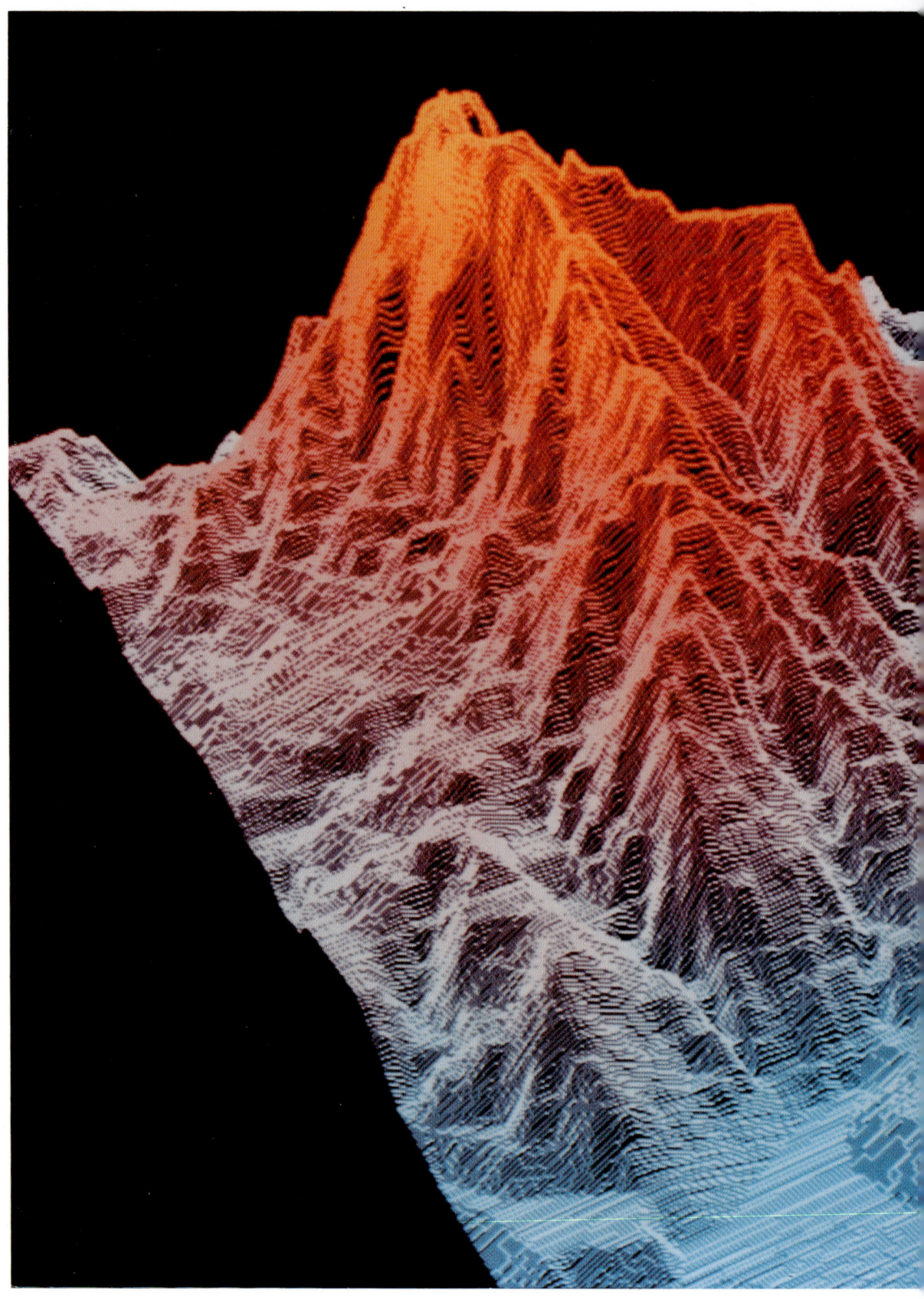

Fig.2. Digital elevation model (DEM) of the east side of Mt. Kinabalu. Colours are scaled from blue to red and represent elevation. Model is exaggerated 3X in the vertical. *Copyright © Reed Beaman.*

KINABALU—Summit of Borneo

Fig.3. Handholds and ropes now assist climbers on the rockface. *(Photo: C.L. Chan)*

Fig.4. A dawn assault. Climbers on the final approach to the summit of Low's Peak. *(Photo: Robert New)*

Only official scientific expeditions tend to be written up properly, so many "first" ascents remain unrecorded. Moreover, many climbers have lacked an overall knowledge of the geography of the mountain due to poor weather and inadequate maps which can result in misleading claims. In particular, Low's Gully has frequently caused confusion. Several parties have abseiled into Commando Cauldron, which is the dramatic cleft between the Donkey's Ears to the west and Tunku Abdul Rahman Peak to the east which lies above Sayat-Sayat Hut, and climbed a first descent into Low's Gully. One party, at great effort, abseiled off the west cliffs below King George Peak into Easy Valley and laboriously climbed their ropes back out again. Little did they know that the point they reached is but an easy walk to the col between Tunku Abdul Rahman Peak and the Lion's Head and thence diagonally down to Sayat-Sayat Hut.

This lack of systematic information may add to the mystique of the mountain, but improved route information will enable future visitors to plan more worthwhile expeditions within their ability. More really skilled climbers might also be tempted to explore the many untamed rock faces. Such climbers have spurned Kinabalu in the past, partly because the larger mountain ranges beckon so strongly, but also because the standard route suggests to the uninformed that this is an easy mountain. Never underrate Mt. Kinabalu, for beyond the standard route lie many challenges and a whole unique world to wonder at and enjoy.

APPROACH ROUTES

These are routes by which the mountain can be climbed to the summit area be it the western or eastern plateau areas. Study of available maps shows that gradients only become steep above about 2500 m, so that anywhere below this level is reasonably accessible, subject of course to the problems of dense vegetation. Above this 2500 m level the terrain becomes increasingly precipitous with the exception of a few lines of weakness, the most obvious of which have now been exploited.

To identify these principle lines of weakness it is convenient to visualise the summit area like a horseshoe pointing northwards. The most commanding feature of the mountain is Low's Gully which descends steeply northwards between the points. The right-hand point leads off along the north ridge, which is the only obvious line of weakness for an approach route which has yet to be achieved. Several attempts at this ridge have been made by British Army parties and by Mrs. Sheila Collenette in the 1960's but this ridge penetrates probably the least developed sector of the lower mountain so that access is difficult. Water problems have also been reported.

Leading off from the base of the right-hand point is the east ridge which has been successfully climbed from Poring Hot Springs. The left-hand point of our horseshoe is more broken and forms into a steep valley with rocky peaks along either side, Victoria and No Name Peak to the east and Alexandra and Dewali Pinnacles to the west. This valley provides a line of weakness to the peak area from the north-east. Running southwards

KINABALU—Summit of Borneo

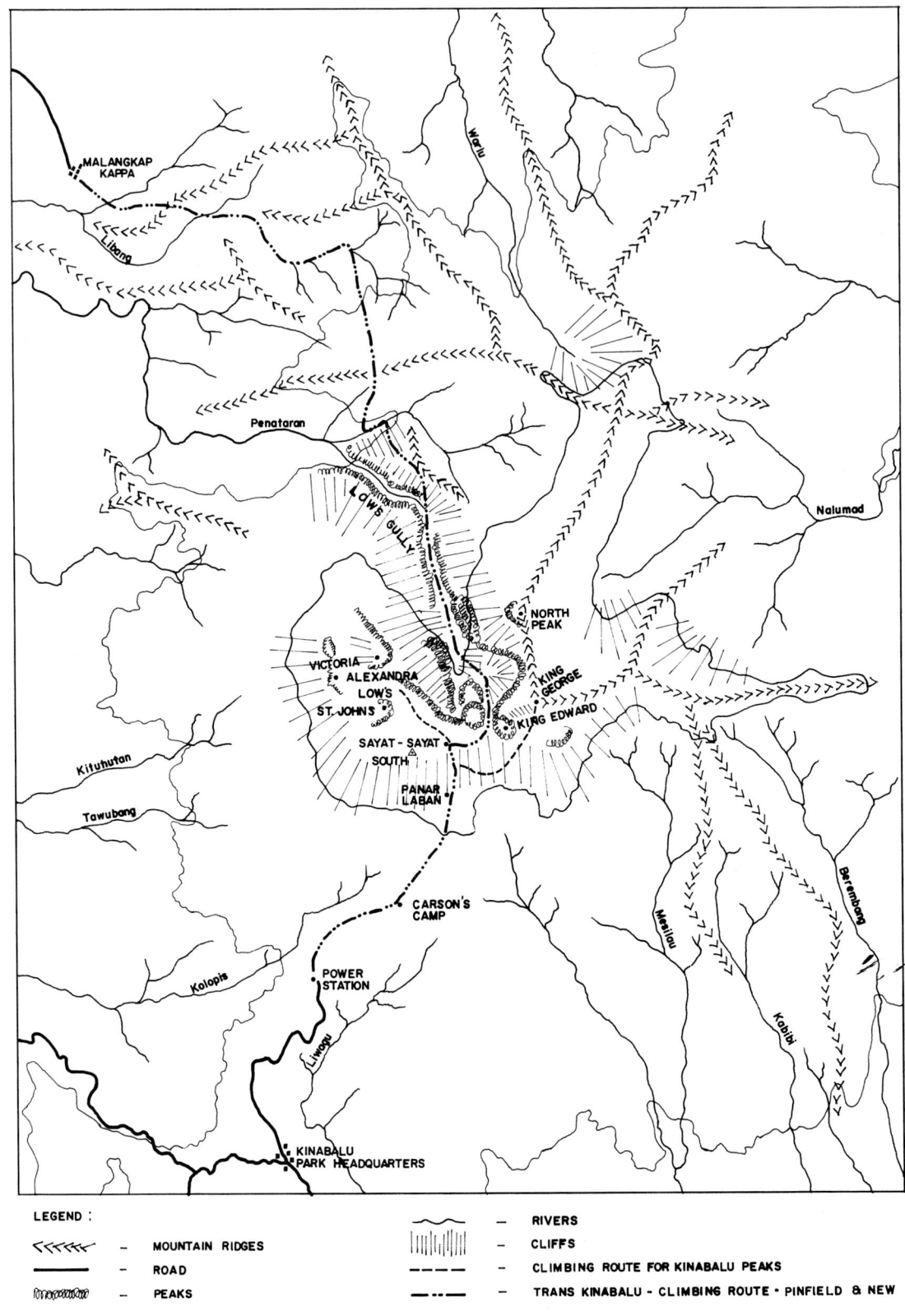

Fig.5. Mt. Kinabalu.

Fig.6. Paka Cave. *(Photo: Albert Teo)*

from the base of the horseshoe is the south ridge which offers the gentlest gradients and which provides the route for the standard trail of today.

The notes below provide basic background on the various approach routes explored and documented to date, commencing with the standard route and working clockwise around the mountain.

SOUTH RIDGE ROUTE (Standard Route)

Hugh Low, 1851 (from Kampung Kiau)
R.F. Evans and C.R. Sarel, 1924 (from Tenompok Pass)
This was formerly called the Paka Route and follows the south ridge which forms the watershed between the Kadamaian river to the west and the Liwagu river to the east. Early ascents were made from Kampung Kiau of which there were at least two variations. Just where these routes climbed on to the main ridge we are not sure but probably around the 2500-m mark a little above Kamborangoh.

A bridle path was developed in the early 1900's from the west coast to Ranau and its route over the Tenompok Pass provided easy access to a higher altitude than Kampung Kiau and a natural route up the South Ridge avoiding the awkwardly steep trail from Kiau to Kamborangoh. This in fact is the route used today.

Over the last ten years the number of climbers on this route has multiplied tremendously and it has become necessary to provide a safe trail to minimise accidents. The route is strenuous and sustained but not in any way difficult. Much of the route is a series of staircases with hand rails in steep sections and fixed ropes over sections. The upper summit area is heavily cairned to avoid losing the way in bad weather and ropes have now been fixed along this section following the recent disappearance of two climbers.

Huts along the route provide accommodation at approximately 2700 m (Layang-Layang staff quarters, formerly Carson's Camp) and 3670 m (Sayat-Sayat), but it has now become normal to use the accommodation around 3300 m at Panar Laban which is the most comfortable and able to accommodate large numbers. Although the record time for the climb from the road head to the summit and back is only 2 hours 20 minutes, it is normal to spend one night at Panar Laban making the ascent to the summit and down on the second day. Most climbers find this second day quite demanding because of the early start in the dark and the long descent. It is recommended for a more pleasurable climb, giving time to take in the beautiful scenery and flora, to spend two nights at Panar Laban so that the climb to the summit on the second day can take place in daylight. Data on this route is given in an Appendix.

The Park Authorities are presently developing a new alternative mountain centre to the existing park headquarters just above the Kinabalu Golf Club beside the Mesilau River. In conjuction with this project, a new trail has been cut from the new Mesilau Lodge site to join the south ridge a short distance above Layang-Layang. The trail is yet to be opened to the public but it is described as easy, though overall probably a little steeper than the existing trail below Layang-Layang. The climbing time is estimated to be no different than the standard trail.

MARAI PARAI ROUTE

Stephen Pinfield, Robert New and Ansow Gunsalam, 1987

Marai Parai is a delightful meadow on a small sloping plateau at a little over 1500 m, on the north-west side of Kinabalu. The first recorded visit was in 1858 by Spenser St. John and Hugh Low and the location is particularly known as one of the few sites for the magnificent *Nepenthes rajah*. Subsequent visits have almost exclusively been of a botanical nature and it was only very recently that a way to the summit via Marai Parai was found. Permission from the Park authorities is required to use this route.

The route starts from the road head at Kampung Kiau and traverses northwards along the flank of the mountain following well-used local paths. The trail is strenuous as it climbs and descends over a series of ridges and involves four river crossings. After the last crossing the path is taken up a prominent ridge line until the vegetation opens out to the grassy area of Marai Parai.

The trail continues up the ridge and peters out a little beyond another clearing. From here it is necessary to forge a route through the dense mossy forest upwards and to the left, the target being a prominent ramp which rises up and left to the north-west corner of the mountain. On the only occasion that this route has been travelled, a bivouac for the night was made in this area of mossy forest.

When the ramp is eventually reached it is followed to its upper limit. A rocky gully leads down to the north from this point for about 12 m (40 ft) from where it is possible to gain access to slabs on the right beneath the towering rock buttresses of the mountain. These slabs provide easy friction climbing which, if followed upwards and to the right, lead naturally into the valley below the West Cwm from where it is an easy walk and scramble to the West Gurkha Hut and the summit peaks. Under present conditions, two days are required for this route but, if a trail is ever cut through the mossy forest on the north-west mountain slopes, the route could certainly be accomplished in one day by a fit party setting out at dawn.

PENATARAN ROUTE

Eric Wong Hon Fui, Alim Biun, Benedict Gangku and Langa bin Langkuan, 1988 (to East Plateau via North Peak)

The classic line for this route is to follow the bed of Penataran river up into Low's Gully from where it has always been hoped a route could be found up into Easy Valley and thereby gain access to the summit area. Many attempts have been made to achieve this route from the north with the earliest recorded being by an R.A.F. Mountain Rescue Team from Hongkong in 1957. Mrs. Sheila Collenette made an attempt in 1959 and British Army expeditions made further attempts in 1983 and 1988.

The problem with this route is that the river mainly follows a confined bed set within a gorge with sheer rock sides. The bed is strewn with large boulders. In wet weather the volume of water makes travel along the river impossible and in dry weather the boulders pose endless and strenuous technical climbing problems. The adjoining ridges are difficult to attain because of the steepness of the terrain and dense vegetation and the ridge lines suffer from a lack of water sources, vital for such a long expedition.

The scenery is dramatic in places and a major risk is to be threatened by flash floods, which are frequent. This river responds quickly to rainfall in the summit area because of its steep and rocky terrain. Accordingly, this route is believed impossible during any prolonged wet period.

As yet, a classic route up the Penataran valley continues to elude expeditions and the final climb from Low's Gully up into Easy Valley looks likely to remain a problem for some time to come. However, North Peak and thence to the Eastern Plateau was climbed in 1987 via the lower portion of the Penataran Route, commencing at Kampung Melangkap Kapa, and leaving the route for North Peak at about 1300 m. This point is the confluence of the rivers from Low's Gully and the west side of the North Ridge where both tributaries are marked by high waterfalls.

ROYAL SOCIETY ROUTE (East Ridge)

Royal Society Expedition and Sheila Collenette, 1961

This route follows the true East Ridge from Poring Hot Springs at 500 m to a little over 3150 m where the ridge is blocked by a steep 150-m rock tower known as Mayabau (Mayerbatu, "Matterhorn") and a succession of impassable rock pinnacles. It has been thought that a way around these difficulties may be possible by descending the ridge to the north and traversing below them but this way has never been pursued. However, Sheila Collenette who followed the Royal Society Expedition cut a path down the south side of the ridge to the Bambangan river and then upwards to meet the Mesilau Route (now referred to as Koutal's Route) by which it is possible to climb to King George Peak on the Eastern Plateau.

The Royal Society Expedition was a major scientific expedition involving a large number of people, porters and equipment and requiring prolonged camps for study purposes. Accordingly, all the expedition camps were located off the main ridge line close to available water. Five camps between Poring Hot Springs and Mayabau (Mayerbatu) were established. This section of the East Ridge Route, which links into Koutal's Route, was cut in 1986, and with basic maintenance, the travel time should be reduced to two days.

KOUTAL'S ROUTE

Sheila Collenette, 1960 (as far as col between Rhino Horn and East Ridge Pinnacles)
Koutal, 1963 (onwards from col to King George Peak)

The development of the Pinosuk Plateau for a golf course and dairy farm in the early 1980's has eliminated the first day of the original 1960 route and the Mesilau cave is but a few minutes' walk from the nearest vehicular access. To reach this point it is necessary to drive from Kundasang to the top of the golf course and to take the road which runs along the east bank of the East Mesilau river to the new Mesilau Lodge. The river can easily be crossed at this point and a pathway takes you naturally to the Mesilau cave.

From Mesilau cave a path leads down to the river to what is, except during flash floods, an easy crossing point to an obvious footpath which leads diagonally up and to the right. This path rises steadily to cross the spur between the east Mesilau and Menteki rivers and eventually follows the Menteki valley which becomes increasingly deep until the normal first camp at Ulu Menteki is reached. The Menteki river is labelled as the Kabibi river on the 1 : 50,000 survey map. From here the path climbs steeply northwards to cross the East Ridge west of the Rhino Horn and just east of the first pinnacles, sometimes referred to as Watu Rumau Wariu. The path then drops to about the 3000-m contour and then roughly contours north-west. The path follows a series of small ups and downs with some scrambling and much vegetation work until reaching the upper Letingan valley. It is normal to make a second camp by the third tributary of Letingan river. In the first few ascents of this route the contour section was replaced by a gruelling descent to cross the Letingan river lower down and then a steep climb for about 300 m to reach the normal Letingan campsite.

Fig.7. View towards North Peak from the top of Easy Valley. *(Photo: S. Pinfield)*

The path from Letingan Camp climbs to about 3400 m to cross the spur between the Letingan and Mekado valleys and then drops steeply into the Mekado valley where the third camp site is normally placed. From here it is necessary to follow the valley upwards, initially negotiating areas of scrub and rock gullies, to emerge on to open bare rock which provides easy going on to and along the main ridgeline to King George Peak.

At present this path is rarely used but, with more constant use, the problems of moving through vegetation will diminish and small parties travelling light should be able to accomplish this route in two days. In contrast, a large expedition in 1987 took nine days and eight camps to complete this route.

TRAVERSE ROUTES

These are routes which do not provide a way to the summit area but which contour around the mountain linking between approach routes. Most of these have been developed for the purpose of research into the ecology of the mountain and have not necessarily been kept open.

PINOSUK ROUTE

Royal Society Expedition, 1961
This route was cut by the Royal Society Expedition of 1961 and provided a traverse across the centre of the Pinosuk Plateau from their Poring base camp, starting about 2.5 km along their East Ridge route from the hot springs, to Kundasang village. This route is of no practical significance today as much of it has been obliterated by development on the plateau area. However, the east half could be useful should there be a need for a path from the Kundasang golf course direct to Poring Hot Springs. The original route was 17 km long and took two days to walk.

KUNDASANG ROUTE

Dr. W. Meijer and Prof. Erdtmann, 1960 (first recorded climb)
This is another route which appears to have fallen into recent disuse but which was first recorded by mistake. Two botanists set out to climb the mountain by a prominent spur which they had identified from the Agricultural Station at Kundasang. Their guide misled them and they were taken along a path which joined the standard route just below the Paka cave. It appeared that this was a path well known to the local people and used by them, although the 1960 climb was the first time this route was reported.

BOWEN'S ROUTE

M. Bowen, 1957
This is the only traverse route of importance to-day. It provides the essential link between the West Plateau and the East Plateau and is, therefore, a key to the development of climbing, walking and other activity on the eastern half of the mountain.

Fig.8. Ladders on Bowen's Route just below the Eastern Plateau. *(Photo: Robert New)*

The original route was not documented at the time and Myles Bowen, who was a geologist with the Shell Company of North Borneo, could give no details when asked to recall it some five years later. All he could recall was that he traversed east below the steep rock faces below Tunku Abdul Rahman Peak and King Edward Peak from somewhere between Paka cave and the pinnacles. He made the climb with a partner and they were both experienced mountaineers who used ropes on the more difficult stretches. He reported, however, that only one pitch of about 15m presented any real problem.

Eric Wong, the present Warden of Kinabalu Park, climbed a route in 1973 which appears to follow Bowen's Route. This route has been greatly improved by "Operation Raleigh" in 1987 by fixing ladders in the steep rock sections and fixed ropes in many other sections. This work was the initiative of Tengku Dr D.Z. Adlin, the President of the Sabah Society (See photograph at page 91).

About 50 m before the first ropes on the standard route, which take the route up and right across steep rock slabs, there is a small path into the *Leptospermum* bushes to the right which leads under these rock slabs. This path is now well cut and provides a descending route along the line where vegetation meets rock slabs. After about 1 km the route contours through mossy forest and eventually leads into a rocky stream bed. The route climbs steeply up left on the right-hand bank of the stream and climbs with the aid of a ladder to a small rock saddle with a fine view. The route then traverses right to negotiate a series of partly vegetated ledges leading to the base of a prominent rock buttress. The route through the ledges has now been simplified by the fixing of ropes and of several sections of aluminium ladder.

The rock buttress originally provided four pleasant rock climbing pitches on clean open rock, the last of which was a short but steep wall requiring good delicate technique. These pitches have now been fitted with ropes and ladders as necessary to enable ascent by any unskilled walker. This short buttress gives access to the most southern point of the East Plateau and from here it is a slog up rock slabs of moderate gradient to the summit of King George Peak.

This route from the Panar Laban area to the summit of King George Peak now takes about three hours for a fit lightweight party. Water is always available in the rocky stream bed referred to above but in dry weather may not be available beyond.

A shelf below the summit of King George Peak on the east arm of the mountain provides a suitable camping site from which the East Plateau can be explored. For casual visits to the East Plateau, there is a convenient large overhanging boulder a little below the west side of Echoing Rocks which provides a useful bivouac site, albeit rather sloping.

CLIMBING ROUTES

A few of the peaks in the summit region, besides Low's Peak, are reasonably easy to climb and are climbed by more adventurous visitors. Such climbs are now rarely undertaken due to stringent Park regulations requiring the use of guides for climbing the mountain who are instructed to ensure that their clients do not stray from the normal trail. Accordingly, most of the climbing routes on Kinabalu have been climbed by parties of mountaineers who, after indemnifying the Sabah Parks Trustees, have obtained a special permit to climb where they please.

There are several main bases from which climbers undertake their climbing. The most popular for large groups is Sayat-Sayat Hut at about 3670 m. This hut is located on the standard summit trail immediately below the Donkey's Ears and this places the hut within a short walk of all the peaks on the western arm of the mountain.

Small climbing parties now favour the West Gurkha Hut which is so named as it was built by the writer with the help of Gurkha soldiers stationed at the British garrison in Seria, Brunei in 1985, within the area which may be described as the West Cwm at about 3850 m. This is a small four-man shelter with many comforts but its main attraction is its magnificent quiet setting amongst the high peaks of the mountain. This hut which also provides easy access to all the peaks of the western arm of Kinabalu, is within sight of the summit of Low's Peak and about twenty minutes' walk to the summit.

The compilation of climbing route descriptions is hindered by the fact that the majority of climbers never write up their routes. Many of the summit peaks have evidence of earlier climbs by way of summit cairns, pitons, expansion bolts and slings, but no descriptions are available. Several attempts to track down route descriptions through climbing clubs in Japan have so far merely yielded a number of journal articles which, after translation, turn out to be of a very general nature. Accordingly any attempt to document climbing routes on Mt. Kinabalu will inevitably be incomplete. Emphasis here has been placed on easy routes, together with a brief commentary on the exploration of Low's Gully.

Fortunately, most of the granite on Mt. Kinabalu is layered in such a way that many of the peaks have a scarp and a dip slope with the dip slope providing quite "easy access" to the summit. Although these are described as "easy access" routes, even these are potentially serious. A slip on an exposed slope can lead easily to a fatal fall. As these routes generally follow slabby dip slopes many of the hand holes are undercut and heavy reliance is needed on friction. Furthermore, there is often a lot of unstable loose rock lying around on these slabs. The whole situation becomes worse when the rock is wet and worse still in windy and poor visibility conditions. It should always be remembered that it is easier to climb up than down and so you should never attempt to climb up anything unless you are confident that you can climb back down again. Use of a rope, even on apparently easy terrain, gives tremendous confidence and is much recommended even for these routes.

LOW'S PEAK (4101 m)
The slope of the summit pyramid from south around to north west provides easy scrambling to the summit. The normal ascent route follows fixed ropes but scrambling in any part of this sector provides easy access.

ST. JOHN'S PEAK (4097 m)
If you descend down the north side of the base of this peak in a westerly direction you will find that about 200 m from the col with Low's Peak you can traverse easily to a point on the back of the peak. This spine can then quite easily be followed to the summit ridge using mainly friction and a variety of hand holes. There are a few short steeper and slightly awkward moves which have been protected by early parties by pitons still securely in place. Ropes are recommended for all but more experienced parties. The route is marked by cairns to the summit ridge which offers an exhilarating position particularly exposed to the south and east. The ridge provides easy scrambling to the summit cairn.

VICTORIA PEAK (4003 m)
In the centre of the east face of the peak is an obvious gully in the shape of a 'Y'. From the base of this gully climb up following easy lines which are generally on the left side or centre of the gully. Although this is essentially a scrambling route, some of the moves may be found a little difficult in descent by those unused to climbing. In these circumstances, a rope is desirable.

OYAYUBI IWU (3900 m approx.)
This is the obvious phallic-like rock pinnacle at the head of the West Cwm which juts out northwards from the col linking Alexandra Peak to Low's to loom menacingly over the West Gurkha Hut below. It is easily climbed by scrambling up its easiest gradient along its south spine. Along this spine the rock is broken into large blocks providing easy holds but on unreliably loose material. You can either climb direct to the summit or take slightly easier ground to the left and then up to the summit. The upper portions of the climb are loose and exposed so great care is needed.

UGLY SISTER PEAK (4032 m)
This is not a particularly prominent peak but it provides the most striking summit on the ridge between Low's Peak and the Donkey's Ears and is situated immediately adjacent to the Donkey's Ears. On a sunny day this ridge provides a very pleasant detour on the descent from the summit with views over Low's Gully. The peak can easily be climbed by scrambling up blocks and following the obvious easy ridge line. This is, however, a very exposed route and ropes are recommended for those unaccustomed to exposure. The ridge walk is a little exposed in places along its north-east side so care is needed, particularly in windy conditions.

SOUTH PEAK (3933 m)
When the mountain is viewed from the south this is the most prominent feature so it is a good one to climb and makes an easy small detour on the standard route to the summit. The easiest route takes the dip slope on its south-west side which is reached by traversing around the west side of the peak from the easy ridge to the peak which is a little to your right when descending the normal route. The peak is in fact little more than a point on the end of the ridge so only a few metres of climbing is required. Climbing relies almost entirely on friction up the summit granite blocks to the small top which is dominated by a trigonometrical station. This is quite an exposed position giving magnificent views but requiring care in windy conditions.

CAULDRON GAP (3900 m approx.)
This is not a peak at all but in fact a col which offers a dramatic view of Commando Cauldron, the culmination of Low's Gully in a narrow steep-sided cleft estimated to be some 300 m deep. This is well worth a visit and is but a short walk and scramble from Sayat Sayat Hut. From the hut follow the cairns up towards Tunku Abdul Rahman Peak which start from the latrine about 100 m below the hut. Some cairns take a route to the col to the right of Tunku Abdul Rahman Peak but Cauldron Gap is the gap between Tunku Abdul Rahman Peak on its right and the Donkey's Ears on its left Aim for this gap following easy lines and you cannot go wrong. The last 100 m requires some awkward climbing up steep rock slabs but there are sufficient hand holes. The lip of the gap is abrupt with an exposed edge and a view into a breathtaking, albeit somewhat daunting, feature of the mountain.

PEAKS OF THE EASTERN ARM
There are a number of other peaks accessible from the Eastern Plateau. The most striking is King Edward Peak but this requires climbing skill, and is not included here. Mesilau Peak, Cirque Peak and North Peak are all easily accessible by following the obvious easy ridge routes to each of these. North Peak is relatively far along the North Ridge and the expedition is likely to require a bivouac. King George Peak (4066 m) is also one of the easy summits to climb on the eastern arm of the mountain and provides a wonderful view of the peaks along the east edge of the Western Plateau. To climb this peak it is necessary to first reach the Eastern Plateau by following Bowen's Route referred to earlier under 'Traverse Routes'. From the end of Bowen's Route it is a matter of merely following the slabs upwards. Most of the route is cairned. This is one of those peaks which when it appears on the horizon seems so close but the trudge seems to go on forever. The climb is very easy; just a slog.

LOW'S GULLY
Low's Gully has many times been referred to in articles about Kinabalu and always with reverence as the most dominating, awe-inspiring and unassailed feature of the mountain. Reports of *"that dark abyss"*, *"lightning flashing up gully below"* and such like abound. Many expeditions have attempted to either descend or ascend the gully, but until recently without success. The mystery of the Gully is made greater by the fact that it usually harbours cloud or mist and is difficult to view clearly from all but a few locations on the mountain.

Difficulty in obtaining a clear view of Low's Gully has also resulted in a lot of misunderstanding as to exactly what feature or features of the mountain comprise the Gully. The main gully with high sheer sides dividing the east and west arms of the mountain provides the bed of the upper reaches of the Penataran river. At its head there is a step in the geology creating waterfalls and a divide into two tributaries. The right-hand fork leads into Commando Cauldron, which is the most obvious upper section of the Gully, and the left-hand fork leads into Easy Valley. This name arises because this upper gully area was first explored by abseiling into it by an expedition of British Commandos in the 1960s.

Fig.9. Climbing one of the steep sections of Bowen's Route. *(Photo: S. Pinfield)*

A Japanese party is also believed to have abseiled into the bottom of Commando Cauldron in 1984 but they made no attempt to explore further and it is likely that further abseiling down the stream bed would have been needed to reach Low's Gully proper. Bearing in mind the need to leave fixed ropes in place for the retreat route, an enormous amount of equipment would have been needed for such a venture. Unfortunately, their report was not at all clear and there is doubt as to its authenticity which may be linked to a long abseil into Easy Valley from below King George Peak which was followed by a claim that Low's Gully had been tamed.

First Descent by Pinfield, Alderhalden and Brandli, March 6th, 1987
The first descent into the main gully below Commando Cauldron was made by a party of three very skilled rock climbers who spent four weeks based at the West Gurkha Hut in February/March 1987. They enjoyed beautifully fine weather with no rain and little cloud. They studied Low's Gully from all angles from the east and west arms of the mountain with binoculars and decided that the line of greatest weakness into the Gully lay below and to the north of the bottom of Easy Valley. They followed up on this research with an attempt which on 6th March 1987 yielded success and brought them to the very bottom of Low's Gully.

The route first took them one day to reach the bottom of Easy Valley where they bivouaced under a prominent boulder which is located on the top of a small spur on the right bank of the valley. From here they traversed north through very dense vegetation to a prominent stream bed which they then followed down rock slabs until they reached a ledge with a sheer drop to steeply sloping and vegetated valley sides. They abseiled over the lip and in two rope lengths, with a convenient midway belay point on a ledge, they reached the vegetation below. The ropes were left in place and they descended, first over steep slabs, with thin vegetated turf which tended to peel off, and then through dense mossy forest. The going was laborious but at 11.00 a.m. they reached the bottom. After three hours of exploration in the gully bottom they returned the way they came, climbing back up their ropes and returning the next day to the West Gurkha Hut after a gruelling expedition.

First Major Exploration by Stephen Pinfield and Robert New, April 12th–17th, 1991
This route, so far only undertaken once, followed the 1987 route into the bottom of Low's Gully but this time the abseil ropes were removed for use on the onward descent. The climbers were thus committed to finding a way out and their intention was to descend the Penataran river all the way to Melangkap Kapa.

After spending one whole day descending the Gully to an altitude of about 1570 m they reached a point where the Gully narrowed to a gorge only some 12 m wide with precipitous sides and a series of waterfalls dropping to small lakes filling the full width of the gorge. At this point they traversed right up steep vegetated slopes to meet the ridge which runs north-west to the confluence of the two main tributaries of the Penataran. A route trending generally north was then taken crossing three rivers and intervening ridges to eventually reach Kampung Melangkap Kapa. This route took five and a half days to complete a traverse of the mountain from south to north from the Power Station via Sayat Sayat and Low's Gully to Melangkap Kapa.

In March 1994 a British Army expedition comprising eight soldiers and two officers set out to achieve the first complete descent of the Gully from the top of Easy Valley to the confluence with the main Penataran. In the event, the expedition split into two separate expeditions. The leading party of five comprising the fittest members reached a point believed to be about 500 m below point reached in 1991. However, their route did not follow the gully bottom for the lower section but involved traversing along the sides of the gully and dropping into the gully at several points to make crossings. This leading group of five also became split into two groups who, suffering from exhaustion, stress and lack of food, reached Melangkap Kapa in a very poor state.

The second group, moving very slowly, eventually reached the same point reached in 1991 when they also were low on rations and morale. This group was unable to find a way to climb out and was eventually rescued by helicopter after a massive army effort to find them.

The real challenge of climbing the mountain by way of Low's Gully without fixed ropes in place remains, but the longstanding mystery of it has at last been penetrated. This expedition, however, will never become one for the faint-hearted for it is a steep and sustained route overshadowed by the constant threat of rain. The abseil point takes the route of a waterfall and heavy rain could prevent escape from the gully. Any accident, even of a minor nature, would be extremely serious as evacuation from the gully area would not be possible. Although the gully may have been tamed, it is likely to remain a serious adventure for all time.

MAPPING OF MOUNT KINABALU

The first line of enquiry for any mountaineer contemplating an expedition is for maps. In the case of Kinabalu, the lack of good maps is lamentable and was a source of complaint during the search and rescue operation mounted by the Park authorities when two climbers were lost in November 1988.

At present there are three sources of mapping materials:
1. Freehand sketches by various expeditions, especially that by Capt. Oliver in 1967.
2. Aerial survey by the Directorate of Overseas Surveys plotted at 1 : 50,000 and often enlarged.
3. Plane table survey carried out by B.W. Sandilands and published in Kinabalu Park literature.

Ironically, it is the freehand sketches, particularly that prepared by Oliver on his 1967 expedition, which are the most useful. This is because the sketches do not attempt contours but merely identify symbolically what is actually to be found on the ground. Accordingly, mountaineers can identify with these sketches more easily.

The aerial survey was based on photography at a height chosen for plotting the Crocker Range, which rarely exceeds 2000 m so that Mt. Kinabalu, in climbing rapidly to more than twice that height, suffers severe distortion. This problem is compounded where the many vertical slopes show insufficient detail on the photographs to enable plotting because of deep shadow. In many respects, Bruce Sandilands' efforts are preferable but he also attempts somewhat meaningless contours. The contour intervals on both these professional maps between the summit of King George Peak and the bottom of Low's Gully suggests an easy stroll. Anyone using such a map in bad weather is in for a nasty shock!

The permanent trigonometrical station on the summit of South Peak is a notable feature of the mountain. This station was, and still is, an important primary station in the main triangulation linking the east and west coasts of Sabah. It was built in 1957 by P.M. Sowdas who was then a Senior Assistant Surveyor in the Department of Lands and Surveys and for three weeks he took day and night observations to Mt. Trus Madi, where J.A. Fryer was stationed, and to Masasau, where B.W. Sandilands was stationed. The station itself started with a galvanised steel pipe set into a hole in the summit rock and around which the concrete pillar was cast. The materials were all carried from Bundu Tuhan by twenty porters under the guidance of Gunting Lagadan who was the first official guide to Mt. Kinabalu and who has been immortalised by a plaque on the summit of Low's peak and a hut at Panar Laban named after him.

Sowdas returned again to the summit area with J.A. Fryer, who was then Director of the Department of Lands and Surveys, in 1967 to measure the height of the subsidiary peaks of the summit area. Unfortunately, on the first day at Sayat-Sayat he broke his ankle. A doctor was sent for and Dr. Raybold climbed the mountain, set the ankle in plaster and the patient was portered off.

The next survey effort on the summit area was that undertaken by B.W. Sandilands as a voluntary effort. He laid out a measured base line on the Western Plateau. The north-west end of the line is located on the col between St. John's Peak and Low's Peak whilst the south-east end is on the plateau itself underneath Ugly Sister Peak. These points are marked by painted rings on the rock.

Following the untimely death of Bruce Sandilands in 1976, four staff members at the Department of Lands and Surveys, including the author, commenced a new survey of the summit area, having realised the shortcomings of existing maps and as a tribute to Bruce. A week was spent in the summit area undertaking ground survey work with a view to plotting from oblique photography at the Directorate of Overseas Survey and lack of funds to undertake fresh survey means that this work has yet to be fulfilled. It is very much hoped that recent events will spur the authorities into completing a detailed survey of the summit area, for reasons of both greater safety and more adventurous use of the mountain.

Appendix. Data chart for the standard route.

Location	Altitude		Distance			Time		
	m	ft	km	chains	miles	Fast	Med.	Slow
Power Station	1874	6148	0	0	0	0	0	0
Carson's Falls	1845	6050	0.10	5	0.06	0:01	0:05	0:10
Pondok Kandis	1990	6530	0.91	45	0.56	0:07	0:25	0:35
Pondok Ubah	1085	6840	1.35	67	0.84	0:13	0:45	1:00
Pondok Lowii	2260	7420	2.17	108	1.35	1:21	1:15	1:45
Pondok Mempening	2505	8220	3.12	155	1.94	0:35	1:55	2:45
Layang-Layang Staff quarters (Carson's Camp)	2700	8860	3.88	193	2.41	0:41	2:25	3:30
Pondok Villosa	2950	9680	4.83	240	3.00	0:55	3:10	4:30
Pondok Paka	3100	10,170	5.29	263	3.29	1:00	3:35	5:00
Laban Rata	3280	10,760	5.85	291	3.64	1:09	4:00	5:45
Panar Laban	3330	10,920	6.01	299	3.74	1:11	4:10	6:00
Sayat Sayat	3670	12,030	7.06	351	4.39	1:35	5:25	7:45
Low's Peak	4101	13,455	8.85	440	5.50	2:00	7:00	10:00

Notes
1. Altitude values were measured by hand altimeter commencing on the summit of Low's Peak and travelling down to Park Headquarters. There are known heights at both ends of the traverse so that intermediate heights could be proportionately adjusted to allow for the change in barometric pressure over the period of the traverse. Hand altimeters are not very accurate at the best of times so heights in metres have been rounded to the nearest 5 m and those in feet to the nearest 10 ft. These measurements significantly vary from those marked on the pondoks by the Park but are considered somewhat more accurate. With the advent of heighting by satellite it is now desirable to check the heights of principal peaks and when this is done it is hoped these huts and pondoks on the standard route will also be accurately heighted.

2. Distance values have been based on the chainage markers fixed along the route with intermediate points estimated by pacing.

3. Fast times have been based on the performance of the front runners in recent Climbathon races, although the record betters these significantly. The present record for the climb is 1 hour 41 minutes.

4. Medium times are based on an average climber carrying twenty-five pounds. These times do not include stops; so any stops need to be added when timing one's progress on the route. Reasonably fit climbers carrying light loads should reduce these times by about 25%.

5. Slow times are based on what is considered a reasonable maximum time including brief stops but not including the major stops that most climbers take at pondoks, especially at Layang-Layang staff quarters (formerly Carson's Camp). Climbers who find they are exceeding these times will very likely not make it to the summit and should consider prudent retreat.

Fig.10. Tengku Dr D.Z. Adlin (right), Kinabalu Park Warden Eric Wong Hon Fui, (second from left), Ranger Benedict Gangku (left) and paramedic Donny Kan, on their 1987 traverse of Bowen's Route (See page 82). *(Photo: Sualim Takun)*

Photo: Robert New

PART 2
THE FLORA OF KINABALU

subsequent to elaboration of this theory over the past 20 years. A new analysis is badly needed, but it is doubtful whether fundamental improvement in understanding of plant-geographic relationships would be possible using the same data Stapf and van Steenis worked over, even in the light of tectonic theory. Some of the conclusions undoubtedly would be different, particularly with respect to van Steenis's 'land bridges', but these authors were working with a seriously inadequate data set. In deference to van Steenis, however, it must be noted that he stated (1964) *"My contribution can only be tentative because there is no complete plant list of Mt. Kinabalu."* He emphasized that *"the interest, and **uniqueness of Kinabalu lies largely with its mountain flora*** [bold italics his]*."* Later in the paper he stated *"Plant geographically the foothill zone, though extremely rich in species, yields few problems innate to Kinabalu."*

Lacking a full listing of the species, the earlier authors missed what now seem to be the truly exciting evolutionary aspects of the flora of Mt. Kinabalu. These involve the numerous genera with great numbers of species; 73 genera have ten or more species and 28 genera have 30 or more. The three largest genera are *Ficus* (figs, family Moraceae) with 88 taxa, *Bulbophyllum* (family Orchidaceae) with 77, and *Syzygium* (cloves and *'jambu's* etc., family Myrtaceae) with 66. Important questions concerning plant geography, evolution, and origin of species in the flora thus need to be addressed that were overlooked by Stapf, van Steenis, and other authors because they lacked a sufficient data set.

Another kind of data unavailable to Stapf and van Steenis concerns the nature of the substrate on which individual species occur. From our field work and from specimen data noted while we have been preparing the enumeration, we were greatly impressed with the importance of areas with ultramafic geology that harbour rare or endemic species and the frequency of species in genera with numerous species that occur principally on ultramafic substrates (Beaman & Beaman, 1990). Even the rare epiphytes are often restricted to ultramafic (ultrabasic) areas. Unfortunately, many of the early collection records do not indicate the nature of the geology, but this generally can be established on the basis of the locality at which a particular specimen was collected.

The Kinabalu climate is another factor that must be included in evolutionary and geographic considerations. From base to summit climatic conditions ranging from humid tropical to alpine, prevail. During the Pleistocene the vegetational zones must have been compressed, with alpine and subalpine conditions occurring at considerably lower elevations than at present. Perhaps of as great significance as the different climatic zones is the fact that the climate has undergone striking variations in recent time and probably during the Pleistocene as well. The El Niño/Southern Oscillation Climatic phenomenon, resulting in droughts in Borneo, occurs on average every four years (Cane, 1983). The 1983 drought was a particularly severe one, of once in 100 years magnitude (Beaman *et al.*, 1985) and resulted (among other things) in the death of a number of *Leptospermum* trees on Kinabalu. Plant mortality also has been recorded after other recent droughts (Lowry *et al.*, 1973; Smith, 1979). It seems possible that the model of stimulation of evolutionary selection of new plant forms as a result of catastrophic climatic events and the association of this phenomenon with exceptional soil types as outlined by Lewis (1962) and Raven (1964), could be relevant to the flora of Mt. Kinabalu. Raven noted that this mode of origin of new species has most likely been of greatest importance in areas characterised by extreme climatic fluctuation. Raven & Axelrod (1978) suggest that rapid origin of new species may be most important in annual species of mediterranean climates, but it needs to be examined with respect to the woody species of Mt. Kinabalu.

Mt. Kinabalu is an ideal evolutionary laboratory for other reasons as well. As a result of its geological youthfulness it offers many new habitats which can be occupied by newly evolved plants and where immigrant populations may be effectively isolated from donor populations. In this respect it simulates a new oceanic island system such as Hawaii. Furthermore, conditions on Kinabalu are ideal for the occurrence of very localized populations, particularly on the many small and widely scattered ultramafic outcrops occurring at different elevations. In addition, the physiognomy of numerous sharp ridges and deep valleys results in circumstances that tend to severely limit movement of both pollinators and seed-dispersal agents. Kiester *et al.* (1984) have made a case for the diversification of *Ficus* being promoted by the random origin of particular gene combinations (genetic drift), temporally isolated by differences in flowering time. The importance of genetic drift in speciation on Mt. Kinabalu is intriguing, as is the possibility of catastrophic selection. Both forces may be acting jointly, a possibility suggested by Grant (1971, p. 116).

Van Steenis (1964) asserted that the array of mountain species on Kinabalu is a distinctly relict one. The ideas of Stapf and van Steenis on land bridges and a relict flora stocked from ancient ranges now eroded away no longer seem tenable. Some taxa may be relict (e.g., *Trigonobalanus,* the Trig-oak), but the extraordinary richness of the flora seems better explained mainly on the basis of rapid adaptive radiation, catastrophic selection and drift, and long- (or short-) distance dispersal of propagules from distant and neighbouring mountain systems.

A likely scenario for evolution and diversification of the Kinabalu flora was anticipated by Corner (1964) in discussing fig diversity when he stated *"The evolution of subgenus Ficus seems to have occurred where there has been relatively recent mountain-making, and to have employed regionally the section or series which happened to be on the spot."* It may be possible to generalise this hypothesis to much of the Kinabalu flora, but careful analysis of taxonomic characters and distribution of species in representative genera will be required which will challenge botanists for many years to come.

REFERENCES

Beaman, J.H. & Beaman, R.S. 1990. Diversity and distribution patterns in the flora of Mount Kinabalu. In: Baas, P., Kalkman, K. & Geesink, R. P. Baas *et al.* The Plant Diversity of Malesia, 147–160. Kluwer Academic Publishers, The Netherlands.

Beaman, J.H. & Regalado, J.C. Jr. 1989. Development and management of a microcomputer specimen-oriented database for the flora of Mount Kinabalu. *Taxon* 38: 27–42.

Beaman, R.S., Beaman, J.H., Marsh, C.W. & Woods, P.V. 1985. Drought and forest fires in Sabah in 1983. *Sabah Society Journal* 8(1): 10–30.

Cane, M.A. 1983. Oceanographic events during El Niño. *Science* 222: 1189–1195.

Corner, E.J.H. 1962. Royal Society Expedition to North Borneo, 1961: Reports. *Proceedings of the Linnean Society, London* 175: 9–56.

Corner, E.J.H. 1964. A discussion on the results of the Royal Society Expedition to North Borneo, 1961. *Proceedings of the Royal Society, London, B* 161: 1–91.

Gibbs, L.S. 1914. A Contribution to the Flora and Plant Formations of Mount Kinabalu and the Highlands of British North Borneo. *Journal of the Linnean Society, London, Botany* 42: 1–240.

Grant, V. 1971. Plant Speciation. Columbia University Press, New York & London.

Kiester, A.R., Lande, R., & Schemske, D.W. 1984. Models of co-evolution and speciation in plants and their pollinators. *American Naturalist* 124: 220–243.

Lewis, H. 1962. Catastrophic selection as a factor in speciation. *Evolution* 16: 257–271.

Lowry, J.B., Lee, D.W. & Stone, B.C. 1973. Effect of drought on Mount Kinabalu. *Malayan Nature Journal* 26: 178–179.

Meijer, W. 1965. A Botanical Guide to the Flora of Mt. Kinabalu. In: Symposium on Ecological Research on Humid Tropics Vegetation. Government of Sarawak and UNESCO.

Raven, P.H. 1964. Catastrophic selection and edaphic endemism. *Evolution* 18: 336–338.

Raven, P.H. & Axelrod, D.I. 1974. Angiosperm biogeography and past continental movements. *Annals of the Missouri Botanical Garden*: 539–673.

Raven, P.H. & Axelrod, D.I. 1978. Origin and relationships of the California flora. *University of California Publications in Botany* 72: 1–134.

Smith, J.M.B. 1979. Vegetation recovery from drought on Mt. Kinabalu. *Malayan Nature Journal* 32: 341–342.

Stapf, O. 1894. On the flora of Mount Kinabalu in North Borneo. *Transactions of the Linnean Society, London, Botany* 4: 69–263.

van Steenis, C.G.G.J. 1964. Plant geography of the mountain flora of Mt. Kinabalu. In: Corner, E.J.H., A Discussion on the Results of the Royal Society Expedition to North Borneo, 1961. pp. 7–38. *Proceedings of the Royal Society, London, B* 161: 1–91.

Whitmore, T.C. (ed.) 1981. Wallace's Line and Plate Tectonics. Clarendon Press, Oxford.

Whitmore, T.C. (ed.) 1987. Biogeographical Evolution of the Malay Archipelago. Clarendon Press, Oxford.

Fig.1. *Clethra pachyphylla* (Clethraceae), endemic to Borneo and found on only a few mountain ranges, is common around Park Headquarters. *(Photo: C.L. Chan)*

THE PLANT LIFE OF KINABALU
— AN INTRODUCTION

E.J.H. Corner
with minor revisions by John H. Beaman

Kinabalu is a scenic wonder, a test for mountaineers from the amateur to the skilled rock-climber, a holiday from the hot lowlands, and botanically a paradise. The people of Sabah possess on this famous mountain what I believe is the richest and most remarkable assemblage of plants in the world. It carries lowland, mountain, and alpine vegetation on a scale that is not seen elsewhere between the Himalayas and New Guinea. Not so long ago the lowland dipterocarp forest, which is so rich in Borneo, covered the base of the mountain up to 1200 m (4000 ft). On the west it has been cleared, but it persists to a small extent on the east and north and adds immensely to the value of the Park. How many species of plant occur on the entire mountain is not known, but certainly many thousand. Even the list of flowering plants is inadequate; it runs to many hundred, but hundreds of collections await identification and novelties continually turn up. The result is a complexity of botany that taxes the most professional. I doubt if any botanist ascending the mountain could identify on sight more than a quarter of the flowering plants that he would encounter; the very first might puzzle him. I do not mean to discourage but to show that the botany is harder than the climbing; and who, yet, has ascended the north side?

This account is limited to a few of the more conspicuous genera and species of the dicotyledons and the conifers, such as occur above 1200 m (4000 ft). Although the fungi (with the exception of luminescent fungi, at the end of this chapter), algae and lichens are not here dealt with, there are in this volume specialist accounts of the ferns (by Holttum & Parris), trees (Meijer), the *Rafflesia* family (Kamarudin), the rhododendron and blueberry family (Argent), the orchids (Lamb), the gingers (Smith), bamboos (Wong & S. Dransfield) and palms (J. Dransfield). Three detailed inventories of major vascular plant groups on Kinabalu, the pteridophytes (Parris, Beaman & Beaman, 1992), orchids (Wood, Beaman & Beaman, 1993) and gymnosperms (Beaman & Beaman, 1993) are now published. There is also a recent account of the mosses and liverworts of Kinabalu (Frahm *et al.*, 1990). Sipman (1993) has reported on the Kinabalu lichens and provides a checklist of 286 species; however, he notes that about one-third of his collections were unidentified and the species list probably less than 50% complete. Even so the task has been difficult because of the lack of field-notes on the obvious peculiarities of many of the common plants and because of the lack of handy illustrations. Though local herbaria are now building up their own collections, including one at the Kinabalu Park Headquarters itself, most of the plants are still known botanically only as dried specimens. On Kinabalu we meet the living in all their vital display, and the task now is to vivify the botany with field-studies, photographs, drawings, and paintings of the living. When he was Director of Agriculture in Sabah, E.J.H. Berwick began this task and it is being continued by local botanists. The scope for the amateur botanist is immense and he must translate the technical into ordinary language.

Fig.2. Small, dainty maroon-petalled flowers of *Euonymus glandulosus* (Celastraceae), a treelet. *(Photo: C.L. Chan)*

Kinabalu is a meeting place for western plants of Himalayan and Chinese genera and for eastern plants of Australian, New Zealand, and, even, American affinity; they mingle, of course, at all altitudes with Malaysian upsurgents. Above 1200 m (4000 ft) most of these Malaysian genera begin to disappear and many new genera, unfamiliar in the lowlands, begin to enter. Such are the buttercup (*Ranunculus*, of Australian affinity), the climbing madder (*Rubia* of European affinity), the Rosaceous trees and shrubs of Sino-Himalayan affinity, and *Gunnera* of the southern hemisphere; yet pitcher-plants (*Nepenthes*) of Bornean affinity continue to prosper. This geographical analysis of the Kinabalu flora dominated the discussion held at the Royal Society of London after the Society's first expedition to explore the east ridge of the mountain. I refer to the learned account given by the late Professor C.G.G.J. van Steenis, an authority on Malesian mountain floras (see Corner, 1964, and van Steenis, 1967), to John Beaman's account on evolution and phytogeography of the Kinabalu flora in this book, and to the paper by Beaman & Beaman (1990).

Ecologists have classified the vegetation on Kinabalu by various ways into altitudinal zones. These are, of course, climatic but for lack of meteorological records they cannot be specified. In any case the zones are ideal because the conditions at most altitudes vary. Soils vary, and there is the special case of the forest that occurs on the ultramafic (ultrabasic) rock. Ridges, because of their exposure and thinner or poorer soil, carry plants of upper altitudes at a lower level; seeds are always tumbling down. Alternatively, gorges such as those of the Mentaki and Bambangan carry forest of the lower zones to the higher, or this forest may have persisted in these higher and sheltered places from a previous state of the mountain. Thus, the oak *Lithocarpus havilandii* forms forest at 3050 m (10,000 ft) on the

Introduction to the Plant Life

Fig.3. Rockface on the south side above Panar Laban (about 3600 m, 11,000 ft), with crevices filled with mosses, grasses, sedges, orchids and very few other species. *(Photo: K.M. Wong)*

east ridge whereas the main oak-forest lies between 1200 and 1800 m (4000 and 6000 ft). I prefer the simplest course which recognises the summit zone as that above 11,000 ft where rocks begin to preponderate and the forest becomes scrub. Mossy forest, or the upper montane zone, covers roughly 1800 to 3050 m (6000–10,000 ft) where, at least on the cloudy ridges, mosses drape the trunks and branches. The montane oak-forest, or lower montane forest, lies roughly at 1200 to 1800 m (4000–6000 ft), and below this altitude one may speak of lowland or hill-forest. I refer especially to the outline given by Ho & Poore (1967), but it must not be forgotten that the first analysis, both ecological and geographical, was that of Stapf (1894). Detailed vegetation studies are currently underway by K. Kitayama, who has already published an excellent map of the vegetation of Kinabalu Park (Kitayama, 1991) and an important paper on an altitudinal transect study of the vegetation. Together with D. Brunotte he has also published observations on the relationship between vegetation and ultrabasic (ultramafic) bedrock on the upper slopes of Kinabalu (Brunotte & Kitayama, 1987).

For general assistance in botanical matters I refer to M.R. Henderson's "Malayan Wild Flowers", to my own "Wayside Trees of Malaya", to Hsuan Keng's "Orders and Families of Malayan Seed Plants", and, especially, to van Steenis's book on "The Mountain Flora of Java". This magnificent work is the first thoroughly illustrated and documented mountain flora for Malesia. It includes many Kinabalu plants of unfamiliar genera, and I hope that copies will be available in the public libraries of Sabah; it is the model for the Mountain Flora of Kinabalu.

Fig.4. *Medinilla speciosa* (Melastomataceae), with vividly pink pendulous inflorescences. *(Photo: C. Phillipps)*

Introduction to the Plant Life

Now Java has at Tjibodas a mountain botanical garden where the native mountain plants are grown and labelled for public benefit; it is the living guide to the mountain flora which cannot survive in the lowlands. I hope, therefore, that at Tenompok or Kundasang there will come another such garden where visitors may see most of the plants of Kinabalu with their botanical names. A start has been made with the Mountain Garden at Park Headquarters (1550 m; 5100 ft) and the Orchid Centre at the Poring Hot Springs (500 m; 1700 ft) but these need further development. At present, an expedition to the mountain is still a journey of discovery.

HERBACEOUS PLANTS

Concerning the numerous and unfamiliar herbaceous plants of the summit zone there is the ecological introduction provided by Smith (1968, 1969, 1970). Here I introduce a few of the more conspicuous genera.

The Kinabalu Buttercup *(Ranunculus lowii)*. Buttercups *(Ranunculus)* are found in most parts of the world to the number of some 500 species, especially in temperate regions where they serve as the introduction to floral botany. This cannot be in the tropics because they occur, if at all, at high altitudes, mostly well above 1200 m (4000 ft), and never in the abundance of temperate meadows. However, the tropical botanist can do as well or better with the *'cempaka'* (*Michelia*, Magnoliaceae).

Fig.5. Low's Buttercup, *Ranunculus lowii* (Ranunculaceae), endemic to Kinabalu. *(Photo: K.M. Wong)*

A recent survey of *Ranunculus* in Malesia by Eichler (1958) describes 36 species for the mountains from Sumatra and the Philippines to New Guinea where most occur; there is none in Malaya. One species, *R. lowii*, called after the first scientific explorer of Kinabalu, is found in Borneo and only on this mountain where it ranges from 3000 m to 3950 m (9800–13,000 ft), and it is one of the commoner alpine herbs. Its alliance is not, as one might expect, with the species of east Asia but with those of the mountains of Sulawesi, the Moluccas, and New Guinea; indeed, with the temperate species of New Zealand. It is a westerly pioneer, or stray, of the east Malesian flora and should be a constant reminder that Kinabalu is the meeting place.

Four other genera of the buttercup family (Ranunculaceae) occur in Malesia, namely *Anemone* and *Thalictrum*, each with three Malesian species but none in Borneo, and the woody climbers *Clematis* (19 species in Malesia, one in Borneo) and *Naravelia* (three species in Malesia, two in Borneo). The wide-spread *Clematis smilacifolia* (from Nepal to New Guinea) is not infrequent with purple-brown flowers in the montane oak-forest on Kinabalu.

The Kinabalu Buttercup has been studied in detail by Smith (1972), whose account is a good example of what should be attempted for other herbs of the summit zone. The buttercup favours open boggy slopes but will tolerate a fair degree of shade. It is a little herb with small toothed leaves, generally with purplish leaf-stalks, and bright yellow flowers set singly at the ends of long stalks which continue to lengthen as the fruit sets. A hairy variety occurs on the upper slopes of the Mekado valley leading to Kinabalu East, but it seems also to be that which was described originally by Stapf from Kinabalu West. At the Mentaki camp of the second Royal Society Expedition there was a low flat rock, splashed with flood-water, on which the Kinabalu Buttercup grew in abundance with other herbs; the altitude was 2750 m (9000 ft) and this seems to be its lowest occurrence. Here it either grew from seeds washed down from a higher level or it is the remains of a colony from more glacial times.

Potentilla (**Rosaceae**). There are many species of this rather buttercup-like genus in Europe and Asia, and a few reach on to the mountains of Malesia as far east as New Guinea. Thus, unlike the Kinabalu Buttercup, they appear to have spread eastwards. In a recent revision of the Malesian species, Kalkman (1968) describes nine species of which three occur in Borneo and only on the summit zone of Kinabalu. They are small rosette herbs which produce stalked clusters of light yellow flowers from the axils of the pinnate leaves. The most striking is *P. borneensis* (also called *P. leuconotis*) which has silvery hairy foliage. Kalkman distinguishes the three in the following way, though it is possible that hybrids may occur between *P. parvula* and *P. polyphylla* (sometimes called *P. mooniana*) :

Leaves silvery beneath .... *P. borneensis*
Leaves dark green, not silvery hairy,
    Leaves usually up to 10 cm long; upper leaflets mostly less than 10 mm long. Stamens as many as the petals or twice as many .... *P. parvula*
    Leaves 10–35 cm long; upper leaflets 10–30 mm long. Stamens at least four times as many as the petals .... *P. polyphylla*

None of these species is endemic to Kinabalu but the form of *P. polyphylla* on the mountain is distinguished as var. *kinabaluensis*. *P. polyphylla* is spread from Assam, Nepal, and Sri Lanka to Java and Borneo. *P. parvula* occurs in the Philippines, Sulawesi, and New Guinea. *P. borneensis* occurs also in Sumatra. The genus is absent from Malayan mountains.

Eyebright (*Euphrasia*, Scrophulariaceae). This is a large genus of herbs which are semiparasitic on the roots of various other herbaceous plants, though one would not suspect this from their green leaves. They grow, often, on grasses, to the roots of which, those of the eyebrights attach themselves with minute suckers. This habit has not been ascertained for the endemic species on Kinabalu, *Euphrasia borneensis*. It is a frequent herb, often prostrate, in grassy places from 2450 m (8000 ft) upwards, even to the summit of King George's Peak. The small leaves are toothed or notched and the flowers occur singly on stalks from the leaf-axils. The white corolla has an upper lip of two short lobes and a larger lower lip of three lobes, and there may be yellow spots in the throat. *E. borneensis* is said to be related to species of Australia and New Zealand.

Fig.6. *Euphrasia borneensis* (Scrophulariaceae), Kinabalu's own eyebright. *(Photo: A. Phillipps)*

Gentians. Two species of *Gentiana* have been described as endemic to Kinabalu, but they are close to *G. quadrifaria* of Java and we await a revision of the genus for the Malesian region. Both are small herbs with small leaves closely set in pairs and with single terminal flowers. *G. lycopodioides* has rigid reflexed leaves and white flowers with purple spots, whereas *G. borneensis* has purple flowers. They can be found in open grassy and boggy places in cracks in the granite rocks from 2300 m (7500 ft) upwards to 3950 m (13,000 ft), often in company with *Haloragis micrantha*. The allied genus *Swertia* seems not to occur in Borneo.

Trigonotis **(Boraginaceae)**. From 3050 m (10,000 ft) upwards, even to the top of King George's Peak, a little plant with narrow blunt leaves creeps through the dwarf scrub and coarse turf, especially in boggy places, and catches the eye with its small white flowers. The leaves are narrowly obovate, slightly hairy, and not an inch long. The solitary flowers in the leaf-axils have a corolla with five blunt lobes and short tube. This is *Trigonotis borneensis*, which is an ally of the blue-flowered forget-me-nots *(Myosotis)*. It was described as a genus *(Havilandia)*, endemic to Kinabalu but it is now referred to the larger Malesian genus *Trigonotis*.

Umbelliferae. Four genera of this family occur on Kinabalu, each with one species, and they illustrate the geographical complexity that centres on the mountain. The little 'pegaga' *(Hydrocotyle javanica)* with small, rounded, often five-to eight-angled or lobed leaves creeps in gravel and on rocks by streams up to 2900 m (9500 ft); it is extremely wide-spread in the tropics of the Old World. The Sanicle *(Sanicula europea)* with larger, rounded leaves divided more or less deeply into three toothed segments creeps with erect flowering stems in the forest and on rocks at 1500–2900 m (5000–9500 ft); its bristly little

Fig.7. *Trachymene saniculifolia* (Umbelliferae), common in rock-crevices and in the open dwarf forest on Kinabalu. *(Photo: K.M. Wong)*

fruits stick to one's clothing. The form on Kinabalu was distinguished as *S. elata* but it is regarded now as, at most, a subspecies of *S. europea* of temperate Europe and Asia and of tropical mountains from Africa to the Moluccas. Both of these are illustrated by van Steenis (1972). Then, more conspicuous from its red stems, leaf-stalks, and flower-stalks, *Trachymene saniculifolia* (or red sanicle) creeps in the open dwarf forest, on ridges, and in rock-crevices from 2150 m (7000 ft) up to the summit peaks; its flowers are usually pinkish and the lower leaves are more divided than in the sanicle. *Trachymene*, in contrast, is an Australian genus reaching as far west as Borneo and the Philippines. According to the Flora Malesiana, 18 species occur in Malesia, mostly in New Guinea, several in Sulawesi, and only *T. saniculifolia* reaches Kinabalu; its distribution is from New South Wales through east New Guinea to Mindoro and Kinabalu. Lastly, in the summit zone, there are the softly hairy rosettes, cushions, or spreading circles of the little *Oreomyrrhis borneensis* with small, narrow, and once or twice pinnate leaves. Three other species occur in New Guinea. *Oreomyrrhis* exemplifies what is called, in plant distribution, the south Pacific track which, by way of Antarctica, linked South America with Australasia, and is to be read into continental drift as the separation of these lands from the Mesozoic period onwards. Thus this tiny plant tells a long story of snow-capped mountains.

Compositae. Various introduced herbs of this ubiquitous family spring up in the clearings on and around Kinabalu. I refer only to *Pseudognaphalium luteoalbum* because of its charming appearance along road-cuttings where it enjoys the steep and wet banks. It grows to a foot or so high with greyish white woolly stems and linear leaves, and small heads of minute yellow flowers. It is illustrated along with many other of these composites by van Steenis (1972). Then the tree-vernonia *(Vernonia arborea)* of the lowlands extends into the gullies of the mountain forest up to 2450 m (8000 ft), if not more, where it can be distinguished by the fresh green leaves. Above 2750 m (9000 ft), indeed right to the summit of King George's Peak, there can be found on rocks and screes, even in the forest, a rosette herb with lax inflorescences of rather large daisy-like heads of flowers; the ray-florets are white and the disc-florets green with yellow pollen. This is *Myriactis cabrerae*. My impression is that the rosette-leaves wither at the time of flowering.

Violets (Violaceae). Two species occur on Kinabalu in more open places in the upper forest from 1400 to 2750 m (4500–9000 ft). The recent account of *Viola* in the Flora Malesiana (Moore, 1971) gives *c*. 400 species for the world, mainly in temperate regions, and 16 wild species on the mountains of Malesia. Both Kinabalu species occur also in Sumatra and Malaya. They are related to Sino-Himalayan species and they have been referred to *V. serpens*, which Moore does not recognise in Malesia. Perhaps what is most interesting is the absence from Kinabalu of several species found on the mountains of Sumatra, Java, Sulawesi, and the Philippines. Both Kinabalu species have violet petals, but plants with white petals veined or striped purple are not uncommon. *V. sumatrana* has dark green or purplish, heart-shaped leaves, glabrous or slightly hairy, and slightly larger flowers than *V. curvistylis* with pale green, hairy leaves about twice as long as broad. They are small perennial herbs with rosettes of stalked toothed leaves and they spread with slender runners.

Fig.8. Almost orchid-like, the purple-violet blooms of *Lobelia borneensis* (Campanulaceae) are a common sight at the start of the climb from Park Headquarters. *(Photo: C.L. Chan)*

Fig.9. *Dichroa febrifuga* (Hydrangeaceae), with pink downturned petals in the open flower. *(Photo: C.L. Chan)*

Astilbe rivularis (**Saxifragaceae**). This unmistakeable herb is not infrequent at about 2750 m (9000 ft). It is a robust, brown-hairy perennial with hollow stem. The large basal leaves are twice pinnate with toothed leaflets but they diminish in size and complexity up the stem, which can reach 2 m (6 ft) high to end in a large terminal panicle of small white flowers turning pinkish in fruit. It is the only species of the genus in Malesia where it is widespread on mountains from Sumatra to New Guinea. It is illustrated by van Steenis (1972), to whose account I am indebted.

Rubiaceae. This family, recognised from the paired leaves with interpetiolar stipules, the corolla-tube, and the inferior ovary, such as *Ixora* typifies, has a great number of trees, climbers, shrubs, and herbs on Kinabalu. I draw attention to a few of the better known herbs because we lack, as yet, a critical botanical revision of the family in Malesia. In the lower mountain forest there are several local species of 'ghost-flower' *(Argostemma)*, easy to recognise as a genus and calling for field-study. Then, by streams in the mountain forest up to 2750 m (9000 ft) or so, there occur two unexpected, yet wide-spread, species of general familiar to temperate botanists. The slender little bed-straw *Galium rotundifolium* with broad leaves in whorls of four is locally common in gravel and on rocks along with *Viola, Sanicula, Cardamine,* and *Hydrocotyle*. It is distributed from the Mediterranean

Fig.10. The white, star-shaped downturned flowers and cup-like fruit capsules are characteristic of the little herb, *Argostemma hameliifolium* (Rubiaceae), found scattered amid mossy patches in the forest around 1400-2000 m. *(Photo: C.L. Chan)*

Fig.11. *Mussaenda frondosa* (Rubiaceae), a climber common around the Park Headquarters, with brilliant orange-coloured corolla and white, enlarged calyx lobes in the flower. *(Photo: C.L. Chan)*

region over the mountains of South-east Asia and Malesia. By the same streams, scrambling up trees to heights of 6 m (20 ft) or more, there are the slender brittle stems of its ally, the madder *Rubia cordifolia*, the Dusun name of which is *'tarambulad'*. It has rather long-stalked, oblong or lanceolate leaves, also in fours, and the tiny bristles on stem and leaf cause them to adhere to one's clothing. Both *Galium* and *Rubia* have phyllodic leaves with longitudinal veins and the stipules are enlarged to resemble the leaves which thus appear in whorls of four. Except for the leaf-stalk, the leaves of *R. cordifolia* suggest at first a monocotyledon. This species is distributed from Africa through South-east Asia to Borneo and the Philippines; it stops at Wallace's line, the well-known boundary between Borneo and Sulawesi in biogeography (van Steenis, 1972, who illustrates both the *Galium* and *Rubia*).

Of *Hedyotis* with several species on the mountain, recognised from the hairy mouths of the short white trumpet-shaped corolla, the endemic *H. macrostegia* is common in the dwarf forest at 2750–3650 m (9000–12,000 ft) and extends in rock-crevices up to 4000 m (13,200 ft). It is a herb up to 1.5 m (*c*. 5 ft) high with long-stalked heads of flowers. Then at similar heights there is the ally *Phyllocrater gibbsiae* which has relatively large flowers borne singly in the leaf-axils. *Phyllocrater* is one of the few endemic genera that appear to have arisen from the intrinsic flora of Kinabalu; yet I doubt if it is more than a part of *Hedyotis*.

Fig.12. *Nertera granadensis* (Rubiaceae), a creeper with tiny leaves and bright red fruits around 2000 m on Kinabalu. *(Photo: C.L. Chan)*

Creeping on paths, rocks, and tree-trunks in damp shady places at 3050–3350 m (10,000–11,000 ft) there is the little *Nertera granadensis*, conspicuous from its red berries among the light green ovate leaves. This plant, illustrated by van Steenis (1972), is distributed from Central and South America, Polynesia, New Zealand, and south Australia, through the mountains of Malesia to south China and Madagascar. Kinabalu is regarded by van Steenis (Corner, 1964) as a stepping stone in this long excursion.

***Haloragis* and *Gunnera* (Haloragaceae).** *Haloragis* is an Australasian genus of which one species reaches Kinabalu and, indeed, west Java. Actually its distribution extends from New Zealand to Japan and south China through New Guinea and the Philippines. *Haloragis micrantha* is a delicate little creeping plant with small toothed leaves withering red, tiny pinkish orange flowers set in terminal panicles with upwardly directed branches, and with white feathery stigmas. It is common in open places along the ridges and in rock-clefts at 2150–3650 m (7000–12,000 ft). How it is pollinated or distributed seems not to be known. It is illustrated by van Steenis (1972), who dwells upon its curious distribution.

The other member of this family on Kinabalu is the massive herb *Gunnera macrophylla*, also illustrated by van Steenis (1972), and there is a photograph of it given by Meijer (1971). With toothed, heart-shaped leaves 30–60 cm (1–2 ft) wide, succulent leaf-stalks, and massive branched spikes of minute flowers it occurs in large tufts at the foot of waterfalls and along seepages at the base of screes at 1500–2750 m (5000–9000 ft). *Gunnera* is a genus of the southern hemisphere, absent from the Asian mainland. *G. macrophylla* is distributed from Sumatra and Borneo to the Solomon islands.

Cruciferae. Growing on the gravel by streams at 1500–2450 m (5000–8000 ft), along with *Viola, Galium,* and *Sanicula,* there is a little herb with a rosette of small pinnate leaves and slightly hairy, toothed leaflets; from the rosette slender racemes arise with reduced leaves and tiny white flowers which set into slender pods about 2.5 cm (1 ft) long. The whole plant varies from 3 or 4 cm (*c.* 1.5 in) to almost 30 cm (1 ft) or so high. This is *Cardamine hirsuta*, known in England as Hairy Bitter-cress. It is wide-spread in the north temperate regions and occurs through the mountains of Malesia. It appears to be the only crucifer in Borneo and it has been suggested that it has been introduced but, having found it many times, I see no reason to doubt its truly wild status. It is illustrated by van Steenis (1972).

***Impatiens* (Balsaminaceae).** The common balsam with large pink flowers, that grows by streams and waterfalls, has been confused with another widely distributed species and has not yet had its formal botanical description and name published.

***Drosera* (Droseraceae).** One species of sundew *(Drosera spathulata)* occurs in the more open and boggy forest on the ultramafic rocks of Kinabalu, up to 2300 m (7500 ft). The sundews are little herbs with rosettes of leaves which catch and digest insects on the stout hairs with sticky drops that occur on the upperside of the leaf. Two of the six species recorded for Malesia by van Steenis (1953) occur in Borneo. *D. burmannii* with sessile

Fig.13. The Kinabalu Balsam. *(Photo: C.L. Chan)*

Fig.14. Like tiny jewelled crowns, rosette sundews (Droseraceae) display leaves covered in glandular hairs that are a potential death-trap for small insects. The Kinabalu species is *Drosera spathulata*. (Photo: A. Lamb)

rounded leaves is found in the lowlands, and *D. spathulata* with stalked spathulate leaves is the mountain species, though it, too, has been found in the lowlands on *'kerangas'* (podsol) soil, as at Bako National Park in Sarawak: it has racemes of white pendent flowers.

***Sonerila* (Melastomataceae).** This large genus of charming forest herbs, distinguished by their three pink petals, the three-angled truncate capsule, and opposite leaves, has at least 12 species on Kinabalu. They are known mainly from dried specimens and the field-botanist must come forward for their appreciation as living plants. They are seldom more than 15–60 cm (1/2–2 ft) high; the leaves vary in depth of green, thickness or succulence, hairiness, variegation with pale spots, and in the nature of each pair because in many species they are unequal and, in not a few, one leaf is so reduced as to seem, at first sight, to be absent. Then pink-flowered species may have white-flowered varieties, not as yet recognised systematically. They grow in humus, on rocks, on fallen tree-trunks, and by streams in the forest. Commonest, perhaps, is *S. tenuifolia*, illustrated by van Steenis (1972), though its leaves may be in unequal pairs and the flowers may be pink or white. About 2750 m (9000 ft) the endemic *S. crassiuscula* is not uncommon with rather thick and fleshy leaves, purple beneath, set in very asymmetric pairs.

Gesneriaceae. Numerous shrubs and herbs of this family occur on Kinabalu but I mention only the spectacular *Agalmyla tuberculata* which comes as a surprise festooning tree-trunks or hanging from boulders at 2750–3050 m (9000–10,000 ft). It has copious aerial roots and large carmine-red to scarlet, almost trumpet-like, flowers.

PITCHER-PLANTS *(NEPENTHES)*

Paths on forested mountains ascend usually by ridges where trees are fewer and less dense and walking is easier and drier. On Kinabalu these paths from 1500 to 3350 m (5000–11,000 ft) lead through galleries of pitcher-plants, most of which seem to enjoy the poor soil and to climb on the shrubs and trees. Descend into the valleys and few, if any, pitcher-plants will be met, but two or three kinds grow on screes and landslips before they have been re-covered with forest. The pitchers are modified leaves. The stalk becomes a narrow blade; the true blade is the pot with its lid; and the length of midrib between the two becomes a sensitive stalk that twines as a tendril round objects of support. The young pitcher, while closed by its lid, secretes a thinly slimy, digestive juice into its cavity. When the lid opens, inquisitive insects enter and descend but, unable to surmount the peristome or corrugated rim round the mouth of the pitcher, they cannot escape and eventually slither down the smooth sides and drown in the liquid. They are digested; the water becomes a stinking soup from which the base of the pitcher absorbs nourishment for the growth of the plant. Thus, on the poor open soils where their tiny brown slip-like seeds germinate, pitcher-plants can thrive through this insectivorous habit; even the first tiny leaf above the cotyledons has a minute, if imperfect, pitcher.

Nepenthes is a Greek word meaning 'removing all sorrow'. It was the epithet given by Homer in the Odyssey to an Egyptian drug thought now to have been opium. It was

Fig.15. A rather spectacular find, the slender-waisted pitchers of *Nepenthes lowii* (Nepenthaceae), with widely flared mouths, are unmistakable. *(Photo: C.L Chan)*

Introduction to the Plant Life

applied fancifully to the liquid in the pitchers of the pitcher-plants and was adopted by Linnaeus as the name for the genus. The Dusun word for *Nepenthes* is *'kuku-anga'*.

Of some 65 species of *Nepenthes* described by Danser (1928) in his well-known monograph, 29 or 30 occur in Borneo, often very locally, and of these, nine occur in the upper part of Kinabalu. An excellent account of the Kinabalu species, with fine colour photographs, has been written by Kurata (1976) and additional information and photographs can be found in Phillipps & Lamb (1988). Some of these plants on Kinabalu have the most astonishing pitchers and, since the time when J.D. Hooker first described them in 1859, the mountain has been famous for their variety. Records of *N. alata, N. boshiana,* and *N. macfarlanei* from Kinabalu are incorrect according to B.E. Smythies, to whom I am greatly indebted for much critical information after he had consulted all the Bornean specimens in the Kew herbarium. Those endemic to the Kinabalu Park are *N. burbidgeae, N. rajah,* and *N. villosa*. However, little is known about their natural history, such as how long the plants live, how quickly they grow, how long a pitcher lasts, how the pitchers on the basal leaves differ from those on the climbing leaves, whether all are dioecious or not, how the flowers are pollinated, the seasons of flowering and fruiting, and what factors determine the survival of seedlings. Then hybrids may occur, such as between *N. rajah* and *N. villosa* and they must be expected when searching on Kinabalu.

Lower pitchers, from the lower or rosette leaves, are commonly wider and more sack-like than the characteristic shapes of those hanging freely from the upper leaves. There are

Fig.16. The enormous leaf pitchers of *Nepenthes rajah* (Nepenthaceae) have a capacity of up to 4 litres. *(Photo: Robert New)*

recent accounts of the development of the *Nepenthes* leaf by Roth (1953) and Schmid (1970). The life-history of the lowland *N. gracilis* is described by Lim & Prakash (1973). Because it is difficult to obtain, one is apt to overlook Hooker's original account (1859) where he enquired into the development of the pitcher.

The species commonly seen on the ascent routes are *N. lowii* at 1500–2450 m (5000–8000 ft), *N. edwardsiana* at 2450–2900 m (8000–9500 ft), and *N. villosa* at 2900–3350 m (9500–11,000 ft). The western ascent has been much depleted by persons who have removed the plants to sell or in the hope that they would grow in the lowlands, which they do not, but on the east ridge it is possible to walk for long distances through this succession of pitchers. In the early morning there is a ringing gonging which we traced to tupaias (tree-shrews) scampering over the pitchers of *N. lowii* and banging the old, empty and resonant, pitchers together. The late Professor J. Harrison, of Singapore, discovered that a snail laid its eggs in the hairs under the lid and that the tupaias came to eat them. The pitchers of *N. edwardsiana* and *N. villosa* are often eaten on one side, evidently by mountain rats in search of food or water.

Fig.17. *Nepenthes fusca* (Nepenthaceae) pitchers with maroon mottling on the outside and a pale green, waxy inner surface. *(Photo: A. Lamb)*

Fig.18. Bloated aerial pitcher of *Nepenthes burbidgeae* (Nepenthaceae). *(Photo: A. Phillipps)*

Introduction to the Plant Life

N. burbidgeae was found on the ultramafic soil of the Marai Parai spur at 900 m (3000 ft). Then it was found during the second Royal Society Expedition on the ultramafic soil of the slopes of Pig Hill on the Pinosuk Plateau at about 2300 m (7500 ft). Dr. Chew Wee Lek recorded the pitchers as yellow with blotches of red. Danser cites no illustration and omits the species from his key, but remarks that it seems nearest to *N. pilosa*. The pitcher is like that of *N. villosa* but with a median flange on the underside of the round lid and with much finer corrugations on the peristome; the stem has two wings.

N. edwardsiana is recognised at once from its cylindric pitchers with very strongly corrugated peristome. The pitchers vary from olive green to reddish (Corner, 1963; 1966, with colour photograph). It has been suggested that this species is the better developed and climbing state of *N. villosa* with similar peristome but funnel-shaped pitchers. I looked into this possibility on the east ridge but I saw no intermediate states and consider that the two should be regarded as distinct.

N. fusca, of Borneo, has been collected several times on Kinabalu at 1500–2450 m (5000–8000 ft). According to Smythies it is very like *N. maxima*, the upper pitchers of which are not so funnel-shaped, and the lid in *N. maxima* has a downward pointing tooth at the tip which is lacking from *N. fusca*. According to Danser, the leaf-blade of *N. fusca* is widest at the middle and in *N. maxima* it is usually widest near the apex. The inflorescences of *N. fusca* are said to appear as if lateral, which is not the case with *N. maxima*.

N. lowii is probably the commonest species on Kinabalu. The lopsided pitcher has an oblong and more or less erect lid, hairy on the reddish-purple underside, and a wide funnel-shaped mouth with a smooth and deep reddish-purple lining leading to a waist above the curved pot. One of our Dusun companions on the first Royal Society Expedition, Momin by name, explained to the others who had never seen this strange object before how the plant had made a belly, a mouth, and an ear (the lid) out of a leaf, and concluded rhetorically *"Isn't our forest wonderfully clever to be able to do these things?"* Ever so in my wanderings have I found that botany is the last subject to reach, if ever, the incisive minds of villagers. I noticed that the hard purple mouth-pieces of the pitchers persisted in the peaty humus long after other parts had decayed, and wondered what the palaeobotanist would make of them if they occurred in his material. A revised description of *N. ephippiata* of south and east Borneo suggests that it is allied with *N. lowii* (Danser, 1931). A study should be made of the pitchers of the lower leaves and their transition to the hanging pitchers because it seems that these juvenile pitchers may have been mistaken for those of other species.

N. maxima has been found on screes and landslips in the upper part of the Bambangan river at 1500–2750 m (5000–9000 ft). Compare *N. fusca* with which hybrids may occur.

N. rajah has large and very striking red pitchers (up to 45 cm, 18 in long), a strongly toothed purple peristome, and long arched lid. Like *N. burbidgeae* it occurs on the ultramafic soil of the Marai Parai spur and on the slopes of Pig Hill. Hooker (1859) wrote of it *"This wonderful plant is certainly one of the most striking vegetable productions hitherto discovered, and in this respect is worthy of taking place side by side with the Rafflesia arnoldii"*.

Fig.19. Delicate pitcher of *Nepenthes tentaculata* (Nepenthaceae), with tentacle-like bristles on its lid, resting on a moss sod. *(Photo: W.M. Poon)*

N. stenophylla is not infrequent in swampy places by the Mesilau and Bambangan rivers about 1500 m (5000 ft). The cylindric green pitchers are blotched with red upwards; the peristome is narrow, and the lid is orbicular.

N. tentaculata is the common species with rather small, green or purple-blotched pitchers in the mossy forest at 1500–3050 m (5000–10,000 ft). The lid is oblong and more or less tentacular-hairy, though not so strongly as the two wings that descend the pitcher. In the upper leaves the base of the blade clasps round the stem.

N. villosa grows only at the higher altitudes of the forest where it is often epiphytic though, apparently, it never climbs. The brown-hairy olive-yellowish pitchers are funnel-shaped and the peristome is more closely, yet less strongly, corrugated than in *N. edwardsiana*. It has been thought to be a juvenile state of *N. edwardsiana*.

PARASITIC FLOWERING PLANTS

Mistletoes are parasites with green photosynthetic leaves. They are ubiquitous in the tropics, growing on the upper branches of trees and shrubs, well exposed to light, unlike the complete parasites which, devoid of chlorophyll, are found in the depths of the forest. Most mistletoes have no ordinary roots. They get their water by means of one or more suckers which tap the sap-wood of the host and, by interrupting its water-supply cause its branches to die back; hence the appearance of *'api-api'* which is their common Malay name. Over two dozen species have been collected from Kinabalu, including the genus *Viscum*. It is distinguished by the fact that it develops only the basal sucker which began with the seedling. In other genera creeping branches develop other suckers and, in some cases, they can form massive thickets of entangled stems; heavy attacks kill the host. The flowers are pollinated by birds seeking the honey in the flower-tubes; in some cases it is known that the mature flower-buds, on being touched, pop open and scatter the pollen. Other birds eat the berries and drop the sticky seeds to infect new plants or branches. Little, however, is known of the natural history of the mistletoes on Kinabalu. Among the more striking there is *Dendrophthoe longituba* around 1200 m (4000 ft), which has greenish yellow flowers in racemes on the twigs behind the leaves, and the flower-tube is nearly three inches long. *Macrosolen* has long scarlet flowers. From 2450 m (8000 ft) upwards to the summit zone the endemic *Lepidella sabaensis* may be conspicuous with long yellow flowers in a head of red bracts (Jacobs, 1961).

The stem-parasite *Rafflesia* and the root-parasites *Rhizanthes*, *Balanophora* and *Mitrastemon,* all of which occur on Kinabalu, have no roots or foliage leaves. They are attached to their hosts by a sucker, much as that of *Viscum*, which in the case of *Balanophora* develops a small, closely warted, tuber up to an inch or so wide. From these tubers the short inflorescences with brightly coloured bracts arise; the tubers are often in clusters and may project through the humus to appear, when sterile, like a fungus. The inflorescences of *Balanophora* are many-flowered, though the flowers are solitary in the other two genera. The bracts vary from pink, orange, and red in *Balanophora* to yellowish in *Mitrastemon* and dull brown in *Rafflesia*.

Rafflesia is perhaps Kinabalu's most spectacular parasitic plant. In the demarcation of Kinabalu Park the eastern side was deliberately included both for the virgin forest at low altitude and for the conservation of the habitat of *Rafflesia*. The genus is named after Stamford Raffles and the first species to be discovered was the gigantic *R. arnoldii*, found by the botanist Joseph Arnold, who accompanied Raffles on his Sumatran journey. It was one of the great moments in biology, and I have often wondered why this epic is not related in Malaysian school-books. There is a modern and most detailed version by John Bastin (1973). The Malay name for *Rafflesia* is *'bunga patma'*. Kamarudin (this volume) discusses *Rafflesia* and the other parasites related to it, *Rhizanthes* and *Mitrastemon*.

Very little is known about *Rhizanthes*, of which *R. zippelii* is known on Kinabalu. *Mitrastemon*, also in the Rafflesiaceae (though some authorities prefer to put it in its own family, the Mitrastemonaceae), is found in Japan, Formosa, Cambodia, Sumatra, and New Guinea. It was found on Kinabalu during the second Royal Society Expedition after a careful search on the advice of Professor van Steenis, who thought that it must occur on the mountain. It was, in fact, locally common in the oak forest at 1200–1500 m (4000–5000 ft) on the trail from Kundasang to the Mesilau base camp; at Park Headquarters it is parasitic on *Quercus subsericea*. Five species are figured by Corner & Watanabe (1969). The Kinabalu species, *M. yamamotoi*, is shown in colour in my account of the mountain for the Straits Times Annual (1966).

For *Balanophora* (Balanophoraceae) there is a monograph by Bertel Hansen (1972, 1976), where 15 species are recognised for the tropics and subtropics of the Old World. At least

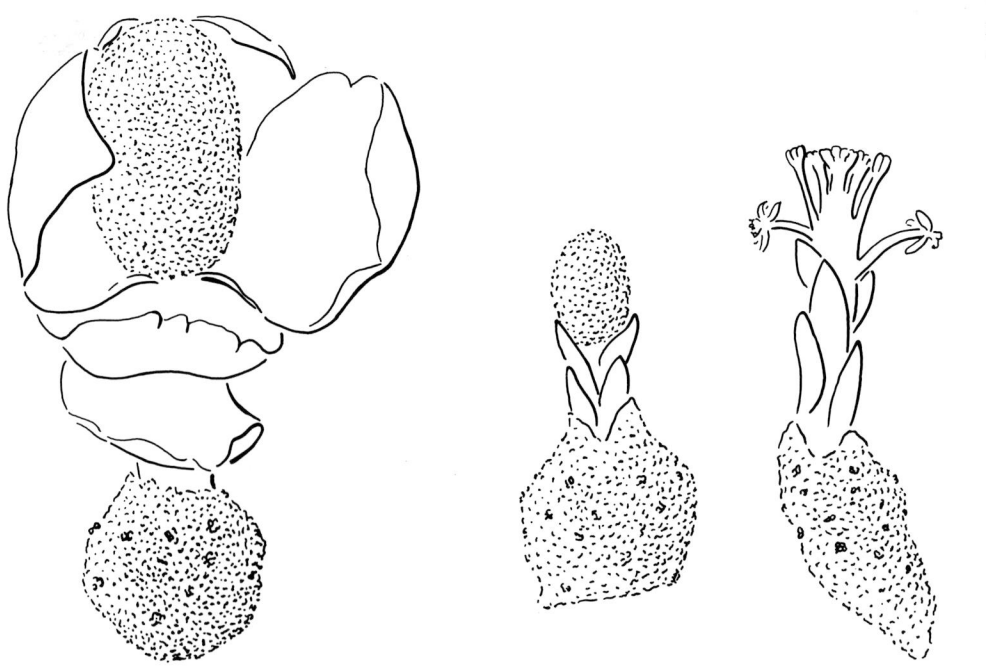

Fig.20. *Balanophora lowii* (left), female plant. *B. reflexa* (right), female and male plants.

three have been found on Kinabalu, though none is endemic. Several species have been illustrated by Corner & Watanabe (1969), but the names must be correlated with those used by Hansen. The species are root-parasites on a variety of host-trees, though the limitations of any one species have not been defined. The inflorescences emerge singly from the warted tubers that form on the roots and the minute seeds are evidently washed into the soil where, in contact with a suitable root, they will penetrate into it with a minute sucker and develop another tuber. *B. lowii* and *B. reflexa* (Fig.20), which has been mistakenly identified with *B. elongata* of Sumatra and Java, are not infrequent on Kinabalu at altitudes from 900 to 2750 m (3000–9000 ft). The third species, *B. papuana*, is either much less common or has been mistaken for *B. lowii*. All three are dioecious but tubers bearing male inflorescences may be mixed with those producing the female, at least in the case of *B. reflexa*. The male flowers are stalked and have conspicuous pale pollen. The female flowers are minute and set in compact heads. The short stems bear scale-leaves which in the Bornean species are as brightly coloured as the flowers. *B. lowii* (Sabah, Sarawak) grows from solitary tubers up to an inch wide, and the stems bear six to eight pairs of pale rose-apricot scale leaves enlarging regularly from below upwards. The flowers are rose-apricot but the stalks of the male ones and the axis of the male inflorescence are yellow. *B. reflexa* (Borneo, east Malaya) grows from rather dense clumps of tubers on a variety of hosts among which species of *Eugenia* have been noted. Its scale-leaves are smaller than in *B. lowii* and are spirally arranged; like the flowers, they are orange-red, scarlet, or crimson in different colonies; in some they are merely yellow with pinkish tips to the scale-leaves. The male flowers open fairly early in the morning when they have a strong foxy smell, reminiscent of *'pandan wangi'*, but this disappears by the afternoon; the stalks of the flowers then become reflexed. *B. papuana* resembles *B. lowii* and differs in the fewer pairs of scale-leaves which are nearly equal in size along the stem; its host-tree on Kinabalu appears to be always *Macaranga rostrata* (Euphorbiaceae). Pollinating insects have not been recorded. In the case of *B. papuana* the male flower-buds have been observed to burst open on touching in the same way as those of the mistletoes; yet it seems unlikely that these lowly plants are bird-pollinated.

BLACKBERRIES AND RASPBERRIES *(RUBUS)*

Eight or more species of this complicated genus in the Rosaceae can be found above 1200 m (4000 ft) on Kinabalu. They fall roughly into the blackberries with scrambling, often thorny, stems that eventually root at the ends and thus extend their thickets, and the raspberries which produce tufts of canes up to 5 m (15 ft) high, commonly without thorns. Blackberries have palmate or digitate leaves and black or red fruits; raspberries have pinnate leaves and yellow or red fruits. Field-notes on the species are unfortunately very inadequate and much more study is needed for their ready identification. The high mountain species at 2750–3950 m (9000–13,000 ft) is the small blackberry *R. lowii*. It is a low, thornless, straggling climber between the dwarf trees and shrubs, with digitate trifoliate leaves purple beneath, and solitary white or pinkish flowers. At mid-altitudes there are three common species, all of which are illustrated by van Steenis (1972), namely, the raspberry *R. fraxinifolius* with red fruits, said to be inedible; *R. lineatus* with orange-red and tasty berries, distinguished by the silvery white undersides to the leaflets which number five on each pinnate leaf and have numerous and closely set veins; the complex blackberry species *R. moluccanus*, which Kalkman (1984) recognizes as having three varieties on Kinabalu, is very abundant round Kundasang. Other species are *R. alpestris, R. benguetensis, R. elongatus,* and *R. rosifolius.*

I draw attention to what we called the 'tree-strawberry', possibly *R. fraxinifolius.* It was fairly abundant on screes and in breaks in the forest about 1500–1800 m (5000–6000 ft). With the habit of a raspberry, it had lax hanging sprays of watery red, insipid, strawberries; that is to say, the dry pips occurred on the outside of the fleshy receptacle, not as individually fleshy pips as in *Rubus.* The true strawberry *(Fragaria)* is allied with *Potentilla* and the flowers of both have the double calyx which is single in *Rubus* and, if I recall rightly, also in the tree-strawberry.

COMMON TREES AND SHRUBS

Heather-family (Ericaceae). The beautiful new publication by Argent *et al.* (1988), "Rhododendrons of Sabah", exemplifies the value of field research on Kinabalu plants. Illustrations in spectacular colour and the clear key and descriptions in this book will greatly enhance further work with these striking plants. Research for the Rhododendron book has been built on the great monograph in the Flora Malesiana (Sleumer, 1966), written with a personal knowledge of the Kinabalu plants and with unequalled authority. Sleumer's keys to identification, however, include a very great many species outside Borneo and are not easy to use because they often require fruit and seed, as well as flower; this is where the botanists of Sabah come in.

Rhododendron has about 280 species in Malesia, with 35 in Sabah, of which 24 occur on Kinabalu. Five species are endemic to the mountain. Seven named hybrids and several others without names occur, particularly in open disturbed habitats at high elevations.

Foremost among the Kinabalu species of *Rhododendron,* I place the Heather rhododendron, *R. ericoides.* It is the shrub with needle-leaves set closely round the twig, as in many heathers, or indeed as in *Dacrydium,* and scarlet flowers just over 1 cm long, solitary or in pairs, that begins to appear on ridges at about 2450 m (8000 ft) and continues abundantly almost to the summit peaks where it is dwarfed to a bush scarcely 30 cm high. This abundant plant is endemic to the mountain. It has allies in Sumatra and Sulawesi, but I have often wondered through what curious circumstances it should have remained unknown to science until Kinabalu had been ascended. *R. lowii,* which is found also on Mt. Trus Madi, is the other extreme with thick twigs, large leaves up to 22.5 x 12.5 cm (9 x 5 in), and clusters of large, funnel-shaped, waxy, yellow or pinkish-yellow flowers up to 10 cm (4 in) wide; it is common, especially in gullies, at 2750–3200 m (9000–10,500 ft). *R. javanicum* subsp. *brookeanum,* found widely in Borneo, even in the lowlands, has rather smaller leaves and flowers which are yellowish-red to bright red and often fragrant of lemon; it occurs at lower altitudes than *R. lowii* and, like many species of the genus, is often epiphytic. Another endemic, occurring from 2750 m (9000 ft) up to the bases of the summit peaks, is *R. buxifolium* with small, blunt, leathery leaves not 2.5 cm long, densely set on the ascending twigs, and crimson flowers much larger than the leaves. A shrub, common on ridges from 1500 m (5000 ft) upwards, is *R. fallacinum* with brown undersides to the nearly sessile leaves and coppery orange flowers. Two species on the ridges also catch the eye because of their narrow lanceolate leaves in apparent whorls. Of these, *R. stenophyllum* has the leaves up to 7.5 cm (3 in) long and orange-scarlet flowers, solitary or paired, while the endemic *R. abietifolium,* found only on the Eastern Ridge, has leaves half as long and somewhat larger pinkish-mauve flowers 3 cm long. *R.* ×*sheilae*, named in honour of Mrs. Sheila Collenette, who has collected many species of *Rhododendron* on Kinabalu, is a hybrid between *R. abietifolium* and *R. buxifolium.*

Further notes on the family and its other genera are given by Argent (this volume). White or pinkish-white flowers are found in three shrubby species, often epiphytic in the mossy forest. *R. orbiculatum* has leaves about 5 cm (2 in) wide. Narrow leaves with revolute margins distinguish *R. himantodes* (linear leaf 0.5 cm wide, flowers with brown dots) and *R. stapfianum* (leaf 1 cm wide).

The Malayan Heath *Styphelia malayana* (**Epacridaceae**) is common on the upper slopes of Kinabalu. A second species, *S. suaveolens*, grows in the summit zone and is distinguished by the shortly stalked leaves in which the side-veins curve and fork towards the margin, by the sweet-scented flowers with shorter sepals and longer corolla, and by the fact that it is dioecious with male and female plants. A close ally, *Trochocarpa celebica*, occurs as a prostrate shrub in rock-crevices in the summit zone, but at 2750–3350 m (9000 –11,000 ft) it is a small tree; it has very small leaves (0.5–2.5 cm long), reddish sepals, and bluish purple (not orange to red) fruits.

Drapetes ericoides (**Thymelaeaceae**). This shrubby little plant, 30–60 cm (1–2 ft) high, occurs in wet places and in cracks in the rocks on the summit zone. It has stiffly ascending branches clothed with tiny leaves and capped with small heads of four to nine white flowers without petals. It is one of the many surprises on Kinabalu because it has been found elsewhere only on the mountains of New Guinea. The three other species of the genus occur in Australia, New Zealand, and temperate South America.

The Trig-oak (*Trigonobalanus verticillata,* **Fagaceae).** This massive tree, recognised from its hollow base and the multitude of sucker-shoots arising from it, occurs rather frequently on steep slopes and broad ridges in a belt about 1200–1500 m (4000–5000 ft) on the south, east, and probably north flanks of Kinabalu. It is a guide to one climatic, or soil, zone of the mountain. It was discovered during 1961 by the Royal Society Expedition and it has turned out to be one of the great botanical discoveries of this century. It can be called the beech-oak because it has the triangular nuts of the north temperate beech trees *(Fagus)* borne in acorn-cups, with the leaves and timber of tropical oaks *(Quercus, Lithocarpus)*, and the seedlings of the beech. It adds the peculiarity of bearing the leaves in tiers, or whorls, of three. Thus a large tree with many suckers bearing the leaves in threes (often with six stipules) is certain proof of the trig-oak. A species of chestnut *(Castanopsis acuminatissima)*, to be found in the same forest, has a similar habit of suckering but its leaves are borne singly and it does not lose the main trunk to form a hollow hole; its

Fig.21. The trig-oak, *Trigonobalanus verticillatus* (Fagaceae). Distributed in Peninsular Malaysia, Borneo and the Celebes, this species was only described in 1962. In Sabah, it is found on Kinabalu at 1200–1800 m. *(Photo: K.M. Wong)*

Fig.22. The long scrolls of bark shed, *Tristaniopsis bilocularis* (Myrtaceae) trees are left with distinctive trunks streaked in hues of grey and pink; they are common in the lower montane forest on Kinabalu. *(Photo: K.M. Wong)*

rounded nuts are covered by a shortly spiny cup. The strange little inflorescences of the Trig-oak, as figured in the Flora Malesiana (Soepadmo, 1972), can often be found among the fallen leaves.

At first the Trig-oak grows a single stout trunk up to 27 m (90 ft) high, from the base of which the sucker shoots sprout. Then for some unknown reason, this large trunk dies, moulders away completely, and is replaced by some of the larger suckers which have grown into saplings. Instead of one trunk, there is a cluster round a hollow. Then, some of these stems die to be replaced by other suckers, and the hollow enlarges. How massive old trees may become or how long they can live, if indeed they die, are not known. The largest tree that I saw was near the Mesilau base-camp of the second Royal Society Expedition, on the opposite side of the river; into its hollow base several people could clamber.

Much has been written about the possible origin and evolution of the beech-oak family without knowledge of the Trig-oak which draws them closer together. The hub of the distribution of the family is in South-east Asia where this unifying genus *Trigonobalanus* occurs; it is now reported from the mountains of Sarawak, Malaya, Sumatra and Sulawesi, as well as from Kinabalu. In 1961 and 1964, I searched for the Southern-beech, *Nothofagus* on Kinabalu and am confident that it does not occur, but I am by no means persuaded that some other trees linking more closely with *Nothofagus* and *Trigonobalanus* may not be discovered somewhere between Kinabalu and New Guinea. The one known locality for the Trig-oak in Malaya is Fraser's Hill, where the trees are not as large as on Kinabalu.

For a detailed botanical account of the Trig-oak I refer to the original article by Forman (1964), to the account in the Flora Malesiana by Soepadmo (1972), and to exciting new work by Nixon & Crepet (1989) linking fossil and modern forms of the genus. These authors distinguish the related genera *Formanodendron* in Thailand and *Colombobalanus* in north-western South America. The species in both new genera previously had been placed in *Trigonobalanus*. Trigonobalanoid fossils are found in the early Tertiary of Europe and North America, demonstrating an ancient and very wide former distribution of these plants.

From Soepadmo's Flora Malesiana treatment we learn of the richness of Borneo, particularly Kinabalu, in species of oak and chestnut. Thus, *Castanopsis* has 34 species in Malesia, 21 in Borneo (ten endemic), and 12 on Kinabalu; *Lithocarpus* has 110 species in Malesia, 73 in Borneo (23 endemic), and about 35 on Kinabalu; *Quercus* has 19 species in Malesia, 18 in Borneo (eight endemic), and 11 on Kinabalu.

These oaks and chestnuts can mostly be recognised from their fallen fruits. We must look forward to such an illustrated account as I attempted in the "Wayside Trees of Malaya". I note especially two of the oaks; *Lithocarpus havilandii* with brown undersides to the leaves and pinkish brown new leaves, which seems to have the greatest altitudinal range from 1200 to 3200 m (4000–10,500 ft) of all the oaks on the mountain; and the deciduous *Quercus pseudoverticillata*, endemic to Kinabalu, with large, light green leaves appearing almost to be whorled (or verticillate) at the ends of the twigs and with large oblong acorns up to 5 x 3 cm (2 x 1.3 in).

Dusun names for *Quercus* and *Lithocarpus* are *'tikalud'* or *'tenkalus'*, for *Castanopsis* *'kegapan'*, and *'turug'* for *Trigonobalanus*.

Drimys (Winteraceae). Sooner or later during the ascent of Kinabalu sombre small trees or shrubs with red new leaves begin to appear. With upstanding glabrous foliage, their identity is clinched by the white flowers, often in threes from the base of the current twig. The petals vary from five to twelve (or more); the stamens are numerous, and the number of carpels varies from three to twelve; each develops into a black, oblong, stalked berry marked by the long stripe of the stigma. This is *Drimys piperita,* first described from Kinabalu, where it is abundant from 1500 to 3350 m (5000–11,000 ft), but now known to occur in the Philippines, Sulawesi, Flores, the Moluccas, New Guinea and Australia. Borneo is its western limit where it probably occurs on all the high mountains. A recent study of the genus (Vink, 1970) gives nine species, four of which are limited to South America, five to Australia, and only *D. piperita* extends into Malesia. *Drimys* is another example of the south Pacific track. It was formerly included in Magnoliaceae but details of flower and seed, the lack of stipules, and the structure of the wood without vessels have led to the distinction of Winteraceae. The genus *Wintera* is a synonym of *Drimys*.

Fig.23. *Drimys piperita* (Winteraceae), with male flowers. *(Photo: C.L. Chan)*

Magnoliaceae. In the discussion of the results of the first Royal Society Expedition to Kinabalu in 1961, held at the rooms of the Society, the authority on this family, J.E. Dandy, remarked *"I know of no other massif of comparable size which has so many species of this family"* (see Corner, 1964). From the lowlands on the eastern side up to 3200 m (10,500 ft) there occur the genera *Magnolia*, *Manglietia*, *Michelia* and *Elmerrillia*, totalling about 10 species. The family is well illustrated by the *'cempaka' (Michelia alba*,

M. champaca), and the white-flowered *M. montana* occurs on Kinabalu at about 900–1500 m (3000–5000 ft) as a tree up to 30 m (100 ft) high. I draw attention to two species of *Magnolia*. One, *M. candollii* is a sprawling shrub with very fragrant, creamy yellow flowers; it grows on the rocky banks of streams up to 2150 m (7000 ft). The other is *M. persuaveolens* subsp. *rigida* which occurs abundantly in steep valleys at 2750–3200 m (9000–10,500 ft) where it is a conspicuous tree up to 24 m (80 ft) high with large, stiff, bright green leaves. It stands well above the general level of the forest and is at times conspicuous from the purplish young leaves. The white petals turn creamy yellow and have a purple base. The flowers are very fragrant in a strange manner that reminded me of strawberries and the better class of durians. The compact green fruits are tessellated from the numerous carpels which adhere together; they reach 12.5 cm (5 in) long and, at maturity, the outer shell peels off to expose the mass of pink pulpy seeds. At the Ulu Mentaki camp of the second Royal Society Expedition I kept several fruits to ripen, so that I could distribute seeds to botanical gardens, but on my return to the camp about a week later from King George's Peak I found that the seeds had all been eaten, presumably by mountain rats which come to infest these camps. To obtain botanical specimens in 1961, we had to fell a large tree because, in the wet weather, the straight trunk was too slippery to climb; the wood was so tough that three hours of continuous axing were required. I would not be surprised if the fallen trunk and the stump, in the valley just west of Camp 4 on the east ridge, persist for many years. Dandy compared the distribution of these Magnoliaceae on Kinabalu with that of *Trigonobalanus*, thereby linking the occurrence of an ancestral family with that of an ancestral genus.

Photinia, Prunus (Rosaceae). Among the small trees conspicuous for their pink new foliage and the scarlet of their withering leaves, two common species of this family occur along the ridges. Both have white flowers and berry-like fruits ripening orange to red. One, *Photinia davidiana* (also known as *Stransvaesia davidiana* or *S. integrifolia*) occurs from 2750 to 3350 m (9000–11,000 ft), and has the flowers in terminal branching clusters; its fruits are round and just over 1 cm wide. The other, *Prunus javanica* (or Java Plum), occurs from 1500 m (5000 ft) upwards and has the flowers on unbranched lateral racemes, mostly from the bare parts of the twigs behind the leaves; its larger fruits are ovoid and about 2 cm long. The fruit of *Photinia* is described botanically as inferior (below the insertion of petals and stamens) while that of *Prunus* is superior. As a detail, the leaf stalk of *P. javanica* has two minute glands at the top on the upperside.

Prunus is the large, north temperate, genus of plums, cherries, apricot, almond, and peach. Four wild species are recorded for Malesia by Kalkman (1965). Kinabalu has also the endemic *P. mirabilis*, found on the East Ridge and distinguished from *P. javanica* by its much larger flowers. *Photinia*, with some 50 species, mostly in the Sino-Himalayan region, has five species in Malesia. Both genera represent the continental element from Asia in the flora of Kinabalu. The Fig-pear *(Pyrus granulosa)* of Malayan mountains has not been found in Borneo.

Weinmannia (Cunoniaceae). This genus of small trees, abundant on ridges and in dwarf forest on the upper slopes of Kinabalu, is easily recognised from the opposite pinnate leaves with paired orbicular stipules, reddish-pink new leaves, and scarlet withering leaflets. A recent revision of the genus by Bernardi (1964) gives 17 species for Malesia, four of which occur on Kinabalu and one of them *(W. clemensiae)* is endemic. The distinctions which he gives concern mainly the foliage; thus—

Lateral leaflets small, 15 x 5 mm, thick, with strongly recurved edges ....*W. clemensiae*
Lateral leaflets larger, flat or the edges slightly recurved,
    Leaflets thick, glabrous, leathery .... *W. aphanoneura*
    Leaflets thin,
        Leaf-rachis dilated; leaflets hairy beneath; stipules persistent .... *W. borneensis*
        Leaf-rachis not dilated; stipules caducous on adult twigs ....*W. blumei*

There is a general description of *W. blumei* in "Wayside Trees of Malaya", and it is illustrated in colour by van Steenis (1972). The genus occurs in tropical America (most species), Madagascar, Malesia, Polynesia, and New Zealand; thus it follows the largely southern distribution of its family.

Ardisia and Rapanea (Myrsinaceae). Numerous species of *Ardisia* occur as small trees and shrubs on Kinabalu. The genus is much in need of revision and, as most of our collections are still unidentified, I can offer no ready specific guide, but recommend the genus to the field-botanist. *Rapanea*, allied with *Myrsine*, has nine species of small tree or shrub on Kinabalu, mostly above 1500 m (5000 ft). In the summit zone, above 3350 m (11,000 ft), *R. dasyphylla* is conspicuous from its short columns of closely set, dark green leaves among which one or more old, dead, leafless stems usually persist. The other species on the mountain are *R. affinis, R. aralioides, R. avenis, R. cruciata, R. forbesii, R. hasseltii, R. penibukana,* and *R. salicina*; we have no ready key to their distinction.

Hollies (*Ilex*, Aquifoliaceae) (being revised by S. Andrews). Some 14 species grow in the Kinabalu area, but some are not sufficiently known for ready distinction in the field. Five species, namely *I. clemensiae, I. oppositifolia, I. zygophylla, I. revoluta* and *I. havilandii* are endemic to Borneo, while the first two are found only in Sabah. They occur as trees, shrubs or lianas in the mountain forest from 900 to 3350 m (3000–11,000 ft), and those which survive in the dwarf forest become flat-topped little trees or bushes. Such is the common *Ilex havilandii* which is very abundant on the ridges with *Rhododendron ericoides* and extends almost to the summit of King George's Peak. It has small, leathery, recurved leaves, rosy red when young, racemes of white flowers tipped pink with crimson calyx, and red to purple berries. Around 900 to 3400 m (3000–11,000 ft) it may be epiphytic and develop a basket of roots round the trunk of its host in the manner of a small strangling fig. *I. clemensiae* from the Penibukan (or Peniguppan) ridge is another epiphytic shrub but has not been sighted for years.

On Kinabalu, *I. spicata* is a few-stemmed shrub with stiffly upstanding, dark green leaves growing mainly at the ends of branches where masses of purplish-red berries are produced. The inner bark of *I. havilandii* is pale yellowish but, on exposure, it quickly turns bluish green. The *Ilex* of Mt. Kinabalu can often be confused with other taxa especially when sterile. *Myrica javanica, Eurya, Rapanea* and *Polyosma hookeri* can all be very misleading.

Introduction to the Plant Life

Mountain *Schima* and other Theaceae. The Mountain *Schima* is a conspicuous bush or small tree with reddish-brown or purple new leaves in the upper forest on Kinabalu, on ridges and in open places from 1800 to 3350 m (6000–11,000 ft). It is considered to be made up of three subspecies on Kinabalu. *S. wallichii* subsp. *brevifolia* occurs at higher elevations than the other two subspecies, and has smaller leaves and larger flowers.

Five species of *Eurya* have been recorded from Kinabalu, though none is endemic. *E. trichocarpa* is a common small tree in the upper oak forest from 2450 to 3050 m (8000–10,000 ft), distinguished by its hairy twigs. *E. obovata* var. *reticulata* (*E. reticulata*) has glabrous twigs and is a common shrub in the dwarf forest from 3350 to 3950 m (11,000–13,000 ft). *E. nitida* differs from *E. obovata* mainly in details of the small flower. I refer to the revision by de Wit (1947).

Gazing from some eminence over the slopes of Kinabalu, one sees streaks of greener forest. They are the younger or secondary forest growing up on screes or where falls of rock have decimated the original forest. In these places species of *Adinandra* abound, but through what succession they lead to the re-establishment of the primary forest is not known; nor indeed, does one understand why so many species of the genus participate. Here is a great opportunity to study the ecology of the forest as it is returning, and a good region for choice is that below the pinnacles on Kinabalu East. A monograph of *Adinandra* (Kobuski, 1947) gives about 70 species distributed from eastern Asia to New Guinea, with two species in tropical Africa. For Borneo 17 species are given, of which 16 occur on Kinabalu. My field-notes do not always agree, however, with Kobuski's descriptions and I am doubtful if the Kinabalu species are yet fully understood; I note particularly the

Fig.24. *Schima wallichii* subsp. *brevifolia* (Theaceae), distinctive by its large white flowers with many stamens. *(Photo: K.M. Wong)*

distinction between *A. impressa* and *A. verrucosa*. I list the Kinabalu species as follows: *A. anisobasis, A. caudatifolia, A. clemensiae, A. collina, A. colombonensis, A. cordifolia, A. dumosa, A. excelsa, A. impressa, A. magniflora, A. nunkokensis, A. quinquepartita, A. sarcosanthera,* and *A. verrucosa*. At Camp 5 of the first Royal Society Expedition, below the Rhino Horn, there was the sound of dropping fruits of *Adinandra* all through the night, probably as they were taken by nocturnal rats or, indeed, by bats. *Ternstroemia lowii*, with very tough leaves, deep dull yellow flowers, and reddish fruits is a common tree of the mossy forest from 2450 to 3350 m (8000–11,000 ft). In the forest near Tenompok and elsewhere *Pyrenaria tawauensis* occurs as a small tree with beautiful light yellow flowers.

Myrtaceous trees. *Leptospermum* ('gelam'), *Tristaniopsis*, and *Syzygium* are three common genera in the mountain forest. Except the first, they are exasperating for the field-botanist because the field-characters by which most of the species can be recognised have not been tied up with the descriptions of the dried specimens. Moreover *Tristaniopsis* and, especially, *Syzygium* are complicated genera for which we lack comprehensive monographs. There are over 60 species of *Syzygium* on Kinabalu, some of which are endemic, but I refrain from singling out any for brief description and recommend their study as a challenge to the local botanist. *Tristaniopsis* has four species on the mountain but it is difficult to pin-point them. They are evergreen trees in which the leaves wither

Fig.25. *Leptospermum recurvum* (Myrtaceae), endemic to Kinabalu. *(Photo: K.M. Wong)*

red. They have the characteristic grey flaky bark which peels in scrolls to expose the smooth orange-brown trunk of vivid and almost red colour in wet weather; such are the ridge species *T. bilocularis* and *T. elliptica* at 1500–2900 m (5000–9500 ft).

The *'gelam'* is represented by the wide-spread *Leptospermum flavescens* from 1500 to 2600 m (5000–8500 ft) and the endemic *L. recurvum* which occurs at higher altitudes, even to the summit peaks where it is dwarfed into a little shrub. In both the leaves wither dull red, but those of *L. recurvum* are smaller, stiffer, and thicker, and have recurved sides. This species appears to be one of the examples where a wide-spread mountain species (*L. flavescens*) has evolved the local endemic (Lee & Lowry, 1980). Yet, further, *L. recurvum* seems to be dividing into glabrous and hairy (silky tomentose) varieties. Stapf remarked on this in his observations under *L. flavescens* (as *L. javanicum*) and it has been the subject recently of detailed investigation by Lowry (1969) and Lee & Lowry (1980) who found that the hairy variety occurred only on Kinabalu West where its presence could be related with the drainage pattern of rain washing the seeds over the granite slopes. *L. recurvum* sometimes exhibits andromonoecy (having both bisexual and functionally male flowers on the same plant); the functionally male flowers do not develop proper stigmas (Wong, 1982).

Fig species (*Ficus*, Moraceae). Borneo has 135 species of wild figs and more than half (78 species) can be found on Kinabalu (Corner, 1962). The mountain has 13 endemic species and five endemic varieties of other species; yet neighbouring mountains have not been sufficiently explored to ascertain how local this endemism may be. The fact is that Kinabalu has the richest fig-flora of any comparable area in the world. As soon as one enters the forest and begins to study trees, epiphytes, shrubs, and climbers, the figs appear. Most, it is true, do not ascend above 1400–1500 m (4500–5000 ft), but some reach 1800 m (6000 ft), and one, *F. deltoidea* var. *kinabaluensis*, can be found on rock-slabs at 3250 m (10,600 ft) near the "Matterhorn" on the East Ridge. This is the highest altitudinal record for the genus, though it seems to be too high for reproduction; neither fig-insects nor seeds appear to develop at this elevation. Perhaps no more species remain to be discovered on the mountain, but there is much need of enquiry into their natural history.

The lowland epiphyte, *F. deltoidea*, extends into the lower mountain region and is easily recognised from its small blunt leaves with brown or olive undersides, the midrib which forks about the middle of the blade and has a conspicuous brownish gland at the fork, and the small orange figs with slender stalks. It is a very variable species and Kinabalu may yet have some undetected varieties; I have written a botanical account of it (Corner, 1969). Seedlings and young plants growing on rocks have ordinary pointed leaves which pass through many transitions to the adult form. The pointed leaf persists, apparently without the blunt form and dichotomous midrib, in var. *kinabaluensis* which has a short thick stalk to the fig. In habit this variety seems to be variable; it may be epiphytic about 1500 m (5000 ft) but, more often, it is a bush or a creeping shrub on exposed ridges. It is known also from Sarawak. Accompanying var. *kinabaluensis* up to 1800 m (6000 ft), there are two varieties of the closely allied *F. oleaefolia*, namely var. *memecylifolia* with small pointed leaves (1–2.5 cm wide) and var. *myrsinoides* with equally small blunt leaves. They are elegant shrubs or small trees, often epiphytic, in the ridge-vegetation. Their little

Fig. 26. Massive columns of root firmly anchoring an established strangling fig (*Ficus* sp., Moraceae) in the Poring area. (*Photo: A. Lamb*)

stalked figs, just over 0.5 cm wide, ripen red to purple-black and the seed-figs have merely one to three rather large seeds, just as in *F. deltoidea*. *F. oleaefolia* is as variable as *F. deltoidea* and some of its narrower leafed forms may occur on Kinabalu.

Two lowland species of strangling fig extend up to 1500 m (5000 ft). *F. sumatrana*, with small leaves and small red figs, seems to be even more devastating at this altitude where it may send roots around neighbouring trees and strangle them as well as its original host. *F. stupenda*, with larger leaves and massive woody orange-red figs (5 x 4 cm), is limited to one main descending root and is, therefore, less destructive. A third and endemic species in the *Trigonobalanus* forest is *F. palaquiifolia*; it seems to fruit rarely and is by no means satisfactorily known. At these altitudes *F. disticha* is a conspicuous and lofty climber; its slender twigs with small leaves (2.5–7.5 x 1–4 cm) brighten the canopy with a multitude of small and shortly stalked figs (1 cm wide) which ripen reddish-brown to purple. This and *F. deltoidea* are illustrated by van Steenis (1972). About 1200 m (4000 ft) one may come across the very large fallen figs of two other climbers. *F. carrii* (endemic) has stiffly hairy, oblong, figs up to 11.5 cm long, and *F. dens-echini* (known also from Sarawak) has almost round, reddish brown, glabrous figs, up to 6.5 cm wide, with five tooth-like scales set round the orifice.

Fig.27. Luscious red figs produced along runners from the stem base of the earth-fig, *Ficus uncinata* var. *strigosa* (Moraceae). *(Photo: C.L. Chan)*

Fig.28. *Ficus cf. endospermifolia* (Moraceae), common at Park Headquarters and the first part of the summit trail, one of Kinabalu's many fig species. *(Photo: C.L. Chan)*

The vegetation which covers the 'erratic blocks' that, as huge boulders, have fallen from the mountain and crashed through the trees to some resting place, has an unusual interest because it shows how, as soil develops on the rock from fallen leaves and other detritus, the forest gradually re-forms and even large trees may stand on the tops of the boulders. Here occurs characteristically a little fig-bush *F. setiflora* with thin, toothed, hairy leaves and scarlet figs 1 cm wide; it is endemic to the mountain but other varieties of it occur in Sarawak and Indonesian Borneo. It belongs in a group of the genus which is mainly Bornean and has five other species on Kinabalu, one of which, *F. endospermifolia,* is a tree of considerable size (Corner, 1970). On screes and landslips, however, at about 1500 m (5000 ft) the little *F. subsidens* creeps as a dwarf shrub through the incipient vegetation. It has surprisingly large leaves, up to 20 x 10 cm (8 x 4 in), for such a habit; the stalked figs ripen rose-red. It is endemic to Kinabalu and its origin is puzzling; it seems to be allied with the lowland *F. montana* of which there are few records from Borneo and none from Kinabalu.

The most interesting places to explore for figs are the streams in deep gullies at 900–1500 m (3000–5000 ft). Here one meets the coarse sapling-like *F. cereicarpa* with large leaves, up to 55 x 15 cm (10 x 6 in), and twice as big in its saplings, which seems always to be sterile until one looks at the base of the stem and discovers, partly hidden by fallen leaves, a mound of scaly brown figs, reach 5–7.5 cm (2–3 in) wide. It thrives in steep gorges or

Fig.29. Draped in moss and ferns, the gnarled trunks and branches of trees in the moist upper montane forest reach only as high as 20 m. *(Photo: A. Lamb)*

chasms where it projects from ledges in the rock and extends horizontally until, with increasing weight, it hangs down and eventually falls off; the big leaves continually flutter in the breeze that blow along these clefts. Now this peculiar plant, of general occurrence in north and central Borneo, is accompanied along the streams by a close ally *F. francisci* which has smaller leaves and smooth figs borne on stout woody spikes from the lower part of the trunk. Then, on the valley-sides, there occurs, if rarely, another ally, namely the endemic *F. virescens*, which in turn leads to the geocarpic *F. treubii* (endemic to Borneo). Geocarpic trees are those which bear the fruit underground. Geocarpic fig-trees clearly belong to *Ficus*, because of their latex, stipules, and leaves, but they appear sterile until one notices rather slender runners issuing from the lower part of the trunk and sagging into the soil; on pulling on them, clusters of figs come to the surface from under the humus and, indeed, out of the firm soil. *F. treubii* is one of these, distinguished by the long tip to the medium-sized and symmetrical leaves. It is common on the valley-sides, especially on the Pinosuk Plateau where the soil is churned up beneath the trees by pigs in search of the fruits.

Here is an instance, of which there must be many on Kinabalu, of living steps in an evolutionary sequence from one growth-habit to another with corresponding change in twig, leaf, flower, fruit, and habitat. Kinabalu is not just a natural meeting place for plants of Asia and Australia, remarkable as this is, but a store-house of evolution which makes one wonder how many of these supposed immigrants may not, in fact, have originated on the earlier massifs of north Borneo. The sequence to geocarpy leads on to other geocarpic species with very asymmetric leaves, such as *F. megaleia,* with leaves up to 1 m (3 ft) long, and *F. uncinata*, both frequenting the streams of Kinabalu. I doubt if anyone knowing but *F. cereicarpa* and *F. treubii* or *F. uncinata* would connect them in the course of evolution; as a specialist in the genus, I did not until I discovered the intermediate steps in these exciting valleys where so few explorers have descended. No wonder Borneo is the focus of the geocarpic figs of Malesia! The botanical study of wild figs is now to be related with that of the insects which pollinate them. It seems that most species of *Ficus* have their particular species or genus of pollinating insect and, therefore, hybrids of *Ficus* are rare, if they occur at all. I have collected the insects from a dozen or so species on Kinabalu, but all the rest remain to be found, and one cannot have too many collections, even from the same species, for verification. I hope that an ardent entomologist will take up this fascinating study. Nearly ripe figs should be placed in a bottle or wide tube, lightly stoppered, until the insects emerge. Then the bottle or tube is turned with its base to the light, where the insects will gather, unstoppered, and the insects transferred by a small paint-brush dipped in 70% alcohol to a small preserving tube with the same liquid. I waited nearly a week for the insects of *F. stupenda* to emerge from figs that had been thrown down by gibbons, and I collected from the bottle not one species of fig-wasp but eight, as well as several other kinds of insect (Wiebes, 1966); the last to emerge was a fearsome fly that darted so quickly that it nearly escaped; I think that even gnats occur in some figs.

Conifers. The genera *Agathis, Dacrydium,* and *Podocarpus* occur in the mountain forest of Kinabalu very much as in Malaya, but there is another and truly characteristic genus,

Phyllocladus. Agathis lenticula or *'dammar puteh'* (Dusun *'tungilan'*) is a locally common big tree at 1150–1800 m (3500–6000 ft), from the Mesilau river across the Pinosuk Plateau. Its bark peels in thin angular flakes and the white dammar can generally be seen oozing from cracks or wounds; many trees are tapped for this dammar. Of *Dacrydium* there are five species, namely *D. beccarii, D. gibbsiae, D. gracilis, D. pectinatum,* and *D. xanthandrum*. Related to these are *Dacrycarpus* with two species, *D. imbricatus* and *D. kinabaluensis* (formerly placed in *Podocarpus*), and *Falcatifolium falciforme*, with curved lanceolate leaves (formerly included in *Dacrydium*). *D. kinabaluensis* becomes dwarfed to a few feet high on the ridges at 3050–3350 m (10,000–11,000 ft). The conifers have been monographed recently for Flora Malesiana by de Laubenfels (1988). On Kinabalu, *Dacrydium xanthandrum* sometimes produces root suckers, thought to assist an individual tree in spreading itself elonally into sites with sparse tree cover (Wong, 1994).

Podocarpus is represented by eight species; they are *P. brevifolius, P. confertus, P. gibbsii, P. globosus, P. laubenfelsii,* and *P. neriifolius*. *P. brevifolius* is common along the east ridge at 2750–3200 m (9000–10,500 ft) as a small tree with ascending twigs. Similar to *Podocarpus* is the large tree *Prumnopitys amara*, recently removed from *Podocarpus* by de Laubenfels. It is found commonly at 1500 m (5000 ft) on the south and east sides.

Fig.30. *Phyllocladus hypophyllus* (Podocarpaceae), the Celery Pine with ovules (left) and male cones (right) from different trees. *(Photo: K.M. Wong)*

Phyllocladus hypophyllus is an Australasian element in the Kinabalu flora. It is distributed from New Guinea to Sarawak, across the north of Borneo, and to the Philippines, but it does not reach the Asian mainland. There are five or six other species in south Australia and New Zealand, though it is strangely absent from New Caledonia. On Kinabalu it occurs from 1500 to 3650 m (5000–12,000 ft), and is one of the common trees on the ridges from 1800 to 2750 m (6000–9000 ft). At lower altitudes it is a tree over 30 m (100 ft) high and, at the higher, it is dwarfed to a bush. It is recognised easily from the rather leathery, fern-like sprays of what appear to be wedge-shaped leaflets with notched edges. The apparent leaflets wither red and the young shoots are pinkish or covered with a glaucous bloom. I warn campers on the mountain that, of all trees likely to crash without warning, even in calm weather, *Phyllocladus* is the most likely. Such a disaster nearly terminated the second Royal Society Expedition when a big tree on the top of the rocks above the Mesilau cave fell lengthwise into the camp on the one still night. The foliage is usually regarded as that of a phylloclade or flattened branch with the leaves reduced to scales in or below the notches, much as can be seen in cactuses. Recently, however, the problem has been re-examined by Hsuan Keng (1963, 1973, 1974), who puts forward the proposition that the phylloclade is a reduced leaf-system such as is found in the early Devonian, fossil seed-ferns. He regards *Phyllocladus* as the most primitive living conifer or, indeed, gymnosperm.

TREES AND SHRUBS OF PARTICULAR INTEREST

I mention the following because of their interest to botanists, either for their structural peculiarities or for their geographical distribution.

Acer laurinum (**Aceraceae**). This species of maple is recorded by Meijer (1971) from the Pinosuk Plateau as, probably, the only known locality in Borneo.

Borneodendron aenigmaticum. This monotypic genus of Euphorbiaceae is endemic to Sabah and has been found on Kinabalu up to 950 m (3200 ft) on ultramafic soil to the north of Ranau. It is a large tree, up to 30 m (100 ft) high, with whorls of three entire, somewhat obovate, stiff leaves and bark that gives out a red sap in the blaze (Meijer, 1971). Its nearest ally is said to be *Cocconeuron* in New Caledonia (Airy Shaw, 1975). This is, indeed, a taxonomic and geographical problem.

Buxus rolfei (**Buxaceae**). This Philippine species has been found on Bukit Hampuan, north of Ranau.

Casuarinaceae. Two species occur on Kinabalu. That which accompanies *Agathis* on the Pinosuk Plateau and is common by the Bambangan river, where it may be seen to advantage from the "Matterhorn" on the East Ridge, is *Ceuthostoma terminale*; the rough brown bark peels in long broad strips. *Gymnostoma sumatranum* is common at about 900–1200 m (3000–4000 ft) by the Mesilau river; it has larger cones and very finely fissured, not scaling, bark. How these species regenerate is problematical. I found, as with the seashore *Casuarina equisetifolia*, no seedlings or saplings beneath the big trees of *C. terminale*, which seem, therefore, to be survivors on re-afforested screes where the seedlings had grown initially in the open. In contrast there were abundant seedlings and saplings of *G. sumatranum* in the mountain oak-forest.

Chloranthaceae. I note *Ascarina philippinensis* and *Sarcandra glabra*. The first is a common little tree up to 12 m (40 ft) high in the forest at 1500–1800 m (5000–6000 ft), especially on the Pinosuk Plateau; it is recognised from the very brittle twigs and the glandular-crenate leaves. The second is a small shrub up to 1.5 m (5 ft) high with red berries, frequent in the forest at 1200–1500 m (4000–5000 ft).

Clethra. The account of Clethraceae in the Flora Malesiana (Sleumer, 1971a) gives 64 species for *Clethra* (America, East Asia, Malesia, Macronesia) with 13 species in Malesia three of which occur on Kinabalu, namely *C. canescens* var. *clementis*, *C. longispicata*, and *C. pachyphylla*. They have rusty brown hairy shoots, at least when young, by which they are first noticed, and white (sympetalous) flowers in axillary and terminal racemes. *C. canescens* occurs up to 1700 m (5500 ft) as a small to fairly large tree with glaucous undersides to the leaves. *C. pachyphylla*, which is illustrated by Sleumer, is a shrub or small tree at 2150–3050 m (7000–10,000 ft), common in the forests of *Lithocarpus havilandii*. *C. longispicata* has been found on Kinabalu only at three localities, near Park Headquarters, on the Pinosuk Plateau, and near Kundasang.

Daphniphyllum borneense. This endemic of Kinabalu is a meagre little tree up to 6 m (20 ft) high, with Terminalia-branching, quite common in gullies at 2750–3350 m (9000–11,000 ft) especially in *Lithocarpus havilandii* forest. It is dioecious—male flowers have mauve-purple stamens and the greenish female flowers develop drupes or berries ripening dull red to purplish-blue with one, rarely two, seeds about 0.5 cm long. The genus was placed in Euphorbiaceae because of the unisexual flowers without petals, but the absence of stipules and the structure of the seed relate it to Buxaceae (Corner, 1976).

Dendrocnide (**Urticaceae**). There are two fairly common species of stinging tree on Kinabalu (Chew, 1969). *Dendrocnide oblanceolata* is common on the Pinosuk Plateau and is known from the more or less obovate leaf decurrent on to the short petiole and the dull purple, hanging, inflorescences; the Dusun name is *'tahipoi'*. *D. stimulans* with white stinging hairs on the inflorescences and with leaves not decurrent on the petiole is common at lower levels up to 900 m (3000 ft). A lower elevation species, *D. elliptica*, has been found at Poring and Nalumad.

Duabanga moluccana (**Sonneratiaceae**). This large tree, abundant on all rocky river banks in Borneo, extends up to 1800 m (6000 ft) on Kinabalu. Large paired leaves and loose clusters of green fruits with four, thick, star-like sepals distinguish it. A sharp gap, which is mainly that of the Riouw pocket, separates the continental *D. grandiflora* (*D. sonneratioides* of "Wayside Trees of Malaya") from *D. moluccana* of central and eastern Malesia. It is, I think, a prime mark of the former easterly connections of Borneo. When we reached the Bambangan river in 1961, on our journey across the Pinosuk Plateau from the Mamut river, it was in flood. Two of our Dusun assistants got across and began to fell a large tree of *D. moluccana* on the east bank to serve as a bridge but, before they had finished, we had found a passage higher up across the rocks. Nevertheless I was worried lest this tree, slightly leaning and half chopped through, should fall. I was astonished, therefore, in 1964 to find this tree still standing in full leaf as if it had suffered no inconvenience. I suppose that these valleys are well protected from the fierce squalls that drive over the flanks of the mountain.

Oil-fruit trees *(Elaeocarpus)*. The common species, *E. congestifolius*, in the upper mountain forest at 2750–3050 m (9000–10,000 ft), is a very bushy, often flat-topped, tree with white flowers, greyish-pink to dull purplish-blue fruits, and old leaves that wither red. The Dusun name for the genus is *'konkurad'*.

Engelhardia. This is the one genus of the walnut-family (Juglandaceae) in Malesia, where nine species occur (Jacobs, 1960; Gasis, 1993). There are six are on Kinabalu. The commonest, up to 2150 m (7000 ft), is *E. serrata*. Closely allied is *E. rigida*, distinguished by the entire leaflets. *E. roxburghiana* has been found only on the south and west sides. *E. apoensis* has been found only once, on the ultramafic hill north-east of Ranau. The large *E. spicata* is common in the lower forest of the East Ridge up to 1150 m (3800 ft). The recently described *E. kinabaluensis* is known from the Mesilau and Mamut areas.

Icacinaceae. Nineteen species of this difficult family have been collected on Kinabalu. The following occur below 1500 m (5000 ft): *Citronella suaveolens*, *Gomphandra cumingiana*, *Iodes philippinensis* (climber, frequent by streams), *Phytocrene macrophylla* var. *caudigera* (climber, endemic around Dallas), and *Stemonurus umbellatus* (in *Agathis* forest at 1150 m, 3500 ft). Above this altitude there are *Apodytes dimidiata* (*c.* 1600 m, 5300 ft, Bambangan river), *Platea excelsa* var. *kinabaluensis* (*c.* 1200 m, 4000 ft, endemic), *Platea sclerophylla* (east ridge at 2450–2850 m or 8000–9400 ft, endemic), and the woody climber *Miquelia caudata* which extends up to 1800 m (6000 ft). The occurrence of *P. excelsa* var. *kinabaluensis* is noteworthy because *P. excelsa* is a species of lowland peat-swamp forest; an analogy is the occurrence of *Stemonurus umbellatus*. *P. sclerophylla* is remarkable in its genus for the dark red petals. *Apodytes*, with a very strange fruit, possibly bird-distributed, is illustrated by Sleumer (1971b).

Myrica **(Myricaceae)**. Two species are recorded for Malesia, namely the lowland *M. esculenta* and the mountain *M. javanica,* which could be called the Mountain Gale. On Kinabalu it is a tree up to 30 m (100 ft) high at 1500 m (5000 ft), but it becomes smaller at higher elevations and on the summit of King George's Peak it is barely 30 cm (a foot) high. Such dwarfing appears so gradually and naturally that it is a surprise that many more trees are not so adaptable. *M. javanica* has the same general features as *M. esculenta* but its leaves are always more or less toothed and glabrous. When searching for *Nothofagus*, unsuccessfully, on Kinabalu, I was constantly arrested by two species of tree; one was *M. javanica* and the other was *Engelhardia serrata*.

Nyssa javanica **(Nyssaceae)**. This rather rare tree of the Himalayas and the Sunda Shelf is reported by Meijer (1971) as occurring at Sosopodon and on the Pinosuk Plateau about 1200–1500 m (4000–5000 ft). It is illustrated in the Flora Malesiana (series 1, vol. 4, p. 29).

Introduction to the Plant Life

Oleaceae. *Olea decussata*, first described as an *Ilex*, is a common tree at 2450–3500 m (8000–11,500 ft) on the East Ridge of Kinabalu. It reaches 15 m (50 ft) high in gullies, and it is recognisable from the upstanding leaves and green twigs with large buds. The small flowers are yellowish white.

***Rhamnus borneensis* (Rhamnaceae)**. This tree was found on Kinabalu at 1500 m (5000 ft) near the Mesilau river during the second Royal Society Expedition in 1964.

***Perrottetia* (Celastraceae)**. The one Malesian species, *P. alpestris*, is divided by Ding Hou (1962) into three subspecies, that in Borneo being ssp. *philippinensis*. On Kinabalu it is a small tree up to 6 m (20 ft) high at altitudes from 1200 to 3050 m (4000–10,000 ft), commonly by streams. In habit it resembles the Myrsinaceous *Maesa ramentacea* with straggling, even subscandent, branches and distichous, delicately toothed, leaves; when young, the veins and petioles are characteristically reddish brown. The short axillary panicles of greenish white flowers produce bunches of little berries which ripen pink to red and, finally, purplish black. It is not an attractive plant, but it is common, and I mention it because the seed-structure seems to forbid its position in Celastraceae (Corner, 1976).

***Scaevola* (Goodeniaceae)**. The common member of this genus is the seashore 'merambong' (*S. frutescens*, or, *S. sericea* as it must now be called). It is a great surprise, therefore, to meet three other species on Kinabalu at 900–2300 m (3000–7500 ft). *S. micrantha* occurs on the ultramafic soil above Layang-Layang staff quarters (Carson's

Fig.31. *Scaevola chanii* (Goodeniaceae), a shrub or small tree endemic to Kinabalu and so far known only from one population on ultramafic soil around 2000–3000 m on the mountain. *(Photo: C.L. Chan)*

Camp), on the Gurulau spur, on Bukit Hampuan, at Marai Parai and on Pig Hill at the east end of the Pinosuk Plateau. It much resembles the seashore *'merambong'* but it is a rather small shrub with smaller leaves and flowers. Another, *S. chanii*, is common at the ultramafic sites just above Layang-Layang staff quarters, and is not known from elsewhere; it is a much smaller bush or small tree, with smaller leaves and inflorescences (Wong, 1993). The third species, *S. verticillata*, has the leaves in whorls of four and has been found on Mt. Tambuyukon to the north of Poring.

Schefflera (**Araliaceae**). One member of this family to be found at high altitudes on Kinabalu is *Schefflera rachyphlebia*. It is a straggling climber growing quite commonly over bushes and small trees in the ridge-forest at 3050–3350 m (10,000–11,000 ft). Over 20 other species of *Schefflera* occur on the mountain, but their taxonomy still is not well worked out.

Scyphostegia borneensis. This small lax tree of disputed affinity is found only in Borneo but is widely distributed on the island. On Kinabalu it is known from the rivers in the south and west up to 1200 m (4000 ft). It is figured in the Flora Malesiana (series 1, vol. 5, p. 297, and vol. 6, p. 967), where alliance with Flacourtiaceae is suggested. From its seed-structure I have indicated alliance with Celastraceae, particularly the Bornean endemic *Sarawakodendron* (Corner, 1976).

Distyliopsis dunnii. No member of Hamamelidaceae had been found in Borneo until a single tree of this species was discovered at 1500 m (5000 ft) by the Mesilau river on the second Royal Society Expedition. It is known from the mountains of Malaya, Sumatra, Sulawesi, Palawan, Luzon, and New Guinea; thus the Kinabalu record was not unexpected. The family has been monographed in the Flora Malesiana (series 1, vol. 5) where seven genera, each with one species, are recorded.

Symplocos (**Symplocaceae**). This is an abundant genus of concern to the botanist on Kinabalu. There has been confusion and uncertainty with the species, but there is now a very welcome revision of the genus (Nooteboom, 1975). Nineteen species are known from Kinabalu, four of which are endemic, namely *S. buxifolia, S. colombonensis, S. trichomarginalis,* and *S. zizyphoides*. For the wide-spread *S. laeteviridis* Nooteboom records six varieties on Kinabalu, but for the more wide-spread *S. cochinchinensis* he gives 34 varieties of which only one occurs on Kinabalu. With this monograph the ecology of the genus should now be studied on the mountain.

REFERENCES

Airy Shaw, H.K. 1975. The Euphorbiaceae of Borneo. *Kew Bulletin Additional Series* 4.

Argent, G., Lamb, A., Phillipps, A. & Collenette, S. 1988. Rhododendrons of Sabah. Sabah Parks Publication No. 8, Kota Kinabalu.

Bastin, J. 1973. Dr. Joseph Arnold and the discovery of *Rafflesia arnoldii* in West Sumatra in 1818. *Journal of the Society for the Bibliography of Natural History (British Museum, Natural History)* 6: 305–372.

Beaman, J.H. & Beaman, R.S. 1990. Diversity and distribution patterns in the flora of Mount Kinabalu. Pp. 147–160 in P. Baas et al. (eds.) The Plant Diversity of Malesia. Kluwer Academic Publishers.

Beaman, J.H. & Beaman, R.S. 1993. The gymnosperms of Mount Kinabalu. *Contributions from the University of Michigan Herbarium* 19: 307–340.

Bernardi, L. 1964. *Revisio generis Weinmanniae*. Pars 3. *Botanisches Jahrbuch* 83: 126–184.

Brunotte, D. & Kitayama, K. 1987. The relationship between vegetation and ultrabasic bedrock on the upper slopes of Mount Kinabalu, Sabah. *Warta Geologi* 13(1): 9–12.

Chew, Wee-Lek. 1969. A monograph of *Dendrocnide* (Urticaceae). *Gardens' Bulletin, Singapore* 25: 1–104.

Corner, E.J.H. 1952. Wayside Trees of Malaya. Government Printer, Singapore.

Corner, E.J.H. 1962a. Royal Society Expedition to North Borneo 1961: Reports. *Proceedings of the Linnean Society, London* 175(1): 9–56.

Corner, E.J.H. 1962b. The Royal Society Expedition to North Borneo 1961. *Empire Forestry Review* (1962): 224–233.

Corner, E.J.H. 1963. Exploring North Borneo. *New Scientist* 366: 488–490.

Corner, E.J.H. 1964. A Discussion on the Results of the Royal Society Expedition to North Borneo, 1961. *Proceedings of the Royal Society, London, B* 161: 1–91.

Corner, E.J.H. 1966. Kinabalu. *The Straits Times Annual* 1966: 34–37.

Corner, E.J.H. 1969. The complex of *Ficus deltoidea*; a recent invasion of the Sunda Shelf. *Philosophical Transactions of the Royal Society, London, B* 256: 281–317.

Corner, E.J.H. 1970. *Ficus* subgenus *Ficus*. *Philosophical Transactions of the Royal Society, London, B* 259: 353–381.

Corner, E.J.H. 1976. The seeds of Dicotyledons. 2 vols. Cambridge University Press.

Corner, E.J.H. & Watanabe, K. 1969. Illustrated Guide to Tropical Plants. Hirokawa Publishing Co., Tokyo.

Danser, B.H. 1928. The Nepenthaceae of the Netherlands Indies. *Bulletin du Jardin Botanique, Buitenzorg,* series 3, 9: 249–438.

Danser, B.H. 1931. Nepenthaceae. *Mitteilungen aus dem Institut fur allgemeine Botanik in Hamburg* 3: 217–221.

de Laubenfels, D.J. 1988. Coniferales. Flora Malesiana, series I, 10: 337–453.

de Wit, H.C.D. 1947. A revision of the genus *Eurya* (Thunb.) Theaceae in the Malay Archipelago. *Bulletin of the Botanical Garden, Buitenzorg,* series 3, 17: 329–375.

Eichler, H. 1958. *Revision der Ranunculaceen Malesiens. Bibliotheca Botanica* 124: 1–110.

Forman, L.L. 1964. *Trigonobalanus,* a new genus of Fagaceae, with notes on the classification of the family. *Kew Bulletin* 17: 381–396.

Frahm, J.P., Frey, W. Kurschner, H. & Menzel, M. 1990. Mosses and liverworts of Mt. Kinabalu. Sabah Parks Publication no. 12. 91p.

Gasis, E.J.F.C. 1993. Four new species of *Engelhardia* (Juglandaceae) from Borneo. *Sandakania* 3: 1–9.

Hansen, B. 1972. The genus *Balanophora* J. R. and G. Forst. A taxonomic monograph. *Dansk Botanisk Arkiv* 28: 1–188.

Hansen, B. 1976. Balanophoraceae. Flora Malesiana, series I, 7: 783–805.

Henderson, M.R. 1954. Malayan Wild Flowers. 2 vols. Malayan Nature Society, Kuala Lumpur.

Ho, Coy-Choke & Poore, M. E. D. 1967. The value of the Mount Kinabalu National Park, Malaysia, to plant ecology. *Malayan Nature Journal* 19: 195–202.

Hooker, J.D. 1859. On the origin and development of the pitchers of *Nepenthes,* with an account of some new Bornean plants of that genus. *Transactions of the Linnean Society, London* 22: 415–424.

Hou, Ding. 1962. Celastraceae. Flora Malesiana, series I, 6: 227–291.

Jacobs, M. 1960. Juglandaceae. Flora Malesiana, series I, 6: 143–154.

Jacobs, M. 1961. Plant life on Mount Kinabalu. *Malayan Nature Journal* 15: 134–139.

Kalkman, C. 1965. The Old World species of *Prunus* subgenus *Laurocerasus,* including those formerly referred to *Pygeum. Blumea* 13: 1–115.

Kalkman, C 1968. *Potentilla, Duchesnia,* and *Fragaria* in Malesia (Rosaceae). *Blumea* 16: 325–354.

Kalkman, C. 1973. The Malesian species of the subfamily Maloideae (Rosaceae). *Blumea* 21: 413–442.

Kalkman, C. 1984. The genus *Rubus* (Rosaceae) in Malesia, II. The subgenus *Malachobatus*. *Blumea* 29: 319–386.

Kamarudin Mat Salleh. 1991. *Rafflesia: Magnificent Flower of Sabah.* Borneo Publishing Co., Kota Kinabalu.

Keng, H. 1963. Aspects of morphology of *Phyllocladus hypophyllus*. *Annals of Botany, London, new series* 27: 69–78.

Keng, H. 1969. Orders and Families of Malayan Seed Plants. Singapore University Press, Singapore.

Keng, H. 1973. On the family Phyllocladaceae. *Taiwania* 18: 142–145.

Keng, H. 1974. The phylloclade of *Phyllocladus* and its possible bearing on the branch systems of Progymnosperms. *Annals of Botany, London, new series* 38: 757–764.

Kitayama, K. 1991. Vegetation of Mount Kinabalu Park, Sabah, Malaysia: Map of Physiognomically Classified Vegetation, Scale 1: 100,000. East-West Center, Honolulu, Hawaii.

Kitayama, K. 1992. An altitudinal transect study of the vegetation on Mount Kinabalu, Borneo. *Vegetatio* 102: 149–171.

Kobuski, C.E. 1947. Studies in Theaceae, XV. A review of the genus *Adinandra*. *Journal of the Arnold Arboretum* 28: 1–98.

Kurata, S. 1976. *Nepenthes* of Mount Kinabalu. Sabah National Parks Publications No. 2, Kota Kinabalu.

Lee, D.W. & Lowry, J.B. 1980. Plant speciation on tropical mountains: *Leptospermum* (Myrtaceae) on Mount Kinabalu, Borneo. *Botanical Journal of the Linnean Society, London* 80: 223–242.

Lim, Ah-Lan & Prakash, N. 1973. Life history of *Nepenthes gracilis*. *Malaysian Journal of Science* 2(A): 43–53.

Lowry, B.M. 1969. Distribution of two varieties of *Leptospermum recurvum* Hook. *f.* on Mount Kinabalu. *Malayan Nature Journal* 22: 75–80.

Meijer, W. 1971. Plant life in Kinabalu National Park. *Malayan Nature Journal* 24: 184–189.

Meijer, W. 1984. New species of *Rafflesia* (Rafflesiaceae). *Blumea* 30: 209–215.

Moore, D.M. 1971. *Viola.* Flora Malesiana, series I, 7: 298–212.

Nixon, K.C. & Crepet, W.L. 1989. *Trigonobalanus* (Fagaceae): taxonomic status and phylogenetic relationships. *American Journal of Botany* 76: 828–841.

Nooteboom, H.P. 1975. Revision of the Symplocaceae of the Old World. Universitaire Pers, Leiden.

Parris, B.S., Beaman, R.S. & Beaman, J.H. 1992. The Plants of Mount Kinabalu. 1. Ferns and Fern Allies. Royal Botanic Gardens, Kew.

Phillipps, A. & Lamb, A. 1988. Pitcher-plants of East Malaysia and Brunei. *Nature Malaysiana* 13(4): 8–27.

Roth, I. 1953. *Zur Entwicklungsgeschichte und Histogenese der Schlauchblätter von Nepenthes. Planta* 42: 177–208.

Schmid, R. 1970. *Nepenthes—Studien I. Botanisches Jahrbuch* 90: 275–296.

Sipman, J.J.M. 1993. Lichens from Mount Kinabalu. *Tropical Bryology* 8: 281–314.

Sleumer, H. 1966. Ericaceae. Flora Malesiana, series I, 6: 469–914.

Sleumer, H. 1971a. Clethraceae. Flora Malesiana, series I, 7: 139–150.

Sleumer, H. 1971b. Icacinaceae. Flora Malesiana, series I, 7: 1–87.

Smith, J.M.B. 1968. Further exploration and observations on Mount Kinabalu East. *Malayan Nature Journal* 22: 29–40.

Smith, J.M.B. 1969. Cambridge Kinabalu Expedition 1967. *Sabah Society Journal* 5: 27–42.

Smith, J.M.B. 1970. Herbaceous plant communities in the summit zone of Mount Kinabalu. *Malayan Nature Journal* 24: 16–29.

Smith, J.M.B. 1972. Natural history of the Kinabalu buttercup. *Malayan Nature Journal* 25: 90–100.

Soepadmo, E. 1972. Fagaceae. Flora Malesiana, series I, 7: 265–403.

Stapf, O. 1894. On the Flora of Mount Kinabalu in North Borneo. *Transactions of the Linnean Society, London, Botany* 4: 69–263.

van Steenis, C.G.G.J. 1953. Droseraceae. Flora Malesiana, series I, 4: 377–381.

van Steenis, C.G.G.J. 1967. The age of the Kinabalu Flora. *Malayan Nature Journal* 20: 39–43.

van Steenis, C.G.J. 1972. The Mountain Flora of Java. E.J. Brill, Leiden.

Vink, W. 1970. The Winteraceae of the Old World. I, *Pseudowintera* and *Drimys*. *Blumea* 18: 225–354.

Weber, B.E. 1967. *Rafflesia*, the largest flower in the world, in Kinabalu National Park. *Sabah Society Journal* 3(3): 111–112.

Wiebes, J.T. 1966. Bornean fig-wasps from *Ficus stupenda* Miq. (Hymenoptera, Chalcidoidea). *Tijdschrift voor Entomologie* 109: 163–192.

Wong, K.M. 1982. Mountain gelam of Kinabalu. *Nature Malaysiana* 7(3): 4–7.

Wong, K.M. 1993. Two new species of *Scaevola* (Goodeniaceae) endemic to Borneo. *Sandakania* 3: 11–16.

Wong, K.M. 1994. A note on root sucker production in the conifer, *Dacrydium xanthandrum* (Podocarpaceae) on Mount Kinabalu, Sabah. *Sandakania* 4: 87–89.

Wood, J.J., Beaman, R.S. & Beaman, J.H. 1993. *The Plants of Mount Kinabalu. 2. Orchids.* Royal Botanic Gardens, Kew.

Fig.1. *Platycerium coronarium*, a rarely collected epiphyte in hill forest on Kinabalu. (Photo: B.S. Parris)

FERNS

R.E. Holttum
revised by B.S. Parris

In the wet tropics ferns are abundant everywhere but, as the great majority of them are not very large plants, they rarely dominate the landscape; they adapt themselves to the various types of growing-places afforded by the trees and other large plants which form the bulk of the natural vegetation, which, in Sabah, is a very mixed evergreen forest. Ferns growing on the ground in the shade of the forest are adapted to permanent weak light and rather high humidity. Where forest has been felled, or in such open places as river-banks, a different set of ferns, which will tolerate strong light and (from time to time) drying winds, establish themselves; these sun ferns would not flourish in permanent shade. In the wet tropics ferns and other plants (especially orchids) are also able to live on the branches of trees. Such plants are called epiphytes; they are adapted in various ways to their habitat which involves exposure of their roots to the air and thus to frequent short dry periods. In Kinabalu Park about two fifths of the total number of species of ferns are epiphytes. Tree-ferns form a special group, as their trunks can raise the crown of fronds some distance above the ground into less humid air and brighter light.

There is one basic character, common to all ferns, which limits the kinds of places where they can grow, and that is their method of reproduction. Ferns produce spores, which are single cells of microscopic size, comparable to the pollen grains of flowering plants; they are produced in organs called "sporangia", which grow in groups (called "sori") forming dark patches of various shapes on the underside of fern fronds. The sori are often protected by coverings of distinctive form called 'indusia'. Spores are dispersed by wind in very large numbers; those which alight in suitable places germinate and produce small green growths called 'prothalli'. The prothalli need quite humid conditions for growth, as they have no protection against drought, and the presence of water is also necessary to allow the free-swimming male reproductive cells to reach and fertilise the egg-cells. After such fertilization a new fern plant can grow. Each prothallus needs to be adapted to grow in the kind of place where the ultimate fern plant can grow.

In Kinabalu Park 608 species of ferns have been found. The total number of known fern species in the whole world is about twelve thousand. To make another comparison, there are more species of ferns in this park than in the whole of mainland tropical Africa. This comparatively large number in a small land area is due partly to the uniformly humid climate, partly to the range of habitats for ferns provided by the forest, as indicated above, and partly to the fact that each species of fern has an adaptation to a particular range of temperature, and temperature ranges on different parts of Mt. Kinabalu are very varied, though they have this in common—that at any one place the daily range of temperature changes little through the year; this may be compared with the often strong seasonal changes in subtropical and temperate regions.

From the point of view of fern classification, Kinabalu provides a very representative set of species, almost all of the principal genera of the Old World being represented, so that a student of ferns can find much of interest within a small area. But the subject of fern classification is very complex and still imperfectly understood, so that new ideas about it are still developing, based partly on the collections of dried specimens (some from Mt. Kinabalu) stored in the world's herbaria. Those who wish to understand the subject more fully are referred to the recent publications listed at the end of this article.

In general, the ferns at altitudes up to 900 m (3000 ft) on Mt. Kinabalu and its foothills are also found in Peninsular Malaysia and Sumatra, many also in the Philippines. Above 900 m (3000 ft) a considerable proportion of species have more restricted distributions, many being confined to Borneo although there may be closely related species in Peninsular Malaysia. At altitudes of over 2150 m (7000 ft) are some species which have a wider distribution to the east and south, to the mountains of New Guinea and to New Zealand. This latter type of distribution also is found in the conifers and some herbaceous plants of high levels on Kinabalu. A few high-altitude ferns are related to those of north temperate regions.

Flowering plants are classified on the characters of their flowers and fruits, which together provide a large range of characters. Ferns provide a much smaller range of characters in their reproductive organs, and a higher magnification is necessary to see them clearly. To see sporangia a X10 hand-lens is necessary; to see details of their structure a binocular of at least X50; to see details of spores one needs a magnification of X400 or more. But it is found that examination of various vegetative structures is also necessary, because ferns not very closely related have evolved rather similar types of fronds and sori. So one must look with a hand lens at the patterns of veins, at the structure of branches of fronds and the way in which they are joined together, at the hairs on various parts of a frond, at the scales on its stalk and on the growing tip of the rootstock; also at the arrangement of vascular strands in the stalk of a frond. All these can be seen sufficiently well by use of a X10 lens, which is the minimum equipment needed for field work on ferns.

ROADSIDE FERNS AT LOWER ALTITUDES

Beside the approach roads to Kinabalu the most conspicuous ferns are those which form thickets; they belong to the *Gleichenia* family and are known by the Malay name *'resam'*. These ferns branch in a repeated forking pattern, sometimes symmetric and sometimes zig-zag by alternate unequal forkings. If one examines one of the forks, one finds a tuft of hairs or scales in the angles; this represents a dormant growing point, and the pattern is caused by the enforced dormancy of these growing-points. The method by which this is controlled is unknown, but if the branches of a fork are cut off at an early stage the growing-point between them will develop. Without this pattern of dormant apices the fronds of these ferns would have a much more normal aspect. The main axis of a frond of the *Gleichenia* family has a temporary dormancy, during which a pair of branches grows to its fullest development; only when this development is completed will the main axis

Fig.2. *Blechnum fraseri* has the habit of a dwarf tree-fern and occurs in lower montane forest. *(Photo: A. Lamb)*

resume growth. This feature enables the ferns to form dense and tangled thickets, as each frond is of indefinite growth in length. Higher up on the mountain, on exposed ridges and other open places, different members of the family occur, having different branch-patterns, and some have only periodic dormancy of the main axis of fronds. There are also ferns of other families which have this type of periodic dormancy and can thus form thickets.

The commonest roadside fern with a tufted growth of pinnate fronds is *Blechnum orientale*, often conspicuous by the red colour of its young fronds. *Blechnum* is a genus of the southern hemisphere; in north temperate regions there is only one species. Its characteristic feature is that the sori lie along each side of the undersurface of the midrib of each leaflet. High on the mountain are quite different species of *Blechnum*.

Also in areas cleared for cultivation, but not conspicuous elsewhere, are plants of a species closely related to the thicket-forming fern called bracken in England, of the genus *Pteridium*. This fern has a rather thick creeping rootstock some distance below the surface of the ground and this is not killed when the fronds are burnt in the process of clearing for cultivation. *Gleichenia* plants, in contrast, have a more slender rootstock creeping on or near the ground surface and they are quite destroyed by burning.

TREE-FERNS

Large tree-ferns can be seen near the roads in and around the Park, often in groups. These all belong to one species, *Cyathea contaminans*, which is very widely distributed in the Malesian region. The young leaf-stalks have a pale bluish waxy surface, with many light brown scales at their bases; the scales conceal sharp thorns. Tree-ferns of this kind occur up to about 1500 m (5000 ft), above which other species appear, mostly of smaller stature. In all, 22 species of tree-ferns of the genus *Cyathea* have been found on Kinabalu and in neighbouring lowland forest. All have a more or less persistent mass of scales protecting the young fronds; details of scale-character, both of the large basal scales and of smaller ones on upper parts of fronds, are important for distinguishing the species. Sori are sometimes protected by an indusium, sometimes not. One species *(C. tripinnata)* has more deeply divided fronds than the others, the ultimate leaflets being of the third order; its sori are covered by overlapping scales, not by a single indusium, though the latter condition was reported by earlier observers. It belongs to a small group of species in the eastern part of the Malesian region, extending to Queensland.

A tree-fern which belongs to the genus *Dicksonia* occurs occasionally in forest at 1350 to 2400 m (4500 to 8000 ft). Its young fronds are covered with a dense mass of reddish hairs, some thick and bristle-like, not flat scales as in *Cyathea*. This species of *Dicksonia* is only known from Borneo and the Philippines; there are related species in New Guinea and Australasia. Another fern which has fronds even larger than tree-ferns, 3.5–4.5 m (12–15 ft) long has a massive prostrate rootstock instead of a trunk; this is covered with soft yellow-brown hairs which have the quality of staunching a bleeding wound. The name of this giant fern is *Cibotium arachnoideum*. Its rootstock survives the burning of trees when

Fig.3. *Humata subvestita* is a common epiphyte of hill forest and oak forest. *(Photo: C.L. Chan)*

Fig.4. *Cheiropleuria bicuspis*, a common montane fern, displays its characteristically ovate, often 2-cusped green fronds and narrow, spore-bearing brown fronds. *(Photo: K.M. Wong)*

land is cleared for cultivation, and it may be conspicuous at 900–1200 m (3000–4000 ft) altitude outside the Park where cultivation persists on steep ground.

HIGH-ALTITUDE THICKET-FERNS

At about 1500 m (5000 ft) the character of the thicket-forming sun-ferns changes, with more variety. Beside the *Gleichenia* family, two other quite different ferns belonging to the *Dennstaedtia* family form thickets by periodic dormancy of their main axes. One is *Hypolepis brooksiae*, which has quite small leaflets, its main branches covered with small prickles; the other is *Histiopteris stipulacea* which has elongate simple leaflets with reflexed edges covering the sporangia. At 2000 m (6500 ft) and above, on the ridges, the *Diplopterygium* (*Gleichenia* family) with periodically dormant apices is *D. bullatum;* it is very rigid, with densely scaly young parts, the upper surface convex between veins. *D. bullatum* occurs eastwards to New Guinea. At altitudes of 1400–2900 m (4500–9500 ft) there are three other species of this habit which do not form conspicuous thickets and have not been well studied. There is still field work to be done on these thicket-ferns.

SHADE FERNS OF FOREST

Inside the forest in the neighbourhood of the Park Headquarters at 1550 m (5100 ft), one finds quite a number of terrestrial ferns among the smaller plants of the forest floor. Probably the most abundant have tufted fronds which have more or less deeply lobed pinnae (leaflets of the first order) and small round sori on their lower surface; these belong to the *Thelypteris* family, a very large one in the wet tropics. They are rather similar in general habit, but show many differences in detail, and 52 species are known in the Park. Of similar habit, but sometimes with more deeply divided fronds (bipinnate) are plants of the genus *Diplazium*, which have sori along the veins, protected when young by rather thin narrow indusia. Ferns with broader, less deeply lobed pinnae, an elaborate network of veins, and small round sori belong to the genus *Tectaria*. Occasionally near streams one may find very large plants of *Angiopteris*, which may be recognized by the swollen fleshy bases of their frond-branches, also by sori consisting of rather large sporangia of unusual form along the veins near the edges of leaflets. This genus and its allies are very different in sporangia and anatomy to most other ferns; they are considered to be related to some palaeozoic fossils, but the relationship is not very certain. There are also some quite small ground ferns of several genera, including *Asplenium* and *Lindsaea* (see below for further notes on these).

In the forest one may occasionally see ferns climbing up tree-trunks; they have roots by which the scaly rootstocks of the ferns (up to finger thickness) are attached to the bark of a

Fig.5. *Gleichenia dicarpa*, an Umbrella Fern found in open lower montane ridge forest. *(Photo: A. Phillipps)*

tree. The fronds project horizontally or are sometimes pendulous. The normal fronds of these ferns have simple elongate pinnae, jointed to the main axis of the frond and bearing no sporangia. Sporangia are formed on special (fertile) fronds with very narrow leaflets, the lower sides of which are quite covered with sporangia; they are not often found. These ferns belong to the genus *Teratophyllum*. Young plants of *Teratophyllum* have small fronds with many leaflets of a shape different from those of old plants; they may sometimes be seen on the lower parts of a tree-trunk.

On rocks by streams in the shade of forest other kinds of ferns may be found, of several different genera. Some of them have sterile and fertile fronds of different shape, the fertile with narrower leaflets. To distinguish these ferns one must look at their vein pattern. At lower altitudes some species of *Asplenium* grow in such places; their elongate sori (along the veins) with rather firm translucent indusium are distinctive, though fronds may vary considerably in different species, from simple to variously branched.

Beside the path up the Summit Trail ridge below Kamborangoh two species of *Lindsaea* are distinctive ground ferns in the forest. The fronds are only 30 cm (1 ft) or so tall, with rather few branches each bearing several small leaflets. The sori are near the edges of the leaflets and are protected by indusia attached below the sori, open towards the edge of the leaflet. *Lindsaea* species are all rather small; the genus occurs throughout the wetter parts of the tropics but with different species in different regions. One of the two species by the path below Kamborangoh occurs also in both Peninsular Malaysia and Sumatra, the other only in Borneo and Sumatra. *Lindsaea* and its allies are a rather isolated group of ferns and undoubtedly old, but little is known of their fossil history.

FERNS OF MOUNTAIN RIDGES

In more open places along the Kamborangoh ridge may be found two ferns which do have fossil relatives which were almost world-wide, dating from Jurassic times. These ferns both have fronds of a peculiar branch-pattern which results in an almost circular outline, the main veins bearing successively smaller branches on their lower sides only. One of these ferns is called *Dipteris*. The divisions of its fronds are broad, with an elaborate network of veins; the main veins fork in their distal parts. Sporangia are borne in small sori on the lower surface, without any indusia. *Dipteris* occurs only in the Malesian region, with isolated species in north-east India and southern China. In addition to the mountain species (two on Kinabalu) there are two others which grow beside rocky streams in forest in the low country locally in Borneo, Sumatra and Peninsular Malaysia.

The other fern with successively smaller branches on the lower side (each branch arising near the base of the last one) is called *Matonia*. The individual branches of the frond are 30 cm (1ft) or more long and deeply lobed, rigid in texture and glossy dark green on the upper surface. The sori on the lower surface are protected by rather thick umbrella-shaped indusia. This fern is only found locally on exposed high ridges in Borneo, Peninsular Malaysia, Sumatra and New Guinea. The plants spread by means of a creeping rootstock and thus form colonies; young plants grown from spores are rarely seen.

In more or less shaded places on the ridges from 1800 m (6000 ft) upwards are three other peculiar fern genera. First, there are a few species of the genus *Coryphopteris* in the *Thelypteris* family which have small trunks like miniature tree-ferns but with simply pinnate fronds only 30 cm (1 ft) or so long. Allied species are found in washed-out peat or sandy soil near the crests of mountain ridges throughout Malesia, about 40 species in all, with the greatest abundance in New Guinea; a few also occur in north-east India and south China. Second, ferns of a genus called *Plagiogyria* are also found which have tufted, simply pinnate fronds with entire pinnae, their rootstocks and leaf-stalks quite lacking hairs or scales, and sterile and fertile fronds of different form, the latter with very narrow pinnae. Young fronds (at their early stages of uncoiling) are covered with slime, through which project small white breathing organs. The biological significance of the layer of slime is not clear, but the breathing organs certainly have the function of allowing access of air to the tissues below the slime. The third fern is very different, having simple rigid brittle pale green fronds on slender stalks, the fertile again much narrower than the sterile; sterile fronds sometimes have a simple pointed apex, sometimes two points more or less widely separated, but fertile fronds are always simple. This species is called *Cheiropleuria bicuspis*; its creeping rootstock has soft hairs on it. The netted venation of the fronds is similar to that of *Dipteris*, and the two genera are probably related.

In more open places on the ridge may occur plants of a large species of *Blechnum* which has narrow fertile pinnae much like those of *Plagiogyria* but always with many scales on them when they are young; young fronds, both fertile and sterile, are bright red. This species, called *Blechnum vestitum*, is closely related to species in both Australia and South Africa.

FERNS OF HIGH ALTITUDES

At about 2900 m (9500 ft) a small tree-fern, *Cyathea havilandii*, with a short trunk (sometimes no evident trunk) and all branches densely scaly, is common on the ridges. In open places on the higher ridges a very peculiar little fern, looking like a dwarf rush, with a tuft of small sporangia-bearing branches at the top of each slender stem, is fairly common; it is called *Schizaea fistulosa* and has a distribution which includes Peninsular Malaysia, New Zealand, New Caledonia and Fiji. There are other species of *Schizaea* at somewhat lower altitudes.

In the valley forest at 3000 m (9750 ft) where the soil is much richer than on the ridges, some fine terrestrial ferns of temperate-latitude type occur, including a *Polystichum* with much-branched fronds 1.25 m (4 ft) or more tall, bearing small rounded leaflets and sori protected by circular indusia; also a true *Dryopteris* with kidney-shaped indusia.

In the summit area some ferns may be found growing under the shelter of projecting rocks which shelter them from the sun. These include species of *Asplenium* (with elongate sori covered by indusia) and also *Athyrium* (with sori of varying shape from kidney-shaped to J-shaped or linear); they are all rather small plants, tougher than is usual in these genera.

Also in such situations are very small ferns of the *Grammitis* family, with simple fronds; this group is mentioned below, in the section dealing with epiphytes, as most of them are epiphytes.

A small species of *Blechnum, B. fluviatile*, with pinnae only 2.5 cm (1 in) or so long, occurs among rocks in more or less sheltered places at 3000 m (9750 ft) or more. It is otherwise known only from New Guinea and Australasia.

EPIPHYTES

Epiphytic ferns are abundant on almost all large trees at all altitudes. Those on the branches of the crowns of tall trees at lower altitudes may be seen by use of binoculars, or may occur nearer the ground on smaller trees on open river banks. They are very varied but belong mainly to the *Polypodium, Davallia* and *Asplenium* families. At high altitudes species of the *Grammitis* family are also abundant.

Members of the *Polypodium* family have a creeping, usually scaly, rootstock to which the stalk of each frond is jointed; when the frond is old it falls and leaves a smooth scar (no-one has ever observed the length of life of a single frond of an epiphytic fern in Malaysia). Fronds are almost always tough or fleshy; this means that they have a thick cuticle which checks the loss of water; also that they are thick enough to store some water (epiphytic orchids have leaves of similar texture, but also store water in fleshy stems). The fronds are simple or at most, pinnate, rarely very large, though there is one species, *Drynariopsis* (or *Aglaomorpha) heraclea*, which has fronds up to 2 m (6 ft) long. All these ferns have sporangia in round or more or less elongate sori which have no indusia. All of them have veins which form an elaborate network, with branching free small veins in the meshes of the net, but often the fronds are so thick that the veins cannot be seen either on the surface or by holding the frond up to the light. The best way to see the veins is to boil a bit of a frond (killing it and expelling internal air), bleach it and soak it in dilute glycerine. The different genera of the *Polypodium* family are classified partly on the nature of the scales on the rootstock, partly on sori and venation; one genus, *Belvisia* (or *Hymenolepis* of older books) has simple fronds with the sporangia on a narrow apical portion, the sporangia being protected when young by small overlapping scales. Another peculiar member of the family is called *Lecanopteris*. Its fleshy rootstock develops internal hollows and these are colonized by ants. The ants carry small seeds to their nest as food and some of these germinate between the crevices in the old parts of the fern's rootstock (which dies away at its base while the tip keeps on growing). In this way a colony of epiphytes is formed which gradually increases in bulk, the old dead parts of each plant decaying and helping to form a mass of humus which can act as a sponge to hold water after rain.

In contrast to *Polypodium*, ferns of the *Davallia* family have much-divided fronds with small leaflets, though their creeping rootstock with jointed frond-bases is very like that of the *Polypodium* family. At altitudes of 500 to 1600 m (1700 to 5300 ft) species of *Davallia*

Fig.6. One of the 22 Kinabalu species of tree-fern belonging to the genus *Cyathea*. *(Photo: Robert New)*

and *Davallodes* may be found as epiphytes, or sometimes on rocks in more open places. The main branches of a frond bear leaflets which are progressively smaller from base to apex of a branch, and the individual leaflets have asymmetric bases. In *Davallia* the scales are uniformly thin, and the sori are protected by indusia attached at base and sides (like a pocket sewn on to a coat) and which open towards the edge of the frond. The shape of the sori varies from species to species and the scales of the rootstock also. Plants of *Davallodes* have scales with a small flat base which bears a dark bristle 1 cm or more long. The form of the indusia in *Davallodes* varies; one Kinabalu species *(D. borneense)* has almost kidney-shaped indusia rather like *Thelypteris* or *Dryopteris,* the other *(D. burbidgei)* has indusia exactly as in *Davallia. Davallodes* differs from *Davallia* also in the branching pattern of its fronds which are always elongate, narrowed towards their bases, whereas *Davallia* fronds are usually widest at the base. There is one species of a third genus, *Araiostegia*, which occurs as a rather low-level epiphyte in shaded places from 1400 m to 2100 m (4600 to 7000 ft); its rootstock and fronds are much as in *Davallia* but the frond is thinner and the indusium is attached only at the base of the sorus. At higher altitudes plants of the genus *Humata*, similar to *Davallia* but smaller and often tougher, grow on small trees in rather open places. As in *Araiostegia*, the indusia are attached at the base of the sorus.

As mentioned above, plants of some species of *Asplenium* grow on rocks by streams or on the ground in forest at medium altitudes, but a large number are epiphytes; in all, 37 species in the genus are known on or near Kinabalu. The commonest species at lower altitudes is the nest-fern *A. nidus*, with simple broad fronds to 1 m (3 ft) or more long and over 10 cm (4 in) wide. The sori can be seen on the basal half of each of the closely parallel veins. These plants catch fallen leaves from trees and hold them; the mass of decaying leaves held between the bases of the fronds and the roots of the fern forms a sponge which holds water and can form the base of a colony of other epiphytes. At the other extreme, some species have bipinnate or even tripinnate fronds which may hang downwards, the largest having fronds 1.25–1.5 m (4–5 ft) long. It is difficult in some cases to understand the difference between young plants of a species which will grow larger, and mature plants of another species which will not. More field study is needed to distinguish species clearly. In other countries it is known that many natural hybrids of *Asplenium* occur. These can be detected by cytological examination and experimental cultivation, neither of which has been undertaken in Sabah.

An interesting genus of epiphytes which always has simple fronds with free veins is called *Elaphoglossum*. Fertile fronds are usually narrower than sterile ones and sometimes on longer stalks. They are always quite covered beneath with sporangia which lack indusia. The fertile fronds are probably produced seasonally, perhaps in response to dry weather; observations on this are lacking. *Elaphoglossum* plants have a short creeping scaly rootstock which has outgrowths 1–2 cm long to which the fronds are rather imperfectly jointed. Species differ in the details of the scales on their surfaces, in the shape of the fronds and the relative shape of fertile and sterile fronds. In the whole Malesian region 50 species of *Elaphoglossum* are known; on Kinabalu eight are recorded. Where

Fig.7. *Dipteris conjugata*, a common but decorative fern along trailsides and on ridges in Kinabalu Park. *(Photo: Robert New)*

Elaphoglossum plants grow with other epiphytes, their fronds at a distance look much like the leaves of orchids, so they are easy to overlook. The species of Kinabalu still need more study.

The *Vittaria* family is represented by seven species on Kinabalu. They are epiphytes or rock plants with simple fronds. *Vittaria* fronds are relatively long and narrow, and the larger ones are pendulous. Sporangia are produced either in marginal grooves or in a narrow band on each side of the midrib; they are accompanied by short hairs which have peculiar enlarged reddish or brown terminal cells. *Antrophyum* species have broader fronds, with sporangia in grooves along the veins, forming a more or less continous network; they also have characteristic hairs with the sporangia, differing in the different species. The smallest plants of the family belong to the genus *Vaginularia* and have thread-like fronds 5–10 cm (2–4 in) long.

FILMY FERNS

Filmy ferns occur everywhere on the upper part of the mountain, where clouds gather every night so that the mass of epiphytes and mosses on trees are dripping wet for a considerable part of each 24 hours. At lower altitudes they are confined to the most humid places in the forest, often near streams. These ferns have the peculiar character that each frond, apart from its veins, consists of a single layer of cells. In all other ferns, and in all higher plants, leaf-blades have a layer of cells (epidermis) on each surface and between these two layers a system of green cells with air-spaces between them; there are openings (stomata) in the epidermis which allow exchange of gases, including water vapour, with the atmosphere.

This internal leaf-structure is lacking in filmy ferns, all green cells of which are in direct contact with the air. They can only exist if the air is very humid most of the time, although many of them can withstand some drying for short periods if not exposed to strong sunlight and drying winds. On Kinabalu there are about 56 species of this family. Most of them have a slender creeping rootstock with small fronds spaced along it, but the larger ones have fronds in a tufted arrangement, the largest 30 cm (1 ft) or more long. The sori of filmy ferns are at the ends of veins, and the sporangia are borne on a slender prolongation of the vein, called a receptacle, which may continue to grow by cell division in its basal part (with continuous production of sporangia also) for some time; its tip, from which old sporangia have fallen, projects as a tiny thread. Broadly speaking, there are two types of sori. In *Hymenophyllum* each sorus is protected by two equal outgrowths at the base of the receptacles. In *Trichomanes* the receptacle grows in the base of a funnel or short tube, the mouth of which may be dilated or sometimes two-lipped. These broad divisions are not quite sharp, and there is much diversity in both *Hymenophyllum* and *Trichomanes* as so defined; for these reasons a number of separate genera have been distinguished, especially in *Trichomanes*, which has a great diversity in frond form.

HIGH-ALTITUDE EPIPHYTES

The most abundant family of epiphytes on the higher parts of the mountain is the *Grammitis* family; they also grow on rocks in rather open places. Altogether 76 species are known on Kinabalu, many occurring from 1800 m (6000 ft) upwards. Nearly one third of them belong to the genus *Grammitis*, with simple fronds 3–30 cm (*c.* 1–12 in) long and 0.5–2 cm wide, with free (usually branched) veins. They nearly always have slender stiff hairs (usually reddish) on their stalks and often on the fronds themselves. The sori are usually round and have no indusia. Thus they have some of the characters of the *Polypodium* family and in the past most have been included in *Polypodium*, but certainly they are a quite distinct group which merits family rank and their relationship to other fern families is uncertain. Apart from *Grammitis* itself most other members of the family have more or less deeply lobed simple fronds and differ in the nature of their hairs, scales, venation and position of the sori. In some cases the sporangia have stiff little hairs on them which can be seen by careful examination with a hand-lens. One genus of the family, *Scleroglossum*, has the sporangia developed in shallow grooves near the edges of the small simple narrow fronds. They resemble *Vittaria* superficially, but are very different in frond structure, spores and scales.

REFERENCES

Christensen, C. & Holttum, R.E. 1934. The Ferns of Mt Kinabalu. *Gardens' Bulletin, Straits Settlements* 8(3): 191–324.

Holttum, R.E. 1954. Plant Life in Malaya. Longmans Berhad, Kuala Lumpur.

Holttum, R.E. 1963. Ferns of Malaya (2nd edition). Government Printer, Singapore.

Holttum, R.E. 1959. Gleicheniaceae, Schizaeaceae. Flora Malesiana, series II (Pteridophyta), 1(1).

Holttum, R.E. 1963. Cyatheaceae. Flora Malesiana, series II, (Pteridophyta) 1(2).

Holttum, R.E. 1978. The *Lomariopsis* group of genera. Flora Malesiana, series II (Pteridophyta), 1(4).

Holttum, R.E. 1982. Thelypteridaceae. Flora Malesiana, series II (Pteridophyta), 1(5).

Holttum, R.E. 1991. The *Tectaria* group of genera. Flora Malesiana, series II (Pteridophyta), 2(2).

Kramer, K.U. 1971. The *Lindsaea* group of genera. Flora Malesiana, series II (Pteridophyta), 1(3).

Parris, B.S., Beaman, R.S. & Beaman, J.H. 1992. The Plants of Mt. Kinabalu 1. Ferns and Fern Allies. Royal Botanic Gardens, Kew.

Fig.1. The forest on ultramafic soil at 3000 m. *(Photo: Robert New)*

NOTES ON THE TREE FLORA OF KINABALU

Willem Meijer

To me as a botanist, born in a temperate country with a very limited tree-flora, to come to Kinabalu was like entering the promised land, a cornucopia of a flora nearly as rich as the whole of Europe with more than a thousand orchids, the richest oak-chestnut flora of any place in the world, the only place where floras on ultramafic (ultrabasic) soils could be studied at altitudes between 450 to 2750 m (1500 to 9000 ft) and a great centre of speciation of all kinds of Ericaceae, Melastomataceae, and many other families and genera, including some of the most archaic woody flowering plants like *Drimys, Ascarina* and *Magnolias*. In 1959, when I first came to Sabah, along the road from Ranau to the Poring Hot Springs at 500 m (1700 ft), many trees, palms, bamboos, aroids, gingers and woody climbers from the lowland dipterocarp forests still could be observed. Higher up near Kundasang and Tenompok it was clear that you were in the midst of the oak-chestnut forests, rich in trees of the laurel family and magnificent Magnoliaceae, Theaceae and all kinds of trees of the Myrtle family, with a smattering of conifers (some like *Podocarpus, Dacrydium, Agathis* and *Phyllocladus* with southern distribution patterns), and an increasing number of ferns and bryophytes on the ground as well as the tree-branches. Above this we saw a rhapsody of rhododendrons and for me as a bryologist the most marvellous mossy forests, laden with epiphytic orchids and ferns.

THE ZONATION OF THE TREE FLORA ON KINABALU

At a few places the boundary of the Kinabalu park goes down to around 150 m (500 ft), but most of the lowland forest included within it is secondary regrowth. One interesting tree found in secondary forest on degraded soils north-west of Kampung Kiau is *Cratoxylon arborescens*. There is more old and young secondary forest around Poring, which has turned out to be a rich source of plants with active compounds that have potential against AIDS and cancer. Remnant patches of fairly good lowland forest could still be found in 1981 near Kampung Nalumad and Kampung Manggis. However these forests have never been properly explored. As we go higher, to around 900 m (3000 ft) species in the lowland families of dipterocarps, figs and fruit trees start to decrease and they usually peter out completely between 1500–1700 m (5000–5500 ft). In agricultural terms this means that here we are above the zone of the tropical lowland fruit trees such as mango, rambutan, durian, jackfruit, *'cempedak'* and *'tarap'* which do not thrive in cool tropical montane climates. However there is another group of mainly lowland trees which is not so temperature-sensitive and which is typical of coastal *'kerangas'* (podsol) and peat soils. These find a niche near Tenompok at 1500 m (5000 ft) on the acid mountain podsol soils : *Agathis, Mezzetia leptopoda, Garcinia bancana, Blumeodendron tokbrai, Fagraea fragrans, Aromadendron elegans, Tristaniopsis whiteana, T. bilocularis, Xanthophyllum affine, Xanthophyllum palembanicum* and *Dehaasia caesia*. Another example of such a tree is *Leptospermum flavescens* which occurs near Kudat and Sandakan near the coast on sandy soils, and which on Kinabalu dominates along some wind and cloud swept ridges up to at least 2450 m (8000 ft) altitude. These may have found refugia here from inundated coastal regions during the warm intervals of the Pleistocene.

The montane families which take over from the dipterocarps and other lowland groups between 900 to 1800 m (3000 to 6000 ft) are the Myrtaceae, Ericaceae, Fagaceae, Theaceae, Magnoliaceae, Podocarpaceae, Cornaceae, Juglandaceae, Clethraceae, Araliaceae and Symplocaceae. Most of these also have representatives in the lowlands, especially on poor soils like those in the Leila Forest Reserve near Sandakan or Bukit Padang near Kota Kinabalu.

The upper limit of trees on Kinabalu is below Sayat-Sayat at about 3350 m (11,000 ft) altitude. Little pockets of forest creep up some of the gullys, but the scouring water keeps many of the steep granite cliffs bare of trees. Apart from the woody Ericaceae, *Schima brevifolia, Drimys piperita, Phyllocladus hypophyllus, Dacrycarpus kinabaluensis* and some *Eugenia* are the species reaching the highest elevations (Meijer, 1965).

Some of the outstanding trees at different altitudes and on the different soils, are highlighted in the following sections.

SECONDARY FOREST NEAR PORING HOT SPRINGS, 150–500 m (500–1700 ft)

Pterygota horsfieldii (Sterculiaceae) has been previously collected in East Kalimantan, East Java, Ceram and New Guinea. It was found as a very large tree in the middle of a burnt field just outside the Park boundary at Poring by Meijer and Beaman in 1983 and 1987. Young sterile specimens were collected in nearby secondary forest, and a few trees may still survive inside the Park near the hot springs.

Hibiscus macrophyllus (Malvaceae). This ornamental tree is the only wild species of hibiscus known from Kinabalu. It occurs around Poring, but is not protected there.

Cinnamomum parthenoxylon (Lauraceae). A tree with very fragrant timber and bark which contains saffrol. Old stumps are very durable and the timber does not lose its fragrance over time.

Cinnamomum burmanii (Lauraceae), 'keningau', 'kulit manis'. People from villages around Kinabalu, especially Kampung Nalumad, still go up the mountain slopes to collect the bark of this wild cinnamon tree. In West Sumatra, long ago, it became a frequent constituent of the homestead gardens and an important export product (Heyne, 1927).

Octomeles sumatrana (Datiscaceae), *'binuang'*. This very fast-growing large tree finds its niche in the hot soggy soil around the hot springs at Poring. It is gregarious along rivers in the lowlands, and can also be seen in the regrowth of old rubber estates along the Sibuga road, Sandakan. Trees are either male or female and the flowers are pollinated by bats during the evening.

Duabanga moluccana (Sonneratiaceae), *'magas'*. Another fast-growing secondary-forest tree which reaches its upper limit near Poring. It should be tried as a fast-growing tree in plantations.

Baccaurea macrocarpa (Euphorbiaceae). A rather spectacular cauliflorous species of the *'tampoi'* genus.

Oroxylum indicum (Bignoniaceae), the Midnight Horror Tree. A magnificent description of this striking and unusual tree is found in Corner (1988).

Litsea garciae (Lauraceae), *'pangalaban'*. According to Burgess (1966) this species is identical with *L. sebifera*. In some parts of Indonesia this tree is considered an attractive fruit tree. It should be tried out in mixed plantations in buffer zones around the park. Heyne (1927) cites a paper by Greshoff who reported many uses of this tree. It deserves renewed study.

Wikstroemia tenuiramis (Thymelaeaceae). A shrub with very strong silky bark fibers. It should be tested for paper manufacture.

THE UPPER DIPTEROCARP FORESTS ABOVE PORING HOT SPRINGS, 500–1200 m (1700–4000 ft)

Elmerillia mollis (Magnoliaceae). This is one of the most valuable trees in the flora of Kinabalu. We once found a large specimen of this tree in an area that was being relogged near Mt. Silam, Lahad Datu. It turned out to be the most excellent furniture timber the local sawmillers had ever seen. This is one of the botanical treasures of Kinabalu which should be saved and propagated in plantations. It might become extinct before its value is realized.

Shorea platyclados (Dipterocarpaceae). This dark red *'seraya'* is being grown in local plantations by village people in Sumatra. It could be grown with *Elmerillia, Duabanga* and *Octomeles*, in abandoned coffee estates, together with all sorts of native durians, *Artocarpus, Baccaurea* and *Nephelium*, rattans and other palms, bamboos and local spices like wild gingers, Marantaceae, wild bananas, *Amorphophallus* and *Rafflesia*. Such a buffer-zone plantation would be of enormous economic value for future development of Sabah and also serve as a tourist attraction.

BUKIT KULUNG – BUKIT HAMPUAN, 450–1400 m (1500–4500 ft)

These ultramafic hills are part of the ultramafic mountain complex which ranges through the eastern part of Sabah from Mt. Silam near Lahad Datu through the upper reaches of the Kinabatangan river to the Labuk river catchment. The whole range marks the place where an old continental plate shifted against the rest of Borneo. These two adjacent ultramafic hills form the most accessible parts of the range being only a few miles from Ranau, but there are a few other ultramafic outcrops that flank the base of Kinabalu.

The tree flora of these areas is still not completely known. From the air the forest on this type of geological formation can always be recognised by its small-crowned appearance. These forests were left untouched by the local Dusuns who had learned that the red-brown soils were unsuitable for growing rice and tapioca. There is always an abundance of small-leaved climbing bamboos in these forests and several rare rattans have also been noticed in them according to field work by Drs. J. and S. Dransfield (pers. comm.). These included *Calamus amplijugus, C. gonospermus, C. laevigatus var. mucronatus, C. zonatus, Daemonorops sabut* and the dwarf palm *Pinanga pilosa*. However, during 1990, large areas were burnt. The most remarkable trees here are the Sabah endemic *Borneodendron aenigmaticum* with red, bleeding bark and two trees shared with the adjacent Philippines:

Fig.2. *Leptospermum recurvum* (Myrtaceae) on ultramafic soils on Kinabalu. *(Photo: K.M. Wong)*

Fig.3. Upper montane forest at 2500 m. *(Photo: K.M. Wong)*

Buxus rolfei and *Excoecaria philippinensis*. The white latex of the latter is extremely dangerous to the eyes and it apparently contains cancer-inducing agents. *Buxus* has some specially bitter substances in its bark. The forest at this altitude on Bukit Hampuan is a mixture of dipterocarps, oaks and conifers with some tropical lowland tree families like Anacardiaceae and Burseraceae. Among the dipterocarps the dark red *'seraya' Shorea venulosa* is and was common as it is in the Labuk mountains and on Mt. Silam. Far rarer is *Dipterocarpus ochraceus* which was found here new to science. It might now be close to extinction. In the genus *Hopea* there was a whole series of rather rare species collected here, only known from this site in the park: *Hopea argentea, H. beccariana, H. dryobalanoides, H. ferruginea, H. pedicellata* and *H. vesquei*.

Towards the summit of Bukit Hampuan we found *Shorea platyclados, Shorea parvistipulata* ssp. *nebulosa* and *Shorea monticola,* none of which is restricted to the ultramafics. A selection of further lowland elements in the tree flora include the giant *Canarium pseudodecumanum*, various Sapotaceae *(Palaquium beccarianum, Planchonella obovata, Pouteria malaccensis)*, *Koompasia excelsa, Scorodocarpus borneensis,* with bark smelling like onions, some nasty *'renghas'* trees *(Gluta wallichii, Melanochyla fulvinervis,* and *Semecarpus cuneiformis)*, with the more innocent *Parishia maingayi* (unique on Kinabalu from this locality) representing the same family, the Anacardiaceae. Among the wild nutmegs (Myristicaceae) are *Gymnacranthera contracta*,

Fig.4. Seed cones of the conifer *Agathis lenticula* (Araucariaceae), endemic to Sabah's Crocker Range and Mt. Kinabalu. *(Photo: A. Lamb)*

G. farquhariana and *Horsfieldia punctatifolia*. In the Annonaceae are trees like *Monocarpia marginalis, Polyalthia cauliflora, P. rumphii* and *P. sumatrana* and in the Tiliaceae, the medium-sized *Pentace discolor* and *P. laxiflora*. Meliaceae is represented by *Aphanamixis borneensis*, Moraceae by *Artocarpus nitidus, A. rigidus* and *A. tamaran*, and Opiliaceae by *Urobotrya parviflora*.

Towards the summits of both hills we found *Borneodendron, Gymnostoma sumatranum,* and *Agathis dammara*, as very large trees and also *Engelhardia, Tristaniopsis, Falcatifolium falciforme, Dacrydium* cf. *beccarii, Drimys piperita, Podocarpus neriifolius, Trigoniastrum hypoleucum* and some Magnoliaceae *(Michelia montana* and *Magnolia sarawakensis).*

The forest here is rather rich in Lauraceae *(Actinodaphne* sp., *Alseodaphne oblanceolata, Cryptocarya crassinervia, Lindera bibracteata, Litsea* (four species) and species of 'obah' *(Syzygium alcinae, S.* cf. *bankense, S. brachirachis, S. fastigiatum, S. sandakanensis, S.* cf. *tenuicaudatum* and one undescribed species). Fagaceae are represented by some 30 species including *Lithocarpus bennettii, L. cantleyanus, L. caudatifolius, L. ferrugineus, L. nieuwenhuisii,* and *L. sericobalanus,* and several species of *Castanopsis* and *Quercus*. I made the first record here for Sabah of the Rubiaceae *Cinchona*-like tree *Mussaendopsis beccariana.* Also in the Flacourtiaceae, *Homalium panayanum, Hydnocarpus woodii, Osmelia philippina* and *Xylosma luzonense* have been found only here on Kinabalu. The lower margin of Bukit Kulung near Ladang Tintululunang is a peculiar shrubby grazing area with several low-growing Flacourtiaceae, *Guioa, Buchanania* and the rare representative of the Boraginaceae *Pteleocarpa lamponga*.

We had hoped that Bukit Kulung–Bukit Hampuan could become a Research Forest with a special Research Station in close proximity to Ranau. Without such a provision, illegal land clearing and further burning could make it vanish. Increased visitation by students and scientific tourists would also benefit the local economy.

THE FOREST AROUND PARK HEADQUARTERS, 1550 m (5100 ft)

During the early 1960's a network of walking trails was put into place in the submontane oak forests around Park Headquarters between 1200 to 1800 m (4000 to 6000 ft). Many trees, certainly over 500, were labelled and specimens collected from them with the purpose of finding out more about the forest composition (Meijer, 1975). Unfortunately, many of these trees have now disappeared. Basically the forest here is a continuation of the Crocker Range vegetation, stretching all the way from Sarawak and west Kalimantan into Sabah. In order to grasp the forest structure of this place one has to become familiar in the first place with the oak family (Fagaceae) and with the genera *Quercus, Castanopsis, Lithocarpus,* and *Trigonobalanus*. Probably more species could be located here. *Castanopsis acuminatissima*, almost looking like a *Lithocarpus, Castanopsis costata,* and *C. microphylla,* were all collected years ago by the Clemenses near Tenompok, now bare of forest. The same is true for *Lithocarpus elegans, L. encleisocarpa, L. luteus,* and *L. porcatus.* Any threat to the integrity of the forests here can potentially cause the extinction of these species.

Fig.5. *Pteleocarpa lamponga* (Boraginaceae). *(Photo: K.M. Wong)*

Fig.6. *Bhesa paniculata* (Celastraceae). *(Photo: K.M. Wong)*

Fig.7. *Borneodendron aenigmaticum*, a large tree unusual in the Rubber-tree family (Euphorbiaceae) for having a red sap, is endemic to Sabah's ultramafic areas and also occur on Kinabalu. *(Photo: J. Kulip)*

Fig.8. Beccari's Tree-Mussaenda, *Mussaendopsis beccariana* (Rubiaceae), in flower. *(Photo: K.M. Wong)*

Fig.9. The long, sword-shaped pods and thin winged seeds are distinctive of the Midnight Horror Tree, *Oroxylum indicum* (Bignoniaceae), found in lowlands and around Poring. *(Photo: K.M. Wong)*

Fig.10. Numerous long-stalked, brightly yellow fruit follicles developed from a single flower of a *Polyalthia rumphii* tree (Annonaceae). *(Photo: K.M. Wong)*

A survey of 455 numbered trees and some collections from this area showed that there is a tree flora of about 150 species, belonging to about 50 families. Only at one place did we try to enumerate a one-acre plot. It was around a rich stand of *Agathis* along the southern boundary of the Park. The main families were Fagaceae (with 28 species), Guttiferae (about 20), Lauraceae (about 26), Myrtaceae (about 20), Theaceae (15), Symplocaceae (11), and Magnoliaceae (4). The most frequent conifers were *Dacrycarpus (Podocarpus) imbricatus, Agathis* sp. and *Phyllocladus hypophyllus*. Among the dicot trees only the following species occured more than three times in the sample : *Dacryodes macrocarpa, Calophyllum aureum, Garcinia "ramiflora", Shorea monticola, Blumeodendron, Quercus subsericea, Elaeocarpus mastersii, Tristaniopsis bilocularis, Aglaia ignea, Magnolia carsonii, Horsfieldia glabra, Knema kinabaluensis, Palaquium gutta* and *Adinandra clemensiae*. The forest here is poorer in species than the upper dipterocarp forests near Poring but the majority of species are widely scattered and only a few conifers and some oaks are locally gregarious. About 20 families which have tens of species in the lowlands peter out here with only one to three species at very low frequencies. A most peculiar archaic tree here is *Ascarina philippinensis*. This tree is also known from the Pinosuk Plateau and from the eastern shoulder of Kinabalu. The genus is also known from New Zealand. Pollen of this family is among that of the oldest flowering plants known so far.

Fig.11. Seedling of the Celery Pine, *Phyllocladus hypophyllus* (Podocarpaceae). *(Photo: K.M. Wong)*

Fig.12. Fine, fern-like foliage of *Dacrycarpus imbricatus* (Podocarpaceae), a common conifer on Kinabalu and other Bornean mountains. *(Photo: K.M. Wong)*

THE PINOSUK PLATEAU AND SOSOPODON, *c*. 1500 m (5000 ft)

It is difficult to describe in detail the flora of this unique area at about 1500 m (5000 ft) along the southern flank of the mountain facing Kundasang and Ranau. It has been largely destroyed now, but a few remnant patches might possibly be refugia for a number of species. The small Sosopodon Forest Reserve contains more than 30 species of Fagaceae, much more than the several found on the whole Pinosuk Plateau. Jacobson (1978) describes this plateau as the result of massive glacial erosion and re-deposit dating from the late Pleistocene after the uplift a few million years ago of the Kinabalu intrusion. The summit cone north of the plateau was covered with a 5.5 sq. km ice-cap. No other side of the mountain shows a relative flat area like this one, dissected by rivers and with thick sandy gravels derived from granite. The main soil type missing from Sosopodon is the larger boggy gravel deposits, often with lots of *Tristaniopsis bilocularis* and two other species of *Tristaniopsis*, which still persist near the golf course site on the Pinosuk Plateau.

Two trees which were found on the Pinosuk Plateau and have never yet been discovered near Park Headquarters are *Acer niveum* and *Sycopsis dunnii* (Meijer, 1968). Both species, witnesses of the ancient evolution of the flora are also known from Sulawesi, but they may now be extinct in Sabah.

The Pinosuk Plateau, especially the lower parts close to Ranau must have been the mainstay of the figs so well described by Corner (1978) who hunted here for species and who came up with almost half of the whole Bornean fig flora from this one mountain, 78 in total of which 13 are endemic, the richest fig flora of any comparable area in the world. The same could be said of the montane oaks and the twelve or so Magnoliaceae and the scores of species of *Syzygium (Eugenia)*, besides many undescribed species which have been collected only in a sterile state. Other examples are *Garcinia* and *Elaeocarpus*.

Among my old notes I found a handwritten report on the Flora of the Sosopodon Forest Reserve dating from December 3, 1966 and it runs as follows:

"Sosopodon Reserve is only 11 hectares (about 26 acres) in size at about 1200 m (4000 ft) altitude just west of Kundasang along the Tamparuli–Ranau road. The terrain is well drained and not too steep, dissected by some small streams and with a well developed topsoil. The forest here has a somewhat different structure from the flatter parts of the nearby Pinosuk Plateau and from areas around Park Headquarters near Tenompok (altitude 1200–1800 m; 4000–6000 ft) because of lack of sandy acid soils. As a consequence *Agathis* is quite scarce here and *Tristaniopsis* is almost absent. The flora of oaks and chestnuts in this reserve is very rich. It also includes the Trig-oak *Trigonobalanus*. Among the largest trees, nearly 2 m in girth, occurs *Palaquium gutta*, the famous *'gutta percha'* tree, which produces latex used for billiard balls and undersea cables and a new species of *Magnolia* named *M. carsonii*. This reserve has a rich population of this new species and it should be considered the type locality. Besides the oaks which are still not all described botanically there exist here a fairly large number of species of *Syzygium (Eugenia)*, *Garcinia* and Lauraceae which are still unknown to science or incompletely described. The

Fig.13. Gigantic acorns of the oak, *Lithocarpus revolutus* (Fagaceae). *(Photo: A. Lamb)*

'*kundasang*' tree, *Coelostegia griffithii*, a relative of the durian, occurs at the southern margin of the reserve just near the garbage pit of the old Forest Bungalow. Only two collections of this tree have been made so far in Sabah. I have also seen it on Mt. Alab in the Crocker Range. The name of Kundasang village probably comes from this tree. Another very rare tree at Sosopodon is *Nyssa javanica*, along the rather steep trail above the bungalow not far from the plantations surrounding this site. So far this is the only tree of this genus found in Sabah. Fossils of it have been found all over the northern hemisphere and it still occurs in eastern North America. The representation of lowland tree families at Sosopodon is somewhat greater than near Park Headquarters because the altitude is about 300 m (1000 ft) lower. The presence of various Euphorbiaceae (*Baccaurea* for example), Celastraceae like *Bhesa paniculata*, the legumes *Parkia roxburghii*, *Milletia* and *Pithecellobium havilandii*, one *Microcos* species (Tiliaceae), some *Artocarpus*, *Meliosma*, *Aglaia* and *Sandoricum*, *Ixonanthes reticulata*, *Sterculia parvifolia* and *Phaeanthus ophthalmicus* (Annonaceae) demonstrate this. The only dipterocarp known from the reserve is *Shorea monticola*. *Planchonella maingayi* is one of the valuable '*nyatoh*' timber trees here. Along the southern boundary occur some trees typical for secondary forests on the slopes of Kinabalu and the Crocker Range including species of *Ficus*, *Macaranga*, *Ardisia copelandii*, and *Ilex cissoidea*. The latter tree should be tested for pulping qualities and as a possible source of timber for the match industry. Quite a number of trees (over 800) have been permanently labelled in this reserve to follow up sterile collections with those of flowers and fruits. Unfortunately at many times the fruiting and flowering of new species of *Eugenia* and *Garcinia* have passed unnoticed. In the undergrowth some tree ferns and the rare terrestrial orchid *Macodes* occur and nearby is the only known locality of a species of the parasitic *Balanophora*."

THE TREE FLORA ABOVE KAMBORANGOH, 1800–3200 m (6000–10,500 ft)

This is the cloudforest zone, where the rhododendron family and some conifers, ferns and bryophytes are dominant together with the festoons of *Nepenthes* and the *Embelia* climbers. Along some ridges there is dominance of *Leptospermum flavescens*, replaced on the ultramafics at about 8000 ft altitude by *L. recurvum* and joined there by *Dacrydium gibbsiae*, *Castanopsis* and some oaks like *Lithocarpus turbinatus*, *L. havilandii*, *L. bullatus* which are among the highest-reaching Fagaceae. *Daphniphyllum*, *Myrica*, *Xanthomyrtus*, some *Magnolia*, *Elaeocarpus*, *Prunus*, *Polyosma*, *Adinandra*, *Schima*, high- altitude species of *Syzygium (Eugenia)*, various *Ilex* species and *Drimys* are also regulars here, besides a sprinkling of *Tristaniopsis*, *Ardisia*, *Schefflera*, *Symplocos* and Lauraceae. The total tree flora recorded at this altitude is about 50 species. At the highest forest altitudes some species of *Rapanea*, *Polyosma* and *Myrica* still occur and the rocky ultramafic summit of Mt. Tambuyukon, (2634 m, 8652 ft) is crowned with the local endemics *Scaevola verticillata* and *Rhododendron meijeri*.

Patches of mossy forests creep up in some gullies to 3200 m (10,500 ft), largely dominated by Ericaceae, conifers and some *Photinia*. *Phyllocladus* finds company there with other more herbaceous plants of southern affinity: *Drapetes*, *Coprosma* and *Trachymene*.

It is too early to publish a tree flora for Kinabalu. Too many species are still undescribed. It cannot be stressed too much that we need a system of permanent plots and permanently labelled and located trees as a living inventory of the tree flora of this park. A specimen in a herbarium becomes like a fossil when nobody can find the species it represents any more at any place in its natural habitat. Its bark may contain a cure for cancer but what is the use if nobody can find a living tree for further propagation? We can now process data on forest communities and forest regeneration with computers, but all this technology is in vain if we cannot properly collect and identify these trees anymore. In this way we can go back to the stone-age in the midst of modern technology.

REFERENCES

Burgess, P.F. 1966. Timbers of Sabah. Sabah Forest Records no. 6. Forest Department, Sabah, Malaysia.

Corner, E.J.H. 1978. The Plant Life. In: Luping, M., Chin, W. & Dingley, E.R. (eds.) Kinabalu—Summit of Borneo. The Sabah Society, Kota Kinabalu.

Corner, E.J.H. 1988. Wayside Trees of Malaya (3rd edition). 2 vols. Malayan Nature Society, Kuala Lumpur.

Heyne, K. 1927. *De nuttige planten van Indonesie* (2nd edition). 3 vols. Batavia, Indonesia.

Jacobson, G. 1978. The Geology. In: Luping, M., Chin, W. & Dingley, E.R. (eds.) Kinabalu—Summit of Borneo. The Sabah Society, Kota Kinabalu.

Meijer, W. 1965. A Botanical Guide to the Flora of Mt. Kinabalu. In: Symposium on Ecological Research on Humid Tropics Vegetation. Government of Sarawak and UNESCO.

Meijer, W. 1968. Botanical Bulletin no. 10. Illustration of *Sycopsis dunnii* opposite page 39. Forest Department, Sabah, Malaysia.

Meijer, W. 1975. The montane forest zone on Mount Kinabalu near the National Park Headquarters. Annual Report, Sabah National Park Trustees, 1974. p. 12–18.

Fig.1. Fresh after a shower, the waxy white blooms of *Rhododendron suaveolens* maintain their elegance. *(Photo: C.L. Chan)*

THE RHODODENDRON AND BLUEBERRY FAMILY

George Argent

The Ericaceae is a fairly large family of flowering plants which is technically characterised by distinctive free stamens whose anthers turn upside down during development and have the rather unusual feature of shedding pollen through pores and not slits (Fig. 2). The family Epacridaceae shares the peculiarity of stamen structure but has the stamens attached to the corolla, not free, as in the Ericaceae. The leaves of the two families are also quite different, Ericaceae usually having a well-developed midrib and network of smaller veins whereas Epacridaceae usually have fine parallel veins more like those of a monocotyledon.

The Ericaceae are distinctive ecologically in being best developed in cool, moist, acid situations. This is probably associated with the root system having an endotrophic mycorrhiza which gives the family a competitive advantage in poor peaty soils. Thus in South-east Asia the Ericaceae are most common on the mountains, being rare at sea level.

The Ericaceae is a family notable in contributing many species which make attractive garden plants in temperate and subtropical areas. Of these *Rhododendron* is probably the best known and the most widely grown.

RHODODENDRON

Rhododendron is the largest genus in the family with about 900 species worldwide of which about one third occur in South-east Asia. Borneo is the second richest island with about 50 species described, 35 of which have been recorded from Sabah and 24 from Kinabalu. The Kinabalu species all belong in section *Vireya*, the predominant group in South-east Asia, which are characterised by their long-tailed seeds. Kinabalu remains one of the most accessible places to see a relatively large number of '*Vireya*' species in one place. A minimum of six species should be seen in flower by a careful observer climbing from Park Headquarters to the summit and back, and at a good time of year, 10–15

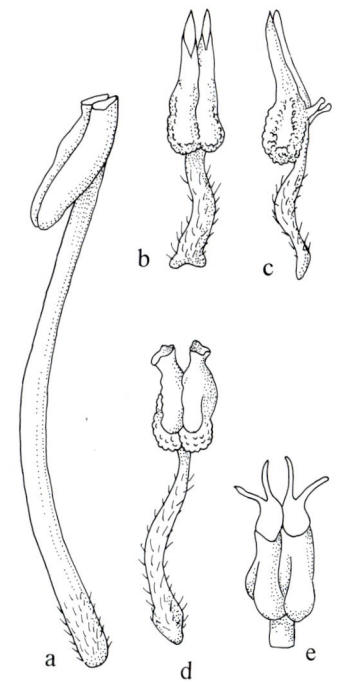

Fig.2. Stamens of *Rhododendron* (a), *Vaccinium* sect. *Rigiolepis* (b & c), *Gaultheria* (d), and *Vaccinium* sect. *Bracteata* (e).

Fig.3. *Rhododendron crassifolium*, a common epiphyte in the lower montane forest. *(Photo: C.L. Chan)*

species can be seen. Only in parts of New Guinea, mostly much less accessible, can this number be equalled or bettered. Corner's treatment (this volume) provides an overview of this spectacular genus on the mountain. For a detailed account see "Rhododendrons of Sabah" by G. Argent, A. Lamb, A. Phillipps & S. Collenette, Sabah Parks Publication No. 8, 1988.

GAULTHERIA

This is an interesting genus of about 150 species with a curious distribution around the rim of the South Pacific and across from South-east Asia into the Himalayas. The genus is very closely related to *Diplycosia* differing essentially in the stamen structure, but the only species occurring in Borneo (and on this island only known from Kinabalu) is easily separated by its racemose inflorescence (Fig. 3a).

G. borneensis Stapf
The habit of this varies from small prostrate plants to erect shrubs up to 120 cm high. It occurs in open rocky areas from about 3300 to 3800 m and can be recognised by its dainty white flowers in small but distinct racemes with a well-developed peduncle which does not occur in *Diplycosia* species. A close look at the position of the ovary may be needed to distinguish it from *Vaccinium* species but in fact the only common *Vaccinium* species of the open granite are *V. coriaceum* and *V. stapfianum* both of which usually have pink flowers. It has been suggested that the prostrate and erect forms of this species may represent separate taxa but more work is needed to refute or establish this suggestion. *G. borneensis* is also known from central Luzon in the Philippines.

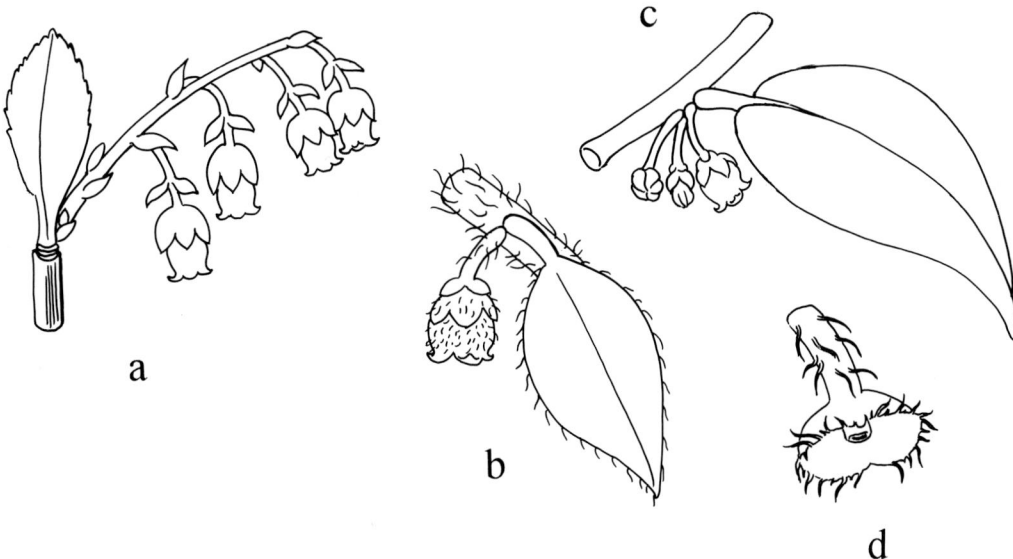

Fig.4. Inflorescence type in *Gaultheria* (a) and *Diplycosia* (b, c), and the distinctive persistent pair of bracteoles at the base of the flower in *Diplycosia* (d).

Fig.5. *Rhododendron brookeanum* var. *kinabaluensis* (Red form). *(Photo: C.L. Chan)*

Fig.6. *Rhododendron brookeanum* var. *kinabluensis* (Orange form). *(Photo: C.L. Chan)*

Fig.7. Rather disproportionate, the brilliant red flowers of the diminutive *Rhododendron ericoides* are larger than its leaves. *(Photo: C.L. Chan)*

Fig.8. *Rhododendron rugosum*. (Photo: C.L. Chan)

DIPLYCOSIA

This is a genus of which just over 100 species have been described, about half from Borneo, and from Kinabalu 27, which is rather more than one quarter of the total. *Diplycosia* is poorly known as its small flowers are easily overlooked and it is not sought nearly so keenly as the more showy Ericaceae.

Many members of this genus have conspicuous brown bristles especially on the young stems and leaves but this is not true of all the species. The genus is probably best identified in the field by the distinctive pair of bracteoles at the base of the flower which usually persist on the dead flower stalk after both flower and fruit have gone (Fig. 4b). *Diplycosia* is closely related to *Gaultheria* but the solitary or fasciculate inflorescence of *Diplycosia* will distinguish it (Fig. 4c & d). A great deal of field study needs to be carried out on details of flowering time, the structure of the 'fruit' which because it is fleshy is not clearly preserved in dried specimens, and the altitude and other ecological limits of the different species.

Descriptions of nearly all the species will be found in Flora Malesiana Vol. 6, pp. 696–740 by H. Sleumer, 1967. When seeking to seriously study *Diplycosia* young shoots should be examined for full details of the different hairs which may be present and fruits should be measured and described fresh unless they are to be pickled in alcohol.

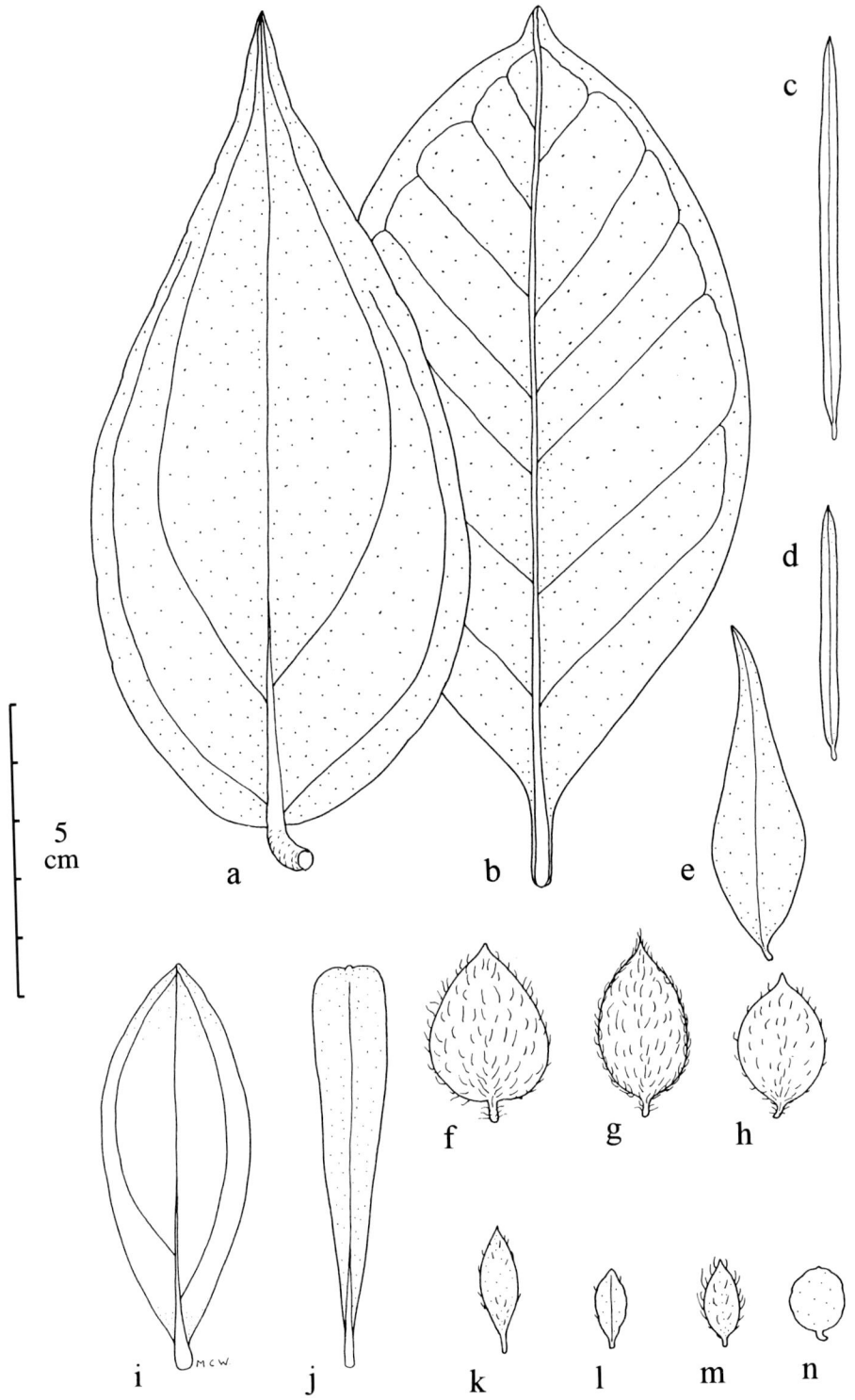

Fig.9. *Diplycosia* leaves.
a. *D. cinnamomifolia.* b. *D. punctulata.* c. *D. rosmarinifolia.* d. *D. pinifolia.* e. *D. caudatifolia.*
f. *D. carrii.* g. *D. chrysothrix.* h. *D. pseudorufescens.* i. *D. commutata.* j. *D. sphenophylla.*
k. *D. myrtillus.* l. *D. ciliolata.* m. *D. abscondita.* n. *D. crenulata.*

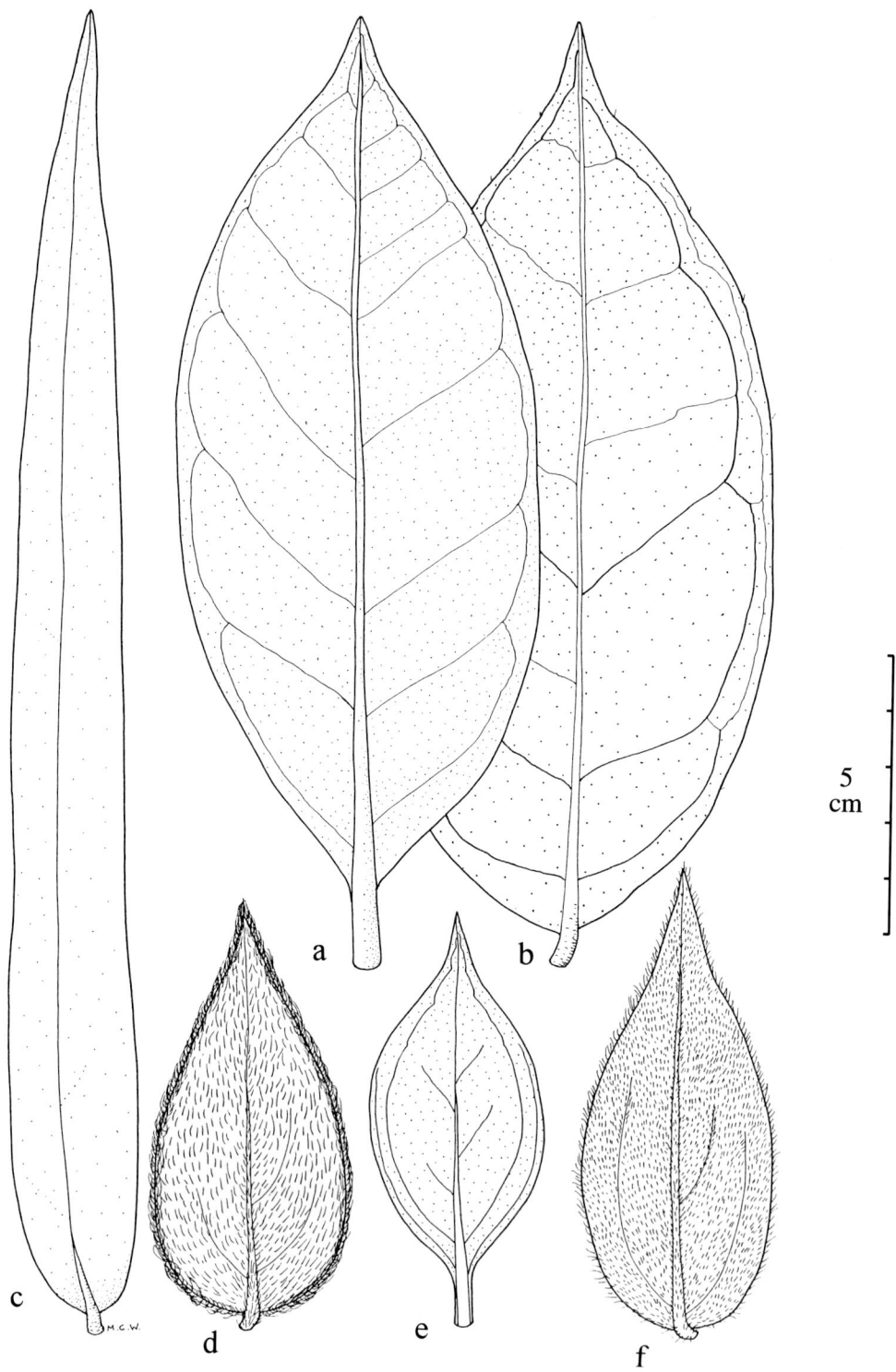

Fig.10. *Diplycosia* leaves, lower side.
a. *D. heterophylla.* b. *D. penduliflora.* c. *D. ensifolia.* d. *D. aurea.* e. *D. memecyloides* f. *D. rufa.*

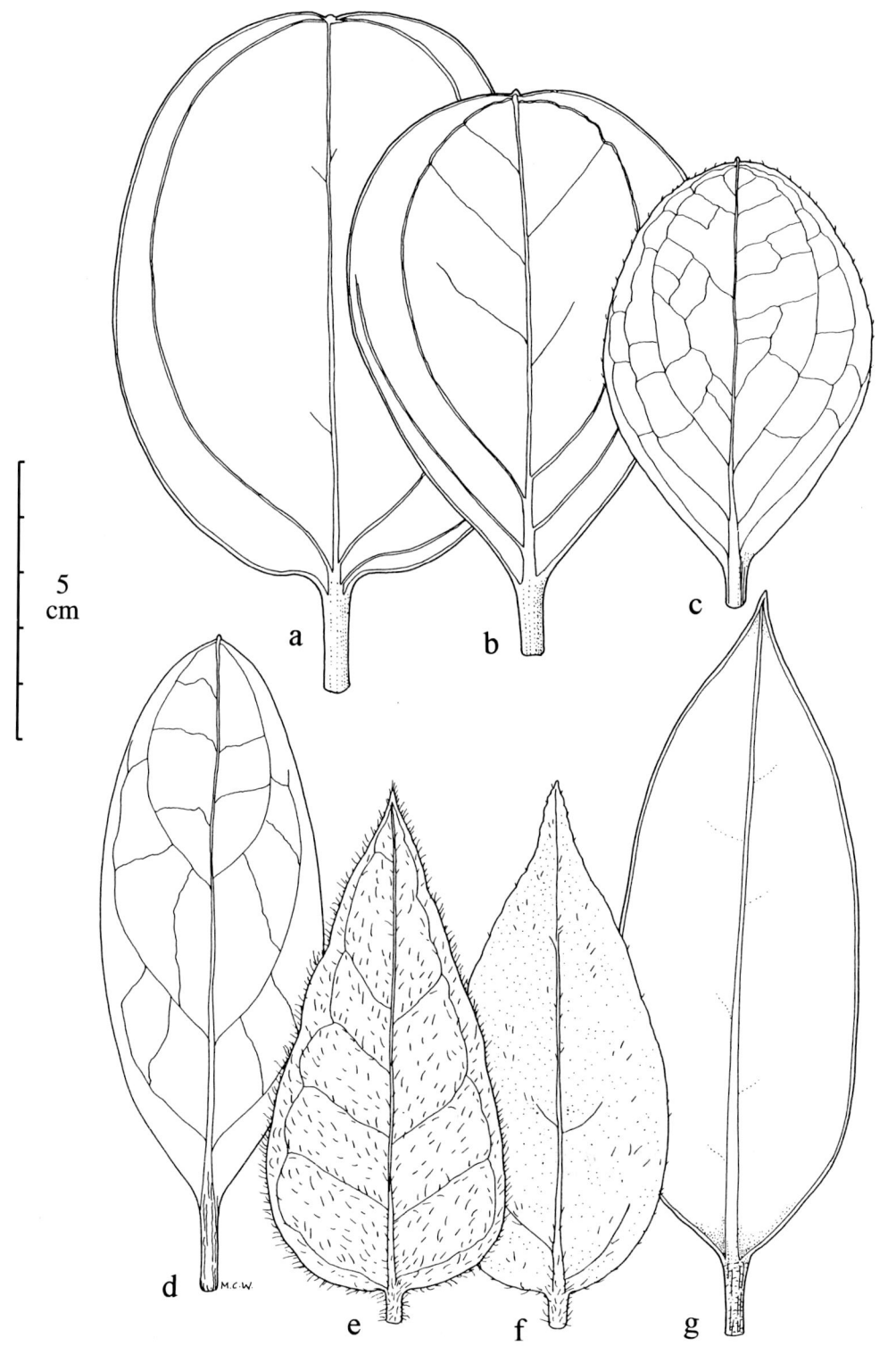

Fig.11. *Diplycosia* leaves, lower side.
a. *D. sanguinolenta.* b. *D. urceolata.* c. *D. kinabaluensis.* d. *D. pittosporifolia* var. *punctiloba.*
e. *D. clementium.* f. *D. hirtiflora.* g. *D. viridiflora.*

Notes on the species

D. abscondita Sleumer (Fig. 9m)
This is an apparently rare species which is poorly known from open rocky ridges between 2400 and 3200 m.

D. aurea Sleumer (Fig. 10d)
A fairly common species, it is distinctive amongst the very bristly species in that the leaf bristles are flattened against the leaf underneath, not erect. It grows as an epiphyte mostly on the bases of trees in ridge forest between 1200 and 1500 m.

D. carrii Sleumer (Fig. 9f)
A small leaved, uncommon species with translucent pink flowers, this has been reported from swampy forest at 1500 m but probably grows as an epiphyte in other types of vegetation. It is very similar to *D. chrysothrix,* but differs from it in the glabrous ovary.

Fig.12. *Diplycosia chrysothrix. (Photo: C.L. Chan)*

Fig.13. *Diplycosia memecyloides. (Photo: C.L. Chan)*

D. caudatifolia Sleumer (Fig. 9e)

A common small-leaved species without bristles and with long attenuate leaf apices, it usually grows between 2000 and 3000 m in shaded situations, often hanging from trunks and large branches in valley forest but is easily overlooked.

D. chrysothrix Stapf (Fig. 9g)

Small-leaved and densely bristly plants, this is found creeping on mossy ground or hanging from branches between 1400 and 3000 m. They are common and easily seen on the hills and ridges around Park Headquarters. The flowers are most commonly white but are also described as violet and green. It differs from *D. carrii* in the hairy ovary.

D. ciliolata Hooker (Fig. 9l)

This is an erect shrub which is usually terrestrial in open areas on the granite dome from 1800 to 3500 m where it is abundant. The foliage is very attractive, small, dense and moderately bristly, but the flowers are small, usually white and inconspicuous.

D. cinnamomifolia Stapf (Fig. 9a)

This is a common, hairless large-leaved species with the leaves ending in acuminate points. It grows as an erect shrub or climber which can be quite conspicuous and very attractive when in full flower, with masses of the lilac flowers clustered like little beads along the stems, in the upper tongues of forest between 2400 and 3600 m.

D. clementium Sleumer (Fig. 11e)

This is a common species in the group of very bristly species occurring between 1300 and 2900 m with large acuminate leaves. The flowers are described as cream, pale green, slate-blue to pink or purplish. More careful observation will probably reduce this apparent variation. The corolla is very hairy in this species and open flowers can be difficult to find.

D. commutata Sleumer (Fig. 9i)

A fairly common species, this is an erect, glabrous shrub with fleshy, white or pink flowers recorded between 1300 and 1500 m, probably mostly epiphytic but with very poor records of observation in the wild. The hairs on the pedicels are sparse, rather thick and glandular and are very quickly shed leaving the pedicel more or less glabrous.

D. crenulata Sleumer (Fig. 9n)

A rare species, this is distinctive with its small rounded leaves but imperfectly understood in its relationship with other small species such as *D. acuminata* and *D. elliptica* and it may well turn out to be a form of *D. elliptica*. Recorded from 1200 to 1700 m, it is mostly an epiphyte high in trees and only seen on recently fallen branches.

D. ensifolia Merrill (Fig. 10c)

A rare species, this has highly distinctive long glabrous leaves. It is reported from between 1370 and 2440 m but there have been no recent collections.

D. heterophylla Blume (Fig. 10a)

An uncommon, but widespread and variable species, this is poorly understood and probably frequently confused with *D. punctulata* which occurs at higher altitude. It is a coarse glabrous plant with large leaves. All Bornean records are probably referable to variety *latifolia* which has been recorded between 700 and 3315 m but altitude records for Kinabalu are incomplete and it is most doubtful if it has anything like this range on the mountain. It occurs as an epiphyte around park headquarters but usually grows high in large trees and is difficult to observe.

D. hirtiflora Argent (Fig. 11f)
This is a rare bristly species related to *D. clementium* but with smaller flowers, so far only collected once from Bukit Hampuan at 1330 m.

D. kinabaluensis Stapf (Fig. 11e)
A common, low, creeping species with fairly large obovate or elliptic leaves, this is a characteristic feature of granite crevices at higher elevations, often sharing these with *Rhododendron ericoides*. The large flowers, about 1 cm in diameter, are usually green but sometimes flushed with red. It ranges from 2500 to almost 4000 m and certainly at upper elevations the identity of this species cannot be confused.

D. memecyloides Stapf (Fig. 10e)
A fairly common species, this is an erect glabrous shrub with broadly elliptic, rather sharply pointed leaves growing both terrestrially and epiphytically. The flowers are small and green, often with a purple flush. It occurs from 900 to 2900 m in open places amongst boulders in the Mesilau river but is also found on ridges along the main Summit trail.

D. myrtillus Stapf (Fig. 9k)
This rare species is somewhat reminiscent of the abundant *D. ciliolata* but is distinguished by having short hairs as well as bristles on the stems. Reported from 1500 to 2650 m, it is still very poorly known.

D. penduliflora Stapf (Fig. 10b)
This is not an easy species to find for the first time, though it is fairly common, but easily recognised by the extraordinary long thin pedicels 2.5 to 4 cm long. It grows terrestrially, mostly in valley forest but occasionally can be found on ridges. It is found from 1000 to 2000 m and can be seen by a careful observer along the Liwagu Trail close to Park Headquarters.

D. pinifolia Stapf (Fig. 9d)
A well-named species, this is common and easy to recognise with its slender pine needle-like leaves. It could be confused with the much rarer *D. rosmarinifolia* which has longer leaves or, when without flowers, with the slender-leaved *Rhododendron stenophyllum*. This, however, has minute multicellular glands visible on the undersides of the leaves when viewed with a lens. *D. pinifolia* can be found on fallen branches around Park Headquarters, occurring from 2000 to 2300 m but mostly it grows as an epiphyte high in large trees where it flowers and fruits freely. Sterile seedlings, however, come up on roadside banks and mossy boulders in streams.

D. pittosporifolia J.J. Smith (Fig. 11d)
This plant has characteristic broad rounded leaves and bristly stems. The Kinabalu forms are referable to variety *punctiloba* but this species is uncommon and poorly known. It is said to grow in low forest and as an epiphyte from 2100 to 2750 m.

D. pseudorufescens Sleumer (Fig. 9h)
A rare, poorly known, small-leaved, bristly species, this is somewhat similar to *D. chrysothrix* and *D. carrii* but differs in the hairs on the calyx as well as the smaller leaves. It is reported from rocky ridges between 2300 and 2900 m. A narrower-leaved form has been described as variety *elliptifolia* Sleumer.

D. punctulata Stapf (Fig. 9b)
This is a large-leaved, glabrous species with more pointed leaves than the closely related *D. heterophylla* and with a fine covering of grey or black punctate dots on the undersides of the leaves. It is reported to occur between 1200 and 2750 m but there is some confusion between this species and *D. heterophylla*. On Kinabalu it is fairly common but it does not appear to occur below about 1800 m.

D. rosmarinifolia Sleumer (Fig. 9c)
A rare, very poorly known species, this is only known from the type locality, the Penataran river on the north-west side of Kinabalu at about 2000 m, presumably an epiphyte. It is very similar to *D. pinifolia* but has longer leaves and quite glabrous stems without the fine tomentum found in that species.

D. rufa Stapf (Fig. 10f)
A common species with densely bristly stems and leaves, the flowers of this have been reported as pink, red or purple with bristles on both calyx and corolla. It grows mostly in mossy ridge forest between 2000 and 3000 m. The species could be confused with *D. clementium* but it has shorter leaves with fewer lateral veins.

D. sanguinolenta Sleumer (Fig. 11a)
A rare, large-leaved glabrous species, this has large bright, or blood-red, fleshy flowers which are probably the largest in the genus being up to 15 mm long. It grows as an epiphyte on forest ridges between 1500 and 1800 m but has rarely been collected recently. It is a Kinabalu endemic and is not known from any other locality.

D. sphenophylla Sleumer (Fig. 9j)
This is a very distinct species with its slender leaves broadening upwards. It is rare on the main trail but common both on the ground and as an epiphyte in low 'pole forest' on the Marai Parai ridge and may be associated with the ultramafic (ultrabasic) areas. It occurs from 1200 to 2300 m and is only known from Kinabalu.

D. urceolata Stapf (Fig. 11b)
It is a species similar to *D. commutata* from which it is difficult to distinguish. A hand lens is needed to observe the different kinds of hairs. It is, however, much less common than *D. commutata*. In *D. urceolata* the pedicels are densely covered with short reddish, non-

glandular, persistent hairs. It is reported from a good deal higher up the mountain than *D. commutata,* growing between 2100 and 3350 m. It would be nice to get further observations to confirm this difference in range.

D. viridiflora Sleumer (Fig. 11g)
A rare, glabrous species with lanceolate pointed leaves and a single pair of lateral veins curving from the base to high up the leaf. Occurring between 1200 and 1700 m it is probably an epiphyte high in large trees and difficult to find. There are very few collections of this species and only one in recent years but it is highly distinctive and, if found, should not be confused with anything else.

VACCINIUM

The leaves of *Vaccinium* are glabrous or with simple, white or often brownish, glandular hairs, often with glands on the edges of the leaf which secrete nectar when the leaves are young. The ovary is inferior and grows into a fleshy berry with a distinct junction at the top of the pedicel. The small genus *Costera*, not so far recorded from Kinabalu, is distinguished by the lack of this junction, the pedicel expanding gradually into the fruit.

This is a large genus of between 400 and 500 species of which about 40 have so far been described from Borneo and of these, 14 species (almost a third) are recorded from Kinabalu. Two sections of the genus are represented:

(a) Section *Rigiolepis,* a very largely Bornean section, is characterised by its small flowers with stamen tubules opening by proportionately long oblique slits (Fig. 2c & d). All the species so far studied have fruits which change from green to orange and finally ripen bright red but more observation is needed on this characteristic. It is represented on Kinabalu by just two species, *V. moultonii* and *V. uroglossum.*

(b) Section *Bracteata,* the largest section in South-east Asia, is best developed in New Guinea but contains about half the known Bornean species and is represented on Kinabalu by 12 species. These species in general have larger flowers than those of section *Rigiolepis,* and have the stamen tubules opening by almost round pores and in all the species on Kinabalu, with the exception of *V. cordifolium*, the fruits change from green to blue or black.

Species of the genus *Vaccinium* are used commercially for fruit in North America and northern Europe but none of the Kinabalu species have potential in this respect, the fruit not being particularly sweet or juicy. Although not as attractive as those of *Rhododendron,* the flowers of some species can look extremely beautiful and several of them are powerfully scented. Young growth can also be very eye-catching with flushes of bright red leaves which can be particularly striking in the open vegetation of the upper granite crags.

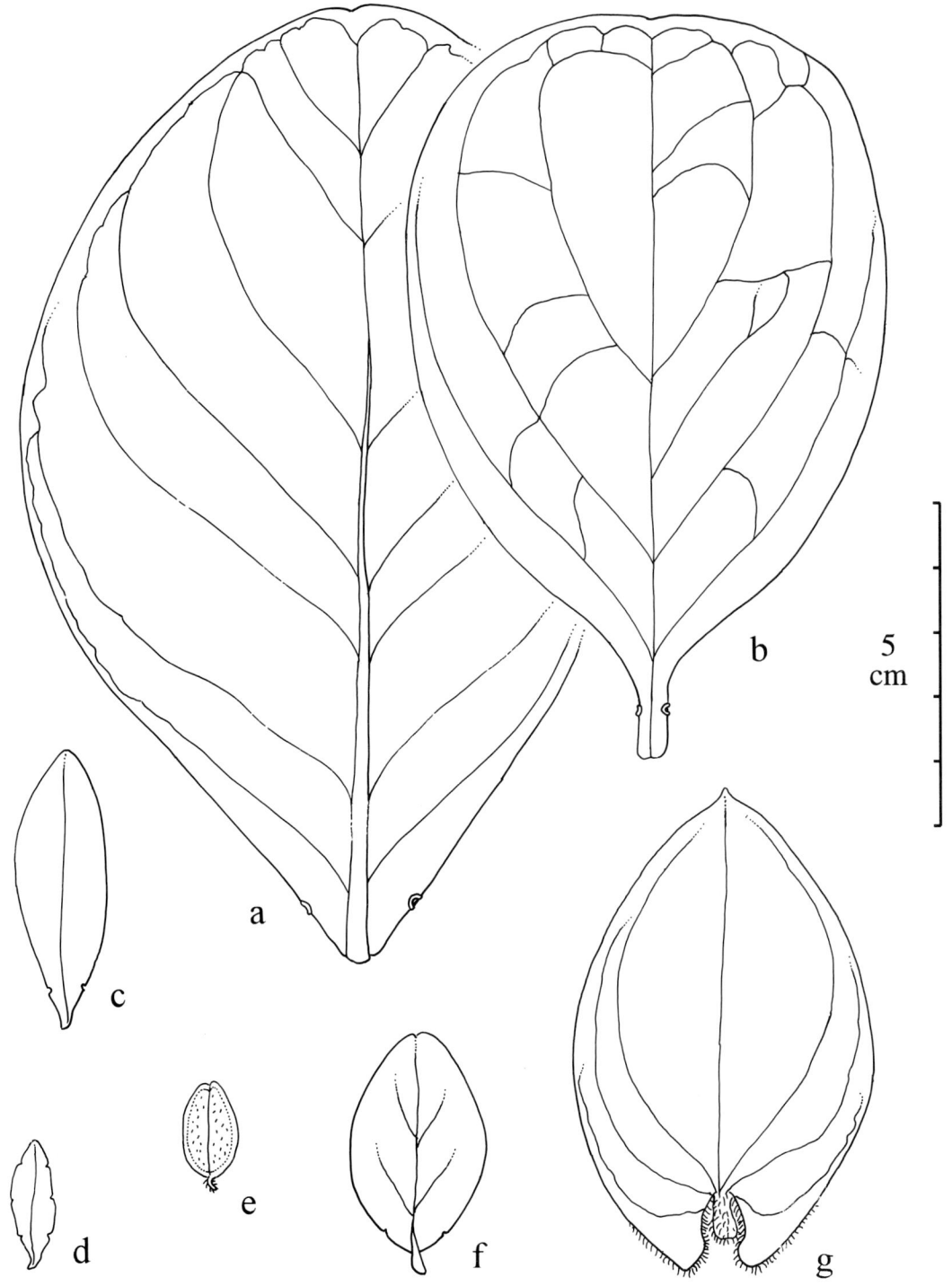

Fig.14. *Vaccinium* leaves.
a. *V. claoxylon*. b. *V. pachydermum*. c. *V. clementis*. d. *V. coriaceum*. e. *V. stapfianum*.
f. *V. elliptifolium*. g. *V. cordifolium*.

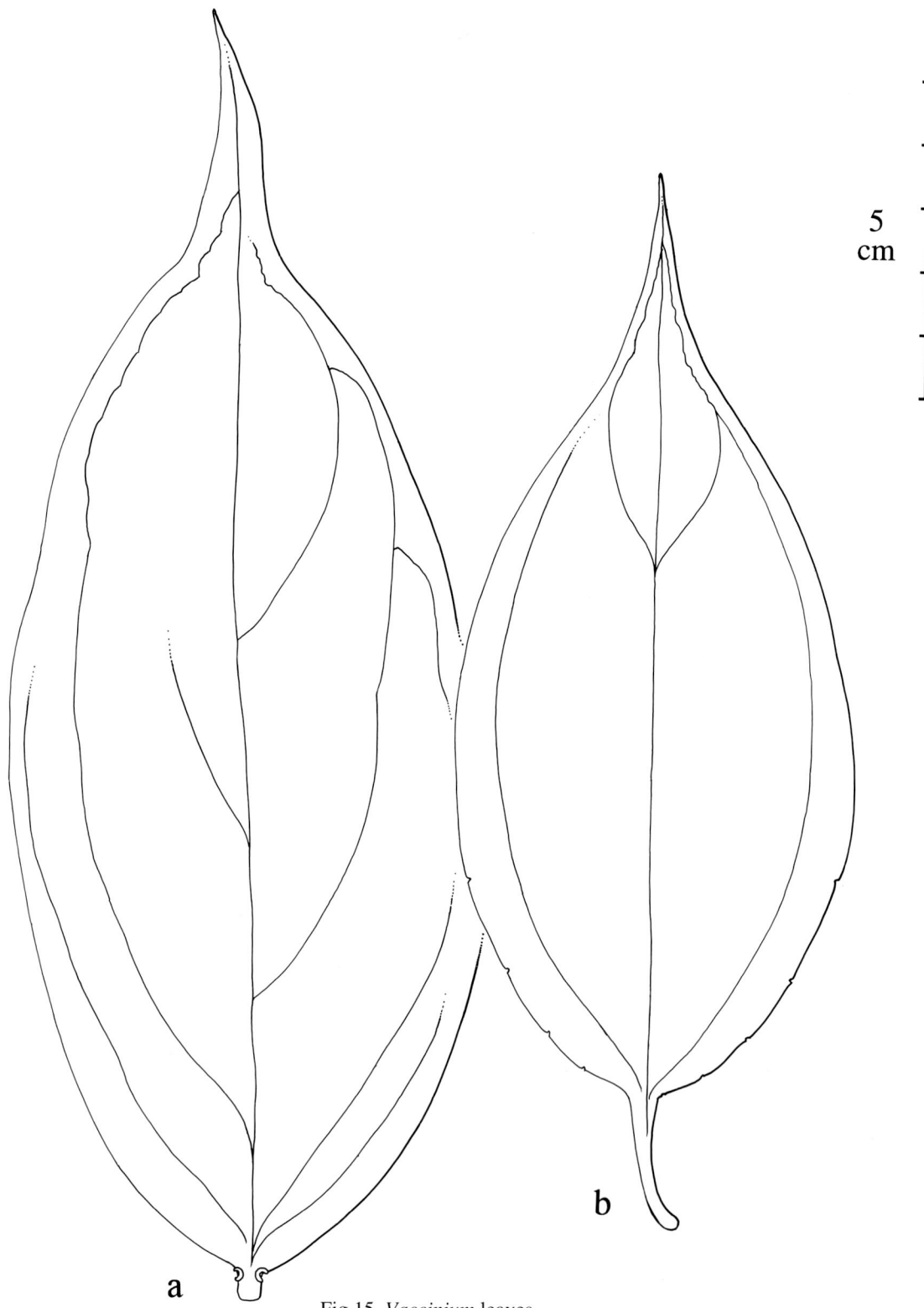

Fig.15. *Vaccinium* leaves.
a. *V. moultonii*. b. *V. retivenium*.

Notes on the species

V. bancanum Miquel (Fig.18e)

Though uncommon, this is a very widespread and variable species often growing into a small tree. The flowers are in delicate white or pink, scented racemes. This species occurs in several varieties, two at least of which occur on Kinabalu: variety *tenuinervium* J.J. Smith is distinguished by its narrow leaves and glabrous or almost glabrous disk; variety *kemulense* J.J. Smith has more typical ovate elliptic leaves and a disk which is densely hairy. This species is generally lowland in distribution occurring down to sea level in a number of places in Borneo. On Kinabalu it is likely to be found up to 2000 m.

V. claoxylon J.J. Smith (Fig.14a)

A common large-leaved, glabrous species, this is easily recognised by the raised lenticels on the twigs which are more conspicuous than in any other species. The leaves have distinctive red veins near the base, the midrib in particular being broad and raised for some distance above the petiole. The flowers are usually cream or pink and pleasantly scented of vanilla. It grows as an erect or sprawling shrub up to 4m and is easily seen on the ridges along the main trail, occurring between 1000 and 3000 m.

V. clementis Merrill (Fig.14c)

A fairly common shrub or small tree occurring between 1500 and 1800 m, this is terrestrial on montane ridges but occurs epiphytically at lower altitudes. It is usually distinctive with its medium-sized blunt leaves and racemes of mostly pink flowers but is by no means always easy to distinguish from *V. bancanum*. Technically *V. bancanum* has glands on the anthers which are lacking in *V. clementis* but these are difficult to see in old flowers and

Fig.16. *Vaccinium clementis*. (Photo: K.M. Wong)

Fig.17. *Vaccinium cordifolium*, common between 2400 and 2900 m along the usual summit trail on Kinabalu. *(Photo: A. Lamb)*

can easily be missed. Although the altitudinal ranges of the two species appear to overlap considerably, *V. clementis* seems to be more common in montane situations and V. *bancanum* in lowland areas. More fieldwork is needed to establish the ecological limits of these species and whether or not they do occur together.

V. cordifolium **Stapf** (Fig.14g)
It is a common species easily recognised by the auriculate leaf bases. This species often catches the eye of climbers up the main trail with its long arching, softly hairy stems ending in a raceme of white flowers which turn pink with age and are followed by glistening red fruits. It is most frequent between 2400 and 2900 m.

V. coriaceum **Hooker *f.*** (Fig.14d)
A fairly common species, this is easily recognised by its small rounded or oval leaves indented with glands around the edge. Only *V. stapfianum* has similar leaves but they lack the indented glands at least in the upper part of the leaf. It is an attractive plant whose young pink or red leaves often look more eye-catching than the white or pink flowers.

V. elliptifolium **Merrill** (Fig.14f)
This is an erect shrub with broadly elliptic leaves with rounded or minutely retuse tips. It is distinct in the long and finely pointed bud scales to be found in the axils of the leaves and the short white hairs of the petiole running along the midvein on the underside of the leaf. Found rarely, it occurs in mossy forest from 1500 to 2300 m.

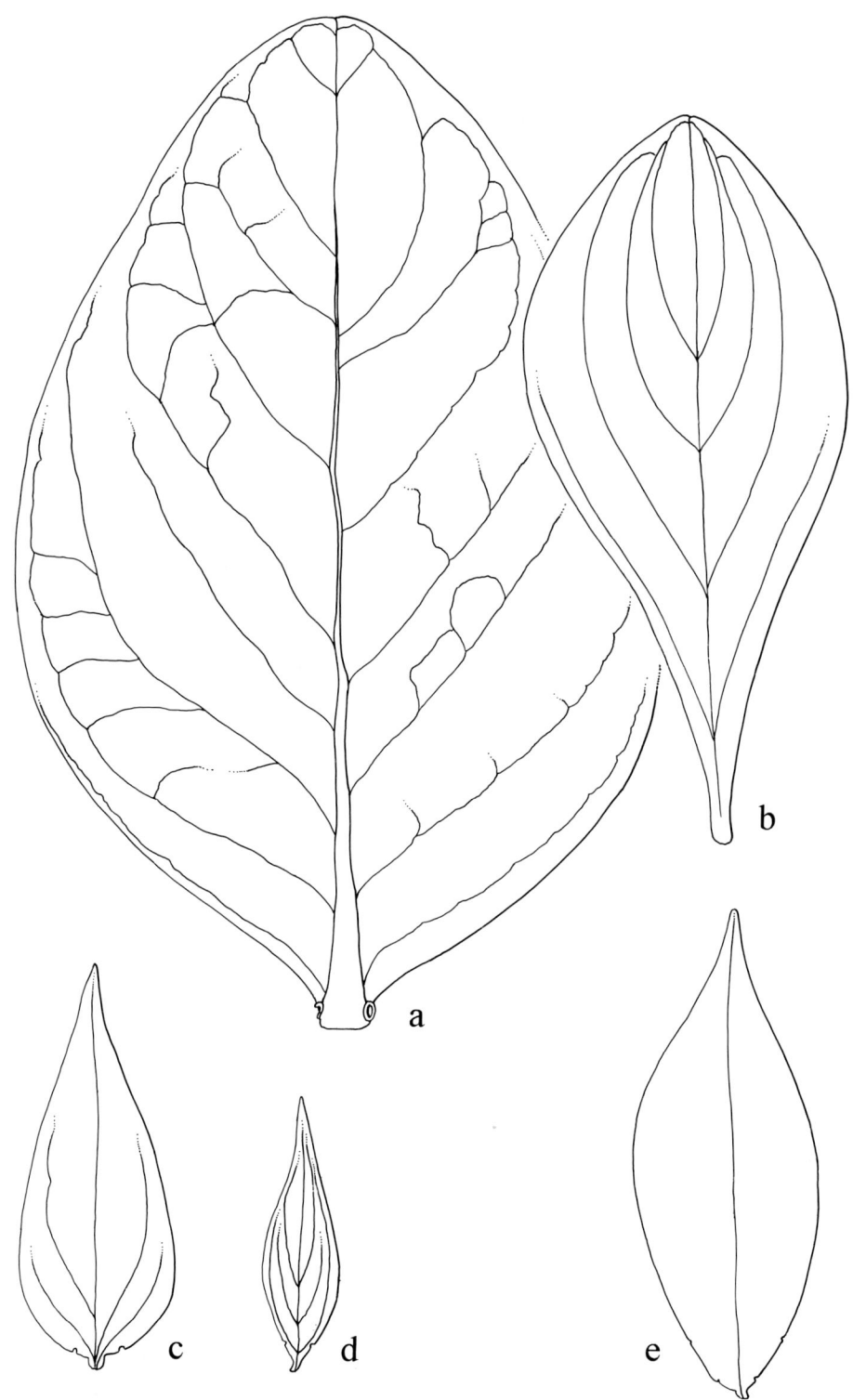

Fig.18. *Vaccinium* leaves.
a. *V. laurifolium.* b. *V. simulans.* c. *V. uroglossum.* d. *V. phillyreoides.* e. *V. bancanum.*

V. laurifolium (Blume) Miquel (Fig.18a)
It is a fairly common, large-leaved species with glabrous branches and glossy leaves. The young growth can look exceptionally attractive and the flowers are handsome pink bells which are generally sweetly fragrant although they have been described as smelling like sour apples. Probably all the Bornean material is referable to the variety *sarawakense* (Merrill) Sleumer which differs from the typical variety in having the rachis and pedicels densely covered in brownish glandular hairs. It occurs between 800 and 1600 m and often grows on large trees where it may be difficult to see but flowering can be on a massive scale, making the plants stand out from the surrounding forest.

V. moultonii Merrill (Fig.15a)
This is a rare species with the small flowers typical of section *Rigiolepis,* and relatively large acuminate leaves. There is only a single record for Kinabalu collected by W. Meijer above Poring Hot Springs between 600 and 800 m and described as a woody climber with yellow flowers.

V. pachydermum Stapf (Fig.14b)
An uncommon species, this has distinctive large, rounded, leathery leaves and racemes of rather fleshy white or pink scented bells. It may be confused with *V. simulans* which has a glabrous rachis, not hairy as in this species, and leaves which also tend to be smaller and more tapering at the base. *V. pachydermum* occurs mostly between 2000 and 3000 m usually as a terrestrial shrub on exposed ridges.

V. phillyreoides Sleumer (Fig.18d)
This species is difficult to see as it occurs as an epiphyte high in large trees and rarely flowers in the Park at ground level. It is an attractive small-leaved, highly branched shrub which can produce masses of red or pink flowers. The acuminate leaves are unlike those of any other species of *Vaccinium* on Kinabalu and are similar to those of *Diplycosia caudatifolia* but the latter is more hanging in habit, does not have glands on the leaf margin and usually has a few persistent pedicels with the bracteoles that characterise *Diplycosia* species. *V. phillyreoides* is recorded between 700 and 1900 m but is often overlooked and is no doubt under-recorded.

V. retivenium Sleumer (Fig.15b)
A common, very distinctive species, this has large leaves on long petioles and with a long acuminate apex. The white flowers although quite large are not very showy and the black fruits are not juicy. It is easily seen on the roadside banks near the power station at 1900 m, where it appears to flower and fruit during most of the year. It is reported as growing between 1100 and 2450 m and is probably most often epiphytic although rarely collected as such.

V. simulens Sleumer (Fig.18b)
Another species which is probably under-recorded, it is easily overlooked when not in flower and is probably epiphytic in large trees where it is inaccessible in many cases. The obovate rounded leaves are most similar to *V. pachydermum* but the leaves are generally smaller and the plants less hairy. The altitudinal range from 1000 to 1850 m is also lower

than that of *V. pachydermum* but the glabrous rachis is the surest way of distinguishing these two species. A variety *leptopodium* has been described from Kinabalu with more slender pedicels and smaller calyx than in the type variety. Both forms are said to grow together.

V. stapfianum **Sleumer** (Fig.14e)
This is a neat erect shrub with a very similar habit to *V. coriaceum* but differs in the absence of glands around the upper part of the leaf margin. Two varieties have been described: the type variety is commonly terrestrial growing between 1800 and 3600 m, where it is abundant, with a corolla 5-6 mm long; while in variety *minus* Sleumer the corolla is up to 3 mm long and the plants are more commonly epiphytic and growing between 1500 and 2500 m. The strongly scented flowers are not so conspicuous as the new leaves but often occur at the same time when the plants can look very attractive.

V. uroglossum **Sleumer** (Fig.18c)
It is an uncommon species which is easily overlooked with its small yellowish-green or cream flowers typical of section *Rigiolepis* being only up to 5 mm long. It has a rather distinctive habit growing long, often hanging branches, which can produce large numbers of the small racemes from the leaf axils along the greater part of the stem. It also often forms a woody tuber at the base which can become quite large. It is usually epiphytic growing in montane forest between 1500 and 1850 m. It is closely related to *V. tenerellum* which occurs in Sarawak but appears to be much more vigorous and always has basal glands on the leaves which are lacking in that species. It is easily distinguished from *V. moultonii,* the only other '*Rigiolepis*' recorded from Kinabalu, by its much smaller leaves.

Fig.1. Kinabalu's largest flower, *Rafflesia keithii*. *(Photo: A. Phillipps)*

THE RAFFLESIA FAMILY

Kamarudin Mat Salleh

Spectacular and gigantic in comparison to other flowers, the totally parasitic *Rafflesia* flowers are considered one of the greatest wonders of the botanical world. *Rafflesia* was first made known to botanical circles through a description in a letter written by Dr. Joseph Arnold to a friend shortly before Arnold died of malaria. Dr. Arnold, a surgeon by training, was a well-known naturalist and a fellow of the Royal Society of London. He was invited to Sumatra by Sir Thomas Stamford Raffles, then the Lieutenant-Governor of Bencoolen, a protectorate of the British East India Company in Sumatra, to study the natural history of Sumatra, which was then little-known. He accompanied Sir Stamford Raffles, better known as the founder of Singapore, and Lady Sophia Raffles, on an expedition to south-western Sumatra in May 1818, where he was shown the *Rafflesia* flower by a local porter. This plant is famous for holding the record as the largest flower known in the plant kingdom. It was named *Rafflesia arnoldii*, commemorating both naturalists. The flower was so huge, that according to them, it measured a full yard across, weighed fifteen pounds and held an estimate of one-and-a half gallons of water!

According to Meijer (1985), the average size of *R. arnoldii* is 70 cm (27.5 inches) in diameter but the largest flower he once measured was a record 92 cm (36 inches) across. It is a specialised parasitic plant, producing flower buds only at certain intervals. The buds need more than a year (19 to 21 months) to develop into the full *"blooming colossus"* of the spectacular five-lobed flower.

The genus *Rafflesia* is believed to consist of 14 species (Mat Salleh & Latiff, 1989.) They are very rare plants, found in a handful of localities in Borneo, Sumatra, Java, Peninsular Malaysia, Thailand and the Philippines. Four species of *Rafflesia* were first recorded from Borneo (Koorders, 1918). These are *R. borneensis, R. ciliata, R. witkampii,* and *R. tuan-mudae. R. ciliata* and *R. witkampii* are imperfectly known, and they may now be extinct as there have been no new reports since the second World War (Meijer, 1985). *R. borneensis* is also little known since it was only once collected from Kutai, in north-eastern Kalimantan in 1917. It may never be found again. *R. tuan-mudae* from Sarawak is related in several aspects to *R. arnoldii* (Meijer, 1958) but the exact relationship remains uncertain.

Recent studies on Bornean *Rafflesia* have led to the discovery of three new species from Sabah, *viz., R.pricei* and *R. keithii* from the Crocker Range and Mt. Kinabalu (Meijer, 1984) and *R. tengku-adlinii* from the Trus Madi Range (Mat Salleh & Latiff, 1989).

BIOLOGY

Rafflesia spp. are extremely specialised plants parasitic on wild forest vines of the genus *Tetrastigma*. The only visible part of the plant is a single flower without leaves, stems and roots. The vegetative parts of the plant are fine filaments that penetrate into the host vine, seemingly without causing any harm to the host. The flowers are unisexual.

Some *Rafflesia* flowers are said to emit *"a penetrating smell more repulsive than any buffalo carcass in an advanced stage of decomposition"* (Mjoberg, 1928). However, Weber (1967) stated that the *Rafflesia* flower *"... never seems to possess a foul odour, in fact sometimes no odour at all can be detected."* Beaman & Adam (1983) and Mat Salleh & Latiff (1989) further noted that even though almost no odour was perceptible from *R. pricei* and *R. tengku-adlinii*, a faint unpleasant smell could be detected when one took a deep sniff from the mouth of the flower. Whichever is the case, Meijer (1985), the world authority on *Rafflesia*, wrote emphatically: *"In my 30 years' experience with R. arnoldii, I found that people fortunate enough to see this fleeting spectacle are overwhelmed not by its scent but by its beauty."* Unfortunately, in spite of its titanic proportions, a *Rafflesia* flower in bloom does not last long enough for its beauty to be appreciated by many. *R. pricei*, for instance, begins to show signs of deterioration within 2 or 3 days after it bursts open (Beaman & Adam, 1983).

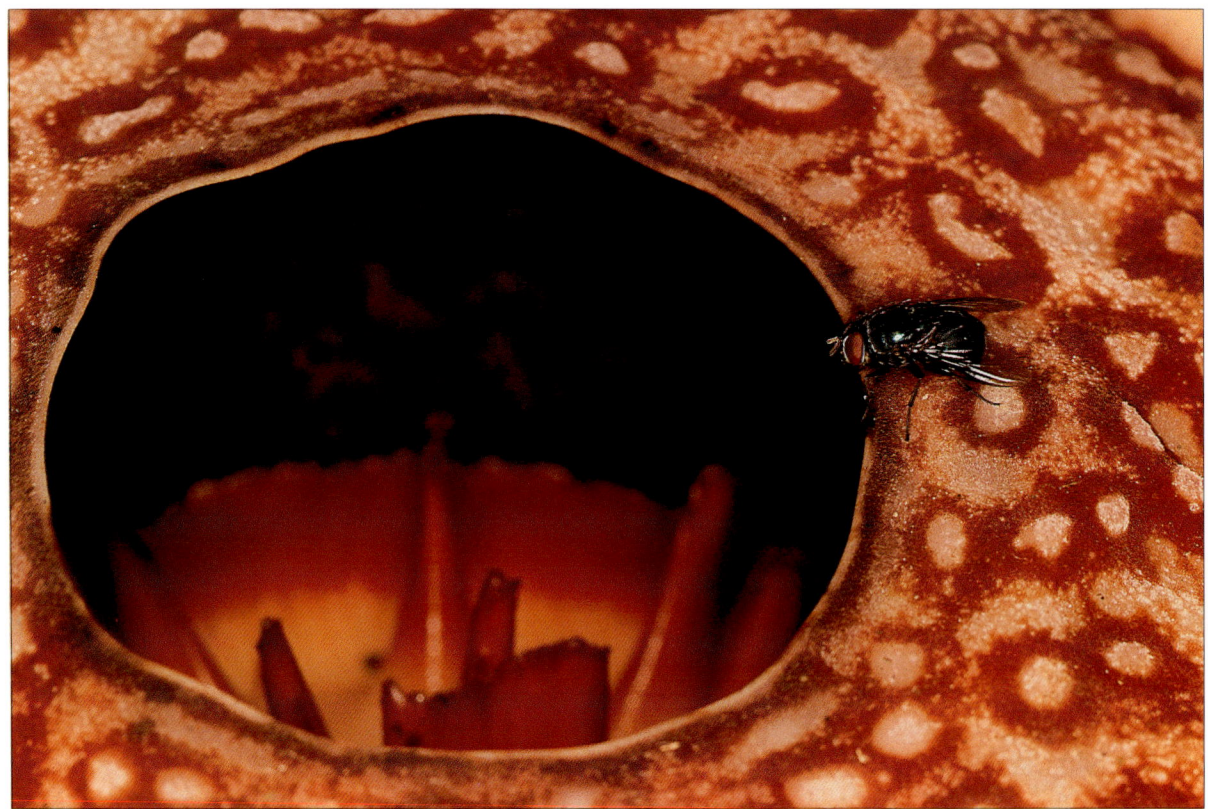

Fig.2. A Bluebottle fly peers into the central aperture of a *Rafflesia pricei* flower. *(Photo: W.M. Poon)*

The pollination biology of *Rafflesia* was discussed in detail by Beaman *et. al.* (1988). The flowers have been observed to attract flies, especially the Bluebottle or Carrion flies of the genera *Lucilia* and *Chrysomya,* by smell as well as by visual cues. These visual cues resemble the pollination mechanisms of certain species of the families Aristolochiaceae and Apocynaceae which have large, obvious flowers and which smell of rotten meat. The flies are lured into hairy grooves on the side of the column which force the insects up against the anthers. Laden with pollen on their backs, they are then guided out by white spots or 'windows' on the underside of the diaphragm, around the mouth. For successful pollination male and female flowers must be in bloom in the same area at the same time.

Many suggestions have been put forward on the possible dispersal agents of *Rafflesia*. Interestingly, these include wild pigs and ground squirrels (Meijer, 1985), ants, termites and even elephants (Kuijt, 1969). Previous attempts in propagating *R. arnoldii* by inserting pollinated seeds in the bark of the host vine were tried as early as 1854. More recently, in 1981, a fresh effort was made by the Singapore Botanic Gardens, using seeds gathered from Sumatra (Meijer, 1985).

There are many factors that make *Rafflesia* vulnerable to extinction, including its parasitic habit and specialised habitat requirements. The loss of habitat and exploitation of the forests where it grows are also at least partly responsible for its rarity.

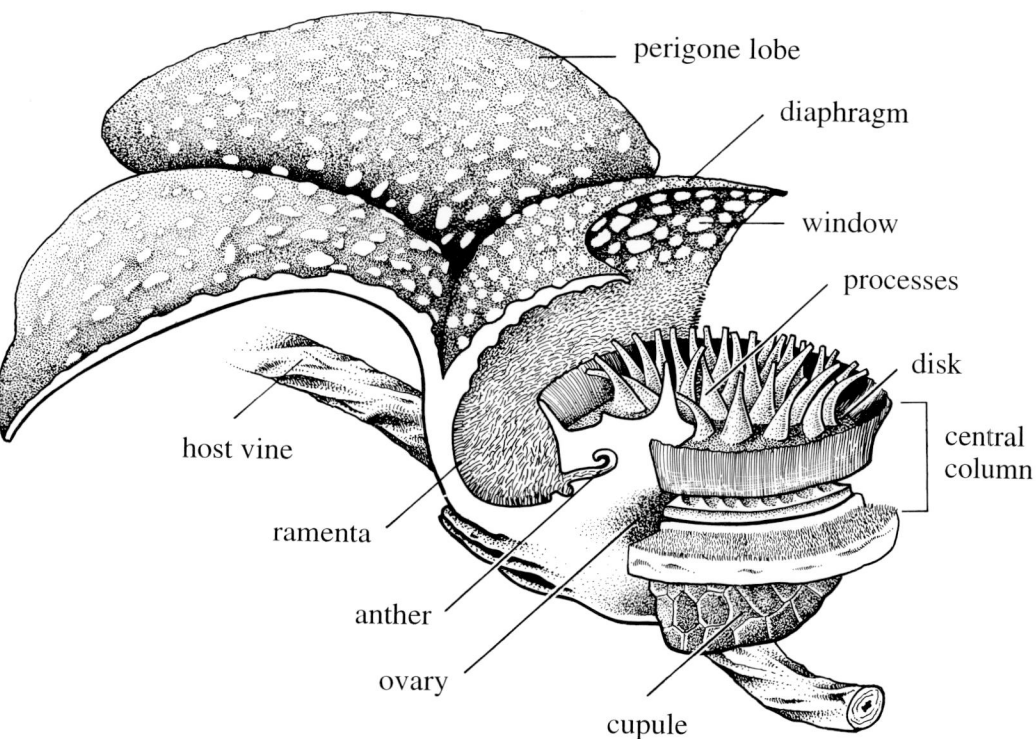

Fig.3. A diagrammatic section through a *Rafflesia* flower showing the different parts. For convenience, parts of both male and female flowers are included in the same drawing, though in nature the flowers are always either male or female. *(Drawn by Lucy F.L. Liew, after Meijer 1985)*

RAFFLESIA AND ITS RELATIVES ON KINABALU

The Rafflesiaceae, the family to which the *Rafflesia* belongs, is mainly a tropical family (with a few temperate species) with 8 genera and about 50 species. Besides *Rafflesia*, the other genus that is represented in the Malesian region is *Rhizanthes* which is easily distinguished by having much smaller flowers with 14 to 18 petal-like lobes instead of only five as in *Rafflesia*. The small amphipacific genus *Mitrastemon* is often included in the family since it has the same general appearance and habit. Though it is indeed closely related to *Rafflesia* it is now being treated as a separate family on its own (Mitrastemonaceae) on the basis of its bisexuality and the hypogynous nature of its flowers (Cronquist, 1981). *Mitrastemon* is a rather small plant, only a few centimetres high, parasitic on oaks and chestnuts in the cloud forests. The inflorescence consists of several pairs of leafy scales surrounding a single small cylindrical flower.

The identity of the two *Rafflesia* species found around Kinabalu was uncertain for years. The flowers were thought to be closely similar to *R. tuan-mudae* then known only from Sarawak, but they also appeared to be close to *R. schadenbergiana* from the southern Philippines (Weber, 1967; Corner, 1978; Beaman & Adam, 1983). Only recently, after careful study on the material available, Meijer (1984) positively determined these two plants as new species, naming them *R. pricei* and *R. keithii*.

Rafflesia pricei is named in honour of Price, who made a collection from the Mamut area in 1967 and deposited the specimen at the Kew herbarium in England. This has flowers 25–37 cm across, or slightly larger, and grows at higher altitudes, around 1200–1400 m. Weber (1967) reported *"a population of some 10 buds in an area of about half-an-acre in the Pinousok* [Pinosuk] *Plateau"* on the eastern side of Kinabalu. Unfortunately, this important site was destroyed when the area was degazetted and excluded from Kinabalu Park in 1984. It was later developed as a golf course and copper mine. However, new sites have been discovered at Bukit Lugas, near Bundu Tuhan (Masni, 1981) and recently at the Tenompok Pass, near Kampung Kiau on the slopes of Kinabalu. There are also several populations of *R. pricei* protected in the Rafflesia Sanctuary Forest Reserve between Km 61 and 64, on the eastern slopes of the Crocker Range below the Sinsuran Pass on the Kota Kinabalu–Tambunan road.

Rafflesia keithii, named after Mr. H.G. Keith, former Conservator of Forests in Sabah (then British North Borneo) is the only other species found around Kinabalu. It grows at lower altitudes (around 400 m) in the Lohan valley, especially near the Poring Hot Springs on the eastern side of the Park. It is a much bigger species than *R.*

pricei, reaching a diameter of 80 cm. *R. keithii* can be distinguished from *R. arnoldii* by its numerous small white warts, on the petal-like perigone lobes, interspersed with bigger warts. This feature is lacking in the true *R. arnoldii*.

Apart from growing in different habitats, the two species are also easily distinguished by the warts on the perigone lobes, the diaphragm, and the size of the central aperture. In *R. keithii* there is always a large aperture, which often exposes the entire disc inside the flower. *R. pricei* has a smaller aperture, exposing only half the disc. *R. keithii* is also found growing outside the Kinabalu area. According to reports, it is found on slopes along the eastern part of the Crocker Range from Tambunan to Tenom. So far, there are no authentic records of *Rafflesia* from the western slopes of the Crocker Range or from the western side of Mt. Kinabalu, though there are unverified reports of *Rafflesia* growing on the western slopes of Kinabalu between Kampung Kiau and Kota Belud.

Fig.4. A rare sighting of twin blooms of *Rafflesia pricei*, in different stages of opening.
(Photo: W.M. Poon)

R. tengku-adlinii, the third species of *Rafflesia* discovered in Sabah, is known only from the eastern slopes of the Trus Madi Range. However, it would not be surprising to find it in the Kinabalu area, especially in the unexplored eastern part of the Park. This species, which is golden orange in colour, is very distinctive and easily recognised. Although it has a small aperture, just like *R. pricei*, the ramenta (the hairy appendages inside the flower) grow right up to the edge of the aperture. These ramenta replace the white spots normally found in both *R. keithii* and *R. pricei*.

Besides *Rafflesia* there is one species of *Rhizanthes* which has been reported from Mt. Kinabalu. *Rhizanthes zippelii* has been reported to occur in the Mt. Kinabalu area but according to a recent account by Meijer & Veldkamp (1988) there is only one specimen collected by Meijer from Poring in September 1981. This rare species has often been confused with *R. lowi,* the only other species in the genus, which has not been reported from Sabah so far although several specimens have been collected from Sarawak and Kalimantan. With further searching, it may yet be found on Kinabalu.

Fig.5. The gaudy pattern of colour and warts on the perigone lobes of *Rafflesia pricei* is distinct from that of the diaphragm that hides a good portion of the central disc inside the flower. *(Photo: W.M. Poon)*

REFERENCES

Beaman, J.H. & Adam, J. 1983. Observations on *Rafflesia* in Sabah. *Sabah Society Journal* 7(3): 208–212.

Beaman, R.S., Decker, P.J. & Beaman, J.H. 1988. Pollination of *Rafflesia*. *American Journal of Botany* 75(8): 118–1162.

Corner, E.J.H. 1978. The Plant Life. In: Luping, M., Chin, W. and Dingley, E.R. (eds.) Kinabalu— Summit of Borneo. The Sabah Society, Kota Kinabalu.

Cronquist, A. 1981. An Integrated System of Classification of Flowering Plants. Columbia University Press, New York.

Koorders, S.H. 1918. *Botanisch Overzicht Der Rafflesiaceae Van Nederlandsch–Indie*. G. Kolff & Co., Batavia.

Kuijt, J. 1969. The Biology of Parasitic Flowering Plants. University of California Press, Berkeley and Los Angeles.

Masni Jubil. 1981. *Kajian Ekologi dan Taksonomi Rafflesia di Sabah khususnya di Tambunan*. B.Sc. (Hons.) thesis, Universiti Kebangsaan Malaysia, Sabah (Unpublished).

Mat Salleh, K. 1991. Rafflesia—Magnificent Flower of Sabah. Borneo Publishing Company, Kota Kinabalu. viii + 48 pp.

Mat Salleh, K. & Latiff, A. 1989. A new species of *Rafflesia* and notes on other species from Trus Madi Range, Sabah (Borneo). *Blumea* 34: 111–116.

Meijer, W. 1958. A contribution to the taxonomy and biology of *Rafflesia arnoldii* in West Sumatra. *Annales Bogoriensis* 3(1): 33–41.

Meijer, W. 1984. New species of *Rafflesia* (Rafflesiaceae). *Blumea* 30: 209–215.

Meijer, W. 1985. Saving the world's largest flower. *National Geographic* 168(1): 136–110. July.

Meijer, W. & Veldkamp, J.F. 1988. A revision of *Rhizanthes* (Rafflesiaceae). *Blumea* 33: 329–342.

Mjoberg, E. 1928. Forest Life and Adventures in the Malay Archipelago. Oxford University Press, Oxford & New York.

Weber, B.E. 1967. *Rafflesia*, the largest flower in the world, in Kinabalu National Park. *Sabah Society Journal* 3(3): 111–112.

Fig.1. Flower of *Nephelaphyllum pulchrum* var. *latilabre*, adorned by their broad, deep lilac petals bearing orange-red median ridges. *(Photo: C.L. Chan)*

ORCHIDS

A. Lamb

The aim in this chapter is to reveal simply both the diversity and fascination of the orchid flora that can be observed by those who visit the mountain, and the historical aspects of the early collectors who searched for them. Orchid flowers are differentiated from those of other flowering plants by having the stamens fused to the style and stigma to form the column. They also have one petal modified to form what is called the labellum or lip, which in some orchids is a landing platform for the visiting insects. In other orchids the lip is developed as a sac or pouch-like trap allowing the insect to exit only past the stigmas and anthers, thus achieving pollination. Many orchid flowers have both nectaries and scent glands, and all sorts of devices have evolved to attract insects. Some flowers even mimic the insects themselves. The pollen occurs in sacs or as pollinia, being specially packaged for transport by insects to another flower.

Orchid seeds are minute and produced in the thousands, dispersed by wind. Germination can only proceed if the right symbiotic fungus is present and invades the embryo providing it with sugars and other nutrients for growth. In the orchid this symbiotic relationship with fungi continues throughout the establishment of the plant, even in the mature plants, and in particular saprophytic orchids.

On Mt. Kinabalu with its different geological features, different rocks such as granite, sandstone and serpentine, different altitudinal zones and forest types, an enormous range of species and forms have arisen within different genera. River valleys, peat forests, or exposed ridges all produce different microclimates at the same altitude. With altitudinal changes come changes in light, temperature and moisture giving rise to even more variable microclimates. Such a range of habitats has hence given rise to a remarkable diversity of species on the mountain.

There are very many epiphytic orchids and a number of terrestrial orchids on Mt. Kinabalu. In considering the habitats and distribution of orchids, competition from other plants is also important. For example, if ferns have colonised a tree branch first, then epiphytic orchids may not always be able to establish there. However in many cases both are found together and in the case of nest ferns such as *Asplenium nidus* and also some *Platycerium* species certain orchids will be found growing in them. Many epiphytic orchids will grow on rocks and cliffs or in gullies but they are not like true lithophytes which will be found growing on mossy rocks only. Some truly lithophytic orchid species may well exist on the large exposed rocky areas on Kinabalu where mosses have established. Some terrestrial orchids such as *Arundina* and *Spathoglottis* species have adapted to colonising disturbed areas, exemplified by landslips and road-cuttings. In the tall forest most species are found on the branches, high up in the tree canopy, and along river banks where light is more abundant. The availability of both light and moisture in stunted mountain forests allows orchids to grow in great abundance.

In 1893 Henry Ridley remarked that few places so rich in orchids as Borneo "have been so much neglected in the elucidation of these plants". However, in the last ten years many more collections and studies have been made and checklists of the orchids of Borneo and of Mt. Kinabalu have been compiled (Wood, Beaman & Beaman, 1993; Wood & Cribb, 1994). Kinabalu orchids also receive attention in the "Orchids of Borneo" series under the editorship of P.J. Cribb of Kew and the coordination of C.L. Chan and the author based in Sabah. In addition, several living orchid centres have been set up at the Agricultural Park, Tenom; the Kinabalu Park and Poring Hot Springs; the Sepilok Forest Research Centre, and currently at the Sinsuran Road in Tambunan District. These centres have realised an important goal in orchid conservation and providing material for many studies on orchids.

These developments created a tremendous interest and awareness of the wealth of native orchid species, especially on Mt. Kinabalu, and the impending dangers that could result in the irretrievable loss of some species. Furthermore, the first trial of reintroducing a rare slipper orchid back into the Kinabalu Park has been attempted (Grell *et al.,* 1988).

One fascinating aspect that has hardly been studied on Kinabalu is the pollination of orchids by insects and other fauna. During the day when most of us usually search for orchids we probably only see half the answer. On Kinabalu one sees very few butterflies at orchid flowers, and most insect visitors are bees, wasps, and flies. In some cases when flowers of *Eria* species are handled many small beetles and bugs fall out of the compact inflorescences. Many of these are probably feeding on the flowers, but in doing so pollinate the flowers that remain. At night however, Kinabalu is noted for the abundance of moths that come to light, and insects that are nocturnal may play a much larger role in orchid pollination than is generally realised. Many Kinabalu orchids have white flowers, and are also scented; these features may indicate pollination by night-flying insects. The amazing range of flower form, colour and scent makes these plants most interesting and worthy of further study.

HISTORICAL NOTES

Hugh Low's discoveries of the amazing plants of Mt. Kinabalu, first in 1851, and later in 1858, set the botanical world alight by all accounts of the day. His reports and those of subsequent explorers came at a time when the interest in new orchid species had reached a fever pitch in England and later Europe. At this time, the nurseries of Veitch, and of Frederick Sanders, greatly influenced the interest in orchids, as apart from producing many hybrids, they financed large numbers of expeditions. The formal establishment of Kew as a State Garden in England in 1842 was also a significant event and the interest in orchids led botanists to start herbarium collections, from which an enumeration of species and subsequently the classification of the orchids began. It was to John Lindley of the London University and Sir Joseph Hooker at Kew, that Hugh Low sent his plants for study. Gustav

Reichenbach, a close friend of Lindley, described in his *"Xenia Orchidaceae"* many new species from Borneo.

Thomas Lobb, the earliest botanical collector to visit Kinabalu after Low, became a well known orchid collector, but many of his collections did not give the localities, or were misleading to safeguard his profession as a collector for Messrs. Veitch Nurseries. F.W. Burbidge, another collector for Veitch, mentions many of the orchids he discovered on Mt. Kinabalu, together with Peter Veitch, in his delightful book, "The Gardens of the Sun" (1880). John Whitehead, who first reached the true summit of Mt. Kinabalu in 1888, mainly collected birds but also some orchids which were sent to the Natural History section of the British Museum in London. This included the famous slipper orchid *Paphiopedilum rothschildianum* known only from Mt. Kinabalu. J. Waterstradt, a professional insect collector who visited Kinabalu in 1894, 1899 and 1908, was, according to Gibbs (1914), also an orchid collector for Rothschild, based in Frankfurt, Germany.

In 1893 the Orchid Review was started by R.A. Rolfe of Kew Herbarium, an orchidologist who described many orchid species from Borneo and Kinabalu. The first flora of Mount Kinabalu, published in 1893 by O. Stapf of the Kew Herbarium, covered the plants collected by Hugh Low, F.W. Burbidge, and G.D. Haviland, then curator of the Sarawak Museum. The orchids in these collections were first described by H.N. Ridley at the Botanic Gardens in Singapore. Ridley also produced an enumeration of Orchidaceae recorded from Borneo in 1893.

The collection of orchids in 1910 by Miss Gibbs was described in detail by R.A. Rolfe of Kew. She collected 48 species in Sabah, many of which were new at that time. Rolfe also covers two previously undescribed species, collected by Haviland. Of these species, 42 were collected on Kinabalu. Together with Haviland's collection, described by Ridley, the orchids from Kinabalu then totalled 61 species of which 53, or 80%, were considered endemic to the mountain.

In 1913 J.C. Moulton, the curator of the Sarawak Museum, spent six weeks collecting plants and insects. *Coelogyne moultonii* is named after him. The next major collection was that of Joseph Clemens in 1915; of 155 species, 100 were new to science. The collection was deposited in the Herbarium in Manila and duplicates sent to the Oakes Ames Herbarium at Harvard in America, and the British Museum. G.A. Haslam collected orchids in 1916 and his specimens were mostly sent to Manila (destroyed in the 1945 war) although some were sent to the Singapore Herbarium.

Joseph Clemens and his wife returned to collect on Kinabalu again from 1931, and the collection was deposited in the British Museum, with duplicates sent to several herbaria including Bogor, Leiden, the Arnold Arboretum, Edinburgh Royal Botanic Garden, and the herbarium in Manila. A total of 427 orchids was collected which were studied by Oakes Ames, at Harvard University. Together with his assistant, Charles Schweinfurth, he published "The Orchids of Mount Kinabalu, British North Borneo" in 1920. Some orchids in Borneo are also covered by E.D. Merrill's "Enumeration of Borneo Plants" in 1921,

Fig.2. *Chelonistele amplissima*, an epiphyte that blooms from October to November on Kinabalu. *(Photo: A. Lamb)*

Fig.3. Exciting, large flaming red flowers of *Renanthera bella*, an epiphyte endemic to areas with ultramafic soils in Sabah. *(Photo: A. Lamb)*

which covers the Clemens collection of 1915. The Clemens collection in Bogor was studied by another well known botanist, J.J. Smith. Clemens was visited by R.E. Holttum in 1931. Holttum's publication of the "Flora of Malaya Vol. I, Orchids" in 1953 covers many Borneo species, and has now been revised by Gunnar Seidenfaden and J.J. Wood.

The next most important collection was that of Cedric E. Carr in 1933. Before visiting Kinabalu to collect for the Singapore Botanic Gardens, he spent some time working at Kew Herbarium. During six months on Kinabalu he collected about 700 species; some were not in flower, but were brought into flower after being collected, in a small garden established on the mountain. Subsequent to this, Carr studied the Clemens collections at the British Museum of Natural History together with his own. In 1935 he published part I of a series on Kinabalu orchids, including 137 species of which 39 were new and 41 were first records for Sabah. Carr died before he could complete the series, and the Singapore Botanic Gardens were allowed to have his collections, notes, and drawings, now kept in the herbarium there and still largely unstudied.

Other studies of orchids that are of relevance to Kinabalu and Borneo are the three volumes of "Orchids of Java" by J.J. Smith, first published in 1905, and his several other papers (Smith, 1912; 1927; 1931). An enumeration of Philippine orchids by Merrill also covers species found in Sabah. Useful references to Borneo orchids are also found in the issues of the Malayan Orchid Review. Gunnar Seidenfaden, in his many volumes dealing with the orchid flora of Thailand, Indochina and Malaya, also covers many Borneo species.

In the 1960's, collections made by Mrs. Sheila Collenette were sent to Kew, and she rediscovered the localities of several rare slipper orchids. In the 1961 and 1964 Royal Society expeditions to Mt. Kinabalu E.J.H. Corner and Chew Wee Lek also collected orchids. In the 1970s and 1980s the author, C.L. Chan, Shim Phyau Soon, P.J. Cribb, J.J. Wood, J.B. Comber, John Beaman, E. de Vogel, J.J. Vermeulen, A. Phillipps, Kiat W. Tan, J.A. Fowlie, and other orchidologists made further collections and studies, in addition to collections made by the staff of the Sabah Forestry Department Herbarium, the Sabah Parks Ecology Section and the UKM(S) Herbarium.

Due to changes in the classification of orchids many species have been renamed and synonyms enumerated. Many new records of species and genera, particularly on the lower slopes of Kinabalu, have been reported. Many of these discoveries are documented in "Orchids of Java" by Comber (1991), "Orchids of Borneo Vol. 1" by Chan, Lamb, Shim and Wood (1994) and "Orchids of Borneo Vol. 2" by Vermeulen (1991). Several new species and records are also enumerated in "The Plants of Mt. Kinabalu, 2, Orchids" by J.J. Wood, R.S. Beaman and J.H. Beaman (1993).

DIVERSITY AND DISTRIBUTION OF BORNEAN AND KINABALU ORCHIDS

The orchids as a family have amazed botanists by the beauty of their flowers, the great diversity of their form and their very wide distribution. They have adapted to a very great range of habitats, and in many cases 'niches' with very particular microclimates of their own. In extreme cases these are so select that certain orchid species will be found in one locality only.

It is estimated by Heywood (1978) that there are 250,000 species of flowering plants in the world, excluding ferns, mosses, fungi, etc. The Orchidaceae are also considered by most to be the largest family of plants in the world, with between 20,000 and 30,000 species. A figure of 25,000 species is considered to be close to the true total. One could add to this that after only 134 years man has today created over 85,000 registered hybrids from only a proportion of these wild species. Excluding these hybrids, the orchids form 10% of all the species of flowering plants in the world. Whitmore (1984) gives an estimate, based on the work of van Steenis, of 25,000 species of flowering plants in the Malesian region, 10% of the world's total flora, of which 3000–4000 are Orchidaceae. Orchids thus make up 14%–18% of the flowering plants in the Malesian region.

The author estimates that Borneo has 2500–3000 species of orchids in 150 genera, with Sabah having about 1500–2000 species in 143 genera, of which at least 30% are endemic species. Thus Borneo has nearly 70% of the Malesian region's orchid species, many of which, however, are also found in neighbouring countries.

Beaman & Beaman (1990) estimates that Mt. Kinabalu has over 4000 species of vascular plants (of which approximately 600 are ferns) in 180 families with 950 genera. For orchids, the author estimates over 1000 species in 121 genera on Mt. Kinabalu with still another two or three genera to be recorded. This means that based on our present knowledge at least 25% of all the vascular plant species on Mt. Kinabalu are orchids, and the orchid flora of Kinabalu contains over 30% of the total orchid species in Borneo!

One genus, *Neoclemensia* is endemic to the mountain. Some genera have only one species whilst others like *Bulbophyllum, Dendrobium, Eria* and *Coelogyne* have nearly 50, or more than 50, species on the mountain. Only one genus, *Nabaluia*, has been named after the mountain, so far. Several more genera are also thought to occur on the mountain but await proper collections or confirmation of the species. In fact, 126 genera for Kinabalu might be closer to the final total.

The orchids are found on all the land masses of the world except those perpetually covered by ice and snow; there are fewer species in the more northern and southern latitudes, and these are nearly all terrestrial species. This may be so because speciation or the rate of evolutionary expansion was slowed down particularly by the Ice Ages, and by the fact that since then, the colder climate in temperate zones has produced a far more restricted range of habitats. In contrast, more complex forests near the equator, in combination with large altitudinal ranges, have increased the diversity of habitats which encourages speciation. Therefore in the tropical belts with high montane ranges the proportion of orchid species to other flowering plants is even higher than in the lowland tropics, probably well over 15%.

Geologically, however, it appears that much of Malesia and Borneo was under the sea only 30 million years ago, and that it was not until 15 million years ago that the great mountain chains started forming. The fauna and flora from the more ancient forests on older land masses to the north and south must have colonised the newly emerging lands of Malesia during this period. During the Pleistocene Ice Ages, the climate in Malesia was much less affected and the tropical forest belt continued to evolve. The Ice Ages, in locking up water as ice, caused the ocean level to drop by more than 100 m and most of the South China Sea became dry land.

Thus Borneo became connected to much of the rest of the Malay archipelago, comprising what is known as Sundaland. This meant that many plant species were able to migrate and the whole area became greatly enriched in species, and it explains why many of the present orchid species are found in all these places today. Plants considered to have retained evolutionarily primitive characters with a longer history and which are found in Borneo on Kinabalu (e.g., the Celery Pine *Phyllocladus*, the Winteraceae and Magnoliaceae) must have migrated into Borneo and Malesia from the continents to the north and south. This is probably reflected by species found on Kinabalu which have close relatives in the Himalayan and Sino-Indian region to the north, and the Australian region to the south.

During this period the deep seated batholith of Mount Kinabalu continued to push up through the Crocker Range. Some of the plant formations from the then much higher Crocker Range transferred to this new mountain, which being of a much harder material, did not weather down as quickly as the softer sandstones of this Range. At the end of the last Ice Age, the ice receded, the seas rose, and Borneo became isolated again as an island. The isolation saw further development of plant form, as species evolved to fill the many available habitats and niches.

THE CLASSIFICATION OF KINABALU ORCHIDS

The most recent generally accepted classification of the estimated 25,000 orchid species worldwide is by Dressler (1981; 1983; 1990a, b, c, d), who grouped the orchids into five subfamilies, all of which are represented on Mt. Kinabalu. Based on evolutionary relationships these have been grouped into tribes, subtribes and genera under each subfamily. Wood, Beaman & Beaman (1993) provide a check-list of Kinabalu orchids.

Most genera are grouped into sections or alliances, but these are not usually used in general literature. For species however, subdivision into subspecies, varieties and forms is quite common. For such subdivisions at least one or two clear distinctive characters are necessary, but for forms, different flower colour is one of the most common criteria. It is in the characteristics of the flower, particularly the reproductive parts, in which the main diagnostic similarities are found among species of the same genus. Within genera, species variation can be great, particularly in the vegetative habit and form of the plants. This is due to different species becoming adapted to different microclimates and habitats. Hence

Fig.4. Long pendulous chains of flowers with snow-white sepals and petals are characteristic of *Coelogyne rhabdobulbon*, common around the Park Headquarters. *(Photo: A. Lamb)*

some species in a genus might be saprophytic (having no leaves), while others may be adapted to growing terrestrially in deep shade with large plicate leaves to absorb what little light penetrates the canopy of trees above. Still others are adapted to exposed sunny habitats where water storage or retention is essential for survival, adopting pseudobulbs or thick fleshy leaves.

ADAPTATIONS AND GROWTH HABITS OF KINABALU ORCHIDS

Primitive-type orchids retain the basic sympodial habit (lateral production of new stems from the base of the plant) of the Monocotyledons. They have terrestrial fleshy roots without a velamen, and have either slender underground rhizomes or corms with several internodes; elongate stems with several spirally arranged thin or plicate leaves and a terminal inflorescence. The most primitive group of orchids living today are the apostasioid orchids. They have a partly fused column, with three stamens and anthers with powdery pollen. They are widely distributed on Mt. Kinabalu, and have the basic habit of fleshy roots, elongate stems with spirally arranged, broad, plicate leaves and terminal inflorescences. The thin broad leaves reflect the need to catch what little light is reaching the forest floor. They are found in the taller forests of the lower slopes of Mt. Kinabalu up to 1000 m.

In more exposed rocky areas in the lowlands by rivers, and on ridges at elevations up to 2000 m the next most primitive group with a similar sympodial habit, the cypripedioid or slipper orchids, can be found, represented by the genus *Paphiopedilum.* They depend on humus that has accumulated between the rocks, and have developed more fleshy or leathery leaves that resist dessication from exposure to occasional drier conditions. One species has adapted this terrestrial habit to growing in the forks of the largest trees near to rivers where similar moist humus pockets exist. Others have adapted to grow as lithophytic orchids on rock faces or boulders where moisture is abundant, such as on cliffs by rivers, or in very mossy forest.

In the more primitive genera of the other subfamilies, such as *Spiranthes, Tropidia, Corymborkis, Goodyera,* and *Cryptostylis* in the spiranthoid orchids, *Habenaria* and *Peristylus* in the orchidoids, and members of the Arethuseae of the epidendroid orchids such as *Calanthe,* all have similar non-specialised vegetative habits. They are terrestrial, and many have the more primitive feature of two stigmas on either side of the column and a rostellum that points upwards. All are adapted to life in the shade.

Certain more primitive terrestrial orchids have evolved completely saprophytic species, without leaves, as they can depend solely on the breakdown of organic matter in association with mycorrhizal fungi for the supply of nutrients, and no longer need leaves for photosynthesis. Many saprophytic species have been found, on different soils, up to 1500 m on Mt. Kinabalu. In the spiranthoid orchids saprophytic species have been found in the genera *Tropidia, Cystorchis,* and *Goodyera.* Of the orchidoid orchids, *Platanthera saprophytica* occurs on the Penibukan ridge. However, it is in the more primitive genera of the epidendroid orchids that most saprophytic orchids have evolved. The genera *Aphyllorchis, Cyrtosia, Lecanorchis, Didymoplexiella, Gastrodia, Epipogum,* and *Stereosandra* are all purely saprophytic, well represented on Mt. Kinabalu, and the monotypic genus *Neoclemensia* is endemic to this mountain. There are only a few saprophytic orchids in the more recently evolved genera such as *Eulophia* in the Cymbidioid orchids.

On the more exposed ridges, and cliffs, and in the stunted heath or ericaceous forests of Mt. Kinabalu some terrestrial orchids have adopted more specialized features such as succulent stems, tuberoids, bulbs or pseudobulbs; thickened stems that can store moisture, and narrow leaves, as they are more exposed to sunlight. The more advanced members of these terrestrial orchids, generally without staminodes, and with pollinia, appear to have developed specialisations such as cane or reed-like stems and narrow leaves, enabling them to grow taller and compete with other vegetation on natural landslide areas. *Arundina graminifolia* is typical, and has adapted very well to roadside cuttings.

A next advancement or level of specialisation appears to be epiphytism. The essential mycorrhizal fungi with which orchids are associated and which are necessary for germination and seedling growth are also found in the rotting bark and moss clumps on tree branches and trunks. Many advanced features appear to have developed in the epiphytic orchids, especially pseudobulbs to store moisture and carbohydrates over dry

Fig.5. *Paphiopedilum rothschildianum*, the "aristocrat of all slipper orchids", is a rare endemic on Mt. Kinabalu. *(Photo: A. Lamb)*

periods. The exposed roots developed two purposes; one to attach the plant strongly to the tree, the other to absorb moisture and nutrients. In the latter only the root tip is absorbent, the rest of the root being protected from dehydration and heat on the exposed trees by an insulating layer of cells called the velamen, although the velamen can also absorb moisture to some extent. For the more exposed orchids in drier areas the leaves evolved to become thicker and more leathery, terete (round) or succulent to store or conserve moisture. Most epiphytic orchids appear to have evolved at a later stage and are found in the subfamily Epidendroideae. The majority of the orchid species on Mt. Kinabalu have evolved within this group.

There is another variation of sympodial growth that represents further specialisation, seen in some terrestrial orchids but obviously of adaptive advantage to epiphytes. In typical sympodial growth, old stems or pseudobulbs are replaced by new shoots arising from basal buds, usually after flowering. The mature, old pseudobulbs provide the nutrients for this new growth, before becoming exhausted and rotting away. Flowering occurs when the pseudobulbs are fully grown, or as the new shoots are formed. However in many species the basal new growth produces a creeping leafy stem along the ground before producing an erect shoot with the inflorescence, and then repeats the process. Some of the primitive terrestrial orchids such as *Goodyera* have this habit. Among sympodial orchids adapted to being epiphytes, this habit is widespread and whole tree branches could be colonized by such orchids which do not remain as discrete clumps.

This habit is found in many species of *Bulbophyllum*, and wonderful examples can be seen around the Park headquarters area, with *B. lobbii* forming thick masses ascending around the smaller tree trunks, or in the lowlands where *B. vaginatum* forms creeping masses along branches on tall dipterocarps. Similarly many species of *Eria* such as *E. ornata* and species of *Coelogyne*, e.g., the common lowland species, *C. foerstermannii, C. rochusseni,* and *C. pandurata* have the same habit. In the smaller genera *Epigeneium longirepens* and *Flickingeria fimbriata* are good examples on Mt. Kinabalu.

Of the creeping terrestrial epidendroid orchids, *Claderia viridiflora* is the best example, and it often makes a start climbing up the base of trees. The clumping or clustering sympodial habit in epiphytic orchids is seen in large genera such as *Dendrobium, Dendrochilum,* many species of *Coelogyne* (e.g., *C. hirtella*), *Cymbidium* (e.g., *C. bicolor*), *Pholidota* (e.g., *P. imbricata*), *Nabaluia, Liparis, Phreatia, Ceratostylis, Thelasis,* and *Agrostophyllum*. In *Dendrochilum,* with more than 30 species in the stunted moss forest on Kinabalu, plants are often found on the ground as well as on the branches of the low *Leptospermum* trees. In genera with many epiphytic species terrestrial representatives are nearly always still found. For instance, in *Cymbidium, C. ensifolium* and *C. borneense* are found on granitic and ultramafic soils, *Pholidota ventricosa* is often terrestrial, and several examples are also found in *Liparis*. But in *Malaxis* many species are terrestrial, and very few have become epiphytic.

Monopodial growth is often regarded as a further specialisation or advancement, allowing plants to go on growing from a terminal point, and so produce elongating stems that can climb up trees. These plants produce roots along the stems at the internodes which are able to both attach the orchid to the tree as well as absorb moisture and nutrients from the bark or moss on the trees. Hence their growth is not restricted and they can go on continually growing and producing flowers, usually laterally. They also produce lateral stems, and so branch. These orchids are typified on Kinabalu by species of *Arachnis*, *Renanthera* and *Trichoglottis*. Intermediate forms with more leathery, strap-like leaves and shorter stems are the *Vanda* and *Aerides* species. The latter typify monopodial species that have completely evolved as epiphytes and no longer need to climb up into the canopy. In some cases such species have very short stems but have soft leathery leaves for storing moisture, and very long root systems. Another genus, *Phalaenopsis,* has even shorter stems with usually broad, fleshy leaves and long root systems; in the more shaded conditions, broader leaves are necessary to catch the little light that gets through the overhead canopy. All these monopodial-growth types belong to the vandoid orchids, except the Cymbidioid *Dipodium* species in the Cymbidieae tribe with climbing stems and adventitious roots, and also the rather remotely related *Vanilla* species. Several species of the latter genus exist on Kinabalu with soft fleshy leaves and long branched climbing succulent stems. Closely allied to them is *Galeola*, a saprophyte with leaves reduced to small bracts along the creeping stems, which depends on symbiotic fungi to break down organic matter to supply their nutritional needs.

Of the 35 genera of monopodial orchids of the Vandeae tribe on Kinabalu, one, *Taeniophyllum,* has very reduced structures. They have very short, hardly visible stems with leaves reduced to minute scales, but they have a mass of long round or flattened green roots that both photosynthesise and absorb moisture and nutrients. They usually have minute flowers, and appear to be amongst the most evolved orchids, in relation to the habitats they occupy, and the insects that pollinate them.

SOME INTERESTING ORCHIDS ON KINABALU

Mt. Kinabalu includes quite large areas of the lower slopes below 1500 m that fall outside the present boundaries of the Park. Many early records came from the lower slopes near Ranau in the south-east, Bundu Tuhan, and Kaung on slopes reaching down to the Tempasuk river to the west. The Pinosuk Plateau and Bukit Hampuan are areas taken out of the park more recently, that contained many rare species, and new records for Mt. Kinabalu. Many of these records are still the only ones. Very little is known of the orchid flora from the northern slopes of the mountain; from the lower reaches of the Penataran river in the west, and the ridges facing Mt. Tambuyukon down to Poring in the east. Here, only species of particular interest, rarity or those which represent a genus in each of the main subfamilies are included.

The Apostasioid Subfamily
The Apostasioideae, revised by de Vogel (1969), is well represented on Mt. Kinabalu by both genera in the subfamily. Borneo, with nine species in the two genera, can be considered the centre of diversity for the subfamily. *Apostasia wallichii* with bright yellow flowers is widespread in Sabah and the Crocker Range, on sandstone ridges up to 1500 m.

Orchids

Fig.6. The bright yellow flowers of *Apostasia wallichii* are typical of their group, which have less elaborate floral parts compared to other orchids. *(Photo: A. Lamb)*

Fig.7. *Coelogyne radioferens*, another distinctive necklace orchid. *(Photo: A. Lamb)*

A. odorata was recorded by Clemens (during 1931–33) from 1000 m at Dallas to nearly 2500 m at Kamborangoh and was also found by Corner at Mesilau. It has white or yellow flowers. *A. nuda* from Bukit Hampuan has probably been lost in recent fires there. Most people could hardly recognise plants of this genus as orchids, with their whorls of leaves and small lily-like flowers, and they are often mistaken for *Dracaena* species.

Neuwiedia, which is much more showy and has larger flowers, in which the free anthers are clearly visible, is also well represented. Three species were found on the lower slopes of Bukit Hampuan (600 m), on ultramafic (ultrabasic) soils, all in the area that was unfortunately burnt in 1990. *N. veratrifolia* with bright yellow inflorescences stands about 1 m in height in flower. It has rather erect leaves with long pointed leaf tips, and was also recorded by Carr on sandstone at Dallas at 1300 m. *N. zollingeri* var. *javanica* on Bukit Hampuan is a shorter plant with a hairy inflorescence, and larger pale yellow flowers and white fruits, and very broad plicate leaves. The third species, *N. borneensis* is also a short plant, but with narrow leaves. It has white flowers but seems to be very rare.

The Cypripedioid Subfamily

The next primitive subfamily, the Cypripedioideae, an early offshoot in orchid evolution, is represented in Borneo by one of the four known genera of slipper orchids, *Paphiopedilum*. Cribb (1987) groups the 60 species into two subgenera. Subgenus *Brachypetalum* is not represented in Borneo. For subgenus *Paphiopedilum* 12 out of 51 species are found in Borneo, of which five species are found on Mt. Kinabalu alone, with another two species, *P. barbatum* (syn. *P. nigritum*) and *P. lawrenceanum*, being dubious records.

This genus with its fascinating flowers has received tremendous attention over the last century from growers and orchid hunters, as well as scientists. The most famous orchid from Mt. Kinabalu, and also with the distinction of being called the "aristocrat of all the Slipper Orchids" is *P. rothschildianum*. It was discovered by the zoologist John Whitehead who sent plants to the famous nursery of Sander and Company, and it was described by the renowned taxonomist H.G. Reichenbach. It is found only on this mountain.

Although protected within a State Park, orchid hunters in recent years have illegally collected and smuggled plants of this and other species out of Sabah. However, recent arrests, court cases, and the publicity surrounding them should dampen such activities, which has made these plants both rare and endangered in their natural habitats. *P. rothschildianum* usually has three to four (rarely up to six) flowers on a tall stem with wide sweeping petals spreading up to 13 cm from tip to tip, which can be likened to the graceful position of the outspread arms of a Kadazan girl during the traditional Sumazau dance. Atwood (1985) studied the pollination in the wild, and discovered that the glandular hairs on the bent staminode, likened to a "spider's leg", mimic colonies of aphids which are the natural brood sites for the syrphid fly *Dideopsis aegrota*. The fly, in laying its eggs on the staminode, usually falls into the slippery shoe-like lip, from which it can only exit by climbing up the hairs, and passing under the stigma and sticky anthers in turn, so that, after repeating the performance on another flower, transmitting the pollen, and pollinating the flowers, fertilization is achieved.

Another very beautiful species endemic to the mountain is *P. dayanum* with beautiful tessellated leaves and large showy flowers. It grows in the same areas as *P. rothschildianum* but in more shaded situations on the ultramafic soils. *P. virens* is now considered as merely a variety of *P. javanicum*. It used to be common and widespread on Mt. Kinabalu and the Crocker Range, and is still found in the Park Headquarters area, and can be often seen in flower in the Mountain Garden at Park Headquarters.

Burbidge and Veitch also collected two other slipper orchids, which were described as *P. burbidgei* and *P. petri,* after them. The first is now considered a form of *P. dayanum* and the latter a natural hybrid of *P. dayanum* and *P. javanicum* var. *virens*. *P. lawrenceanum,* a Sarawak species, was reported from along the Tempasuk river on the lower slopes of Mt. Kinabalu growing along the river bank, as far as Kota Belud. It seems it no longer occurs here and this remains a doubtful record.

A further showy species with tessellated leaves is *P. hookerae,* widespread in Borneo, and scattered over many localities on Mt. Kinabalu from 600 m up to 2100 m. A distinct variety previously described as *P. volonteanum* with narrow leaves is now considered to be *P. hookerae* var. *volonteanum* (Cribb, 1987). Another species, *P. lowii,* discovered by Hugh Low on his early expeditions to Borneo, was found at 1000–1500 m on the Pinosuk Plateau, but this population has probably been lost with the clearing of the forest there. It has very recently been collected on the north-western slopes of the mountain. Growing in the forks of huge trees, this is Borneo's only epiphytic slipper orchid, and it has very beautiful flowers. It is still found in other parts of Sabah and Borneo.

The Spiranthoid Subfamily
The Spiranthoideae has three tribes, all represented on Mt. Kinabalu. The tribe Tropidieae consists of terrestrial orchids with woody stems and plicate leaves and several distinct primitive features. Both genera in the tribe are represented on Mt. Kinabalu. *Corymborkis veratrifolia,* a lowland species found up to 1000 m on Mt. Kinabalu, is a tall plant which produces clusters of beautifully scented white flowers at intervals throughout the year. It grows in heavy shade, and has potential for landscaping. Clemens found plants over 2 m tall at Lobang Cave. *Tropidia* are generally rather inconspicuous plants looking like small bamboo seedlings with rather dull small cream or white to yellow flowers. *T. pedunculata* was found at Dallas. The saprophytic *T. saprophytica,* without any leaves and small white and yellow flowers, has been found on the Penibukan ridge. *T. curculigoides,* with yellow flowers, occurs on ultramafic soils at Bukit Hampuan.

The Tribe Cranichideae with fleshy roots has three subtribes found on Mt. Kinabalu and is only represented by one species in the subtribe Spiranthinae. *Spiranthes sinensis* (syn. *S. lancea*) has been seen from 1000 m at Kampung Kiau to 1500 m at Park Headquarters, where it can often be found on grass verges along the roads. It has a rosette of lance-like leaves and a scape of spirally arranged small pink and white flowers. It is widespread throughout Malesia.

A second subtribe Cryptostylidinae has only one genus, *Cryptostylis* with about 15 species. Three species are recorded from Mt. Kinabalu. *Cryptostylis acutata* appears to be rare, though found by the Clemenses, and Carr, from 1000 m at Menetendok gorge to over 2000 m at Kamborangoh. *C. arachnites* is common along the Park Headquarters trails whereas *C. clemensii* (*C. tridentata*) is rare. The flowers of this genus mimic female ichneumon wasps, or related species, and pollination is effected by the pseudocopulation of the male wasps.

The subtribe Goodyerinae has mostly small herbs, many of which are called "jewel" orchids on account of the beautifully coloured veins in the leaves. Thirteen of the 36 genera are found on Mt. Kinabalu. The largest and most primitive looking is *Lepidogyne longifolia* which is still found near Kiau. Tall plants nearly 1 m or more in flower, they have typical spirally arranged whorls of plicate leaves. The genera with species described as jewel orchids are quite numerous. The flower spikes of small, usually hairy flowers are generally uninteresting except in a few cases. *Macodes lowii* is probably the most outstanding with its bright golden veins and it was once common on Bukit Hampuan. *M. petola* was also common on the ridges below 1000 m but is now rare.

Goodyera kinabaluensis with pink to red veins on dark velvety leaves is rare, but it has also been found on the Crocker Range. *G. ustulata*, *G. reticulata* and *G. procera* both have more lanceolate leaves with silver to pink veins on greenish-purple leaves. *G. reticulata* with white veins is also found along the Crocker Range and from Java to Thailand. There are several other species with either plain green leaves, or which have green leaves with white veins, like *G. rostellata* near the power station. *G. rubicunda* is found from Dallas to Tenompok. *Anoectochilus longicalcaratus* is another species with dark velvety leaves and golden veins which has rather spectacular white flowers and is found quite often in the Park Headquarters area.

Cystorchis variegata has beautiful dark and light green variegated leaves, and is sometimes seen along the trail from Poring Hot Springs to the Langanan falls. This genus has several saprophytic or leafless species in Borneo, and *C. aphylla* (with pink and white flower spikes) has been recorded on Mt. Kinabalu, and more recently from Bukit Hampuan.

Kuhlhasseltia kinabaluensis with yellow flowers has not been seen since it was found by the Clemenses on the Marai Parai Spur. However, *K. javanica* (which has been confused with *K. kinabaluensis*) is quite common, but has white flowers. This species is common along trails at Park Headquarters.

Pristiglottis is represented by the beautiful purple-leafed *P. hasseltii* with its large white flowers, which is also found along the Crocker Range. A small creeping plant found in wet moss up to 3000 m at Kamborangoh, *Myrmechis kinabaluensis* with similar but smaller white flowers is also the only representative for that genus so far. Similarly *Hylophila kinabaluensis*, a taller, more succulent herb, with a showy head of pink flowers is also the only species of its genus found so far and is endemic. It grows naturally in a section of the Mountain Garden at Park Headquarters.

The genera *Erythrodes, Hetaeria, Vrydagzynea,* and *Zeuxine* are all represented on Mt. Kinabalu by two to several species in each genus. All are terrestrial orchids mostly with green leaves, and small white to cream flowers. *Hetaeria grandiflora* is found along the Mesilau (west) river. *H. angustifolia* was first described from Mt. Kinabalu by Carr. *Erythrodes* is often found near streams and rivers and in moss forest. *E. triloba* was first described by Carr from Tenompok. *Vrydagzynea bicostata* and *V. grandis* have been seen on the trail to Marai Parai near the Haya Haya river, and have also been recorded at the Mesilau river by Chew and Corner. *V. bicostata* and *V. argentistriata* from Bundu Tuhan were described by Carr from Kinabalu. *Zeuxine papillosa* was collected near the Menetendok Gorge. *Z. strateumatica* and *Z. gracilis* are two other widespread species also recorded on Kinabalu. *Cheirostylis*, growing in moss on rocks in streams in the Crocker Range, is another genus that is expected will one day be found at lower altitudes on Mt. Kinabalu.

The Orchidoid Subfamily
The Orchidoideae is not closely related to the Spiranthoideae and is characterised by an erect anther that projects beyond the stigma, and also by the root-stem tuberoids found in many species.

The Tribe Diurideae, characterised by root-stem tuberoids, is represented on Kinabalu by one of its six subtribes, the Acianthinae. The genera *Corybas* and *Acianthus* (the latter Australian) are reportedly pollinated by fungus flies and the *Corybas* or helmet orchids are thought to mimic fungi. In recent years, a species of *Pantlingia* has also been discovered in two or three localities on Mt. Kinabalu, tiny plants growing in leaf litter in mixed montane conifer/oak forest, particularly where there are *Dacrydium* trees. It has beautiful jade blue-green flowers, and colonies of plants have been found growing naturally in the Mountain Garden at Park Headquarters. The genus *Corybas* is represented by three species, often found in areas with ultramafic soils, and usually in valleys by streams or rivers where there are mossy rocks or banks. *C. pictus* with heart-shaped leaves with a beautiful reticulate pattern of silver or deep pink veins, and a large purple and white flower is widespread, and can be found at Park Headquarters along the Silau Silau trail. *C. kinabaluensis* has only been found in the Marai Parai area and appears to be rare. The widespread *C. carinatus* with little pink and white flowers often in banks of sphagnum-like mosses is not very commonly seen on the mountain but has been recorded from the Mamut river. All the *Corybas* have characteristic spherical root-tuberoids.

The Tribe Orchideae has two out of its three subtribes represented on Mt. Kinabalu. The subtribe Orchidinae is represented by only one genus, *Platanthera,* on Kinabalu. These terrestrial plants look a bit like a *Spiranthes* in habit with a 'whorl' of spiky grass-like green leaves. They are mostly found on the higher montane slopes especially in the more open shrubby *Leptospermum* forest at 1500 m on the Marai Parai ridge, and above Kamborangoh and Layang Layang to 3000 m at Laban Rata. The tall spikes of yellowish-green to green flowers are often hard to spot amongst the other herbs and sedges. *P. kinabaluensis* can be often spotted when in flower on the trail from the Paka cave area to Laban Rata and has green to yellowish-green flowers. A saprophytic species, *P.*

saprophytica, with white flowers, was found by Carr on the Penibukan ridge en-route to Marai Parai, where both *P. stapfii* and *P. kinabaluensis* occur also in the open sedge areas. Another species, *P. angustata,* was found in the area around Kamborangoh. This genus, with more than 150 species, is mostly found in north temperate zones and hence its preference for the high altitudes of Mt. Kinabalu.

Two genera on Mt. Kinabalu represent the subtribe Habenariinae. *Habenaria* with over 600 species is widely distributed in all the continents, and it has spherical to oblong root-stem tuberoids. *Platanthera* was at one time placed with *Habenaria* but while *Habenaria* has two distinct convex, long, cylindrical to club-shaped stigmas, *Platanthera* has a flat stigma surface under the rostellum of the column like most orchids. Like *Platanthera,* many *Habenaria* are found in northern temperate areas, and so most species frequent mid-montane altitudes. These terrestrial orchids usually have succulent stems with a whorl of leaves that can be quite large and broad, as they often grow in moist, shady habitats. The inflorescence is often quite tall bearing a few to many flowers some of which can be very showy. The flowers are usually easily recognised by the erect median sepal forming a hood over the column with a very complex lobed lip and even the petals in some species are lobed. Despite the large numbers of species found worldwide only two or three have been identified on Mt. Kinabalu. The most surprising is *H. damaiensis* which was found in the Damai Beach area at the foot of Mt. Santubong near Kuching in Sarawak. It was also found by Carr and Clemens near Kundasang and Tenompok at over 1000 m. The plants have a whorl of broad leaves near the ground and a spike of creamy-white flowers with olive green lobes on the lip, and a long spur. Another Kinabalu species, *H. setifolia*, has a

Fig.8. The cinnamon-scented flowers of *Paraphalaenopsis labukensis*, a "rat-tail orchid" found only in areas of ultramafic geology. *(Photo: A. Lamb)*

Fig.9. A sparkling translucent white, the delicate bloom of the very rare *Ceratochilus jiewhoei* resembles an evanescent snowflake. *(Photo: C.L. Chan)*

whorl of large broad leaves, and large plants have been found in the Haya Haya river area, one reaching 1.6 m in height. The tall flower spike bears many vivid green flowers with intricately lobed lip and petals.

The genus *Peristylus* was also confused with *Habenaria* in the early accounts for Borneo and Kinabalu by Ames & Schweinfurth (1921) and Masamune (1942), but Carr (1935) more or less correctly sorted out the species. The seven species he listed included *P. brevicalcar, P. ciliatus,* and *P. kinabaluensis,* all collected in the Tenompok and Bundu Tuhan areas from 1000 to 1500 m, and all with fairly small flowers. *P. hallieri,* commonly seen along the roadside and forest trails at the Park Headquarters, is a small plant with a rosette of grass-like leaves, and an inflorescence up to 20 cm tall with many small greenish-yellow flowers, the lobed lip having two very narrow thread-like lateral lobes. *P. goodyeroides,* a widespread species from the Himalayas to New Guinea, has broad leaves and small flowers, and occurs at over 1000 m in the same Bundu Tuhan to Dallas area. Its occurrence on the mountain overlaps with two other species, *P. grandis,* also with green flowers, and distributed from Malaya to New Guinea, and *P. candidus* with a distribution from Cambodia and Malaya to the Indonesian islands and Borneo. *Peristylus* is also characterized by oblong stem-root tuberoids but has two convex cushion-like stigmas united to the base of the lip. Like the previous genera it is widely distributed, but mainly in northern temperate areas and so tends to inhabit higher montane areas in the tropics.

The Epidendroid Subfamily

The four subfamilies covered so far include a total of 25 genera but this is less than a quarter of the total genera recorded for Mt. Kinabalu. The remaining 96 genera all fall within the fifth subfamily, Epidendroideae, which can be subdivided further into five groups, the vanilloid, epidendroid, cymbidioid, dendrobioid and vandoid orchids. In fact more than half of all the orchids in the world fall into this sub-family. Since it has followed a different evolutionary pathway this subfamily also has several primitive species, and some of the more primitive vanilloid orchids have, according to Dressler (1981), more primitive features than the spiranthoid and orchidoid orchids, especially in terms of fruits and seeds. With such a large and diverse group fewer examples can be given in this account for some of the very large genera.

The main features of the subfamily according to Dressler (1981 & 1983) include the clearly defined pollinia with the more primitive species having soft, mealy pollen compared to the distinct hard pollinia of the vandoid orchids. Another feature found particularly in the more primitive species is that the anther is erect in the young flower buds, but later bends down over the apex of the column until it is at right angles to the axis of the column.

The Vanilloid orchids

The most primitive group in the subfamily comprises the vanilloid orchids, particularly the genus *Vanilla,* which has a pantropical distribution and which must have spread onto the different continents before they drifted apart.

On Mount Kinabalu the subtribe Limodorinae of the tribe Neottieae is represented by species of the saprophytic *Aphyllorchis* of which *A. pallida* is commonly seen along the trails at Park Headquarters, though it is hard to spot with its pale purple-streaked stems and small white flowers. *A. montana* has also been recorded at Park Headquarters.

The tribe Vanilleae has pollen grains reminiscent of the Slipper orchids, and the genera in the subtribe Vanillinae are considered very primitive. The subtribe Vanillinae is represented on Kinabalu by *Vanilla*, mainly in the mixed hill dipterocarp forest on the lower slopes. *Vanilla sumatrana*, collected only by Carr near Kaung at 500 m has yellow tepals and a white lip with red veins and a pale green apex. This appears to be very rare in Sabah. These lower slopes are now cleared of most of the original forest. *V. pilifera* was found on Bukit Hampuan and are long hanging vines covered in creamy white flowers having a pink lip with a tuft of white hairs. This species occurs also in Pahang, and appears to be common in the Crocker Range and is widespread in Sabah.

V. kinabaluensis was described by Carr from the Menetendok Gorge at 900 m and was also collected by the Clemenses at 1000 m at Dallas. This magnificent species is also found in the Crocker Range at about 800 to 900 m, often climbing huge dipterocarps to 30 m or more. Its large pendulous leaves, and many flower spikes, with one or two large showy yellow flowers open at a time on each, are quite an amazing sight. No doubt other vanilla species recorded from the Crocker Range may also be found on the mountain.

The genera of the subtribe Galeolinae are saprophytic. *Cyrtosia javanica* is a small fleshy, leafless herb usually noticed because of the mass of pinkish brown fruit (fleshy 'beans' or seed pods) or the short pinkish stems bearing several hairy white flowers, with a cup-shaped yellow lip hidden by the tepals. This species is found in the Crocker Range and was recorded by Carr and the Clemenses near Bundu Tuhan and Dallas-Tenompok, at 1400 m. *Galeola nudiflora* was seen on the lower slopes between Poring and Ranau on the old jeep track, with thick brown succulent stems scrambling over a large rotten tree stump and bearing small brown scale leaves. It had a mass of branching flower spikes, with masses of flowers with hairy yellow lips. This widespread species is found in the Crocker Range and elsewhere in Sabah and is distributed from Thailand through Indonesia to the Philippines. It is considered one of the largest saprophytic orchids.

It is probable that *Erythrorchis altissima* with glabrous brown to orange-brown stems, and inflorescences of white flowers also occurs on Kinabalu since it was recorded in the Crocker Range by J. Comber (pers. comm.) and to the north of Kinabalu in the Bengkoka Peninsula. This species has interesting winged seeds.

The remaining subtribe in the Vanilleae, Lecanorchidineae has a single genus, *Lecanorchis*. This also is a genus of primitive saprophytic orchids that are hard to spot. *L. multiflora* has brownish black wiry stems that rise about 20–40 cm above the leaf litter. It was collected by Carr on the Sg. Kinataki at *c.* 1000 m and is common and widely distributed in hill forest in Sabah and widespread from Indonesia to Thailand. The flowers are not very conspicuous with olive brown sepals and a cream lip with the apex bent down and covered in white hairs.

Fig.10. *Nabaluia angustifolia*, one of two species on Kinabalu, of a genus named after the mountain and endemic to Borneo. *(Photo: A. Lamb)*

Another vanilloid tribe, Gastrodieae, also contains mostly saprophytic species with fleshy tubers and coralloid underground stems. The subtribe Gastrodiinae, with only saprophytic genera, is represented by three genera on Mt. Kinabalu, including one endemic to this mountain and named after the Clemenses, *Neoclemensia,* by Carr. *N. spathulata* was collected by the Clemenses on the Penibukan Ridge at *c.* 1000 m. It has a stout cylindric rhizome from which an erect inflorescence grows to about 10 cm tall with 3 laxly arranged, trumpet-shaped purplish flowers about 2.5 cm long. It differs from *Gastrodia* in that though the sepals are joined to form a tube, the bright orange petals are free and only joined to the lateral sepals at the base, and are much shorter than the purple sepals.

The genus *Gastrodia,* entirely saprophytic and centred in South-east Asia, is represented by one endemic species on the mountain, *G. grandilabris.* It has a tuberous rhizome 8 cm or longer, lying horizontally in peaty organic matter. From this arises an olive brown inflorescence, usually in January, which is about 20–30 cm tall with four to six rather ugly, warty olive-brown, ball-shaped flowers. This was found at Tenompok and also occurs on ridges around Park Headquarters. It appears to be restricted to this part of the mountain.

Closely related to *Gastrodia,* the saprophytic *Didymoplexiella* has the petals and sepals joined but only from near the base to midway along the sepals. *Didymoplexiella kinabaluensis* is another Mt. Kinabalu endemic and was found by Carr at 900 m at the Menetendok Gorge. It has an erect, slender brown-purple peduncle to 39 cm tall and a densely flowered rachis of over 13 cm. The flowers have purple-brown tepals that are slightly warty, and a three-lobed lip that is white suffused dull purple.

The saprophytic subtribe Epipogiinae has two genera. Both are represented on Mt. Kinabalu by a single species. *Epipogium roseum* was collected near the Mamut Copper Mine in deep leaf litter under mixed dipterocarp forest by the Lohan river. This has branched, tuberous rhizomes and produces a cluster of leafless, white to cream flower stalks over 30 cm tall with many white flowers spotted and streaked with pinkish purple. The sepals and petals are all free but do not open widely, and the lip is spurred. This species is widespread from Africa through India to South-east Asia and Australia.

Stereosandra is represented by a single species, *S. javanica,* widespread in South-east Asia including Borneo, and found by a stream near Poring. It is closely related to *Epipogium,* but the flowers have no spur. This has a tuberous rhizome and produces a single tall inflorescence with a cream, purple-streaked stem.

The tribe Nerviliae contains one genus *Nervilia* and is the only Vanilloid tribe with leafy species. They are terrestrial orchids with round underground tubers produced from runners (stolons). The plants produce a single suborbicular to heart-shaped, plicate leaf. The leaf usually dies down in the dry season, and when the rains come a simple terminal inflorescence is produced. Most species occur in countries such as Thailand with well-defined dry seasons. On Mt. Kinabalu only one species, *Nervilia punctata,* is known, found by Carr at Ulu Kagitang at over 1000 m, and also seen on the trail to Marai Parai near the Haya-Haya stream. This is also found in Java, Sumatra, Peninsular Malaysia and Thailand.

The Epidendroid orchids

The Epidendroid tribes usually have hard pollinia, and mostly lack the stipes and viscidium associated with the pollinia of the more advanced vandoid tribes.

Of five subtribes in the tribe Arethuseae, only the Bletiinae which is pantropical, and the Arundinae are found in Borneo. The subtribe Arundinae is characterised by slender, cane-like stems and grass-like conduplicate leaves (having one central fold in the leaves). The genera *Arundina* and *Dilochia* are similar in that they are large sympodial orchids forming a cluster of tall, cane-like leafy stems, and unlike other species of the tribe, they do not have corms or pseudobulbs. *Arundina* has only one very variable species, *Arundina graminifolia*, distributed throughout South-east Asia. It has tall canes that can reach over 2 m, with many grasslike leaves. Hence it is often called the Bamboo orchid. The inflorescences are terminal, and sometimes branched. The plants colonise landslides, and can never establish in undisturbed shady forest. In recent times they have become a major coloniser of roadsides and roadside cuttings, from sea level to over 3000 m and they are used as landscape plants in the Mountain Garden at Park Headquarters. On Mt. Kinabalu three forms can be seen. The most showy is the lowland form with pinkish tepals and a large purple lip and a deep yellow patch in the midlobe. The canes have plain green leaves, and it is rarely found except on the very lower slopes. The second form is most common, found from 1000 to nearly 2000 m, with purple-tinged leaves, smaller flowers with white tepals, and a less showy deep mauve and white lip with some yellow in the midlobe. This is common along the roads up to and within the Park Headquarters. A pure white peloric form (i.e. in which the lip looks like the other petals) can also be found around Park Headquarters.

Dilochia is a genus of about eight species of which five occur on Mt. Kinabalu. Two of the species are mostly recorded as epiphytes, but can also be terrestrial plants. The largest species is *D. cantleyi,* seen as a terrestrial plant at Marai Parai (1500 m) with leafy canes climbing in shrubby forest to nearly 3 m. The large showy terminal inflorescence has white flowers with a conspicuous yellow lip speckled with some purple. It appears restricted to this area of the mountain. *D. wallichii*, recorded by Carr and the Clemenses at 800–1000 m near Dallas, was also seen along the road to the Power Station, growing terrestrially, although it is also often recorded as an epiphyte. This species has a large, often showy, branched terminal inflorescence with all flowers facing in one direction. The flowers do not open widely, the cream tepals of the flowers are suffused pinkish-purple, and the hidden lip is reddish-purple with yellow edges. Also in the Park Headquarters area and Tenompok is a similar species, *D. parvifolia* with a yellower lip. This is endemic to Borneo. One of the most common orchid species seen by visitors climbing the mountain is *D. rigida,* initially mistaken for a *Bromheadia* (J.J. Wood, pers. comm.) This is a much shorter plant with thin erect stems with shorter stiffer leaves growing to 40 to 60 cm tall. Frequently epiphytic, it is equally common as a terrestrial in open areas along ridge tops from Park Headquarters to above Layang-Layang at 3000 m. This is also a Borneo endemic. It has a smaller terminal infloresence of few flowers, that are variable in colour but with generally creamy white tepals suffused purple on the back, with a cream purple-spotted lip and a yellow base to the midlobe.

The nine genera of the Bletinae found on the mountain are more typical sympodial terrestrials, with corms, and pseudobulbs and often broad plicate leaves, and many of the species are found on the shaded forest floor. A genus with the strangest flowers is *Acanthephippium,* distributed from the Himalayas to New Guinea, with the widespread *A. javanicum* recorded from the lower slopes of Kinabalu. The species has a cluster of thick pseudobulbs about 12 cm tall and about 2 cm thick, enclosed by long bracts each bearing three broad plicate leaves. Very short inflorescences with six or (seldom) more flowers are produced from the lower part of the pseudobulbs so the flowers are close to the ground. The flowers are very unusual in that they have a bulbous urn-like shape, this being formed by the three sepals being joined along the edges to form an urn, the base being a pronounced, slightly bilobed mentum, and the apex forming a narrow opening. On the outside the flowers are creamy yellow suffused with purple. The lip has two erect, rounded white and purple side lobes, at the base of which are bright yellow forked teeth or calli on the two yellow keels that extend to the small downbent, red apex of the lip.

Phaius is represented by six species on Kinabalu, including the widespread *P. tankervilleae* which is among the largest terrestrial orchids on the mountain. Two newly recognized species of this genus are endemic to Kinabalu, occurring on ultramafic substrate. Some of the most interesting orchids are found among species of *Plocoglottis* which are well known for the "mousetrap" action of the lip petal, which is held forward by one of the lateral sepals and is released like a spring when the sepal is disturbed by an insect. This spring action throws the insect against the column and the pollinia. The most common is *P. lowii,* but the prettiest is perhaps *P. acuminata* which has yellow patches on its leaves. Four species of *Plocoglottis* are known on the mountain.

About half a dozen *Spathoglottis* occur on Kinabalu, mostly in disturbed sites. *S. microchilina,* related to the widespread *S. aurea,* is common around Park Headquarters and along the Kamborangoh road; both are distinct by their plicate leaves and yellow flowers on a long inflorescence stalk. There are only a handful of *Taenia* species on the mountain, of which *T. purpureifolia,* a small orchid often found on moss sods and with purple to almost black lower leaf surfaces, deserves mention.

On Kinabalu, the subtribe Coelogyninae is represented by six genera, among which is the genus of the necklace orchids, *Coelogyne.* Among the necklace orchids themselves, in section *Tomentosae* of the genus, is the frequently encountered *C. rhabdobulbon* (common around the Park Headquarters area) which has long pendent inflorescences bearing flowers with snow-white petals and sepals and a creamy white lip with side lobes having a brown patch on the outside. This species is commonly epiphytic on tree trunks and branches but also grows on moss-covered rocks. The limp long inflorescences of *C. moultonii* can have up to 50 medium-sized white flowers which are almost covered by the very large yellowish boat-shaped bracts. The species of *Coelogyne* on Kinabalu are classified into several sections, and number nearly 40 in all. *Chelonistele* has a handful of species, all epiphytic and nearly as attractive. The most commonly seen species around the Park Headquarters is *C. amplissima* which has an erect inflorescence bearing up to eight pale brownish cream flowers. It is usually seen blooming in October to November. Far more diverse is *Dendrochilum,* with more than 30 species on Kinabalu and some 70 in Borneo, usually epiphytic, terrestrial, or lithophytic. The Kinabalu species have erect swollen pseudobulbs which are borne close together, and the inflorescences are curved with a drooping tip. Common along the main trail to the summit are *D. grandiflorum,* with pinkish brown flowers and a greenish column, and *D. kamborangense,* with greenish to lemon-yellow flowers. There are quite a few species, many endemic, at the upper part of the mountain; rather conspicuous are *D. alpinum,* growing by rocks near stunted trees around Panar Laban and slightly higher and with pinkish yellow flowers, and *D. stachyodes,* easily seen in crevices in the granite rock faces above Sayat Sayat and with creamy white flowers.

Another genus in the Coelogyninae is *Pholidota,* with six species on the mountain. *P. ventricosa* is the most common species with erect inflorescences bearing many translucent flowers. The pale green bracts drop off before the flowers open. This species is easily identified by its very robust habit and very large leathery leaves. The salmon flowers borne in two ranks on the pendulous, zig-zag inflorescence stalk of *P. gibbosa* are distinctive. Two other genera, *Entomophobia* and *Nabaluia,* are endemic to Borneo. *Entomophobia,* literally meaning "fear of insects", has but a single species, *E. kinabaluensis.* The genus is so named because the flower is more or less closed as it develops, the stigma being quite inaccessible to any insect visitors because of a transverse callus on the lip. *Nabaluia,* related to *Pholidota,* is named after the mountain and includes only two species on Kinabalu. Both species have greenish yellow flowers with a white to pinkish lip with brown patches, but *N. angustifolia* has linear leaves, those in *N. clemensii* being broader.

The subtribe Glomerinae is represented on Kinabalu by *Agrostophyllum,* a genus of mostly small-flowered orchids, with long stems and leaves regularly arranged in two ranks. The inflorescence is terminal, a dense cluster of small flowers. The sepals and petals are similar and the lip is basally sac-shaped. There are a dozen or so species on the mountain. Another subtribe, Polystachyinae is represented by one species *Polystachya concreta,* epiphytic, with short stems bearing a few leaves and terminal racemes of small flowers which have the lip on the upper side.

The Cymbidioid orchids
These include the tribes Malaxideae and Cymbidieae. The former is represented by three genera, *Liparis, Malaxis* and *Oberonia. Liparis* has more than 20 species on Kinabalu, either epiphytic or terrestrial. The pretty crimson to purple blooms of *L. atrosanguinea,* a species with broad leaves to about 25 cm long, are worthy of note. Some 14 species of *Malaxis* occur on Kinabalu, mostly terrestrial orchids with creeping or short fleshy stems and attractive leaves often with crisped or wavy, purplish or brownish margins. *M. calophylla* has coppery leaves with green-spotted edges, *M. metallica* has leaves which are dark purple and appearing amethyst in sunlight, and *M. lowii* has leaves which are purple-brown with a green central zone on the upper side. Only about a dozen species of *Oberonia* are found on the mountain. They are epiphytes with laterally compressed leaves and flattened broad sheaths that overlap neatly at the base, and very small flowers frequently in whorls on a slender terminal inflorescence. *Oberonia* orchids appear to be more diverse in the lowlands.

Four subtribes of the Cymbidieae are represented on Kinabalu. Eight species of *Bromheadia* represent the subtribe Bromheadiinae here; they are either terrestrial or epiphytic. Some have leaves which are laterally compressed, such as *B. brevifolia* where the leaves are just a centimetre long or so, and *B. scirpioidea* which has longer leaves to 10 cm long or more. Others have normal leaves not laterally compressed, as in the familiar *B. finlaysoniana*, a terrestrial orchid to 1 m high or so, usually in open or disturbed sites at lower elevations. The flowers of the different species share a very similar structure, differing mostly in size and colour, but all are short-lived, opening in the morning and fading by the afternoon.

The subtribe Eulophiinae on Kinabalu includes *Dipodium*, *Eulophia*, *Geodorum* and *Oeceoclades*. *D. pictum* and *D. scandens* are both climbing orchids with long monopodial stems bearing two rows of long narrow leaves which overlap at the base. The erect inflorescences bear up to about a dozen medium-sized flowers with conspicuous speckles on the lower side of the petals and sepals. *Eulophia* on the mountain includes three species; one, *E. zollingeri*, is a leafless saprophyte with dull red-brown flowers while the other two, *E. graminea* and *E. spectabilis*, are leafy terrestrial orchids of open places. Unlike *Eulophia* which has erect inflorescences, *Geodorum* has a drooping inflorescence, as seen in its sole representative on the mountain, *G. densiflorum*. *Oeceoclades pulchra* is also the only species of its genus on Kinabalu, again a terrestrial orchid of open places.

Among the several genera of the subtribe Cyrtopodiinae on Kinabalu, *Grammatophyllum* is familiar through *G. speciosum,* an epiphyte that forms immense tufts on the tallest trees at lower elevations. As in the only other species, *G. kinabaluensis,* the flowers are easy to recognize by the purple-brown spots and blotches on the sepals and petals. *Claderia viridiflora,* a common creeping orchid which grows over logs and a short distance up tree bases in the lowlands and mid-montane forests, is distinctive by its long slender rhizome bearing erect leafy shoots with strongly plicate leaves. Nine species of *Cymbidium* are found on Kinabalu, the most distinctive being *C. finlaysonianum, C. atropurpureum* and *C. dayanum,* epiphytes building up large tufts of pseudobulbs and long grassy leaves. The first two species have limply hanging inflorescences whereas *C. dayanum* has somewhat erect inflorescences.

Thecopus maingayi and *Thecostele alata* are the only representatives of the subtribe Thecostelinae on Kinabalu. *Thecostele alata* is a widespread species with single-jointed, one-leaved, flattened pseudobulbs with a few ridges, leaves to around 30 cm long and a pendulous unbranched inflorescence bearing many well-spaced flowers. The sepals and petals are pale yellow at the base, white in the middle and purplish at the tips, with a few purplish spots. It occurs at lower elevations on Kinabalu.

The subtribe Acriopsidinae is represented by *Acriopsis,* with three species on the mountain. Though by no means spectacular, these epiphytic orchids are easily recognised by their small pseudobulbs bearing narrow leaves, the profusion of branched white roots, downturned inflorescences (in most species), and tiny flowers with united lateral sepals and a tube formed by the lip and the column.

The Dendrobioid orchids

Five subtribes found on Kinabalu constitute this group, of principally epiphytic sympodial orchids. The subtribe Eriinae includes *Ascidieria* (one species, *A. longifolia*), *Ceratostylis* (seven species, including *C. ampullacea* generally found in ultramafic areas), *Porpax* (a single species), *Trichotosia* and *Eria*. *Trichotosia*, with a dozen species, is typically red-brown hairy on the stems, leaves and inflorescences; the inflorescences are lateral and burst through the leaf sheaths, with rather large concave hairy bracts held at right angles to the inflorescence axis, and the sepals are red-hairy on the outside. *T. ferox* is very common around the Park Headquarters.

Eria is a large genus, on Kinabalu represented by nearly 60 species, many poorly understood or named, and divided into a number of sections. The lateral sepals are joined at their base to the column-foot, forming a mentum; the lip is often more or less 3-lobed with a narrowed base joined to the column-foot and forming a spur; the column is short with two lateral horns; and there are eight pollinia in the flower, distinguishing this genus from *Dendrobium* which has four pollinia in the flower. The leaves in some taxa are found throughout the length of the stem except at the very base, as in *E. biflora*, *E. rigida* (with lateral inflorescences) and *E. obliqua* (with terminal inflorescences). In most, the single or few leaves are found toward the apex of the stem, the lower part of which is covered with sheaths. In *E. ornata* the inflorescences develop from the base of short fleshy pseudobulbs although in many other species the inflorescences are terminal or lateral but arise away from the base. The inflorescence in *E. javanica* reaches 60 cm long, bearing many flowers, and is quite exceptional. In many other species the inflorescences are very much shorter

Fig.11. *Paphiopedilum lowii*, Borneo's only epiphytic slipper orchid, is found on Kinabalu. *(Photo: W.M. Poon)*

and some bear only one to several flowers (as in *E. nutans, E. leiophylla* and *E. pannea*), while others have many flowers (as in *E. robusta* and *E. floribunda*).

The subtribe Podochilinae includes *Podochilus,* with about half a dozen species, characteristically small plants with tiny leaves in two rows along the stem, some looking more like mosses and liverworts than orchids. They can be difficult to pick out when growing among mosses on tree trunks. *Appendicula,* in the same subtribe, has close to 20 species on Kinabalu and has larger leaves than *Podochilus;* the inflorescences are terminal or lateral but many species can be recognised by the leaves which are usually held obliquely to the stems and which usually have an obvious joint at the base of the blade. Some species have pendulous stems, e.g., *A. pendula*. The stems can also be markedly flattened, as in *A. anceps*. In one species, *A. foliosa*, the leaf sheaths and lower side of the leaf base have conspicuous dense dark-brown dots. *Poaephyllum*, represented by several species on Kinabalu, is a closely related genus with the habit of *Appendicula* but differing in flower structure. The stems of *P. pauciflorum*, found at lower elevations on Kinabalu, can grow to around half a metre in length; the flower has eight pollinia and the lip base is joined to the sides of the column-foot to form a sac.

The species in subtribe Thelasiinae are not very attractive at all. This subtribe includes the curious small genus *Octarrhena*, with laterally compressed leaves and petals and lip smaller than the sepals. There are on Kinabalu six species of *Thelasis* and nine species of *Phreatia*, not all properly known. *T. carnosa* has leaves which are somewhat cylindrical.

The large genus *Dendrobium*, with some 60 species on Kinabalu, is the chief genus of the subtribe Dendrobiinae which includes two other smaller genera, *Epigeneium* (five species on Kinabalu) and *Flickingeria* (nine species on Kinabalu). In *Dendrobium* is found a number of species with pretty, conspicuous flowers, including the white-flowered *D. spectatissimum, D. parthenium* and *D. singkawangense*, and the greenish-flowered *D. olivaceum*. Most *Dendrobium* species on Kinabalu occur at lower to mid-montane elevations. Several *Epigeneium* species are found in the upper montane forest on Kinabalu; these are *E. kinabaluense, E. longirepens* and *E. tricallosum*. They are not very showy orchids at all, as is the case with *Flickingeria* species which have rather short-lived flowers.

The remarkable genus *Bulbophyllum* is placed in its own subtribe Bulbophyllinae. Almost 90 species of *Bulbophyllum* have been recorded for Kinabalu. These sympodial orchids show an amazing variation in habit, inflorescence form and flower structure. Most species are recognizable as members of the genus as their pseudobulbs are conspicuous, each with a single joint and bearing one leaf at the top; however, in a number (in section *Aphanobulbon*, such as the common *B. flavescens*) the pseudobulbs can be very small and quite inconspicuous. The flowers can be arranged on a raceme (as in *B. coriaceum*, with pretty yellow flowers), in a fan-shaped formation (as in section *Cirrhopetalum*, exemplified by *B. vaginatum*, with some 15 long-tailed yellow flowers) and also in tight clusters (e.g., in *B. salaccense*, section *Globiceps*, with several small purplish flowers). Some species produce but a single flower in the inflorescence. Around Park Headquarters can easily be seen *B. lobbii* and *B. microglossum* (in section *Sestochilus*), distinctive from the short chains of pseudobulbs attached to tree trunks and producing from the rhizome protruding inflorescences with stout stalks on each of which a single large flower is produced. Many species have also distinctive vegetative characters. *B. montense* is one of those which are peculiar because its pseudobulbs are often flattened and appressed to the substrate (as is typical of its section, *Monilibulbus*), and a chain of such pseudobulbs partly covering the rhizome can look distinctive; it grows among mosses or on bark. The strongly 4-angled, yellow pseudobulbs of *B. biflorum* are characteristic of the species. In *B. macranthum* the sheaths disintegrate into groups of bristles along the rhizome bearing well-spaced pseudobulbs. *B. undecifilum* is typical of section *Epicrianthes*, characterised by pendulous rhizomes with the growing end curved forwards, a one-flowered inflorescence and petals with a number of linear appendages. *B. teres* is one of several species with leaves that are terete or somewhat circular in cross-section. Some species have foul-smelling flowers, believed to attract pollinating flies, as in *B. foetidolens*, where the drooping inflorescence bears closely clustered flowers with purple-blotched sepals and petals.

The Vandoid orchids

These monopodial orchids with lateral inflorescences are classified as a single subtribe, Aeridinae, in the sole tribe Vandeae. In them, pseudobulbs are entirely absent, and the two or four pollinia are borne on a distinct, usually flattened stalk or stipes and attached to a disc. Seidenfaden (1988) arranged the genera into groups according to the number of pollinia and their characteristics. The diversity within this subtribe is amazing and includes flower forms from large, as in *Arachnis*, to minute, as in *Schoenorchis* or *Microsaccus*. Vegetatively, there are long climbing plants as in *Arachnis* ranging to tiny *Taeniophyllum* plants which are almost leafless.

The genera are allied into groups, based on characters of the inflorescences, pollinia and column. Group 1 and Group 2 genera have four pollinia. In Group 1, including *Microsaccus* and *Taeniophyllum*, the pollinia are nearly equal and free from one another. *Microsaccus* has laterally compressed leaves and *Taeniophyllum* is almost leafless, the leaves reduced to tiny scales. These plants are mainly twig epiphytes, not easily observed except on twigs blown down from tree crowns.

Group 2 genera have the four pollinia developing as two pairs. In this group, 16 genera are recorded on Kinabalu, including the showy orchids in *Arachnis*, *Dimorphorchis* and *Renanthera*. Popularly called the Scorpion Orchids, *Arachnis* is represented by three species on Kinabalu, which are climbing species typically with long stems and large flowers with a movable lip and curved lateral sepals recalling the claws of a scorpion, the upper sepal being its tail. *A. flos-aeris* is a rather widespread species with the distinctive yellowish green sepals and petals which are blotched purple-brown. *Dimorphorchis* is curious because of its long pendulous inflorescences which bear flowers of two different colour patterns; two species, *D. lowii* and *D. rossii*, occur on the lower slopes of the mountain. Two species of *Renanthera* are found on Kinabalu. *R. bella* is unmistakable by its large, flaming red flowers while the Bornean form of *R. matutina* has light orange flowers which are open over a long period, two to three at a time, on an elongate inflorescence. *Thrixspermum* is another genus in this group, with 11 species on Kinabalu. *T. triangulare* is a frequently encountered epiphyte between Park Headquarters and Paka Cave; its flowers, unfortunately, last only a day. The genus is distinguished by the firmly attached lip, which is sac-shaped with a callus on its front wall. *Trichoglottis* is not properly known on Kinabalu, and there may be a dozen species or so on the mountain. The lip of the flower, which is always hairy, characteristically has a tongue-like structure at the back. Of the other genera in this group, *Schoenorchis,* the species of which have very narrow leaves, is also worth mentioning; in *S. juncifolia t*he leaves are terete (circular in cross-section).

Genera in the remaining three groups have only two pollinia. Group 3 genera include those with elongate, often branched inflorescences, many with large flowers and often a distinct column-foot in the flower. Groups 4 and 5 are characterised by genera with comparatively short inflorescences bearing small to medium-sized flowers often with a short or no column-foot.

Group 3 includes such well known or spectacular genera as *Aerides, Paraphalaenopsis, Phalaenopsis, Robiquetia* and *Vanda*. On Kinabalu, *Aerides odorata*, a widespread species, is the sole representative of its genus. Its sepals and petals are white with purplish blotches at the tips, and the medium-sized flowers are sweetly fragrant. Also with only one species on Kinabalu, *Paraphalaenopsis* is represented by *P. labukensis*, which is a pendent epiphyte with whip-like terete leaves and a short inflorescence bearing up to five or six, large, cinnamon-scented flowers with purplish speckled petals and sepals. *Phalaenopsis*, the genus of the Moon Orchid, has three species on the mountain. The flowers do not have any spur, but the column-foot is distinct and the firmly attached lip bears several appendages. *P. amabilis*, a well known garden plant, is naturally found on Kinabalu. Five species of *Robiquetia* are found on Kinabalu, a few only recently recognized as distinct species. These are usually pendulous epiphytes with unbranched pendent inflorescences bearing many small flowers. The flowers have a firm immovable lip with short side-lobes, a slender spur, and an erect column without any distinct column-foot. There are two species of *Vanda, V. hastifera* var. *gibbsiae* and *V. helvola*, known on Kinabalu. The moderately large flowers of *Vanda* are distinctive by a relatively small spur without any calli, an immovable lip with simple lobes, and pollinia which are only slightly shorter than the broad stipes. *V. helvola* is not among the most beautiful of *Vanda* species, many of which are horticulturally important.

Two curious genera, *Gastrochilus* and *Luisia*, are placed in Group 4. *Gastrochilus*, with only one species on Kinabalu, has a lip with a broad rounded sac without any internal callus. *Luisia* is represented on the mountain by two species, both with terete leaves and short, dense inflorescences.

The remaining seven genera of vandoid orchids on Kinabalu are placed in Group 5. These are *Chamaeanthus* (one species), *Chroniochilus* (two species), *Malleola* (three species), *Microtatorchis* (two species), *Pennilabium* (one species), *Porrorhachis* (one species), and *Tuberolabium* (one species). Of these, only a few deserve mention. The *Chamaeanthus* and *Chroniochilus* species are rare hill-forest orchids on Kinabalu. Of the *Malleola* species, *M.witteana* has leaves that are purplish on the lower side. The species of *Microtatorchis* have leaves which are tiny or reduced to scales, as in *Taeniophyllum*, and *Pennilabium* has short stems with few leaves that are unequally bilobed at the tip and somewhat twisted at the base.

REFERENCES

Ames, O. & Schweinfurth, C. 1921. Studies in the Family Orchidaceae, Vol. 6. The Orchids of Mount Kinabalu, British North Borneo.

Atwood, J.T. 1985. Pollination of *Paphiopedilum rothschildianum*: brood-site deception. National Geogr. Research, Spring 1985: 247–254.

Beaman, J.H. & Beaman, R.S. 1990. Diversity and distribution patterns in the flora of Mount Kinabalu. In: Baas, P., Kalkman, K. & Geesink, R. (eds.), The Plant Diversity of Malesia. Kluwer Academic Publishers, The Netherlands. Pp. 147–160.

Burbidge, F.W. 1880. The Gardens of the Sun. John Murray, London.

Carr, C.E. 1935. Two collections of orchids from British North Borneo, Part 1. *Gardens'. Bulletin, Straits Settlements* 8: 165–240.

Chan, C.L. 1994. A new species of *Dendrobium (Orchidaceae: Epidendroideae: Dendrobieae)* from Mount Kinabalu, Sabah. *Sandakania* 5: 67–71.

Chan, C.L., Lamb, A., Shim, P.S. & Wood, J.J. 1994. Orchids of Borneo, Vol. 1. The Sabah Society, Kota Kinabalu, in association with Royal Botanic Gardens, Kew.

Comber, J.B. 1990. Orchids of Java. Royal Botanic Gardens, Kew.

Cribb, P. 1987. The genus *Paphiopedilum*. Royal Botanic Gardens, Kew.

Dressler, R.L. 1981. The Orchids. Natural History and Classification. Harvard University Press, Cambridge, Mass., U. S. A.

Dressler, R.L. 1983. Classification of the Orchidaceae and their probable origin. *Telopia* 2 (4): 413–424.

Dressler, R.L. 1990a. The Orchids. Natural History and Classification. Harvard University Press. Revised edition.

Dressler, R.L. 1990b. The Neottieae in orchid classification. *Lindleyana* 5(2): 102–109.

Dressler, R.L. 1990c. The Spiranthoideae—Grade or Subfamily? *Lindleyana* 5(2): 110–116.

Dressler, R.L. 1990d. The Major Clades of Orchidaceae—Epidendroideae. *Lindleyana* 5(2): 117–125.

Grell, E. 1988. Reintroduction of *Paphiopedilum rothschildianum* in Sabah. *American Orchid Society Bulletin* 57(11): 1238–1246.

Heywood, V.H. (ed.). 1978. Flowering Plants of the World. Oxford University Press.

Gibbs, L.S. 1914. A Contribution to the Flora and Plant Formations of Mount Kinabalu and the Highlands of British North Borneo. *Journal of the Linnean Society (Botany)* 42: 1–240.

Masamune, G. 1942. *Enumeratio Phanerogamarum Bornearum*. Tokyo.

Seidenfaden, G. 1988. Orchid Genera in Thailand. XIV. Fifty Nine Vandoid Genera. *Opera Botanica* no. 95. Copenhagen.

Smith, J.J. 1912. Orchidaceae. In: Winkler, H., *Beitrage zur Kenntnis der Flora und Pflanzengeographie von Borneo* 2. *Engl. Bot. Jahrb.* 48: 96–106.

Smith, J.J. 1927. Orchidaceae. In: Irmscher, E., *Beitrage zur Kenntnis der Flora von Borneo. Mitt. Inst. allg. Bot. Hamb.* 7: 9–76.

Smith, J.J. 1931. On a collection of Orchidaceae from Central Borneo. *Bull. Jard. bot. Buitenz.* 3. s. 11: 83–160.

Vermeulen, J.J. 1991. Orchids of Borneo. Vol. 2, *Bulbophyllum*. Royal Botanic Gardens, Kew and Toihaan Publishing Company, Kota Kinabalu.

Whitmore, T.C. 1984. Tropical Rain Forests of the Far East. 2nd Edition. Clarendon Press, Oxford.

Wood, J.J., Beaman, R.S. & Beaman, J.H. 1993. The Plants of Mount Kinabalu. 2. Orchids. Royal Botanic Gardens, Kew.

Wood, J.J. & Cribb, P.J. 1994. A Checklist of the Orchids of Borneo. Royal Botanic Gardens, Kew.

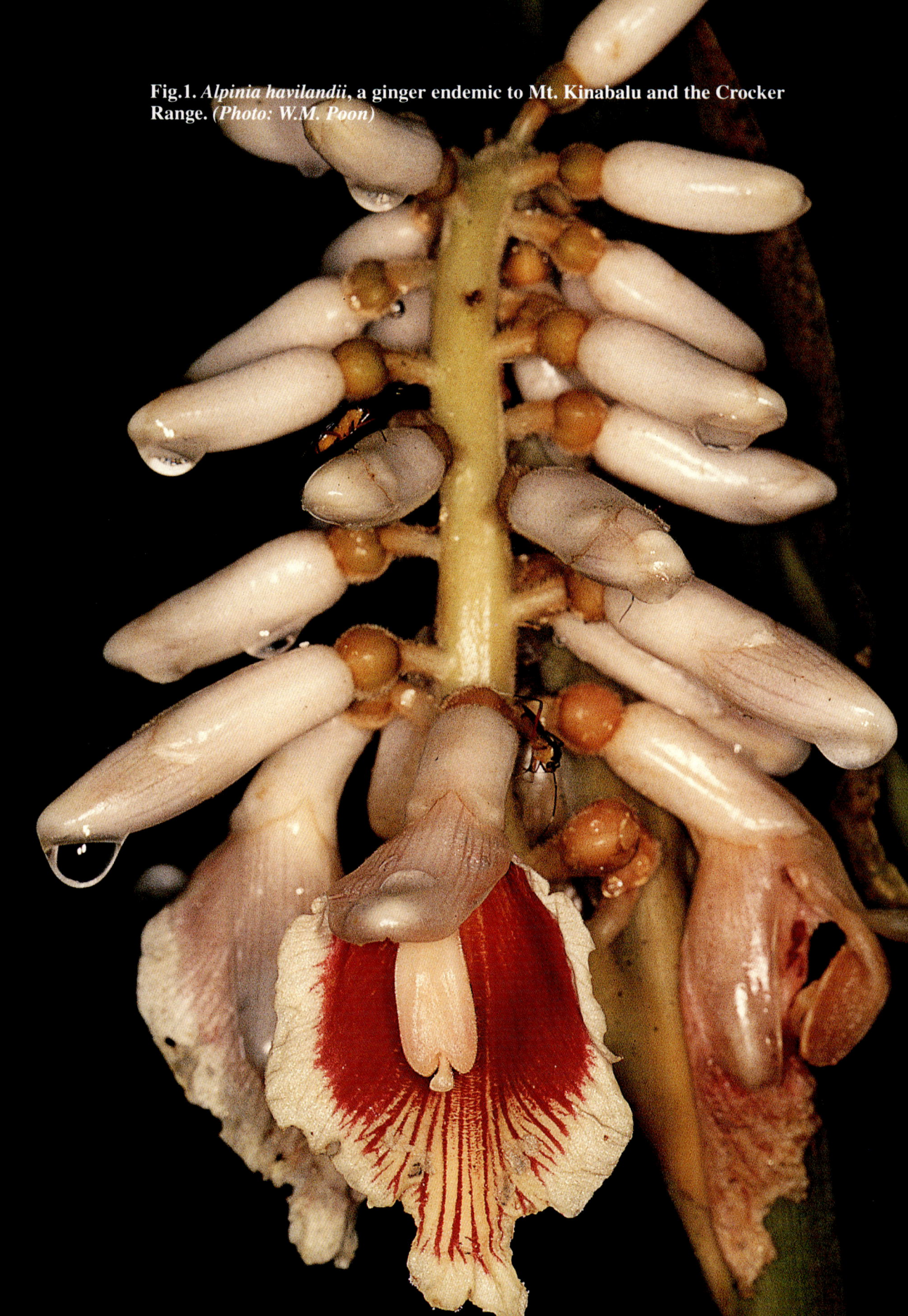

Fig.1. *Alpinia havilandii*, a ginger endemic to Mt. Kinabalu and the Crocker Range. *(Photo: W.M. Poon)*

GINGERS

Rosemary M. Smith

Before discussing these interesting and often spectacular plants, any possible confusion must be avoided by pointing out that the name 'ginger' is used in two ways: for the genus *(Zingiber)* which gives us the commercial product and for the whole family (Zingiberaceae) to which it belongs. The Zingiberaceae contains several important spice plants and many of its members are rich in volatile oils. The best known is the root or stem ginger *Zingiber officinale;* one of the oldest spices used by man. Confucius wrote of it in the 4th century B.C.; it is mentioned in the Koran, and was highly prized by the ancients of Greece and Rome who obtained supplies from Arab traders who travelled the old silk road between India and the West. The true country of origin of *Z. officinale* is today unknown, as is also the case with turmeric *(Curcuma longa),* an essential ingredient of curry powder and important too as a dye plant. Ginger and turmeric come from the rhizomes, or underground stems, of the plant, but in another ginger of commerce, cardamom *(Elettaria cardamomum),* it is the aromatic seed which is used. Details of the history of these, and other gingers, in trade and cultivation, can be found in H.N. Ridley's famous (1912) book "Spices", and a more modern account is given in the similarly titled volumes of the Tropical Agriculture series by J.W. Purseglove *et al.* (1981).

Over 30 species of Zingiberaceae are to be found in Kinabalu Park. They are particularly abundant around Poring Hot Springs (500 m) but may occur at altitudes of up to about 2000 m. The majority of Kinabalu gingers have tall, very distinctive, leafy shoots—often called fronds—which are sometimes over 3 m tall. While some gingers, such as the common white-flowered *Hedychium cylindricum*, are readily seen and recognised, several genera produce their flowers at ground level in the litter of the forest floor and such inflorescences may be easily overlooked. A tall frond lacking flowers at the top should not be dismissed as a sterile plant, as a downward glance may be rewarded by the sight of a brilliant orange *Amomum* or scarlet-bracted *Zingiber* inflorescence. Much work has still to be done on the Zingiberaceae and not all those which occur in the Park have been named precisely as yet.

The ginger flower is superficially like that of an orchid in that it possesses but a single stamen, and in both families the lip usually provides the most showy part of the flower. There is, however, an important botanical distinction; the orchid lip is a true petal, in the Zingiberaceae it is a modified stamen.

The gingers of Kinabalu Park may be conveniently divided into two groups: plants in which the flowers arise at the top of the leafy shoot, or are occasionally pushed out sideways from it *(Hedychium, Globba, Alpinia, Burbidgea, Plagiostachys)* and plants in which the inflorescence is quite separate from the leaves, held well above ground on a leafless stalk, or near ground level and sometimes embedded in the soil *(Zingiber, Hornstedtia, Etlingera, Amomum)*. In the latter group, the inflorescence is almost always protected by an outer layer of large, sometimes brightly coloured, bracts.

HEDYCHIUM

The name *Hedychium* is derived from the Greek *hedys* (sweet) and *chion* (snow), a reference to the sweetly scented white flowers of *H. coronarium,* the first species to be described. A single species, *H. cylindricum*, is recorded from many localities in the Park and is extremely common there. Up to 2 m in height, but often much less, it has predominantly white flowers with a large bilobed lip and long slender reddish stamens. In fruit it is spectacular as the ripe capsules burst open to reveal an orange interior containing bright red seeds, each of which is partially covered by a white appendage known as the aril. *H. cylindricum* may be found growing on tree trunks as an "air plant" or epiphyte, a growth habit adopted by many orchids and ferns. The species also occurs in Java and Sumatra.

Fig.2. Delicate white blooms of the usually epiphytic *Hedychium cylindricum*, a common ginger of Kinabalu Park. *(Photo: C.L. Chan)*

GLOBBA

The globbas, which get their generic name from the Amboinan word *'galoba'*, rarely exceed 1 m in height and are characterized by their delicate small flowers with long arching stamens. The leafy shoots are not always obviously frond-like.

G. atrosanguinea found along the old road to the Mamut mine, above Ranau, is easily recognised by its bright red bracts, and the yellow-flowered, green-bracted *G. propinqua* is recorded from several localities, below 1500 m. *G. tricolor* var. *gibbsiae,* a variety named for Miss Lilian Gibbs, first European lady to reach the summit of the mountain, has white and yellow-orange flowers. In *G. pendula* and *G. franciscii* the flowers are plain orange, sometimes with a darker spot on the lip. The latter is readily distinguished by the widespreading inflorescence, each branch of which may bear over 20 flowers. This species commemorates A.B.C. Francis, Resident of the Interior in North Borneo early this century.

Globbas produce fruit infrequently and often reproduce vegetatively by means of bulbils. These small organs are formed, instead of flowers, in the lower part of the inflorescence, and eventually fall to the ground where they may grow into new plantlets which will resemble the parent exactly.

ALPINIA

Alpinia was named in honour of Prosper Alpinio, a 16th century Italian botanist. Of the half dozen or so species known in the Park, *A. latilabris* is much the most spectacular. Reaching a height of at least 3 m, the large pink and white flowers are up to 8 cm long and well set off by the rich yellow lip which is heavily marked by deep crimson spots and stripes. It occurs in the forest behind the hot springs at Poring, and is perhaps one of the less common gingers of the Park. Equally easy to recognise and much more likely to be encountered is *A. havilandii*, a dominant ginger around Park Headquarters at 1550 m. Until recently it was believed to be restricted to Mt. Kinabalu but is now known to occur in the Crocker Range also. It was named after the English naturalist, G.D. Haviland, who collected plants in Borneo in the late 19th century. This species has the curious habit of pushing out its inflorescence laterally, just below the top of the leafy shoot; this feature, plus the golden-brown hairs on the flower stalks, make its recognition easy. The flowers of *A. havilandii* are white with red markings on the lip and are only a little smaller than those of *A. latilabris*. An equally attractive species, but a much rarer one, is *A. glabra* (Fig.10). It has been found on the road to Kampung Kiau on the southern boundary of the Park. The flowers are red and orange, and, as the name indicates, the plant is quite without hairs.

By comparison with *A. latilabris, A. havilandii* and *A. glabra,* the three remaining Kinabalu alpinias are smaller flowered and less brilliantly coloured. *A. ligulata* and *A. nieuwenhuizii*—the latter honours the Dutch explorer Dr. A.W. Nieuwenhuis—are closely related to each other, and future research may indicate that they are not distinct. Both have pinkish green flowers, copiously produced and borne on strongly branching inflorescences.

Fig.3. The flower heads of a Kinabalu *Zingiber* species emerge through the forest-floor litter, producing dainty pale yellow blooms. *(Photo: C.L. Chan)*

Fig.4. *Alpinia glabra.*

They are very tall plants, often reaching over 3 m, and are frequently found by streamsides or in more open, disturbed areas.

There remains *A. galanga* which, like turmeric and root ginger, is an ancient spice plant and provides the medicinal and culinary spice galangal. This species is widely cultivated throughout South-east Asia and often becomes naturalised; it is uncertain if it is truly wild in Borneo, but a plant growing just inside the entrance to Poring Hot Springs is reputed to have a local wild origin. *A. galanga* is about 2 m tall with a hairy inflorescence and 2–3 cm-long greenish white flowers, usually with some red stripes on the lip.

BURBIDGEA

This small genus of five or six species, which is not known outside Borneo, reminds us of F.W. Burbidge, an Irishman who came to Borneo in the late 19th century to search for plants of horticultural merit. His travels, which included two collecting trips on the slopes of Mt. Kinabalu in the days when the buffalo provided a convenient, if insecure mode of transport, are vividly described in his book "The Gardens of the Sun".

Burbidgea is almost unique in the Zingiberaceae in that it is the petals which form the most conspicuous part of the flower, the lip being reduced to a narrow upright organ which is held against the stamen. The flowers are orange yellow, often with a pink tinge which increases in intensity as the inflorescence matures. *B. schizocheila* (syn. *B. pubescens*) is the sole Park representative. It is a small herb, generally well under 1 m in height, and, like the other members of this genus, produces narrowly elongate capsules which are quite distinctive. Plants can be seen in the Mountain Garden at the Park Headquarters.

Fig.5. In an ornate arrangement on the inflorescence, the orange-yellow flowers of *Burbidgea schizocheila* each has three conspicuous perianths. *(Photo: C.L. Chan)*

PLAGIOSTACHYS

Plagio (oblique) *stachys* (spike) is aptly named and quickly recognised. The densely congested, small-flowered inflorescence is pushed out from the side of the leafy shoot *below* the lowermost leaves. In some species the inflorescence produces copious amounts of mucilage through which the opening flowers develop. This mucilage, which occasionally occurs in *Amomum,* was well described by the great Italian naturalist Odoardo Beccari in his "Wanderings in the Great Forests of Borneo" (*"Nelle Foreste di Borneo"*) as a *"sort of putrescent slime ... in which an enormous number of Coleoptera (beetles) seek refuge."*. One species of *Plagiostachys* has been found in the Park. It is most nearly related to the non-mucilaginous *P. strobilifera* and a fruiting example is shown in Fig.6.

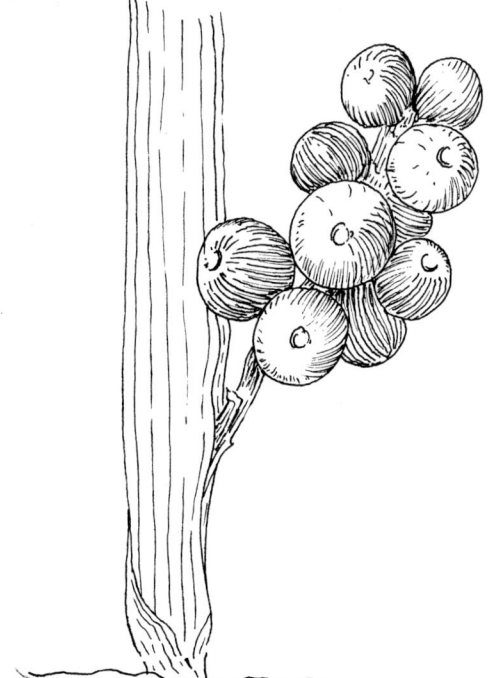

Fig.6. *Plagiostachys* in fruit.

HORNSTEDTIA

This genus commemorates Claes Frederic Hornstedt, an 18th century surgeon and naturalist who was born in Sweden. The hornstedtias are quickly recognised by the spindle shape of the flower heads, which are covered by rigid bracts. The commonly red and white flowers appear, a few at a time, from the top of the inflorescence. Sometimes this inflorescence is held on a long erect stalk, as in *H. gracile* (Fig.7 left) and in the more robust *H. havilandii;* but in *H. scyphifera,* which has rough bracts with hairy cross pieces, and the smooth-bracted *H. incana* the head is almost stalkless. The latter (Fig.7 right) is a common species within the Park and grows with its rhizome raised above ground on vertical aerial roots (stilt roots). The leafy shoots of *Hornstedtia* are often very tall, sometimes as much as 5 m.

Fig.7. *Hornstedtia gracile* (left) and *H. incana* (right).

Fig.8. Glossy red flowers protrude from the short spindle-shaped inflorescence of *Hornstedtia incana*. (Photo: C.L. Chan)

ZINGIBER

The name Zingiber derives from the sanskrit *'singabera'* meaning a root. While *Z. officinale* is the only species which is cultivated extensively, two others, *Z. zerumbet* and *Z. pupureum* (syn. *Z. cassumunar*) are well-known village plants in Penisular Malaysia and much used medicinally. Two species inhabit Kinabalu Park; *Z. coloratum*, which has bright red bracts and white flowers, and *Z. pseudopungens,* which has shaggy, reddish-brown bracts. Both are to be found at Poring and have fronds up to 2 m high.

AMOMUM

The name amomum comes from an old Greek word *(amomom),* once used for a spice plant—of unknown identity—which was reputed to have anti-toxic properties.

A. kinabaluense is common on the forest trails and is not, as yet, recorded from outside the Park. It is a yellow-orange, mucilaginous, few-flowered species and the rather slender fronds are sometimes less than 1 m tall. Of a much deeper orange hue and a considerably larger plant, is *A. oliganthum* (Fig.9 centre) which has a dense many-flowered inflorescence.

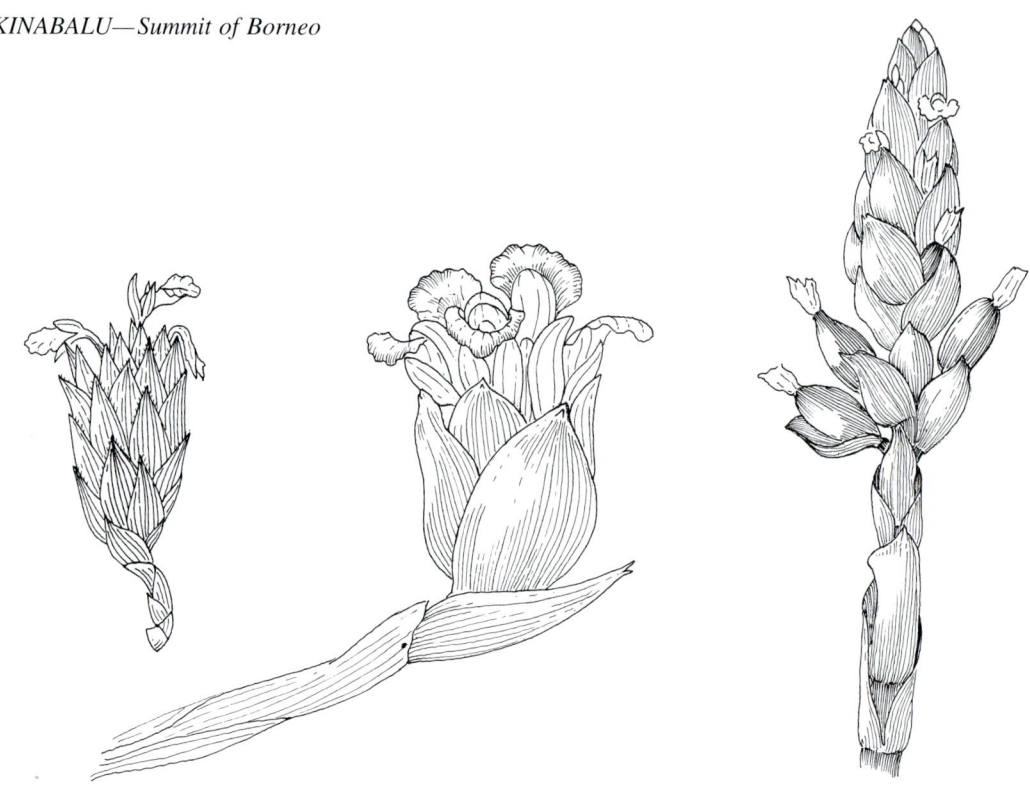

Fig.9. *Amomum compactum* (left), *A. oliganthum* (centre) and *A. anomalum* (right).

Both these species have the flower heads embedded in the litter and both produce spiny fruit. *A. compactum* (Fig.9 left) is of similar habit, but here the capsules are spherical and more or less smooth. This is the 'round cardamom of Java' and is cultivated on that island for its aromatic seeds. The small white and yellow flowers have some red lines on the lip and the bracts are thin-textured and papery.

Two further *Amomum* are known in the Park—but more will surely be found—and both have their inflorescence stalks above ground. They are the cream-flowered *A. longipedunculatum*, which has a long prostrate stalk and produces some stilt roots, a rare occurence in *Amomum*, and the much more robust *A. anomalum* (Fig.9 right). This species, so named because two flowers are usually produced within each bract

Fig.10. The flower heads of *Amomum kinabaluensis*, endemic to Mt. Kinabalu, are embedded in the forest-floor litter. *(Photo: C.L. Chan)*

instead of the customary one, has small dull yellow flowers; the inflorescence lengthens considerably with age and bright red oblong fruits are formed.

ETLINGERA

This genus commemorates the 18th century German botanist Andreas Ernst Etlinger. Until recently *Etlingera* was split into three genera, *Achasma, Nicolaia* and *Geanthus*, but botanically these three have important characters in common. When it was decided to unite them, it was found that *Etlingera,* although unused for many years, was the oldest correct name for the group.

At least six species grow in the Park and all of them produce tall robust leafy shoots. The best known is the Torch ginger, *E. elatior*, whose flower heads are a common sight in the markets of Malaysia; the young buds are often added to spicy dishes. Here the inflorescence is held well above ground on a 1–1.5-m stalk and the many small flowers are surrounded by showy, spreading, pink or red bracts. Only one other Kinabalu *Etlingera* has the inflorescence held above ground, but here the stalk is much shorter and the bracts do not spread. This plant is probably a variety of the Sarawak species *E. muluensis*; it has reddish bracts and yellow-orange flowers. Several clumps grow only a few metres from the Park Administration building and there are plants in the Mountain Garden at Park Headquarters as well. A closely related species, *E. fimbriobracteata*, can be seen at Poring; the base of its inflorescence is embedded in the ground and the many flowers are bright yellow with a reddish anther-crest and dark red stigma.

Amongst the most spectacular *Etlingera* are those in which the lip has become elongated. The number of species in this group is uncertain but the plants fall into two distinct flower types; that of *E. littoralis* which (in the plants found in the Park) have plain red flowers and, because the petals are short, the back of the stamen is clearly visible and *E. punicea,* which usually has some yellow in the centre of the lip, and in which the stamen is completely hidden by the hooded uppermost petal. In these species the inflorescence is deeply embedded in the ground. At the height of flowering, when several flowers open at a time, the elongated lips may form a radiant pattern of exceptional beauty. Lastly, there is *E. brevilabris* (Fig.11) a striking species with deep red flowers, a large, but not elongate lip and white, shining stigma. The inflorescence is few-flowered and partially embedded in the ground.

Fig.11. *Etlingera brevilabris.*

Fig.12. *Etlingera punicea*, with brilliantly coloured lip-petals that radiate outwards from an inflorescence embedded in the ground. *(Photo: A. Lamb)*

COSTUS

Finally, a word on *Costus* is relevant. This large pantropical genus is often placed in a separate family, the Costaceae, but some authors continue to treat it as a subfamily of the

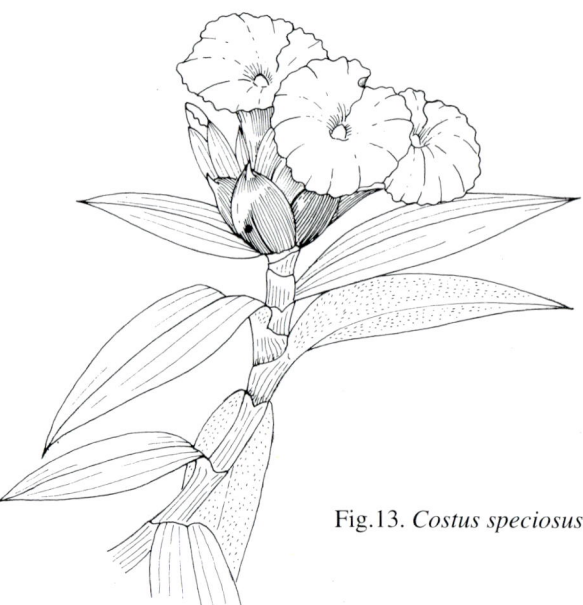

Fig.13. *Costus speciosus*.

Zingiberaceae, Costoideae. The most obvious distinguishing feature of *Costus* is the arrangement of the leaves which is spiral and quite unlike the two-ranked arrangement of other Bornean gingers. Furthermore, the stems are often branched. *C. speciosus* (Fig.13) may be found in the Park in the lowland areas; this cream-flowered species is widespread throughout Malaysia and Indonesia.

REFERENCES

Beccari, O. 1904. Wanderings in the Great Forests of Borneo (transl. Dr. E.H. Giglioli, rev. and ed. F.H.H. Guillemard). Archibald Constable and Co., London.

Burbidge, F.W. 1880. The Gardens of the Sun. John Murray, London.

Purseglove, F.W., Brown, E.G., Green, C.L., & Robbins, S.R.J. 1981. Spices. 2 vols. Longman Scientific and Technical, London.

Ridley, H.N. 1912. Spices. Macmillan and Co., London.

Fig.1. The *poring* bamboo, *Gigantochloa levis*. (Photo: A. Phillipps)

BAMBOOS

K.M. Wong & Soejatmi Dransfield

Bamboos are a distinct lifeform in any forest and certainly on Mt. Kinabalu as well. This specialised group of grasses exhibits an amazing range of habits. They can be erect, clambering to scrambling, or climbing in habit (Wong, 1986). Some species as known now are unique to Kinabalu, whereas others occur also in other localities in Sabah, but certainly on a regional scale all species of bamboo found naturally within the Park can be considered rare, and a few are extremely localised.

In terms of the number of species, there are not that many bamboos on Mt. Kinabalu. Only six are so far known within the Park and four other species have been recorded just outside. The abundance of several species on Mt. Kinabalu, especially evident along the usual climbers' approach, reflects the relative importance of bamboos as a component of montane forests. This is not restricted to Mt. Kinabalu, for bamboos are also a significant component in the montane and ridge flora elsewhere in South-east Asia, although perhaps this aspect has been much ignored in accounts of the vegetation. They are naturally abundant on some mountains and, although they can be relatively invasive, they are not, in the first place, present due to habitat disturbances and canopy opening.

Kinabalu also represents an important locality in bamboo biogeography, partly by virtue of its height and partly because its massif is situated at the northernmost end of the Crocker Range system. Hence we find that *Racemobambos,* a genus of 17 species of mainly montane bamboos in Malesia (Peninsular Malaysia, Borneo, Palawan, Sulawesi, Seram, New Guinea extending to New Ireland), is significantly represented (by four species) on this northernmost high massif on the island of Borneo (Dransfield, 1983). Also, *Yushania tessellata,* known only from Kinabalu, Mt. Alab in the Tambunan area of Sabah, and the Meligan Forest Reserve in south-west Sabah, is a sister-species of *Y. niitakayamensis* which is known from the highlands of Luzon and Taiwan (Dransfield, 1983). Kinabalu, then, is an important locality for the distribution of certain genera and for speciation, in relation to other highland chains and islands in Malesia.

AN ANNOTATED CHECKLIST

Within the Park, six species are known:

Racemobambos hepburnii S. Dransfield
A clambering/scrambling species with thin-walled and rather flexible pencil-thin culms and fine-leafed branches which can clamber onto and drape itself over the surrounding plants. This is common around the Park Headquarters at 1550 m up to *c.* 2250 m around

Kamborangoh. Elsewhere it occurs on the Crocker Range at *c*. 1000 m. *R. hepburnii* and *R. gibbsiae* typically have leaves less than 1 cm broad (often not more than 0.5 cm) and three glumes in the spikelet, whereas *R. rigidifolia* and *R. hirsuta* have broader leaves and two glumes in the spikelet. This species was described only as recently as 1983, when it was realized that it differed significantly from the next species. It is locally known as *'kobong kobong'* in the Dusun language in Bundu Tuhan.

Racemobambos gibbsiae (Stapf) Holttum
A species also clambering/scrambling in habit and closely related to *R. hepburnii*, this differs chiefly in the larger, hairy spikelets of the inflorescence and its occurrence within a higher altitudinal range. It is common in mossy forest from around Kamborangoh to Layang-Layang staff quarters (formerly Carson's Camp), on the Summit Trail (*c*. 2250 to 2700 m), and on the Marai Parai spur from 1500 to 2000 m. This was first collected by Miss Lillian Gibbs, who made the first recorded ascent of Kinabalu by a woman in 1910. It is a Kinabalu endemic.

Racemobambos rigidifolia Holttum
Also clambering/scrambling in habit, this species characteristically has rigid narrow leaves and glabrous spikelets. This has a more restricted distribution, and occurs on ultramafic (ultrabasic) soil on Marai Parai on the western slope of the mountain. It also seems to be a Kinabalu endemic.

Racemobambos hirsuta Holttum
This clambering/scrambling bamboo is related to *R. rigidifolia* but its leaves are smaller and not as rigid; also the spikelets are hairy. It occurs on Kinabalu on ultramafic soil on the western slope of the mountain, and has been documented from Penibukan (or Peniguppan) to Marai Parai (at *c*. 1200 m). This species has the widest distribution of the four Kinabalu species of *Racemobambos*; it has also been documented in Sabah on Mt. Silam and Mt. Nicola.

Yushania tessellata (Holttum) S. Dransfield
This elegant erect bamboo grows only to about 7 m tall and occurs in the forest along the Kiau View Trail at Park Headquarters, around the Power Station (at 1900 m) and below Kamborangoh. Its slender culms are medium green to yellowish-green and are characterised by the frequent occurrence of root-thorns at the lower nodes and 3–5 branches developing at about the same level at each of the upper nodes. It is known only from Kinabalu, Mt. Alab in the Tambunan district further south, and the highlands in the Meligan Forest Reserve in south-west Sabah.

Kinabaluchloa nebulosa Wong
The last bamboo known growing naturally within the Park confines is a slender-culmed, rather elegant bamboo with a sister species on the Main Range mountains of Peninsular Malaysia (Wong, 1993). The Kinabalu bamboo has thin-walled culms that grow very long and which get entangled in the tree-canopy or sometimes flop over in a semi-scrambling habit. The young culms are characterised by a ring of fine spreading bristles at the nodes. Fully developed culms have internodes which are unusually long (60 to 100 cm) and as

Fig.2. Fine-foliaged, slender culms of *Racemobambos hepburnii* entangle with the surrounding vegetation at Park Headquarters. *(Photo: K.M. Wong)*

Fig.3. Young culm of *Kinabaluchloa nebulosa*, with a ring of fine spreading bristles at the nodes. *(Photo: K.M. Wong)*

Fig.4. The long, slender culms of *Kinabaluchloa nebulosa* are frequently entangled in tree crowns in the forest around Park Headquarters. *(Photo: K.M. Wong)*

Fig.5. *Yushania tessellata*, an elegant erect bamboo, has its nearest relative in the highlands of Luzon and Taiwan. *(Photo: K.M. Wong)*

Fig.6. *Yushania tessellata* has a distinctive branch complement, with 3-5 main branches developing at about the same level at the node. *(Photo: K.M. Wong)*

such resemble those of the Malayan *K. wrayi*, which are used for constructing blow-pipes. At each branching node there are relatively few subequal branches bearing relatively large leaves (*c.* 2 x 20 cm). The Kinabalu taxon also occurs in other parts of Sabah, Brunei and Sarawak, where the internodes are sometimes used for making musical instruments, such as the *'sompoton'* (Sabah) and the *'engkrui'* (Sarawak). On Kinabalu, this species can be seen easily in the forest around the Park Headquarters and on the Penibukan (or Peniggupan) ridge. The botanical name *Kinabaluchloa* means "grass of Kinabalu" and *nebulosa* means "in the clouds".

Four other species have been documented just outside Park limits. These are :

Dinochloa sublaevigata **S. Dransfield**
This species belongs to one of very few climbing genera of bamboos and has characteristically twining culms, and has been documented from the eastern shoulder of Kinabalu and along the road to Poring. It is a resident of hill dipterocarp forest and is also known from the Sandakan and Tawau areas (Dransfield, 1981). Its large leaves (to *c.* 6 x 40 cm) give it a resemblance to *D. trichogona* but its culm-sheath bases are hairless and its fruits are rugose, unlike those in that species. Many *Dinochloa* species are potentially highly invasive plants (Wong, 1986) and cleared areas on the fringe of the Park may in time be colonised by this species. The leaves of this species, like those of *D. trichogona*, are used for wrapping Hokkien Chinese glutinous-rice dumplings locally called *'bak chang'*. Both species are frequently known as *'wadan'* in Sabah.

Gigantochloa levis **(Blanco) Merrill**
This large erect bamboo is known in Sabah as *'poring'* and is one of the most useful bamboos in the state. It grows to 30 m tall and the culms are used for many purposes including house construction. It is cultivated in villages but is more often wild or naturalised in groves on hill slopes above 500 m altitude. There is a large grove about 10 minutes' walk above the hot springs at Poring. This bamboo differs from *Schizostachyum* in the lack of a white-waxy ring below the node, and in having a clearly dominant central branch at each branching node.

Schizostachyum brachycladum **Kurz**
This widely distributed species probably grows wild in Sabah but is also often cultivated. It is an erect bamboo with erect culm-sheath blades, many subequal branches at each node and a white-waxy zone just below the node. Internodes, of 7 to 10 cm diameter, of this species are used for cooking glutinous rice called *'lemang'* and as water-containers and tapai-drinking vessels, and the split culms are used in basketry and flooring. It is locally called *'buloh nipis'* or *'buloh lemang'*, or *'tulu'* in the Dusun language in Ranau.

Schizostachyum lima **(Blanco) Merrill**
This is common in Sabah but also occurs in the Philippines. It is a smallish erect bamboo with culms to *c.* 1.5 cm diameter and drooping tips. In this species, the culm-sheath blades are reflexed, there are many subequal branches at each node and a white-waxy zone just below the node. The culms are used as fishing-rods and sometimes as straws for drinking *'tapai'*, a local wine. The local name of ths species is *'sumbiling'*.

NOTES ON THE NATURAL HISTORY OF KINABALU BAMBOOS

It is always tempting to surmise on the "strategies" of dispersal and spread in bamboos. In Kinabalu Park, we can distinguish two principal forms of growth habit in bamboos. One is that of a tightly clumped, basically erect bamboo, such as in *Yushania tessellata* and

Fig.7. Following mass flowering and death in April 1981, the curtains of senesced culms of *Racemobambos gibbsiae* were replaced by high-climbing culms of a new seed generation only after many years. The species is a Kinabalu endemic with intervals of 10–20 years between flowering episodes. *(Photo: K.M. Wong)*

Kinabaluchloa nebulosa (although the very long culms of the latter have a tendency to droop over and appear somewhat scrambly), accompanied by a branching habit that produces relatively short subequal branches at the nodes. The other is a truly clambering habit, seen in *Racemobambos*, accompanied by the development of a dominant branch at most nodes which can grow quite long to recapitulate the form and function of the original culm. The first type of growth habit occupies less space and, where a clump is quite erect, packs most of its mass into a cylinder-like space; spreading occurs by the production of new culms growing outwards from the clump edge and is slow. In contrast, the clambering habit disperses the mass of the plant over a much larger ground area through the reiterative branching of culms and branches alike, although the actual base of a clump is still quite concentrated at one spot. This has the effect of directly dispersing seeds over a larger area than in the case of clumped erect forms, although spreading may be similarly slow. Given that *Yushania tessellata* and *Kinabaluchloa nebulosa* are not known to flower and seed frequently, it is perhaps no surprise that they are not commonly found in the area. Hence we find, with the exception of *Racemobambos rigidifolia* and *R. hirsuta* which are perhaps restricted to ultramafic substrates, that clambering bamboos are generally commoner in the Park. Indeed, *R. hepburnii* and *R. gibbsiae* cannot be missed during the hike up Kinabalu.

Racemobambos hepburnii and *R. gibbsiae* have been known to flower gregariously, when grand displays of simultaneous flowering are shown by a large proportion of the population and are interspersed by periods of complete sterility (Wong, Chan & Phillipps, 1988). In recent times *R. hepburnii* has been documented in flower in 1962–65 and 1986–88, and *R. gibbsiae* in 1910, 1933, 1957, 1967 and 1979–81. Each occasion of gregarious flowering may last two to three years and may take over a year to build up in intensity, i.e., for more and more individuals to come into flower. The interval between episodes of gregarious flowering may be in the order of ten to twenty years. A clump can continue to be in a flowering state for a year or more before all its culms die down completely. Clumps that have flowered normally die and are replaced by a new cohort of seedlings, although some regenerate new culms from their rhizome systems. Following gregarious flowering and mass senescence, the dying curtains of brown culms draped over the vegetation in the mist forest presents a most uncanny impression.

The known flowering episodes of *R. hepburnii* (the most recent one during 1986–88) and *R. gibbsiae* (most recently 1979–81) have so far not coincided. This may be a reflection of a temporal segregation in reproduction between the two species, which otherwise are closely related and share an overlap in distribution on the mountain.

These montane clambering bamboos are an inherent component of the vegetation on Kinabalu and their growth does not seem restricted only to gaps and open sites in the forest. Seedlings and young clumps of *R. gibbsiae* appear to establish as well in comparatively open sites, frequently on moss and liverwort sods, as in darker conditions in the undergrowth of the forest. The distribution of clambering bamboos, however, does seem patchy and there are sites where they are definitely commoner. This may be due to other factors influencing the comparative establishment success from site to site, e.g., the pattern of seed fall and dispersal, predation, site conditions and competition with other plants.

The relationships between bamboos and animals on Kinabalu have not been studied. For example, we do not know if the sudden abundance of seeds (and correspondingly sudden dearth of vegetative mass) accompanying an episode of mass flowering has any effect on herbivore populations. Ants have sometimes been observed to frequent spaces enclosed by culm sheaths, but whether this constitutes a random event requires more careful investigation. The lucky visitor may spot the Greater Bamboo Bat *(Tylonycteris robustula)* leaving narrow slits in the internodes of the larger erect bamboos, where it sometimes roosts.

A KEY TO IDENTIFYING KINABALU BAMBOOS

Culms frequently twining up tree stems; culm-sheaths with a leathery wrinkled basal zone .... *Dinochloa sublaevigata*

Culms erect or clambering/scandent but never twining; culm-sheath bases smooth,

    Culms pencil-thin (or not much thicker), clambering; main branch at a node evident, often growing very long and behaving like a culm,

        Leaves typically less than 1 cm broad (often not more than 0.5 cm); glumes in the spikelet often three,

            Leaves generally 4–6 cm long; spikelets with hairy lemmae (1600–3000 m altitude) .... *Racemobambos gibbsiae*

            Leaves generally 6–12 cm long; spikelets with hairless lemmae (1000–2000 m) .... *R. hepburnii*

        Leaves typically broader; glumes in the spikelet usually two,

            Leaves to *c.* 15 cm long, those on the flowering branch rigid; spikelets hairless (above 1500 m) .... *R. rigidifolia*

            Leaves to 20–32 cm long, those on the flowering branch not rigid; spikelets hairy (lowlands to 1200 m) .... *R. hirsuta*

    Culms thicker, erect or even very much arching or drooping over but not truly clambering; main branch at a node evident or not,

        Young shoots with a ring of spreading bristles at each node; mature internodes 60–100 cm long .... *Kinabaluchloa nebulosa*

        Young shoots without such a hair-ring; mature internodes usually not exceeding 60 cm,

Basal culm nodes frequently developing recurved root thorns... *Yushania tessellata*

Basal culm nodes without root thorns,

> Culms with a white-waxy zone just below each node; hairs on the internode pale; branches at a node all subequal,
>
>> Internodes reaching 7–10 cm diameter; culm-sheath blades erect and slightly inflated like a dome .... *Schizostachyum brachycladum*
>>
>> Internodes to only *c.* 1.5 cm diameter; culm-sheath blades reflexed and linear .... *S. lima*
>
> Culms without any special white-waxy zone below each node; hairs on internode dark; branch complement at each node with a central dominant branch .... *Gigantochloa levis*

REFERENCES

Dransfield, S. 1981. The genus *Dinochloa* (Gramineae—Bambusoideae) in Sabah. *Kew Bulletin* 36(3) : 613–633.

Dransfield, S. 1983. The genus *Racemobambos* (Gramineae—Bambusoideae). *Kew Bulletin* 37(4) : 661–679.

Wong, K.M. 1986. The growth habits of Malayan bamboos. *Kew Bulletin* 41(3) : 703–720.

Wong, K.M. 1993. Four new genera of bamboos (Gramineae—Bambusoideae) from Malesia. *Kew Bulletin* 48(3) : 517–532.

Wong, K.M., Chan, C.L. & Phillipps, A. 1988. The gregarious flowering of Miss Gibbs' bamboo *(Racemobambos gibbsiae)* and Hepburn's bamboo *(R. hepburnii)* on Mount Kinabalu, Sabah. *Sabah Society Journal* 8(4) : 466–474.

Fig.1. Fruits of *Pinanga pilosa*. *(Photo: C.L. Chan)*

PALMS

John Dransfield

Around Park Headquarters palms are a conspicuous feature of the forest undergrowth and most visitors to the Park will have little difficulty in recognising the feathery leaves of many of the plant species as belonging to palms. Many of the Kinabalu palms are climbers beset with spines; these are, of course, rattans and rattans are responsible for making it difficult or unpleasant to wander off the path in places, especially in the mid-montane forest near Park Headquarters at 1550 m. So far about 52 different species of palm from ten genera have been recorded within the Park boundary. Some of these are lowland species which are at the upper end of their range in the lowest parts of the Park near Poring Hot Springs at 500 m, while others are strictly montane species, rarely if ever found below about 1000 m. It is perhaps surprising that only two of the palms, *Salacca dolicholepis* and *Calamus mesilauensis* are endemic to Kinabalu—that is, they are found nowhere else in the world. All other species can be found either elsewhere in Sabah or in Borneo; even the slender rattan, *Calamus gibbsianus*, which is such a feature of the forest between the Park Headquarters and Layang-Layang staff quarters (formerly Carson's Camp) at 2700 m, for long thought to be endemic, has recently been recorded for the Crocker Range and the Kelabit Highlands in Sarawak.

The palms of Kinabalu with one or two exceptions are relatively well known. The exceptions are to be found in the undergrowth genus *Pinanga*. Pinangs are abundant in almost all of the forest types up to about 3000 m above sea level; they are very variable in leaf form and in degree of branching of the inflorescence. *P. lepidota*, *P. keahii*, *P. variegata*, *P. pilosa* and *P. aristata* are easily distinguished, but there remains a confusing array of often very handsome palms which are very difficult to name with certainty. Some forms have already been named, but the so-called species seem to run into each other. It seems preferable to refer to all these as members of the *Pinanga capitata* complex, until they are better understood.

PALMS OF THE LOWER PARTS OF KINABALU

Two large palms which are particularly striking at Poring are *Arenga undulatifolia* with its short stocky trunk and large leaves with wavy leaflets and *Caryota no,* a huge palm with doubly pinnate leaves—perhaps the most massive of all Bornean palms. Both these palms present their inflorescences in an unusual way, starting at the top of the trunk followed by inflorescences produced down the trunk. Eventually the stems die after flowering and fruiting. Although *A. undulatifolia* is widespread throughout Borneo, the southern

Philippines and eastern Sulawesi, *Caryota no* is a very local palm which is threatened with extinction in many parts of Borneo. *Arenga brevipes*, related to *A. undulatifolia* but with shorter stems and flat leaflets occurs in small valleys at altitudes up to about 1000 m. It is now nowhere common because of forest clearance—it is much less tolerant of disturbance than *A. undulatifolia*. Several widespread lowland rattans are also to be found in the forest at Poring—most handsome of these is *Korthalsia jala* with its curious net-like extension to the leaf sheath. Species of *Korthalsia* are not found above about 1000 m above sea level. *Calamus acuminatus,* or *'rotan padas'*, is common near Poring; it is a very slender species with reddish-tinged young leaves. The stems of this species are frequently collected for basket weaving. The largest *Calamus* species at Poring is *C. ornatus* which produces very long stems up to 5 cm in diameter when bare; these stems can be used in the manufacture of furniture.

PALMS OF THE LOWER MONTANE FOREST

There is no doubt that the richest assemblage of palms in the Park is to be found in the lower montane forest, especially around the Park Headquarters. Here are to be found several species of rattan, pinang and a handsome mountain salak, all growing in abundance. Perhaps the commonest of the rattans is *Daemonorops longistipes*; it has relatively short stems, the leaf sheaths yellowish and covered with a fierce array of black spines, while the leaves end in climbing whips. This species has very short inflorescences. In marked contrast is the commonest species of *Calamus*, *C. marginatus*; it has separate climbing whips arising from the hideously spiny leaf sheaths rather than from the ends of the leaves, and the inflorescences are immensely long, sometimes as much as 6 m. It can climb into the forest canopy where it becomes extremely difficult to dislodge. *Calamus javensis*, on the other hand, is an elegant slender species with short leaves bearing few very broad leaflets and sheaths which are not nearly as spiny. *C. tenompokensis* is closely related to *C. javensis* but has a short, often subterranean stem and large rosette leaves with broad leaflets. *C. mesilauensis* is a slender species with a whip borne at the leaf tips—it has unusually large reddish brown fruits. Endemic to Kinabalu, it is nowhere common on the mountain, and much of the area of the Pinosuk Plateau where it grew well has now been cleared. The largest of the mountain rattans is *Plectocomia elongata*, an infrequent giant, which tends to occur in large light gaps or old land slips; its huge leaves, often 5 or more metres long bear leaflets in groups. It flowers once only and then the stem dies; the strange pendulous inflorescence branches which appear like plaits of hair, are unmistakable.

Salacca dicholepis is endemic to Kinabalu; it is a plant of the lower part of steep valleys and can be seen beside the Liwagu Trail at Park Headquarters. It has a very short subterranean stem and large leaves very heavily armed with long spines pointing in all directions. The leaflets are chalky-white beneath. The fierce spines no doubt protect the excellent edible fruit which are borne down among the dead sheaths. Like most of the rattans, *Salacca* is dioecious—that is, there are separate male and female plants—and this accounts for part of the difficulty of finding ripe fruit.

Fig.2. *Plectocomia elongata*, the largest rattan on Kinabalu, flowers only once in its life before dying. *(Photo: K.M. Wong)*

Fig.3. *Areca kinabaluensis*, a common montane palm in Borneo, in the forest around Park Headquarters. *(Photo: J. Dransfield)*

Fig.4. Fruit-bunch of one of the forms of *Pinanga capitata* on Kinabalu. *(Photo: C.L. Chan)*

The pinangs common in the lower montane forest belong to two genera—*Areca,* the genus of the true cultivated pinang, *Areca catechu,* and *Pinanga.* There is as yet only one species of *Areca* in the park—this is *A. kinabaluensis* which, despite is name, is common in montane forest throughout Borneo. It has dark green leaves and a highly branched inflorescence in which the female flowers are confined to the very bases of the branches while the male flowers are found throughout. In contrast the inflorescence of *Pinanga* has far fewer branches and the female and male flowers are found along the entire length of all the branches. The daintiest of the pinangs is *P. pilosa* which scarcely exceeds 1.5 m tall and forms clumps in the undergrowth. Although it is common around Park Headquarters, it also occurs much higher on the mountain. The closely related *P. aristata* (Fig. 6) which has exquisitely mottled young leaves is a larger plant, occurring in valley bottoms at slightly lower elevations than *P. pilosa. P. keahii* is a very short-stemmed species which forms thickets; it has an unbranched inflorescence and large fruit which are pointed when young, but become bloated and round at maturity. Throughout the montane forests occur pinangs with branched inflorescences and usually with well developed trunks to 2 or more meters tall; the flowers may be borne spirally or in two rows and the trunk may be solitary or clustered. Individual plants can appear very distinctive and, indeed some of these have been given names such as *Pinanga dallasensis, P. lumuensis, P. gibbsiana* and *P. capitata.* However, if one looks carefully in forest at many elevations, on the ultramafic and off, it becomes increasingly difficult to apply these names. At present we may refer to all of them, as mentioned above, as the complex of *P. capitata.*

Fig.5. *Pinanga capitata* in the forest at Kamborangoh. *(Photo: J. Dransfield)*

Fig.6. *Pinanga aristata*. *(Photo: J. Dransfield)*

KINABALU—Summit of Borneo

PALMS OF THE UPPER MONTANE FOREST

Pinanga capitata, in one of its forms and *Calamus gibbsianus* are the palms which reach the highest elevation in Kinabalu (and indeed in the whole of South-east Asia). These two palms peter out at about 3000 m above Layang-Layang staff quarters (Carson's Camp). Like *P. capitata*, *C. gibbsianus* is a very variable species for which several names have been published. Nevertheless, the described forms run into each other. Around Park Headquarters this rattan is at the lower end of its range and has slender stems with rather

Fig.7. *Calamus gibbsianus*, easily seen in the forest between the Park Headquarters and Layang-layang at 2700 m. *(Photo: J. Dransfield)*

large leaves with lax leaflets, while higher up the plant has a more stocky appearance with much shorter and closer leaflets. On the ridge of Mt. Tambuyukon there is a particularly handsome form with very short leaves with crowded very stiff leaflets.

If the palm flora of the Kinabalu Park is compared with that of the Gunung (Mt.) Mulu National Park in Sarawak or that of Taman Negara in Peninsular Malaysia, then it has to be admitted that it is not particularly diverse; this is probably due in part to the paucity of lowland habitats included within the park boundary. Nevertheless palms are a conspicuous and important component of the forests of Kinabalu and the diversity of forms within the complexes of *Pinanga capitata* and *Calamus gibbsianus* suggest the incipient evolution of forms which are not yet sufficiently isolated to be distinguished as species. Clearly these two groups would repay careful study.

Photo: Robert New

PART 3
THE FAUNA OF KINABALU

Fig.1. Carrying its translucent shell, the green-bodied *Rhinocochlis nasuta* begins its nocturnal foray. *(Photo: C.L. Chan)*

LAND SNAILS

J.J. Vermeulen

Borneo has a rich fauna of terrestrial molluscs (the land snails and dito slugs), comprising some 500 different species. In all surrounding islands, as well as the Malay Peninsula, fewer species occur. Particularly among the smaller species there are many which are endemic to a small area only: a mountain range, or even a single hill. Terrestrial molluscs are often very selective where environmental requirements are concerned. Certain habitats are favoured, while others are avoided. The habitats richest in species are:

a) Areas with a limestone soil, such as isolated limestone hills and hill ranges, particularly in the northern and eastern part of Borneo. A bucketful of soil from a single limestone hill may contain from 30 to 70 different species. Limestone areas are usually also rich in endemic species.

b) Areas with ultrabasic soil, or with a young volcanic soil, which may sometimes yield a moderately diverse fauna of approximately the same composition as limestone areas. No species have been found so far on these soils which are endemic to a small area.

c) Coastal areas such as densely vegetated uplifted coral reefs, coastal dunes consisting of slightly calcareous sand and other habitats which are close to the sea, but not under its immediate influence. These harbour a fauna entirely of terrestrial molluscs. The animals usually occur much more scattered. Hardly any endemic species occur here, most species are ubiquists extending their ranges with the shifting of the coastlines.

The fact that so many species prefer these habitats can probably be explained by the abundant presence there of calcium, which the animals need to build up their shells.

All other habitats in Borneo are poor in species, as large areas have soils derived from sandstones and shales, or from igneous rocks. In a wet tropical climate, and covered with primary forest, such soils tend to develop very acid conditions which are poisonous to most snails. Only those species which live on trees can survive here.

DIVERSITY OF LAND SNAILS ON KINABALU

Mt. Kinabalu, with no limestone outcrops and only limited tracts of soils derived from ultrabasic rock, does not seem a very suitable habitat for terrestrial molluscs at first consideration. In spite of this, the checklist below is quite substantial, with distinctly more species than can be found in other areas in Borneo which seem equally unsuitable for many molluscs. The reasons for this unexpected diversity may be several. First, the Kinabalu area consists of rugged, mountainous terrain with many steep slopes. On these slopes the drainage is very efficient, mechanical erosion predominant, and the chemical leaching of the rock by stagnant water, which causes an increase in the acidity of the soil, minimal. In such circumstances plant litter on the forest floor, on a bedrock of alternating sandstone and shale, may harbour a small fauna of snails. Second, at a higher altitude, and at lower temperatures, the chemical leaching is less intense anyway. A third reason may be that species living in the Kinabalu area have responded, just as many other groups of animals have, to the Tertiary and Quaternary uplift of the area to alpine altitudes by increased speciation. Indeed, particularly at about 3000 m and higher up most species found are endemic to Mt. Kinabalu. Lower down, the number of endemic species decreases, and more widespread species occur. A last reason for the comparatively large number of species occurring on Mt. Kinabalu may be that soils derived from ultrabasic rock occur and these support a number of widespread species.

In areas where the vegetation has been cleared or otherwise disturbed, a number of species not indigenous to the area have been recorded: *Subulina octona* and *Bradybaena similaris*. These species apparently do not survive easily in primary forest. On the other hand, a number of species which are certainly endemic to the Kinabalu area have been observed on weathered rocks on cleared roadsides in the Headquarters area: *Diplommatina rubra* and *D. electa*. Possibly these species are used to living on rock outcrops and are therefore able to colonise such disturbed environments.

Very little else is known about the ecological requirements of the various species. Tillier & Bouchet (1988) observed no living snails on, or near, the forest floor at 3000 m. However, they hesitate to conclude that all the species collected by them are arboreal, because the incessant rains during their collecting activities may have rendered the forest floor temporarily too wet for the animals. Some certainly live in trees, on leaves or on bark. At least two phylogenetically unrelated species have adapted to living among leaves. In *Rhinocochlis nasuta* and *Leptopoma undatum* the shell is thin, white and translucent. The soft tissue is pale green, visible through the shell as a brilliant bright green.

In the older literature a number of species are recorded from Kinabalu which have not been recollected in recent years. It is most likely that these species were found in forests on the hills around Mt. Kinabalu, at medium and low altitudes, and have disappeared with the clearance of forest. Because they may still occur further to the north in the Kinabalu Park, where more forest at lower altitudes is preserved, they have not been deleted from the list.

STRUCTURE AND CLASSIFICATION

It may be useful to explain in few terms, which are often used to describe the shape of the shells. All terrestrial molluscs belong to one class, the Gastropods. Usually, the shell of these molluscs consist of a coiled tube, which is closed at one end, and which widens towards an opening at the other end. If one holds a shell in front between thumb and index finger, with the closed end of the coiled tube pointing upwards, and the aperture facing the observer, in many cases the opening (called *aperture*) is to the right side. Such shells are called *dextral*. If it is to the left side, the shell is called *sinistral*. The upward-pointing end of the shell is called the top, or *apex*. The coils (called *whorls*) together form a more or less conical body, the *spire*. Between the whorls a furrow is visible, in many cases called the *suture*. The widest circumference of the last whorl is called the *periphery*. The apeture often has a thickened rim called the *peristome*. In many cases the living animal can retract into the shell through the aperture, and those belonging to the subclass *Prosobranchia* often bear on the back a corneous or calcareous lid, or *operculum*, which fits into the aperture and serves to protect the animals from the outside. On the underside of the shell, the last whorl encircles the *umbilicus* which may, however, be sealed off in many species.

The species can in most cases be recognised by their shell. However, to arrange the species into genera and into families in such a way that their classification reflects their phylogenetic relationships, knowledge of the anatomy of the animal is indispensable. If the soft parts are studied, it often shows that species with very similar looking shells must be classified in entirely different families. Examples of this can be found among the Kinabalu molluscs: without knowledge of the soft parts one would be tempted to place *Trochomorpha rhysa* and both *Geotrochus* species in one genus. All three have low conical shells with a more or less sharp periphery and a closed umbilicus. However, on account of the anatomy of the generative organs the first must be classified with the *Trochomorphidae*, and both *Geotrochus* species with the *Helicarionidae*. Another example is that the true slugs (molluscs without a shell, or with a much reduced shell) on Kinabalu can be found in the *Ariophantidae*, the *Euconulidae*, as well as in the *Philomycidae*. Such observations lead to the idea that evolution of the shape of the shell in molluscs (or its presence of absence) is highly sensitive to environmental influence, and that adaptations may easily lead to parallel developments in the shells of species which are otherwise only remotely related.

Unfortunately the first traces one finds of snail life in a forest are usually empty shells, and it is only incidentally that one finds a living animal. Most species are known from their shells only. This has serious consequences for the existing classification into genera and families. Often, the anatomy is known of only a single or a few species in a genus. All other species, of which only shells are available, are grouped in that same genus on account of similarities in the shell. It is feared that much of the present classification is not natural and will have to be adjusted once specialists have been able to dissect more terrestrial mollusc species. In fact the anatomical dissections of a number of Kinabalu species by Tillier & Bouchet (1988) has already led to the description of no less that three new genera.

A CHECKLIST OF KINABALU LAND SNAILS

The terrestrial mollusc fauna of Mount Kinabalu has so far attracted little attention. Laidlaw (1937) and Tillier & Bouchet (1988) give checklists of the species, but none of these include all species so far recorded. The list below compiles all the data I could find in the literature as well as a small number of species present in collections. A revision of the Bornean species of the genus *Diplommatina* is provided by Vermeulen (1993). Undoubtedly more species occur. In particular the forests at higher altitudes still must harbour more endemics, yet undiscovered.

Subclass: **PROSOBRANCHIA** (shell with operculum)

CYCLOPHORIDAE

Cyclophorus kinabaluensis E.A. Smith, 1895
Shell brownish with darker blotches, dextral, large, low conical, 4–5 cm wide. Mt. Kinabalu, once collected. Occurs in scattered localities in East Sabah, at low altitude, on limestone.

Lagocheilus alticola Laidlaw, 1937
Shell whitish with brown blotches, dextral, conical, with fine spiral ribs, up to 0.9 cm wide. Umbilicus open, narrow. Mt. Kinabalu, at 3000 m and higher. Endemic.

Lagocheilus conicus E.A. Smith, 1895
As *L. alticola*, but with a somewhat higher spire, and an almost closed umbilicus. Mt. Kinabalu, once collected. Occurs in scattered localities throughout Sabah, at low altitude, on limestone.

Lagocheilus kinabaluensis E.A. Smith, 1895
As *L. alticola*, but with very distinct spiral ribs. Mt. Kinabalu, at 1000 m, once collected. Possibly endemic.

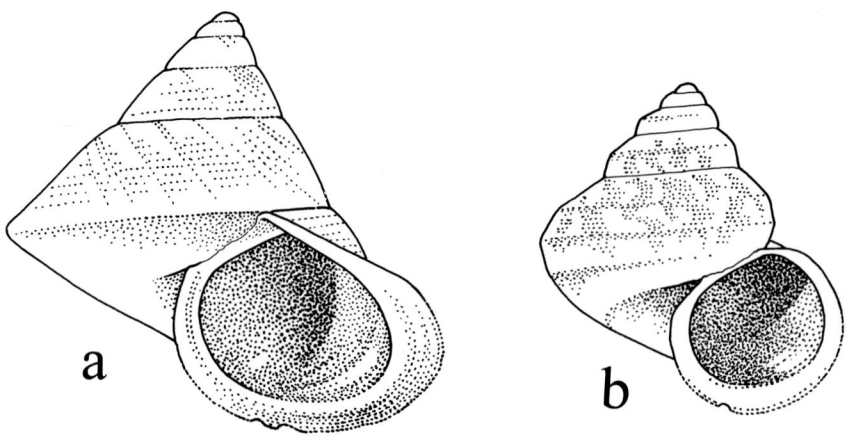

Fig.2. a. *Leptopoma undatum*. b. *Lagocheilus conicus*.

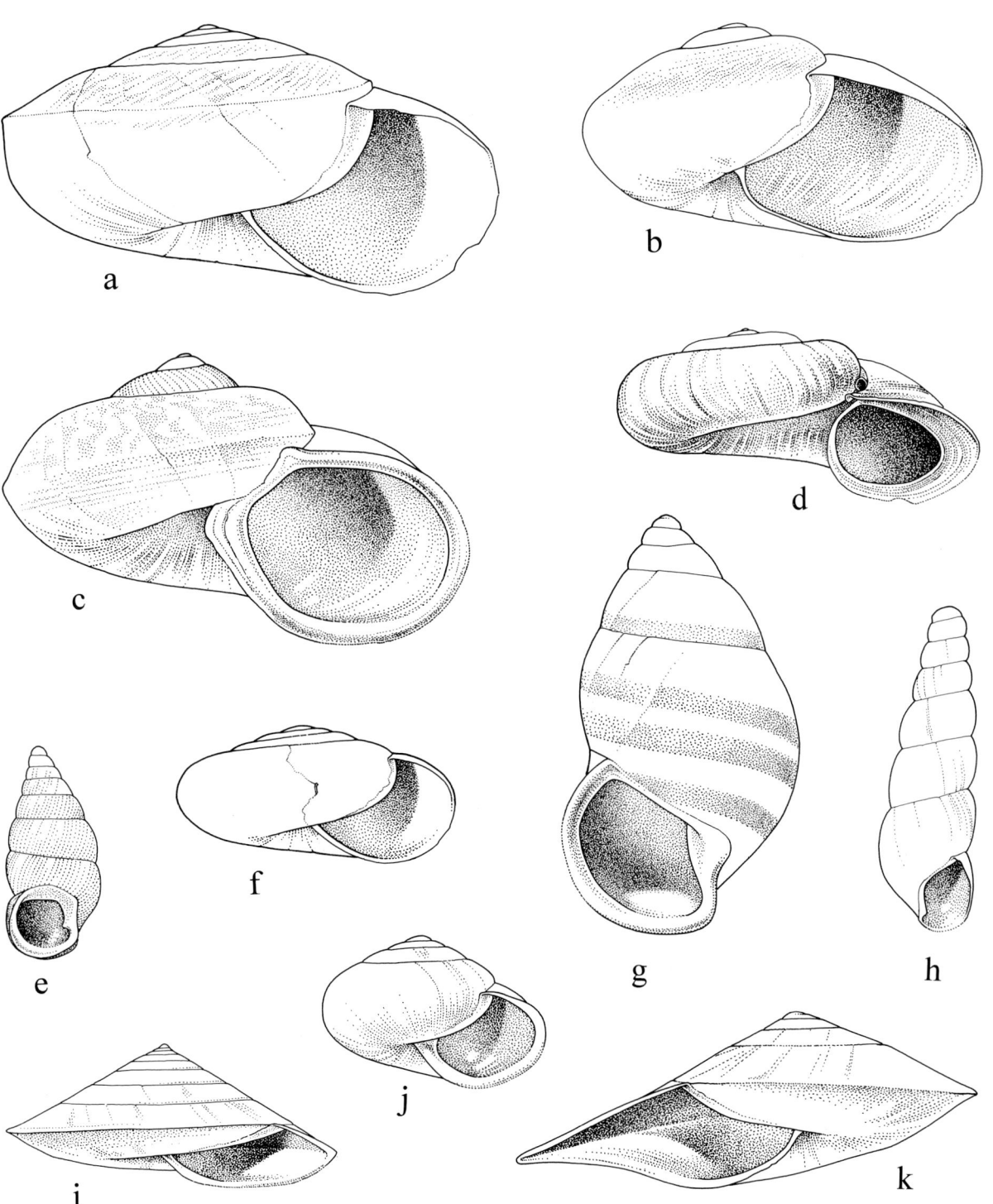

Fig.3. a. *Hemiplecta cf. egeria*. b. *Kalamantania whiteheadi*.
c. *Cyclophorus kinabaluensis*. d. *Opisthoporus boxalli*. e. *Diplommatina electa*.
f. *Everettia subconsul*. g. *Amphidromus martensi*. h. *Subulina octona*.
i. *Geotrochus kinabaluensis*. j. *Bradybaena similaris*. k. *Rhinocochlis nasuta*.

Leptopoma sericatum (Pfeiffer, 1853)
As *L. undatum* but with a shell with brownish or pink spiral bands as well as fine spiral ribs. Mt. Kinabalu, at 1300 m. Widespread throughout Borneo.

Leptopoma undatum (Metcalfe, 1852)
Shell white, dextral, conical, with flat whorls, up to 1.5 cm wide. Mt. Kinabalu, at 1500 m. Wide-spread throughout.

Leptopoma whiteheadi E.A. Smith, 1887
Very close to *L. sericatum* and possibly identical with that species. Differs mainly in having radial blotches of brown on the shell, instead of spiral colour bands. Mt. Kinabalu, at 600–1200 m alt.

Opisthoporus boxalli (Godwin Austen, 1893)
Shell with brown blotches, dextral, almost discoid, 2 cm wide. Aperture round, with a small notch where it touches the preceding whorl. This notch is so deep that it forms a second opening, close to the suture of the shell. Mt. Kinabalu, once collected. Widespread throughout Borneo.

Pterocyclos amabilis (Fulton, 1905)
Differs from *Opisthoporus boxalli* in having a much shallower notch, which does not form a second opening near the suture. Mt. Kinabalu, foothills at low altitude. Possibly endemic.

Pterocyclos sp. (sensu Laidlaw, 1937)
As *P. boxalli*, but with a still lower spire, and smaller. Mt. Kinabalu, at 1600 m.

DIPLOMMATINIDAE

Diplommatina electa Fulton, 1905
Shell dull yellowish or brownish, sinistral, spindle-shaped, with fine radial ribs, about 7 mm high. Mt. Kinabalu, at 1800 m. Endemic.

Diplommatina plecta Fulton, 1901
Shell dextral, spindle-shaped, with rather inconspicuous ribs, about 3 mm high. Mt. Kinabalu, once collected. Endemic.

Diplommatina recta E.A. Smith, 1895
As *D. plecta*, but shell more conical, with more conspicuous, densely placed transverse ribs. Mt. Kinabalu, once collected. Also found on Balabac.

Diplommatina rubra Godwin Austen, 1889
As. *D. electa*, but shell bright orange red, with more distinct, densely placed radial ribs. Mt. Kinabalu, at 1700–2300 m. Endemic; a record from Niah hills is probably not correct (in spite of extensive collecting the species has not been found there again).

Diplommatina whiteheadi **E.A. Smith, 1898**
Shell sinistral, almost cylindrical, with distinct ribs, about 1.3 mm high. Mt. Kinabalu, once collected. Occurring in the Crocker Range on sandstone soil, in leaf litter, at 1800 m; and in east Sabah on limestone, in lowland conditions. Very rare.

Subclass: *PULMONATA* (shell without operculum)

ARIOPHANTIDAE

Everettia corrugata **Laidlaw, 1937**
Shell glossy brown, dextral, lenticular, whorls transversely wrinkled below the suture. Shell about 2 cm wide. Mt. Kinabalu, at 2200–3400 m. Endemic.

Everettia subconsul **(E.A. Smith, 1887)**
As *E. corrugata*, but whorls not transversely wrinkled below the suture. Mt. Kinabalu, at 1800 m. Also found on Banggi Island, in lowland conditions.

Hemiplecta cf. *egeria* **E.A. Smith, 1895**
Shell dull brown above, yellowish below the periphery, dextral, lenticular, periphery

Fig.4. *Chloritis kinabaluensis*, a petite snail with fine spiral ribs on its shell, extends its feelers. *(Photo: C.L. Chan)*

keeled, obliquely wrinkled above and slightly below the periphery. Shell up to 6 cm wide. Mt. Kinabalu, at 1800 m. Also found on Palawan.

Ibycus sp. (sensu Laidlaw, 1937)
A slug. Animal pale yellow, leaden grey on the back, very long and slender. Shell with about $2^{1}/_{2}$ whorls. Specific status uncertain. Mt. Kinabalu, at 1600 m.

Kalamantania whiteheadi (Godwin Austen, 1891)
Shell whitish, pink or light brown, dextral, more or less globose, last whorl distinctly widened, periphery rounded, obliquely wrinkled above the periphery, about 4 cm wide. Mt. Kinabalu, at 1600 m. Occurring in the Crocker Range on sandstone soil, at 1800 m; and in the interior of Sabah on limestone, at 500 m.

Microparmarion pollonerai Simroth, 1893
A slug. Animal dark bluish grey, crest of the tail and the rugae yellow. Mantle yellowish grey, partly covering the shell, without lobes extending over the shell, with three longitudinal ridges. Shell thin, flat, with $1^{1}/_{2}$ whorls. Mt. Kinabalu, at 1600–3300 m. Endemic.

Microparmarion simrothi Collinge & Godwin Austen, 1895
As *M. pollonerai*, but animal yellow, mottled with dark brown. Head with three longitudinal black bands. Mantle mottled with brown, with two longitudinal rows of warts. Mt. Kinabalu, at 1100–2600 m. Endemic.

Microparmarion sp. (sensu Laidlaw, 1937)
As *M. pollonerai*, but animal grey, darker on the back. Mantle grey, mottled with small, pale blotches. Specific status uncertain. Mt. Kinabalu, at 3300 m.

Rhinocochlis nasuta (Metcalfe, 1851)
Shell pure white, sinistral, discoid, periphery very sharp, surface smooth, peristome drawn out into a spur at the periphery. Shell about 4 cm wide. Mt. Kinabalu, at 1800 m. Widespread throughout Borneo, but only locally common.

BRADYBAENIDAE

Bradybaena similaris (Ferussac, 1822)
Shell whitish or brownish, dextral, more or less globose with a low spire, periphery rounded, peristome thickened, umbilicus open, narrow. Shell up to 2 cm wide. Mt. Kinabalu, introduced in areas with a disturbed vegetation. Widespread.

CAMAENIDAE

Amphidromus martensi Boettger, 1894
Shell bright yellow, sometimes with brown or greenish spiral bands, sinistral or dextral, spindle shaped. Height up to 5.5 cm. Mt. Kinabalu, at 1600 m. Widespread in East Sabah, found in lowland conditions on limestone as well as sandstone soil.

Amphidromus pictus Fulton, 1896
As *A. martensi*, but white, with large, purplish transverse blotches, always sinistral, conical. Mt. Kinabalu, up to 3200 m. Widespread in Borneo and the Phillippines.

Chloritis dulcissima E.A. Smith, 1898
As *Bardybaena similaris*, but shell dark purplish brown with three white spiral bands. Surface of the shell densely covered with small pits. Endemic to Mt. Kinabalu, once collected.

Chloritis kinabaluensis (Kobelt, 1894)
As *Bradybaena similaris*, but shell light brownish. Surface of the shell densely covered with small pits. Mt. Kinabalu, at 1800 m. Widespread in East Sabah, usually on limestone in lowland conditions.

EUCONULIDAE

Gunongia dendrobates Tillier & Bouchet, 1988
Shell corneous, small, conical with rather flat whorls. Top whorls with a very fine, inconspicuous spiral striation. Periphery not carinate. Aperture less than half the height of the shell. Shell about 3 mm high. Mt. Kinabalu, at 3000 m. Endemic.

Fig.5. *Leptopoma sericatum*, widespread in east Sabah and usually found in the lowlands on limestone. *(Photo: C.L. Chan)*

Gunongia gregaria Tillier & Bouchet, 1988
As *G. dendrobates*, but periphery carinate, and aperture more than half the height of the shell. Shell about 5 mm high. Mt. Kinabalu, at 3000 m. Endemic.

Kionghutania humilis Tillier & Bouchet, 1988
Shell corneous, small, conical with rather flat whorls. Top whorls with some ten rather coarse spiral cords. Spiral striation present above as well as below the periphery. Shell about 3 mm high. Mt. Kinabalu, at 3000 m. Endemic.

Kionghutania kinabaluensis Tillier & Bouchet, 1988
As *K. humilis*, but spiral striation on the top whorls only, the last whorl with rather distinct transverse growth lines instead. Shell about 5.5 mm high. Mt. Kinabalu, at 3000 m. Endemic.

Kionghutania nephelophila Tillier & Bouchet, 1988
As *K. humilis*, but spiral striation on the last whorl above the periphery only, absent below. Shell height about 4 mm. Mt. Kinabalu, at 3000 m. Endemic.

Sabalimax cyanantyx Tillier & Bouchet, 1988
A slug. Animal greyish blue, pink on the back, rather short. Mantle with small lobes which do not cover much of the shell. Shell with 3 whorls. Mt. Kinabalu, at 3000 m. Endemic.

Sabalimax pantherina Tillier & Bouchet, 1988
As *S. cyanantyx*, but animal dark blue, yellow on the back, rather long. Mantle with large lobes covering part of the shell. Mt. Kinabalu, at 3000 m. Endemic.

HELICARIONIDAE

Geotrochus kinabaluensis E.A. Smith, 1895
Shell pale brownish, slightly darker at the periphery, dextral, discoid with a very sharp periphery, with very fine spiral striation above the periphery, up to 2 cm wide. Mt. Kinabalu, at 1000–1500 m. Widespread in East Sabah on limestone soil in lowland conditions.

Geotrochus whiteheadi E.A. Smith, 1895
As *G. kinabaluensis*, but smaller, and with a slightly higher spire. Mt. Kinabalu, at 1800 m. Widespread in Sabah, on the Crocker Range on sandstone soil at 1800 m, elsewhere on limestone soil in lowland conditions.

Geotrochus sp. (V 1191)
As *G. kinabaluensis*, but with the spire almost flat. Spiral striation above the periphery absent. Mt. Kinabalu, at 1800 m. Endemic.

PHILOMYCIDAE

Meghimatium striatum **(Van Hasselt, 1823)**
A slug. Animal orange yellow, usually with five almost black longitudinal bands. No shell present. Mt. Kinabalu, at 1700–2400 m. Widespread throughout Southeast Asia.

Meghimatium uniforme **Laidlaw, 1937**
As *M. striatum*, but animal uniform greyish brown. Mt. Kinabalu, at 3000–3300 m. endemic.

SUBULINIDAE

Subulina octona **(Brug, 1793)**
Shell white or corneous, dextral, with a high conical spire and a rounded top. Mt. Kinabalu, introduced in areas with a disturbed vegetation. Widespread.

TROCHOMORPHIDAE

Trochomorpha rhysa **Tillier & Bouchet, 1988**
As *Geotrochus kinabaluensis*, but with fine, transverse ribs near the top, elsewhere with fine spiral striation above the periphery. Mt. Kinabalu, at 3000 m. Endemic.

REFERENCES

Laidlaw, F.F. 1937. Notes on land mollusca from Mount Kinabalu, British Borneo. *Bull. Raffles Mus., Singapore* 13: 177–189.

Tillier, S. & Bouchet, P. 1988. Land snails and slugs from the upper montane zone of Mt. Kinabalu (Sabah, Borneo), with descriptions of new species and genera. *Indo-Mal. Zool.* 5: 255–293.

Vermeulen, J.J. 1993. Notes on the non-marine molluscs of the island of Borneo 5. The genus *Diplommatina* (Gastropoda, Prosobranchia, Diplommatinidae). *Basteria* 57: 3–69.

Fig.1. Brown and suitably patterned, an adult of *Tagora asclepiades* (Eupterotidae) rests imperceptibly against the forest-floor litter. This is a lowland species restricted to the Sundaland. *(Photo: C.L. Chan)*

BUTTERFLIES AND MOTHS

J.D. Holloway

Since writing this chapter for the first edition of this book I have had the opportunity to study butterflies and moths from Bornean mountains other than Mt. Kinabalu, collected by myself and colleagues. These studies can now be contrasted with the survey that I and two others conducted on Kinabalu in 1965, collecting butterflies and sampling moths on an altitude transect from 1000 m almost to the summit.

Kinabalu shares with other Bornean mountains most of its moth and butterfly fauna and hence most of the observations made in this chapter are common to all of them. However, because of its greater altitude and greater expanse of habitat at the altitudes of the summit zones than that of the other mountains, Kinabalu supports a number of unique species. Recent surveys in the Gunung (Mt.) Mulu National Park in Sarawak and on mountains in neighbouring Brunei have served to pinpoint these species more accurately, as have taxonomic studies arising from all the surveys (Holloway, 1976, 1983, 1985, 1986a, 1987a, 1988, 1989). They are listed in an Appendix.

Mt. Kinabalu is one of the many geological structures that have arisen at the compression zone of the westward moving Pacific tectonic plate and the northward moving Indian Ocean tectonic plate. The zone extends from South-east Asia through Indonesia and round the north and east of Australia to New Zealand. It is characterised by earthquakes and volcanoes and has a long history of land uplift and depression. Over the past forty million years, Australia, as part of the Indian Ocean Plate, has been drifting northwards relative to mainland Asia, having originally been joined to Antarctica along the South-east Indian Ridge (McKenzie & Sclater, 1971; see also Holloway, 1979). It is thought (MacArthur & Wilson, 1967) that the major centres of species richness, and therefore probably evolution for plants and animals have been associated with the larger land areas and, in biological interaction between two areas, spread of organisms is predominantly from the larger to the smaller. Thus, biogeographic plant and animal distribution patterns on the Sunda Shelf and through the Indonesian archipelago must be seen as resulting from the spread and interaction of floral and faunal elements from centres in Asia and Australia, the nature of this interaction being determined also by the complex geological history of the intervening area. As shown in Holloway & Jardine (1968) and Holloway (1969, 1984a, 1987b), present-day patterns of faunal or floral distribution may reflect past geological events.

In general, distribution patterns are controlled by disposition of land, not only in the two dimensions of the geographical map, but also in the third dimension of altitude. The lowlands and foothills of Kinabalu are close to those of South-east Asia but more isolated from those of Australia and New Guinea. At higher altitudes Kinabalu is part of an upland archipelago of montane habitat incorporating central Borneo, much of Sulawesi and Seram, and a large area of New Guinea. These montane areas are roughly equidistant from montane habitats in the south-eastern Himalayas and the temperate zone of eastern Australia. Thus it might be predicted, if long-distance dispersal from these mainland centres contributed the majority of the Bornean flora and fauna, that the lowland plants and animals in Borneo would be predominantly Asian but that of montane areas such as Kinabalu would consist of a blend of Himalayan and temperate Australian elements.

Such a scenario follows from the geological indications of increase of numbers and area of islands in the Indo-Australian archipelago through the Tertiary. New land presents a biological vacuum to be filled by dispersal from already existing land areas; changing geography in this new land through the processes of plate tectonics means that distribution patterns establish on a "moving canvas", those reflecting recent geography overlying those reflecting past geography (Holloway, 1982).

This long-range dispersal prediction holds for the flora, and the mixture of eccentric elements (representatives of genera with centres of species richness far away in northern or southern temperate areas) on Kinabalu has been well documented, but for other groups, such as birds and moths, the upland species are almost entirely of Himalayan affinity. In Holloway (1970) I suggested that the relative richness in each group in the source areas might be important, the Australian moth and bird faunas being relatively much poorer in species. Richness is generally associated with efficiency and competitiveness in evolutionary terms. A similar phenomenon was described for the Lesser Sunda island chain in Holloway & Jardine (1968). In arid savannah-type habitats in Australia the bird fauna is much richer than the butterfly fauna. In the Lesser Sunda chain, where such habitats are also extensive, there is a correspondingly greater representation of Australian birds.

There has been much controversy in the literature as to when Kinabalu derived its Australian floral element, but theories of an ancient, broad mountainous belt connecting Asia and Australia and serving as a centre of evolution for flora and fauna must be refuted on grounds of contrary geological evidence (land stepping stones between the two areas were much less in the past), the pollen record (southern elements did not appear in Borneo until the Pliocene) and ecological considerations (montane floras of the East Indies are disharmonic: they lack many families and genera represented in Australian and Himalayan associations, suggesting the filtering effect of dispersal along island chains). The disparity between floral and faunal affinities mentioned in the previous paragraph is not what would be expected in an ancient relict community where plants and animals would have shared a common history. Further discussion of this may be found in Holloway (1970), Raven & Axelrod (1972) and Smith (1980). The break-up of a continuous belt of mountainous land by erosion and fragmentation into the modern Indo-Australian archipelago would also have led, at least for organisms with a limited means of dispersal, to a single common pattern of vicariant endemism and area relationships as suggested by biogeographers such as Nelson & Platnick (1981) and Schuh & Stonedahl (1986). Ancestral species widespread

Butterflies and Moths

over such a hypothetical mountainous belt would become fragmented in range and speciate progressively in a common manner that would reflect the process of fragmentation of the land through erosion and other processes. Thus study of relationships between the descendant species will yield a common pattern of relationship between the areas in which these species occur. Modern taxonomic treatments of plant and animal genera occurring in the Indo-Australian tropics are revealing a complexity of patterns that are counter to the concept of a single pattern of area relationships (e.g., Holloway, 1982, 1984a, 1987b and references therein).

Fig.2. *Monosyntaxis trimaculata* (Arctiidae: Lithosiinae), a Bornean montane endemic. *(Photo: C.L. Chan)*

Fig.3. *Ruttellerona lithina* (Geometridae: Ennominae), a montane species that occurs also in Sulawesi, the Moluccas and New Guinea. *(Photo: C.L. Chan)*

BUTTERFLIES

Very few butterflies are recorded above 2000 m on Kinabalu and there is little in their distribution unique to the mountain. The majority of species are found in similar lowland and mountainous localities throughout the lands on the Sunda Shelf. Moths are far more abundant at high altitudes and many species are recorded only from Kinabalu as will be seen later.

A detailed account of the Kinabalu butterflies may be found in Barlow, Banks & Holloway (1971). In the Table given below, the representation of the various butterfly families at different altitudes is shown. The altitude elements in the Table follow those recognised for the moths in Holloway (1970) but several species are characteristic of more than one element, being found from the lowlands to 2200 m. Thirty-seven species were taken above 2000 m but only sixteen were characteristically upper montane, ten of these being from the family Lycaenidae. The family Pieridae (especially the genus *Delias*) is also strongly represented at high altitudes, contrasting with the primarily lowland Hesperiidae. The list of species for higher altitudes is comparable to that of Corbet & Pendlebury (1978) for Peninsular Malaysia, but does not give comprehensive cover of lowland species, except those most commonly found at Poring Hot Springs, at 500 m.

The butterfly fauna of Borneo is very similar to that of Peninsular Malaysia, Sumatra and Java, in fact more so than would be expected considering the ocean gaps between these lands today. But during the Ice Ages (when much water accumulated at the poles as ice) the sea level fell, exposing all the Sunda Shelf (Sundaland), enabling plants and animals to pass freely from one land to another (Holloway & Jardine, 1968).

Borneo has strong zoogeographical links with rainforest areas in mainland Asia but much weaker ones with the Philippines, Sulawesi and the Lesser Sunda chain (Lombok to Timor). The Lesser Sundas support an impoverished butterfly fauna allied to that of Java and Sumatra, but the Philippines and Sulawesi, with a long history of isolation, support a large number of endemic species, though these are generally of Asian affinity. Despite the proximity of Sulawesi to Borneo today, the butterfly faunas are distinct. The water gap between the two has never been broken by land, and there is evidence to suggest that Sulawesi has drifted closer to Borneo from a position further east in recent geological time (Holloway, 1973a, 1987b). Its Asian fauna has been derived through the Philippines rather than directly from Borneo.

The Moluccas, New Guinea, eastern Melanesia and north-eastern Australia form a zoogeographic region separated from the Oriental Region by a major discontinuity along Weber's Line (Holloway & Jardine, 1968). This Papuan Region supports numerous, characteristic butterfly genera, with a higher proportion related to the Asian fauna than to the long-isolated Australian fauna. Papuan genera have contributed a handful of species to the Bornean fauna which have spread from east to west, contrary to the general pattern. *Tenaris horsfieldii* (Nymphalidae: Amathusiinae) is such a species, often encountered on Mt. Kinabalu.

Kinabalu butterflies: number of species in the different altitude elements.

	Lowland	Foothill	Lower montane	Upper montane	Total species	Malaya
Papilionidae	15	8	7	–	22	44
Pieridae	18	19	15	1	35	44
Nymphalidae	46	38	25	2	97	227
Lycaenidae	34	28	33	10	92	332
Hesperiidae	13	11	2	1	33	209
Others	2	4	3	–	11	42
Singletons, all families	45	37	33	2		
Total species	171	141	115	16	290	898

Some species are represented strongly in more than one element. Also shown are the number of species in each family with the numbers for Peninsular Malaysia for comparison (Corbet & Pendlebury, 1978) and the approximate placing of singleton species with altitude. The species numbers for Kinabalu refer only to those taken by Barlow, Banks & Holloway (1971), and these are much lower than those for Peninsular Malaysia. The total Bornean fauna is closely comparable in size; our collecting of lowland species was extremely restricted. Nymphalidae here includes as subfamilies Satyrinae, Danainae and Amathusiinae. The total species number recorded for Peninsular Malaysia now exceeds one thousand.

A further exception to the general west to east spread of species is the presence on Kinabalu of *Ptychandra talboti* (Satyrinae), a montane species also recorded from Mt. Dulit, Mt. Mulu and Mt. Trus Madi. It represents a fairly old link with the Philippines, where the rest of the genus, six much larger and more ecologically diverse species, occurs (Banks, Holloway & Barlow, 1976).

The rest of the Bornean fauna is associated with the main centres of butterfly diversity in South-east Asia (Holloway, 1969 and 1973a). These range from widespread, lowland genera, broadly centred from north-east India to Sundaland, to genera centred strongly on the mountainous areas of Burma, north-east India and west China. On Kinabalu, lowland species, and species characteristic of secondary vegetation tend to fall into the former category and montane species into the latter. One of the highest Kinabalu butterflies, the Bornean endemic lycaenid *Austrozephyrus borneanus*, belongs to a genus of many species centred on the mountains of Assam and west China. [Terms such as 'lycaenid', 'hesperiid', etc. refer to moth or butterfly families and those such as 'ennomine' and 'amathusiine' refer to subfamilies. Thus an ennomine geometrid is a species in subfamily Ennominae of family Geometridae. Readers wishing to familiarise themselves with the classification of butterflies and moths should refer to Corbet and Pendlebury (1978), Barlow (1982) or

Holloway, Bradley and Carter (1987). The Bornean butteflies have recently been covered in a fully illustrated, comprehensive catalogue with keys by Otsuka (1989, 1991)].

Bornean butterfly species can be divided roughly into three groups on the basis of distribution (Holloway, 1973a). The first group contains species widespread in the Oriental and Australasian tropics. They are usually mobile, opportunist species, often migratory and characteristic of open habitats of secondary growth. Examples of these are *Eurema hecabe*, *Catopsilia* species, *Danaus chrysippus*, *Melanitis leda*, *Zizina otis* and *Lampides boeticus*. All these species are found as far east as New Caledonia and many extend further into the Pacific or to the African tropics.

The other two groups are more restricted in distribution. The first extends throughout Sundaland and South-east Asia, weakly to the Philippines, Sulawesi and the Lesser Sundas and is centred on South-east Asia. The second is largely restricted to Sundaland. In Holloway (1973a) I presented an hypothesis that this distribution pattern resulted from two invasions of the East Indies during periods of low sea level in the Pleistocene. An intervening period of population fragmentation, isolation and speciation occurred in the longest warm interglacial when the sea level was much higher than it is today and significantly separated the islands on the Sunda Shelf. This fragmentation of the earliest invasion usually resulted in species in each of mainland Asia, Sundaland, the Philippines and Sulawesi, the Lesser Sundas and the Papuan Region (see also Holloway, 1982, 1987b). In the second invasion the mainland Asian species often spread again into the East Indies. Thus in Sundaland, duplexes (closely related pairs of species) are frequent. Several examples may be observed on Kinabalu such as (naming the mainland species first) *Symbrenthia lilaea* and *S. anna*, *Cyrestis nivea* and *C. maenalis*. Corbet & Pendlebury (1956: 54) drew attention to several examples of species duplexes found in Malaya, in many cases where the mainland species has not re-invaded Sundaland. The duplexes have interesting local distributions on Kinabalu. In each case mentioned above, the Sundaland species is more local, usually restricted to wetter or more montane localities. It would appear that the species from the larger, richer area of the South-east Asian mainland are more competitive and ecologically versatile than those characteristic of the fragments of Sundaland.

The duplex of *Eurema tominia* and *E. nicevillei* found on Kinabalu (Holloway, 1973a) is interesting for two reasons. Firstly, it would appear to have resulted initially from an east to west invasion from Sulawesi and secondly the genetic isolation of the two species would appear to be incomplete. Both species have the blackening along the posterior edge of the forewing that characterises forms of the genus found in Sulawesi and hence it is a strong possibility that the complex of species originated there, spreading to Sundaland and Burma in the first period of invasion. Fragmentation then led to distinctive forms evolving in Sumatra with Malaya and Burma, in Java, in Bali, in the Lesser Sundas and in Borneo as well as in Sulawesi. In the second period of spread the Sumatran species *(nicevillei)* invaded Borneo where *tominia nabalua* already occurred. The *nicevillei* population appears to have spread through drier lowland forest in Borneo, ousting *tominia* everywhere except in montane localities where it held its own. But the two forms can still interbreed and on Kinabalu one finds pure *tominia nabalua* in the lower montane zone,

Fig.4. *Asota kinabaluensis* (Noctuidae: Aganainae), a Bornean montane endemic. *(Photo: C.L. Chan)*

especially on the Pinosuk Plateau, and *nicevillei* in dry forest localities in the lowlands. In areas of wet lowland forest on the fringe of Kinabalu, such as at Poring, intermediate forms occur. Similar intermediates have been taken in the past in mountainous areas of Sarawak and Kalimantan.

Butterflies exhibit a variety of behaviour patterns (see Holloway, 1984b). Many, especially lycaenids and females of *Trogonoptera brookiana*, fly in the forest canopy, rarely coming down to ground level except over exposed ridges and during very windy conditions. Others, such as *Eurema*, *Mycalesis*, *Ypthima* and *Neptis* species, are found most commonly at ground level, settling on low herbage in clearings and at forest margins. These genera contain a number of species of secondary vegetation. Other species visit damp mud and silt (e.g., *Lamproptera*, *Graphium*, *Appias*, *Symbrenthia anna* and some lycaenids) or dung and rotting carcasses *(Vagrans, Rohana paristatis)*. Another group of genera and species characterises deep undergrowth in forest and woodland, broken only by shafts of sunlight *(Euthalia* and *Tanaecia*, most amathusiines and several other satyrines and nymphalines) and a few fly most readily at dusk *(Lethe, Melanitis* and several hesperiids). Hence butterfly collecting tends to take account of these facts and is highly subjective and selective.

MOTHS

Quantitative sampling is essential for a statistical analysis of local distribution patterns such as altitude zoning. Most moths come readily to light, especially that with a high proportion of ultra-violet emission. This property can be used to collect large samples for statistical analysis. Even so there is some contrast between samples taken from below the canopy and those taken from above. Several species of lymantriid, especially *Euproctis*, and two species of *Ectropis (ischnadelpha* and *longiscapia*, ennomine geometrids frequently seen at water soon after dusk on the forest floor) are much commoner in sub-canopy samples from the lower montane zone on Kinabalu. Nevertheless our 1965 survey, sampling mainly from sites overlooking the forest canopy, collected material that gave valuable indications of altitude differences in the moth fauna when analysed numerically. This work is described at length in Holloway (1970). The altitude elements found in the distribution of Kinabalu moths showed good correlation with the zones for plants and birds described in the literature.

A similar survey was conducted in the Gunung (Mt.) Mulu National Park in Sarawak (Holloway, 1984c). This covered the lowland fauna more comprehensively. It gave a more complete zonation at lower altitudes that has somewhat different terminology from that used on Kinabalu (see below). The lower montane element, centred at about 1000 m, is equivalent to the Kinabalu foothill element but excludes species of disturbed habitats. The upper montane element more or less corresponds to the lower montane one on Kinabalu (at around 1900 m). A few species from this element and those taken only at the summit of Mt. Mulu are assigned to the upper montane (1970 m to 2500 m) and "Radio Sabah" (relay station at 2600 m, just below the Layang-Layang staff quarters) elements of Kinabalu.

Butterflies and Moths

In the lowlands and foothills of Kinabalu up to around Bundu Tuhan and Kundasang, the situation resembles that for the butterflies. The moth species are also mainly of widespread Oriental distribution, many extending throughout the Indo-Australian tropics, often characteristic of secondary growth. Species restricted to Sundaland are also numerous but in the foothills rather than the lowlands. Sundaland species are also well represented in the lower montane element (characterising a zone from 1200 m to 1900 m) but widespread species are rare. One third of the lower montane species are recorded only from Kinabalu and another third are also found in the Himalayas. The endemic species are mainly of Himalayan affinity and many may be recorded from other Indonesian mountains when these have been collected thoroughly.

Passing from the upper montane element (1970 m to 2500 m) on Kinabalu to the "Radio Sabah" element and the summit element (characteristic of the sub-summit dwarf forest round Panar Laban and Sayat-Sayat) endemism increases to more than fifty percent and most other species are of Himalayan or north temperate derivation. Several species (about five percent) are found only in the broadly mountainous area from Kinabalu and Sulawesi to New Guinea. The high-altitude moth fauna has much in common with that of high mountains of Luzon, Sumatra and central Seram (southern Moluccas). More collecting is needed in the mountains of Sulawesi and on Gunung (Mt.) Tahan in Peninsular Malaysia.

The summit element (3000 m and above) contains only four species. One is a noctuid from the genus *Diarsia*. This genus is strongly centred in west China and six more species occur

Fig.5. *Lassaba acribomena* (Geometridae: Ennominae), a montane species shared with Sumatra. *(Photo: C.L. Chan)*

Fig.6. *Plutodes flavescens* (Geometridae: Ennominae), a montane species also known from mainland Asia. *(Photo: C.L. Chan)*

Fig.7. Moths widespread in the Oriental Region. Top: *Daphnusa ocellaris* (Sphingidae), found commonly in the lowland forest understorey. Centre left: *Macrocili maia* (Drepanidae), a montane species that occurs as far north as Korea. Centre right: *Tridrepana flava* (Drepanidae), a lowland to montane species that ranges from the Himalaya to Sulawesi. Bottom: *Neochera marmorea* (Noctuidae: Aganainae), a lowland species found from India to Borneo.

Fig.8. Moths more or less restricted to the Sunda Shelf. Top: *Cossus kinabaluensis* (Cossidae), ranging from the lowlands to 1700 m. Upper centre left: *Pachyodes rubroviridata* (Geometridae: Geometrinae), found from 1000 m to 1600 m. Upper centre right: *Paectes roseovincta* (Noctuidae: Euteliinae), taken mainly from 1600 m to 2000 m though rare in the lowlands. Lower centre left: *Callidula jucunda* (Callidulidae) (1000–2000 m). Bottom: *Psaphis camadeva* (Zygaenidae: Chalcosiinae), rare at around 1700 m.

Fig.9. Montane species of Himalayan affinity. Top: *Sarcinodes* sp. near *aequilinearia* (Geometridae: Oenochrominae). Upper centre left: *Sabaria* sp. near *incitata* (Geometridae: Ennominae). Upper centre right: *Horithyatira decorata* (Thyatiridae). Lower centre left: *Arichanna maculata* (Geometridae: Ennominae). Lower centre right: *Borbacha altipardaria* (Geometridae: Ennominae). Bottom: *Rhagastis castor* (Sphingidae).

Fig.10. Montane moths with northerly or easterly affinities. Top left: *Hypochrosis herois* (Geometridae, Ennominae), also in Sulawesi. Top right: *Macrobarasa xantholopha* (Noctuidae: Sarrothripinae), Himalaya to New Guinea. Centre left: *Thysanoplusia bipartita* (Noctuidae: Plusiinae), also in Sulawesi. Centre right: *Micromia latistriga* (Geometridae: Larentiinae), also in New Guinea. Bottom left: *Anisodes flavissima* (Geometridae: Sterrhinae), also in S. Moluccas and New Guinea. Bottom right: *Risoba avola magna* (Noctuidae: Sarrothripinae), also Philippines, S. Moluccas, New Guinea.

Fig.11. Montane moths restricted to Kinabalu or endemic to Borneo. Top: *Episteme conspicua* (Noctuidae: Agaristinae). Upper centre left: *Milionia pendleburyi* (Geometridae: Ennominae). Upper centre right: *Agathia succedanea* (Geometridae: Geometrinae). Lower centre left: *Fascellina albicordis* (Geometridae: Ennominae). Lower centre right: *Histia nivosa* (Zygaenidae: Chalcosiinae). Bottom: *Othreis kinabaluensis* (Noctuidae: Catocalinae).

Fig.12. Four moths from the summit zone and a rare high altitude lymantriid, the first two and the last endemic to Kinabalu, the third endemic to Borneo and the fourth shared with Java. Top: *Hypocometa titanis* (Geometridae: Larentiinae). Upper centre left: *Diarsia barlowi* (Noctuidae: Noctuinae), Upper centre right: *Poecilasthena nubivaga* (Geometridae: Larentiinae). Lower centre: two forms of *Chloroclystis oribates sayata* (Geometridae: Larentiinae). Bottom: *Euproctis kamburonga* female (Lymantriidae); the male is smaller, brown rather than white.

in the "Radio Sabah" and upper montane elements. A *Xestia*, close to the Palaearctic *c-nigrum*, in the "Radio Sabah" element is also from a large west Chinese noctuid genus. Related species occur on Mt. Korintji in Sumatra and in the mountains of Luzon. Two other species in the summit element belong to genera strongly represented in the central Indonesian mountains, both larentiine geometrids. *Hypocometa titanis* is endemic to Kinabalu and is part of the *Phthonoloba-Hypocometa* complex characteristic of the mountains of South-east Asia and the Papuan region. The other species belongs to a more widespread genus of mainly temperate environments, *Chloroclystis*. It is probably the Javan montane *C. oribates*. The fourth species, another larentiine, is the only representative of a south temperate genus to be found on Kinabalu, *Poecilasthena nubivaga*. The genus is centred in south-eastern Australia, with a single representative in many mountain ranges throughout the Papuan and Oriental regions to as far north as Burma and Luzon. Noel McFarland, with experience of the genus in Australia, suggested that it might feed as a larva on *Leptospermum*.

A few high-altitude species may have been derived from New Guinea, where much recent evolution and speciation has occurred at all altitudes. *Horisme labeculata* ("Radio Sabah" element) and two new species belong to a morphologically distinct section of the genus

Fig.13. *Antheraea celebensis* (Saturnidae). *(Photo: C.L. Chan)*

with numerous high-altitude species in New Guinea (Larentiinae). The ennomine genus *Myrioblephara* has numerous species in New Guinea with two species complexes that include *simplaria* and *flexilinea* extending to Kinabalu and beyond. Morphologically the genus is very close to the Palaearctic *Aethalura* .

There are several duplexes to be found at high altitudes on Kinabalu; the higher species usually restricted to Kinabalu (see the Appendix) and the lower more widespread. An example is the upper montane arctiid *Agylla bisecta* (endemic), derived from the lower montane *Agylla divisa* which extends to the Himalayas. The isolation of Kinabalu from the central Bornean mountains has led to a duplex arising within the island: apart from *Hypocometa titanis* in the summit element, the very similar but much smaller *H. leptomita* occurs in the upper montane element and also in the mountains of Sarawak. These duplexes can also be attributed to climatic fluctuations in the Pleistocene Ice Ages, which resulted in the increase and decrease of areas of montane habitat more than once.

A more general discussion of montane moths in the Indo-Australian tropics and their biogeography can be found in Holloway (1986b). This discussed the representation of various moth families (also in Holloway, 1987c) at higher altitudes and describes the distribution patterns in certain key groups and genera.

As might be expected, the elements are progressively poorer in species with altitude (lower montane—220; upper montane—73; "Radio Sabah"—26; summit—4), reflecting the increasing isolation of the altitude zones from areas of similar habitat. The decrease in species richness with altitude and the decrease in the evenness with which individuals from an element in the samples we made are distributed amongst the species (an indication of the degree of species packing in the environment) both testify to the youth of the upper parts of Kinabalu (Holloway, 1973a). The lower montane element is rich and ecologically mature, probably almost saturated with species; the greatest moth diversity in Borneo occurs at 1000 m (Holloway, 1984c, 1986b). Measurement of the decline of diversity with altitude is presented by Holloway (1987c); figures for New Guinea, with a larger high montane area than Borneo, are, altitude for altitude, consistently higher. It is therefore important that the Kinabalu Park should remain intact with at least its present area to conserve diversity in all its zones so that its potential benefit to mankind may be fully studied from all aspects.

REFERENCES

Banks, H.J., Holloway, J.D. & Barlow, H.S. 1976. A revision of the genus *Ptychandra* (Lepidoptera). *Bulletin of the British Museum Natural History (Entomology)* 32: 217–252.

Barlow, H.S. 1982. An Introduction to the Moths of South-east Asia. The author, Kuala Lumpur.

Barlow, H.S., Banks, H.J. & Holloway, J.D. 1971. A collection of Rhopalocera (Lepidoptera) from Mt. Kinabalu, Sabah, Malaysia. *Oriental Insects* 5: 269–296.

Corbet, A.S. & Pendlebury, H.M. 1978. The Butterflies of the Malay Peninsula. (3rd edition, revised J.N. Eliot). Malayan Nature Society, Kuala Lumpur.

Holloway, J.D. 1969. A numerical investigation of the biogeography of the butterfly fauna of India, and its relation to continental drift. *Biological Journal of the Linnean Society, London* 1: 373–385.

Holloway, J.D. 1970. The biogeographical analysis of a transect sample of the moth fauna of Mt. Kinabalu, Sabah, using numerical methods. *Biological Journal of the Linnean Society, London* 2: 259–286.

Holloway, J.D. 1973a. Problems with small islands. In: Organisms and Continents through Time. Palaeontological Association Special Publication.

Holloway, J.D. 1973b. The taxonomy of four groups of butterflies (Lepidoptera: Rhopalocera) in relation to general butterfly distribution in the IndoAustralian area. *Transactions of the Royal Entomological Society, London* 125: 125–176.

Holloway, J.D., 1976. Moths of Borneo with special reference to Mount Kinabalu. Malayan Nature Society, Kuala Lumpur.

Holloway, J.D. 1979. A survey of the Lepidoptera, Biogeography and Ecology of New Caledonia. Series Entomologica 15. W. Junk, The Hague.

Holloway, J.D. 1982. Mobile organisms in a geologically complex area: Lepidoptera in the IndoAustralian tropics. *Zoological Journal of the Linnean Society, London.* 76: 353–373.

Holloway, J.D. 1983. The moths of Borneo: family Notodontidae. *Malayan Nature Journal* 37: 1–107.

Holloway, J.D. 1984a. Lepidoptera and the Melanesian Arcs. In Radovsky, F.J., Raven, P.H. & Sohmer, S.H. (eds.) Biogeography of the Tropical Pacific. Bishop Museum Special Publication 72.

Holloway, J.D. 1984b. Notes on the butterflies of the Gunung Mulu National Park. In: Jermy, A.C. & Kavanagh, K.P. (eds.) Gunung Mulu National Park, Sarawak, Part II. *Sarawak Museum Journal 30, Special Issue 2*.

Holloway, J.D. 1984c. The larger moths of Gunung Mulu National Park; a preliminary assessment of their distribution, ecology and potential as environmental indicators. In: Jermy, A.C. & Kavanagh, K.P. (eds.) Gunung Mulu National Park, Sarawak, Part II . *Sarawak Musuem Journal 30, Special Issue 2*.

Holloway, J.D. 1985. The Moths of Borneo: Family Noctuidae: Subfamilies Euteliinae, Stictopterinae, Plusiinae, Pantheinae. *Malayan Nature Journal* 38: 157–317.

Holloway, J.D. 1986a. The Moths of Borneo: Key to families; families Cossidae, Metarbelidae, Ratardidae, Dudgeoneidae, Epipyropidae and Limacodidae. *Malayan Nature Journal* 40: 1–166.

Holloway, J.D. 1986b. Origins of Lepidopteran faunas in high mountains of the IndoAustralian tropics. In: Vuilleumier, F. & Monasterio, M. (eds.) High Altitude Tropical Biogeography. Oxford University Press, New York.

Holloway, J.D. 1987a. The Moths of Borneo: Superfamily Bombycoidea: families Lasiocampidae, Eupterotidae, Bombycidae, Brahmaeidae, Saturniidae, Sphingidae. Southdene, Kuala Lumpur.

Holloway, J.D. 1987b. Lepidoptera patterns involving Sulawesi: what do they indicate of past geography? In : Whitmore T.C. (ed.) Biogeographical Evolution of the Malay Archipelago . Oxford Monographs on Biogeography 4. Clarendon Press, Oxford.

Holloway, J.D. 1987c. Macrolepidoptera diversity in the IndoAustralian tropics: geographic, biotopic and taxonomic variations. *Biological Journal of the Linnean Society, London* 30: 325–341.

Holloway, J.D. 1988. The Moths of Borneo: Family Arctiidae, Subfamilies Syntominae, Euchromiinae, Arctiinae: Noctuidae misplaced in Arctiidae (Camptoloma, Aganainae). Southdene, Kuala Lumpur.

Holloway, J.D. 1989. The Moths of Borneo: Family Noctuidae. Trifine subfamilies: Noctuinae, Heliothinae, Hadeninae, Acronictinae, Amphipyrinae, Agaristinae. *Malayan Nature Journal* 42: 57–226.

Holloway, J.D., Bradley, J.D. & Carter, D.J. 1987. Lepidoptera. Vol 1. Commonwealth Institute of Entomology. Guides to Insects of Importance to Man. C.A.B. International, Wallingford.

Holloway, J.D. & Jardine, N. 1968. Two approaches to zoogeography: a study based on the distribution of butterflies, birds and bats in the IndoAustralian area. *Proceedings of the Linnean Society, London,* 179: 153–188.

MacArthur, R.H., & Wilson, E.O., 1967. The Theory of Island Biogeography. Princeton University Press, Princeton, New Jersey.

McKenzie, D. & Sclater, J.G. 1971. The evolution of the Indian Ocean since the Late Cretaceous. *Geographical Journal of the Royal Astronomical Society.* 25: 437–528.

Nelson, G. & Platnick, N. 1981. Systematics and Biogeography, Cladistics and Vicariance. Columbia University Press, New York.

Otsuka, K. (ed.) 1989, 1991. Butterflies of Borneo. 2 vols. Tobishima, Tokyo.

Prout, L.B. 1932. On the Geometridae of Mt. Kinabalu. *Journal of the Federated Malay States Museum* 17: 39–111.

Raven, P.H. & Axelrod, D.I. 1972. Plate tectonics and Australian palaeobiogeography. *Science,* 176: 1379–1386, New York.

Schuh, R.T. & Stonedahl, G.M. 1986. Historical biogeography in the IndoPacific: a cladistic approach. *Cladistics* 2: 337–355.

Smith, J.M.B. 1980. The vegetation of the summit zone of Mount Kinabalu. *New Phytologist* 84: 547–573.

Appendix. Moths recorded only from Kinabalu.

112 'macro' moth species are currently only recorded from Kinabalu. No doubt many of these will be found elsewhere in Borneo when more entomological exploration is undertaken. Nevertheless it is likely that all the noctuine and apameine noctuids, a high proportion of the larentiine geometrids and all higher-altitude members of duplex pairs (e.g., several ennomine geometrids) are genuinely restricted to the mountain. Most of these are commonest at 2000 m and above.

A number of species are known only from the vicinity of the old Mesilau Royal Society Base Camp (1500 m) on the Pinosuk Plateau. Unfortunately the majestic montane forest in this area has been destroyed so the conservation status of these species is uncertain. Some of the Lymantriidae may be very localised and specific to forest type.

ZYGAENOIDEA

Zygaenidae (2 species)
Two dayflying Chalcosiinae, *Histia nivosa* Rothschild and *Opisoplatia grandis* Jordan, appear restricted to Kinabalu. No altitude data are available.

Limacodidae (2 species)
Nagodopsis parvimargo Holloway and *Griseothosea kinabaluensis* Holloway are known only from single specimens, taken at 1200 m and 1930 m respectively.

BOMBYCOIDEA

Bombycidae (1 species)
Penicillifera purpurascens Holloway is only known from four specimens taken at Mesilau.

Lasiocampidae (2 species)
Paradoxopla cardinalis Holloway is known only from the holotype taken at 2600 m. *Trabala rotundapex* Holloway is frequent from 1500 m to 2110 m.

GEOMETROIDEA

Epiplemidae (4 species)
Epiplema caerulimargo Holloway is frequent from 1500 m to 2110 m, but *Epiplema transgrisea* Holloway is known only from a singleton taken at 1760 m. *Dirades rufinervis* Holloway was taken singly at 1620 m and 1970 m but *Gathynia mesilauensis* Holloway is known only from a Mesilau singleton.

Geometridae (35 species)
The oenochromines *Ozola prouti* Holloway and *Ozola submontana* Holloway are only known at present from Kinabalu but belong to a complex that needs taxonomic revision. Their status may therefore change. Only one species of the predominantly lowland subfamily Geometrinae can be listed, *Idiochlora berwicki* Holloway, known singly from 1970 m. The Sterrhinae include *Anisodes melantroches* Prout and *Scopula brookesae* Holloway, rare at 1970 m.

Most endemic Geometridae are in the subfamily Larentiinae: *Xanthorhoe mesilauensis* Holloway (frequent at Mesilau, found as high as 2110 m); *Cosmorhoe moroessa* Prout (singleton, 1700 m); *Ecliptopera zaes* Prout (singly at 1620 m, 2110 m); *Ecliptopera furvoides* Thierry Mieg (infrequent, 1620–2600 m); *Horisme maerens* Holloway (singleton 2110 m); *Chloroclystis luteata* Holloway (frequent, 1620–2600 m); *Chloroclystis coelica* Prout (infrequent, 2690–2970 m); *Chloroclystis discisuffusa* Holloway (frequent, 1620–2600 m); *Chloroclystis layanga* Holloway (2110 m, common at 2600 m); *Chloroclystis eurystalides* Prout (rare, 2110–2600 m); *Chloroclystis turgidata* Walker (frequent, 1200–2110 m); *Chloroclystis punctinervis* Holloway (singleton, 2110 m); *Gymnoscelis transapicalis* Holloway (infrequent, 1760–1930 m); *Hypocometa bathylima* Prout (rare, 1620–1970 m); *Hypocometa titanis* Prout (1970 m to summit, common at 2600 m and above); *Phthonoloba stigmalephora* Prout (infrequent, 1970–2600 m); *Phthonoloba caliginosa* Holloway (singleton, 2600 m); *Phthonoloba bracteola* Holloway (rare, 1200–1970 m); *Sauris quassa* Prout (singleton, 1550 m); *Acolutha altipunctata* Holloway (infrequent, 1970–2600 m).

The Ennominae come second to the Larentiinae in endemism on Kinabalu: *Garaeus altapicata* Holloway (frequent, 2110–600 m); *Dasyboarmia isorrhopha* Prout (common, 1500–2600 m); *Ectropis geniculata* Prout (frequent, 1200–1970 m); *Catoria proicyrta* Prout (frequent, 1620–1970 m); *Diplurodes refrenata* Prout (infrequent, 1970–2600 m); *Apophyga altapona* Holloway (frequent at 2600 m); *Synegia punctinervis* Holloway (1970–2600 m, abundant at higher parts of this range); *Synegia potenza* Holloway (frequent, 1620–1970 m); *Milionia pendleburyi* Prout (rare, dayflying, 1500–1800 m).

NOCTUOIDEA

Notodontidae (1 species)
The only endemic notodontid is *Quadricalcarifera trioculata* Holloway, common from 1200 m to 1970 m.

Arctiidae (12 species)
Many Syntominae are dayflying and infrequently collected, so some of the species listed may occur elsewhere: *Amata megista* Hampson, *Amata teinopera* Hampson, *Amata kinensis* Hampson, *Amata pseudextensa* Rothschild and *Streptophlebia obliquistria* Hampson (no altitude data); *Amata trifascia* Holloway (rare, 1620–1750 m); *Caeneressa robusta* Holloway (rare, 1620–1970 m); *Caeneressa lutosa* Holloway (singleton, 1500 m).

Endemics in the Arctiinae are restricted to one genus that contains species that are partially or wholly dayflying. The first two listed are of this nature, the last two being taken only at light: *Nyctemera kiauensis* Holloway (singleton, 1000 m); *Nyctemera tenompoka* Holloway (singleton, 1500 m); *Nyctemera kinabaluensis* Reich (frequent, 1200–2110 m); *Nyctemera montana* Holloway (rare, 1970 m–2110 m).

Lymantriidae (22 species)
Many endemics from this family are rarities known only from Mesilau on the Pinosuk Plateau. The species are: *Redoa sp.* 7 (an undescribed species (Holloway, 1976) from 1620 m); *Pellucens kinabaluensis* Strand (rare, 1760 m); *Euproctis cina* Strand (infrequent, 1050–1620 m); *Euproctis rufibasis* Holloway (singleton, 1970 m); *Euproctis tuhana* Holloway (singletons at 1200 m, 1620 m); *Euproctis altilodra* Holloway (infrequent, 1500–1970 m); *Euproctis biflava* Holloway (rare, 1200–1620 m); *Euproctis sabahensis* Holloway (singleton, 1970 m); *Euproctis anna* Swinhoe (no altitude); *Euproctis vespertilionis* Holloway (singleton, Mesilau); *Euproctis viridoculata* Holloway (infrequent, 1050–1620 m); *Medama spatulidorsum* Holloway (two from Mesilau); *Lymantria sexspinae* Holloway (rare, 1500–1620 m); *Aroa transflava* Holloway (dayflying, infrequent, 1500–1760 m); *Aroa cinerea* Holloway (dayflying, infrequent, 1620–2110 m); *Aroa biformis* Holloway (dayflying, common, 1200–1660 m).

Noctuidae (31 species)
The Noctuinae are all montane and include the following Kinabalu endemics: *Agrotis kinabaluensis* Holloway (common at 2600 m, ranges over 1620–3750 m); *Xestia isolata* Holloway (common, 2110–2600 m); *Diarsia banksi* Holloway (frequent at 2600 m); *Diarsia serrata* Holloway (rare at 2600 m); *Diarsia barlowi* Holloway (common from 2110 m to summit).

Amphipyrinae include several endemics from the tribe Apameini: *Phlogophora styx* Holloway (rare at 2600 m); *Phlogophora triangula* Holloway (two from 1970 m); *Phlogophora viridivena* Holloway (two from 2600 m); *Phlogophora lignosa* Holloway (two from 1970 m); *Phlogophora kinabalua* Holloway (infrequent, 1620–2110 m); *Feliniopsis kinabalua* Holloway (infrequent, 1200–2600 m); *Callopistria montana* Holloway (infrequent, 1500–2110 m).

There are three endemic Acontiinae, all represented by single specimens: *Corgatha nabalua* Holloway (1620 m); *Corgatha griseicosta* Holloway (1620 m); *Lithacodia potens* Holloway (1970 m). The Euteliinae also have endemics represented by singletons: *Atacira waterstradti* Holloway (no altitude); *Chlumetia kinabalua* Holloway (1760 m).

Nolinae are represented by *Nola harthani* (infrequent, 3000–3750 m). The Chloephorinae include four endemics: *Carea albimargo* Warren (common, 1200–2600 m); *Carea argentipurpurea* Holloway (infrequent, 1620–1970 m); *Carea ferrinigra* Holloway (frequent, 1200–1970 m); *Tortriciforma tamsi* Holloway (frequent, 1500–2110 m).

The Catocalinae (including Ophiderinae), through rich in species in Borneo, contribute only three endemics: *Parallelia flavipurpurea* Holloway (rare, 1200–1620 m); *Catephia susanae* Holloway (singleton, 1620 m); *Platyja crenulata* Holloway (two, at 1970 m).

There are five endemics in the hypenine/herminiine group: *Hadennia subapicibrunnea* Holloway (singleton, 1620 m); *Epizeuxis ocellata* Holloway (two, at 1500 m and 1620 m); *Badiza rufosa* Holloway (three, 1500–1970 m); *Adrapsa thermesia* Swinhoe (singleton, Mesilau); *Hypena tristigma* Holloway (singleton, 1970 m).

Fig.1. *Batocera victoriana*, a strikingly coloured longhorn beetle. *(Photo: C.L. Chan)*

BEETLES

C.L. Chan, Akira Ueda & Fatimah Abang

The order Coleoptera which consists of beetles and weevils, is the largest order in the animal kingdom. It has approximately as many species as the entire plant kingdom (Arnett, 1985) and estimates of the number of species so far described in the world vary between 277,000 and 350,000 (Britton, 1979). Beetles are easily distinguished from other insects by having leathery or hardened fore-wings developed into the elytra which protect the membranous flight (hind) wings when not in use. Some beetles have wings which are much reduced and a very few are absolutely wingless. It has been suggested that the possession of the elytra which provide protection, and the ability to fold the hind-wings, are features which contributed to the successful evolution of the beetles. Apart from that, the ability to exist in almost any known habitat is another factor increasing their chances of survival, which also accounts for their diversity.

The mouthparts of beetles are designed principally for chewing but some rare species in the Australian region have piercing-sucking mouthparts (Arnett, 1985). Beetles are also characterised by having large compound eyes and an abdomen which lacks appendages on the tenth abdominal segment. The antennae are highly variable and usually have 11 or fewer segments and the legs are modified in many different ways, for digging, swimming and running.

Beetles are extremely varied in shape and form, but normally their bodies are stout and hardened. Sexual dimorphism is sometimes obvious, for instance in the stag beetles (family Lucanidae) and in the trilobite beetles (family Lycidae). Beetle colour varies as much as shape and form. A very large number of species are black or dark brown. Some families such as the ladybirds (family Coccinellidae), the longhorn beetles (family Cerambycidae), the leaf beetles (family Chrysomelidae) and a few others are brightly coloured but the jewel beetles (family Buprestidae) and the flower-chafers (family Scarabaeidae: subfamily Cetoniinae) are perhaps the most brilliant. Size also varies considerably, ranging from 0.25 mm (family Ptilidae) to 150 mm (e.g., *Xixuthrus* sp.) in length.

Beetles undergo complete metamorphosis. The eggs are of various sizes and shapes, laid on, or near, the larval food source. The larvae are highly diverse in structure and this stage is often the most destructive, feeding on plant tissues and stored organic material, e.g., grains, wood, paper and so on. Some are carnivorous, living in humus and forest litter where they attack and consume other insects and invertebrates. The adults are mostly terrestrial, living above ground, or under bark and a number bore into wood. Several families, however, are aquatic both as larvae and as adults. Comparatively little is known of the life history of beetles as most are difficult to rear. The whole life cycle can be as short as a few weeks as in the leaf beetles or as long as several years as in the stag beetles.

Beetles are either herbivores, carnivores, parasites or scavengers. A number of them are crop pests. However, many species are very useful especially the predatory species which actually help in pest control. Although a number of studies have been done on the beetle fauna of Kinabalu, a thorough survey and checklist of the order as a whole is still lacking.

So numerous and diverse is the beetle fauna of Mt. Kinabalu that in a short chapter of this kind it is impossible to deal with every family represented. Below we provide notes on some of the more interesting groups.

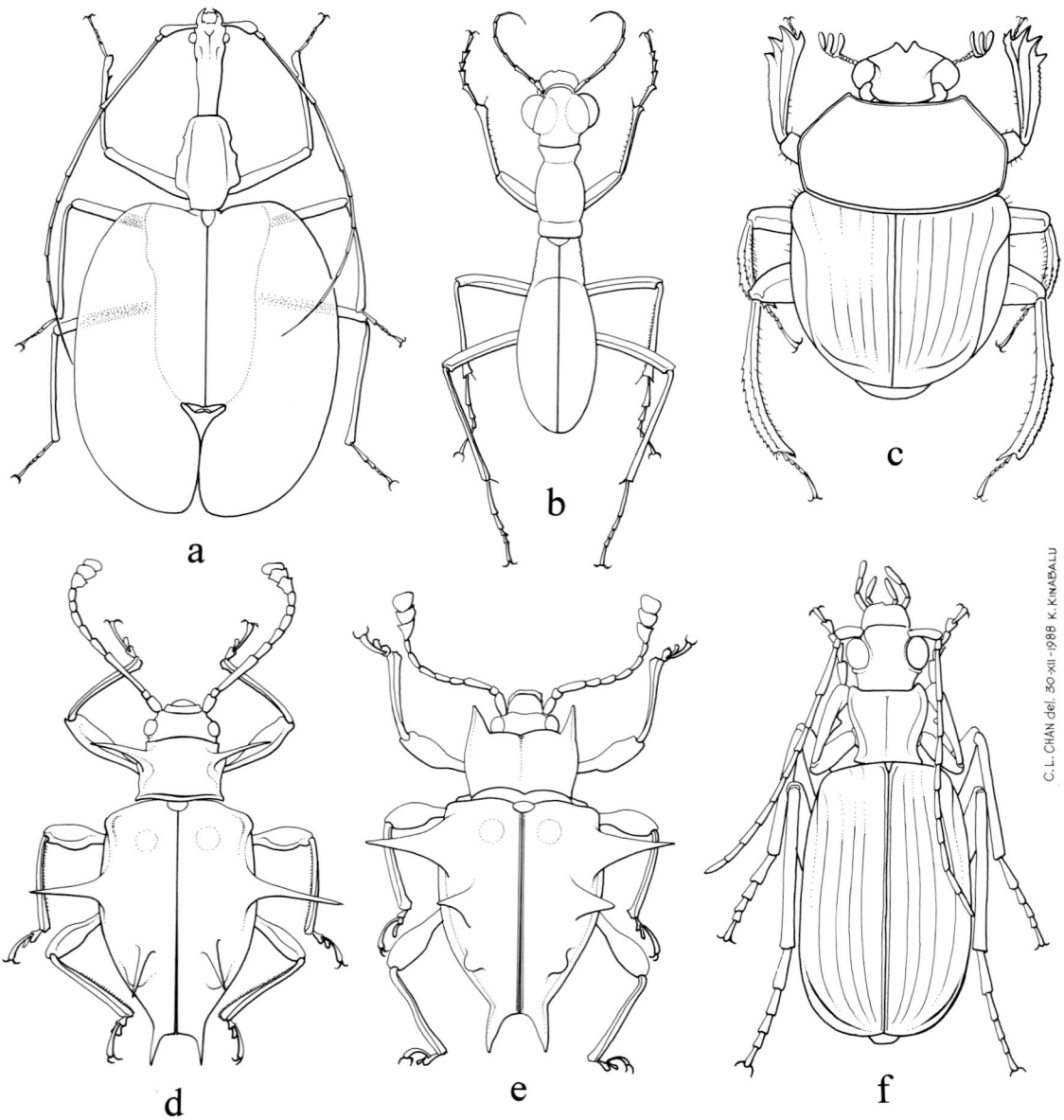

Fig.2. *a. Mormolyce phyllodes.* *b. Tricondyla cyanipes.* *c. Gymnopleurus marus.*
d. Cacodaemon spinicollis. *e. Cacodaemon spinosus.* *f. Brachinus biguitticeps.*

TIGER BEETLES

The tiger beetles (family Cicindelidae) are carnivorous and prey on small insects with their razor sharp mandibles. Eighty species have so far been recorded from Borneo. Most of the species belong to the large genus *Cicindela*. Among them, *Cicindela aurulenta* is a typical example. Its elytra are decorated with three pairs of yellow spots and it is very common on the dry ground at Poring Hot Springs (500 m).

Like insects found on islands, some species of tiger beetles on Kinabalu have lost their power of flight. An example is a *Cicindela* sp. with a shining brown marbled pattern on the elytra. It is usually found running about on the gravel along the Kamborangoh road between Park Headquarters (1550 m) and the Power Station (1900 m) and mimics a large brown ant. The male is carried above the larger female during mating.

Some species prefer an entirely different habitat. A beautiful, metallic green *Cicindela* sp. is found in very shady wet areas. Perhaps the most attractive of all the tiger beetles, this species is not uncommon along the Silau-Silau Trail around the Park Headquarters. It has also been found at the Dahobang river at the base of the Peniguppan (or Penibukan) ridge, on the south-west side of the mountain.

Though many tiger beetles are terrestrial, some arboreal forms are also encountered in the Park area. The genera *Trycondyla* and *Collyris* are typical examples. They have vestigial wings and are incapable of flight. A perfect example of mimicry is exhibited by a green longhorn grasshopper *Condylodera tricondyloides* (family Tettigoniidae). It looks exactly like *Collyris sarawakensis* in its earlier immature stage and mimics *Trycondyla cyanea* in its later stage in general form, and also, amazingly, in behaviour.

The larvae of the tiger beetles are carnivorous. They burrow into claybanks with their heads just below the surface. They are very specialised, armed with bristles and with a strangely humped back which effectively secures them to the sides of their tunnels. They prey on passing insects, seizing them with their powerful jaws at lightning speed and dragging them into the tunnel where the prey is then consumed.

GROUND BEETLES AND BOMBARDIER BEETLES

Closely related to the tiger beetles, the ground beetles (family Carabidae) are richly represented on Mt. Kinabalu although most of our species are very small and lack the striking colouration of their relatives from China—the home of the most beautiful carabid beetles. Most ground beetles are carnivorous and as the common name implies, these beetles are usually found scavenging on the forest floor among leaf litter for food. The most bizzare of all carabid beetles is the genus *Mormolyce* of the subfamily Harpalinae, the fiddle beetles. The body of this most unusual insect is flattened, the slender head is very elongated, with the elytra broadened at the sides, giving the general outline of a violin. Only five species are known. Three species, *Mormolyce phyllodes*, *M. quadraticollis* and *M. tridens* are found in Borneo. The latter two are endemic to the island. They are often found resting motionless on the underside of bracket fungi.

Fig.3. *Diamesus osculans*, a widespread species of Carrion beetle of the family Silphidae. *(Photo: C.L. Chan)*

Fig.4. A female *Odontolabis femoralis*, like in all Stag beetles, lacks the prodigious development of the mandibles in the males. *(Photo: C.L. Chan)*

Some ground beetles, together with the fiddle beetles, emit a foul-smelling fluid from the abdomen when attacked by predators. This defensive mechanism is especially well-developed in the notorious bombardier beetles (family Brachinidae). When threatened, they belch out a pungent volatile fluid with an audible bursting sound. The temperature of the fluid may reach up to 100°C as the result of a chemical reaction. Among the three species recorded from Borneo, *Bruchinus bigutticeps* can be commonly seen around Poring Hot Springs. Caution must be taken not to touch them.

CARRION BEETLES

The carrion beetles (family Silphidae) are represented in the Park by a few species. They are moderately large, more or less flattened, and oblong, sometimes with very short elytra exposing the abdomen. Both the adults and larvae feed on carrion, fungi and vegetable detritus. A large species, *Diamesus osculens* measuring up to 4.5 cm, is found occasionally attracted to the lights, making a loud noise in flight. The general colour is brownish black with dull orange markings on the elytra. It emits an unpleasant odour when disturbed. It is a cosmopolitan species, widely distributed in the Indo-Australian region. The genus *Necrophorus* is also found in the Park. It is a smaller beetle than *Diamesus* but has very similar colour patterns on the elytra. The carrion beetles are mainly confined to the temperate countries in the northern hemisphere. In the tropics they are very poorly represented.

STAG BEETLES

The stag beetles are among the most interesting of the wood-feeding beetles. Many very large and beautiful species are endemic to Mt. Kinabalu. They are characterised by their elbowed antennae and the over-sized mandibles which, in the males, are often as long as the entire body, as in the genus *Cyclommatus*. The females, on the other hand, have very small mandibles. *Odontolabis femoralis* is a common species and frequently seen attracted to lights at Park Headquarters. The male beetle is dark chestnut brown in colour with the light yellow elytra and measures up to 8 cm long. The much smaller female is similarly coloured except that the elytra are marked with an inverted black triangle. The size of the adult male is extremely variable.

BESS BEETLES

Beetles in the family Passalidae are generally known as the bess beetles. About forty species are found in Borneo. They vary from small to large, glossy black beetles with very constant form and sexes looking very much alike. They live in or under decaying wood in the forest. They are sub-social insects which demonstrate higher social behaviour than the carrion or dung beetles. The larvae are incapable of crunching dead wood due to their weak mandibles. Hence the mature beetles feed their young at all stages including the newly hatched adults. The adult beetle produces a hissing sound by rubbing the abdomen against a file-like process on the underside of the wing while the larvae stridulates by rubbing its midlegs and the vestigial hind legs together. This sonic communication is very effective in the nest.

The genus *Aceraius* is most interesting and fifteen species have been recorded from Borneo. Some of them are very large and may attain a length of 45 mm as in *Aceraius kinabaluensis*, an endemic species not uncommon around the Park Headquarters and often attracted by lights. It is coated with beautiful, long, silky reddish hairs on the sides of the body.

RHINOCEROS AND DUNG BEETLES

Hundreds of species of scarab beetles (family Scarabaeidae) are found within the Park. They are extremely varied in size, shape and habit. The subfamily Dynastinae, commonly known as rhinoceros beetles are represented in the Park by a few, very conspicuous species. This subfamily reaches its greatest diversity in South America where the longest beetle in the world, *Dynastes hercules* is found. The well developed male can reach the amazing length of 16 cm, measured from the tip of the forward pointing horn of the prothorax to the posterior margin of the abdomen.

About eight species of rhinoceros beetles are found within the Park. The most common species encountered is *Xylotrupes gideon*, the Two-Horn Rhinoceros Beetle. The general colour is a shining dark chestnut brown but those found in the lowlands are smaller in size

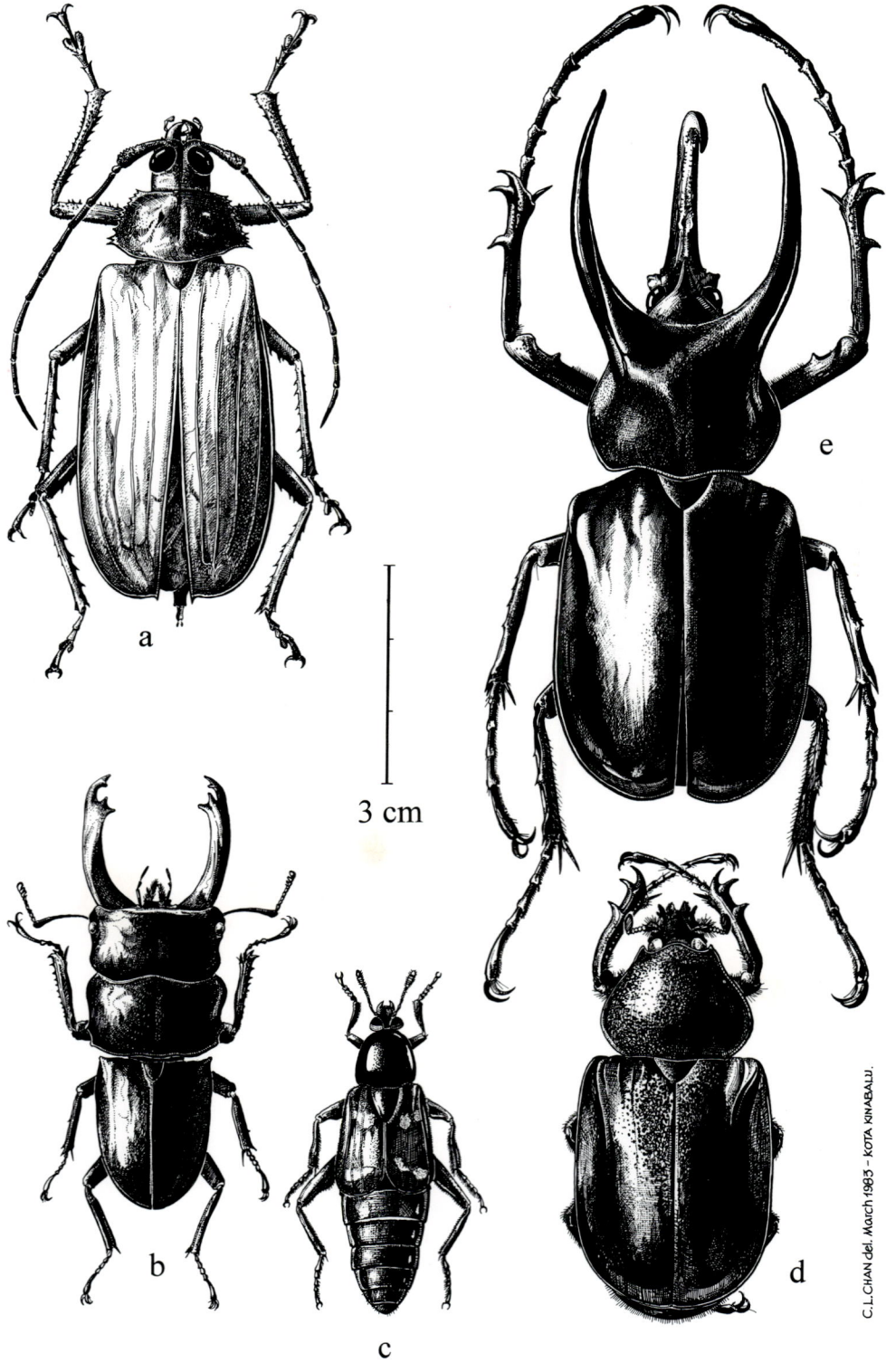

Fig.5. *a. Xixuthrus microcerus.   b. Eurytrachellelus reichei* (male).   *c. Diamesus osculans.*
d. Chalcosoma mollenkampi (female).   *e. Chalcosoma mollenkampi* (male).

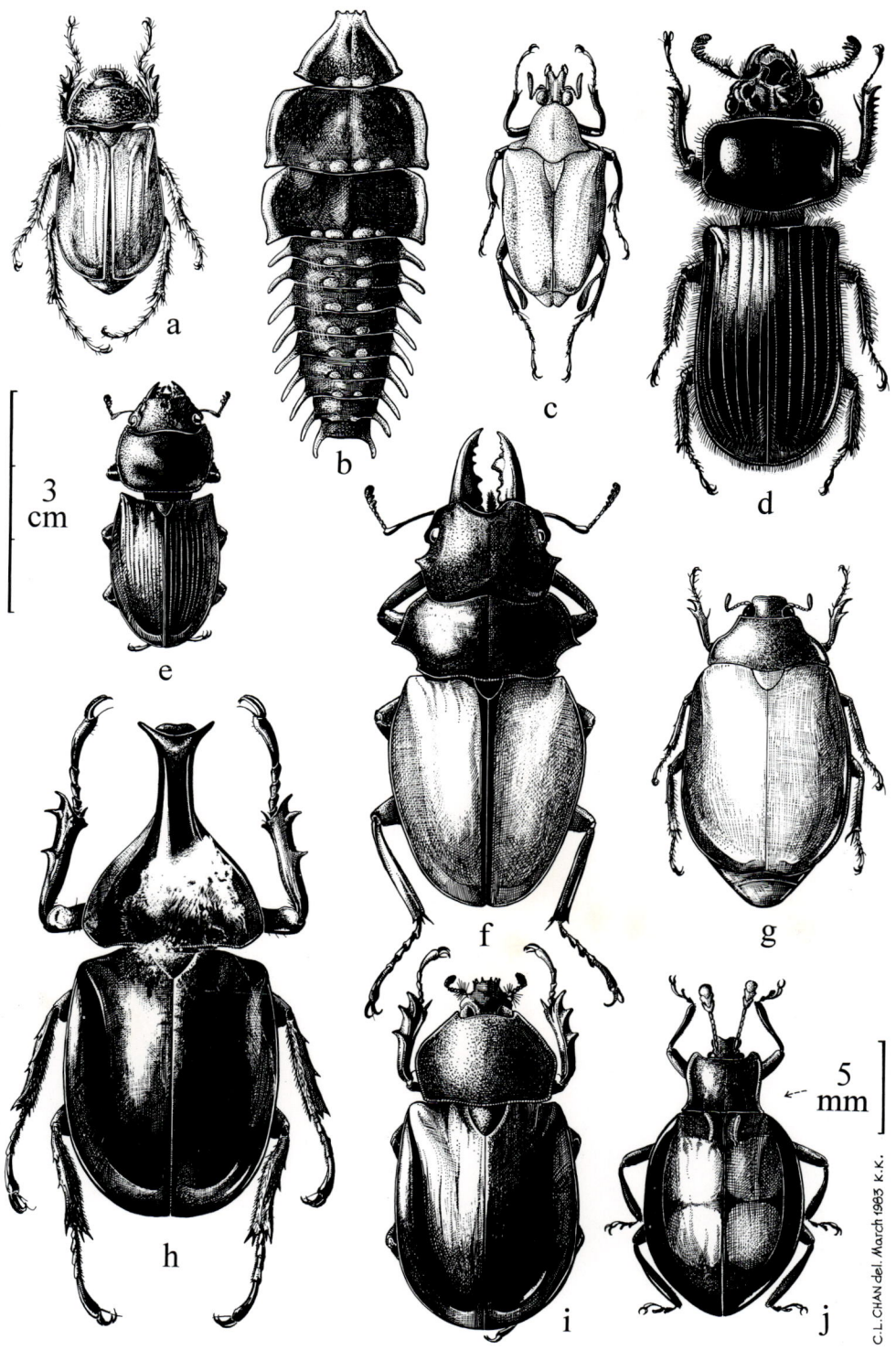

Fig.6. *a. Phyllophaga* sp. *b. Duliticola* sp. *c. Pseudochalcothea spatulifera.*
d. Aceraius kinabaluensis. *e. Eurytrachellelus reichei* (female). *f. Odontolabis femoralis.*
g. Leucopholis sp. *h. Xylotrupes gideon* (male). *i. Xylotrupes gideon* (female).
j. Eumorphus felix.

Fig.7. The female *Chalcosoma mollenkampi* is beautifully coated in a layer of golden-red hairs. Like in all members of the Dynastid subfamily, sexual dimorphism is marked. *(Photo: C.L. Chan)*

Fig.8. A handsome, brick-red male Stag-beetle *(Cyclommatus giraffa). (Photo: C.L. Chan)*

Fig.9. A mating pair of *Xylotrupes gideon* (Scarabeidae). *(Photo: C.L. Chan)*

and much lighter in colour. They are very common and during the mating season from September to October, numerous specimens are seen attracted to lights around Park Headquarters. The female stridulates violently if molested. Three species are known in the genus *Chalcosoma*. *Chalcosoma mollenkampi* is a very large glossy black beetle about 9.5 cm long. It is occasionally seen attracted to lights, and is endemic to Borneo. The male of this magnificent beetle is armed with two long, forward-pointing horns on the prothorax while the head is also armed with a large horn curving upwards. The legs are long and very strong. The female is very common and devoid of the armaments which are characteristic of this subfamily. It has a green shield over the granulated elytra and is covered by a coat of reddish hairs especially where the wing-covers meet. The legs are also proportionally shorter. *Chalcosoma atlas* is smaller than *C. mollenkampi* and is found in Malaya, the Philippines and Indonesia. It is rarely seen at the Park Headquarters, being more common at the Poring Hot Springs. The females of both *Chalcosoma atlas* and *C. mollenkampi* are very similar and difficult to distinguish from each other. Other genera recorded from the Park are *Trichogomphus, Dichodontus* and *Clysters*.

The dung beetles (subfamily Scarabaeinae) feed exclusively on animal droppings. They often roll the dung into balls and push them to an appropriate spot where they bury them in a hole which they dig with relative ease. They lay their eggs in the dung balls which are used as a food source for their offspring when they hatch. The Poring Hot Springs is one

Fig.10. *Pseudochalcothea spathifera*, a Flower beetle. *(Photo: C.L. Chan)*

Fig.11. A Melolonthid beetle of the genus *Phyllophaga* sp., a common species found around the Park Headquarters. *(Photo: W.M. Poon)*

Fig.12. Totally white except for the edges of its elytra, *Leucopholis* sp., belonging to the Melolonthinae, is a leaf-feeder. *(Photo: C.L. Chan)*

of the richest areas for this group of scavenging beetles. They are generally rather small in size and almost uniformly dull black in colour.

Many of the male dung beetles are armed on the prothorax and head with fantastic horns and tubercles that are extremely varied in size and shape. Like the dynastids, the females are almost completely devoid of these structures; when present, they are very weakly developed. *Gymnopleurus marus* is a species with a flattened body having a pair of elongated hind legs specialised for dung-ball rolling. The genus *Sisyphus* consists mainly of small beetles with long mid- and hind-legs. *Cantharsius molossus* is the largest dung beetle in Borneo and is commonly found flying around in the forest after dark. A vast number can be collected by using the pitfall trap with dung as bait. This beetle often digs a deep hole 2 cm in diameter under the dung pats of water buffalo and cattle. It is extremely common in the forests at Poring Hot Springs.

FLOWER-CHAFERS AND MELOLONTHINES

The flower-chafers (subfamily Cetoniinae) are a group of moderate-sized, diurnal, nectar-feeding beetles. Some of them are the most attractive of beetles having an exceedingly glossy body in hues of metallic blue, green, red and gold, literally glittering like jewels. When they take flight, the elytra are merely raised up a little to allow the hind wings to spread out from within. They are the best flyers among the beetles and are sometimes found in large numbers feeding gregariously on flowering trees.

The flower-chafers attracted much attention from the famous ornithologist John Whitehead during his ascent of Mt. Kinabalu in 1888. He collected many species during his expedition of which a large proportion proved to be new to science. One of these was *Pseudochalcothea spatulifera*, a metallic coppery green beetle about 3 cm long. The male is armed with a spoon-shaped appendage at the inner side of the hind legs. The female completely lacks this feature. This is the only known species of flower-chafer in the Park that is commonly attracted to lights.

An exceptionally handsome species found in the Park is the very rare *Theodosia westwoodi*. This metallic, golden-green beetle flies during the day in search of nectar. The armament of the male is similar to that in *Xylotrupes gideon*. Four species of this montane genus are known from Borneo.

Numerous species of the subfamily Melolonthinae have been recorded from Mt. Kinabalu. One of the most common is *Phyllophaga* sp., a dark reddish brown beetle with very hairy legs. It stridulates violently when disturbed. There is a *Leucopholis* sp. which is less commonly seen. The larvae of both species feed on roots of plants.

Fig.13. *Cyclommatus montellelus* is endemic to the mountains of Sabah and in the male has exceptionally long mandibles that are often the length of its entire body. *(Photo: C.L. Chan)*

Fig.14. A Hispine beetle of the family Chrysomelidae. *(Photo: C.L. Chan)*

Fig.15. A Lycid beetle, diurnal in habit, is often seen resting on foliage. *(Photo: C.L. Chan)*

Fig.16. An adult Trilobite beetle of the genus *Duliticola*, commonly seen feeding on rotten tree trunks along trails in Kinabalu Park. *(Photo: C.L. Chan)*

TRILOBITE BEETLES

A telescopic-eyed and fearsome-looking creature, *Duliticola* belongs to the family Lycidae but it is commonly known as the trilobite beetle, a name derived from the strange shape of its larvae which resembles that of the extinct, ancient trilobites. Most trail walkers at Park Headquarters will not miss these sluggish insects moving slowly over the moist forest floor, feeding upon rotten wood. All these are the females and when they reach maturity, they remain in their larval form and do not undergo a complete metamorphosis. All the males are small beetles with a pair of fully functional wings, quite unlike their partners. *Duliticola paradoxa* can be seen in the lowland forest at Poring Hot Springs.

The female of a beautiful species with bright red spots on the back can be commonly encountered at the Park Headquarters, but the male of this gorgeous beetle still remains unknown. The biology of these amazing trilobite beetles is still largely clouded in mystery.

MUSHROOM BEETLES

Many beetles are mushroom feeders, such as some ground beetles, the fiddle beetles, the majority of the pleasing fungus beetles (family Erotylidae) and the fungus beetles (family

Endomychidae). Beetles in the genus *Cacodaemon* are small fungus beetles. Despite their small size, their bodies are usually armed with spines like those of a porcupine. Twenty-three species of *Cacodaemon* are known mainly from the Oriental region with only two which are Indo-Chinese in distribution. *Cacodaemon spinicollis* and *C. spinosus* are two of the sixteen species found in Borneo. They are often found on the underside of mushrooms.

Members of the genus *Eumorphus* are beautiful black beetles often ornamented with four large yellow spots on their elytra. Some species have broadened elytra similar to those of the fiddle beetles. A typical example is *Eumorphus felix* from the Park Headquarters area. *Eumorphus marginatus* has even more extended elytra. They are usually found together with their larvae on the undersides of bracket fungi.

Fig.17. *Eumorphus fryanus* seen feeding on a *Ganoderma* Bracket fungus. *(Photo: Akira Ueda)*

LONGHORN BEETLES

A large proportion of the species of the longicorn or longhorn beetles (family Cerambycidae) are timber pests. They are especially destructive during the larval stage.

Fig.18. Newly emerged Longicorn beetle with the elytra still white, which will turn into a light brown in a day. *(Photo: C.L. Chan)*

The adults are distinguished by the antennae which are usually longer than the body. The larvae of all longhorn beetles, on the contrary, have very short antennae consisting of two, rarely three segments.

The subfamily Laminae has some large attractive species belonging to the genus *Batocera*. *Batocera thomsoni* is often attracted to lights at the Park Headquarters. The elytra of this beautiful species are conspicuously marked with creamy yellow spots while the prothorax is handsomely decorated with two large, bright red spots. The red colour fades soon after the beetle dies. It produces a hissing sound by rubbing the hind edge of the prothorax over a file-like process on the mesothorax. They are ferocious insects with strong and sharp mandibles, which bite readily. Other less common species found in the park are *Batocera parryi* and *B. rubus*. Some of the host plants of *Batocera* are several species of *Ficus, Artocarpus* and wild mangoes.

Hoplocerambyx spinicornis, a coppery-gold-coloured species with serrate antennae is also sometimes seen in the Park Headquarters area although it appears to be more abundant in the lowland forests. These beetles are unerringly able to find newly felled or dying trees in the forest where the male and the female mate. The eggs are laid randomly in the crevices of the bark. A similar but much larger species is the rare but beautiful *Neocerambyx paris* which attains a length of 9 cm. The larvae have been found in the trunks of rubber trees.

Members of the subfamily Prioninae are all very large beetles. The margin of the prothorax is always armed with some kind of spine. *Xixuthrus microcerus* is quite commonly found in the Park.

CHRYSOMELIDS

Hundreds of species belonging to the family Chrysomelidae live within the Park. Many of them are active during the day and feed on leaves or flowers. Some of them are very beautifully coloured in metallic blue or green. Some are more specialised and armed with sharp spines on the body.

REFERENCES

Arnett, R.H. 1985. American Insects. A Handbook of the Insects of America North of Mexico. Van Nostrand Reinhold Co, New York.

Britton, E.B. 1979. Coleoptera. The Insects of Australia. CSIRO. Melbourne University Press, Melbourne.

Duffy, E.A. 1968. A Monograph of the immature stages of Oriental Timber Beetles (Cerambycidae). British Museum (Natural History), London.

Johki, Y. & Kon, M. 1987. Passalidae in Sabah. Studies on the behaviour and life-cycle strategies of arboreal insects in the humid tropics. Vol 1: 64–81. Department of Zoology, Kyoto University, Kyoto.

Klots, A.B. & Klots, E.B. 1975. Living Insects of the World. Doubleday & Co., New York.

Morimoto, K. & Hayashi, N. 1986. The Coleoptera of Japan in colour. Vol. I. Hoikusha Publishing Co., Osaka. (in Japanese).

Sakaguchi, K. 1979. Insects of the World. Vol. 1. Hoikusha Publishing Co., Osaka. (in Japanese).

Sakaguchi, K. 1981. Insects of the World. Vol. 2. Hoikusha Publishing Co., Osaka. (in Japanese).

Stork, N.E. 1986. An annotated checklist of the Carabidae (including Cicindelinae, Rhysodinae and Paussinae) recorded from Borneo. British Museum (Natural History), London.

Strohecker, H.F. 1964. A synopsis of the Amphisternini (Coleoptera: Endomychidae). *Pacific Insects* 6 (2): 319–357.

Strohecker, H.F. 1968. A synopsis of the genus *Eumorphus* (Coleoptera: Endomychidae). *Pacific Insects* 10 (1): 79–112.

Fig.1. From Kinabalu's forests is gradually released enough water to sustain fascinating habitats and life in the streams. *(Photo: W.M. Poon)*

FRESH-WATER FISHES OF KINABALU AND SURROUNDING AREAS

Chin Phui Kong

The systematic documentation of the fresh-water fishes of Borneo, as well as of the entire East Indies, began with the work of the Dutch ichthyologist Pieter Bleeker. In a series of papers which appeared during the period 1851–1860, Bleeker recorded most of the fresh-water fishes now known from Borneo. Even in Vaillant's summary of the fauna in 1893, as many as 111 of the 152 fresh-water species listed had already been reported by Bleeker. All of Bleeker's fishes were documented from Indonesian Kalimantan (then Dutch Borneo). Except for the description of *Gastromyzon borneensis* Gunther (in 1874), Vaillant's paper is the first to cite Sabah (then North Borneo) localities for fresh-water fishes; he listed five from Mt. Kinabalu. Subsequently, Inger & Chin's (1959, 1961 and 1962) papers have been devoted wholly to the Sabah fauna.

Sabah's land area comprises 73,711 sq. km or about one-tenth of Borneo's total of 719,775 sq. km, yet it has a much richer fish fauna than other parts of the island—it has more than one-third of the fresh-water fishes now known from Borneo. In Sabah, Mt. Kinabalu is the source of many important rivers. The Liwagu flows eastward from the southern slope of the mountain to join the Labuk which drains into the Labuk Bay. The Mamut, Lohan and Langanan flow from the east side to join the Sugut which drains into the Sulu sea. The Sirensing and Kinarom flow from the north side to join the Bongon before draining into the Marudu Bay. The Kadamaian (the lower course of the Kadamaian is also known as the Tempasuk) flows from the north-western slope into the South China sea. And the Pegalan flows southward from south of the Liwagu and along the Tambunan valley to join the Padas before draining into the Brunei bay. The Kinabalu area is thus important to the study of fresh-water fishes.

In more recent years, during the Royal Society Expedition to Mt. Kinabalu in June and August, 1961, Chin (1962) recorded nine species of fish from the streams and rivers on the east and south sides of Mt. Kinabalu. H.M. King Leopold of Belgium recorded 15 species, also from the east and south sides of the mountain, during his expedition to Mt. Kinabalu in October, 1971 (Gosse, 1972). Chin (1978), summarising the fish fauna from the Kinabalu Park, reported a total of 32 species. From July 1985 to January 1986, Abdullah (1986) made extensive collections of fresh-water fishes from 17 localities in and around the Park, including the Kinarom river (north of Mt. Kinabalu) and the Penataran river (east of Mt. Kinabalu) where the fish fauna had not been previously collected. He listed 23 species, seven of which were newly listed for the Park.

The present report covers 40 species records, mainly taken from the records of Chin (1978) and Abdullah (1986). Fishes from the Kaingeran (a tributary of the Pegalan) and the upper course of Kadamaian in Inger and Chin's works are also included in this report.

THE FISH FAUNA

The names of the 40 species of fish covered in this report, the localities and habitats where they were found, and their recorded local names are listed in Appendix 1. Fishes are not found in all the streams of Mt. Kinabalu. At high altitude especially, on many occasions of collecting, only tadpoles have been found. The highest point where fishes have been collected is at 1580 m on the Silau-Silau stream, and the lowest point was at 200 m on the Kinarom river. Water temperatures recorded at collecting stations, at the time of collection, are listed in Appendix 2. Since 1950 some 3800 fish specimens have been collected from the Kinabalu drainage for scientific studies (see Appendix 3). The present collection represents the major fish fauna of the Park.

Nine families of fresh-water fishes are found in this region, *viz.*, Mastacembelidae, Anguillidae, Cyprinidae, Gastromyzontidae, Cobitidae, Bagridae, Sisoridae, Anabantidae and Cichlidae. Although there are more species of Cyprinids than any other family of fishes in the fauna, in the clear mountain streams the Gastromyzontids are by far the most common fishes to be found, either in pools or in the riffles. *Gastromyzon* and *Protomyzon*, which are known to the local people as *'ikan rokot'* and *'ikan dalat-dalat'* respectively, can usually be seen grazing on algae growing on the surface of rocks and gravel. If they are not disturbed, one can observe them moving slowly over the surface of the boulders, leaving narrow trails where they have scraped away the algae. *Gastromyzon* is confined to Borneo. So far there are ten species of Gastromyzontids reported from Borneo, of which four species are found on Mt. Kinabalu. *Gastromyzon* has evolved a most specialized and efficient ability to cling to substrates in swift waters, through a combination of adaptations to its pectoral and pelvic fins, and the lower surface of its body.

Glaniopsis is only known from Borneo, where it lives in clips and holes among rocks and gravel, and is not so spectacular as *Gastromyzon*. But these little fishes (seldom attaining 100 mm in length) are unique in their appearance by having a head structure as in that of a *Clarias* (a catfish) and a body resembling that of a *Nemachilus* (a loach). Local people call the fish *'ikan tengalus'* or *'lauos'*. In 1982, when Roberts examined the old specimens collected from Mt. Kinabalu deposited at the Natural History Museum, London; at the Institut Royal des Sciences Naturelles de Belgique and at the Field Museum of Natural History, Chicago, he described one new species, namely, *Glaniopsis denudata*, and added two new records *(Gastromyzon fasciatus and G. monticola)* to the list of Kinabalu fishes (Roberts, 1982).

Among the Cyprinids, *Hampala macrolepidota bimaculata* or *'ikan barap'* is perhaps the only game fish in this region which takes a baited hook readily; the fish may attain 60 cm in length. *Tor douronensis* or *'ikan belian'* and *Lobocheilus bo* or *'ikan serauyi'* are much liked as food by local people, and are therefore very much sought after; the former usually reaches over 40 cm and the latter about 25 cm in length. *'Ikan seluang' (Rasbora sumatrana)* is a small Cyprinid which is most common in small streams with slow-flowing water over a silt and gravel bottom. *Puntius gonionotus* or *'lampam jawa'* was introduced into Ranau in about 1960 for culture in ponds; it is now also found in the drains and streams near the fish ponds.

All the catfishes of the families Bagridae and Sisoridae are quite common in this region, but they are never found in abundance. They occur as small schools or are individually scattered in their natural habitat. *Anabas testudineus* or *'ikan karok'* and *Trichogaster trichopterus* or *'ikan sepat-sepat'* are common in the small muddy streams in padi fields in Ranau. They are used by local people for food. *Tilapia mossambica*, which is originally from Africa, was introduced into Sabah around 1950 for culture in ponds. It is now to be found in Ranau in all ponds, padi fields, streams and rivers with slow-flowing water. Being a warm-water fish, it is not found above 1000 m altitude. The fish is used for food and the small individuals are favoured by the local people for making *'jarok'* or fermented fish. *Mastacembelus,* the Spiny eel or *'ikan salan'* and *Anguilla*, the fresh-water eel or *'ikan sinsilud'* are not commonly seen in this region, although they can be found if looked for hard enough.

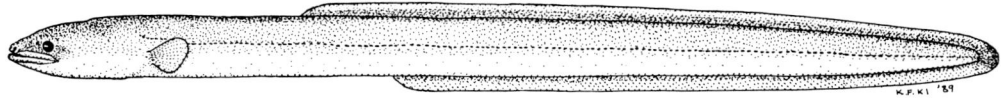

Fig.2. *Anguilla borneensis* Popta

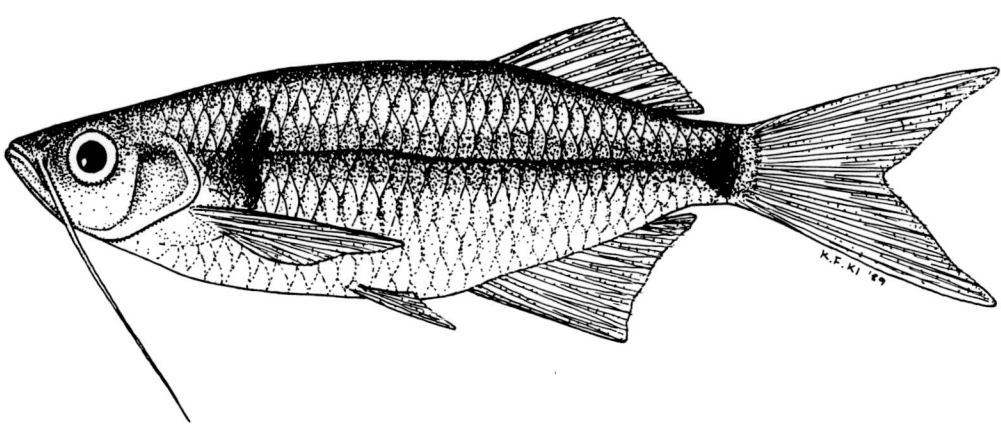

Fig.3. *Nematabramis everetti* Boulenger

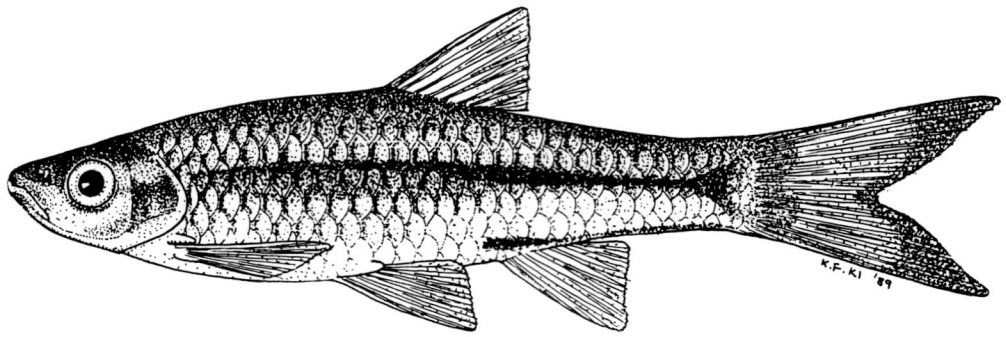

Fig.4. *Rasbora sumatrana* (Bleeker)

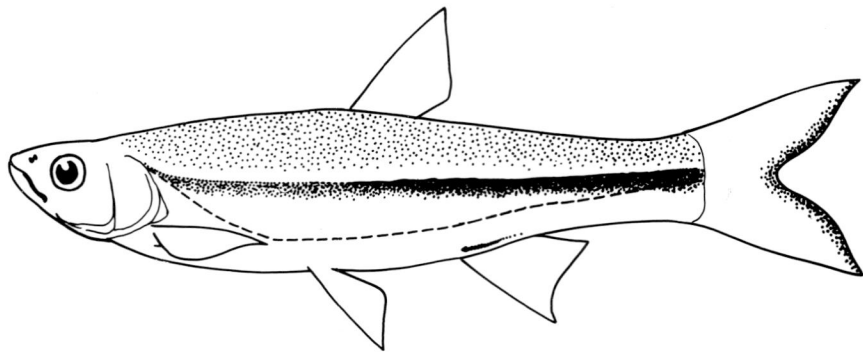

Fig.5. *Rasbora argyrotaenia* (Bleeker)

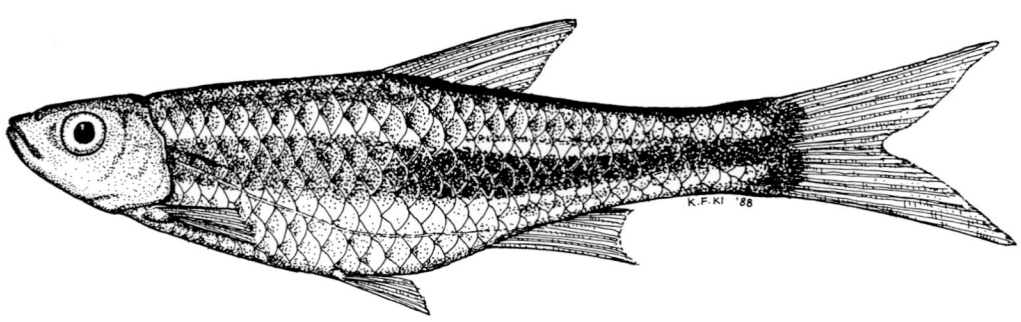

Fig.6. *Rasbora hubbsi* Brittan

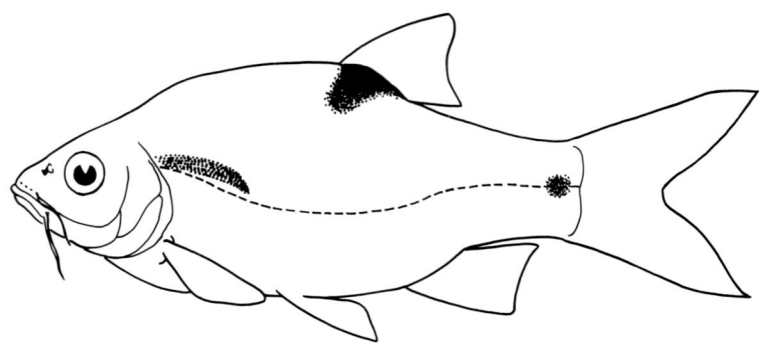

Fig.7. *Puntius binotatus* (Valenciennes)

Fresh-water Fishes

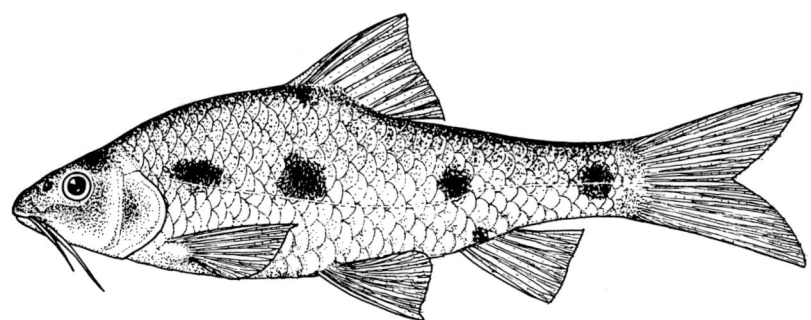

Fig.8. *Puntius sealei* (Herre)

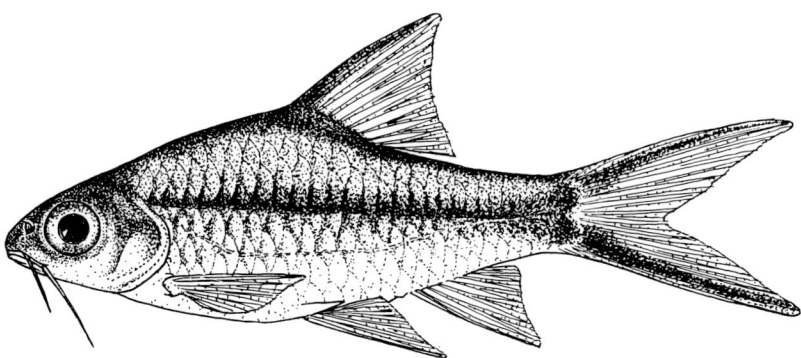

Fig.9. *Puntius collingwoodi* (Gunther)

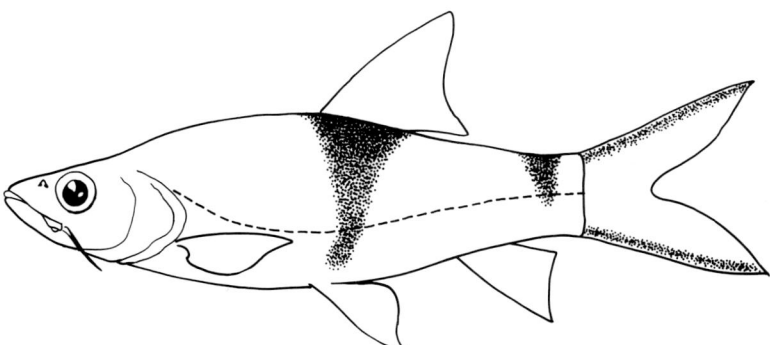

Fig.10. *Hampala macrolepidota bimaculata* Popta

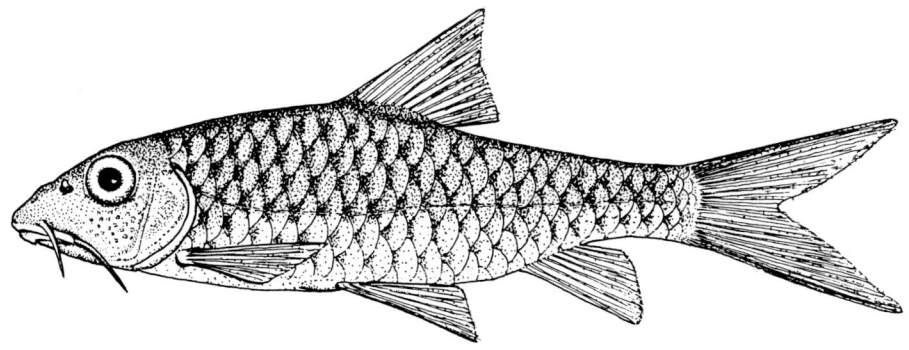

Fig.11. *Tor douronensis* (Valenciennes)

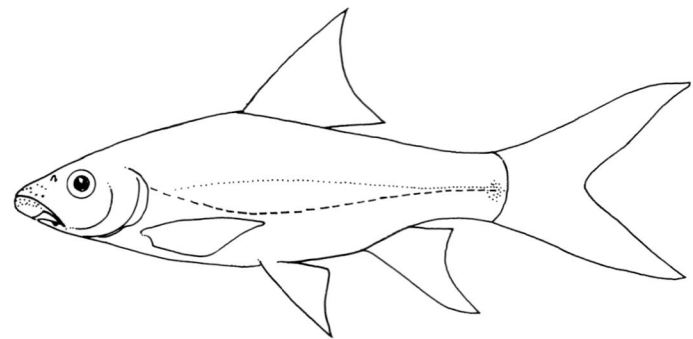

Fig.12. *Lobocheilus bo* (Popta)

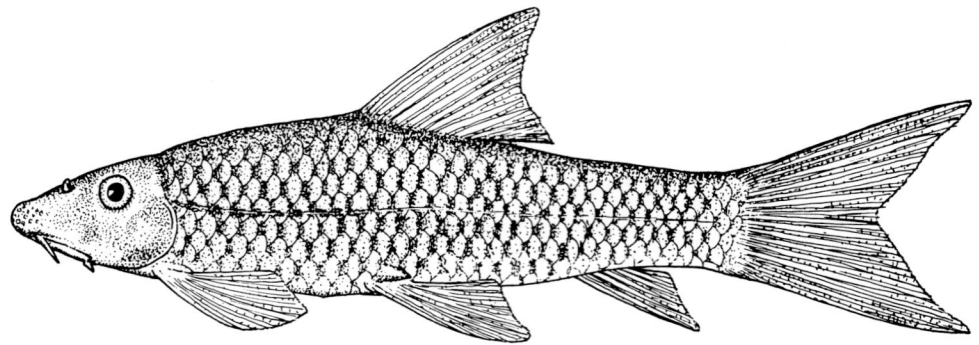

Fig.13. *Garra borneensis* (Vaillant)

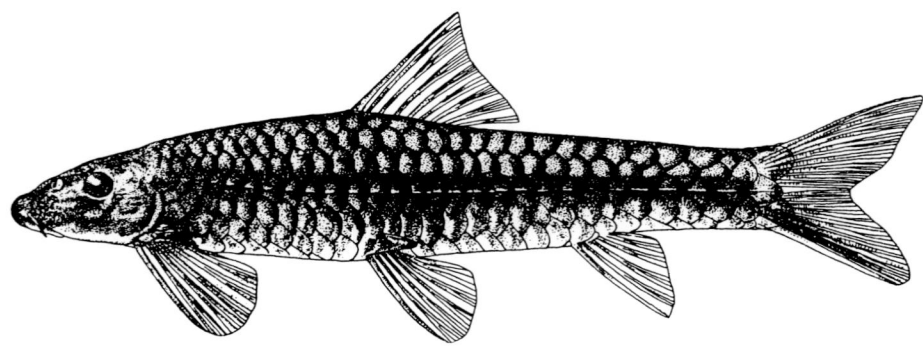

Fig.14. *Paracrossochilus acerus* Inger & Chin

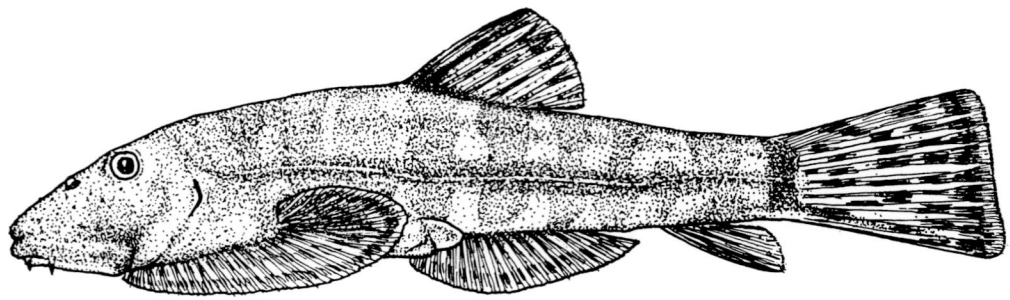

Fig.15. *Gastromyzon borneensis* Gunther

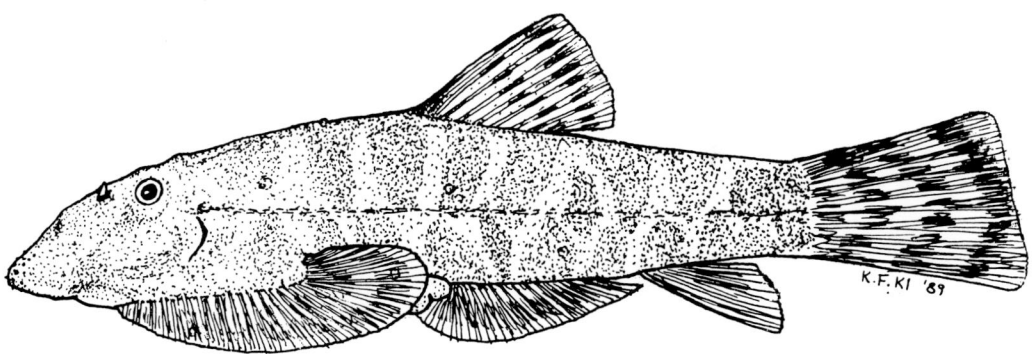

Fig.16. *Gastromyzon lepidogaster* Roberts

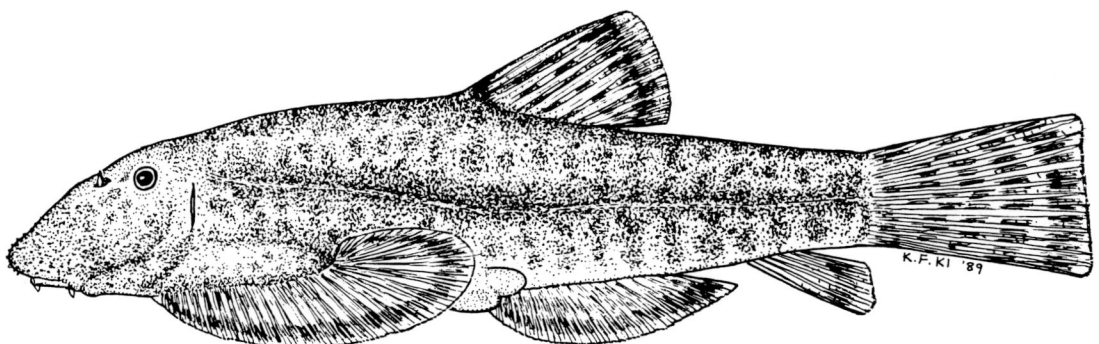

Fig.17. *Gastromyzon monticola* (Vaillant)

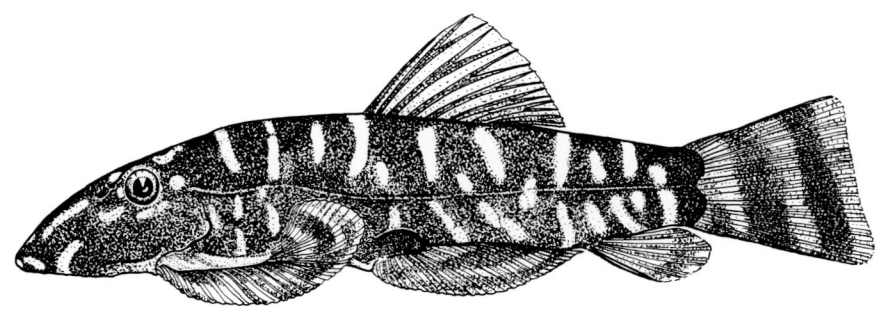

Fig.18. *Gastromyzon fasciatus* Inger & Chin

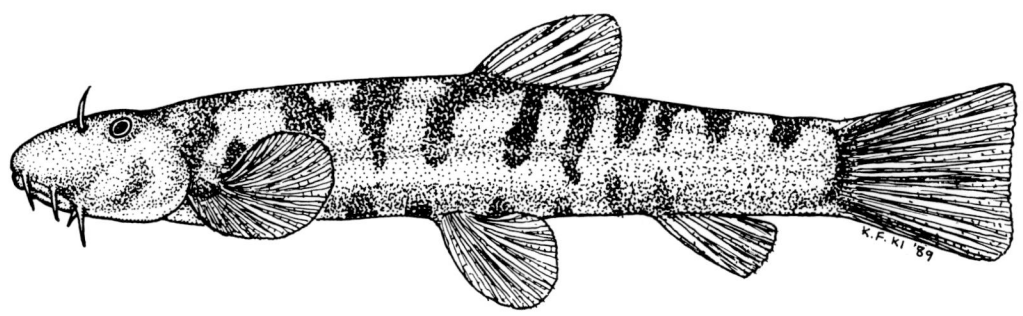

Fig.19. *Glaniopsis hanitschi* Boulenger

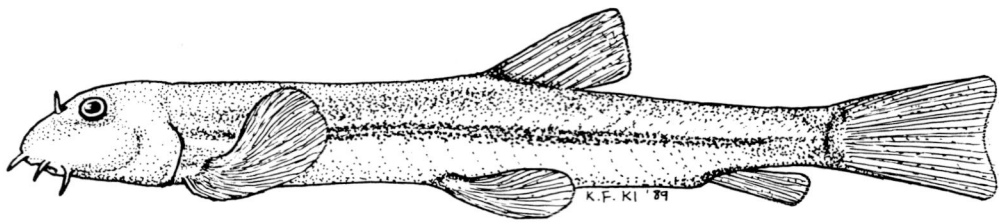

Fig.20. *Glaniopsis denudata* Roberts

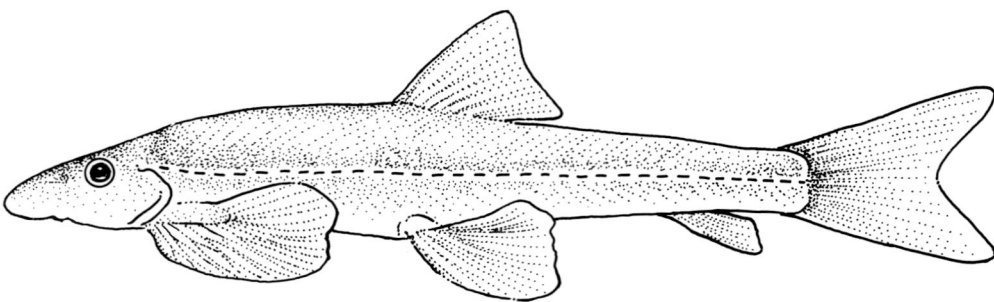

Fig.21. *Parhomaloptera microstoma* (Boulenger)

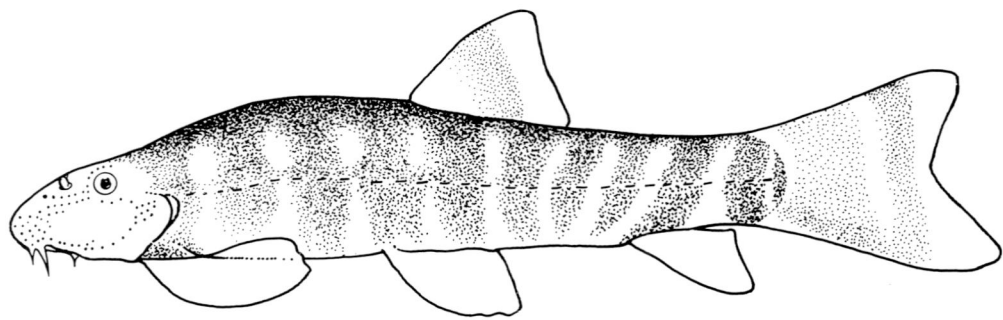

Fig.22. *Protomyzon griswoldi* (Hora & Jayaram)

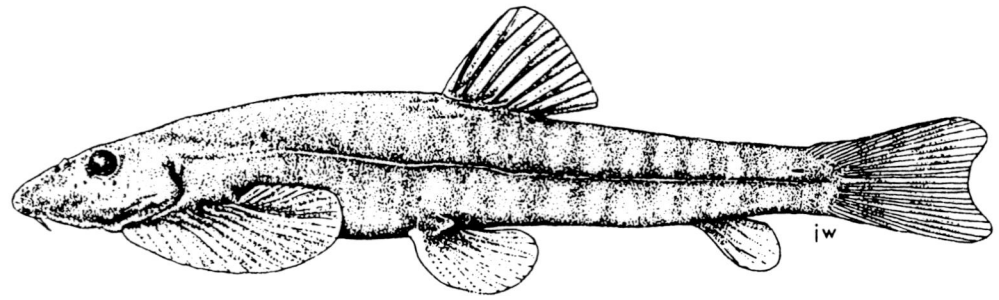

Fig.23. *Protomyzon aphelocheilus* Inger & Chin

Fresh-water Fishes

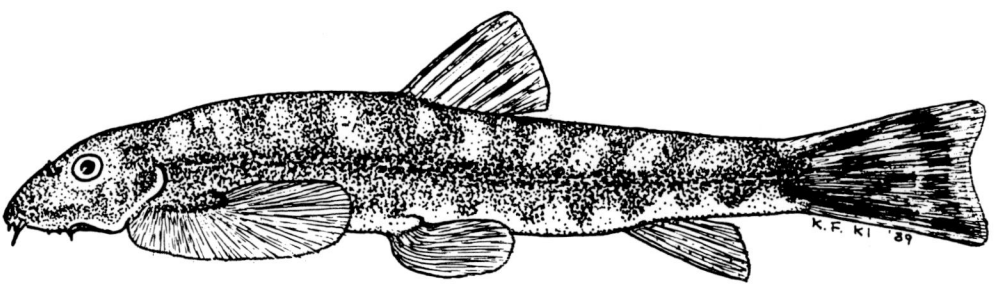

Fig.24. *Protomyzon whiteheadi* (Vaillant)

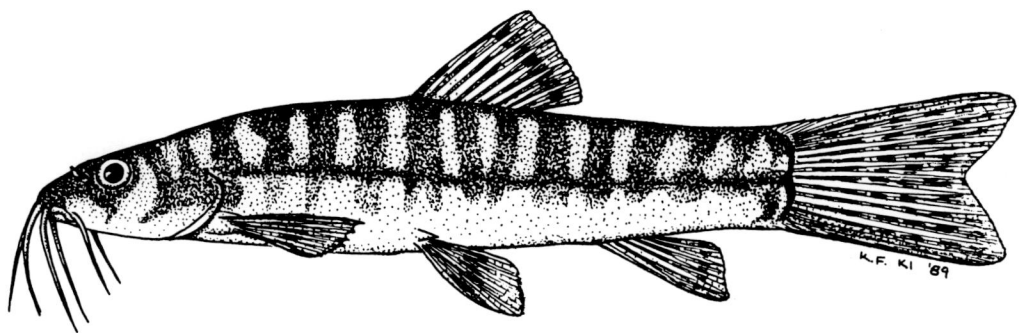

Fig.25. *Nemachilus olivaceus* Boulenger

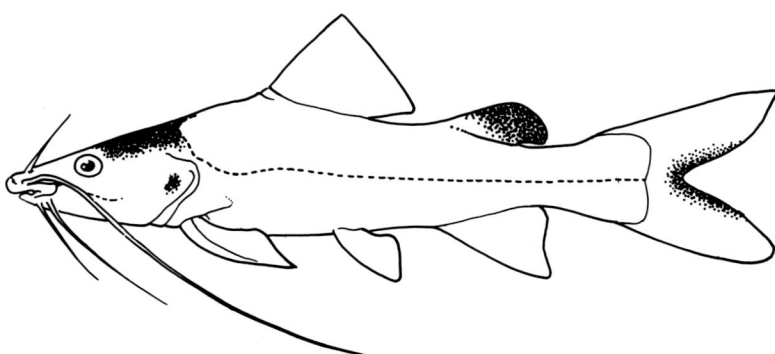

Fig.26. *Mystus nemurus* (Valenciennes)

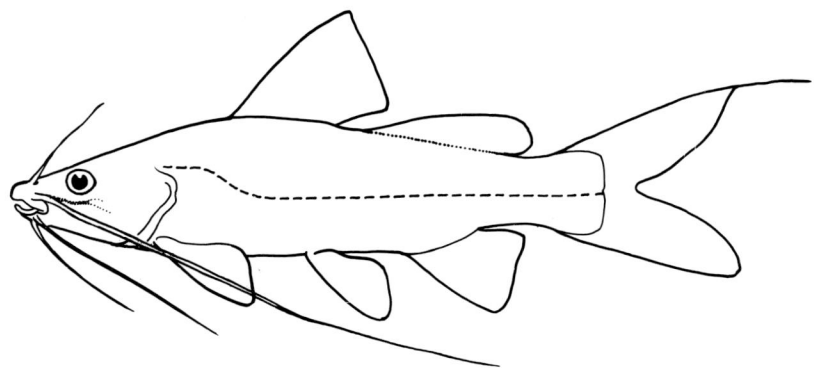

Fig.27. *Mystus baramensis* (Regan)

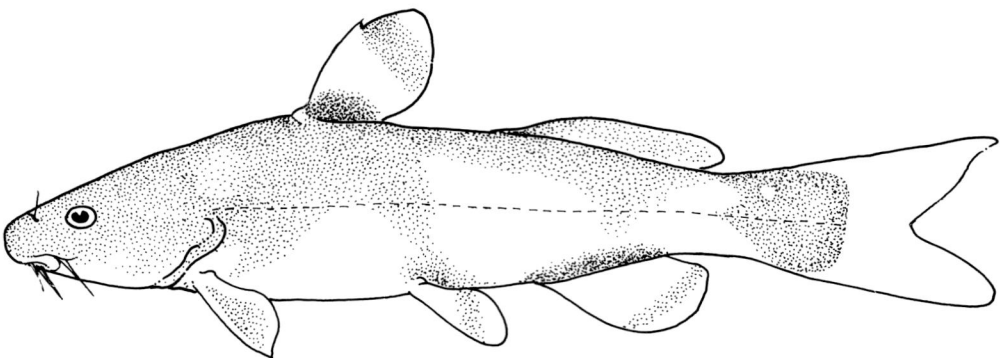

Fig.28. *Leiocassis micropogon* (Bleeker)

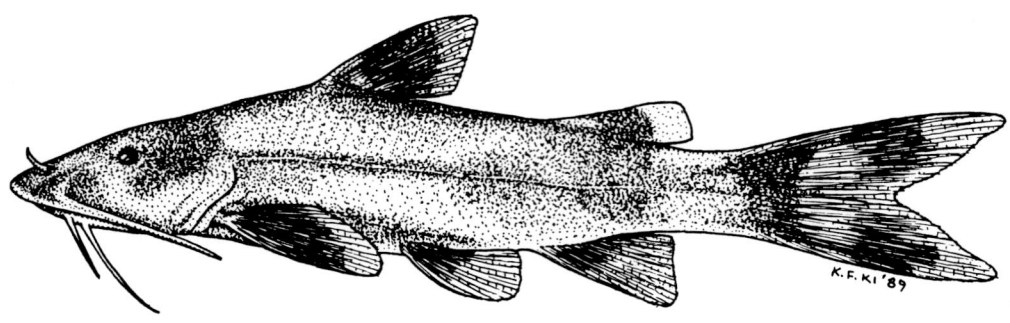

Fig.29. *Glyptothorax major* (Boulenger)

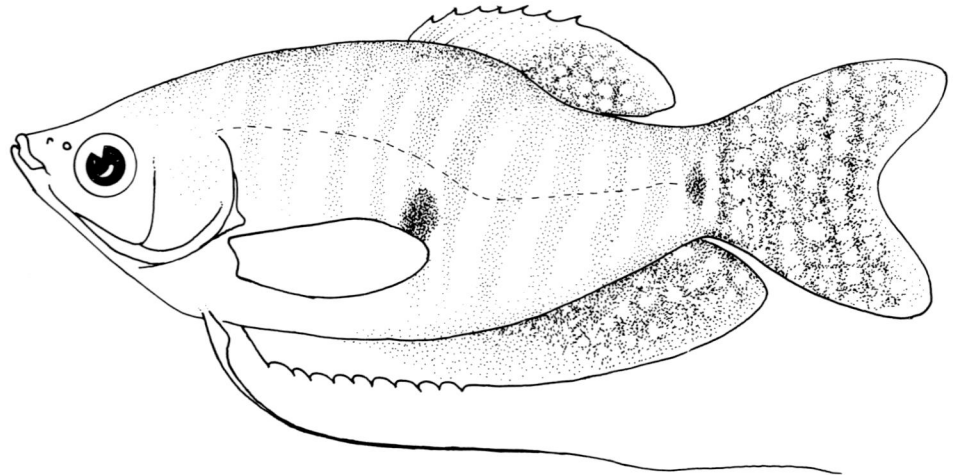

Fig.30. *Trichogaster trichopterus* (Pallas)

REFERENCES

Abdullah Samat. 1986. A survey of fresh-water fishes and their ecology at various altitudes in Kinabalu Park. Unpublished B.Sc. (Hons.) thesis, Universiti Kebangsaan Malaysia, Sabah.

Chin, P.K. 1962. Special Reports—Fish. In: Corner, E.J.H. Royal Society Expedition to North Borneo 1961: Reports. *Proceedings of the Linnean Society, London,* 175 (1): 35–36.

Chin, P.K. 1978. Fresh-water fishes of Kinabalu National Park and its vicinities. In: Luping, M., Chin, W. & Dingley, E.R. (eds.) Kinabalu—Summit of Borneo. The Sabah Society, Kota Kinabalu.

Chin, P.K. & Inger, R.F. 1989 A New Species of Gastromyzontine Fish, *Gastromyzon danumensis* from Sabah, Borneo. *Mal. Nat. J.* 43 : 53–58

Gosse, J.P. 1972. Fishes of Kinabalu National Park (North Borneo). *Bull. Inst. R. Sci. nat Belgium, Biologie.* 48:3.

Inger, R.F. & Chin, P.K. 1959. New species of fresh-water catfishes from North Borneo. *Fieldiana, Zoology* 39: 279–296.

Inger, R.F. & Chin, P.K. 1961. The Bornean cyprinoid fishes of the genus *Gastromyzon* Gunther. *Copeia*: 166–176.

Inger, R.F. & Chin, P.K. 1962. The fresh-water fishes of North Borneo. *Fieldiana, Zoology* 45: 1–268.

Roberts, T.R. 1982. The Bornean Gastromyzontine fish genera *Gastromyzon* and *Glaniopsis*, with descriptions of new species. *Proceedings of the California Academy of Sciences* 42 (20): 497–524.

Appendix 1. A checklist of fishes known from Kinabalu and surrounding areas.

SPECIES	LOCALITIES	ALTITUDE (m)	LOCAL NAMES	HABITATS
I. **MASTACEMBELIDAE**				
1. *Mastacembelus maculatus* Valanciennes	Sungai (S.) Pengakatan Ranau	520–640	'salan'	In turbid water over gravel or silted bottom.

II. ANGUILLIDAE

2. *Anguilla borneensis* Popta (Fig.2)	S. Mamut S. Pengakatan S. Kipungit S. Mantukungan	420–520	*'butul'* or *sinsilud'*	In clear or turbid water over gravel or silted bottom.

III. CYPRINIDAE

3. *Nematabramis everetti* Boulenger (Fig.3)	Ranau S. Mantukungan S. Kinarom	200–550	*'lallang,'* *'gepeng,'* *'dumpis'*	In clear or turbid water over gravel or silted bottom.
4. *Nematabramis alestes* Brittan	S. Penataran	240–400		Rock and sand bottom.
5. *Nematabramis steindachneri* Popta	S. Pengakatan S. Penataran	370–640	”	”
6. *Rasbora sumatrana* (Bleeker) (Fig.4)	Ranau	500	*'seluang,'* *'buntong'* or *'londoi'*	”
7. *Rasbora argyrotaenia* (Bleeker) (Fig.5)	S. Kadamaian S. Kinarom	200–600	”	In clear water over gravel bottom.
8. *Rasbora hubbsi* Brittan (Fig.6)	S. Kinarom	200	”	Rock, sand and slightly silted bottom.
9. *Rasbora myersi* Brittan	S. Kinarom	200	”	”
10. *Puntius binotatus* (Valenciennes) (Fig.7)	S. Kepongoh S. Langanan S. Pengakatan Ranau S. Kaingeran S. Penataran S. Kapadsaan	240–640	*'turungau'* or *'puteh'*	In clear and turbid slow running waters over silted bottom.

11. *Puntius sealei* (Herre) (Fig.8)	S. Mamut S. Kepongoh S. Mantukungan S. Kinarom	200–550	"	"
12. *Puntius collingwoodi* (Gunther) (Fig.9)	S. Kadamaian	600	'puteh' or 'selap'	In clear waters over gravel and rock bottom.
13. *Puntius gonionotus* (Bleeker)	Ranau	500	'lampam jawa'	Introduced species in fish ponds.
14. *Hampala macrolepidota bimaculata* Popta (Fig.10)	"	500	'barap' or 'gorap'	In clear water over gravel and rock bottom.
15. *Tor douronensis* (Valenciennes) (Fig.11)	S. Pengakatan S. Mamut S. Kaingeran S. Langanan S. Kadamaian S. Kinarom S. Kipungit S. Mantukungan S. Penataran	200–800	'belian'	In clear or turbid water over silt, gravel or rock bottom.
16. *Lobocheilus bo* (Popta) (Fig.12)	S. Kadamaian	600	'kalauis' or 'serauyi'	In clear water over gravel or rock bottom.
17. *Osteochilus vittatus* (Valenciennes)	"	600	'alangoi', 'toros', 'logau' or 'orongol'	"
18. *Osteochilus spilurus* (Bleeker)	S. Kinarom	200	"	Open country with bushes.

19. *Garra borneensis* (Vaillant) (Fig.13)	S. Kadamaian S. Penataran S. Kinarom	200–620	'*bat-duan*' or '*tunjungan*'	In clear or muddy waters over gravel or silted bottom.
20. *Paracrossochilus acerus* Inger & Chin (Fig.14)	S. Kadamaian S. Kaingeran	240–600	"	In clear water with rocky or gravel bottom.

IV. GASTROMYZONTIDAE

21. *Gastromyzon borneensis* Gunther (Fig.15)	Bundu Tuhan S. Kadamaian S. Liwagu S. Mamut S. Langanan S. Mantukungan S. Pengakatan S. Kaingeran S. Kipungit	440–1070	'*rokot*'	"
22. *Gastromyzon lepidogaster* Roberts (Fig.16)	S. Kipungit	635–645	"	Rocky bottom.
23. *Gastromyzon monticola* (Vaillant) (Fig.17)	S. Kadamaian S. Mamut S. Kipungit S. Mantukungan S. Kinarom	200–620	"	Rock and sand bottom.
24. *Gastromyzon fasciatus* Inger & Chin (Fig.18)	S. Kaingeran S. Parutan	640	"	Rock and sand bottom.
25. *Glaniopsis hanitschi* Boulenger (Fig.19)	S. Silau-Silau S. Liodan S. Langanan S. Brakakis S. Mamut	380–1580	'*tengkalus*'	In clear water with rocky or gravel bottom.

Fresh-water Fishes

		S. Lohan S. Mantukungan S. Liwagu S. Mesilau S. Bambangan S. Kipungit S. Taralasak			
26.	*Glaniopsis denudata* Roberts (Fig.20)	S. Silau-Silau S. Liwagu S. Mesilau S. Bambangan	1380–1580	"	Rock and sand bottom.
27.	*Parhomaloptera microstoma* (Boulenger) (Fig.21)	Bundu Tuhan	1130	'dalat-dalat'	In clear water with rocky or gravel bottom.
28.	*Protomyzon griswoldi* (Hora & Jayaram) (Fig.22)	S. Kadamaian S. Penataran S. Taralasak S. Kapadsaan	240–620	'dalat-dalat'	"
29.	*Protomyzon aphelocheilus* Inger & Chin (Fig.23)	S. Kaingeran S. Liwagu S. Kipungit S. Penataran	370–1430	"	"
30.	*Protomyzon whiteheadi* (Vaillant) (Fig.24)	S. Silau-Silau S. Liodan S. Langanan S. Brakakis S. Bambangan S. Liwagu S. Kadamaian S. Mamut S. Mesilau S. Kipungit S. Kapadsaan S. Mantukungan S. Taralasak S. Kinarom	200–1580	"	In clear hill streams with rock, gravel or sand bottom.

31. *Protomyzon borneensis* Hora & Jayaram	Mt. Kinabalu S. Kaingeran	640–1220	"	"

V. COBITIDAE

32. *Nemachilus olivaceus* Boulenger (Fig.25)	S. Mamut S. Mantukungan S. Langanan S. Pangakatan S. Kepongoh S. Penataran S. Kinarom	200–640		In clear or turbid waters over gravel, sand or mud.

VI. BAGRIDAE

33. *Mystus nemurus* (Valenciennes) (Fig.26)	S. Kaingeran S. Kadamaian S. Mantukungan S. Penataran S. Kinarom	200–640	'baung' or 'sobong'	"
34. *Mystus baramensis* (Regan) (Fig.27)	S. Langanan S. Pengakatan	520–640	"	"
35. *Leiocassis micropogon* (Bleeker) (Fig.28)	S. Pengakatan	640	"	In turbid water over gravel and mud bottom.

VII. SISORIDAE

36. *Glyptothorax major* (Boulenger) (Fig.29)	S. Kadamaian S. Pegalan S. Pengakatan	520–640	'songar' or 'payuntong'	In clear or turbid waters over rocky, gravel or mud bottom.
37. *Glyptothorax platypogon* (Valenciennes)	S. Pengakatan	640	"	In turbid water over gravel and mud bottom.

VIII. ANABANTIDAE

38. *Anabas testudineus* (Bloch)	Ranau	520	'karok'	In small streams and padi fields with slow flowing water over mud bottom.
39. *Trichogaster trichopterus* (Pallas) (Fig.30)	Ranau	520	'sepat-sepat'	"

IX. CICHLIDAE

40. *Tilapia mossambica* (Peters)	S. Pengakatan Ranau	520–640	Tilapia or 'kalapia'	Introduced species. Found in rivers, padi fields.

Appendix 2. Water temperature at the various collecting stations.

STATION	ALTITUDE (m)	WATER TEMP. (°C)	REMARKS
Carson's Falls	1840	15.2	Under primary forest, shaded.
Silau-Silau	1540–1580	17.3–17.9	"
Liwagu	1430–1540	16.1–16.7	Under primary forest, partly shaded.
Mesilau	1460–1470	15.8–16.6	Open country with bushes.
Bambangan	1380–1400	16.7–17.4	Bushes, most partly exposed.
Kipungit	480–645	21.5–23.7	Under low Keruing primary forest, shaded.
Mamut	520–850	19.8–24.5	Open country with bushes.
Kepongoh	510–520	26.2	"
Mantukungan	440–470	22.7–22.9	"
Penataran	240–400	22.3–23.8	Under primary forest, partly exposed.
Taralasak	380	24.0	Open country.

Kapadsaan	350	23.7	Under primary forest, shaded.
Liodan	1220	16.0	Under thick forest.
Lohan	730	22.5	Open country.
Pengakatan	640	21.0	”
Kaingeran	640	20.0	Mostly covered by trees.
Langanan	520	18.0	Partly covered by small trees.
Kadamaian	615–620	21.3–21.4	Open country with bushes.
Kinarom	200	24.5–25.3	”

Appendix 3. Records of fish collections from the Kinabalu drainage.

DRAINAGE	LOCALITIES	ALTITUDE (m)	DATE	NO. OF SPECIMENS COLLECTED
Liwagu / Sugut	Silau-Silau	1520	7/10/71	101
	”	1540–1580	11–14/7/85	91
	Liodan	1220	7/10/71	32
	Pengakatan	640	8/10/71	161
	Liwagu	1060–1160	Aug. 61	543
	”	1430–1540	11–14/7/85	269
	Komawanan	1060	Aug. 61	12
	Mesilau	1460–1470	11–14/7/85	46
	Pengakatan	550	June 61	19
			Total:	1274
Mamut / Labuk	Langanan	520	8/10/71	149
	Mamut	430–850	June 61	953
	”	520	27/8–1/9/85	4
	Bambangan	1380–1400	30/9/85	99
	Mantukungan	470	June 61	93
	”	440–450	27/8–1/9/85	97
	Buluntungan	520	June 61	6
	Kipungit	480–650	27/8–1/9/85	187
	Lohan	730	June 61	36
	Kepongoh	520	27/8–1/9/85	11
			Total:	1635

Kinarom / Bongon	Kinarom	200	2–4/1/86	198
Kadamaian	Kadamaian	610	Feb. 50	38
	"	620	12/8/85	267
	Penataran	240–400	20–21/11/85	301
	Taralasak	380	"	10
	Kapadsaan	350	"	69
			Total:	685
Pegalan / Padas	Kaingeran	640	July	59
	Purutan	610	"	44
			GRAND TOTAL:	3836

Fig.1. Masked Tree Frog (*Rhacophorus acutirostris*), one of the many species collected by John Whitehead. *(Photo: W.M. Poon)*

FROGS AND TOADS

Robert F. Inger, Robert B. Stuebing & Tan Fui Lian

As it has long been known that animal species usually live within relatively narrow altitudinal ranges (for example, below 1000 m, or between 1200 and 1700 m), naturalists have been attracted to Kinabalu for years expecting to find species restricted to its higher levels. The main burst of exploration, as it relates to frogs and toads, took place between 1885 and 1930. The principal persons were John Whitehead and A.H. Everett, whose names became attached to species of amphibians (e.g., *Amolops whiteheadi* and *Pedostibes everetti*), and F.N. Chasen and H.M. Pendlebury, whose names were latter attached to species of snakes *(Trimeresaurus chaseni* and *Calamaria pendleburyi)*. These early explorers found many species that were new to science as well as some already known from other places in Borneo at low elevations. At first, it was thought that all or most of the new species were restricted to Mt. Kinabalu, if not to its highest levels, then at least to its middle zones. As we will see later, that turned out not to be true.

At any rate, by 1931, when M.A. Smith published his paper, "The Herpetology of Mt. Kinabalu, North Borneo, 13,455 ft", 40 species of frogs and toads were known from the mountain. At the time of the previous review for the Sabah Society in 1978, 43 species were included. The faunal count now stands at 68 (see Appendix 1). Two factors account for this significant increase. First, we have included the entire Park, in this report, departing from the precedent set by Smith in 1931 of dealing only with the fauna above 900 m. Lowering the elevational limit to 200 m adds 14 lowland species to the list. Secondly, since 1978 another burst of exploration of the fauna has taken place, most significantly by the Ecology Section of Kinabalu Park, and the Museum of Zoology, Universiti Kebangsaan Malaysia (Sabah Campus), but also joined by workers from elsewhere in Malaysia, Great Britain, Japan and the United States.

Five new species have been described since 1978: *Kalophrynus baluensis* by B. H. Kiew, *Meristogenys amoropalamus* and *M. orphnocnemis* by M. Matsui, *Leptolalax pictus* by R. Malkmus, and *Philautus bunitus* by Inger, Stuebing, and Tan. These include forest floor species, conspicuous stream-side frogs, and one bush frog. One of the things that is supposed to happen when specialists study a group of animals (or plants) intensively is an improvement in understanding of the relationships of species and of the definitions of species. In the case of the Kinabalu frog fauna, work in the last 10 years has not only led to discovery of the three new species, but also to the recognition that in several groups two or more species were being confounded under a single name. The most conspicuous example of that phenomenon involves the little bush frogs of the genus *Philautus*. These animals are so difficult to separate that no less than three species were included under one name, *P. aurifasciatus*, in the first edition of this book. Mr. Julian Dring used the differences in calls, which he recorded in the field and then analysed with a sound spectograph, to make sense out of Bornean species of this genus.

Other studies have shown that relationships of species are not what we once thought they were, leading to changes in some names. This explains our use of the names *Leptobrachium montanum* (*L. hasselti* in 1978), *Leptolalax gracilis* (for *Leptobrachium gracilis*), *Leptobrachella baluensis* (for *Nesobia mjöbergi*), and *Rhacophorus bimaculatus* (for *Philautus bimaculatus*).

As the study of amphibians of Mt. Kinabalu continues, we may expect discovery of more resident species. These future discoveries, however, are more likely to be of species known from elsewhere in Borneo. After all, a number of the species found originally on Kinabalu—*Micrixalus baluensis, Occidozyga baluensis, Huia cavitympanum,* etc.—have since been discovered at other places in Borneo. Why not the reverse? In 1978, we made the prediction that *"as many as a dozen more species"* would be found on Kinabalu. That number has already been attained, and we now predict that close to 75 species will ultimately be known from the Park.

Fig.2. Large-eyed Litter Frog *(Leptobrachium montanum)*, a montane species now known from appropriate elevations across the entire island of Borneo. *(Photo: C.L. Chan)*

NATURAL HISTORY

Although the total size of the fauna, that is, the species diversity, is interesting, it is more important that we learn more about the lives of the known amphibian residents. That is the main goal of the continuing study of these animals in the Park.

The amphibian fauna of Kinabalu is a sort of microcosm of the fauna of Borneo as a whole. There are species of frogs that never leave the banks of streams, some that appear at streams only by accident and spend their lives widely distributed in the forest, and some that breed at the stream-side but spend most of their lives in the forest. Some species spend their entire lives at ground level, on or under dead leaves, logs, moss, and rocks; some perch on low vegetation, herbs, and shrubs; and some live fairly high in trees. What is known about the local horizontal and vertical distribution of the frogs and toads of Kinabalu is summarized in Appendix 2, though more of the information comes from observations on the same species elsewhere in Sabah.

About half the species disperse widely through forests of several kinds, depending on the altitudes at which the frogs occur. For example, *Rana chalconota* lives at lower elevations in the Park, and therefore is found in the tall, lowland dipterocarp forest and adjacent secondary growth. The small bush frog, *Philautus mjöbergi*, which has been seen only above 1450 m, lives mainly in mossy oak-chestnut forest. At any one place, at low or moderately high elevations, the frogs are distributed in vertical layers, referred to in the preceding paragraph. In places like the forest at Poring Hot Springs (500 m), for example, the ground level is occupied by species such as *Leptobrachium montanum* and *Microhyla borneensis;* the layer of herbs and low shrubs by the small toad *Ansonia spinulifer*, and the tree layer by true tree frogs such as *Polypedates otilophus* and *Rhacophorus pardalis*. We know less about vertical stratification at higher elevations, but not far from Park Headquarters (1550 m) the phenomenon is clear. Ground level is the territory of the horned frog *Megophrys baluensis* and the high-altitude representative of *Leptobrachium montanum*, low vegetation the home of the small bush frogs *Philautus mjöbergi* and *P. petersi,* and trees the zone of several species of *Rhacophorus (R. angulirostris* and *R. everetti)*.

Another large component of the fauna consists of species that never wander far from the margins of streams, emerging from water as transforming tadpoles, then feeding, growing, and breeding on the banks or on vegetation overhanging streams. This group shows the same kind of vertical stratification as the forest species. At lower elevations, the rocks and gravel of the banks are occupied by the giant toad *Bufo juxtasper* and a rock-skipping frog, *Staurois latopalmatus;* and shrubs and small trees by several species of torrent frogs *(Meristogenys orphnocnemis* and *M. whiteheadi)* and the poisonous frog *Rana hosei*. Along the streams at moderate elevations (*c.* 1500 m), for example, the Silau-Silau stream, the same vertical layering takes place, with a small toad *(Ansonia hanitschi)* and rock frog *(Staurois tuberilinguis)* on gravel or rocks and torrent frogs *(Meristogenys kinabaluensis)* perching on shrubs and trees.

Fig.3. Kuhl's Creek Frog *(Rana kuhli)*, widely distributed in Southeast Asia. *(Photo: C.L. Chan)*

Fig.4. Kinabalu Slender Toad *(Ansonia hanitschi)*. *(Photo: C.L. Chan)*

These two segments of the frog community, the forest and stream groups, are not completely separated. Juveniles of a few stream-side frogs, mainly *Rana signata* and *R. hosei*, move away from natal streams into forest to feed and grow and then return to streams as they reach maturity. However, most of the mixing of streams and forest components takes place because many of the forest species breed in streams.

The toad, *Bufo divergens*, for example, breeds where little shallow pools have been cut off from the current of a small stream. The forest floor frogs, *Megophrys nasuta* and *Leptobrachium montanum*, lay their eggs in large open pools where the current is not strong, in moderate-sized streams. Still others, such as *Leptolalax gracilis*, breed where the current is swift, in the riffles and rapids typical of the montane streams of Kinabalu.

Some forest species are independent of flowing water throughout their life cycles. The floor-dwelling *Microhyla borneensis* and the tree frog *Polypedates otilophus* may lay eggs at the same rain pool on the forest floor. Another tree frog, *Nyctixalus pictus*, lays its eggs in water-containing tree holes, and at least one species of *Philautus* (it is not clear which one) puts its eggs in water-filled pitcher plants. Other species of *Philautus* leave their small clutches of relatively large eggs in wet moss, where the young pass through the entire larval period within the gelatinous egg envelop.

Fig.5. Cinnamon frog (*Nyctixalus pictus*). This species has very recently been discovered on Mount Kinabalu. *(Photo: W.M. Poon)*

Fig.6. Kinabalu Tree Frog (*Rhacophorus baluensis*). Originally described from Mt. Kinabalu, the species occurs the length of the Crocker Range. *(Photo: C.L. Chan)*

Distribution of tadpoles of the species that breed at isolated pools in the forest is very simple and obvious: those tadpoles live in pools only. However, tadpoles that live in streams have more complicated distributions. Some, for example, tadpoles of *Bufo divergens* and *Rana chalconota*, are confined to sheltered areas such as small side pools at the edges of small streams. Tadpoles of *Rana kuhli* live in the weak current of the smallest creeks and roadside ditches near Park Headquarters. At lower elevations, tadpoles of *Ansonia leptopus*, *Rana blythi*, and *R. signata* may occur together wherever the current and bottom conformation cause accumulations of dead leaves. Riffles, rapids, and small waterfalls provide home for what we think of as the characteristic tadpoles of the Park. These are tadpoles that have special suctorial devices enabling them to cling to rocks in the strongest current (tadpoles of the genera *Amolops* and *Ansonia*), or that have slender bodies and wriggle under or between the rocks on the bottom (for example, tadpoles of *Leptolalax gracilis* and *Leptobrachella baluensis*). Then there are a few generalists, such as tadpoles of *Leptobrachium montanum* and *Megophrys nasuta*, that live in almost the entire spectrum of stream microhabitats, from sheltered side pools to rapids.

We have more information about Kinabalu's tadpoles than we did in 1978, thanks to recent work on the Park's amphibians. Several of the rock-clinging, torrent-adapted tadpoles can now be associated with species of adults. Prior to 1980 one could only name the tadpoles *Meristogenys A, Meristogenys B,* and so on. Also ten years ago it was not known that some of Kinabalu's tree frogs of the genus *Rhacophorus* had tadpoles that lived in swift water. Being able to put species names on tadpoles makes it possible to understand more fully the ecological relations of species—which ones move from forest to streams or which remain independent of streams; which sets of related species are ecologically separated at adult or

Fig.7. *Philautus* sp., a bush frog, one of three closely related, taxonomically confusing species found on the mountain. *(Photo: C.L. Chan)*

tadpole or at both stages; etc. The anatomy of tadpoles also provides clues to evolutionary relationships, but only if one knows which tadpoles belong to which species of adults.

As to the perennial question of altitudinal stratification, the picture is clearer than ten years ago, but still has serious gaps (Appendix 3). We use the zonation proposed by Corner in 1978 for his chapter on vegetation, recognising, as he did, that it glosses over the complicating effects of slope face and deep gullies. The overall picture provided by Appendix 3 is that this fauna is shaped like the mountain, with a broad base of many species in the lowlands and progressive narrowing of the fauna towards the top. The second point to be made about the distribution of this fauna is that the overlap between montane and lowland species occurs mostly in the "lower montane zone", between 1220

Fig.8. File-eared Tree Frog *(Polypedates otilophus)*, a lowland species found throughout Borneo. *(Photo: C.L. Chan)*

Fig.9. A bush frog, *Philautus mjöbergi*. *(Photo: C.L. Chan)*

and 1929 m. Information is too fragmentary to tell if this amount of overlap is related to slope face and deep gullies. A third point to be made about Appendix 3 is that some groups are clearly lowland in nature, for example, the so-called "true frogs" of the genus *Rana*. On the other hand, there are two genera, the slender toads *(Ansonia)* and bush frogs *(Philautus)*, with species all the way up and down the mountain.

Finally, we must caution readers about the weaknesses of the information concerning certain species from higher elevations. The little frog *Leptobrachella baluensis* was known only from a single locality on Kinabalu, at Kamborangoh, 2250 m, but we have found it recently at Poring, 600 m; it will surely be found at elevations in between. Two species have been seen only from the general location "Kinabalu" (Appendix 1) and have never been found elsewhere. These are the toads *Pedostibes everetti* and *Pedostibes maculatus*. It is most likely that they are montane species occurring above 1800 m. Otherwise they almost certainly would have been found somewhere in Sabah or Sarawak by now, a century after their discovery. Several other species have the single locality "Kinabalu", for example, the toads *Bufo divergens*, and *Leptophryne borbonica*. We place these in the lowland group because of their known altitudinal distributions in other parts of Borneo.

A perhaps obvious summary of our discussion of natural history is that there is much to learn about the frogs of Kinabalu. What is needed the most? Detailed observations on the behaviour and distribution (both altitudinal and local microhabitat) of almost all species are required. Even such a simple thing as detailed descriptions of colouration would be useful; that would give us valuable clues on variation. Another gap to be filled by future work is identification of the tadpoles of many species.

Appendix 1 lists seven species of *Ansonia*. So far, we know only one type of *Ansonia* tadpole from Mt. Kinabalu. Appendix 3 lists four species of *Rhacophorus* from the lower montane zone; there are only two tadpoles from Kinabalu that can be referred to this group. Those are just two examples. There is much to do.

REFERENCES

Smith, M.A. 1931. The Herpetology of Mt. Kinabalu, North Borneo, 13,455 ft. *Bulletin of the Raffles Museum* 5: 3–22.

Appendix 1. List of frogs and toads and their known Kinabalu localities.

Family Megophryidae
Leptobrachella baluensis Smith—Kamborangoh, S. Kipungit
Leptobrachium abbotti Cochran—S. Kipungit, S. Mantukungan, Marak-Parak, Poring
Leptobrachium montanum Fischer—Bundu Tuhan, Kamborangoh, S. Liwagu, S. Silau-Silau
Leptolalax dringi Dubois—Marak-Parak, Poring
Leptolalax gracilis (Günther)—Kamborangoh, Kiau, S. Liwagu, S.Mamut, S. Silau-Silau, S. Tibabar
Leptolalax pictus Malkmus—S. Langanan, Poring
Megophrys baluensis (Boulenger)—Bundu Tuhan, Kamborangoh, Lumu-Lumu, Mempening Trail, Silau-Silau Trail
Megophrys edwardinae Inger—Poring
Megophrys nasuta (Schlegel)—Bukit Ular Trail, Bundu Tuhan, S. Kipungit, Kiau, S. Mamut, S. Mantukungan, Marai-Parai, Marak-Parak

Family Bufonidae
Ansonia albomaculata Inger—S. Kipungit
Ansonia fuliginea (Mocquard)—Kamborangoh, Layang-Layang, Marai-Parai, Mentaki, S. Mesilau, Panar Laban
Ansonia guibei Inger—S. Mesilau
Ansonia hanitschi Inger—S, Kadamaian, Layang-Layang, Lumu-Lumu, Marai-Parai, S. Mesilau, S. Silau-Silau
Ansonia longidigita Inger—Kamborangoh, S. Kadamaian, Kiau, S. Liwagu, Lumu-Lumu, S. Mesilau, S. Pinokok, S. Tibabar
Ansonia platysoma Inger—Bundu Tuhan
Ansonia spinulifer (Mocquard)—S. Kipungit, S. Langanan, Marak-Parak, S. Tananansad
Bufo divergens Peters—"Kinabalu"
Bufo juxtasper Inger—S. Kipungit, S. Langanan, S. Mantukungan, Marak-Parak, Silau-Silau Trail, S. Tananansad
Leptophryne borbonica (Tschudi)—"Kinabalu"
Pedostibes everetti (Boulenger)—"Kinabalu"
Pedostibes maculatus (Mocquard)—"Kinabalu"
Pelophryne misera (Mocquard)—Kamborangoh, Layang-Layang, Marai-Parai, Paka

Family Microhylidae
Chaperina fusca Mocquard—Kiau, S. Liodan, Marak-Parak, Pinokok, Poring
Kalophrynus baluensis Kiew—Kamborangoh, Lumu-Lumu, Mempening Trail, Mesilau, S. Silau-Silau
Kalophrynus pleurostigma Tschudi—Poring
Kaloula pulchra Gray—Park Headquarters
Metaphrynella sundana (Peters)—Poring
Microhyla borneensis Parker—Poring
Microhyla petrigena Inger and Frogner—Poring

Family Ranidae

Huia cavitympanum (Boulenger)—S. Kipungit, S. Langanan
Ingerana baluensis (Boulenger)—Marak-Parak, Poring, Sayap
Meristogenys amoropalamus (Matsui)—S. Penataran, S. Silau-Silau
Meristogenys kinabaluensis (Inger)—S. Kipungit, Kiau, S. Langanan, S. Mantukungan, Marai-Parai, S. Mesilau, S. Silau-Silau, S. Tibabar
Meristogenys orphnocnemis (Matsui)—Bundu Tuhan, Kiau, S. Kipungit, S. Kinataki, S. Langanan, S. Mamut, Mantukungan, Marai-Parai, Marak-Parak, S. Pinokok, S. Tananansad
Meristogenys whiteheadi (Boulenger)—S. Kipungit, Kiau, S. Langanan, Lobong, Pinokok
Occidozyga baluensis (Boulenger)—Bundu Tuhan, Kiau, Marak-Parak, Pinokok, Poring
Rana blythi Boulenger—S. Mamut, S. Mantukungan, Marak-Parak
Rana Chalconota (Schlegel)—S. Kipungit, Kiau, S. Langanan, Marak-Parak, Poring
Rana finchi Inger—Marak-Parak, Poring
Rana hosii Boulenger—S. Liodan, S. Mamut, Marak-Parak, S. Silau-Silau
Rana kuhli Dumeril & Bibron—Bundu Tuhan, Kamborangoh, S. Kipungit, Kiau, S. Kipogoh, S. Langanan, S. Liwagu, S. Mantukungan, Marai-Parai, Marak-Parak. Pinokok, Poring, S. Silau-Silau, Tenompok
Rana luctuosa (Peters)—Bundu Tuhan, Kaung, Kiau
Rana nicobariensis (Stoliczka)—Kiau, Marak-Parak, Park Headquarters
Rana palavanensis Boulenger—Bundu Tuhan, Kiau
Rana signata Günther—S. Kipungit, S. Mamut, Marak-Parak, S. Tananansad
Staurois latopalmatus (Boulenger)—S. Kipungit, Kiau, S. Langanan, S. Liwagu, S. Mamut, S. Mantukungan, Marak-Parak
Staurois natator (Günther)—S. Kipungit, S. Mamut, Marak-Parak
Staurois tuberilinguis (Boulenger)—S. Kadamaian, S. Kipungit, Kiau, S. Liwagu, S. Mamut, S. Mantukungan, Marai-Parai, Pinokok, S. Silau-Silau

Family Rhacophoridae

Nyctixalus pictus (Peters)—Kiau, Lumu-Lumu, Poring
Philautus amoenus Smith—Kamborangoh
Philautus bunitus Inger, Stuebing & Tan—Kiau View Trail, S. Liwagu, Sayap
Philautus hosei (Boulenger)—Bundu Tuhan
Philautus longicrus (Boulenger)—Layang-Layang, S. Tibabar
Philautus mjöbergi Smith—Kamborangoh, Layang-Layang, Lumu-Lumu, Marai-Parai, Mempening Trail, S. Mesilau, Paka, S. Silau-Silau, S. Tibabar
Philautus petersi (Boulenger)—Kamborangoh, Lumu-Lumu, Silau-Silau Trail, S. Tibabar
Polypedates colletti Boulenger—Marak-Parak
Polypedates leucomystax (Boie)—Bundu Tuhan, Kaung, Kiau, Park Headquarters, Poring
Polypedates macrotis Boulenger—Marak-Parak
Polypedates otilophus Boulenger—S. Kipungit, Poring
Rhacophorus angulirostris Ahl—Kiau, S. Liodan, Marai-Parai, Pinokok, S. Silau-Silau
Rhacophorus appendiculatus (Günther)—Marak-Parak
Rhacophorus baluensis Inger—Bundu Tuhan, Marai-Parai, Park Headquarters

Rhacophorus bimaculatus Peters—Lumu-Lumu
Rhacophorus dulitensis Boulenger—Marak-Parak
Rhacophorus everetti Boulenger—Bundu Tuhan, S. Kipungit, S. Liwagu, Marai-Parai, Pinokok, S. Silau-Silau
Rhacophorus gauni (Inger)—S. Kipungit, S. Mantukungan
Rhacophorus harrissoni Inger & Haile—S. Kipungit, Marak-Parak
Rhacophorus pardalis Günther—Marak-Parak

Appendix 2. Microhabitats of Kinabalu frogs and toads.

I Stream-side species
Ansonia hanitschi—on rocks and gravel
Bufo juxtasper—on gravel banks
Huia cavitympanum—on rocks and low vegetation
Meristogenys amoropalamus—on rocks and low vegetation
Meristogenys kinabaluensis—on rocks and low vegetation
Meristogenys orphnocnemis—on rocks and low vegetation
Meristogenys whiteheadi—on rocks and low vegetation
Rana blythi—on gravel and mud banks
Rana kuhli—on rocks or gravel
Rana hosii—on rocks
Rana signata—on mud banks or low vegetation
Rhacophorus gauni—on bank vegetation
Staurois latopalmatus—on rocks
Staurois natator—on low vegetation
Staurois tuberilinguis—on rocks or herbs

II Wide-ranging forest species
Ansonia albomaculata—in litter or low vegetation
Ansonia longidigita—in litter or low vegetation
Ansonia platysoma—in litter or low vegetation
Ansonia spinulifer—in litter or low vegetation
Bufo divergens—in litter
Chaperina fusca—in litter or shrubs
Kalophrynus baluensis—in litter
Kalophrynus pleurostigma—in litter
Leptobrachium abbotti—in litter
Leptobrachium montanum—in litter
Leptolalax dringi—in litter or low vegetation
Leptolalax gracilis—in litter or low vegetation
Leptolalax pictus—in litter or low vegetation
Leptophryne borbonica—in litter
Megophrys baluensis—in litter
Megophrys edwardinae—in litter
Megophrys nasuta—in litter

Frogs and Toads

Fig.10. The Bornean Horned Frog, *Megophrys nasuta*. (Photo: A. Lamb)

Metaphrynella sundana—in tree holes
Microhyla borneensis—in litter
Microhyla petrigena—in litter
Nyctixalus pictus—in trees and shrubs
Occidozyga baluensis—in litter, especially in seepages
Pelophryne misera—in litter
Philautus bunitus—in trees and shrubs
Philautus longicrus—in low vegetation
Philautus mjöbergi—in low vegetation
Philautus petersi—in low vegetation
Polypedates colletti—in trees and shrubs, > 2 m above ground
Polypedates macrotis—in trees and shrubs, >2 m above ground
Polypedates otilophus—in trees and shrubs, >2 m above ground
Rana chalconota—in shrubs and trees
Rana finchi—in litter
Rana luctuosa—in litter
Rana palavanensis—in litter
Rhacophorus angulirostris—in trees and shrubs
Rhacophorus appendiculatus—in trees and shrubs
Rhacophorus bimaculatus—in low trees
Rhacophorus dulitensis—in trees
Rhacophorus harrissoni—in trees >2 m above ground
Rhacophorus pardalis—in trees >2 m above ground

III Forest species with horizontal and vertical distributions uncertain

Ansonia fuliginea—probably as in *A. albomaculata*
Ansonia guibei—probably as in *A. albomaculata*
Leptobrachella baluensis—probably in litter or in low vegetation
Micrixalus baluensis—habits uncertain
Pedostibes everetti—habits unknown
Pedostibes maculata—habits unknown
Philautus amoenus—probably in low vegetation
Philautus hosei—breeds at streams; arboreal; non-breeding habits unknown
Philautus petersi—probably as in *P. mjobergi*
Rhacophorus everetti—probably as in *R. acutirostris*

IV Species associated with man; in villages, clearings, and secondary forests

Kaloula pulchra—a semi-burrower
Polypedates leucomystax—on soil, shrubs, trees, or even in houses
Rana nicobariensis—on soil or low vegetation

Appendix 3. Altitudinal distribution of frogs and toads on Kinabalu.

Summit zone (above 3050 m)

Ansonia fuliginea,
Pelophryne misera,
Philautus mjöbergi.

Upper montane zone (1830–3050 m)

Ansonia fuliginea
Ansonia hanitschi
Ansonia longidigita
Kalophrynus baluensis
Leptobrachella baluensis
Leptolalax gracilis
Meristogenys amoropalamus
Pelophryne misera
Philautus amoenus
Philautus longicrus
Philautus mjöbergi
Philautus petersi

Lower montane zone (1220–1830 m)

Ansonia guibea
Ansonia hanitschi
Ansonia longidigita
Bufo juxtasper
Kalophrynus baluensis
Kaloula pulchra
Leptobrachium montanum
Leptolalax gracilis
Megophrys baluensis
Megophrys nasuta
Meristogenys amoropalamus
Occidozyga baluensis
Philautus mjöbergi
Philautus petersi
Polypedates leucomystax
Rana hosei
Rana kuhli
Rana luctuosa
Rana palawanensis
Rhacophorus acutirostris
Rhacophorus baluensis
Rhacophorus bimaculatus

Meristogenys kinabaluensis
Meristogenys orphnocnemis
Nyctixalus pictus

Rhacophorus everetti
Staurois latopalmatus
Staurois tuberilinguis

Lowland zone (below 1220 m)

Ansonia albomaculata
Ansonia hanitschi
Ansonia longidigita
Ansonia platysoma
Ansonia spinulifer
Bufo divergens
Bufo juxtasper
Huia cavitympanum
Ingerana baluensis
Kalophrynus pleurostigma
Kaloula pulchra
Leptobrachium abbotti
Leptobrachium montanum
Leptolalax dringi
Leptolalax pictus
Leptophryne borbonica
Megophrys edwardinae
Megophrys nasuta
Meristogenys amoropalamus
Meristogenys kinabaluensis
Meristogenys orphnocnemis
Meristogenys whiteheadi
Metaphrynella sundana
Microhyla borneensis
Microhyla petrigena

Nyctixalus pictus
Occidozyga baluensis
Philautus hosei
Polypedates colletti
Polypedates leucomystax
Polypedates macrotis
Polypedates otilophus
Rana blythi
Rana chalconota
Rana finchi
Rana hosii
Rana kuhli
Rana luctuosa
Rana palavanensis
Rana signata
Rhacophorus angulirostris
Rhacophorus appendiculatus
Rhacophorus dulitensis
Rhacophorus gauni
Rhacophorus harrissoni
Rhacophorus pardalis
Staurois latopalmatus
Staurois natator
Staurois tuberilinguis

Fig.1. *Pycnonotus zeylanicus*, the Straw-headed Bulbul. *(Photo: D. Wechsler © VIREO)*

SOME INTERESTING BIRDS OF KINABALU PARK

B.E. Smythies

Kinabalu is a recent mountain; geologists date it as late Pliocene or Quaternary and say it was uplifted one to three million years ago. Much thought has been devoted by a number of authors to the geographical affinities and origins of its distinctive flora and fauna. The recent confirmation of the theory of continental drift, supported by the theory of plate tectonics, has thrown new light on problems of long-range dispersal of plants and animals. Without going into details we can at present guess that the avifauna of Mt. Kinabalu dates back no earlier than the Pleistocene, whereas the flora is of much more ancient origin.

It is a well-known fact that if you climb a mountain of more than 900 m (3000 ft) in the tropics you start seeing birds that are not found in the lowlands. A montane species is defined as one that does not occur on mountains less than 900 m (3000 ft) in height. In recent years a number of species in Borneo that were formerly classed as montane have been found at low elevations far from high mountains, not everywhere but in one or two special places, e.g., Ashy Bulbul at Niah; Sunda Whistling Thrush at Bau; Red-Capped Laughing-Thrush in the Trusan. Nevertheless the distinction between montane and lowland birds is a convenient one.

The birds of Mt. Kinabalu can be divided into four groups:

(1) Birds of the subalpine zone (2450 m or 8000 ft to the summit);
(2) Montane species that are endemic to Borneo;
(3) Montane species that are not endemic to Borneo;
(4) Lowland species.

At one time several species were believed to be endemic to Mt. Kinabalu, but now they are all known to live on at least one other mountain—Mt. Trus Madi 50 km (38 miles) away, and some also occur on Mt. Tambuyukon 20 km (15 miles) to the north. In the notes that follow I have selected the more interesting or distinctive, about 80 in all, with emphasis on the subalpine species and on the montane species endemic to Borneo, because these can be studied in the Park more easily than elsewhere; the other mountains on which they live involve long and arduous journeys to reach them. The names used are those of the author's "The Birds of Borneo" (Smythies, 1981); in the following notes Malaysia is used in its geographical rather than political sense.

BIRDS OF THE SUBALPINE ZONE

MOUNTAIN BLACKBIRD
(Turdus poliocephalus)

A large and friendly blackbird with chestnut belly, yellow eyelids, and deep yellow bill and feet, its voice is a loud whistling. Its food is almost exclusively vegetarian. It builds a heavy and substantial nest, but normally lays one egg only.

Together with the Mountain Blackeye this is much the commonest and most conspicuous bird of the upper slopes of Mt. Kinabalu until the bare rock is reached. Although so successful here, where it seems to be completely at home, it is found on only two other mountains in Borneo (Mt. Trus Madi, 50 km (38 miles) distant and Mt. Tambuyukon, 20 km (15 miles) to the north). To try and determine what ecological factors limit its distribution would be an interesting study.

The species has a wide range in the Asia-Pacific region. It avoids the continental land masses, but extends from the Greater Sundas to Formosa in the north, Samoa in the east, and Lord Howe Island in the south, thus straddling Wallace's line (a feat that few other birds have achieved). In Java and Sumatra it is a montane bird (seven subspecies) living at 1200–3050 m (4000–10,000 ft,) but in the western Pacific islands (another 18 subspecies) it lives at or near sea level.

MOUNTAIN BUSH WARBLER
(Cettia vulcania)

This is a dark brown bird, paler below, with a narrow buff eyebrow. It has a soft but sweet song *witch-a-wee-chee-wee* with emphasis on the last two notes. The food is entirely animal (insects, spiders). It is quite common, but creeps about like a mouse in dense undergrowth and is easily overlooked. The species has a considerable range outside Borneo.

KINABALU FRIENDLY WARBLER or
FRIENDLY BUSH WARBLER
(Bradypterus accentor)

It is a reddish-brown bird with a moderately long tail and a boldly spotted throat. Normally silent, a hissing note, a weak whistle, and a *chuck* note when disturbed have been recorded. The food is animal (insects, spiders). It is usually seen singly, on or near the ground, and owes its name to its habit of hopping about near human feet, flicking its wings and showing no sign of fear. This bird can only be seen on Mt. Kinabalu, Mt. Trus Madi and Mt. Tambuyukon; it has been found nowhere else in the world, and is therefore one of the most exclusive attractions the Park has to offer, but recent reports suggest that it is now uncommon along the trail to the summit.

MOUNTAIN BLACKEYE
(Chlorocharis emiliae)

A small dark olive-green bird, it has yellow eyebrows and ear-coverts, black lores, and a black ring round the eyes; the bill is orange-brown and the feet yellow. The wings make a *brrp brrp* noise in flight. The song is melodious, and has been likened to that of the Song Thrush *(Turdus ericetorum)*, and in the early morning 5.30–6.00 a.m. there is a regular dawn chorus, which was recorded on tape during the 1961 Royal Society Expedition. The call-notes are heard all day and have a twittering finch-like quality. It feeds on both animal and vegetable matter, but insect food is preferred. The nest is usually built in a *Leptospermum* bush, and the eggs laid mostly in January. Towards the summit of Mt. Kinabalu it is easily the most conspicuous and probably the most abundant bird; it goes up to the very limits of vegetation, but normally never descends below the strictly upper-montane moss-forest habitat. Unlike the Mountain Blackbird, this species is restricted to Borneo, extending southwards through the higher mountain ranges.

The above four species are found only on the higher parts of Mt. Kinabalu, i.e., from about 7000 ft upwards, but they are not the only species in this top zone, where many of the birds listed below also appear at times. Most of those seen will belong to the 46 montane species (birds that are not found on mountains below 900 m or 3000 ft high), and the most exclusive of these are the 14 species endemic to Borneo.

Fig.2. A frogmouth (*Batrachostomus* sp.) on Kinabalu. *(Photo: Charles Phillipps)*

ENDEMIC MONTANE SPECIES

RED-BREASTED PARTRIDGE
(Arborophila hyperythra)

This is more often heard than seen, because it is shy and difficult to observe. It has two unmistakable notes: one is a single ringing call repeated three times per second, and answered by a loud double note dropping in pitch, like *cuckoo,* uttered once per second. It is a brown-coloured bird with conspicuous large white spots on a broad band of black along the side of the body; crown black, a broad grey line from eye to nape; chin and throat rufous. The bird's calls are commonly heard up to 3050 m (10,000 ft); it feeds on both animal and vegetable matter.

CRIMSON-HEADED PARTRIDGE
(Haematortyx sanguiniceps)

This handsome dark-coloured partridge with crimson head is unmistakable. High clucking harsh notes and a single short note at intervals have been recorded. It feeds on both animal and vegetable matter. Unlike the Red-breasted Tree Partridge it seems to go about in pairs rather than in coveys, and is found up to 3050 m (10,000 ft). The species probably ranges more or less throughout the higher mountains of Borneo.

Fig.3. *Hypsipetes criniger*, the Hairy-backed Bulbul.
(Photo: D. Wechsler © VIREO)

WHITEHEAD'S TROGON
(Harpactes whiteheadi)

The light grey breast distinguishes this trogon from other species. The male has the forehead, crown, nape and ear-coverts scarlet but in the female these parts are brown; the wing-coverts are finely barred black and white. It is a quiet and static bird, the only note recorded being a peculiar growling one. It generally sits on the higher branches of the lower forest trees and seldom moves. Feeds mainly on insects such as grasshoppers, leaf insects, ants, etc. The species extends southwards along the higher mountain ranges.

WHITEHEAD'S BROADBILL
(Calyptomena whiteheadi)

Its large size and black throat prevent confusion with the Green Broadbill *(C. viridis)*, which may be seen up to 1200 m (4000 ft). The male is iridescent green with black markings, and the female is duller. Generally a very quiet bird, but loud and harsh jay-like calls and a noisy wheeze have been recorded. It is a shade lover, frequenting damp, dark ravines, and living mainly on large fruits. It builds the usual hanging nest of the broadbills and normally lays two eggs. Extends southwards through the higher mountain ranges.

BLACK-COLLARED FRUIT HUNTER
(Chlamydochaera jefferyi)

The male is a grey bird with a buff-coloured head and black breast; the female is reddish-brown where the male is grey; it has a black line through the eye to the nape. Except that it eats nothing but fruit, surprisingly little has been recorded about this species; the voice, nest and eggs are unknown. A local species of old jungle, it occurs here and there in the higher mountain ranges.

EVERETT'S THRUSH
(Zoothera everetti)
and ORANGE-HEADED THRUSH
(Zoothera citrina)

Its chestnut breast and flanks contrast with dark upperparts and white throat and belly; its ear-coverts are whitish; there is a black moustachial stripe. Except that one specimen had fed on insects, this is a rare bird about which nothing has been recorded. An allied species is the Orange-headed Thrush *(Zoothera citrina)*, a distinctive and beautiful thrush with chestnut head, bluish-grey upperparts, and a white patch on the shoulder of the wing. I have seen it on the road below the Tenompok pass, and Whitehead collected several at 900–1200 m (3000–4000 ft). The species is widespread in South-east Asia, but rare in Borneo.

MOUNTAIN WREN-WARBLER
(Napothera crassa)

A dark brown bird with mottled upperparts, this has a whitish throat, and reddish belly and flanks; it is charming and full of curiosity: I have had a party of six come right close up, chirping and peering, and at dusk they set up an attractive warbling. It is common up the East ridge to 3050 m (10,000 ft). It takes animal food, and the nest and eggs are unknown.

SHORT-TAILED BUSH WARBLER OR BORNEAN STUBTAIL
(Urosphena whiteheadii)

This is a small bird with no visible tail, long buff eyebrows, and long noticeably pale legs; a dark line through the eye, whitish throat and breast, and brown upperparts. It utters a scarcely audible high-frequency bat-like note with a shiver in it. It hops along the ground or creeps in dense undergrowth close to the ground, more like a mouse than a bird. It feeds on insects and the nest and eggs are unknown. The species extends southwards along the higher mountain ranges.

Fig.4. "More often heard than seen." The Short-tailed Bush-Warbler *(Urosphena whiteheadi)*, a montane species endemic to Borneo. *(Photo: D. Wechsler © VIREO)*

Fig.5. The Green Broadbill *(Calyptomena viridis)*, known from the lowlands up to about 1200 m. *(Photo: D. Wechsler © VIREO)*

Fig.6. Rufous-winged Flycatcher *(Philentoma pyrhopterum)*, common throughout Borneo's lowlands, sometimes seen at Poring. *(Photo: D. Wechsler © VIREO)*

BORNEAN MOUNTAIN WHISTLER
(Pachycephala hypoxantha)

The olive-green upperparts, yellow underparts, and fair size (length 15 cm or 6 in) are diagnostic. It has a rich *whee whee whee* whistle, followed by a single harsh note, frequents the lower branches of trees, and lives mainly on animal food. Virtually nothing is known of the nest and eggs. The species extends southwards along the higher mountain ranges.

WHITEHEAD'S SPIDERHUNDER
(Arachnothera juliae)

A striking and unmistakable species, it is brown streaked with white, and has conspicuous bright orange on the rump and under the tail-coverts. A long twittering note, a short sharp bleat, and a thin high-pitched squeaky song have been described. It is a bird of the moss forest. To see a party of these lovely birds chasing each other round the bushes in golden evening sunlight is an unforgettable experience.. The nest and eggs are unknown. It extends southwards along the higher mountain ranges of Borneo.

PYGMY WHITE-EYE
(Oculocincta squamifrons)

A tiny bird with a thin white eye-ring, it is olive grey above and yellowish white below; the forehead is speckled with white. It utters a *chit chit chit* note and frequents moss forest, scrub jungle, and village clearings; it keeps low and will approach very closely. The nest and eggs are unknown. It has been collected as low as 180 m (600 ft) on Mt. Kinabalu. The species extends southwards along the higher mountain ranges.

KINABALU SERPENT EAGLE
(Spilornis kinabaluensis)

This is a rare bird formerly thought to be a sub-species of the much commoner Crested Serpent-Eagle. It is distinguished by its black throat.

BARBETS

The last three montane endemics are all barbets, and they are described below together with the non-endemic and lowland species. The Park is an excellent place in which to study barbets; for example, at the Royal Society 1961 base camp above Poring Hot Springs no less than seven of the nine Bornean species were seen or heard, and an eighth was seen higher up the mountain.

From dawn until about 7 a.m. the barbets are busy feeding and are mostly quiet. Then the great barbet chorus rings out, from 7–9 a.m., and is followed by a good deal of calling throughout the day, ending with a second grand chorus at 4–6.30 p.m. when the barbets hand over abruptly to the cicadas. In high forest it is most difficult to see barbets actually calling, and much patience is needed to link a particular call to a particular species. Barbets hum, they do not sing, because the notes are sounded with the bill closed and the throat bulging out; at each note the tail dips.

The biological significance of barbet vocalism remains obscure. Why—alone among the birds of Borneo—do they sit in the tree-tops and call for hours on end, and apparently at all times of the year? There is no reason to suppose that it has anything to do with either breeding or territory. They are not gregarious birds, and (except for the Brown Barbet, which some authorities hold to be no barbet at all) one rarely sees more than two or three of one species together.

BROWN BARBET
(Calorhamphus fuliginosus)

This is the only barbet with no green in the plumage, which is brown above and pale greyish-yellow below from the breast. The note is a curious thin sibilant high-pitched whistle. The species extends throughout Malaysia, and may be seen at the lower elevations in the Park.

GOLD-WHISKERED BARBET
(Megalaima chrysopogon)

Up in the tree-tops this is not easy to distinguish on plumage from the two following species; the grey throat is perhaps the best guide. The largest species, and perhaps the noisiest of all, with a loud quick double note of coppersmith tone, 25 per 10 seconds, in a series of 30–50 double notes. The species extends throughout Malaysia and is a common bird in submontane forest.

MANY-COLOURED OR RED-CROWNED BARBET
(Megalaima rafflesi)

This has the whole forehead and crown crimson, whereas the Gold-whiskered Barbet and the Gaudy Barbet have the forehead yellow; it has its chin and throat blue whereas the Gold-whiskered Barbet has a grey chin, and the Gaudy Barbet a crimson one. The yellow patch below the eye does not extend forward below the eye to the bill as in the Gold-whiskered Barbet. But these niceties are not easy to observe high in the tree-tops. The call is distinctive, *took took* (pause) *took-took-took* ... to 10–15 notes at three per second. One of the best known of the lowland barbets. The species extends throughout most of Malaysia.

GAUDY OR RED-THROATED BARBET
(Megalaima mystacophanes)

For the male, see under the preceding species; the female has the forehead and throat greenish-blue. The call consists of two short notes followed by a series of 10–15 resonant notes at the rate of two per second. The species is found in Malaya, Sumatra, and Borneo, and is abundant in lowland forest to 1400 m (4500 ft).

YELLOW-CROWNED BARBET
(Megalaima henrici)

The fore-crown and sides of the crown are yellow; centre and back of crown blue; and the throat blue with a red spot on the side that nearly joins a crimson collar on the nape. The call is very distinctive, *took-took-took-took-trrrook,* always four *tooks* followed by a rolling note, repeated for 10–20 seconds, each individual phrase lasting just over 1 second. Above the Poring Hot Springs it is noisy and persistent. A common submontane species in Malaya, Sumatra, and Borneo.

GOLDEN-NAPED BARBET
(Megalaima pulcherrima)

The fore-crown, centre of crown, nape, and throat are blue; with a golden collar on the nape. The call is *took-took-trrrook, took-took-trrroook,* etc., always two *tooks*. This is the real highlander among the barbets, ranging from 900–3050 m (3000 to 10,000 ft) on Mt. Kinabalu, but seldom seen or heard below 1500 m (5000 ft). It is one of the three barbets endemic to Borneo, extending southwards along the higher mountain ranges to Mt. Murud and Mt. Mulu.

MOUNTAIN BARBET
(Megalaima monticola)

It is easily confused with the female Gaudy Barbet, even in the hand. There is no red spot in front of the eye, the red on the crown is at the back and not on the top, and there is a small red spot on the side of the throat; the bill is much shorter. The call resembles a metronome gone mad *took-took-took-took...* (hiccup etc. at the rate of five *tooks* per second, so fast that it sounds just as if the bird is giving itself hiccups at intervals). It is endemic to Borneo, but a common montane species almost throughout the island. In spite of its name it is not, on Mt. Kinabalu, nearly such a high mountain bird as the Golden-naped Barbet, and I have not seen it above 1500 m (5000 ft).

BLACK-THROATED BARBET
(Megalaima eximia)

This is a much smaller bird, the size of the Little Barbet, with which it is easily confused on plumage; the main differences are that there is no red immediately above and below the eye, and the chin and upper throat are blue in the Kinabalu subspecies, whereas in the Little Barbet the chin is pale blue and the throat is black. A much quieter bird than the other barbets, its call has not been accurately recorded. This is the third of the barbet species endemic to Borneo, where it is a common montane species throughout. It is not confined to forest, but comes regularly out into the open and cultivated country, especially among groves of fruit trees.

LITTLE OR BLUE-EARED BARBET
(Megalaima australis)

See under the preceding species. Other features are a crimson patch on the crown and a yellow spot below the eye. The usual call is a double *to-rook, to-rook,* etc. It will be heard in the lower parts of the Park. The species is widespread in S.E. Asia and the commonest barbet in Borneo, where it is a familiar bird of rubber gardens and cultivated areas.

NON-ENDEMIC MONTANE SPECIES AND LOWLAND SPECIES

Another group of montane species, about 31 in all, comprises species that are not endemic to Borneo. The more interesting or conspicuous among them are described in the following notes, along with lowlanders that are likely to be seen frequently in the Park.

CRESTED SERPENT EAGLE
(Spilornis cheela)

A large dark-brown eagle, its a black-and-white crest, is very prominent when erected. In flight the wings appear very broad and rounded; a narrow black border and a broad white band behind it running along the whole length of the hind edge of the wing and across the tip of the tail make this bird easy to recognize overhead. Rather noisy, frequently uttering on the wing a plaintive whistling call of several notes, *kuk-kuk-kuk-kuk-kuk-queer-queer-queer,* the *kuks* forming a preliminary run up the scale. Fairly common, and often seen soaring high over Park Headquarters. It feeds mainly on reptiles such as snakes and rock lizards, but has a varied diet. The species is found throughout Borneo, and has wide distribution in S.E. Asia.

MOUNTAIN IMPERIAL PIGEON
(Ducula badia)

This large pigeon has a distinctive call *click-whroom-whroom;* the preliminary *click* is only audible at close range, but the *whroom-whroom* is a melodious booming call that resounds across the mountain valleys. On Mt. Kinabalu it is one of the characteristic bird sounds to be heard around Kundasang in November, whereas in July it is only heard occasionally. The species is widespread in S.E. Asia, and common throughout the mountain ranges of Borneo.

RUDDY CUCKOO-DOVE
(Macropygia emiliana)

This is distinguished from the Little Cuckoo dove *(Macropygia ruficeps)*, which it closely resembles in general colour, by a considerably larger size and longer tail and a purplish-brown breast with inconspicuous black barring; the Little Cuckoo Dove has a brown or buff breast heavily marked with black, a purplish-brown belly, not buff-brown, and a different voice. The call is a mournful *tok-wao* repeated several times. It frequents both primary and secondary forest. The nest and eggs are described by Whitehead. On Mt. Kinabalu it is sometimes seen near the Park Headquarters. The species has a wide range from Malaysia to Australia, and is sparingly distributed through Borneo.

LITTLE CUCKOO-DOVE
(Macropygia ruficeps)

A small purplish-brown dove, the breast is buff (in the male) or brown (in the female) and heavily marked with black. The call is *croo-wuck, croo-wuck...* repeated very rapidly, about 30 times in 15 seconds, then a pause of five seconds, and then repeated again; the *croo* is only audible at close range, and all than can be heard from a distance is *wuck, wuck, wuck,* etc. The booming of the mountain imperial pigeon *(Ducula badia)* and the call of this little dove are among obvious and distinctive sounds of the mountainsides. On the East ridge I have seen a nest with young at 2950 m (9700 ft) in July. The species is widespread in S.E. Asia, and found throughout Borneo as a submontane resident.

LARGE HAWK-CUCKOO
(Cuculus sparverioides)

This is deceptively like a small Sparrow-Hawk or Goshawk *(Accipiter* spp.*)* in plumage pattern and style of flight. The crown, nape and sides of neck are ashy grey, passing into rich ashy brown on the rest of the upperparts; the tail is above brown, banded with blackish and tipped with white or rufous-white; the breast rufous. The call, a loud *brain-fever* or *pipeeah,* is one of the characteristic sounds of the Kundasang–Bundu Tuhan road in the breeding season. Breeding is not recorded in Borneo; in India spiderhunters and laughing-thrushes are among the most popular victims. The species is widespread in S.E. Asia; one subspecies breeds in Borneo along the higher mountain ranges, another subspecies is a rare winter visitor to the lowlands.

ORIENTAL CUCKOO
(Cuculus saturatus)

In plumage this closely resembles the Common Cuckoo *(C. canorus)*. The call of the resident race is heard everywhere on Mt. Kinabalu at 1200–2150 m (4000–7000 ft) in February–March; it consists of a triple hoot *hoop, hoop-hoop*, with the slightest possible pause after the first *hoop*; very like the call of the Hoopoe *(Upupa epops)*, but birds have been watched at close range actually making the call, and the Hoopoe is unknown on Mt. Kinabalu. The species breeds in Siberia, Japan, and the Himalayas to Burma and Formosa and reaches Australia in winter.

MOUNTAIN SCOPS OWL
(Otus spilochephalus)

This little owl is reddish-brown finely speckled all over with black and buff. Whitehead found it in moss forest at 2750 m (9000 ft) and never heard it utter a sound. Needs further investigation. The species is widespread in S.E. Asia, and in Borneo extends southwards along the higher mountain ranges to Mt. Mulu and Mt. Dulit.

COLLARED OWLET
(Glaucidium brodiei)

The small size and absence of ear-tufts distinguish this from the scops owls. It utters a distinctive *tonk-ta-tonk-tonk,* high pitched and rather metallic, often heard during the day as well as at night. Further notes on it in the Park are needed. The species is widespread in S.E. Asia, and is probably found on most of the mountains in Borneo.

MALAYSIAN EARED NIGHTJAR
(Eurostopodus temmincki)

The beautiful three-note whistle *tod tadau* may be heard in the Park at the lower elevations (e.g., round Ranau and above Poring Hot Springs).

LARGE-TAILED NIGHTJAR
(Caprimulgus macrurus)

Everyone in Borneo is familiar with the call of the *tok tok* bird. It is a rich note, deliberate and loud, repeated very steadily at the rate of about 15 toks in ten seconds. It has been collected at Bundu Tuhan, and should therefore be heard around the Park.

WREATHED HORNBILL
(Rhyticeros undulatus)

This is the species of hornbill most likely to be seen in the National Park and has been seen as high as 3350 m (11,000 ft), though the Rhinoceros Hornbill *(Buceros rhinoceros)* is an occasional visitor. The large size, an *all white tail,* and white sides of the head and neck (these parts often stained yellow) are diagnostic. The crown is chestnut in the male, black in the female. The iris and bare skin round the eye are cherry red; the bare skin of the throat yellow or blue or both. I have counted a flock of 12 at 1700 m (5500 ft) on the East ridge. Remarkable for the loud resonant swish of the wings in flight and the deep *rowkh rowkh* of its call resounding over the mountain side. The species is widespread in S.E. Asia and sparingly distributed through Borneo, mainly in submontane areas.

WOODPECKERS

These are mostly birds of the lowland forests. The species most likely to be seen in the Park are:-

CRIMSON-WINGED WOODPECKER
(Picus puniceus)
and CHECKERED-THROATED WOODPECKER
(Picus mentalis)

Both green woodpeckers with a good deal of crimson on the wings and yellow crests at the back of the head. The first has a crimson crown and pale brown throat and breast, whereas the second has an olive-brown crown and a black-and-white checkered throat and rufous-chestnut breast. Both are widespread in Malaysia.

MAROON WOODPECKER
(Blythipicus rubiginosus)

Ivory-white bill and maroon back and wings diagnostic. It has been recorded up to 1500 m (5000 ft) on Mt. Kinabalu. The species occurs in Malaya, Sumatra, Borneo.

ORANGE-BACKED WOODPECKER
(Reinwardtipicus)

As the bird flies away the orange back of the male or the whitish back of the female are diagnostic. Head and crest are crimson in the male, brown in the female. The species is widespread in Malaysia.

PITTAS

These are also mainly birds of the lowland forests. The species most likely to be seen in the Park around Poring are:-

BLUE-BANDED PITTA
(Pitta arquata)

An unmistakable pitta, mostly crimson with green wings, it has a blue band across the chest and a blue line leading back from the eye. Whitehead found it on Mt. Kinabalu at 550–1200 m (2000–4000 ft) in thick bamboo jungle. It is endemic to Borneo.

BANDED PITTA
(Pitta guajana)

It has conspicuous yellow eyebrows from the bill over the eye to the nape. The rest of the head is dark; the back and wings brown, with a white wing-bar; chin and throat pale yellow; rest of underparts closely banded black and yellow; tail blue; and there is a blue patch on the belly of the male but not of the female. It frequents old jungle and goes up to 1500 m (5000 ft) on Mt. Kinabalu. The species is distributed over most of Malaysia.

BLACK-FACED CUCKOO-SHRIKE
(Coracina larvata)

All darkish grey, the crown and throat is black in the male, and grey in the female. It utters a long whistling call. It takes animal food. The nest and eggs are not described from Borneo. Conspicuous at high altitudes in moss forest, it is one of the commonest tree birds there. The species inhabits the Greater Sundas, and in Borneo extends southwards along the higher mountain ranges to the Usun Apau plateau and Mt. Dulit.

BAR-WINGED FLYCATCHER-SHRIKE
(Hemipus picatus)

A small bird, black above, white below, it has a white rump and broad white wing-bar and wing-band; the tail feathers are tipped with white. Its voice is not described from Borneo. Not uncommon on Mt. Kinabalu at 900–1200 m (3000–4000 ft). Takes animal food. Nest and eggs not described from Borneo. The species is widespread in S.E. Asia and a montane resident throughout the mountains of Borneo (rarely also at sea level).

MOUNTAIN OR GREY-CHINNED MINIVET
(Pericrocotus solaris)

The male is black and red, the female grey and yellow. It is the only montane minivet in Borneo. They travel about in small flocks, or in the mixed hunting parties so characteristic of montane forests. Nests and eggs are not described from Borneo. Widespread in S.E. Asia, it is one of the conspicuous birds on Mt. Kinabalu at 900–2150 m (3000–7000 ft), and extends southwards to Mt. Mulu and Mt. Dulit.

BLUE-WINGED LEAFBIRD
(Chloropsis cochinchinensis)

This is the species of leafbird most likely to be seen in the Park, and is distinguished from the others by blue on the wings; both male and female have a black throat in the montane subspecies, which some authorities treat as a separate species. Usually seen in low scrub, the species is widespread in S.E. Asia. The montane subspecies is abundant in the higher mountains of Borneo.

BULBULS

Most species live in the lowlands. The following are the ones most likely to be seen in the Park:—

BLACK-CRESTED BULBUL
(Pycnonotus melanicterus)

A very lively and noisy bird with a long black crest, it is not a forest species, frequenting scrub and hill padi farms, and is common in most of the mountains of Borneo though Whitehead considered it decidedly scarce on Mt. Kinabalu. The species is widespread in S.E. Asia.

PALE-FACED OR FLAVESCENT BULBUL
(Pycnonotus flavescens)

This superficially resembles the Yellow-vented Bulbul *(P. goiavier)*, the common lowland species that is often seen in more open areas, but the under tail-coverts are a deeper richer yellow. This is the real highlander among the bulbuls, in the mornings ranging up to 3500 m (11,500 ft) to feed on berries but found as low as 900 m (3000 ft). The species is widespread in S.E. Asia.

OCHRACEOUS BULBUL
(Criniger ochraceus)

A brown bird, it has a white throat, the feathers of which are frequently puffed out. A common, conspicuous and garrulous bird with loud call-notes, it frequents scrub rather than high forest. It has been seen at 2650 m (8700 ft). The species is widespread in S.E. Asia, and occurs throughout the mountain ranges of Borneo.

ASHY BULBUL
(Hypsipetes flavala)

The contrast of yellowish-green wings and tail with white throat, grey breast, and bright yellow under tail-coverts is diagnostic. The white feathers of the throat are often puffed out, as in the Ochraceous Bulbul. It is widespread in S.E. Asia and abundant throughout the mountains of Borneo, though there seem to be no actual notes from the Mt. Kinabalu area.

BLUE OR WHITE-BROWED SHORTWING
(Brachypteryx montana)

Best identified as a short-tailed long-legged bird of the moss forest or of the bare rock above the tree-line, the male is dark blue with a concealed white eyebrow; female reddish-brown with only the mantle blue. The alarm note is a rich low note, like that made when two pebbles are struck together. Feeds on insects. Nests and eggs are not described from Borneo. The species is widespread in S.E. Asia, but in Borneo (apart from Mt. Kinabalu) it has been recorded only from Mt. Trus Madi, Mt. Mulu, and Bario.

SUNDA WHISTLING THRUSH
(Myophonus glaucinus)

Found along rocky streams 550–2750 m (2000–9000 ft), the male is dark purplish-blue, the female browner. The species is confined to the Greater Sundas, and in Borneo is found more or less throughout in submontane localities.

Fig.7. Grey-and-Brown Laughing Thrush *(Garrulax palliatus)*, a montane resident common around Park Headquarters. *(Photo: D. Wechsler © VIREO)*

BABBLERS

Babblers are mostly birds of the lowland forest in Borneo, and it is only necessary to mention three species here.

TEMMINCK'S BABBLER
(Trichastoma pyrrhogenys)

Its crown is dark greyish-brown with pale streaks; the upper-parts rufous-brown; throat white; and the breast and sides of belly rufous, the centre of belly being white. The voice is not recorded. Eggs have been collected on Mt. Kinabalu in March. Described by Whitehead as fairly common on the lower slopes at 900–1200 m (3000–4000 ft), the species is confined to the Greater Sunda Islands.

CHESTNUT-BACKED SCIMITAR BABBLER
(Pomatorhinus montanus)

Its crown and sides of the head are black with long conspicuous white eyebrows; upperparts rufous; underparts white; it has a long curved bill. The usual call, commonly heard at 1150–1700 m (3500–5500 ft) on Mt. Kinabalu, is a loud but mellow triple hoot. It lives in the undergrowth of the montane forest. The nest and eggs are described by Whitehead. Widespread in S.E. Asia, and found throughout Borneo in submontane localities, it is the only representative of a genus that has many species in the Himalayas, mountains of Burma, etc.

GREY-THROATED BABBLER
(Stachyris nigriceps)

This has rather rich brown plumage, a yellow ring round the eye, a white cheek patch, and a grey crown streaked with white. The voice is unknown in Borneo, but Whitehead described the nest and eggs. It frequents both high forest and scrub. The species is widespread in S.E. Asia.

BLACK LAUGHING-THRUSH
(Garrulax lugubris)

This odd bird has the whole crown and naked face skin of a greenish-yellow colour, yellower at the base of the bill; or as W.S. Gilbert would have put it (hence *lugubris*):

> "A greenery-yallery, Grosvenor Gallery,
> Foot-in-the-grave young man."

The bare skin of the neck is dull bluish green, the bill vermillion; and the plumage blackish. It utters a loud booming note *queer-queer-hoop-hoop-hoop*. It creeps about the trees like the Chestnut-capped Laughing-Thrush, but looks much longer, less fluffy and generally less active. The nest and eggs are not described from Borneo. A forest bird of the 1200 m (4000 ft) zone. The species lives in Malaya, Sumatra, and Borneo.

GREY-AND-BROWN LAUGHING-THRUSH
(Garrulax palliatus)

The wings and tail are reddish-brown; the rest of the plumage blackish; and a patch of blue skin is under the eye. Cheerful and conspicuous with a noisy whistle. Primarily a vegetable feeder, it also takes insects. The nest and eggs are not described from Mt. Kinabalu. The species lives in Sumatra and Borneo, where its range is similar to that of the Black Laughing-Thrush.

CHESTNUT-CAPPED LAUGHING-THRUSH
(Garrulax mitratus)

It has a distinctive chestnut head, grey plumage above, a conspicuous white wing-patch, and a chestnut colour under the tail. It utters a loud whistling note *wu-twuu-twuu-twuu*, the last notes descending in pitch, and strikes up a hearty dawn chorus 6–6.30 a.m. This bird is one of the ornithological features of the lower slopes of Mt. Kinabalu, but it is also found more sparingly up to the limit of tree growth. The nest and eggs are described by Whitehead. The species occurs in Malaya, Sumatra, and Borneo.

WHITE-BROWED SHRIKE-BABBLER
(Pteruthius flaviscapis)

The sexes differ. The male has the top and sides of the head black with a long white eyebrow starting just above the eye, and a chestnut and yellow patch on the wing; the female is grey with an indistinct eyebrow and no yellow on the wing. It has a distinctive call-note *cha-chew, cha-chew* or *cha-cha-chip, cha-cha-chip*. An arboreal bird, it keeps much to the tree-tops, searching the main branches for insects. The nest is a cradle of fine roots slung from a fork. A bird of the moss forest, it is fairly common around 2750 m (9000 ft). The species is widespread in S.E. Asia and a familiar bird of the Himalayas.

CHESTNUT-CRESTED YUHINA
(Yuhina everetti)

A striking gay little bird, easily identified by tit-like habits, an erectile chestnut crest, and white outer tail feathers; the throat is often puffed out. It constantly utters harsh or twittering notes, as the active flocks, that may number 20 birds, flit from tree to tree. This and the Chestnut-capped Laughing-Thrush are the two most characteristic birds of the Kundasang–Bundu Tuhan road. The nest and eggs have been described by several authors. The species is widespread in S.E. Asia, and in Borneo (where it is the only representative of a well-known Himalayan genus) it is common throughout in submontane localities.

WHITE-BELLIED YUHINA
(Yuhina zantholeuca)

A rather nondescript bird with olive-green upperparts, it has white underparts, and a short erectile crest. Though normally silent, it has a characteristic sharp-toned wheezy squeaking note. Whitehead met with it in small parties at 1500 m (5000 ft) on Mt. Kinabalu. The species is widespread in S.E. Asia, and found throughout Borneo in submontane localities.

MOUNTAIN LEAF-WARBLER
(Phylloscopus trivirgatus)

It has an olive-yellow crown with two irregular black bands on the sides; a black line through the eyes; and is olive-green above and pale olive below (not bright yellow in the Kinabalu subspecies). It has a thin high-pitched song and various call-notes. A common bird of Mt. Kinabalu at 1500–3050 m (5000–10,000 ft), and at Park Headquarters, it can usually be found low down in primary forest at the edge of the road in company with other birds. The species is widespread from Malaysia to the Solomons.

YELLOW-BREASTED WARBLER
(Seicercus montis)

This differs from the above in its chestnut crown and double wing-bar. It is described as having an extremely irritating high-pitched song of disjointed notes, starting at first daylight. On Mt. Kinabalu it is most often seen in thick bamboo undergrowth. The nest and eggs are not described from Borneo. The species has a wide range from Malaya to Timor.

WHITE-THROATED FLYCATCHER-WARBLER
(Abroscopus superciliaris)

The grey head with a narrow white eyebrow and white throat, distinguish this from the Mountain Leaf-Warbler and the Yellow-breasted Warbler; it also has the underparts bright yellow. According to Whitehead it has a very pleasing song. Like the Yellow-breasted Warbler it frequents the tangled bamboo thickets on the steep flanks of Mt. Kinabalu. The species is widespread in S.E.Asia, and a common submontane resident in Borneo.

MOUNTAIN TAILORBIRD
(Orthotomus cuculatus)

Its cap is orange, nape grey, upperparts olive-green, throat greyish-white, and the remaining underparts are bright yellow. Its song is unmistakable, consisting of a four-note whistle, the first two notes on the same pitch, the third a trill, and the fourth sometimes higher sometimes lower in pitch than the first two, the whole repeated in a remarkable number of different keys, high and low. It frequents bamboo thickets, but keeps low down and is difficult to see. The nest and eggs are not described from Borneo. The species is widespread in S.E. Asia.

WHITE-THROATED FANTAIL
(Rhipidura albicollis)

This is a dark grey bird with narrow white eyebrow, white throat, and narrow white tips to the outer tail feathers; it has a habit of fanning the tail. (A white-spotted breast and much longer white tips to the outer tail feathers distinguish the Spotted Fantail Flycatcher *(Rhipidura perlata)* which is sighted occasionally.) The song consists of four ascending notes and two or three descending ones, the intervals irregular, rather high-pitched and thin in tone—one of the distinctive sounds around Park Headquarters. Occurs in both primary and secondary forest and scrub, 1200–2750 m (4000–9000 ft). The nest and eggs have been described from Mt. Dulit. The species is distributed from the Himalayas to Malaysia.

GREY-HEADED FLYCATCHER
(Culicicapa ceylonensis)

The grey head, olive-green upperparts and yellow underparts are diagnostic. The constantly uttered call *silly-billy* attracts attention. A bold and friendly bird of the forest undergrowth, it may be seen around the lower slopes of Mt. Kinabalu. Whitehead describes a nest and eggs he found close to his camp. The species is widespread in S.E. Asia, and occurs throughout Borneo in submontane localities, and locally up to 1700 m (5500 ft).

INDIGO FLYCATCHER
(Eumyias indigo)

The male is an indigo-blue flycatcher with some light blue on the forecrown, a black face, and its belly and under tail-coverts are fulvous. The female is described as having a pale ring round the eye; the back is olive-brown with several whitish 'V's formed by the edge of wing primaries and secondaries; the side of throat and belly mottled, the centre of belly white; and the legs are very dark. The tips of wings almost touch the tip of the tail. A very tame bird with a squeaky song, it is a bird of the moss forest, taking both animal and vegetable food; and one of the characteristic birds of the 1500–1800 m (5000–6000 ft) zone. The nest and eggs are not described from Borneo. The species lives in the Greater Sundas.

SNOWY-BROWED BLUE FLYCATCHER
(Ficedula hyperythra)

The male has the upperparts dark bluish-grey with white at the base of the tail (not easy to see in the field); the wings and tail are blackish; eyebrows short and white; chin black; throat and breast rusty; and belly whitish. The female differs in being greyish-brown above and has a buff throat and belly. A very tame bird of the moss forest, it takes both insects and berries. The nest and eggs are described by Whitehead. On Mt. Kinabalu it is fairly plentiful at 1200–2450 m (4000–8000 ft) and goes up to 3350 m (11,000 ft). The species is widespread in S.E. Asia, and in Borneo extends southwards along the higher mountain ranges.

LITTLE PIED FLYCATCHER
(Ficedula westermanni)

The male has its upperparts black; a broad eyebrow, a patch on the wing, basal half of the lateral tail feathers, and the whole underparts white; the female is olive-brown above, with its upper tail coverts rufous, underparts whitish down the centre, and is grey on the sides of the breast. It utters a thin high *pi-pi-pi-pi* followed by a low rattle. A bird of the moss forest, common at 1500–2450 m (5000–8000 ft). The nest and eggs are described by Whitehead. The species is widespread in S.E. Asia, and in Borneo extends southwards along the higher mountain ranges.

PYGMY BLUE FLYCATCHER
(Muscicapella hodgsoni)

Its small size and thin narrow bill are distinctive. The male is bright blue above, with the crown and rump vivid; the forehead and sides of head are black; the underparts rusty. The female is olive-brown above, buffy-white below; with no black on the chin. The species is widespread in the mountains of S.E. Asia, but nothing is known of its habits, etc., in Borneo apart from the fact that it has been collected on Mt. Kinabalu up to 1800 m (6000 ft) and on Mt. Dulit. It is a rare bird on which more notes are needed.

Several other species of blue flycatcher may be seen in the Park, especially at the lower elevations. A number of winter visitors also come to the Park, e.g., **Sooty or Dark-sided Flycatcher** *(M. sibirica)*, **Asian Brown Flycatcher** *(M. latirostris)*, **Ferruginous Flycatcher** *(M. ferruginea)*, **Blue-and-White Flycatcher** *(Cyanoptila cyanomelana)*, **Black-and-Orange Flycatcher** *(Ficidula mugimaki)*, all of which may be seen from about October to April.

WHITE-BROWED JUNGLE FLYCATCHER
(Rhinomyias gularis)

This is an olive-brown flycatcher with a distinct eyebrow; the throat is white, contrasting with and sharply demarcated from the grey breast. A silent bird of the 900–2150 m (3000–7000 ft) zone on Mt. Kinabalu, it is commoner at the higher elevations. The nest and eggs are described by Whitehead. The species is found in the Philippines and Borneo, where it extends southwards along the higher mountain ranges.

BLACK-SIDED FLOWERPECKER
(Dicaeum monticolum)

The scarlet throat and breast of the male is diagnostic; the female is olive-grey. It utters high piercing notes and eats quite large fruit and a variety of insects. It frequents mistletoe flowers on forest trees. The nest has been described from Bario. Fairly common on Mt. Kinabalu around 1200 m (4000 ft), the species is confined to the Celebes and Borneo.

SCARLET SUNBIRD
(Aethopyga mystacalis)

The male is scarlet down to the waist, with a scarlet tail and light grey belly; the female has its head and throat grey, with a greenish tinge on the neck and breast, and the wings and tail are washed with red. Found on Mt. Kinabalu up to 1800 m (6000 ft), it is probably most abundant in the 1200–1500 m (4000–5000 ft) zone, where epiphytes are plentiful. The species ranges through Malaysia, and is found throughout the mountains of Borneo at moderate elevations.

BLACK-CAPPED WHITE-EYE
Zosterops atricapillus)

The black forehead distinguishes this from other white-eyes. Its upperparts are olive-green, throat and breast yellowish, and flanks grey. The habit and voice are not described from Borneo, but Whitehead described a nest found at 1500 m (5000 ft). Quite common round Park Headquarters, the species lives in Malaya, Sumatra, and Borneo.

EVERETT'S WHITE-EYE
(Zosterops everetti)

This differs from the Black-capped White-eye mainly in lacking the black forehead. Fairly common on the lower slopes of Mt. Kinabalu, it ascends to 1700 m (5500 ft) or more. The species lives in Thailand, Malaya, and western Borneo.

BAMBOO MUNIA OR TAWNY-BREASTED PARROTFINCH
(Erythrura hyperythra)

The forehead is black, crown blue, upperparts including tail green; and the underparts are rufous. While on the wing it continually utters its call-note, which is a hissing sound like *tzit-tzit*. It is a rather rare bird of the bamboo thickets at 1500–2750 m (5000–9000 ft) on which more information is needed. The species is widely distributed in the Philippines and Malaysia, but in Borneo known only from Mt. Kinabalu and Mt. Mulu.

GREY OR ASHY DRONGO
(Dicrurus leucophaeus)

The prominent white lores and a light grey plumage are diagnostic; the iris is orange-red. It has various calls. Like the Chestnut-capped Laughing Thrush, one of the ornithological features of the lower slopes of Mt. Kinabalu and round Park Headquarters, it is much more abundant around the Dusun villages and rice fields than in high forest. The nest and eggs are described by several authors. The species is widespread in S.E. Asia, and common in the mountains of Borneo.

SPANGLED DRONGO
(Dicrurus hottentottus)

This has a glossy black plumage, spangled with blue on the head and breast. The shape of the tail is diagnostic, with the outer feathers prominently curved outward and upward. The hairs springing from the forehead, from which the bird derives its name, are not easy to see in the field. It is not as abundant as the previous species and more of a forest bird. The nest and eggs are described by Whitehead. The species is well known in S.E. Asia, and is found throughout submontane Borneo in primary forest.

BLACK-AND-CRIMSON ORIOLE
(Oriolus cruentus)

This is black with a crimson belly. Its call is a nasal mew, like some notes of other orioles. It is a bird of the moss forest. The nest and eggs are not described from Borneo. The species is distributed throughout Malaysia, and in Borneo extends southwards along the higher mountain ranges.

COMMON GREEN MAGPIE
(Cissa chinensis),
and SHORT-TAILED GREEN MAGPIE
Cissa thalassina)

The Common Green Magpie occurs mainly between 300 and 900 m (1000 and 3000 ft) (rarely higher) and the Short-Tailed Green Magpie between 900 and 2450 m (3000 and 8000 ft), so they could both be found in the same area. The plumage is confusingly similar but the second species has a shorter tail, with narrow greenish-white tips to the feathers and the crown is without any trace of yellow. Whitehead could distinguish them by voice, saying that the note of the Short-tailed Green Magpie is not nearly so clear as that of the Common Green Magpie, but is still a feeble attempt at *ton-ka-kis*. Both species are widespread in S.E. Asia and Malaysia, but the Short-tailed Green Magpie only at the higher elevations. In Borneo it extends southwards along the higher mountain ranges.

Fig.8. Feeding on fruits and insects in the forest canopy, the Malaysian Treepie *(Dendrocitta occipitalis)* makes harsh cries and a range of bell-like musical notes sometimes audible from half a kilometre away. *(Photo: Morten Strange)*

MALAYSIAN TREEPIE
(Dendrocitta occipitalis)

An unmistakable bird with a raucous voice, it is common on Mt. Kinabalu up to 2750 m (9000 ft), both in primary and secondary forest. The nest and eggs are described by Whitehead. The species is confined to Sumatra and Borneo, where it inhabits the northern and central mountains.

The above notes should be sufficient to demonstrate that, in modern terms, we know hardly anything about the birds of Mt. Kinabalu, apart from a general idea of what species occur and where. Accurate field descriptions are lacking for many species, both in regard to plumage and to voice. Breeding biology, apart from descriptions of nests and eggs, has hardly been touched.

Modern mist-netting techniques have been little tried, except to trap birds for ringing (banding). Dr. Fogden's studies (Ibis 114(3): 307–343, 1972) based on mist-netting data, on the ecology and population dynamics of forest birds in lowland Sarawak, demonstrate how much can be achieved by these methods, which are invaluable for studying shy and skulking forest birds.

Thus the Kinabalu Park has much to offer the visitor, whether a casual bird-watcher out to see a few interesting species during a short visit, or a serious student out to embark on a doctoral thesis requiring several years' study.

REFERENCES

Various authors. 1961. A discussion on the results of the Royal Society expedition to North Borneo. *Proceedings of the Royal Society, London*, B, 161: 1–91 (1964).

Smith, J.M.B. 1972. Natural history of the Kinabalu buttercup. *Malayan Nature Journal* 25: 90–100.

Smythies, B.E. 1981. The Birds of Borneo (3rd edition). The Sabah Society, Kota Kinabalu, with Malayan Nature Society, Kuala Lumpur.

Whitehead, J. 1893. Exploration of Kina Balu, North Borneo. Gurney & Jackson, London.

Fig.1. Black-naped Monarch Flycatcher *(Hypothymis azurea).*
(Photo: D. Wechsler © VIREO)

AN ANNOTATED CHECKLIST OF THE BIRDS OF KINABALU PARK

D.V. Jenkins & G.S. de Silva,
revised by **D.R. Wells & A. Phillipps**

The purpose of this paper is to provide an easy reference to the scattered works of ornithologists, scientific expeditions, and collectors who have over the years, worked in the Mt. Kinabalu area, which includes Poring Hot Springs, Kampungs Kiau, Kaung, Bundu Tuhan, Nalumad, and Kundasang and the Liwagu and Kadamaian valleys. A checklist of the avifauna of Mt. Kinabalu and in particular of the area presently known as the Kinabalu Park has been a long-felt need and a requirement for the greater appreciation of the park's ecology. The park covers an area of some 753 sq. km (291 sq. miles) and it has been impossible or impractical to cover its whole length and breadth. We have drawn heavily from the literature but further material of difficult accessibility or publications unknown to us may exist. Readers are therefore requested to communicate with the Sabah Society if they are aware of any papers or material unlisted here.

This revised checklist includes only those species of birds recorded by research workers and other reliable observers or collected by scientific expeditions in the area of the mountain and unless indicated to the contrary, citations in the text refer exclusively to Mt. Kinabalu itself. Wherever possible notes have been added by us. Initials indicate the source of data. Except where indicated, we have followed Smythies (1981) for taxonomic order and for English and scientific names but have used common English names from the "Checklist of the Birds of Sabah" by C.M. Francis (1986), while others in common use are also included. We appreciate that others may now disagree with Smythies' systematics, but his book "The Birds of Borneo" remains the only easily accessible reference to the avifauna of the area. We have therefore, in an attempt to avoid confusion, followed his work. Where in a few cases scientific names used in this revision of the Checklist differ from those used in Smythies (1981) this has been indicated. To eliminate confusion, local names (which can vary among villages) have not been used; there is also the possibility that local names are sometimes invented if in doubt, or to please the enquirer.

Sight records have been included in this paper although we realise that such records are unacceptable to some museum-based ornithologists. However, the sightings recorded here are only those made by observers we regard as reliable, of birds which should be present in the park area. Further ornithological work should confirm the presence of the birds so listed.

Some 306 species have now been recorded in the Mt. Kinabalu area. Of these 262 species are resident and 23 are endemic to Borneo. Twenty-seven species are passage migrants and winter visitors, six species are of uncertain status and ten of the resident species also have migrant populations. They are distributed among 46 families.

ALTITUDINAL DISTRIBUTION OF BIRDS

Smythies (1981) recognises four zones of distribution of resident bird species in Bornean mountains, i.e., Higher Montane; Montane; Sub-montane and Lowland, and classified them as follows:

Higher Montane birds are those found only on mountains exceeding 1500 m (5000 ft) but on such mountains may be found well below the 1500 m contour.

Montane birds are those found only on mountains exceeding 900 m (3000 ft), but on such mountains may occasionally be found below the 900 m (3000 ft) contour.

Lowland birds are those found on the plains and foothills, but some species ascend into the montane zone up to 1500 m (5000 ft), or more.

Sub-montane birds are less well defined, but link the lowland and montane zones. They avoid the flat coastal plains, but in mountainous country, they do come down almost to sea level.

All four classes are present in the Kinabalu area, and within the boundaries of the Kinabalu Park.

Though the avifaunal survey of Kinabalu is still incomplete—the north and north-east of the mountain being virtually inaccessible and unexplored—there is little chance that any new species endemic to the mountain will emerge. Several publications show that Kinabalu birds also occur in the mountains of Sarawak and along the spinal chain from Mt. Kinabalu. For instance, the Kinabalu Friendly Warbler (*Bradypterus accentor*), for many years thought to be endemic to Mt. Kinabalu, was found on Mt. Trus Madi, in 1956 by the Cambridge University Expedition, and on Mt. Tambuyukon in 1982.

VEGETATION AND BIRDS

Except for the highest slopes of Mt. Kinabalu, the foothills, valleys and mountains of the Park are covered with secondary and primary forest. Outside the park boundary, shifting cultivation is general, in some areas reaching an elevation of around 1500 m (5000 ft).

There is no indication that the botanical composition of the forest has any effect on the distribution of bird communities (Smythies, 1968), but the form of the forest has an effect. Certain species are strictly confined to primary forest and never emerge therefrom, some shun it and prefer secondary forest. Others live freely in both types of forest, and some prefer the more open environment of cultivated lands and around habitations. As shifting cultivation, roads and open disturbed ground creep closer towards the Park boundary, so do the birds that live in these habitats. The Magpie-Robin *(Copsychus saularis)* and the Chestnut Munia *(Lonchura malacca)* are two examples of generally lowland birds that have been seen on grass verges just outside the Park entrance, in recent years.

MIGRATION

There have been few studies of bird migration in Sabah, and little is known of the subject, but the Tenompok Pass at 1500 m (5000 ft), shortly before Park Headquarters is reached, may with investigation prove to be a route for migratory birds crossing the Crocker Range.

Q. Phillipps (1974, pers. comm.) spent two nights at the head of Tenompok Pass in October 1974 attempting to attract night-flying migrants by shining the lights of his vehicle down the Kadamaian valley. On the first night, which was moonless but clear, five birds were seen which included a wagtail and a warbler. On the second night, the sky was overcast for a period and during the first hour, thirty migrant birds were recorded which included five Blue-winged Pittas *(Pitta moluccensis)*, and an unidentified bittern.

Little is known about local migrations, but records of two bulbuls, usually found in the lowlands, at high altitudes are probably evidence that local migrations are much more extensive than previously realised. In the case of bulbuls, nomadism rather than true migration is more probable. One of the probable migratory routes to Borneo from China, Japan and Korea is by way of the inter-island chain from Japan and Taiwan through the Philippines to Sabah (McClure, 1973). The majority of birds arriving in Sabah from the Philippine islands would enter the country by way of the north and north-east coast, and in progressing south go to the east of Mt. Kinabalu and the Crocker Range. Some, however, go to the west of the Crocker Range and would have to cross the Range to continue southwards to the interior of Sabah and Indonesian Borneo. It has been shown for Peninsular Malaysia that the southern influx of migrants occurs on a broad front, irrespective of topography (Wells, 1973), and the same may be true for Sabah. Nevertheless, the Kadamaian valley which extends from Kota Belud to the Tenompok Pass is the first major valley leading to the Crocker Range that the birds would encounter, and could act as a funnel for migrants. Much more work and investigation is required before the significance of the pass can be ascertained.

SYSTEMATIC LIST

Abbreviations used to indicate sources of data are as follows:

B–Bober
BK–Ben King
BL–Berwick and Lathbury
Bs–Blasius
C–Chuang

K–Kuntz
KNP–Specimens in the bird collection at the
    Kinabalu Park Headquarters
KP–K. Phillipps
M–Medway

D–Dingley	P–Peters
de S–de Silva	PC–Pendlebury and Chasen
DY–D. Yong	PP–Q. Phillipps and J. Phillipps
E–Enriquez	RC–R. Crawford Prentice
F–Fogden	RY–R. Yamie
FL–Frank Lambert	S–Smythies
FR–F. Rosendaal	SH–Sharpe
FS–F. Sheldon	Sk–Sarawak Museum Ringing Records
G–Gore	SM–Sabah Museum Ringing Records
GH–Gibson-Hill	SP–Stella Pierce
H–Harrisson	SJ–S. Jacobson
J–Jenkins	TE–T. Ebenhard
Jn–Johnson	W–Whitehead
JS–J. Schmitt	WE–W. Eddie

Dr. R.E. Kuntz collected birds in Sabah during 1960 for the National Museum of Natural History, Smithsonian Institution, Washington, D.C. In September of that year he collected at Ranau but unfortunately, his collecting areas are not recorded. His Ranau skins (64 in number) are now at the Smithsonian Institution and where they confirm sight records and doubtful or ancient records they have been included.

ARDEIDAE : HERONS, EGRETS AND BITTERNS

1. ***Butorides striatus* (Linnaeus 1758) : Little (Green) Heron**
   A resident race *B.s. javanicus* and a winter visitor *B.s. amurensis*. Typical bird of rivers from tidal reaches to headwaters (S). One obtained by Whitehead in a rocky stream at the foot of Kinabalu.

ACCIPITRIDAE : HAWKS AND EAGLES

2. ***Macheiramphus alcinus* Bonaparte 1850 : Bat Hawk**
   Lone individuals seen at Park Headquarters at 1550 m (5100 ft) at dusk in 1980 (FR) and 1982 (FL).

3. ***Pernis ptilorhyncus* (Temminck 1821) : Crested Honey buzzard**
   Birds of the lowland forest edge. Resident and winter visitors to Borneo. *P.p. torquatus* is the resident race and *P.p. orientalis*, the visitor. Residents collected at 800 m (2700 ft) and 850 m (2800 ft) (Sk). Everett and Whitehead both collected specimens but no details of race given.

4. ***Haliastur indus* (Boddaert 1783) : Brahminy Kite**
   Normally a coastal resident. Irregular visitor to park area; observed by Whitehead at 300 m (1000 ft). Collected at Ranau 550 m (1800 ft) (K).

5. ***Accipiter soloensis* (Horsfield 1821) : Chinese Goshawk**
   A winter visitor. One collected at 300 m (1000 ft) by Whitehead in 1887.

6. *Accipiter trivirgatus* (Temminck 1824) : Crested Goshawk
   Resident lowland species. Whitehead collected specimens at 300 m (1000 ft) in 1887 and 1888. A specimen from 900 m (3000 ft) in 1913 (Sk).

7. *Accipiter gularis* (Temminck and Schlegel 1844) : Japanese Sparrowhawk
   A common winter visitor throughout Borneo (S). Sight record from Poring Hot Springs (500 m, 1700 ft) (BL), and collected by Whitehead at 300 m (1000 ft).

8. *Accipiter virgatus* (Temminck 1822) : Besra
   Sub-montane resident. Collected and many sight records from the mountain between 300 and 1500 m (1000 and 5000 ft).

9. *Butastur indicus* (Gmelin 1788) : Grey-faced Buzzard
   Passage migrant and winter visitor. Collected by Whitehead at 300 m (1000 ft) and also by Burbidge and by Everett (Sh), but no details of locality are available. Sight record at Park Headquarters in 1981 (RC & WE) and from around Kampung Bundu Tuhan, at *c*. 1300 m (4200 ft) 1982 (FS).

10. *Spizaetus cirrhatus* (Gmelin 1788) : Changeable Hawk Eagle
    Resident and sparingly distributed throughout Borneo (S).

11. *Spizaetus alboniger* (Blyth 1845) : Blyth's Hawk Eagle
    Resident; has a preference for mountains and sub-montane localities (S). One record from Poring Hot Springs (BL).

12. *Hieraaetus kienerii* (Geoffroy Saint-Hilaire 1835) : Rufous-bellied Eagle
    Probably resident but rare (G). One collected at 300 m (1000 ft) by Whitehead in 1887.

13. *Ictinaetus malayensis* (Temminck 1822) : Black Eagle
    Resident throughout Borneo from the coast to the hills but not common. Collected on Kinabalu by Everett (Sh) and by Griswold at 950 m (3100 ft) (P). A pair presumed to be of this species seen at Park Headquarters (J).

14. *Spilornis kinabaluensis* Sclater 1919 : Mountain or Kinabalu Serpent Eagle
    Endemic to Borneo and occurring throughout the higher mountains of Sabah, but rare (DY). Seen twice between Park Headquarters and the Power Station at 1900 m (6230ft) (DY). Collected by Whitehead above 1000 m (3000 ft).

15. *Spilornis cheela* (Latham 1790) : Crested Serpent Eagle
    Resident throughout Borneo, and probably the commonest eagle (DY). Seen several times above Park Headquarters (PP). Collected at Tenompok 1500 m (5000 ft) (B) and also by Whitehead.

FALCONIDAE : FALCONS

16. *Microhierax latifrons* **Sharpe 1879 : White-fronted Falconet**
    Confined to Borneo (S). Sight records from Ranau and Poring (BL, DY).

17. *Falco peregrinus* **Tunstall 1771 : Peregrine Falcon**
    Uncommon resident and winter visitor. Whitehead observed this bird at 2450 m (8000 ft). *F.p. ernesti* Sharpe 1894, the resident race, is thought to have been observed on Kinabalu (G); *F.p. japonensis* Gmelin 1788 is the winter visitor.

18. *Falco severus* **Horsfield 1821 : Oriental Hobby**
    Rare and possibly a vagrant. Specimen collected by Everett on Kinabalu (Sh). Sight record from Poring (DY).

19. *Falco tinnunculus* **Linnaeus 1758 : (Eurasian) Kestrel**
    Occasional winter visitor to Borneo. A sight record from Ranau in November 1959 (BL) and December 1972 (Jn).

PHASIANIDAE : QUAILS, PARTRIDGES AND PHEASANTS

20. *Coturnix chinensis* **(Linnaeus 1766) : Blue-breasted Quail**
    Resident. Seen up to 1200 m (4000 ft) on rough grassy slopes on Kinabalu (S). *C.c. lineata* (Scopoli 1786) is the Sabah race. Collected at 300 m (1000 ft) (W), and collected at Ranau (K). Several birds run over at the Park Headquarters complex collected (KNP).

21. *Arborophila hyperythra* **(Sharpe 1879) : Red-breasted Partridge**
    A montane species confined to Borneo, and common on Kinabalu from 1200 m to 1500 m (4000 to 5000 ft) (G). Collected by Whitehead between 600 m and 1200 m (2000 and 4000 ft). The Kinabalu race is *A.h. erythrophrys* (Sharpe 1890).

22. *Rollulus rouloul* **(Scopoli 1786) : Crested (Wood) Partridge**
    Resident in lowland forest (G), ascending to 1050 m (3500 ft) (S). Collected by Johnson in 1951 around Kampung Bundu Tuhan at *c.* 1200 m (4000 ft).

23. *Haematortyx sanguiniceps* **Sharpe 1879 : Crimson-headed Partridge**
    Common montane resident found up to 3050 m (10,000 ft) and confined to Borneo. A group with young observed in primary forest at 1900 m (6200 ft) in April (J). Resident on Kinabalu, usually in pairs (S). Seen and collected on several occasions at 1700 m (5500 ft).

24. *Argusianus argus* **(Linnaeus 1766) : Great Argus**
    A lowland resident. Collected at Ranau (K). Recorded near Poring (S) and call heard at about 900 m (3000 ft) above Poring (de S).

RALLIDAE : RAILS, CRAKES, MOORHENS, GALLINULES AND COOTS

25. *Rallina fasciata* **(Raffles 1822) : Red-legged Crake**
    Status uncertain on the mountain, but resident and migrant populations. Collected by Griswold on Kinabalu at 900 m (3000 ft) (P). No details of race given. A dead bird collected by staff at Park Headquarters, January 1987 (KNP).

26. *Amaurornis phoenicurus* **(Pennant 1769) : White-breasted Waterhen**
    A very common lowland resident. Two birds, possibly migrants, were observed at 1500 m (5000 ft) near Park Headquarters (J). Collected at Ranau (K).

SCOLOPACIDAE : SNIPES AND SANDPIPERS
27. *Actitis hypoleucos* **(Linnaeus 1758) : Common Sandpiper**
    Passage migrant and winter visitor. Collected on Kinabalu at 750 m (2500 ft) by Haviland in 1892 (Sk).

28. *Gallinago stenura* **(Bonaparte 1830) : Pintail Snipe**
    Winter visitor. Common in hill rice at Poring (FS).

COLUMBIDAE : PIGEONS AND DOVES
29. *Treron curvirostra* **(Gmelin 1789) : Thick-billed Pigeon**
    Resident throughout Borneo and collected on local night dispersal at 700 m on the Crocker Range (FS). A dead bird collected by Park staff from the parking lot, Park Headquarters, October 1988 (KNP). Commonest pigeon at Poring (PP). Collected in Ranau (K).

30. *Treron olax* **(Temminck 1823) : Little Green Pigeon**
    Resident and locally common throughout Borneo. Recorded from Poring, 1985 (KP & JS).

31. *Treron vernans* **(Linnaeus 1771) : Pink-necked Pigeon**
    Resident and the commonest pigeon in the lowlands. Found by Whitehead up to 300 m (1000 ft).

32. *Ptilinopus jambu* **(Gmelin 1789) : Jambu Fruit Dove**
    Resident throughout Borneo in the lowlands. Birds on local migration collected on a number of occasions, having killed themselves by flying into walls or windows at Park Headquarters. Nesting recorded at 1550 m (5100 ft) in 1985 (DY, SJ, FL). Also collected at 900 m (3000 ft) (W).

33. *Ducula aenea* **(Linnaeus 1766) : Green Imperial Pigeon**
    Widespread resident in the lowlands of Borneo. One collected by Griswold in 1937 at 950 m (3100 ft) (P). Several collected at Kampung Kiau c. 1300 m (4200 ft) (FS).

34. *Ducula badia* **(Raffles 1822) : Mountain Imperial Pigeon**
    Common resident in the foothills of Mt. Kinabalu, and heard calling between 1050 and 2450 m (3500 and 8100 ft) above Poring (S). Flocks seen daily flying down in the early morning and back in the afternoon from Royal Society Expedition camp, Mesilau river at 1600 m (5200 ft) on Kinabalu in April 1964 (G). Often heard near Park Headquarters (J). Eggs collected by Ryves at Kampung Kiau in February (GH). Many specimens obtained between 800 m (2700 ft) and 2150 m (7000 ft).

35. *Macropygia emilian* **Bonaparte 1854 : Ruddy Cuckoo Dove**
    Submontane species but occasionally found in the lowlands. Common at Kundasang

up to 1350 m (4500 ft) (G). Occasionally seen at Park Headquarters (J). Collected to 600 m (2000 ft) (W). This is *M. phasianella* in Smythies (1981).

36. ***Macropygia ruficeps* (Temminck 1834) : Little Cuckoo Dove**
Submontane resident. Whitehead found them ranging from 300 m to 2750 m (1000 to 9000 ft) on Kinabalu. Seen and heard from 1050 m to 2850 m (3500 ft to 9400 ft) (S). On 9th July, 1961, at 2950 m (9700 ft) a bird was found incubating two recently hatched nestlings in a nest built in a rattan palm about 4.5m (15 ft) above the ground (S). Common at Park Headquarters. Eggs collected at Kiau in February and March (GH). Many specimens obtained.

37. ***Streptopelia chinensis* (Scopoli 1786) : Spotted Dove**
Common resident throughout Borneo in open country. Collected by Everett and Griswold on Kinabalu but no location or height given (Sh, P), but presumably near kampong rice-fields. Collected at Ranau (K), and a sight record from Kundasang (BL).

38. ***Chalcophaps indica* (Linnaeus 1758) : Emerald Dove**
Widespread and reasonably common resident in lowlands and uplands (S). Netted at Poring (PP, FS). Birds on local dispersal killed on several occasions by flying into sides of buildings or lights at Park Headquarters at night (PP, KNP).

PSITTACIDAE : PARROTS
39. ***Loriculus galgulus* (Linnaeus 1758) : Malay Lorikeet or Blue-crowned Hanging Parrot**
Common resident in the lowlands. Observed at 1050 m (3500 ft) above Poring (S), at 1600 m (5300 ft) in 1971 and at Park Headquarters in 1973 (J).

CUCULIDAE : CUCKOOS, MALCOHAS AND COUCALS
40. ***Cuculus sparverioides* Vigors 1832 : Large Hawk Cuckoo**
Resident on Kinabalu and the Crocker Range above 900 m (3000 ft) and quite common (G). Collected between 950 m (3100 ft) and 1350 m (4500 ft) (P, W).

41. ***Cuculus fugax* Horsfield 1821 : Hodgson's Hawk Cuckoo**
One resident race *C. f. fugax* occurs in Borneo and is common on Kinabalu and the Crocker Range above 900 m (3000 ft) (G). Collected at 900 m (W). *C. f. nisicolor* Blyth 1843 is a rare visitor and has been collected once on Kinabalu at 950 m (3100 ft) (P). A young dead bird was collected by Park staff at Park Headquarters in July 1988 (KNP).

42. ***Cuculus vagans* Muller 1845 : Moustached Hawk Cuckoo**
Scattered records throughout Borneo. Recorded from Poring 1985 (KP & JS). Status uncertain (S).

43. ***Cuculus micropterus* Gould 1837 : Indian Cuckoo**
Comparatively common resident in lowlands and mountains. On Kinabalu, up to 1200 m (4000 ft) (S).

44. *Cuculus saturatus* **Blyth 1843 : Oriental Cuckoo**
Two races visit Borneo, *C.s. saturatus* and *C.s. horsfieldii* Horsfield and Moore 1853, where they are passage migrants and winter visitors. The call of a third resident race, *C.s. insulindae,* a triple hoot, is commonly heard at Park Headquarters from January to May (J). Collected at 900 m (3000 ft) (Sk).

45. *Cacomantis sonneratii* **(Latham 1790) : Banded Bay Cuckoo**
Resident and locally common (G). An unconfirmed sighting from 1500 m (5000 ft) (J) and netted at Poring (DY).

46. *Cacomantis merulinus* **(Scopoli 1786) : Plaintive Cuckoo**
Abundant resident of lowlands, ascending hills to 1200 m (4000 ft) (S). Collected at 950 m (3100 ft) on Kinabalu (P).

47. *Cacomantis sepulchralis* **(Muller 1843) : Rusty-breasted Cuckoo**
A single sight record from Poring (BL). This is *C. variolosus* in Smythies (1981).

48. *Chrysococcyx xanthorhynchus* **(Horsfield 1821) : Violet Cuckoo**
Resident and sparingly distributed through the lowlands of Borneo but seldom noted. Recorded from Poring in the hot pools clearing 1985 (KP & JS) and 1986 (DY).

49. *Chrysococcyx minutillus* **Gould 1859 : Malayan or Little Bronze Cuckoo**
A widely distributed rare resident of Borneo. One specimen obtained at 950 m (3100 ft) (P). This is *C. malayanus* in Smythies (1981).

50. *Chrysococcyx russatus* **Gould 1868 : Gould's Bronze Cuckoo**
A specimen collected at 945 m (3100 ft) on Kinabalu, now in the Museum of Comparative Zoology, Harvard. The subspecies is *aheneus.* See Parker, S.A. (1981) Prolegomenon to further studies in the *Chrysococcyx 'malayanus'* group (Aves, Cuculidae). Zoologische Verhandelinge 187: 1–56).

51. *Surniculus lugubris* **(Horsfield 1821) : Drongo Cuckoo**
Common resident of lowlands and uplands. Sight records from Tenompok (S) and Poring (BL). Collected around Kampung Nalumad at *c.* 750 m (2500 ft) (J) and by Whitehead at about 300 m (1000 ft).

52. *Eudynamis scolopacea* **(Linnaeus 1758) : Common Koel**
Winter visitor. Two races—*E.s. chinensis* Cabanis and Heine 1863 and *E.s. malayana* Cabanis and Heine 1863, the latter being the more common (S). Sight record of a bird crossing the track between Ranau and Kundasang (BL).

53. *Clamator coromandus* **(Linnaeus 1766) : Chestnut-winged Cuckoo**
Passage migrant and winter visitor. A sight record from hill rice near Poring (FS).

54. *Phaenicophaeus chlorophaeus* **(Raffles 1822) : Raffles's Malcoha**
A common lowland resident in primary and secondary forest ascending up to 900 m (3000 ft) (S). Observed above Poring at 1050 m (3500 ft) (S) and at 1700 ft (DY).

Collected at 300 m (W) and at above Kampung Kaung at *c.* 650 m (2200 ft) (E), and at Ranau (K).

55. ***Phaenicophaeus diardii* (Lesson 1830) : Black-bellied Malcoha**
    Resident in lowland forest to 900 m (3000 ft). (G). A sight record from Poring (BL) and collected at 300 m (1000 ft) (Bs).

56. ***Phaenicophaeus sumatranus* (Raffles 1822) : Chestnut-bellied Malcoha**
    Resident in lowland forest, ascending to Kinabalu foothills above Ranau (G). An unusual and possibly doubtful record, as this bird is normally a resident of mangoves and the coast. There have been no recent sightings (FS).

57. ***Phaenicophaeus javanicus* Horsfield 1821 : Red-billed Malcoha**
    Resident in lowland forest, up to 1300 m (FS) but preferring the primary forest canopy (G). A sight record from Poring (BL) and collected at Kaung (E) and at 300 m (1000 ft) (W).

58. ***Phaenicophaeus curvirostris* (Shaw and Nodder 1810) : Chestnut-breasted Malcoha**
    Resident and common in both lowland and montane forest (G). Collected at 300 m (1000 ft) (W), 350 m (1100 ft) (E) and by Treacher (Sh). Sight record at 1050 m (3500 ft) (S). Also a record from Ranau (K).

59. ***Centropus sinensis* (Stephens 1815) : Common or Greater Coucal**
    Common resident in lowlands, often in scrub and on roadsides. Regularly seen at Poring at edge of compound (J). Eggs taken by Ryves at Kiau in March (GH).

60. ***Centropus bengalensis* (Gmelin 1788) : Lesser Coucal**
    Resident. Found on the foothills of Kinabalu but higher than *C. sinensis* (G). In 1971, one was taken near Park Headquarters (J). Also collected by Griswold, but no height given (P). Sight record from Poring (FS).

STRIGIDAE : TYPICAL OWLS

61. ***Otus rufescens* (Horsfield 1821) : Reddish Scops Owl**
    Apparently resident but scarce, in lowland and montane primary forest (G). Netted at 1500 m (5000 ft) on Kinabalu in 1964 (M). The identification is doubtful, as confusion with the next species has also occurred on Malayan mountains.

62. ***Otus spilocephalus* (Blyth 1846) : Mountain Scops Owl**
    A montane resident but rarely seen. Collected by Whitehead and at 1800 m (6000 ft) (P). Also occurs along the Crocker Range and on Mt. Trus Madi (FS).

63. ***Otus bakkamoena* Pennant 1769 : Collared Scops Owl**
    Common resident of the lowlands. Collected in the neighbourhood of villages on Kinabalu up to 300 m (1000 ft) (W). Netted at Kampung Kiau (de S).

64. *Otus brookei* (Sharpe 1892) : **Rajah's Scops Owl**
    Resident, but only one Borneo specimen was known, from Sarawak's Mt. Mulu until a dead bird was picked by Park staff on the Summit Trail of Mt. Kinabalu at *c.* 1900 m (6200 ft) in 1986 (KNP).

65. *Bubo sumatranus* (Raffles 1822) : **Barred Eagle Owl**
    Resident and sparingly distributed throughout the lowlands, ascending the mountains to 900 m (3000 ft) (S). Collected by Treacher (Sh) but no altitude recorded, and by Whitehead at 900 m.

66. *Glaucidium brodiei* (Burton 1836) : **Collared Owlet**
    A little known montane resident. Four netted at 1500 m (5000 ft) (M). Collected by Everett at Kinokok, *c.* 1000 m (3300 ft) (Sh). Common in mountain forest throughout Sabah (FS). A dead bird was picked up by Park staff from a parking lot at Park Headquarters in July 1989 (KNP).

67. *Ninox scutulata* (Raffles 1882) : **Brown Hawk Owl or Boobook**
    One race resident and widely distributed in Borneo. Another race visits Sabah and Sarawak in small numbers. *N.s. borneensis* (Bonaparte 1850) is the resident race, *N.s. burmanica* Hume 1876, is the winter visitor (S). Observed at 1500 m (J). Collected at Ranau (K).

PODARGIDAE : FROGMOUTHS

68. *Batrachostomus mixtus* Sharpe 1892 : **Short-tailed Frogmouth**
    A submontane resident in Borneo, but scattered. Calls heard several times at Park Headquarters during 1984 and 1985 are thought to have been this species (DY). *B. poliolophus* in Smythies (1981).

69. *Batrachostomus javensis* (Horsfield 1821) : **Javan or Blyth's Frogmouth**
    Resident in Borneo but only six specimens have ever been collected. Seen and heard at Poring (DY).

CAPRIMULGIDAE : NIGHTJARS

70. *Eurostopodus temminckii* (Gould 1838) : **Malaysian Eared Nightjar**
    Resident in the lowlands. Call heard at 1050 m (3500 ft) above Poring, and also recorded from Tenompok (S).

71. *Caprimulgus macrurus* Horsfield 1821 : **Large-tailed Nightjar**
    A common lowland resident. Collected around Kampung Bundu Tuhan at *c.* 1200 m (4000 ft) (S). One specimen by Whitehead at 600 m (2000 ft) and one by Johnson from around Kampung Kaung *c.* 400 m (1300 ft) in 1951 (B).

72. *Caprimulgus indicus* Latham 1790 : **Grey Nightjar**
    Migrants seen most years since 1982 at Park Headquarters hawking insects at dusk (FR, FL and PP).

APODIDAE : SWIFTS

73. *Aerodramus fugiphagus* (Thunberg 1821) : (Grey-rumped) Edible-nest Swiftlet
    Lowland cave resident, but Griswold obtained a pair on Kinabalu at 950 m (3100 ft) (P). Possibly a doubtful record. There has been no verification of the identity of Griswold's specimens in recent years and there are no other records (FS). This is *Collocalia fuciphaga* in Smythies (1981). See Medway, Lord & Pye, J.D. (1977) Echolocation and systematics of swiftlets. pp. 225-238 in: Stonehouse, B. and Perrins, C.M. (eds), Evolutionary Ecology. Macmillan, London.

74. *Collocalia esculenta* (Linnaeus 1758) : White-bellied or Glossy Swiftlet
    Widely distributed in Borneo (S) and the commonest resident swiftlet in Sabah. Can be seen from the coast to the highest point on Kinabalu (G). Collected at 1500 m (P).

75. *Hirundapus giganteus* (Temminck 1825) : Brown Spine-tailed Swift or Brown Needletail
    Resident and widely distributed through Sabah (G). Small numbers seen at Park Headquarters and observed to mix with *C. esculenta* (J). Sight record from Poring (FS).

76. *Rhaphidura leucopygialis* (Blyth 1849) : Silver-rumped Spinetail
    Resident and abundant in Borneo. Sight records from Poring (BL, DY).

77. *Cypsiurus balasiensis* (Gray 1829) : Asian Palm Swift
    Resident but local. Specimens obtained by Whitehead and Griswold (P) on Kinabalu, but no height recorded.

HEMIPROCNIDAE : TREESWIFTS

78. *Hemiprocne comata* (Temminck 1824) : Whiskered Treeswift
    Resident and common in the lowlands up to 750 m (2500 ft). A sight record from Poring (BL).

79. *Hemiprocne longipennis* (Rafinesque 1802) : Grey-rumped Treeswift
    Common resident throughout the lowlands of Borneo (S). Collected by Burbidge on Kinabalu (Sh) and recorded from Poring (BL, DY).

TROGONIDAE : TROGONS

80. *Harpactes diardii* (Temminck 1832) : Diard's Trogon
    Resident and fairly common throughout Borneo in primary forest up to 1200 m (4000 ft) (S). A sight record from Poring (DY). Collected at Ranau (K).

81. *Harpactes kasumba* (Raffles 1822) : Red-naped Trogon
    Resident throughout Borneo in the lowlands in primary forest. Recent sight records from Poring (FR, TE, KP & JS). Recorded from Mt. Tambuyukon between 550 and 1200 m (1800 and 4000 ft) in 1982 (PP).

82. *Harpactes whiteheadi* Sharpe 1888 : Whitehead's Trogon
    A montane resident confined to Borneo. First discovered by Whitehead on Kinabalu

at 1200 m (4000 ft). A pair presumed to be this species seen at 2000 m (6500 ft) above Poring (S). Many collections between 900 and 1800 m (3000 and 6000 ft). Regularly seen at Park Headquarters (PP).

83. *Harpactes duvaucelii* (Temminck 1824) : Scarlet-rumped Trogon
   A common resident throughout the lowland forest of Borneo and previously overlooked in the Park. Sight records from Poring in 1982 (FR) and from Park Headquarters in 1986 and 1988 (DY).

84. *Harpactes orrhophaeus* (Cabanis and Heine 1863) : Cinnamon-rumped Trogon
   A sub-montane resident, mostly collected between 1050 and 1350 m (3500 and 4500 ft) but has also been obtained in the lowlands. Seen at 1550 m (5100 ft) on Kinabalu (J). Collected by Whitehead but no elevation recorded.

85. *Harpactes oreskios* (Temminck 1832) : Orange-breasted Trogon
   A sub-montane resident in Borneo. Whitehead met with it on Kinabalu from 300 to 900 m (1000 to 3000 ft) (S). Ringed by Medway at 1050 m (3500 ft) and several collected. (Sk, Sh and P).

ALCEDINIDAE : KINGFISHERS

86. *Lacedo pulchella* (Horsfield 1821) : Banded Kingfisher
   An uncommon resident throughout Borneo in primary forest, ranging from the lowlands to 1700 m (5500 ft) in moss forest (S). Scarce in the lowlands, becoming more common above 750 m (2500 ft). Common on the east side of Kinabalu at 1050 m (3500 ft) in 1961 (G). Specimen from 600 m (2000 ft) (W).

87. *Actenoides concretus* (Temminck 1825) : Chestnut- or Rufous-collared Kingfisher
   Resident throughout Borneo in primary forest, in the lowlands (S). Reaches 1700 m (5500 ft) on Kinabalu but nowhere common (G). Collected at Poring at 500 m (1700 ft) and 600 m (2000 ft) (FS). *Halcyon concreta* in Smythies (1981). See Fry, C.H. (1980) The evolutionary biology of kingfishers (Alcedinidae). Living Bird 18: 113–160.

88. *Halcyon chloris* (Boddaert 1783) : Collared or White-collared Kingfisher
   A resident and common bird on the coast and inland to the interior plains (G). A specimen obtained by Treacher on Kinabalu, but no elevation or locality given (Sh).

89. *Halcyon pileata* (Boddaert 1783) : Black-capped Kingfisher
   Abundant winter visitor, found on the Kinabalu foothills (S).

90. *Alcedo euryzona* Temminck 1830 : Blue-banded Kingfisher
   Resident and not uncommon along streams in primary forests, especially on large streams (S). Collected by Whitehead up to 1200 m (4000 ft).

91. *Ceyx erithacus* (Linnaeus 1758) : Black-backed or Oriental (Dwarf) Kingfisher
   A common resident in Borneo in primary forests in the lowlands along jungle streams (S). Netted at Poring (PP) and collected at 900 m (3000 ft) (W).

MEROPIDAE : BEE-EATERS

92. *Merops viridis* **Linnaeus 1758 : Blue-throated Bee-eater**
    Common resident in coastal districts, but a local migrant (S). Sight records from Poring, 1976, in open country (FS).

93. *Nyctyornis amictus* **(Temminck 1824) : Red-bearded Bee-eater**
    Resident in primary and secondary forest in the lowlands and quite common (G). Sight records from Poring (BL, DY). Collected by Whitehead at about 300 m (1000 ft), and at Ranau (K).

CORACIIDAE : ROLLERS

94. *Eurystomus orientalis* **(Linnaeus 1766) : Broad-billed Roller or Dollarbird**
    Two races, *E. o. calonyx* Sharpe 1890, and *E. o. deignani* Ripley 1942 are winter visitors. A third, *E. o. cyanicollis* is the resident race. Collected by Everett (Sh) and Whitehead, but race or locality not indicated. Sight records from Poring, where it is common (PP).

BUCEROTIDAE : HORNBILLS

95. *Anorrhinus galeritus* **(Temminck 1831) : Bushy-crested Hornbill**
    Resident in lowland primary forest. A noisy party was heard at 1050 m (3500 ft) above Poring (S). A specimen from 300 m (1000 ft) (W).

96. *Rhyticeros undulatus* **(Shaw 1811) : Wreathed Hornbill**
    Resident and sparsely distributed in Borneo, in sub-montane localities (S), but locally common (G). Flocks of between 4 and 27 birds seen from 1050 to 2850 m (3500 to 9400 ft) on the mountain. Collected by Griswold but no height given. Birds seen regularly flying high over Park Headquarters (PP).

97. *Anthracoceros malayanus* **(Raffles 1822) : Black Hornbill**
    Resident throughout the lowlands but not noticeably common (S). Collected at 300 m (1000 ft) (W). Eggs taken by Ryves at Kaung in February (GH). Sight record from Poring, 1981 (FS).

98. *Anthracoceros albirostris* **(Shaw and Nodder 1807) : Pied Hornbill**
    A resident of Borneo but chiefly a bird of the coast and offshore islands (S). One seen at Park Headquarters (J). This is thought by some authorities to be a doubtful record. *A. coronatus* in Smythies (1981). See Frith, C.B. and Frith, D.W. (1983) A systematic review of the hornbill genus *Anthracoceros*, Aves, Burotidae. *Zoological Journal of the Linnean Society*, 78: 29–71.

99. *Buceros rhinoceros* **Linnaeus 1758 : Rhinoceros Hornbill**
    Resident throughout Borneo in sub-montane forests. Heard at 1050 m (3500 ft) above Poring (S) and seen at 1750 m (5800 ft) (J). Collected by Griswold but no height given (P).

100. *Rhinoplax vigil* (Forster 1781) : Helmeted Hornbill
   Resident throughout Borneo in sub-montane forest (S). A specimen taken at 900 m (3000 ft) (Sk). Recorded up to 900 m (3000 ft) (W) and at Poring (DY).

INDICATORIDAE : HONEYGUIDES
101. *Indicator archipelagicus* Temminck 1832 : Malaysian Honeyguide
   A rare lowland resident scattered throughout Borneo. A single sight record from Poring (DY).

CAPITONIDAE : BARBETS
102. *Calorhamphus fuliginosus* (Temminck 1830) : Brown Barbet
   A common lowland resident. A small party of five seen twice at 1050 m (3500 ft) above Poring (S). Collected on lower slopes to 300 m (1000 ft) (W).

103. *Megalaima chrysopogon* (Temminck 1824) : Gold-whiskered Barbet
   Common resident in sub-montane forests. Observed at 1050 m (3500 ft) above Poring (S). Collected at 300 m (1000 ft) (Bs) and at 950 m (3100 ft) (P).

104. *Megalaima rafflesii* (Lesson 1839) : Many-coloured or Red-crowned Barbet
   Common resident in primary and secondary forest in the lowlands (G). Collected on Kinabalu by Burbidge (Sh), but no details of altitude given.

105. *Megalaima mystacophanos* (Temminck 1824) : Gaudy or Red-throated Barbet
   An abundant lowland resident of primary forest. Observed at 1050 m (3500 ft) above Poring but more common around the hot springs at Poring (S). Netted at Poring (PP) and specimens taken up to 950 m (3200 ft).

106. *Megalaima henricii* (Temminck 1831) : Yellow-crowned Barbet
   Resident in sub-montane primary forest, observed at 1050 m (3500 ft) above Poring (S).

107. *Megalaima pulcherrima* Sharpe 1888 : Golden-naped Barbet
   Common montane resident confined to Borneo. Found on Kinabalu from 900 m to 3200 m (3000 to 10,500 ft) (S) and common at about 1050 m (3500 ft) above Poring (de S) and at Park Headquarters (J). Many collected between 900 m and 2450 m (3000 and 8000 ft).

108. *Megalaima monticola* (Sharpe 1889) : Mountain Barbet
   Common montane species confined to Borneo. Many collected on Kinabalu from 900 to 2200 m (3000 to 7200 ft). Commonly heard at 1050 m (3500 ft) above Poring (S) and at Park Headquarters (J).

109. *Megalaima eximia* (Sharpe 1892) : Black-throated Barbet
   Sub-montane to montane resident confined to Borneo. Collected at 1050 m (3500 ft) on Kinabalu, and recorded up to 2150 m (7000 ft) though most specimens are between 900 and 1500 m (3000 and 5000 ft) (P). Appears to be rare, and has not

been seen in recent years (FS), except for a single sight record at 900 m (3000 ft) above Poring (DY). The race found on Kinabalu, *M.e. cyanea* (Harrisson & Hartley, 1934) has a blue forehead and throat; elsewhere, the nominate race has a black forehead and throat (S).

110. *Megalaima australis* (Horsfield 1821) : **Little or Blue-eared Barbet**
 The commonest barbet in Borneo and lowland resident (S). Commonly heard on the mountain below 1050 m (3500 ft) (S) and collected at 300 m (1000 ft).

PICIDAE : WOODPECKERS

111. *Sasia abnormis* (Temminck 1825) : **Rufous Piculet**
 Resident throughout Borneo and common in lowland secondary forest. Collected at Poring (FS) and specimens from 300 m (1000 ft) (W).

112. *Picus puniceus* Horsfield 1821 : **Crimson-winged Woodpecker**
 Resident in primary and secondary forest in the lowlands and up to 1500 m (5000 ft) in the mountains (G). Collected at 600 m (2000 ft) (W), 900 m (3000 ft) (Sk) and sight records up to 1700 m (5500 ft) (J, S). Collected at Ranau (K).

113. *Picus mentalis* Temminck 1825 : **Checkered-throated Woodpecker**
 A common resident in primary forest with a wide altitude range. Several collections between 550 m and 1700 m (1800 and 5500 ft), and often seen at Park Headquarters where immature birds were observed in December 1970 (J). Collected at Ranau (K).

114. *Picus miniaceus* Pennant 1769 : **Banded Woodpecker**
 Resident in primary forest from the lowlands to 1700 m (5500 ft) (G). Collected at Poring (FS) and several collected between 300 and 900 m (1000 and 3100 ft) on the west and south-west flanks of the mountain.

115. *Celeus brachyurus* (Vieillot 1818) : **Rufous Woodpecker**
 A common resident in primary and secondary forest with wide altitude range from sea-level to 1750 m (5700 ft) (S). Ringed at Poring (PP). *Micropterus brachyurus* in Smythies (1981). See Short L.L. (1973) Habits of some Asian Woodpeckers (Aves, Picidae). *Bulletin of the American Museum of Natural History* 152 : 257–364.

116. *Picoides canicapillus* (Blyth 1845) : **Grey-capped Woodpecker**
 Resident in lowlands, ascending mountains to 1700 m (5500 ft) (S). Locally common. Collected between 600 and 900 m (2000 and 3000 ft) (W).

117. *Meiglyptes tristis* (Horsfield 1821) : **Buff-rumped Woodpecker**
 Common resident in lowland forests (S). Collected around Kampung Nalumad, at about 600 m (2000 ft) on the east side of Kinabalu (J) and at Ranau (K).

118. *Meiglyptes tukki* (Lesson 1839) : **Buff-necked Woodpecker**
 Common lowland resident (S). Collected at Poring (FS) and by Whitehead at about 300 m (1000 ft).

119. *Hemicircus concretus* (Temminck 1824) : Grey-and-Buff Woodpecker
A lowland resident recorded from Poring 1981 (RC & WE) and 1985 (KP & JS).

120. *Dinopium rafflesii* (Vigors and Horsfield 1830) : Olive-backed Woodpecker
Resident in lowland forest but not common (S). In primary and secondary forest to 900 m (3000 ft) (G). A record from Ranau (BL) and collected at 600 m (2000 ft) (W).

121. *Blythipicus rubiginosus* (Swainson 1837) : Maroon Woodpecker
Common resident in lowland and hill forest with a wide altitude range, going up to 1700 m (5500 ft) on Kinabalu (S). Netted at Poring (PP, DY), and specimens taken at 950 and 1450 m (3200 and 4700 ft) (Sk) and at 1500 m (5000 ft) (W).

122. *Reinwardtipicus validus* (Temminck 1825) : Orange-backed Woodpecker
Common resident in lowland forests; occurs on Kinabalu to about 1500 m (5000 ft) (G). Observed near Park Headquarters (J). *Chrysocolaptes validus* in Smythies (1981). See Short L.L. (1973). Habits of some Asian Woodpeckers (Aves, Picidae). *Bulletin of the American Museum of Natural History* 152 : 257 - 364.

EURYLAIMIDAE : BROADBILLS

123. *Calyptomena viridis* Raffles 1822 : Green Broadbill
A lowland resident, fairly common in old forests (W). Collected up to 1200 m (4000 ft).

124. *Calyptomena hosei* Sharpe 1892 : Hose's Broadbill
Confined to Borneo, where it is a sub-montane bird with a patchy distribution (S). Observed at Poring in 1973 (PP).

125. *Calyptomena whiteheadi* Sharpe 1887 : Whitehead's Broadbill
A montane species confined to Borneo, extending down the Crocker Range from Kinabalu (FS). A single egg taken at Kiau in March (GH). Many specimens from Kinabalu between 900 and 1700 m (3000 and 5500 ft). Whitehead described the nest on Kinabalu.

126. *Psarisomus dalhousiae* (Jameson 1835) : Long-tailed Broadbill
A montane resident with a restricted range on Bornean mountains (S). Resident on Kinabalu around 900 to 1200 m (3000 ft to 4000 ft) (G). Several collections between 900 to 1350 m (3000 and 4500 ft) (Sk) and also at 1700 m (5500 ft) (P).

127. *Cymbirhynchus macrorhynchos* (Gmelin 1788) : Black-and-Red Broadbill
Resident and common in lowlands near water (S). Netted and collected at Poring (PP, FS), where it is common, and at Kaung (E).

128. *Eurylaimus ochromalus* Raffles 1822 : Black-and-Yellow Broadbill
Resident throughout Borneo in the lowlands in primary forest to about 1200 m (4000 ft) (S). Observed at Kundasang (BL) and at Poring (PP). Collected at 300 m and 335m (1000 ft and 1100 ft) (W, E), and by Griswold but no height given (P). Collected at Ranau (K).

129. *Eurylaimus javanicus* **Horsfield 1821 : Banded Broadbill**
Resident in Borneo in the lowlands in primary forest, ascending to about 1200 m (4000 ft) (G). Collected at 300 m (1000 ft) on Kinabalu (W).

130. *Corydon sumatranus* **(Raffles 1822) : Dusky Broadbill**
Resident but sparsely distributed in the lowlands of Borneo in primary forests. Observed above Poring at 1050 m (3500 ft) (S). Obtained up to 600 m (2000 ft) (W) and one collected at 1800 m (6000 ft) (G).

PITTIDAE : PITTAS

131. *Pitta arquata* **Gould 1871 : Blue-banded Pitta**
A bird of primary forest with a preference for sub-montane localities. Confined to Borneo (S). On Kinabalu, Whitehead found it at 600 to 1200 m (2000 to 4000 ft) in true forest, frequenting thick bamboo jungle (S).

132. *Pitta baudi* **Muller and Schlegel 1840 : Blue-headed Pitta**
Confined to Borneo where it is locally common in lowland primary forest (S). A sight record from Poring (P).

133. *Pitta guajana* **(P.L.S. Muller 1776) : Banded Pitta**
A sub-montane resident, confined to old jungle and distinctly local. On Kinabalu Whitehead obtained two at 1500 m (5000 ft) but most records are at altitudes of 600 to 1200 m (2000 to 4000 ft) (S).

134. *Pitta moluccensis* **(P.L.S. Muller 1776): Blue-winged Pitta**
Passage migrant and winter visitor. Several birds seen migrating over the Tenompok Pass at 1500 m (5000 ft) in October (P). Dead birds collected at Park Headquarters by Park staff in April and October (KNP).

HIRUNDINIDAE : SWALLOWS

135. *Delichon dasypus* **(Bonaparte 1850) : Asian House Martin**
A winter visitor in Borneo (S). Recorded at 950 m (3200 ft) in the Liwagu valley above Ranau (F).

136. *Hirundo tahitica* **Gmelin 1789 : Pacific Swallow**
Common resident in open country (S). Seen regularly at Park Headquarters (J).

137. *Hirundo rustica* **Linnaeus 1758 : Common or Barn Swallow**
Holarctic. The race wintering in Borneo breeds in Siberia and Japan. Very abundant in open country as a passage migrant and winter visitor (S). Often seen at Park Headquarters in winter (J). Collected by Everett (Sh).

MOTACILLIDAE : WAGTAILS AND PIPITS

138. *Motacilla cinerea* **Tunstall 1771 : Grey Wagtail**
A passage migrant and winter visitor. Abundant at Park Headquarters where they appear in August and leave by the end of April. Arrive in flocks but winter singly

(J). Collected at 900 m (3000 ft) (Sk, W). *M. caspica* in Smythies (1981). See White, C.M. & Bruce, M.D. (1986) The Birds of Wallacea. *B.O.U. Checklist No.7*. British Ornithologists' Union, London.

139. *Dendronanthus indicus* **(Gmelin 1789) : Forest Wagtail**
    A rare migrant. Harrisson saw one in February 1952 at 900 m (3000 ft) on Kinabalu (S). Another observed at Membakut (Beaufort area) on the west coast lowlands in February 1962 (G). These are the only two Sabah records.

CAMPEPHAGIDAE : FLYCATCHER-SHRIKES, CUCKOO-SHRIKES, AND MINIVETS

140. *Tephrodornis gularis* **(Raffles 1822) : Large Woodshrike**
    Resident and sparingly distributed through the lowlands of Borneo (S). Collected at about 900 m (3000 ft) on Kinabalu (W). *Tephrodornis virgatus* in Smythies (1981). See Raffles (1822) *Transactions of the Linnean Society* 13: 304.

141. *Coracina striata* **(Boddaert 1783) : Bar-bellied Cuckoo-shrike**
    Resident in lowland forest. Ascends to 1200 m (4000 ft) in the hills (S) and recorded at this height on Kinabalu (S). Also sighted at Poring (BL).

142. *Coracina larvata* **(Muller 1843) : Black-faced or Sunda Cuckoo-shrike**
    A montane resident, extremely common at the higher levels. Altitude range about 900 to 2150 m (3000 to 7000 ft) (S). Often seen in primary and secondary forest at Park Headquarters (J). Many collected between 900 and 1500 m (3000 and 5000 ft).

143. *Coracina fimbriata* **(Temminck 1824) : Lesser Cuckoo-shrike**
    Locally common lowland resident in forests. Collected by Whitehead but found no higher than 900 m (3000 ft).

144. *Hemipus hirundinaceus* **(Temminck 1822) : Black-winged Flycatcher-shrike**
    A common resident throughout the lowlands of Borneo in old jungle, more open country and cultivated areas (S). Ascending to 900 m (3000 ft) (G). Collected at Ranau (K).

145. *Hemipus picatus* **(Sykes 1832) : Bar-winged Flycatcher-shrike**
    A lowland to montane resident throughout Borneo to 1800 m (6000 ft). Two were observed above Poring at 1050 m (3500 ft) (S). Collected by Whitehead between 900 and 1200 m (3000 and 4000 ft).

146. *Pericrocotus solaris* **Blyth 1846 : Mountain or Grey-chinned Minivet**
    Very common montane resident in Borneo (S). Variously recorded and collected from 900 to 2450 m (3000 to 8000 ft) and is common at Park Headquarters (J).

147. *Pericrocotus igneus* **Blyth 1846 : Fiery Minivet**
    Resident in Borneo, chiefly in coastal districts, and not common (S). However, (Sh) records *"an adult male, in Mr. Burbidge's collection,"* described as being from an

expedition to Kinabalu. It is possible that this bird was collected early in the expedition while still in the plains. Also collected by Goss and Dodge (B).

148. *Pericrocotus flammeus* **(Forster 1781) : Scarlet Minivet**
Resident in Borneo but patchy in distribution and not common. Whitehead collected it on Kinabalu only at 900 to 1200 m (3000 to 4000 ft) in mixed flocks with *P. solaris* (Sh). Often found in the lowlands (FS).

LANIIDAE : SHRIKES

149. *Lanius cristatus* **Linnaeus 1758 : Brown Shrike**
Common winter visitor, chiefly to coastal districts (S), but has been collected up to 1700 m (5500 ft) on the Crocker Range (FS). Has been obtained on Kinabalu by several collectors at low altitudes.

150. *Lanius tigrinus* **Drapiez 1828 : Thick-billed or Tiger Shrike**
A winter visitor in considerable numbers (G). Sight records from Ranau (BL, DY).

ARTAMIDAE : WOOD SWALLOWS

151. *Artamus leucorhynchus* **(Linnaeus 1771) : White-breasted Wood Swallow**
A common resident in Borneo, especially in coastal districts (S), but ascends to 1500 m (5000 ft) (G). A specimen from Kinabalu obtained by Griswold, but no height or locality given (P) and one at 350 m (1100 ft) by Haviland in 1892 (Sk).

AEGITHINIDAE : IORAS, LEAFBIRDS AND BLUEBIRDS

152. *Aegithina tiphia* **(Linnaeus 1758) : Common Iora**
Common resident of the lowlands. Collected at Poring (FS) and at Ranau (K).

153. *Chloropsis cyanopogon* **(Temminck 1832) : Lesser Green Leafbird**
A common resident in lowland forest (S). Several records from Poring (BL, DY) and collected at Kaung (E).

154. *Chloropsis sonnerati* **Jardine and Selby 1827 : Greater Green Leafbird**
Resident in lowland forest, ascending to 1200 m (4000 ft) (G). Collected at Poring (FS).

155. *Chloropsis cochinchinensis* **(Gmelin 1788) : Blue-winged Leafbird**
A common resident in primary and secondary sub-montane to montane forest throughout Borneo. Several specimens collected (S). Seen above Poring at 1050 m (3500 ft) in association with Bar-winged Flycatcher Shrike *(Hemipus picatus)* and Velvet-fronted Nuthatch *(Sitta frontalis)* (S). Ascends to 2150 m (7000 ft) on Kinabalu (G).

156. *Irena puella* **(Latham 1790) : (Asian) Fairy Bluebird**
A common lowland resident in Borneo, confined to primary forest; occasionally up to 1500 m (5000 ft) on mountains (S). Collected on Kinabalu at 300 m (1000 ft) (W), and at Poring (FS), where it is common. One record from Kundasang (BL).

PYCNONOTIDAE : BULBULS

157. *Pycnonotus melanoleucos* (Eyton 1839) : Black-and-White Bulbul
    A lowland resident. A dead bird picked up at 3050 m (10,000 ft) above Poring during the Royal Society Expedition (S), probably on nomadic dispersal. Also collected by Everett, and Griswold, but no height or locality given (Sh, P).

158. *Pycnonotus atriceps* (Temminck 1822) : Black-headed Bulbul
    Common resident of lowland primary and secondary forest. Sight records from Poring (BL, DY) and collected at Kaung (E). *"The discovery of the remains of a Black-headed Bulbul on the summit of Mt. Tambuyukon* (in 1982) *is further evidence of the extensive local migrations of some fruit-eating species of forest birds"* (PP). This is in fact nomadism, not migration.

159. *Pycnonotus melanicterus* (Gmelin 1789) : Black-crested Bulbul
    Abundant montane resident (S). Fairly common around 900 m (3000 ft) on Kinabalu and the Crocker Range (G). Collected between 750 and 1050 m (2500 and 3500 ft) (Sk, W).

160. *Pycnonotus squamatus* (Temminck 1828) : Scaly-breasted Bulbul
    An uncommon sub-montane resident of primary forest (S). Seen at Ranau and at Poring (DY).

161. *Pycnonotus zeylanicus* (Gmelin 1789) : Straw-headed Bulbul
    In the lowlands (S), ascending to 1200 m (4000 ft) but scarce at this altitude (G). Collected at Poring (FS). Eggs taken at Kiau in March (GH). Collected between 750 and 900 m (2500 ft and 3000 ft) (Sk).

162. *Pycnonotus flavescens* Blyth 1845 : Pale-faced or Flavescent Bulbul
    A montane resident in Borneo from 900 to 3500 m (3000 to 11,500 ft) (S). Many collected between 1600 and 3100 m (5200 and 10,200 ft).

163. *Pycnonotus goiavier* (Scopoli 1786) : Yellow-vented Bulbul
    Abundant lowland resident (S). Seen near Park Headquarters (J) and netted at Poring (PP). Collected by Griswold but no height given (P).

164. *Pycnonotus plumosus* Blyth 1845 : Olive-winged Bulbul
    Common resident in secondary forest (S). Collected at Poring (FS).

165. *Pycnonotus brunneus* Blyth 1845 : Red-eyed Bulbul
    Common lowland resident in primary and secondary forests (S). Netted at Poring (PP).

166. *Pycnonotus simplex* Lesson 1839 : Cream-vented Bulbul
    Common lowland resident (S) and obtained on Kinabalu from 300 to 450 m (1000 to 1500 ft) (W). Collected at Poring (FS).

167. *Pycnonotus erythrophthalmos* (Hume 1878) : **Spectacled Bulbul**
Common lowland resident in primary and secondary forest (S). Netted at Poring (PP). Collected by Goss and Dodge (B), and at Ranau (K).

168. *Criniger bres* (Lesson 1832) : **Grey-cheeked Bulbul**
Resident in primary and secondary forest in the lowlands (S). Collected at Poring (FS), and at 1500 m (5000 ft) (E) and 750 m (2500 ft) (C).

169. *Criniger ochraceus* Horsfield and Moore 1854 : **Ochraceous Bulbul**
Common montane resident from 900 to 2150 m (3000 to 7000 ft) (G). Many collected between 900 and 1050 m (3000 and 3500 ft) and seen at 2650 m (8700 ft) (J).

170. *Criniger phaeocephalus* (Hartlaub 1844) : **Yellow-bellied Bulbul**
Common resident in lowland forests. Collected at Poring Hot Springs (FS). Seen regularly at Poring in 1982 (TE, FR) and 1985 (KP, JS).

171. *Hypsipetes criniger* (Blyth 1845) : **Hairy-backed Bulbul**
Locally common lowland resident in primary and secondary forest (S). Netted at Poring (PP, DY).

172. *Hypsipetes malaccensis* Blyth 1845 : **Streaked Bulbul**
Locally common resident in lowland primary and secondary forest (S). Sight record from Poring (DY).

173. *Hypsipetes flavala* (Blyth 1845) : **Ashy Bulbul**
Montane resident, abundant throughout Borneo, occasionally found at low altitudes (S). Common from 900 to 1800 m (3000 to 6000 ft) (G) and many collected in this range. Netted at Poring (PP).

TURDIDAE : ROBINS, FORKTAILS AND THRUSHES

174. *Erithacus cyane* (Pallas 1776) : **Siberian Blue Robin**
Passage migrant and winter visitor in small numbers (S). Obtained on Kinabalu at 300 m (1000 ft) (W) and seen at Kundasang (BL). A specimen obtained by Everett from Kinabalu but no height or locality given (Sh). Netted at Poring in December (DY), and collected in Ranau on 26th September (K).

175. *Brachypteryx montana* Horsfield 1821 : **Blue or White-browed Shortwing**
Montane resident, with Sabah records from Kinabalu, Mt. Trus Madi (S), Mt. Tambuyukon (PP), and Rinangisan at 1300 m in the Crocker Range (FS). Common above the treeline to 3050 m (10,000 ft) but has been ringed at 1050 m (3500 ft) (M), in primary forest and collected between 1200 and 2950 m (4000 and 9700 ft) (P), (W). Sight record from Tambuyukon around 1800 m (6000 ft) in ultramafic (ultrabasic) forest in 1982 (PP).

176. *Copsychus saularis* (**Linnaeus 1758**) : **Magpie Robin**
Common resident in cultivated lowlands. Seen at 1450 m (4800 ft) near Bundu Tuhan (J) and collected at 500 m (1600 ft) (FS), 950 m (3100 ft) (P) and 850 m (2800 ft) (Sk). The Sabah race *C.s. adamsi* Elliot 1890, has a black belly and white under-tail coverts.

177. *Copsychus malabaricus* (**Scopoli 1786**) : **White-rumped Shama**
Resident in old and secondary jungle in lowlands, ascending to 1200 m (4000 ft) (G). Collected at Poring (FS) and by Whitehead on Kinabalu but no height recorded.

178. *Enicurus leschenaulti* (**Vieillot 1818**) : **White-crowned Forktail**
Two resident races are found in Borneo; one race in the lowlands and the other montane. *E. l. borneensis* Sharpe 1889 with a longer tail, is found throughout the mountains of Borneo; on Kinabalu mostly at 300 to 1200 m (1000 ft to 4000 ft) (S). Seen frequently along the Silau-Silau stream at Park Headquarters in 1985 (SJ), and seen at 950 and 1950 m (3100 ft and 6400 ft) above Poring (S). Fairly common along jungle and mountain streams. Collected between 300 and 900 m (1000 and 3000 ft) (Sk, W).

179. *Enicurus ruficapillus* **Temminck 1832** : **Chestnut-naped Forktail**
Resident throughout Borneo in the lowlands along shady streams of clear water in old jungle. Distribution is patchy (S). Sight and netting records from Poring (BL, DY).

180. *Monticola solitarius* (**Linnaeus 1758**) : **Blue Rock Thrush**
Passage migrant and winter visitor. Collected by Treacher but no altitude given (Sh). One male observed on bare, recently cleared ground at Park Headquarters in January 1975 (J). Another sighting from Kundasang in January 1983 (FS).

181. *Turdus poliocephalus* **Latham 1801** : **Mountain Blackbird or Island Thrush**
A montane resident in Borneo, usually found on the higher levels of Kinabalu from 2150 m (7000 ft) to the limit of vegetation, and on Tambuyukon and Trus Madi (S, PP). Found breeding near the summit of Kinabalu in early February 1952 (S). A common species at high elevation and many collected between 2200 m and 3200 m (7200 and 10,500 ft). Seen regularly around Park Headquarters and Tenompok in small numbers during the drought in 1983 (PP).

182. *Turdus obscurus* **Gmelin 1789** : **Eye browed Thrush**
Passage migrant and winter visitor. Plentiful around Kinabalu up to 2450 m (8000 ft) (S) and flocks common (G). Regularly seen at Park Headquarters in winter, often singly (J). Collected at 2200 and 3100 m (7200 ft and 10,200 ft) (PC).

183. *Zoothera citrina* (**Latham 1790**) : **Orange-headed Thrush**
A rare sub-montane resident known from the lower slopes of Kinabalu, where Whitehead collected five from 900 to 1200 m (3000 to 4000 ft), from Trus Madi where one was obtained at 1300 m (4300 ft) (S), and from the Crocker Range at

1300 m (FS). Seen at Park Headquarters on two separate occasions in July 1983 (PP). A dead bird collected by Park staff at the Park Headquarters in June 1988 (KNP).

184. *Zoothera everetti* **(Sharpe 1892) : Everett's Thrush**
Confined to Borneo. A rare montane resident ranging from 1200 to 2150 m (4000 to 7000 ft) (S). One ringed by Medway at 1800 m (6000 ft) and collected by Griswold (P). A pair seen twice along the Silau-Silau Trail at Park Headquarters in July 1983 (KP & JS). One was killed flying into a window at Park Headquarters, July 1983 (RY).

185. *Zoothera interpres* **(Temminck 1826) : Chestnut-capped Thrush**
A rare and shy bird, resident in the lowlands of Borneo (S). Also recorded as a night-migrant over mountain passes at 1300 m (FS). A specimen from the eastern side of Kinabalu (Sh), but no locality or height given. Seen nesting at Poring in September 1969 (PP), and a dead bird collected by Park staff along the Kota Kinabalu–Ranau road (no altitude given), October 1988 (KNP).

186. *Myiophoneus glaucinus* **(Temminck 1823) : Sunda Whistling Thrush**
Sub-montane resident throughout mountains of Borneo (S). Met with sparingly at 600 to 2750 m (2000 to 9000 ft) on Kinabalu (W). Ringed at 1500 m (5000 ft) (M) and collected by Griswold (P). Not uncommon on the Silau-Silau stream at Park Headquarters (PP).

187. *Chlamydochaera jefferyi* **Sharpe 1887 : Black-collared or Black-breasted Fruit Hunter**
A decidedly local montane resident of old jungle confined to Borneo. Observed above Poring at 2000 and 2850 m (6500 ft and 9400 ft) (S). Collected at 900 and 2750 m (3000 and 9000 ft) (SK). Seen at Park Headquarters (J) and dead birds collected by Park staff at Headquarters in August 1988 and April 1989 (KNP). Birds often appear in one area for a few days in mixed hunting parties, and then will not be seen again in the same area for several months (PP). Called the Black-breasted Triller and placed in the family Campephagidae in Smythies (1981). DNA studies have now shown it to be more closely related to the thrushes. See Alquist, Sheldon and Sibley (1984) *Journal für Ornithologie* 125(2).

TIMALIIDAE : BABBLERS AND LAUGHING-THRUSHES
188. *Eupetes macrocerus* **Temminck 1831 : Malaysian Rail-babbler**
Resident but sparsely distributed through Borneo in primary forest, with a preference for sub-montane localities (S). One sight record from above Poring at 900 m (3000 ft) (DY).

189. *Pellorneum capistratum* **(Temminck 1823) : Black-capped Babbler**
Resident throughout the lowlands of Borneo in primary forest (S). Collected on Kinabalu at 300 m (1000 ft) (W) and at Poring (FS).

190. *Trichastoma pyrrhogenys* (**Temminck 1827**) : **Temminck's Babbler**
 A montane resident, throughout the mountains of Borneo (S). Eggs collected by Ryves at Kiau in March (GH). Fairly common on Kinabalu and the Crocker Range around 900 to 1200 m (3000 to 4000 ft) and collected at these heights (W). Netted at Poring (PP). Tape-recorded around the Park HQ by A.B. van den Berg.

191. *Trichastoma malaccense* (**Hartlaub 1844**) : **Short-tailed Babbler**
 Resident and locally common throughout the lowlands of Borneo in primary forest (S). Collected at Poring (FS).

192. *Trichastoma rostratum* **Blyth 1842 : White-chested Babbler**
 Resident and locally common in primary forest in the lowlands, usually near water (G). Seen at Poring (BL). An odd record which needs corroboration (FS).

193. *Trichastoma bicolor* (**Lesson 1839**) : **Ferruginous Babbler**
 A locally common resident throughout Borneo in the lowlands to primary forest (S). Netted at Poring (PP).

194. *Trichastoma sepiarium* (**Horsfield 1821**) : **Horsfield's Babbler**
 Resident in lowland forest and locally common. Netted at Poring (SM).

195. *Malacopteron magnum* **Eyton 1839 : Rufous-crowned Babbler**
 Common resident in lowland forest where most of its time is spent in the understorey (S). Sight records from Poring (BL, DY).

196. *Malacopteron cinereum* **Eyton 1839 : Scaly crowned Babbler**
 Common resident in lowland forest. Netted, (DY), and collected, at Poring (FS).

197. *Malacopteron magnirostre* (**Moore 1854**) : **Moustached Babbler**
 A common resident of lowland forest (S). Ascends to 1200 m (4000 ft) (G), and ringed at 1050 m (3500 ft) in 1964 (M).

198. *Malacopteron affine* (**Blyth 1842**) : **Plain or Sooty-capped Babbler**
 Common lowland resident. Collected at 550 m (1800 ft) above Poring (FS).

199. *Pomatorhinus montanus* **Horsfield 1821 : Chestnut-backed Scimitar Babbler**
 Resident in sub-montane localities in Borneo, sparsely distributed in primary and secondary forest. Commonly heard on Kinabalu at 1050 to 1700 m (3500 ft to 5500 ft) (S). Eggs taken by Ryves at Kiau in February and March (GH). Collected between 450 and 1700 m (1500 ft and 5500 ft) (W, FS, P).

200. *Kenopia striata* (**Blyth 1842**) : **Striped Wren Babbler**
 Resident in lowland forest but local (G). Observed at Poring (BL). Another odd record which needs corroboration (FS).

201. *Napothera crassa* **(Sharpe 1888) : Mountain Wren Babbler**
A higher montane resident confined to Borneo. Commonly seen from 2000 to 2850 m (6500 to 9400 ft) on Kinabalu (S), and ringed at 1500 and 2750 m (5000 ft and 9000 ft) in 1964 (M, DY). Many collected between 950 and 2350 m (3100 and 7750 ft).

202. *Napothera epilepidota* **(Temminck 1827) : Eyebrowed Wren Babbler**
A sub-montane resident in Borneo. Collected at 900 m (3000 ft) (Sk) and at 1500 m (5000 ft) (W).

203. *Macronous gularis* **(Horsfield 1822) : Striped Tit Babbler**
An abundant resident throughout the lowlands of Borneo in both old and secondary jungle. Common in cultivated areas and around human habitations (S). Found in old clearings on Kinabalu up to 300 m (1000 ft) (W). Collected at 300 m (1000 ft) (Sk, W); 500 m (1600 ft) (FS) and eggs taken by Ryves at Kiau in February and March (GH).

204. *Macronous ptilosus* **Jardine and Selby 1835 : Fluffy backed Tit Babbler**
Resident throughout Borneo in the lowlands in primary and secondary forest (S). Collected at Poring (FS). Collected by Whitehead *"a few hundred feet up the spurs of Kina Balu"*.

205. *Stachyris nigriceps* **Blyth 1844 : Grey-throated Babbler**
A montane/sub-montane resident and fairly common on Kinabalu. Whitehead found it frequenting old rice plantations and true forest from 300 to 1500 m (1000 ft to 5000 ft). Ringed at 1500, 1800 and 3300 m (5000, 6000 and 10,800 ft) in 1964 (M). Several collected at lower elevations.

206. *Stachyris poliocephala* **(Temminck 1836) : Grey-headed Babbler**
Resident and commonest at submontane elevations, in lowland forest, ascending to 1200 m (4000 ft) (G). Collected at Poring (FS), and at 1200 m (4000 ft) (W).

207. *Stachyris nigricollis* **(Temminck 1836) : Black-throated Babbler**
Common resident throughout the lowlands of Borneo in primary forest (S). Netted at Poring (P).

208. *Stachyris maculata* **(Temminck 1836) : Chestnut-rumped Babbler**
Lowland forest resident, locally common (S). Collected at Poring (FS).

209. *Stachyris erythroptera* **(Blyth 1842) : Chestnut-winged Babbler**
A common resident in lowland forests in Borneo (S). Collected at Poring (FS).

210. *Stachyris rufifrons* **Hume 1873 : Rufous-fronted Babbler**
Appears to be a rare sub-montane resident in primary forest (FS). Netted at Poring (PP).

211. ***Garrulax lugubris*** **(Muller 1835) : Black Laughing-thrush**
A montane resident in Borneo. On Kinabalu, Whitehead met with it at 1200 m (4000 ft) in primary forest and considered it to be local and common (S), but Gore regards it as fairly common on Kinabalu at around 1200 to 1800 m (4000 to 6000 ft). Appears in small groups, often mixed with other laughing-thrushes at long, irregular intervals, for a few days at a time at Park Headquarters (PP). Has been observed at Poring (BL) and netted at 1500 m (5000 ft) (M).

212. ***Garrulax palliatus*** **(Bonaparte 1850) : Grey-and-Brown or Sunda Laughing- thrush**
A montane resident common on Kinabalu. Specimens taken at 900 m (3000 ft) (Sk) and at 1200 m (4000 ft) (W). Netted at Park Headquarters (DY), where it is common.

213. ***Garrulax mitratus*** **(Muller 1835) : Chestnut-capped Laughing-thrush**
An abundant montane resident widespread in Borneo. Whitehead described its range on Kinabalu as 200 to 2750 m (700 to 9000 ft). Particularly common on Kinabalu from 900 to 3200 m (3000 ft to 10,500 ft) (S) and has been recorded at 3350 m (11,000 ft) (J). A great number collected from 750 to 3100 m (2500 to 10,200 ft). The bird's 'laughing' song is a common call around Park Headquarters. Eggs taken by Ryves at Kiau in February and March (GH). *G. m. treacheri* (Sharpe 1879), is the Kinabalu race.

214. ***Pteruthius flaviscapis*** **(Temminck 1835) : White-browed Shrike Babbler**
A montane resident in Borneo. Specimens obtained from 1200 to 3050 m (4000 to 10,000 ft) by several collectors.

215. ***Alcippe brunneicauda*** **(Salvadori 1879) : Brown Fulvetta**
A lowland to sub-montane resident in old jungle throughout Borneo. Collected at Poring and at 600 m (2000 ft) (FS). Occurs on the Crocker Range up to 1200 m (FS).

216. ***Yuhina everetti*** **(Sharpe 1887) : Chestnut-crested Yuhina**
A sub-montane resident, confined to Borneo, and common on Kinabalu in active flocks from 500 to 2150 m (1600 to 7000 ft) (S). Nesting in March at Park Headquarters, and eggs collected by Ryves at Kiau in February and March (GH). Obtained by many collectors between 900 and 2600 m (3000 and 8500 ft).

217. ***Yuhina zantholeuca*** **(Blyth 1844) : White-bellied Yuhina**
A sub-montane resident with a wide altitudinal range from sea-level to 1500 m (5000 ft). Collected at 1500 m (5000 ft) (W).

ACANTHIZIDAE : AUSTRALIAN WARBLERS

218. ***Gerygone sulphurea*** **Wallace 1864 : Flyeater**
Resident in Borneo but more often heard than seen. Collected on the lower slopes of Kinabalu by Everett (Sh). Included in the Sylviidae in Smythies (1981). See White, C.M.N. and Bruce, M.D. (1986) The Birds of Wallacea. *B.O.U. Checklist 7*, British Ornithologists' Union, London.

SYLVIIDAE : WARBLERS

219. *Urosphena whiteheadi* **(Sharpe 1888) : Short-tailed Bush Warbler or Bornean Stubtail**
A montane species confined to Borneo, more often heard than seen. Found above 900 m (3000 ft) (G). Collected between 1200 and 2150 m (4000 and 7000 ft) (W). In April 1982 a nest with 2 eggs was found along the Silau-Silau Trail at Park Headquarters. (SP). *Cettia whiteheadi* in Smythies (1981). See White, C.M.N. & Bruce, M.D. (1986) The Birds of Wallacea. *B.O.U. Check-list 7*. British Ornithologists' Union.

220. *Cettia vulcania* **(Blyth 1870) : Mountain or Sunda Bush Warbler**
A montane resident with a restricted range. Whitehead obtained it from 2150 to 3650 m (7000 to 12,000 ft) and Harrisson found it common above 2900 m (9500 ft) (S). Gore regards its range as being from 1350 to 3650 m (4500 ft to 12,000 ft). There are two races: *C. f. oreophila* Sharpe 1888 on Kinabalu and the darker *C. f. banksi* Chasen 1935 elsewhere. Collected between 1500 and 3350 m (5000 and 11,000 ft) (Sk, P). *C. montanus* in Smythies (1981). See Wells, D.R. (1982) Biological species limits in the *Cettia fortipes* complex. *Bulletin of the British Ornithologists' Club* 102: 57–62.

221. *Bradypterus accentor* **(Sharpe 1888) : Kinabalu Friendly Warbler or Friendly Bush Warbler**
Confined to Borneo on the higher slopes of Kinabalu, Mt. Tambuyukon and Mt. Trus Madi. Seen singly from 2150 to 2850 m (7000 to 9300 ft) above Poring. Whitehead found it from 2150 to 2750 m (7000 to 9000 ft) and Harrisson regards it as common from 3050 to 3650 m (10,000 to 12,000 ft) (S). All collections made above 2200 m (7200 ft). A sight record from Tambuyukon at *c*. 1800 m (6000 ft) in 1982 (PP).

222. *Prinia flaviventris* **(Delessert 1840) : Yellow-bellied Wren Warbler or Prinia**
A common resident of the lowlands in the open (S) and up to 1100 m (3600 ft) (FS). Collected at Poring (FS), also by Everett (Sh) and Griswold (P), but no height recorded.

223. *Locustella ochotensis* **(Middendorff 1853) : Middendorff's Warbler**
Rare passage migrant and winter visitor to Borneo. One record from Kinabalu at 300 m (1000 ft) by Whitehead.

224. *Phylloscopus borealis* **(Blasius 1858) : Arctic Warbler**
Common passage migrant and winter visitor to all parts of Borneo (S). Collected at 300 m (1000 ft) on Kinabalu (W), 900 m (3000 ft) (Sk) and at 2000 m (6500 ft) (FS). A sight record from Poring (BL).

225. *Phylloscopus trivirgatus* **Strickland 1849 : Mountain Leaf Warbler**
A common higher montane resident on Kinabalu from 1500 to 3050 m (5000 to 10,000 ft) (S), and many collected in this range.

226. *Seicercus montis* (Sharpe 1887) : **Yellow-breasted Warbler**
A common resident on Kinabalu above 1200 m (4000 ft) (G), and often seen at Park Headquarters and recorded up to 2450 ft (8000 ft). Several collected between 1050 and 1500 m (3500 and 5000 ft).

227. *Abroscopus superciliaris* (Blyth 1859) : **Yellow-bellied Warbler**
A sub-montane resident. Inhabits the tangled bamboo jungle on the steep sides of Kinabalu at 900 to 1800 m (3000 to 6000 ft) (S, FS), and collected within this range. Eggs taken by Ryves at Kiau in March (GH).

228. *Orthotomus cuculatus* **Temminck 1836 : Mountain Tailorbird**
A high montane resident from 1200 to 1800 m (4000 to 6000 ft) on Kinabalu, where it is common (G). Seen regularly at Park Headquarters, and one sighted at 2650 m (8700 ft) (J). Netted at 1500 m (5000 ft) in 1964 (M) and collected at 1200 m (4000 ft) (W).

229. *Orthotomus sericeus* **Temminck 1836 : Red or Rufous-tailed Tailorbird**
Resident and common in the lowlands. Collected at Poring (FS).

230. *Orthotomus sepium* **Horsfield 1821 : Red-headed or Ashy Tailorbird**
A common resident throughout the lowlands. A specimen obtained by Griswold on Kinabalu, but no height or locality given (P), and collected at 300 m (1000 ft) (W). Occurs up to 1140 m (3750 ft) on the Crocker Range (FS). *O. ruficeps* in Smythies (1981). See Hoogerwerf, A. (1962) Further notes on the Ashy Tailor Bird, formerly known as *Orthotomus ruficeps* (Lesson) and *Orthotomus cinereus* Blyth. *Bulletin of the British Ornithologists' Club* 82: 147–154.

MUSCICAPIDAE : FLYCATCHERS

231. *Rhipidura albicollis* (Vieillot 1818) **White-throated Fantail**
A common montane resident from 1200 to 2750 m (4000 to 9000 ft). Seen occasionally above Poring at 1500 to 1800 m (5000 to 6000 ft) (S). One of the common birds around Park Headquarters. Collected between 900 and 2750 m (3000 and 9000 ft).

232. *Rhipidura perlata* **Muller 1843 : Spotted Fantail**
A common lowland resident in primary and secondary forest up to 1500 m (5000 ft) (S). One observed at 1600 m (5300 ft) (J) and at 1050 m (3500 ft) above Poring (S). Collected at Poring (FS).

233. *Rhipidura javanica* (Sparrman 1788) : **Pied Fantail**
A common resident throughout the lowlands in cultivated country and gardens. Observed at Poring (J) and also ringed at 1500 m (5000 ft) by Medway on the Pinosuk Plateau. Collected at 300 m (1000 ft) (W).

234. *Culicicapa ceylonensis* (Swainson 1820) : **Grey-headed Flycatcher**
A sub-montane resident throughout Borneo locally common to 1700 m (5500 ft).

One observed at 1050 m (3500 ft) above Poring (S). Specimens from 950 m (3200 ft) (Sk) and 900 m (3000 ft) (W).

235. *Muscicapa sibirica* **Gmelin 1789 : Sooty or Dark-sided Flycatcher**
Passage migrant and winter visitor to Borneo in small numbers (S), up to 1500 m (5000 ft) (G). Observed at 1600 m (5300 ft) in September, October and January (J).

236. *Muscicapa ferruginea* **(Hodgson 1845) : Ferruginous Flycatcher**
Passage migrant and winter visitor. Specimens collected from the lower slopes of Kinabalu (S) and from 1500 m (5000 ft) (Bs).

237. *Muscicapa latirostris* **Raffles 1822 : (Asian) Brown Flycatcher**
Passage migrant and winter visitor (S). Small flocks netted at about 1600 m (5300 ft) in February (J). Collected at 900 m (3000 ft) (W). Watson reverts to *M. daurica* Pallas 1811. See Watson, G.E. (1986) Old World, Holarctic and Oriental Phylloscopidae, Muscicapidae, and Monarchidae; in Mayr, E. & Coltrell, G.W. (eds.) *Chick-list of Birds of the World, II.* Cambridge, Mus. Comparative Zoology.

238. *Eumyias thalassina* **(Swainson 1839) : Verditer Flycatcher**
Uncommon sub-montane resident. Whitehead found it only on the lower slopes of Kinabalu below 300 m (1000 ft). A specimen obtained by Griswold on Kinabalu but no height or locality given (P). Occurs on the Crocker Range to 1140 m (3750 ft), (FS). *Muscicapa thalassina* in Smythies (1981). See White, C.M.N. & Bruce, M.D. (1986) The Birds of Wallacea. *B.O.U. Checklist no.7.* British Ornithologists' Union, London.

239. *Eumyias indigo* **(Horsfield 1821) : Indigo Flycatcher**
A montane resident ranging from 1500 to 1800 m (5000 to 6000 ft) and less frequently, down to 900 m (3000 ft) (S). Many collected between 800 and 2450 m (2700 and 8000 ft). Often seen at Park Headquarters and one sighting at 2650 m (8700 ft) (J). *Muscicapa indigo* in Smythies (1981). See Van Marle, J.G. & Voors, K.H. (1988) The Birds of Sumatra. *B.O.U. Checklist no.10.* British Ornithologists' Union, London.

240. *Cyanoptila cyanomelana* **(Temminck 1829) : Blue-and-White Flycatcher**
A passage migrant and winter visitor to Borneo in fair numbers, up to 1350 m (4500 ft) (S). Netted at Poring and Park Headquarters during February and March (PP, J), several collected at 300 m (1000 ft) (W), and 900 m (3000 ft) (Sk). Seen on Kinabalu at 1350 m (4500 ft) (S).

241. *Cyornis concreta* **(Muller 1835) : White-tailed Flycatcher**
A sub-montane resident from 600 to 1200 m (2000 to 4000 ft). Locally common (G). Observed on the road to the Power Station from Park Headquarters at about 1700 m (5500 ft) (J). The local race *C.c. everetti* (Sharpe 1890) has no white in the tail which makes the name 'white-tailed' confusing for Borneo (S).

242. *Cyornis turcosa* (Bruggemann 1877) : **Malaysian Blue Flycatcher**
Common lowland resident in primary and secondary forest (S). Collected at Poring (FS) and also at Ranau (K).

243. *Cyornis banyumas* (Horsfield 1822) : **Hill Blue Flycatcher**
Sparingly distributed as a sub-montane resident in Borneo. Specimens have been collected from Kinabalu (S). Eggs taken by Ryves at Kiau in March (S, GH).

244. *Cyornis superba* Stresemann 1925 : **Bornean Blue Flycatcher**
A sub-montane resident confined to Borneo; most specimens taken between 600 and 1500 m (2000 and 5000 ft) (S), which is anomalously high up and represents possible confusion with *C. banyumas*. A record from Ranau (BL) and netted at Poring (SM).

245. *Ficedula hyperythra* (Blyth 1842) : **Snowy-browed Flycatcher**
Sub-montane resident on Kinabalu. Fairly plentiful at 1200 to 2450 m (4000 to 8000 ft) and goes up to 3350 m (11,000 ft). (S). Common above Poring 1800 to 2900 m (6000 to 9500 ft) (S). Obtained by several collectors between 1700 and 3350 m (5500 and 11,000 ft).

246. *Ficedula mugimaki* (Temminck 1835) : **Mugimaki Flycatcher**
Passage migrant and winter visitor in small numbers, wintering on the mountains (S). Several recorded at Park Headquarters (J).

247. *Ficedula dumetoria* (Wallace 1863) : **Rufous-chested Flycatcher**
A sub-montane resident sparingly distributed throughout Borneo (S). Netted at 1050 m (3500 ft), 1964 (M), 1600 m (5300 ft) (J), and at Poring (DY).

248. *Ficedula narcissina* (Temminck 1835) : **Narcissus Flycatcher**
Passage migrant and winter visitor to Sabah in small numbers (S). Obtained at 300 m (1000 ft) by Whitehead and also by Goss and Dodge early in 1904 but no height or locality given (B).

249. *Ficedula westermanni* (Sharpe 1888) : **Little Pied Flycatcher**
A montane resident of Kinabalu. Common from 1500 to 2450 m (5000 to 8000 ft) (S) and many collections in this range. Regularly seen at Park Headquarters (S).

250. *Muscicapella hodgsoni* (Horsfield and Moore 1854) : **Pygmy Blue Flycatcher**
A rare montane resident in Borneo, collected once on Kinabalu at 1200 m (4000 ft) (W).

251. *Rhinomyias olivacea* (Hume 1877) : **Olive-backed or Fulvous-chested (Jungle) Flycatcher**
Lowland resident. Everett collected one on Kinabalu (S) but no height given.

252. *Rhinomyias umbratilis* (Strickland 1849) : **White-throated or Grey-chested Jungle Flycatcher**
Resident throughout the lowlands of Borneo in primary forest (S). Collected at 300 m (1000 ft) (W), and 500 m (1600 ft) (FS). Also obtained by Griswold but no height given.

253. *Rhinomyias ruficauda* (Sharpe 1877) : **Rufous- or Chestnut-tailed Jungle Flycatcher**
A montane resident recorded on Kinabalu at 900 m (3000 ft) by Whitehead. Collected at 900 m (3000 ft) (Sk).

254. *Rhinomyias gularis* Sharpe 1888 : **White-browed or Eyebrowed Jungle Flycatcher**
A higher montane resident. Whitehead found it at 900 to 2150 m (3000 to 7000 ft) on Kinabalu but more plentiful at the higher elevations (S). Netted at 1500 m (5000 ft) on the Pinosuk Plateau (SM), at Park Headquarters (DY) and at 3300 m (10,800 ft) (M). Collected at 950 m (3200 ft) (Sk) and 1500 m (5000 ft) (Bs).

255. *Philentoma pyrhopterum* (Temminck 1836) : **Rufous-winged Flycatcher**
A common resident throughout the lowlands of Borneo to 1500 m (5000 ft) (S). Netted in Poring in 1971 (PP).

256. *Philentoma velatum* (Temminck 1825) : **Maroon-breasted Flycatcher**
Resident throughout the lowlands of Borneo, but apparently scarce or local in Sabah (S). Occasionally in the mountains up to 1500 m (5000 ft) (G). Obtained on Kinabalu by Whitehead at 600 m (2000 ft), and above Poring (FS).

257. *Hypothymis azurea* (Boddaert 1783) : **Black-naped Monarch**
Resident throughout the lowlands of Borneo (S), but ascending to about 1200 m (4000 ft) in the mountains (G). Collected at Poring (FS), and at Nalumad (J).

258. *Terpsiphone paradisi* (Linnaeus 1758) : **Asian Paradise Flycatcher**
A common resident in the lowlands of Borneo up to 1200 m (4000 ft) (S). Observed at *c*. 1200 m (4000 ft) on the road to the Kinabalu Park Headquarters from the west coast (J). Netted at Poring in 1971 (PP), and collected at Ranau (K).

PACHYCEPHALIDAE : WHISTLERS
259. *Pachycephala hypoxantha* (Sharpe 1887) : **Bornean (Mountain) Whistler**
A montane resident confined to Borneo. On Kinabalu Whitehead found it at 900 to 2450 m (3000 to 8000 ft) but more plentiful at the higher elevation. Several collected between 900 and 2150 m (3000 and 7000 ft). Seen as high as 2900 m (9600 ft) on Kinabalu (J).

SITTIDAE : NUTHATCHES
260. *Sitta frontalis* (Swainson 1820) : **Velvet-fronted Nuthatch**
A resident species common on the coast (G) and up to 2000 m (6500 ft) on Kinabalu (FS). Often seen at Park Headquarters (J). Collected at 900 m (3000 ft) (W).

Checklist of Birds

DICAEIDAE : FLOWERPECKERS

261. *Prionochilus xanthopygius* **Salvadori 1868 : Yellow-rumped Flowerpecker**
 Common lowland resident confined to Borneo (S). Netted at Poring in 1971 (PP).

262. *Prionochilus maculatus* **(Temminck 1836) : Yellow-breasted Flowerpecker**
 Common resident in the lowland forests (S). Netted at Poring (PP) and collected by Everett, but no height given (Sh).

263. *Dicaeum chrysorrheum* **Temminck 1829 : Yellow-vented Flowerpecker**
 Lowland to sub-montane resident and sparsely distributed throughout Borneo (S). One collected at 950 m (3200 ft) by Haviland in 1892 (Sk) and by Whitehead, but no height given.

264. *Dicaeum concolor* **Jerdon 1840 : Plain Flowerpecker**
 One specimen taken on Kinabalu by Griswold, but no height or locality given (P). Resident, but probably overlooked. A record from Poring (BL) and one clutch of two eggs taken by Ryves at Kiau in March (GH).

265. *Dicaeum monticolum* **Sharpe 1887 : Black-sided Flowerpecker**
 Common montane resident on Kinabalu above 900 m (3000 ft) (G). Obtained between 600 and 1700 m (2000 and 5500 ft) by several collectors. *D. celebicum* in Smythies (1981).

266. *Dicaeum cruentatum* **(Linnaeus 1758) : Scarlet-backed Flowerpecker**
 Resident throughout the lowlands (FS) and collected at 300 m (1000 ft) (W).

267. *Dicaeum trigonostigma* **(Scopoli 1786) : Orange-bellied Flowerpecker**
 A common lowland resident (S). Recorded from Kundasang at about 1300 m (4300 ft) (BL) and collected on Kinabalu, but no height or locality given, by Goss and Dodge (B) and Griswold (P). Also collected at 300 m (1000 ft) (W) and at 500 m (1600 ft) (FS).

NECTARINIDAE : SUNBIRDS AND SPIDERHUNTERS

268. *Anthreptes simplex* **(Muller 1843) : Plain Sunbird**
 A common resident throughout the lowlands of Borneo previously overlooked in the Park area. Recorded from Poring 1982 (FR) and 1985 (KP & JS).

269. *Anthreptes malacensis* **(Scopoli 1786) : Brown-throated Sunbird**
 One of the commonest sunbirds, resident throughout Borneo and found up to 950 m (3200 ft) (S). Collected on Kinabalu at 950 m (3200 ft) (P).

270. *Anthreptes rhodolaema* **Shelley 1878 : Red-throated Sunbird**
 Resident in the lowlands of Borneo but previously overlooked in the Park area. Seen at Poring 1982 (FR) and 1986 (DY).

271. *Anthreptes singalensis* **(Gmelin 1788) : Ruby-cheeked Sunbird**
 Lowland resident (S). Collected by Whitehead at 300 m (1000 ft).

272. *Hypogramma hypogrammicum* **(Muller 1843) : Purple-naped Sunbird**
Common lowland resident. Collected at Poring (FS).

273. *Nectarinia sperata* **(Linnaeus 1766) : Purple-throated Sunbird**
Common lowland resident (S). Collected in forest at Poring (FS).

274. *Nectarinia jugularis* **(Linnaeus 1766) : Yellow-breasted or Olive-backed Sunbird**
Resident and collected on Kinabalu at 1020 m (3500 ft) (P), 1050 m (3340 ft) (E) and 1350 m (4400 ft) (C). Recorded on one occasion at Park Headquarters (J).

275. *Aethopyga siparaja* **(Raffles 1822) : Crimson Sunbird**
Common lowland resident. Whitehead obtained it on Kinabalu up to 600 m (2000 ft) above which elevation *A. mystacalis* takes over (S). Collected at Ranau (K).

276. *Aethopyga mystacalis* **(Temminck 1822) : Scarlet Sunbird**
A sub-montane resident throughout the mountains of Borneo at moderate elevations. Collected at Kinabalu from 600 up to 1800 m (2000 up to 6000 ft) (W) and plentiful at about 1200 m (4000 ft) (S). Seen reguarly at Park Headquarters (J).

277. *Arachnothera longirostra* **(Latham 1790) : Little Spiderhunter**
Resident in lowland and scrub jungle ascending to 1350 m (4500 ft) (G). Collected at Poring (FS). Also collected by Griswold but no altitude given (P) and three obtained below 900 m (3000 ft) (W).

278. *Arachnothera robusta* **Muller and Schlegel 1845 : Long-billed Spiderhunter**
A lowland resident, but local and erratic in distribution (S). A female and an immature bird were knocked out while attempting to fly through the window of a cabin at Poring (D).

279. *Arachnothera flavigaster* **(Eyton 1839) : Spectacled Spiderhunter**
Resident but probably the rarest of the spiderhunters. Reaches 1700 m (5500 ft) in Sarawak (S), and one collected on eastern side of Kinabalu but no height or locality given (Sh).

280. *Arachnothera chrysogenys* **(Temminck 1826) : Yellow-eared Spiderhunter**
Resident in lowland forest, but not common (S). Seen at Poring (BL). This record needs to be corroborated (FS).

281. *Arachnothera affinis* **(Horsfield 1822) : Grey-breasted Spiderhunter**
Resident in primary forest (S). Several specimens collected on Kinabalu between 1000 and 1500 m (3100 and 5000 ft).

282. *Arachnothera juliae* **Sharpe 1887 : Whitehead's Spiderhunter**
Common montane resident above 1200 m (4000 ft) on Kinabalu (G), and confined to Borneo. Frequently observed at Park Headquarters and collected at 1700 m (5500 ft) (Sk, P).

ZOSTEROPIDAE : WHITE-EYES

283. *Zosterops atricapillus* **Salvadori 1879 : Black-capped White-eye**
A montane resident on Kinabalu from 900 m (3000 ft) upwards (S). Quite common at Park Headquarters and collected from 1000 to 2150 m (3100 to 7000 ft).

284. *Zosterops everetti* **Tweeddale 1877 : Everett's White-eye**
A sub-montane resident, fairly common on Kinabalu up to 1700 m (5500 ft) (G). Collected at 1500 m (5000 ft) (Bs).

285. *Oculocincta squamifrons* **(Sharpe 1892) : Pygmy White-eye**
A sub-montane resident confined to Borneo. Collected on Kinabalu as low as 200 m (600 ft) (S), and at 750 m (2500 ft) (C). One sighting at 2150 m (7000 ft) (J).

286. *Chlorocharis emiliae* **Sharpe 1888 : Mountain Blackeye**
A high montane resident confined to Borneo and the commonest bird above 3050 m (10,000 ft) on Kinabalu. On Kinabalu's East Ridge it was the commonest bird seen from 1700 to 2850 m (5500 to 9400 ft) (S). Specimens obtained from 1400 to 3650 m (4500 to 12,000 ft) by many collectors. Seen regularly around Park Headquarters during the drought in 1983 (PP).

STURNIDAE : STARLINGS

287. *Aplonis panayensis* **(Scopoli 1783) : Philippine (Glossy) Starling**
Abundant resident of coastal districts. One collected by Everett described as being *"procured on Kinabalu"* but no location or height given (Sh). Also collected at Ranau (K).

ESTRILDIDAE : MUNIAS

288. *Erythrura prasina* **(Sparrman 1788) : Long-tailed Munia or Pin-tailed Parrotfinch**
A bird of obscure status that seems subject to local movements. Whitehead observed large flocks in the Dusun rice fields on Kinabalu in January, specimens being collected by him. The following month there was no trace of the birds (S). A record from Park Headquarters in 1988 (BK).

289. *Erythrura hyperythra* **(Reichenbach 1862) : Bamboo Munia or Tawny-breasted Parrotfinch**
A higher montane resident in Borneo where it is scarce and rarely encountered. Whitehead collected three specimens on Kinabalu at 2450 m (8000 ft) and observed them at 2750 m (9000 ft). Several were seen by the Royal Society Expedition in 1964 (G) and were ringed at 1800 and 3300 m (6000 and 10,800 ft) by Medway. A dead bird was collected by Park staff at about 2600 m (8500 ft) near the Summit Trail in April 1988 (KNP).

290. *Lonchura fuscans* **(Cassin 1852) : Dusky Munia**
Abundant resident in fields and open grassy country but confined to Borneo. Collected at Poring (FS) and netted at 1050 m (3500 ft) on the Kinabalu East Ridge (M). Seen along the roadside at Park Headquarters more frequently in recent years (PP).

291. ***Lonchura malacca*** **(Linnaeus 1766) : Chestnut Munia**
Abundant resident and local nomad in Borneo. Collected at 1700 m (5500 ft) on Kinabalu (P), but scarce above 1200 m (4000 ft) (G). Netted at Poring (PP).

DICRURIDAE : DRONGOS

292. ***Dicrurus annectans*** **(Hodgson 1836) : Crow-billed Drongo**
Migrant wintering in lowland forests, but Burbidge collected two on Kinabalu at low altitude (S). One record from Poring in November (BL).

293. ***Dicrurus leucophaeus*** **Vieillot 1817 : Grey or Ashy Drongo**
A common montane resident throughout the mountains of Borneo. Abundant on Kinabalu around 1200 m (4000 ft) (G), and one of the most conspicuous birds at Park Headquarters. Nesting recorded in March at Park Headquarters (J) and eggs collected by Ryves at Kiau in the same month (GH). Many specimens obtained from 750 to 1800 m (2500 to 6000 ft).

294. ***Dicrurus aeneus*** **Vieillot 1817 : Bronzed Drongo**
Common lowland resident confined to primary forest (S). Netted at Poring (PP).

295. ***Dicrurus hottentottus*** **(Linnaeus 1766) : Spangled or Hair-crested Drongo**
A sub-montane resident throughout Borneo in primary forest (S). Frequents more open spaces in the neighbourhood of clearings from 750 to 1500 m (2500 to 5000 ft) (W). Seen and netted at Park Headquarters (J) and on the Pinosuk Plateau (M). Specimens from 750 and 900 m (2500 and 3000 ft) (Sk). Eggs collected by Ryves at Kaung in February (GH).

296. ***Dicrurus paradiseus*** **(Linnaeus 1766) : Greater Racket-tailed Drongo**
Common lowland resident in secondary and primary forest (S). Collected at Poring (FS) and at Kampung Nalumad (J).

ORIOLIDAE : ORIOLES

297. ***Oriolus chinensis*** **Linnaeus 1766 : Black-naped Oriole**
Rare in Borneo (S). A single record from Kinabalu in 1893 when a specimen was obtained by Everett (Sh) at Kampung Melangkap at over 600 m (2000 ft). Status unknown.

298. ***Oriolus xanthonotus*** **Horsfield 1821 : Dark-throated Oriole**
Resident throughout Borneo in lowland forests (S). Not found above 300 m (1000 ft) on Kinabalu by Whitehead. However, there are sightings from Poring and Ranau (BL, DY). Seen twice in mixed hunting parties on Mt. Tambuyukon at 550 m (1800 ft) and at 750 m (2500 ft) in 1982 (PP).

299. ***Oriolus cruentus*** **(Wagler 1827) : Black-and-Crimson Oriole**
Common montane resident. Several collected between 800 and 1350 m (2600 and 4500 ft) (Sk) and common at Park Headquarters (PP).

CORVIDAE : JAYS, MAGPIES, TREEPIES AND CROWS

300. *Platylophus galericulatus* (Cuvier 1817) : **Crested Jay**
   Common resident throughout the lowlands of Borneo (S). Sight record from 1300 m (4300 ft) (BL) and collected at 500 m (1600 ft) (FS) and 900 m (3000 ft) (W, Sk). Commonly seen at Poring (PP).

301. *Cissa chinensis* (Boddaert 1783) : **Common Green Magpie**
   Resident on Kinabalu from 300 to 1800 m (1000 to 5000 ft) (S) and several specimens collected. Eggs taken by Ryves at Kiau in February (GH).

302. *Cissa thalassina* (Temminck 1826) : **Short-tailed Green Magpie**
   A montane resident ranging from 900 to 2450 m (3000 to 8000 ft) (S). Scarce, but several collected within these limits.

303. *Dendrocitta occipitalis* (Muller 1835) : **Malaysian or Sunda Treepie**
   A montane resident and common on Kinabalu from about 300 to 2750 m (1000 to 9000 ft). Always seen around Park Headquarters. A large number collected between 800 and 2150 m (2700 and 7000 ft).

304. *Platysmurus leucopterus* (Temminck 1824) : **Black Magpie**
   A fairly common resident throughout the lowlands of Borneo (S). One specimen was procured on Kinabalu at nearly 300 m (1000 ft) (W).

305. *Corvus macrorhynchos* (Wagler 1827) : **Jungle or Large-billed Crow**
   Only four specimens known from Borneo (S), one of which was collected by Everett on Kinabalu (Sh). Status unknown.

306. *Corvus enca* (Horsfield 1821) : **Slender-billed Crow**
   Fairly common throughout the lowlands and interior. Collected on Kinabalu by Treacher (Sh) but no height or locality given; and by Whitehead at 300 m (1000 ft). Also recorded from Poring (BL).

REFERENCES

Anon. 1977. Borneo Birds—Yale Expedition 1976–77. Unpublished mimeograph.

Berwick, E.J.H. & Lathbury, Sir G. 1959. List of birds seen in North Borneo, 8th–17th November, 1959. Unpublished mimeograph.

Blasius, W. 1901. *Vogel vom Kina-Balu (British Nord Borneo). Journal für Ornithologie:* 1901: 68–69.

Bober, T.S. 1973. Personal communication (List of birds collected on Mt. Kinabalu and presented to the Smithsonian Institution, Washington D.C. by the following collectors: P.S. Bourns and D.C. Worcester, 1892–93; G.A. Goss and H.D. Dodge, 1904; D.H. Johnson, 1951; R.E. Kuntz, 1960).

Chuang, S.H. 1974. Personal communication. Being a list of bird skins from the Kinabalu area housed in the Department of Zoology, University of Singapore, formerly the Singapore National Museum collection.

Enriquez, C.M. 1927. Kinabalu, the Haunted Mountain of Borneo. H.F. & G.Witherby, London.

Everett, A.H. 1889. A list of the Birds of the Bornean Group of Islands. *Journal of the Straits Branch, Royal Asiatic Society* 20: 91–212.

Fogden, M.P.L. 1965. Borneo Bird Notes, 1963–65. *Sarawak Museum Journal* 12(25–26, new series): 395–414.

Francis, C.M. 1986. Checklist of the Birds of Sabah. Western Foundation of Vertebrate Zoology, U.S.A.

Gibson-Hill, C.A. 1950. A collection of Bird's Eggs from North Borneo. *Bulletin of the Raffles Museum Singapore* 21: 106–115. (Notes on a collection of bird's eggs taken by V.W. Ryves during 1938 and 1939).

Glenister, A.G. 1971 (2nd edition). The Birds of the Malay Peninsula. Oxford University Press.

Gore, M.E.J. 1964. Notes on nests of the Golden Naped Barbet, Black Throated Barbet and Velvet Fronted Nuthatch. *Sabah Society Journal* 2(3): 138–139.

Gore, M.E.J. 1968. Checklist of the Birds of Sabah, Borneo. *Ibis* 110: 165–196.

Hanitsch, R. 1900. An expedition to Mount Kinabalu, British North Borneo. *Journal of the Straits Branch, Royal Asiatic Society* 34: 49–88.

Harrisson, T. 1955. The mountain black-eye *(Chlorocharis)*. *Sarawak Museum Journal*. 6 (new series): 662–687.

Harrisson, T. 1964. Remarks on the birds of Mt. Kinabalu. In: Corner, E.J.H., A Discussion on the Results of the Royal Society Expedition to North Borneo, 1961. *Proceedings of the Royal Society, London, B.* 161: 80–82.

Ho, C.C. & Poore, M.E.D. 1968. The value of the Mount Kinabalu National Park, Malaysia to Plant Ecology. In: Conservation in Tropical South East Asia. I.U.C.N.

Jenkins, D.V. 1970. Bird notes from the Kinabalu National Park. Annual Report of Sabah National Park Trustees for 1969.

Kinabalu Park Headquarters File: KP(E)/5/21. Bird records and sightings.

Kortekaas, C.M., Rozendaal, F.G. & Schringa, J. 1982. The Birds of the Kinabalu National Park, Sabah, Borneo. Unpublished records filed at Kinabalu Park Headquarters.

Lambert, F. 1985. Bird records at Kinabalu Park, 18–23 June 1985. Unpublished records filed at Kinabalu Park Headquarters.

McClure, H.E. 1973. Some aspects of Bird Migration in Asia. In: Nature Conservation in the Pacific. I.U.C.N.

Medway, Lord. 1964. List of Birds banded on Mt. Kinabalu, Sabah, Malaysia with the Royal Society Expedition 1964. Unpublished mimeograph.

Pendlebury, H.M. & Chasen, F.N. 1932. A zoological expedition to Mt. Kinabalu, British North Borneo (1929). *Journal of the Federated Malay States Museum* 17: 1–38.

Peters, J.L. 1940. Birds from Mt. Kinabalu, North Borneo. *Bulletin of the Museum of Comparative Zoology, Harvard* 87(3): 195–211.

Pierce, S. 1982. Unpublished bird records filed at Kinabalu Park Headquarters.

Pierce, S. 1983. Unpublished bird records filed at Kinabalu Park Headquarters.

Phillipps, A. 1982. Diary report of an expedition to Mt. Tambuyukon. Unpublished report to the Sabah Parks.

Phillipps, Q. 1970. Some important nesting notes from Sabah. *Sabah Society Journal* 5(2): 141–144.

Phillipps, Q. 1973. Kinabalu—Sabah's National Park. *Animals* 15(7): 292–298.

Phillipps, Q. & Phillipps, J. 1970. Bird banding in the Kinabalu National Park. Annual Report, Sabah National Park Trustees for 1970.

Prentice, R.C. & Eddie, W.M. 1981. An annotated list of birds recorded in Sabah and Brunei, (July–Sept. 1981). In: Eddie, W.M.M. (ed.) 1981. Report of the University of Aberdeen Expedition to Mt. Kinabalu (Sabah) 1981. Unpublished.

Sabah Museum. Ringing Records. Unpublished.

Sarawak Museum. 1975. List of bird skins from Mt. Kinabalu in the Museum's collection. Unpublished mimeograph.

Schmitt, J. & Phillipps, K. 1985. Bird list from Poring Hot Springs, 4–8 May 1985. Unpublished records filed at Kinabalu Park Headquarters.

Sharpe, R.B. 1879. On collections of birds from Kinabalu Mountain, in North Western Borneo. *Proceedings of the Zoological Society, London* 1879: 245–249.

Sharpe, R.B. 1893. Bornean Notes I. Additions to the avifauna of Mount Kinabalu. *Ibis* 1893: 560–563.

Sharpe, R.B. 1894. Bornean Notes III (x). Further additions to the avifauna of Mt. Kinabalu. *Ibis* 1894: 538–540.

Sharpe, R.B. 1894. Bornean Notes III (xi). Notes on birds collected in North Borneo by Mr. A.H. Everett. *Ibis* 1894: 540, 531.

Sharpe, R.B. & Whitehead, J. 1893. On the birds of North Borneo. (Being an arrangement of Sharpe's Ibis papers on the Whitehead collections with additional notes by Whitehead). Appendix 2. In: Whitehead, J. The Exploration of Kina Balu, North Borneo. Gurney & Jackson, London.

Sheldon, F. 1977. List of Poring Birds from the Yale Collection. Unpublished mimeograph.

Smythies, B.E. 1959. Bird Notes from Mt. Kinabalu. *Sarawak Museum Journal* 9: 257–262.

Smythies, B.E. 1968. (2nd edition) The Birds of Borneo. Oliver & Boyd, Edinburgh.

Smythies, B.E. 1962. Special Reports—Birds. In: Corner, E.J.H., Royal Society Expedition to North Borneo 1961: Reports. *Proceedings of the Linnean Society, London,* 175(1): 50–54.

Smythies, B.E. 1964. The birds of Mt. Kinabalu and their zoogeographical relationships. In: Corner, E.J.H., A Discussion on the Results of the Royal Society Expedition to North Borneo, 1961. *Proceedings of the Royal Society London, B* 161: 75–80.

Smythies, B.E. 1981. The Birds of Borneo (3rd edition). Sabah Society with Malayan Nature Society.

Stauffer, P.H. 1973. Geology and the Malayan Nature Journal. *Malayan Nature Journal* 25: 161–183 (1971–72).

Thompson, M.C. 1966. Birds from North Borneo. University of Kansas Publications, Museum of Natural History 17: 377–433.

Wells, D.R. 1973. Birds in the Malayan Nature Journal: An Annotated Bibliography for the years 1940–1972. *Malayan Nature Journal* 25: 62–96.

Whitehead, J. 1893. The Exploration of Kina Balu, North Borneo. Gurney & Jackson, London.

Fig.1. The Slow Loris *(Nycticebus coucang)* is a small, nocturnal primate which feeds on ripe, fleshy fruits and small animals including insects. It occurs around Mount Kinabalu to an altitude of about 1300 m. *(Photo: W.M. Poon)*

MAMMALS

Junaidi Payne

This chapter replaces (but owes much to) the chapter on small mammals of Mt. Kinabalu by Drs. Lim Boo Liat and Illar Muul in the first edition of "Kinabalu—Summit of Borneo" (Lim & Muul, 1978). This new chapter attempts to summarise and clarify the main features of the earlier one, while incorporating large mammals and adding some new information on the small ones. Most of the new information comes from that compiled and kindly supplied by Anthea Phillipps (1991). Mr. Quentin Phillipps, who was present at Poring in 1970 when Lim and Muul collected numerous small mammals, kindly clarified some records which in published literature are equivocal, and added some of his own unpublished observations.

GENERAL FEATURES

All the species of mammals which occur on Mt. Kinabalu and its foothills can be assigned to one of two broad groups. Firstly, there are those which are primarily animals of the lowlands and hills, occurring throughout much of Sabah and which extend up the slopes of Mt. Kinabalu to maximum altitudes which vary with species. For convenience, these are called "lowland" species (Appendix 1). At least ninety species in this group have been recorded either within Kinabalu Park, or in the secondary forests fringing the Park boundary. Twenty-one of this group are bats. Further studies undoubtedly would reveal that more than one hundred lowland species occur within the Kinabalu Park. Secondly, there is a group of twenty-two species, which in Borneo are confined to mountain ranges, and which are called "montane" species (Appendix 2).

A number of general comments may be made about the lowland and montane groupings. The two groups of species are not separate on the mountain, and there is a great altitudinal range within which lowland and montane species are sympatric, even amongst pairs of species which are morphologically (and presumably ecologically) very similar. Clear examples are the Plain and Whitehead's Pigmy Squirrels and Prevost's and Kinabalu Squirrels. Possibly, breeding populations of such pairs of species are spatially separate while non-breeding individuals are not similarly confined. The lowest record of a montane species is from dipterocarp forest at 300 m (1000 ft) (Kinabalu Squirrel), while two lowland species (Barking Deer and Sambar Deer) have been recorded in upper montane forest as high as 3350 m (11,000 ft).

For most lowland species, the maximum altitude at which individuals have been recorded on Mt. Kinabalu is higher than the maximum altitude recorded for the same species in other mountain ranges. The dipterocarp forest zone on Mt. Kinabalu extends to about 1200 m (4000 ft) altitude, as compared to about 900 m (3000 ft) elsewhere. Of all the lowland mammal species recorded within or adjacent to the Park, 45 (about 50%) have not been recorded above 1200 m (4000 ft) and these may be presumed to be limited to dipterocarp forest. The remaining species are evidently not limited by the extent of the dipterocarp zone. A few, such as the Plantain Squirrel and *Rattus* species, are rare in, or absent from, dipterocarp forests, and probably have increased their range by moving into secondary growth at high altitudes. The high-altitude records on Mt. Kinabalu of large-bodied, mobile lowland animals such as deer, pig and Sun Bear probably represent non-resident or non-breeding individuals. The highest altitude records for at least six lowland bat species and two lowland-dipterocarp forest rat species were obtained by Allen & Coolidge (1940); they are well above the highest records for those species obtained by other workers either on Mt. Kinabalu or elsewhere. In some taxonomic groups of lowland mammals found in the Kinabalu Park, the species with the largest body size extends to the highest altitude. This is apparent for tree squirrels, rats, tree-mice, deer and carnivores generally, and is in accordance with general trends on a world-wide basis for taxa of large body size to occur in cold climates. However, for some groups (for example, fruit bats, insectivorous bats, primates, flying squirrels and cats), this observation does not hold true.

All montane mammal species known in Borneo occur in the Kinabalu Park, but only two members of this group (Black Shrew and Kinabalu Shrew) are known only from Mt.

Fig.2. The Ferret-Badger *(Melogale personata)* occurs at altitudes between 1070 and 3000 m on Mount Kinabalu. Its diet is believed to include earthworms and small vertebrates. It has close relatives in the mountain ranges of mainland Asia and Java, but in Borneo appears to be confined to Mt. Kinabalu and the Crocker Range. *(Photo: A. Lamb)*

Kinabalu. Thirteen (60%) of the montane species occur only in Borneo, while two (Summit Rat and Mountain Giant Rat) occur only in the mountains of Borneo and Sumatra, and two more (Grey Fruit Bat and Long-tailed Mountain Rat) only in the mountains of Borneo, Sumatra and Peninsular Malaysia. The remaining five (Lesser Gymnure, Sunda Shrew, Himalayan Water Shrew, Spotted Giant Flying Squirrel and Ferret-badger) have a wide distribution encompassing mainland Asia and some of the Sunda islands; in some or all areas outside of Borneo, these species occur in lowland habitats. Bones of the Lesser Gymnure and Ferret-badger have been found at Niah caves in northern Sarawak, not much above present sea level, the latter dating from about 20,000 years ago (Harrisson, 1978). Some montane species cover a large altitudinal range on Mt. Kinabalu, spanning several habitat types. The Mountain Treeshrew, Smooth-tailed Treeshrew, Grey Fruit Bat, Jentink's Squirrel, Bornean Mountain Ground Squirrel, Whitehead's Pigmy Squirrel, Mountain Giant Bat, Long-tailed Mountain Rat, Mountain Spiny Rat and Ferret-badger occur from upper dipterocarp forest into the upper montane mossy forest zone. It would seem likely, therefore, that at least some montane species are not restricted to particular habitats but instead possess physiological and behavioural adaptations permitting them to live in a relatively cold climate. In contrast, the Kinabalu Squirrel and Brooke's Squirrel are listed as montane animals because they are confined to the mountain ranges of north-western Borneo, yet they occur only on the lower part of Mt. Kinabalu in dipterocarp and lower montane forests.

INSECTIVORES

The mammals classified as insectivores feed only or predominantly on invertebrate animals. Superficially, they resemble rodents, but they are characterised by rounded or conical teeth with sharp points, unlike rodents, which have chisel-like front teeth for gnawing hard plant material. Borneo's largest insectivore, the moonrat, has been recorded only on the fringes of Kinabalu Park. The Lesser Gymnure is restricted on Mt. Kinabalu to forest above the dipterocarp level, but on mainland Asia, it extends to lowland forests. Four species of shrews are known from Mt. Kinabalu. They are rarely seen because they are small and do not enter conventional traps used for obtaining small mammals. However, shrews may sometimes be seen running across forest paths, and they can be caught by pitfall traps sunk into the ground. The South-east Asian White-toothed Shrew and Himalayan Water Shrew are widespread through much of Asia. The Black Shrew, known only from one specimen, is the only mammal found on Mt. Kinabalu which is unique to the area and which has no close affinities with any other known member of its taxonomic group (Medway, 1977). The Kinabalu Shrew was classified as a sub-species of the South-east Asian White-toothed Shrew (Medway, 1977; Payne *et al.*, 1985) until Musser (pers. comm. to C.M. Francis) discovered that specimens of both have been collected at the same site, indicating that they represent two closely-related but distinct species.

TREESHREWS

Treeshrews have been classified as both primates and insectivores, but are now regarded as a distinct group of their own, known as Scandentia. They feed primarily on insects and fruits. Borneo has ten species of treeshrews, the greatest number of any region where the order occurs. The Mountain Treeshrew is usually the most commonly seen mammal in the lower montane forest on Mt. Kinabalu, and it is the species which most frequently enters cage traps set for small mammals in this habitat.

DERMOPTERA

There are only two species within this order of mammals, both colugos. The alternative name of Flying Lemur is misleading, because these animals are not related to lemurs, and they travel through the forest mainly by gliding. The Bornean species, believed to feed mainly on leaf shoots and possibly bark and sap, occurs at Poring Hot Springs (500 m; 1700 ft) but has never been recorded above about 900 m (3000 ft) altitude at any location.

BATS

Although all bats are classified under one order, Chiroptera, it has now been established that the grouping is artificial, because fruit bats and insectivorous bats have evolved from different ancestors to become morphologically similar. Of the seventeen species of fruit bats and seventy-five species of insectivorous bats known from Borneo, all except one, the Grey Fruit Bat, are primarily lowland animals. The power of true flight enables individuals to range over relatively large distances in order to feed, unlike flightless small mammals, in which species may cover a great altitudinal range but individuals are generally confined

Fig.3. The Malay Civet or Tangalung *(Viverra tangalunga)* is one of eight species of civets recorded on and around Mount Kinabalu. This species is active mainly on the ground and feeds on small vertebrates and invertebrates. *(Photo: K.M. Wong)*

to ranges of only a few hectares. The Large Flying-fox, which has been observed at Poring, is probably the most mobile mammal in Borneo. It is likely that all individuals spend some of the time in coastal and island habitats, moving according to availability of food supplies.

PRIMATES

Both Bornean species of nocturnal primates, tarsier and slow loris, have been reported from the lower fringes of Mt. Kinabalu (Lim & Muul, 1978). The Red Leaf-monkey has been reported (Tan, F.L, unpublished note) to occur as high as 3050 m (10,000 ft) on Mt. Kinabalu, much higher than any other primate; it is the most widespread monkey on the island of Borneo. The Grey Leaf-monkey is confined to northern and north-eastern Borneo, and has not been recorded above 2000 m (6500 ft). An adult male of this species on the Silau-Silau trail at Park Headquarters (1550 m, 5100 ft) has been seen feeding on the eggs of a babbler, the only reported case of any leaf-monkey taking animal prey (Goodman, 1989). Medway (1977) records a maximum altitude of 2450 m (8000 ft) for the orang-utan, but this is based on a dubious report by Whitehead (1893), and Payne (1988) states that 1450 m (4800 ft) is the highest authentic record, from the Mamut river on the south-east side of Mt. Kinabalu in 1961. In about 1965, a group of Kinabalu Park

Fig.4. Greater Bamboo Bat *(Tylonycteris robustula)* emerging from its roosting site in the internode of a bamboo stem. This insectivorous bat occurs up to 1000 m on Mt. Kinabalu. *(Photo: A. Lamb)*

Fig.5. The Bornean Gibbon *(Hylobates muelleri)* lives in small monogamous groups in dipterocarp forests, sometimes extending into lower montane forests. *(Photo: Loi Pui King)*

staff including Mr. Gabriel Sinit (pers. comm.) found the hairs of what was probably an Orang-utan, but possibly a Red Leaf-monkey, under a ledge on the bare rocky summit area of Mt. Kinabalu. This mysterious record might indicate a stray animal lost far above its normal range, or even the remains of a cloak made by a human climber. Orang-utans occur only in the eastern and northern parts of Kinabalu Park, mainly in the upper dipterocarp zone and lowest part of the lower montane forest zone. It has been suggested that there are between only 25 and 120 orang-utans within Kinabalu Park, and that this population is ecologically different from those in the lowlands of eastern Sabah which are associated with forests on alluvium (Payne, 1988).

PHOLIDOTA

The Pangolin is the only member of this order in Borneo. The species is generally recorded in lowland habitats, but it has been twice recorded between Kinabalu Park Headquarters and the Power Station at 1900 m (6230 ft).

Fig.6. The Pangolin *(Manis javanica)* is a toothless, brownish, scaly mammal which feeds only on ants and termites. It has long, powerful claws for opening the nests of its prey. It has been recorded near Kinabalu Park headquarters but is more usually found in gardens near forest edge at lower altitudes. *(Photo: A. Lamb)*

RODENTS

Rodents in Borneo include tree squirrels, ground squirrels, flying squirrels (which glide), rats, mice and porcupines. The Giant Squirrel is the largest tree squirrel in Borneo, extending from lowland dipterocarp forests to lower montane forest. Prevost's and Kinabalu Squirrels are almost identical by metrical and cranial features, and the variation in colour between different sub-species of Prevost's Squirrel in different parts of Borneo is greater than that between Prevost's and Kinabalu Squirrels in Sabah. Altitudes given on collector's labels indicate that the two forms overlap, and that they must be regarded, therefore, as true species. Related to these squirrels but smaller in size are four species which show an unusual sequence of features. The Plantain Squirrel (hind foot length 42–52 mm, with a pale red belly) is widespread in Peninsular Malaysia and insular Southeast Asia, and typically occurs at greatest abundance in secondary forests and plantations. Slightly smaller (hind foot 36–40 mm) but otherwise very similar is the Ear-spot Squirrel, confined to altitudes below 900 m (3000 ft) in northern Borneo. Smaller still (hind foot 32–35 mm) with a grey belly and differently-shaped incisor teeth is the Bornean Black-banded Squirrel, confined to mountains but at altitudes below about 1700 m (5500 ft) in northern Borneo. And yet smaller (hind foot 27–33 mm) is the Red-bellied Sculptor Squirrel, with grey-tinged red belly and uniquely-shaped incisor teeth, confined to altitudes between 900 m (3000 ft) and 1700 m (5500 ft) in north-western Borneo. It would seem that the three smallest species evolved in the forests of northern Borneo, probably from a single ancestral type. The morphological features of the Bornean Black-banded Squirrel, actually intermediate between the Ear-spot and Sculptor Squirrels, yet superficially resembling the Black-banded Squirrel *(Callosciurus nigrovittatus)* of Peninsular Malaysia, led to its being described under two genera by different zoologists, and it was only recently identified as a single unique, intermediate species (Payne *et al.*, 1985). Five other squirrel species (Jentink's, Brooke's, Four-striped Ground, Bornean Mountain Ground and Whitehead's Pigmy Squirrel) occur only in northern Borneo. Lim & Muul (1978) record the presence of the Slender Tree Squirrel *(Sundasciurus tenuis)* on Mt. Kinabalu, a species otherwise known in Sabah only from Sipitang in the extreme southwest of the state (Medwey, 1977). Studies in dipterocarp forest in Peninsular Malaysia suggest that the height and complexity of forest "architecture" influence squirrel species diversity and permit specialisation into various ecological niches (Payne, 1979). If this is so, the proliferation of squirrel species in northern Borneo, especially in the mountains, which is greater than in any other region of the world, may stem partly from the diversity of forest structure in this relatively small area, as well as from the changing patterns of climate and forest types during the Pleistocene and Quaternary periods.

There has been a similar proliferation of rat and mouse species in the forests of the Sunda shelf, with two species occurring only in the mountains of Borneo and Sumatra, and six (Mountain Spiny, Chestnut-bellied Spiny and Small Spiny Rats, Large and Grey-bellied Pencil-tailed Tree-mice, and Ranee Mouse) confined to Borneo. The Long-tailed Giant Rat exhibits the greatest altitudinal range of any small mammal in Borneo. Specimens from above about 1500 m (5000 ft) on Mt. Kinabalu are larger and darker coloured than those from lower elevations. It is conceivable that the upper form represents a different species, but further collection of specimens is required to resolve this possibility.

CARNIVORES

The carnivores are represented in Borneo by a diverse array of animals, of which the two smallest (Malay Weasel and Ferret-badger) and the largest (Sun Bear) occur in Kinabalu Park. All species eat at least some animal material, but some species of civets feed primarily on fruits. The only record of a Clouded Leopard, Borneo's largest wild cat, in the Mt. Kinabalu area is of footprints on Mt. Madalon, near the northern boundary. The species is known from sightings at above 1200 m (4000 ft) in lower montane forest in the Crocker Range. The unconfirmed sighting by C. Phillipps (pers. comm.) of a Bay Cat on Mt. Kinabalu is of interest because the species is known from only a few specimens, all obtained many decades ago in Sarawak and Kalimantan. Of greatest interest is Hose's Civet, unusual among carnivores in having a restricted distribution at high altitude. It occurs only in the mountains of western Sabah and northern Sarawak at altitudes of between about 600 and 1200 m (2000 and 4000 ft). The Ferret-badger, known in Borneo only from Mt. Kinabalu, also occurs in Nepal, Assam, Burma, Thailand, Indochina and Java.

Fig.7. The Leopard Cat *(Felis bengalensis)* is the most commonly seen species of wild cat in Borneo. It favours forest edges and rural gardens, where it feeds on rats and large insects. *(Photo: A. Lamb)*

LARGE TERRESTRIAL HERBIVORES

The occurrence of Sumatran Rhinoceros in the upper Mekado valley on the east side of Mt. Kinabalu is reported by local residents but the last definite sightings (and hunting) seems to have been during the 1950's. Old, unconfirmed signs of rhinos were reported on the eastern side of the mountain, to the south of Mekado, during the 1961 Royal Society expedition. Since then, there have been no definite reports of the presence of rhinos in the region. Regrettably, even if a very few do still exist in the remote central area north of Mt. Kinabalu, the number would probably be too small to represent a viable breeding population.

Studies in Sarawak (Caldecott, 1986) have shown that Bearded Pigs may move great distances in search of food in the form of fallen fruits of dipterocarp trees and (in the lower montane zone) Fagaceous trees. The pigs can survive and breed in areas lacking both kinds of trees, but it is likely that their numbers and productivity are accordingly lower. Kinabalu Park thus serves as a massive source of pig food, and surrounding human settlements which rely on wild animal meat and fat are well-served by preservation of the Park.

Two species of barking deer are now recognised in Borneo (Groves & Grubb, 1982), although some zoologists believe that these are actually two forms of the same species. Only the larger, darker form in which the male possesses rough, forked antlers, has been reliably observed in Kinabalu Park.

REFERENCES

Allen, G. M. & Coolidge, H. J. 1940. Asiatic Primate Expedition collections: mammals. *Bulletin of the Museum of Comparative Zoology, Harvard* 87: 131–166.

Caldecott, J. O. 1986. Hunting and Wildlife Management in Sarawak. World Wide Fund for Nature Malaysia, Kuala Lumpur.

Goodman, S.M. 1989. Predation by the Grey Leaf Monkey *(Presbytis hosei)* on the contents of a bird's nest at Mt. Kinabalu Park, Sabah. *Primates* 30(1): 127–128.

Groves, C. P. & Grubb, P. 1982. The species of muntjak (genus *Muntiacus*) in Borneo: unrecognised sympatry in tropical deer. *Zoologische Mededelingen (Leiden)* 56(17): 203–216.

Harrisson, T. 1978. Kinabalu, The Wonderful Mountain of Change. In: Luping, M., Chin, W. & Dingley, E.R. (eds.) Kinabalu—Summit of Borneo. The Sabah Society, Kota Kinabalu.

Lim, B. L. & Heynemann, D. 1968. A collection of small mammals from Tuaran and the southwest face of Mt. Kinabalu, Sabah. *Sarawak Museum Journal* 16: 257–276.

Lim, B. L. & Muul, I. 1978. The small mammals. In: Luping, M., Chin, W. & Dingley, E.R. (eds.) Kinabalu—Summit of Borneo. The Sabah Society, Kota Kinabalu.

Medway, Lord. 1977. Mammals of Borneo. Field keys and annotated checklist. Monographs of the Malaysian Branch of the Royal Asiatic Society. No. 7. Malaysian Branch of the Royal Asiatic Society, Kuala Lumpur.

Payne, J. B. 1979. Synecology of Malayan tree squirrels, with particular reference to the genus *Ratufa*. Ph.D. thesis, University of Cambridge (Unpublished).

Payne, J. 1988. Orang-utan Conservation in Sabah. World Wide Fund for Nature Malaysia, Kuala Lumpur.

Payne, J., Francis, C. M. & Phillipps, K. 1985. A Field Guide to the Mammals of Borneo. The Sabah Society, Kota Kinabalu with WWF Malaysia, Kuala Lumpur.

Phillipps, A. (compiled) 1990. Selected mammal notes from Kinabalu Park. *Sabah Society Journal* 9(2): 161–168.

Thomas, O. 1898. Descriptions of new Bornean and Sumatran mammals. *Annals and Magazine of Natural History* 7(2): 245–251.

Whitehead, J. 1893. Exploration of Kina Balu, North Borneo. Gurney & Jackson, London.

Appendix 1. Maximum altitude records (in metres) of Kinabalu's lowland mammals.

(Sources: Lim & Heyneman, 1968; Lim & Muul, 1978; Medway, 1977; G. Musser, personal communication to C.M. Francis; Payne *et. al.*, 1985; A. Phillipps, 1991; C. Phillipps & Q. Phillipps, pers. comm.).

Symbols used:
    * no records available of maximum altitude on Mt. Kinabalu
    # these species recorded only near the boundary of Kinabalu Park
    ? these species recorded only through unconfirmed sightings
    ! probably now extinct on Mt. Kinabalu

South-east Asian White-toothed Shrew *(Crocidura fuliginosa foetida)*	1700
Pentail Treeshrew *(Ptilocercus lowii lowii)*	#
Common Treeshrew *(Tupaia glis longipes)*	#
Slender Treeshrew *(Tupaia gracilis gracilis)*	#

Mammals

Lesser Treeshrew *(Tupaia minor minor)*	1050
Large Treeshrew *(Tupaia tana paitana)*	1010
Colugo or Flying Lemur *(Cynocephalus variegatus natunae)*	*
Large Flying Fox *(Pteropus vampyrus)*	500
Short-nosed Fruit Bat *(Cynopterus brachyotis brachyotis)*	1700
Horsfield's Fruit Bat *(Cynopterus horsfieldi persimilis)*	1460
? Long-tongued Nectar Bat *(Macroglossus minimus lagochilus)*	*
? Dusky Fruit Bat *(Penthetor lucasii)*	*
Tail-less Fruit Bat *(Megaerops ecaudatus)*	900
Greater Sheath-tailed Bat *(Emballonura alecto rivalis)*	700
Lesser False Vampire *(Megaderma spasma kinabalu)*	900
Bornean Horseshoe Bat *(Rhinolophus borneensis borneensis)*	*
Acuminate Horseshoe Bat *(Rhinolopus acuminatus sumatranus)*	1700
Greater Woolly Horseshoe Bat *(Rhinolophus luctus foetidus)*	1500
Whiskered Myotis *(Myotis muricola muricola)*	1490
Black Myotis *(Myotis ater nugax)*	1490
Javan Pipistrelle *(Pipistrellus javanicus javanicus)*	1600
Least Pipistrelle *(Pipistrellus tenuis nitidus)*	1490
Narrow-winged Pipistrelle *(Pipistrellus stenopterus)*	500
Greater Bamboo Bat *(Tylonycteris robustula)*	1050
Gilded Tube-nosed Bat *(Murina rozendaali)*	500
Papillose Woolly Bat *(Kerivoula papillosa malayana)*	1050
Clear-winged Woolly Bat *(Kerivoula pellucida)*	1050
Large Bent-winged Bat *(Miniopterus magnater macrodens)*	500
Slow Loris *(Nyticebus coucang borneanus)*	at least 1280
Western Tarsier *(Tarsius bancanus bancanus)*	below 900
Grey Leaf Monkey *(Presbytis hosei hosei)*	1200
Red Leaf Monkey *(Presbytis rubicunda)*	3050
Long-tailed Macaque *(Macaca fascicularis fascicularis)*	1200
Pig-tailed Macaque *(Macaca nemestrina nemestrina)*	750
Bornean Gibbon *(Hylobates muelleri funereus)*	1500
Orang-utan *(Pongo pygmaeus pygmaeus)*	1450
Pangolin *(Manis javanica)*	1700
Giant Squirrel *(Ratufa affinis sandakanensis)*	1700
Prevost's Squirrel *(Callosciurus prevostii pluto)*	550
Plantain Squirrel *(Callosciurus notatus dilutus)*	1700
Ear-spot Squirrel *(Callosciurus adamsi)*	*
Horse-tailed Squirrel *(Sundasciurus hippurus pryeri)*	*
Low's Squirrel *(Sundasciurus lowii lowii)*	1050
Slender Squirrel *(Sundasciurus tenuis parvus)*	*
Four-striped Ground Squirrel *(Lariscus hosei)*	1500
Tufted Ground Squirrel *(Rheithrosciurus macrotis)*	750
Plain Pigmy Squirrel *(Exilisciurus exilis)*	900

Horsfield's Flying Squirrel *(Iomys horfieldi thomsoni)*	1800
Black Flying Squirrel *(Aeromys tephromelas phaeomelas)*	1050
Thomas's Flying Squirrel *(Aeromys thomasi)*	1600
Temminck's Flying Squirrel *(Petinomys setosus setosus)*	1600
Grey-cheeked Flying Squirrel *(Hylopetes lepidus platyurus)*	1400
Red-cheeked Flying Squirrel *(Hylopetes spadiceus everetti)*	1050
Smoky Flying Squirrel *(Pteromyscus pulverulentus borneanus)*	550
Red Giant Flying Squirrel *(Petaurista petaurista rajah)*	900
House Rat *(Rattus rattus diardii)*	1650
Malaysian Field Rat *(Rattus tiomanicus)*	1650
Ricefield Rat *(Rattus argentiventer)*	1600
Polynesian Rat *(Rattus exulans ephippium)*	1650
Muller's Rat *(Sundamys muelleri borneanus)*	at least 1280
Dark-tailed Tree Rat *(Niviventer cremoriventer kina)*	1500
Red Spiny Rat *(Maxomys surifer bandahara)*	1700
Chestnut-bellied Spiny Rat *(Maxomys ochraceiventer)*	1700
Small Spiny Rat *(Maxomys baeodon)*	1400
Whitehead's Rat *(Maxomys whiteheadi whiteheadi)*	2150
Long-tailed Giant Rat *(Leopoldamys sabanus)*	3100
Grey Tree Rat *(Lenothrix canus malaisia)*	550
Common Pencil-tailed Tree-mouse *(Chiropodomys gliroides pusillus)*	1200
Large Pencil-tailed Tree-mouse *(Chiropodomys major)*	1490
Grey-bellied Pencil-tailed Mouse *(Chiropodomys muroides)*	1050
Ranee Mouse *(Haeromys margarettae)*	900
Long-tailed Porcupine *(Trichys fasciculata)*	900
Common Porcupine *(Hystrix brachyura)*	900
Sun Bear *(Helarctos malayanus euryspilus)*	2300
Yellow-throated Marten *(Martes flavigula saba)*	1500
Malay Weasel *(Mustela nudipes)*	1500
Malay Civet or Tangalung *(Viverra tangalunga tangalunga)*	750
Banded Linsang *(Prionodon linsang gracilis)*	1800
Masked Palm Civet *(Paguma larvata ogilbyi)*	2150
Binturong *(Arctictis binturong penicillata)*	1500
Small-toothed Palm Civet *(Arctogalidia trivirgata stigmatica)*	1500
Banded Palm Civet *(Hemigalus derbyanus boiei)*	750
Clouded Leopard *(Neofelis nebulosa diardi)*	900
Leopard Cat *(Felis bengalensis borneoensis)*	1450
? Bay Cat *(Felis badia)*	1700
Asian Two-horned Rhinoceros *(Dicerorhinus sumatrensis)*	!*
Bearded Pig *(Sus barbatus barbatus)*	2450
Lesser Mouse-deer *(Tragulus javanicus klossi)*	#
Large Mouse-deer *(Tragulus napu borneanus)*	600
Common Barking Deer *(Muntiacus muntjak pleiharicus)*	3350
Sambar Deer *(Cervus unicolor brookei)*	3350

Appendix 2. Altitudinal ranges (in metres) of Kinabalu's montane mammals.

(Sources: Lim & Muul, 1978; Medway, 1977; G. Musser, *in litt.*, Payne *et. al.*, 1985; A. Phillipps, 1991; Thomas, 1898).

* denotes records from Crocker Range and Sarawak

Lesser Gymnure *(Hylomys suillus dorsalis)*	1200–3350
Black Shrew *(Suncus ater)*	1700
Kinabalu Shrew *(Crocidua baluensis)*	1650–3650
Sunda Shrew *(Crocidura monticola)*	1500
Himalayan Water Shrew *(Chimarrogale himalayica phaeura)*	450–1700
Mountain Treeshrew *(Tupaia montana baluensis)*	900–3170
Smooth-tailed Treeshrew *(Dendrogale melanura baluensis)*	900–3350
Grey Fruit Bat *(Aethalops alecto aequalis)*	1050–2750
Kinabalu Squirrel *(Callosciurus baluensis baluensis)*	300–1800
Bornean Black-banded Squirrel *(Callosciurus orestes venetus)*	550–1700
Jentink's Squirrel *(Sundasciurus jentinki jentinki)*	900–3140
Brooke's Squirrel *(Sundasciurus brookei)*	485–1050
Red-bellied Sculptor Squirrel *(Glyphotes simus)*	1400
Bornean Mountain Ground Squirrel *(Dremomys everetti)*	1050–3400
Whitehead's Pigmy Squirrel *(Exilisciurus whiteheadi)*	550–2980
Spotted Giant Flying Squirrel *(Petaurista elegans banksi)*	1050–1700
Summit Rat *(Rattus baluensis baluensis)*	2150–3350
Mountain Giant Rat *(Sundamys infraluteus infraluteus)*	900–2920
Long-tailed Mountain Rat *(Niviventer rapit)*	485–3350
Mountain Spiny Rat *(Maxomys alticola)*	1050–3350
Ferret-badger *(Melogale personata everetti)*	1050–2980
Hose's Civet *(Hemigalus hosei)*	*600–1200

Photo: W.M. Poon

PART 4

PARK FUNCTIONS & LOCALITIES

Fig.1. Silent sentinel of the mysterious summit plateau: the Donkey's Ears.
(Photo: Robert New)

KINABALU PARK: PAST, PRESENT AND FUTURE

Francis S. P. Liew

The National Parks Ordinance of 1962 came into force on 11th May, 1962. The Ordinance provided for the constitution of national parks, following a Resident's enquiry into objections and claims for customary rights and the subsequent management of the national parks by a Board of Trustees. It prohibited certain acts in national parks and provided penalties. Two parks were gazetted under this Ordinance, namely, Kinabalu National Park in 1964 and Tunku Abdul Rahman National Park in 1974.

In September 1977, the National Parks Ordinance of 1962 was repealed and replaced by the National Parks Enactment of 1977. This Enactment empowered the Board not only to preserve and protect national parks in the State but also national reserves. The national reserves are areas, which although deserving of protection, do not for various reasons qualify to be called national parks. Four more national parks were created under the 1977 Enactment, namely, Turtle Islands National Park in October 1977, Pulau Tiga National Park in June 1978, Klias Peninsula National Park in July 1978 and Tawau Hills National Park in May 1979. Unfortunately, in August 1981, the then State Government decided to degazette the whole of the Klias Peninsula National Park and reverted it back to a Forest Reserve.

On 8th March 1984, the State Legislative Assembly passed the new Parks Enactment of 1984 to repeal and replace the old National Parks Enactment of 1977. The objectives of introducing this new enactment were to streamline the control and management of parks in Sabah and to redefine the boundaries of all the parks. Under the new Enactment, the location and extent of each park were clearly shown and a land title for each park for a period of nine hundred and ninety-nine years free of all liabilities and encumbrances was vested in the name of the Board of Trustees of the Sabah Parks. With this new Enactment, all the five existing national parks in the State were reconstituted as state parks and were known thereafter as follows:

Taman Kinabalu (Kinabalu Park)	— 75,370 ha
Taman Tunku Abdul Rahman (Tunku Abdul Rahman Park)	— 4929 ha
Taman Pulau Penyu (Turtle Islands Park)	— 1740 ha
Taman Pulau Tiga (Pulau Tiga Park)	— 15,864 ha
Taman Bukit Tawau (Tawau Hills Park)	— 27,972 ha

In addition, the new Enactment created a new park covering an area of 139,919 ha called the Crocker Range National Park. This new park protects the very important water-catchment area for most of the major rivers of the Interior and West Coast Divisions.

To date the total area gazetted as parks in Sabah stands at approximately 265,794 ha (including land and sea). This represents about 3% of the total land area of the State. Other ecologically significant areas of the State that have been proposed for inclusion in the parks system include the Semporna Islands for the rich marine life, the Lower Kinabatangan river region for its wildlife and riverine ecosystem and possibly the Klias Peninsula for the protection of the nipah palm–mangrove ecosystem. The Board of Trustees is always on the lookout for more areas to be constituted as national parks so that the parks system in Sabah will one day include all the representative ecosystems that are found in the State. The preservation and protection of these valuable assets is a very heavy responsibility entrusted to us and we must account for our use and care of them to those who come after.

POLICY

The greatest problem faced by park managers throughout the world is the mistaken belief held by many that parks are created specially for tourism and recreation, and that development planning should be directed at providing facilities along the line of holiday resorts. Unfortunately, this trend of thought is not only held by the general public but is also often found in the minds of politicians and senior decision-makers in both the public and private sectors. While it is true that tourism is one of the facets of a park's development, it should not be allowed to take precedence over other more important values. These include flora and fauna preservation, watershed and landscape protection, the role of parks in science and education, the conservation of endangered species and gene pools, etc. The obvious solution is to strike a balance between conservation and tourism, and precautionary measures must be adopted so that tourists coming to a park may be satisfied without compromising the interests of nature protection and conservation.

Over the years, since the gazettement of Sabah's first national park in 1964, the lack of a park policy has resulted in the interpretation of the use of Kinabalu Park in different ways. This had caused conflicts in administration and planning and development, and the park's many other roles, particularly in the field of conservation and education, had often been ignored.

Sabah, as a young developing State, with its tourism industry still in its infancy, is not expected to encounter the pressure for development and the damage by overuse, as had happened in parks in other highly populated and developed countries, for many years to come. Nevertheless, whatever development that does take place must be controlled from the start and great care must be taken to ensure that no damaging precedents are created. This requires that a firm policy be laid down not only to guide the park managers and ensure continuity of purpose, but also to guide the planners and developers involved. Parks

History and Future of the Park

are, after all, areas set aside where visitors are allowed to enter, under special conditions, for inspirational, educational, cultural and recreational purposes. A certain amont of development must therefore be provided in the parks, but if allowed to go on unchecked and unplanned this can lead to the lessening, and perhaps eventual destruction of the very values that inspired the original creation of the parks.

This danger was recognised in 1974, when a paper on a "National Parks Policy For Sabah" was prepared by D.V. Jenkins, Francis Liew and Peter Hetch. This was approved and accepted by the Sabah National Parks Board of Trustees, and subsequently by the State Cabinet. Based largely on the Canadian National Parks Policy, the Sabah Parks policy laid down a basis for the control and management of parks in Sabah. However, it must be appreciated that a policy is only of value if the provisions laid down are followed through without fear or favour, and that they should only be changed after thorough and careful study.

ADMINISTRATION

The first Board of Trustees of the Sabah National Parks was appointed in January 1963, chaired by the Conservator of Forests (Mr. G.L. Carson, C.B.E.) with four other members (Mr. E.J.H. Berwick, C.B.E., Mr. J. Comber, Datuk Ganie Gilong, Mr. Y.K. Wong).

On 16th January 1964, the first national park in Sabah, the Kinabalu National Park, was officially gazetted. This was, at least partly, in response to the recommendations of the

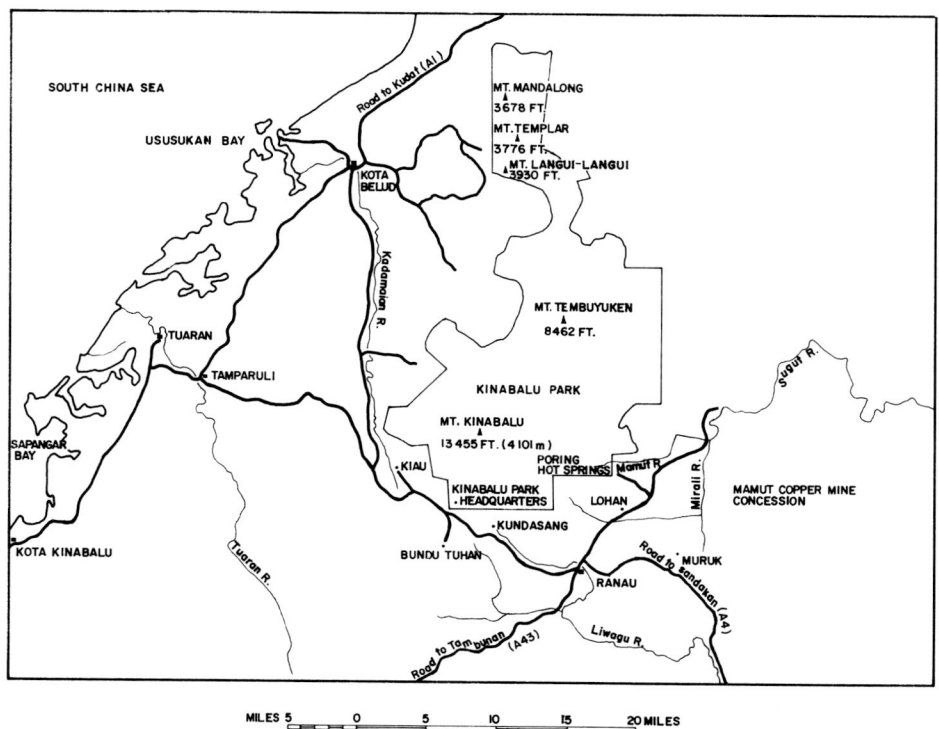

Fig.2. Site and area of Kinabalu park, Sabah.

Royal Society of Great Britain, who, in 1961 and 1964 sent out scientific expeditions to explore the area, though Mt. Kinabalu had been proposed as a National Park some years earlier.

In the early days, the Kinabalu Park was administered from the town of Kota Kinabalu. In 1965, Mr. I. H. Sario, the Senior Forest Officer, Kota Kinabalu was appointed as part-time Park Warden of Kinabalu Park in addition to his departmental duties. He was supported by a staff of five Park Rangers. Great difficulty was encountered in recruiting suitable staff to work in the park mainly because of the arduous nature of the work, the opportunities for easier and more congenial employment elsewhere and the lack of a pension or provident fund for staff on contract terms. In 1966, Mr. F.M. Corpuz, replaced Mr. I.H. Sario as the Senior Forest Officer, Kota Kinabalu.

A new post of Park Warden was established in 1967 and when Mr. G.L. Carson retired from the post of Conservator of Forests and ex-officio Chairman of the Board of Trustees on 1st August, he immediately assumed the office of full-time Park Warden based at the Kinabalu Park Headquarters itself, near Tenompok. Mr. G.L. Carson retired as Park Warden on 31st August, 1969 and was replaced by Mr. D.V. Jenkins, Assistant Director of Forests, on assignment from the Forest Department.

Mr. Jenkins remained on assignment as District Forest Officer, Kota Kinabalu and Park Warden until February 1972, when he proceeded on long leave. He returned to Sabah in September to take up a new appointment as Park Warden, Sabah, in the Chief Minister's Department and was assigned to the Sabah Parks to administer the Kinabalu Park. At the end of 1972, the author was seconded to Kinabalu Park from the Forest Department as Assistant Park Warden and was posted to Kinabalu Park Headquarters, and in March 1973 joined the Parks Service as a full-time officer.

Mr. D.V. Jenkins continued as the Park Warden until May 1974 when he was promoted to Assistant Director of Parks following the gazettement of the Tunku Abdul Rahman Park and was transferred to Kota Kinabalu. Subsequently, the author was promoted to Park Warden in charge of Kinabalu Park, and served in this capacity until April, 1978, when Mr. Jenkins left at the end of his contract. Subsequently, the author was appointed as Acting Assistant Director of Parks and Mr. Eric Wong Hon Fui was appointed as Assistant Park Warden in charge of Kinabalu Park. In 1980, Dr. Janardhanan s/o Swami replaced Mr. Eric Wong as Park Warden when the latter went for a ten-month Diploma Course in Environmental Conservation Management at Ciawi, Bogor, Indonesia. Upon his return from training in October, 1982, Mr. Eric Wong was appointed Acting Park Warden for Kinabalu Park, a post which he still holds.

EXCISIONS AND EXTENSIONS OF KINABALU PARK

As first gazetted in 1964, Kinabalu National Park covered an area of about 711 sq. km with altitudes ranging from 600 m up to the summit of Mt. Kinabalu at 4101 m.

Seven years later, on April 29, 1971, an area of about 25 sq. km was de-reserved from the Kinabalu Park to make way for the Mamut Copper Mine. To compensate for the loss, the State Government, in August 1974, decided to incorporate the Mt. Templar Forest Reserve as an extension to the Kinabalu Park along the northern boundary. This extension covers an area of 93 sq. km, consisting mainly of dipterocarp forest below the 900 m contour line. With this extension the park's area was expanded to 779 sq. km. Under the new Parks Enactment of 1984, however, the boundaries of the Kinabalu Park were redefined, the irregular parts being straightened and streamlined. Consequently, the area of the park was reduced to approximately 753 sq. km. Unfortunately, this meant that two scientifically important areas were excised and designated for other purposes. These were the Pinosuk Plateau and Bukit Hampuan. The Pinosuk Plateau was the main site for the studies carried out by the Royal Society Expeditions under the leadership of Professor E.J.H. Corner in 1961 and 1964. Much of the area has now been clear-felled for various development projects including a dairy-farm, temperate fruit-tree trials, an asparagus farm, and a rose and chrysanthemum farm as well as a golf course. Recently, however, efforts by the Park management to have at least part of the area returned have been successful, and the golf-course and the surrounding area is the site chosen for the proposed Mesilau Nature Resort.

Bukit Hampuan was an extremely valuable site for the study of ultramafic (ultrabasic) vegetation, with many species of plants unrecorded elsewhere in the Park, but a large portion of the hill was burnt in 1989 when efforts were on-going to have this area returned to the Park as well. Nevertheless, some parts do remain intact and the continued value of the area for scientific studies should not be underestimated.

RESEARCH AND EDUCATION

The most fundamental obligation of a park's management is the preservation and wise management of the natural features found within the park area protecting them for the benefit, education and enjoyment of present and future generations. With this objective in mind, a Park Ecology section was established towards the end of 1980. To start off the Ecology Section, Mr. Peter Walpole was appointed as the Park Ecologist based at the Kinabalu Park. Mr. Walpole laid down the nucleus of an entomological collection and a herbarium collection, and he also initiated plans for the Exhibit Centre in the new Administrative Building. Mr. Walpole left the Park Service in 1981; the post was filled by Ms. Anthea Phillipps, later in the same year, and six Park Naturalists were added to the staff.

A major impetus was given to the development of an Education Programme at Kinabalu Park with the arrival of Mr. Tony Pierce, a volunteer from the Canadian Executive Service Overseas in January 1982. Mr. Pierce was a retired Chief Park Naturalist from the Jasper National Park in Canada, and in the six months that he was here, with his wife Stella, Mr. Pierce provided invaluable training in audio-visual and interpretation techniques. With his advice and assistance, the Education Programme was started in Kinabalu Park in July 1982. Under this programme, slide and film shows and free guided nature walks for the public were conducted on a regular basis every week to help make visits to the Park more meaningful and enjoyable. Special programmes were also given to students and other interested groups on request. The response from visitors to this Education Programme was most encouraging.

A major project in 1982 was starting a collection of living plants, including a large number of orchids, from all over Kinabalu Park, in the Mountain Garden, a fenced-in area of about 1.5 ha, near the Administration Building. Mr. Anthony Lamb, Principal Research Officer at the Tenom Agricultural Research Station, served as the consultant for this project.

In February, 1983, Mr. Tony Pierce and his wife returned to Kinabalu Park for another tour of three months to advise on further training for the Park Naturalists and on the development of the Education Programme, and in 1984, the newly established Mobile Unit started regular programmes to the surrounding villages of the park to inform the public on the reason for, and the value of, Kinabalu Park. In 1984 alone, a total of 27 kampongs and schools were visited and an attendance of 4473 was recorded.

In 1985, the Ecology Section was fortunate to have Ms. Susan Jacobson from U.S.A. who spent a year in Kinabalu Park carrying out evaluation and research of the Education Programmes for her Ph.D. thesis. During her spare time, she also conducted refresher

Fig.3. From Park Headquarters: the grey backdrop of Kinabalu challenges the climber. *(Photo: F.S.P. Liew)*

courses for the Park Naturalists who benefitted a great deal from her knowledge and experience.

1986 saw an increased emphasis on the research functions of the Ecology Section as well as continued development of the Education Programme. The herbarium continued to expand and a major research project was started in May on the Kinabalu pitcher-plants. Park Naturalists carried out studies to measure the growth rates and life span of the pitchers of *Nepenthes villosa* and to identify the types of insects living inside the pitchers. Ecology staff also actively participated in various research visits made by scientists and researchers from all over the world.

A pilot project to reintroduce seedlings of the rare orchid *Paphiopedilum rothschildianum* back into certain areas of the Kinabalu Park took place from 4th to 8th April, 1987, with the help of Dr. Ernst Grell from West Germany. Three subsequent check-up visits to the sites showed that the project was initially successful.

Towards the end of December 1987, Ms. Anthea Phillipps resigned as Park Ecologist. As a temporary measure Ms. Tan Fui Lian was put in charge of the Ecology Section. On 1st September 1988, Mr. Jamili Nais, another botanist, joined the Parks' Service as the new Park Ecologist.

In 1989, a *Rafflesia* research project was started by the Ecology Section. This project is an attempt to locate the various *Rafflesia* sites throughout the State and to monitor the blooming of this rare flower. Information is entered into a computerised database, and a total of 34 sites have been recorded so far. One of the largest *Rafflesia* flowers in Sabah, *Rafflesia keithii*, measuring 90 cm (36 in) in diameter was discovered in April 1989, at a site near Ranau. However, this record was broken in June 1991, when another *Rafflesia keithii* flower, measuring 94 cm (37.5 in) across was discovered inside the Poring-Mamut Rafflesia Sanctuary. This sanctuary covers an area of just under 1 ha and is now fenced up to give total protection to the *Rafflesia* population there. The Mamut Copper Mine Sdn. Bhd. bore all the costs for the fencing of this very important conservation area. At one time, more than 250 buds of both *R. pricei* and *R. keithii* were counted within the area.

By the end of 1990, the herbarium collection at Kinabalu Park had grown to a total of 5847 collections (Angiosperms 3792; Gymnosperms 80; Ferns 892; Fungi 62; Mosses and Lichens 169) and a spirit collection of 852 specimens. The park's zoological specimen collection was also enlarged by the acquisition of duplicate specimens from the museum of Universiti Kebangsaan Malaysia (Sabah).

Two volunteer entomologists from the Japanese Overseas Cooperation Volunteers (JOCV) were attached to the Ecology Section in 1990. They are Ms. Keiko Sugimoto who is stationed at Poring Hot Springs to start a Butterfly Farm and Mr. Haruki Sadamori who is stationed at Kinabalu Park Headquarters to identify and collect insect specimens for the park.

VISITOR FACILITIES

Park Headquarters
The first staff-quarters and visitor accommodation at Park Headquarters, consisting of a 20-bed Youth Hostel, was built in 1964. Offices and self-catering visitor chalets gradually followed, so that by 1979, 90 persons could be accommodated each night at Park Headquarters. In 1980, a restaurant and new office facilities, including a conference room, exhibit centre, laboratory, herbarium and library were added, with the completion of the new Administration Building. Visitor figures between 1965 and 1981 rose gradually but steadily, until the sealing of the new road between Kota Kinabalu and Ranau saw visitor figures more than double, shooting up from just over 15,000 in 1981 to nearly 50,000 in 1982. Consequently there was a much increased demand for facilities as well as increased participation in the Education Programmes. Partly in response to this a Mini-Theatre capable of showing 16-projector multi-vision slide-shows was completed in 1987, followed by a Multi-purpose Recreation Hall with indoor sports facilities and a stage for cultural performances in 1988, as well as many more visitor chalets. A well-stocked souvenir shop was also started. Today, 228 people can sleep each night at Park Headquarters. Because the cool atmosphere the Park Headquarters offers is now only 2 hours' drive from hot and humid Kota Kinabalu, and because there are no other highland areas in Sabah that are so easily accessible and provide so much, visitor pressure continues to increase. To accommodate the needs of both tourists and scientists conducting research in the Park, construction of new offices and research facilities was started in 1991. However, it is hoped that development of further visitor facilities at the Poring Hot Springs, and at the proposed Mesilau Nature Resort will channel much of the future visitor pressure away from the Park Headquarters, which will be managed mainly as a base for climbers and researchers.

Summit Trail
Until 1964, all those who climbed Mt. Kinabalu stayed overnight at the Paka cave at 3100 m. At the end of the Royal Society Expedition, their base camp, an aluminium hut called 'Burlington Hut' after the Royal Society's offices in London, was taken up to Panar Laban at 3330 m, to be used as a more convenient base for climbers. This was followed in 1967 by a similar hut erected at Sayat-Sayat at 3670 m, and further basic accommodation at Panar Laban. The need for better facilities was soon felt and in 1983, construction work on the climbers' rest-house of Laban Rata at Panar Laban was started. Every item for this building was either carried up manually or air-lifted by chartered helicopters. The actual construction of the rest-house was carried out by the 5th and 7th Brigades of the Malaysian Armed Forces Engineering Squadron with assistance from the Park's Maintenance Section in plumbing and tiling. The rest-house was finally completed in 1985 and was opened for visitor use in December that year with a capacity for 56 climbers a night in dormitory-style rooms. Electricity was brought up from the TV relay station at Layang-Layang at 2600 m, and all the rooms are heated with electric heaters, and both hot and cold showers are available. In addition there is also a small restaurant serving hot food and drinks. The total accommodation for climbers at Panar Laban can now sleep 120 a night.

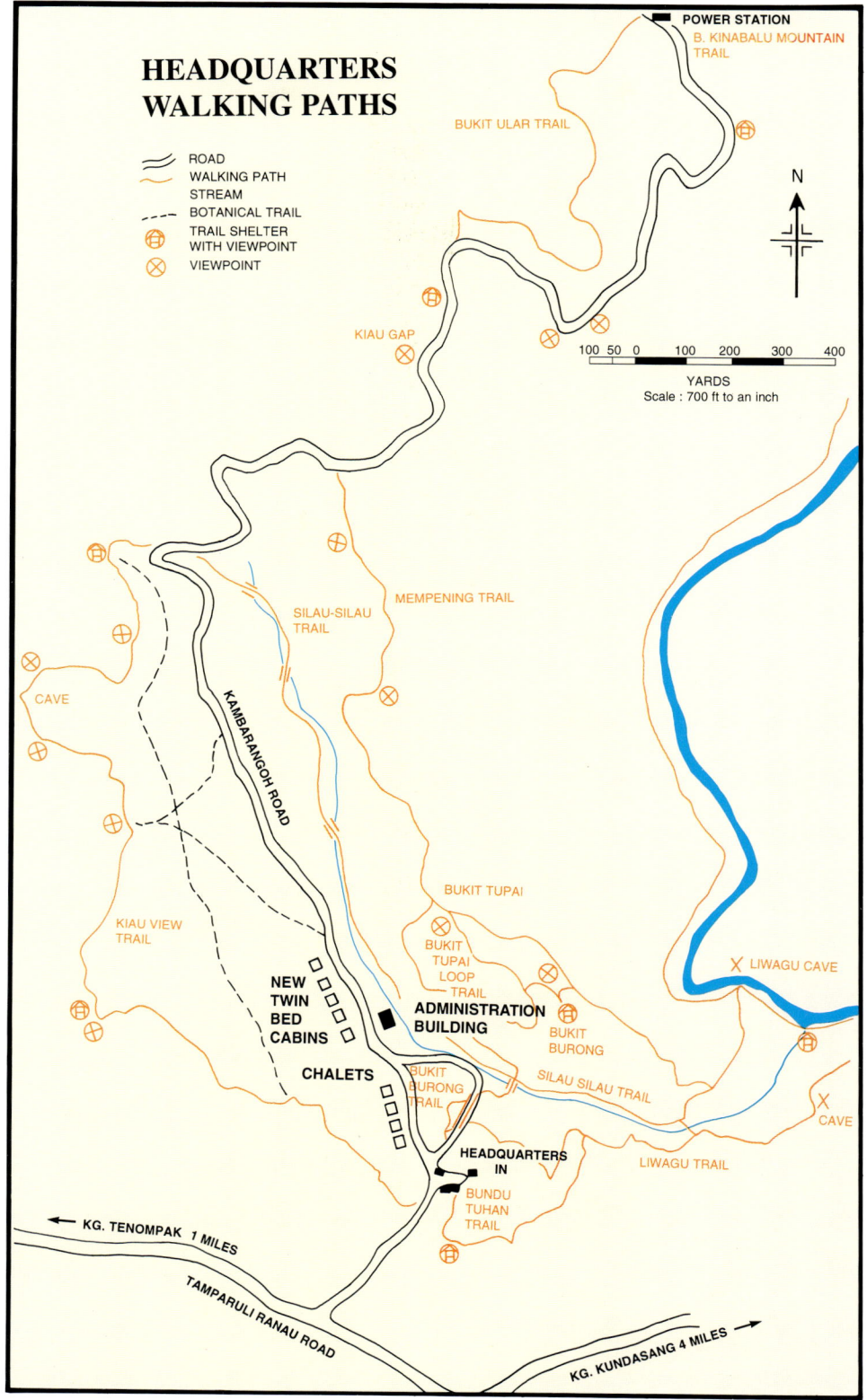

Fig.4. Trails around the Park Headquarters at Kinabalu.

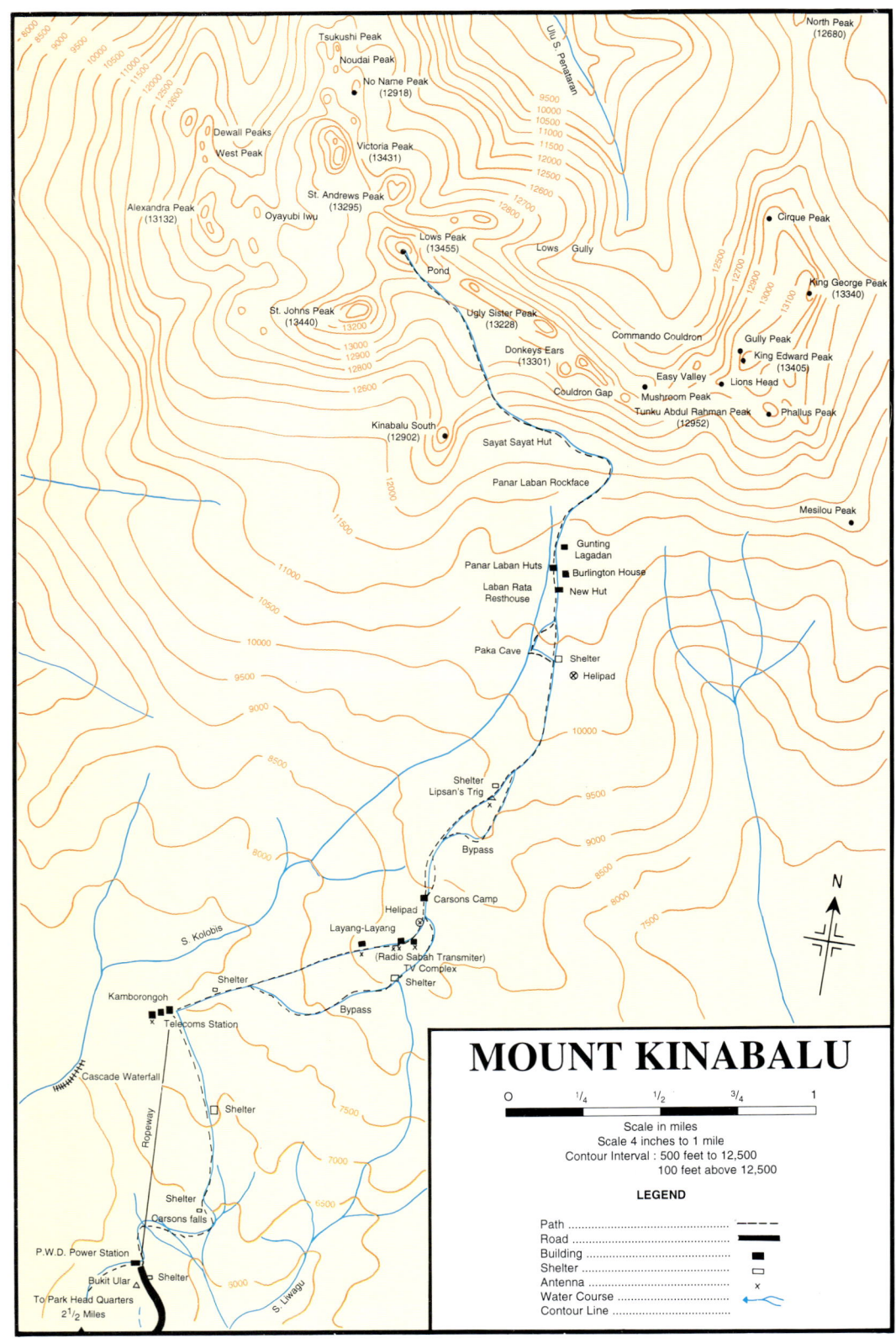

Fig.5. The Summit Trail on Kinabalu.

Fig.6. The usual climbers' trail just above Timpohon, showing Carson's Falls at the background. *(Photo: Robert New)*

Poring Hot Springs

The hot springs at Poring were first developed by the Japanese during World War II, so a rough track was already in place when the Kinabalu Park was gazetted, and it was decided to develop the area further as a Ranger station.

The first staff-quarters at Poring were put up in 1966, followed by a visitor cabin and campground in 1967 and 1968. In 1969 a "heavy-duty" suspension bridge was constructed over the Mamut river to allow visitors easier access to the hot springs and bath troughs. Development at Poring was put on hold from 1970 to 1977 due to uncertainty regarding the possible effects of the opening up of the Mamut Copper Mine on the hot springs. It was only towards the end of 1978 after it had been proven that the mine operation did not adversely affect the hot springs that development of visitor facilities resumed at the station. In 1979 a rock swimming-pool, changing rooms and toilets were constructed near the hot spring area and more bath troughs were built in 1980. A new Youth Hostel which housed 24 persons a night was erected in 1982, and the following year a new office and a proper entrance gate were completed.

Work on a lowland Orchid Centre, to complement the orchid collection in the Mountain Garden at Park Headquarters, started in 1986 and by the end of 1987, 61 genera and 246 species of wild orchids as well as 21 hybrid varieties had been planted in the Orchid Centre. Most of the lowland species were transferred from the Tenom Orchid Centre based at the Agricultural Research Station in Tenom as part of an agreement to split the

Fig.7. Visitors' baths at the Poring hot springs. *(Photo: A. Phillipps)*

collection. In this way the effect of climatic variations on the different species could be observed and the loss of rare plants through disease or other factors could be minimized. A tissue-culture laboratory with micro-propagation facilities is now being built to allow for the propagation of rare species.

In October 1988, construction of a major project, a tree-canopy walkway, was started, with assistance from Dr. Illar Muul, as a joint project between the Sabah Parks, the Smithsonian Institution and the Washington-based Integrated Conservation Research Corporation. Funds were provided by the United Nations 'Man and the Biosphere' programme based in Paris, with assistance from Malaysian Airlines in the transport of freight and personnel. This is the world's first canopy walkway to be opened to tourists, and it is about 15 minutes' walk from the hot spring area. The walkway stretches some 75 m and is suspended about 30 m above the forest floor. It has platforms, linked by horizontal ladders, each built around a large tree, where visitors can sit quietly to watch birds, mammals and insects of the upper strata of the forest.

Another canopy walkway, purely for scientific research, is also being built. This one is being constructed at a slightly higher altitude and will be restricted to scientists only. Sabah is the first tropical rainforest region to feature a canopy walkway with the latest technology and design. This project, designed specifically to study the ecology of the rainforest canopy will eventually lead to more comprehensive research on the birds, insects and animals of the upper strata of the tree canopy.

Fig.8. With some of the richest rain forest life known, the Park caters to more than just a fantastic climb to its summit. *(Photo: Albert Teo)*

A Development Master Plan was completed for Poring in 1988. This plan identifies and lays out locations for the various development projects that are being carried out at this station including new offices, visitor chalets, restaurants, extension and renovation of the hot spring area as well as a road across the Mamut river to the hot pools. Currently an animal treatment centre is being developed to care for animals that have been captured illegally or hurt, as well as a Butterfly Farm. With the sealing of the road from Ranau to Poring in 1989, the number of visitors has increased considerably, as shown in the following table.

Number of visitors to Kinabalu Park annually.

Year	Park HQ	Poring
1965	879	–
1966	1599	463
1967	2163	673
1968	2705	2072
1969	2675	2459
1970	3067	4213
1971	3437	6723
1972	4272	7300
1973	5755	7450
1974	6758	7801
1975	7086	8230
1976	7798	8657
1977	8196	8090
1978	9303	9965
1979	12,326	12,184
1980	13,020	19,571
1981	15,217	23,741
1982	45,948	39,387
1983	56,655	38,387
1984	163,337	30,239
1985	174,077	39,479
1986	210,988	39,664
1987	187,368	38,416
1988	183,865	33,966
1989	173,459	75,103
1990	233,965	129,520
1991	210,862	114,526
1992	191,456	110,456
1993	181,142	112,952
1994	200,907	117,994

Figures from 1984 onwards are more accurate as they were based on head counts at the entrance gate. Figures before 1984 were based on the number of visitors who signed the Visitor's book.

Fig.9. The forest canopy walkway at Poring. *(Photo: Albert Teo)*

Fig.10. The climbers' rest-house of Laban Rata at Panar Laban, 3330 m. *(Photo: Albert Teo)*

Fig.11. At the West Gurkha Hut, just below the summit peaks. *(Photo: Robert New)*

THE FUTURE

In 1990, the Sabah Parks Board of Trustees commissioned Sun Chong & Wong (Sabah) and Coopers & Lybrand Malaysia to carry out a Management and Development Masterplan for Sabah Parks with emphasis on Kinabalu Park. The terms of reference of the consulting teams were:

(a) To develop a coherent conservation strategy and accompanying manpower requirements for Sabah Parks for the next ten years;
(b) To prepare a detailed development plan for Kinabalu Park; and
(c) To prepare a broad concept, design and development plan for the proposed Kinabalu Nature Resort (Mesilau Nature Resort and Golf Club Resort Areas).

The Management Plan is basically a set of guidelines which identifies how the Kinabalu Park is to be managed. It is the basic working document for the park managers because it identifies the long-term direction in which the managers must head. More specifically, it identifies the purpose of the park and its natural values (e.g., outstanding features, wildlife, vegetation communities, etc.); it provides the objectives of management of the park and determines the development and management strategy to be followed to meet the basic management objectives; and it details the work that needs to be carried out to attain the basic management objectives.

The final report covers 3 volumes. Volume 1 covers the Executive Summary, Organisation and Manpower, while Volume 2 covers the following features: conservation, research, education, recreation/tourism, management of natural values, management of areas of outstanding natural and scenic value, management of areas of special scientific value, management of wilderness and conservation values, management of cultural and historical values and management of visitor use for recreation and tourism. Readers who are interested in the detailed descriptions of the above-mentioned features are welcome to refer to Volume 2 of the final report. Volume 3 covers the proposed Kinabalu Nature Resort at Mesilau on the Pinosuk Plateau and the proposed Golf Club Resort. This area is about 5 km from Kundasang and is accessible from an existing track which can be easily upgraded to a tarred road.

The most important factor that should be taken into consideration in the planning of this resort is the effect that development may have on the natural environment of the area. With this in mind, it has been rightly emphasised that the concept of the resort should utilise the natural characteristics of the area as much as possible, create minimal disturbance, and should not contravene the image of the park as a conservation area.

The Mesilau Resort site has a number of significant physical features which can be used and emphasised in the conception, design and development of the resort. For a start, the proposed site is at the base of a large, imposing mountain range, which gives it a distinct 'highland' image. This rugged mountain range is covered with dense forest conveying an impression of wilderness. Above the tree line, the massive exposed rocks of Mt. Kinabalu produce a panoramic view not found in any other part of Malaysia. Thus the resort site is part of a natural setting which has dramatic scenic qualities. These special attributes set the Mesilau Resort site apart from all other major resorts in South-east Asia and will definitely appeal to certain tourist markets, namely those who seek mountains, or more secluded environments and those with a liking for nature and a sense of adventure.

Various nature-based educational and recreational activities and programmes will be provided. Among the facilities proposed are a Nature and Outdoor Education Centre and Interpretative Centre where nature can be appreciated and outdoor skills can be developed. This centre will provide an avenue for educating present and future generations for tomorrow's conservation efforts. Riverside chalets and jungle lodges will be built unobtrusively along the Mesilau river and further in along the jungle edge.

The proposed Mesilau Resort will basically divert an increasing number of visitors away from the main focal point of the Park, the Headquarters which will be developed as a climber's base. Poring Hot Springs, the second focal point of the Park, is hot and humid and will be developed mainly as a research area. The Mesilau Nature Resort will portray a very different atmosphere, that of leisure and adventure in cool natural surroundings.

The present golf course will be integrated within the nature resort providing quality accommodation and a variety of recreational activities, yet respecting the scenic beauty and natural integrity of the surrounding area. The Kinabalu Golf Course already has nine holes and a further nine holes are under construction. It has been suggested that the management of the Mesilau Nature Resort be under the control of the current management of Kinabalu Park with additional staff.

CONCLUSION

Nature tourism is fast becoming an important industry in the changing world of international tourism today. This trend has emerged mainly because of an increasing appreciation of plants and animals in their natural habitats and there is also an increasing general awareness of the great biological diversity of the tropical rain forest. This biodiversity cannot be created or duplicated in places outside the tropics and it is this very character that draws large groups of tourists from the more developed countries to our shores.

Besides being there for the people to see and appreciate, natural parks in Sabah have many other scientific values. The potential use of tropical plants for medicines, pharmaceuticals, and as gene-pools for plant-breeding is being realised more and more by scientists and researchers. Hence there is increased emphasis on basic research into the biodiversity of the natural forests. Other ecological functions are performed by the parks as well. The vegetation on the steep terrain in the Kinabalu Park area protects the soil against severe erosion and also acts as an absorbent sponge for rain water. It therefore supplies water for most of the major rivers on the west coast of Sabah.

Despite the efforts by the management of Sabah Parks to educate the public about the importance and value of parks, there will always be pressure from the surrounding village folk who apply for land to be excised from the Park for various purposes. However, any incursion or demand on any of the parks must be totally resisted by government because the parks belong to the people in perpetuity.

On a more positive note, to curb illegal activities such as logging and stealing of rare plant or animal species from parks, a Task Force has been set up to review and amend the existing Parks Enactment of 1984. Special emphasis will be placed on more stringent measures to be taken against the offenders. Serious offences may warrant a mandatory jail sentence plus a deterrent fine. Another step taken by the Management to help reduce illegal activities is to get the park's boundaries properly surveyed.

This survey work requires time and a great amount of funds, hence it will be carried out in stages over the years. In addition, more ranger stations will be established at strategic points around the boundaries to enforce the park's regulations. Construction work on a ranger station has started already at Kampung Sayap near Kota Belud and another one will be set up at Kampung Sirinsim near Kota Marudu. It is hoped that with the setting up of more ranger stations, illegal activities within the Kinabalu Park will be reduced, if not totally eliminated.

Kinabalu Park is one of the few places in Malaysia where one can enjoy and experience a pristine environment within a short distance from an international airport. It takes only two hours to drive on a tarred road from the airport to the Park Headquarters. It is therefore crucial that the uniqueness of the flora and fauna of the park should remain undisturbed. All of Sabah's existing six parks help to preserve and protect the animal, plant and marine life as well as the mountains and rivers. Though the parks only cover about 3% of Sabah's total land area, they nevertheless play a very important and significant role in the conservation of nature and in the tourist industry in the State. Parks constitute a priceless part of our natural heritage which we hold in trust for our future generations.

Fig 1 View west from Water Point, Mount Kinabalu *(Photo: Robert New)*

KINABALU PARK: RESEARCH AND CONSERVATION

Ghazally Ismail & Lamri Ali

The importance of Kinabalu Park to the international scientific community has long been recognised. The unique biological features of the Park include tropical lowland, montane and sub-alpine forests—an altitudinal range of habitats unmatched elsewhere on the island of Borneo. Virgin forest within the Park is home to many animal and plant species that could disappear within our lifetime if not protected. Indeed, in a world where tropical forests are disappearing at an alarming rate, Kinabalu Park stands as a natural monument for scientific research, conservation, and the aspirations of future generations for a better world.

RESEARCH

The need for research as a base for managing the flora and fauna of the Kinabalu Park has been recognised for a long time. In general, research data can be used in three ways: firstly, to monitor the changes in abundance and distribution of the Park's flora and fauna; secondly, to assist the Park managers in understanding the biological processes and interactions occurring among species and communities; and finally, to provide a base for the Park's interpretation services, so that the visiting public can learn as much as possible about the interaction of plants and animals in their natural habitats within the Park.

Kinabalu was the first park established in the state of Sabah, and it has been extensively studied by scientists from all over the world. As a result the flora and fauna of the Kinabalu Park is probably one of the best known of any area of comparable size in Malaysia. To date, more than 300 research projects have been completed and the findings published in scientific journals, both locally and internationally.

The highly diverse plant life of Mt. Kinabalu has received particular attention ever since Stapf's first enumeration of the flora in 1894. A list of major expeditions and projects on the flora of Kinabalu is given in the Appendix. In the post-war era, both the Forestry Department and the Royal Society expeditions in 1961 and 1964 made major contributions to our knowledge of the flora. More recently, much work has been carried out by the Kinabalu Park staff and the Universiti Kebangsaan Malaysia (Sabah) who have also directed their attention to documenting the diversity of insects, frogs and small mammals. Studies conducted in the Kinabalu Park have not only resulted in numerous scientific publications, but also in a series of more popular books published by the Sabah Parks. Titles to date include "Nepenthes of Mount Kinabalu", "Rhododendrons of Sabah", "Mosses and Liverworts of Mt. Kinabalu" and "Frogs of Sabah". Despite all these efforts,

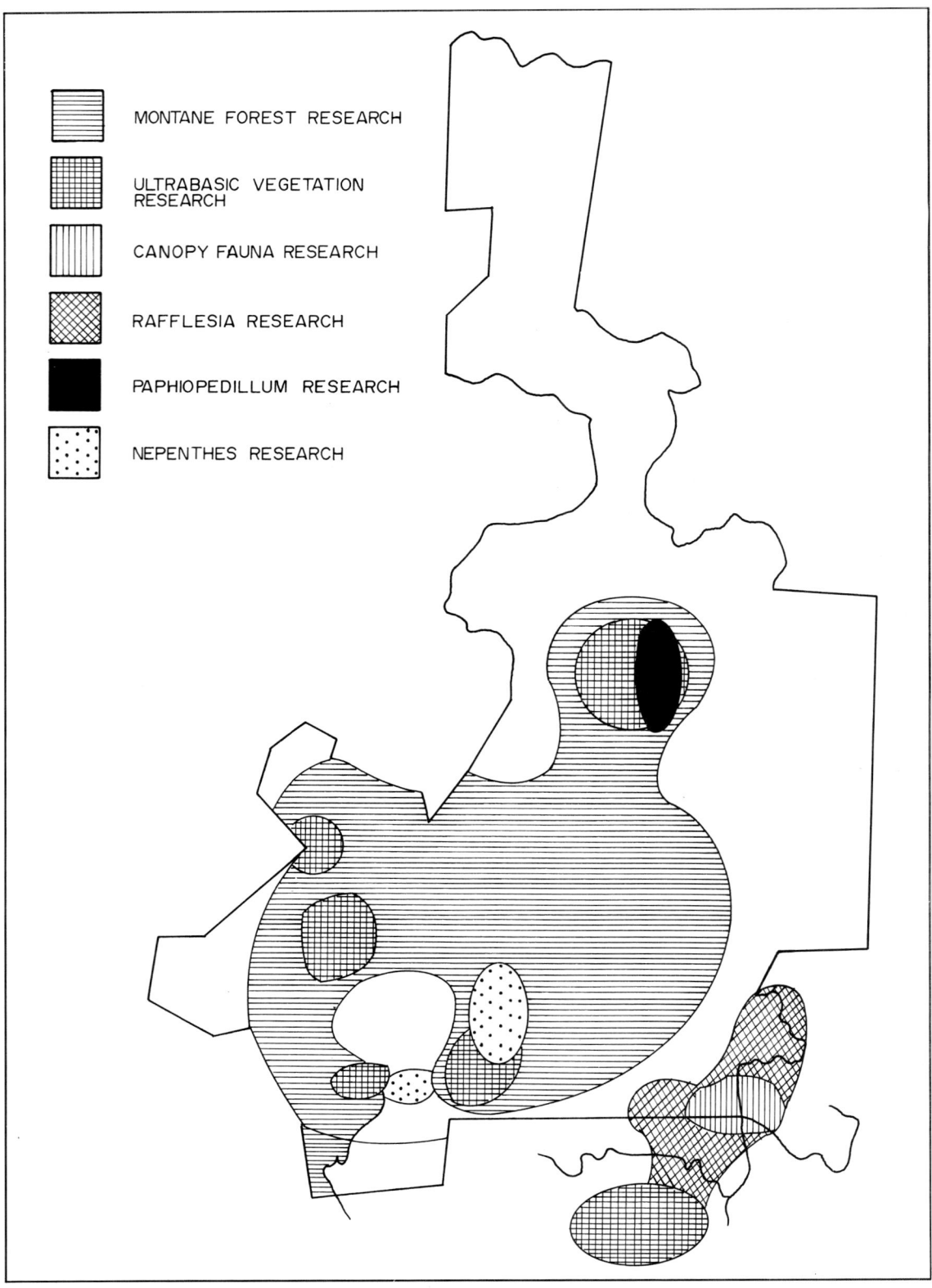

Fig.2. Zoning of areas of special scientific value in Kinabalu park.

much work still remains to be done: a recent review of research to date revealed some major gaps in our knowledge of the Park's flora and fauna.

FAUNAL DIVERSITY

There are two broad categories of mammals that occur in the Kinabalu Park: the lowland and the montane species. The lowland species are found primarily in the foothills and valleys within the Park boundary. There are about 90 lowland species, of which 21 are bats (Payne, this volume). The montane species are confined to the higher mountain ranges, with at least 22 species. Both the montane and lowland zones of Mt. Kinabalu are known to harbour a great diversity of mammals, but the reproductive biology of most of these mammals is still largely unknown. Especially critical research needs are studies on the population biology of the 21 species of bats and their role in pollination and seed dispersal in the Park. In-depth studies into these areas ought to be encouraged.

The birds of Kinabalu Park can be categorized into 4 groups: (i) species of the subalpine zone, (ii) endemic montane species, (iii) non-endemic montane species and (iv) lowland species (Smythies, this volume). Four species of birds are found mainly in the sub-alpine from about 2150 m upwards, and there are about 46 montane species of birds on Mount Kinabalu that are not found below 900 m in height. Of these 46 species, 14 are endemic to Borneo. Unfortunately, accurate field descriptions for many of these species are generally lacking. Breeding biology, apart from descriptions of nests and eggs, has hardly been touched.

To-date, nine families of fishes have been recorded from the Kinabalu Park region (Chin, this volume). Species of the Gastromyzontidae are by far the most common fishes in the clear mountain streams of the Park and they are only found in Borneo. Some of the fishes are likely to be adversely affected by any increase in suspended solids in the stream waters of the Park which may occur, as a result of rapid infrastructure development and other human activity, but the reproductive biology of most of the fish in Kinabalu Park is still largely unknown.

The species list for the frogs and toads of Kinabalu Park now stands at 61 (Inger *et al.*, this volume), but as the study of amphibians of Mt. Kinabalu continues, more discoveries of new resident species will be recorded. Since 1978, for example, three new species have been described, but detailed observations on the behaviour, distribution and habitat of almost all species is lacking. Yet the occurrence of different frogs and toads can serve as biological indicators of environmental change, since changes in the water quality at streams and rivers can render them unsuitable for the breeding of these species.

With the exception of butterflies and moths, the diverse insect fauna of Kinabalu Park has also received little attention from either taxonomists or ecologists. Very few of the 290 species of butterflies reported from the Park are recorded above 2000 m (Holloway, this volume). Moths, on the other hand, are far more abundant at high altitudes and many species are recorded only from Kinabalu Park. Much more knowledge of the invertebrate fauna of the Park is needed for a full appreciation of its importance, and selected insect groups found within Kinabalu Park may also be useful as biological indicators of localized ecological changes associated with increased development and recreational activity.

FLORAL DIVERSITY

On the whole, the flora of Mt. Kinabalu has received much more attention from the scientific community than the fauna. Many major expeditions and scientific studies have increased our knowledge of the plant communities of Mt. Kinabalu. Mt. Kinabalu is considered to be a convergent point where Himalayan and Chinese genera meet with those of Australian, New Zealand and even American affinity; and mingle at all altitudes with the Malaysian flora (Corner, this volume). Most of the Malaysian genera start to disappear at altitudes of about 1,200 m where other genera, not found in the lowlands, begin to enter.

In terms of plant diversity, Mt. Kinabalu is reputed to be one of the richest areas in the world. In an area of about 700 sq. km, some 4000 species of vascular plants occur at different altitudinal zones (Beaman, this volume). There are over 600 species of ferns that have been documented in the Park, more than occur in the whole of mainland tropical Africa (Holttum, this volume).

The flora of Kinabalu exhibits a high degree of endemism. For example, Borneo has 135 species of *Ficus* and more than half (78 species) can be found in the Park. Further, the Park has 14 endemic species and five endemic varieties of other fig species making Kinabalu Park one at the richest areas for figs in the world (Corner, this volume). The insectivorous plants *Nepenthes* occur in the Park at altitudes ranging from about 1500 m to 3350 m thriving on the nutrient-poor soils on the mountain. Of some 81 species of *Nepenthes*, 36 occur in Borneo and of these ten species exist in the Park. However, only four species are endemic to Kinabalu Park, namely *N. burbidgeae, N. kinabaluensis, N. rajah* and *N. villosa.*

The number of orchid species in Borneo has been estimated to be more than 2000 and more than 700 species belonging to 121 genera exist in Kinabalu Park; i.e., over 30 percent of all the orchid species in Borneo (Lamb, this volume). The famous Slipper Orchids of the genus *Paphiopedilum* are represented by at least five species in the Park including the endemic *P. rothschildianum.*

Botanically, many gaps remain to be filled in. Of particular relevance to the Park management would be ecological studies of the differences in the vegetation between the western and the eastern slopes of the mountain which differ in climatic exposure and visitor use. Information is also lacking on nutrient cycles, particularly in relation to weathering, rainfall, leaching, runoff and biomass-removal over differing geological substrates, for example, on granite as compared with the ultramafic (ultrabasic) rocks that occur on both the western and eastern sides of Mt. Kinabalu. Hydrological studies would help to define the Park's role as a major water-catchment area for the region. Does most of this water originate from the bare upper reaches of the mountain or from lower down, and how quickly does it reach rivers in the lowlands outside the Park?

Many of the research projects suggested above will be both time-consuming and costly. Further, the Sabah Parks in its present set-up does not have the resources to carry out projects which require long periods of field research and input from experts in varied disciplines. Therefore, the Park authorities have sought to encourage researchers from local universities and from overseas, provided that the results can be utilised in a way that benefits the Park management as well as society as a whole.

CONSERVATION

The conservation of the Kinabalu Park's flora and fauna is necessary for the preservation of Sabah's natural heritage for future generations. A major emphasis has been laid on conserving the habitats of particularly rare or endemic plant or animal species that occur within the Park boundaries. Among the vulnerable species within Kinabalu Park that are protected are the Slipper Orchids (*Paphiopedilum*), the *Rafflesia*, famous for producing the biggest flowers in the world; the carnivorous plants *Nepenthes* and the showy rhododendrons. Measures have been taken to protect these rare and endangered species *in situ* from habitat disturbance and commercial exploitation. Development projects have been avoided in habitats of rare species. The Park management authorities have also adopted a policy of banning the introduction of exotic plants that may compete with, or cause the decline of, rare species in the Park.

Conservation strategies for plants and animals in Kinabalu Park are based on the following: (i) identification and scientific understanding of plant and animal species of special concern; (ii) identification of the specific factors threatening the continued survival of the species in their natural habitats and (iii) organization of resources to protect rare and endangered species from further disturbance. This requires caution in all decisions that may alter habitat, since the margins for error are small.

It must be recognised that a rare species is not necessarily an endangered one. Many plants or animals that are restricted in range or habitat on Mt. Kinabalu may be rare but they are reasonably well protected. Thus some species which occur in the montane zone may be relatively rare or absent elsewhere, but are not necessarily threatened or endangered within the Park. Conversely, some species that are distributed over a relatively large area throughout Sabah, such as the species of *Rafflesia* must be placed high on the list of endangered plants. Although *Rafflesia* is known to occur in at least 34 different sites within and around Kinabalu Park, densities are always low and sites outside the Park are usually highly vulnerable to human disturbance or forest clearance. Identification of the actual degree of threat to the plant or animal species, habitat or community is therefore of real importance when drawing up strategies for conservation. Although the threats are themselves complex and difficult to characterize, the decline of a species is generally caused by a combination of several activities. The degazettement of the Pinosuk Plateau in 1984 and the partial destruction by fire of Bukit Hampuan in 1990, are examples of the destruction of a once-protected habitat that may result in the disappearance of many plants of scientific importance. The clearance of primary forest for infrastructural development in and around the Poring Hot Springs recently is another human activity which may have reduced the numbers of the *Tetrastigma* vines thus depriving the parasitic *Rafflesia* of its host plant.

Once the threat (or threats) to a species has been clearly determined, there is a need to assess the resources available for conservation. The traditional approach to conservation of rare species or habitats in the Kinabalu Park has been through zoning of specific land areas (Map 5). Of course, it must be realised that different species or habitats possess different tolerance levels to disturbance.

In recent years, the Sabah Parks authorities have seriously considered venturing into the conservation of rare and endangered species through *in vitro* cultivation. A case in point is that of the Slipper Orchids. Orchid-growing today is both a popular past-time and an important industry throughout the world. A few years ago, there were several exciting discoveries of new *Paphiopedilum* species in the South-east Asian region. If orchid seeds are collected instead of the wild plants, it does not take long to raise many thousands of seedlings through tissue culture techniques. Yet, unscrupulous collectors have been known to enter the Kinabalu Park and collect wild plants of *P. rothschildianum* from the few known localities within the Park. The Sabah Parks management intends to develop laboratory facilities and provide training for their staff to acquire competence in orchid tissue culture techniques. Once it is possible to propagate rare species of orchids in the laboratory in considerable quantity and make them available to orchid growers, it should be easier to protect the wild populations. These techniques also allow for the possibility of re-introduction, back into the wild, of species of rare orchids that have been successfully propagated in the laboratory.

EDUCATION

Education is widely regarded as the most effective long-term means of ensuring the protection of Kinabalu Park. The Park has long recognized the need for an information centre and has also developed a range of other interpretative material and programmes, including brochures, self-guided tour pamphlets, videos and slide shows.

Visitors to Kinabalu Park come from diverse backgrounds and include students, biologists and the interested public. Nature trails in the Park have given them the opportunity to explore the diverse plant and animal life. Daily guided nature walks conducted by knowledgeable Park Naturalists have aroused in all participating visitors a better knowledge and appreciation of the tropical forest and, more importantly, a concern for its future. The future of Kinabalu Park is only as safe as the commitment of the people of Sabah to its protection for the benefit and wonderment of future generations.

Appendix. Major explorations and contributions to understanding the flora of Mt. Kinabalu.

Year	Person(s)	Contribution
1892	G.D. Haviland	Collected plant specimens from Mt. Kinabalu.
1894	O. Stapf	Published an enumeration of 364 plant species; 140 of them published for the first time.
1910–1914	L.S. Gibbs	Added to the plant lists published by Stapf from her own collection.
1915	J. Clemens & M. Clemens	Collected plant specimens from Mt. Kinabalu over 2 months.
1915	E.D. Merrill, O. Ames & C. Schweinfurth	Worked on the plant collections made by the Clemenses.
1931–1933	J. Clemens & M. Clemens	Returned to Mt. Kinabalu for plant collection for a period of approximately 2 years.
1933	van Steenis	Preidentified plant specimens collected by the Clemenses.
1960–present	Sabah Forestry Department	Many plant collectors from the Department made several trips to Mt. Kinabalu.
1961	E.J.H. Corner	Led the first Royal Society Expedition to Mt. Kinabalu.
1964	E.J.H. Corner	Led the second Royal Society Expedition to Mt. Kinabalu.
1965	W. Meijer	Published an account of the Kinabalu flora.
1981–1983	T. Sato & Jumaat Adam	Collected specimens for the Universiti Kebangsaan Malaysia Sabah (UKMS) Herbarium.
1983–1984	J. Beaman & R. Beaman	Collected specimens for the UKMS Herbarium.
1983–1986	Kamaruddin M. Salleh & Sukup Akin	Collected specimens for the UKMS Herbarium.
1989	J. Beaman & R. Beaman	Made available the first computer database for plants of Mt. Kinabalu.

Fig.1. Entrance to the Kinabalu National Memorial. *(Photo: W.M. Poon)*

THE KINABALU NATIONAL MEMORIAL, KUNDASANG

J.C. Robinson

The National Memorial at Kundasang lies just outside Kinabalu Park, but the origins of both are linked and owe much to the inspiration of one man, Major G. S. Carter, D. S. O. Toby Carter was a New Zealander employed in Borneo as a surveyor by the Shell Oil Co. between 1935 and 1940. In 1942, he enlisted in the Royal Australian Engineers and after service in New Guinea, was parachuted, in 1945, into the Kelabit Highlands of Sarawak to gather military intelligence and organise native resistance to the Japanese occupation. In this task he was deeply impressed by the trust and bravery of the Bornean peoples, on whom he was completely dependent.

During the flight to Sarawak, Major Carter glimpsed Ranau, but was not to know that the last of 2400 Australian and British prisoners of war sent there on a Death March from Sandakan must have looked up in despair. For the Japanese had decided to destroy all prisoners. They sent them loaded, but naked, to walk a distance of 240 km (150 miles), on a ration of 70 g (2.5 oz) of rice a day. Since there were to be no survivors or witnesses to this crime, the few who reached Ranau were simply shot.

But there were survivors; two men escaped early on the march and four from Ranau. Too weak to walk, they crawled at night and hid in the day, until not far from the memorial site, they could go no further. It was here that they were found by a Dusun farmer. Knowing the penalty, if caught, he nevertheless hid and fed these strangers and when they were a little stronger, though not yet able to walk, he and his friends, carried them 24 km (15 miles) through the hills to an Allied detachment operating in the area. The two men each weighed just over 27 kg (60 lb) and the spark of life was nearly gone. Barega died in 1988. He remained a simple farmer, lived his life like his ancestors and died in sight of Kinabalu. Who will remember his bravery, his compassion? And what of the many others, simple village folk who, in those dark days, offered their little to those with less, and were seen, caught and killed; for that was the penalty for giving a half-coconut of water to a dying prisoner.

After the war, Toby Carter returned to his old job but his war experiences had left their mark; he could not forget the waste of youth in the Death March nor the honour and decency of the hill people. He wanted a memorial for the former but he also wanted a practical way of helping the latter attain a higher standard of living. He believed that *"around a commemorative symbol of deep historical significance there could arise a project of direct and indirect benefit to the loyal-hearted people of Borneo."* The project was to be at Kundasang and, in 1957, his plans were put to Government.

The reply was equivocal—the Government approved of the scheme, but would give no financial support. However, they did agree to make all of Kinabalu above 1800 m (6000 ft) a Forest Reserve, to provide land for a memorial garden at Kundasang free-of-charge and also to provide jeep-track access. Consideration, but not money, would also be given to the development of a tourist centre, by commercial enterprise, in the vicinity of the memorial park.

Carter was probably not surprised by this reply for at this time there was only an earth track from Ranau—where there was a small airfield built by the Japanese with P.O.W. labour. The jeep track from Tamparuli was being constructed but had some miles to go. Government funds were desperately short for the roads, water supplies, schools and medical facilities that were needed everywhere.

Without delay Carter established "The Kinabalu National Memorial Fund" with His Excellency the Rt. Hon. Malcolm MacDonald, P.C., formerly U.K. Commissioner for South-east Asia, as Patron. The Committee of ten included the expatriate managers of all the major companies operating in British Borneo at that time. The Hon. Philip Lee Tau Sang C.B.E., Member of the Executive and Legislative Councils of North Borneo was the only local member. Toby Carter was the Secretary.

The Committee set about fund-raising with an initial target of M$25,000 (in the local currency), which was to be used to construct a memorial garden. A well-written brochure, titled "A Tragedy of Borneo 1941–45" was published in 1958 and sold for M$2.00, with profits devoted to the fund. The key article "Historical Background" was written by Carter who gave a quietly factual account of the ghastly story of Borneo during the war years. Kidman-Cox, of the North Borneo Agricultural Department, contributed a paper on the "Agricultural potential of the Ranau District" and Tom Harrisson (a fellow Allied Officer and later Curator of the Sarawak Museum) wrote a broad-ranging article entitled "The Wildlife of Kinabalu."

But this was not the only source of funds. Toby solicited and obtained donations from many sources but especially from relatives of those Australian servicemen who died in Borneo. This later created some embarrassment since contributors, not suprisingly, were concerned that nothing had been built—they were not to know the difficulties of access, a matter which Toby and the Committee had greatly underestimated.

In July 1960, Max Haymes, the Chairman of the Fund, and a member of the Legislative Council, raised the question, in Council, of the formation of a National Park at Kundasang. He was concerned with the preservation of land in its natural state between 1200 m (4000 ft), the level at Kundasang, and 1800 m (6000 ft), the level at which the Forest Reserve started.

But it was not to be until May 1962, that a "National Park Bill" was put before the North Borneo Legislative Council. In introducing it the Chief Secretary, said *"the Bill owes its origin to the vision and proselytising zeal of Major Carter"* and went on to say that at the

Fig.2. In the shadow of Kinabalu: the town of Kundasang, today benefitting from both tourism and highland agriculture. *(Photo: Albert Teo)*

request of the Kinabalu Memorial Committee, the Central Town and Country Planning Board met in June 1960 to discuss problems associated with the Memorial scheme. This was the first occasion the Board had exercised its functions in respect to country development.

Copies of the report prepared by Professor Corner, leader of the Royal Society Expedition to Kinabalu in 1961 had been made available to members. Clearly the exciting descriptions of the mountain (which none of the members had climbed) and its animals must have appealed, for the Bill was passed without dissent. The outcome was the appointment of the North Borneo National Parks Trustees. This did not in itself set up Kinabalu or any other park but it enabled that action to be taken when desired.

In the meantime, the composition of the Memorial Committee had changed. Toby Carter left Borneo in 1961 and Joe Berwick, Director of Agriculture for North Borneo, took over as Secretary. Representatives of the main racial groups, Ganie Gilong, the Dusun Native Chief of the Ranau District, O.K.K. Datu Mustapha and Ngui Ah Kui became committee members, joining Tony Grier, Donald Stephens, Maurice Lerner (Treasurer) and P. Lintan. Max Haymes of the Hong Kong and Shanghai Bank remained as Chairman. By March 1961, the fund had reached M$150,000, the design had been agreed and Donald Stephens took over from Max Haymes as the latter was leaving on retirement.

Some time previously Toby Carter had plans drawn for the memorial by an overseas architect. The scheme was large and "Victorian heroic" in style. The trouble was that it could not be built at Kundasang due to transport limitations. It was therefore decided to ask resident architects to submit new ideas for which the only design guide was that they should be physically feasible and not exceed the budget sum available. All work was to be on a voluntary basis without fees. (Mr. J.C. Robinson's design was chosen by the Committee—Eds.)

The chosen design, quickly dubbed a "fort" from its external appearance, consisted of four interlocking but separate gardens set at different levels on the small hill that formed the site. The walls gave privacy to each garden and shelter from the wind. The planting of the gardens was to represent the homelands of those who died; a formal rose garden with ivy-covered walls for Britain; sun-reflecting white walls with "hot" coloured flowers for Australia; and rough stone walls with logs and wild flowers from Kinabalu for Borneo. At the top level lay the "Contemplation Garden" with a long pool and pergola; from here the visitor can pass out to a viewing platform with a superb view of the mountain.

Work started in 1961 and proceeded steadily, albeit slowly for a few years, until the contractor stopped, claiming that he had already constructed more walling than that shown on the drawings. Investigations showed that either the original survey, or the setting out must have been in error, but it mattered little for the committee had no more funds to disburse, and could only appeal to Government for help. The Memorial Committee was dissolved in 1970 when Government finally took over the site. Funds for completing the project were allocated in 1971, and in 1973 responsibility for looking after it was transferred to the National Parks Trustees, a logical solution since the newly established Park Headquarters was only 6 km (4 miles) away.

Kinabalu National Memorial

The Kinabalu Memorial bears no names for it is not strictly a war memorial but one dedicated to the brotherhood of man as exemplified by the trust and respect the people of Borneo, Australia and Britain had for each other during those dark days. To the men on the Death March, Kinabalu was not a thing of beauty but a granite tomb that came closer each weary day. But they need no memorial for the spirits of the mountain that bore witness to their pain live on while man passes on his way. It is all history now, but as we scan the mountain slopes it will do no harm to think back to those times of sadness that were to be the seed from which the Memorial grew:

> Look up in awe,
> to where the misty peaks meet heaven
> where the spirits of the mountain dwell
>
> Remember those who came this way before
> saw those same rocks thru' weary eyes
> before they died. Remember them.

Fig.1. Narrow gorge with lakes, Mount Kinabalu. *(Photo: Robert New)*

KINABALU PLACE NAMES IN DUSUN AND THEIR MEANING

John H. Beaman, Rajibi Haji Aman, Jamili Nais, Gabriel Sinit & Alim Biun

---

"Most Borneo names have their roots buried in prehistory, beyond any hope of further disentanglement. Some writers have been bold enough to wade in the swamp of terminology, nevertheless." Harrisson and Harrisson, 1971.

In the course of exploration of Mount Kinabalu, beginning with the first expedition of Hugh Low in 1851 (Harrisson, 1978), a large number of place names has accumulated in the scientific literature. Most of these are from the Dusun language, with a smaller number in Malay and English. The Dusun names generally have been recorded by persons with limited or no command of that language, with the result that many variant spellings have accumulated. Dusun place names often have a special meaning concerning a particular locality, and collectively represent a rich lore about Kinabalu. The first author, with the assistance of the other authors, is in the process of preparing a location map of Mount Kinabalu that will be used in connection with a botanical inventory of the mountain. The inventory is being produced with the aid of a computerised specimen database (Beaman & Regalado, 1989), which requires that plant collection localities be standardised. Variant spellings of many localities have presented a challenge in the preparation of both the map and the database. It is beyond the scope of this chapter to produce a full synonymised list of variant spellings and other expressions for particular localities as there are over 3000 of these for herbarium specimens. However, such a list for the plant collections is in preparation as a separate project.

The participation of native speakers of the Dusun language has been essential to produce standardised spellings of place names that are meaningful in that language. The present account, therefore, is the result of collaboration between a botanist who has examined over 20,000 plant specimens on which many of the localities have been recorded and four persons whose first language is Dusun (of the Ranau group *sensu* Rutter (1929, p. 38), but who also have excellent command of English and Malay. In this respect we have been more fortunate than the Royal Society expeditions, about which Corner (1964, p. 14) lamented "... we certainly needed a scientific member of the expedition conversant with their [Dusun] language which has so much to tell in its own names about wild things." Even with the competence in the Dusun language of four of the authors of this chapter, however, the task of standardisation and derivation of meanings is daunting because, as noted by Rutter (1929, p. 262), Dusun has a great many local variations and idiosyncrasies of pronunciation. St. John (1986, vol. 1, p. 322) commented on the problem as follows: "In making vocabularies here [Kiau] we found the villagers very careless of their pronunciation: for instance, the word 'heavy' was at different times written down, *magat, bagat, wagat,* and *ogat*; for 'rice,' *wagas* and *ogas*; for 'to bathe,' *padshu, padsiu,* and *madsiu,* and indifferently pronounced in these various ways by the same people." We note that although St. John was correct in noting the carelessness of pronunciation of some words, much of the variation is readily explainable by the native speakers. The differences are caused by, firstly, the different pronunciation or word derivation in different phrase construction (e.g., *medsu* [not *madsiu* as noted by St. John] is a verb, the act of bathing, while *pedsu* is the root word or alternatively, could mean asking one 'to bathe'; *wagat* is the root word while *magat* means 'getting heavier'). Secondly, some of the variant pronunciation is from a neighbouring community (e.g., *awagat* is the Kiau proper pronounciation for 'heavy' while *a'agat* (not *ogat* as noted by St. John) is from the neighbouring Kampung Bundu Tuhan. We note the tendency of immitating the pronunciation of a neighbouring community when confronted by an outsider.

For purposes of conducting this study the five authors have had the opportunity to travel together around Mount Kinabalu to document the position of particular localities and to interview local kampung residents in 15 kampungs, whose knowledge of their area has made it possible to put place names on the map, and, in cases not already known to the Dusun-speaking authors, to determine the meaning of these names. As a result of the interviews we have accumulated a list of many more place names for Mount Kinabalu than are represented in the botanical database or are on any published map. We believe that the standardisation of the spelling of these names, definition of their meaning, and representation of them on the location map will significantly facilitate future research concerning Mount Kinabalu and will also increase the appreciation of both scientists and casual visitors to one of the earth's most remarkable biological, geological, and physiographic features.

Most of the persons interviewed for the study in August, 1990, and July, 1992, were advanced in age, and it is unlikely that much of their knowledge about Kinabalu localities will be passed on to future generations. We therefore feel fortunate to have been able to obtain this information before it is lost. In cases of discrepancies about the spellings and acceptance of particular names, we have attempted to recognise the local usage based on information from the informants.

The major informants, listed by kampung, are as follows: Kundasang—Koutal Bendial @ Norman (a guide for E. J. H. Corner, Sheila Collenette, and Willem Meijer); Kiau—Meguring Sombout (presently a regular Kinabalu guide); Takutan—Lemudin Tadong (uncle of Jamili Nais); Nalumad—Medili Gunad (a Kinabalu Park employee); Pinawantai Pahu—Nasip Pungut (helped survey the Kinabalu Park boundary with George Mikil; Keung—Done Sawal, Muyou Limbana, and Sumbin Binua; Sayap—Baruk bin Kiaku, Pendingau bin Gendihan, Lasius Tingkawan, and Penimbul bin Serunggal; Melangkap Kapa—Tempuling Sidan and Sindi Sarabun; Melangkap Tomis—Garog bin Koko; Bundu Tuhan—Masalin bin Penyon; Cinta Mata Kundasang—Sumbing Banggaloi; Mamut Copper Mine—Mohamad Hidil Ramli (Environmental Superintendent, Mamut Copper

Mine Sdn. Bhd.); Poring—Sian Lagas; Kilimu Ranau—Kupin Gangkut; Kituntul Ranau—Sinit Gimbaran (father of Gabriel Sinit), Patuk Gijaran.

The Dusun people originally populated most of the northern half of what is now known as Sabah, except for certain coastal areas. They are classified by Rutter (1929, pp. 37–40) into two main branches, inland and coastal, which he further divides into 15 groups. The Dusun language is of Austronesian (Malayo-Polynesian) origin, consists of a number of local dialects, and belongs to the North Indonesian subgroup of Philippine languages (Dyen, 1965; Rutter, 1929, pp. 262–263). Significant language variations on different parts of Mount Kinabalu were noted by the Dusun-speaking authors of this paper, for example, between Takutan and Sayap. According to Rutter's classification, Dusuns populating various areas of Mount Kinabalu would include the Ranau, Kiau, and Tempasuk groups, the latter further divided into a Sayap subdivision.

A Kadazan-English and English-Kadazan dictionary has been published (Antonissen, 1958) which includes only a few of the words listed below. Kadazans are the urban people while Dusun is the more general ethnic term, sometimes used to specifically refer to the rural population. The words included in the present work might be expected to be under-represented in Antonissen's dictionary because of its urban emphasis. His work also includes a section on Kadazan grammar. A grammar and vocabulary of Dusun also has been published by Gossens (1924), but this relates principally to the Papar dialect and thus is of limited relevance. The vocabulary by St. John (1986, vol. 2, Appendix D, pp. 407–416) for 'Tempasuk Dusun' is of some interest, although most of the words he listed do not seem to be associated with place names.

The Dusun pronunciation (at least to the Dusun living around Kinabalu covered in this study) do not contain the letter "o" (as pronounced in oven or moth). Thus, although there are efforts among some Dusun/Kadazan orthographers to standardise the spelling from "E" to "O" to approach the sound "uh" (as pronounced in merge), we have preferred the letter "E" instead of "O" in this paper to approach this sound ("uh" as pronounced in merge). We do not use this system in an authoritative linguistic way, but propose it to avoid confusion as to how a word should be properly pronounced. Further, this is to clarify the incompatibility of using various spelling norms for particular sounds in this language, and (in the face of different spelling used for important place names on Kinabalu) endeavour to provide a system of standardisation.

Some place names, however, are so well known and have been so frequently represented with a variant spelling that we accept them but indicate in brackets the correct spelling. Among these are Poring (Pering), Tenompok (Tenempek), and Pinosuk (Pineusuk). We have not been able to determine the meaning of all place names of Mount Kinabalu, but we take a less pessimistic view of this endeavour than would Harrisson and Harrisson (1971), whom we quote in the prologue. Many place names where the meaning is not included probably originated from classical Dusun words, no longer understood by the present generation of Dusuns. For example, hardly even half the words uttered in the classical Dusun rites/spells are understood by the present generation. Some of the unresolved place names may have originated from stories that we can no longer trace.

This is not a complete list of places on Mount Kinabalu. An additional problem is that we cannot precisely position certain place names on the map, and therefore cannot give the latitude-longitude coordinates. The reason for this difficulty is that during the interviews it was not always possible to be certain that we had correctly related precise map locations to places the informants described, particularly in the case of some small tributaries (almost all of which seem to have names) to the rivers into which they flow. In spite of this incompleteness, we believe it preferable to make available at this time the information presently known rather than wait until a more perfect list can be produced.

A few place names are nonsense but nevertheless are so well established that it seems necessary to accept them. Thus, Nonohan Mountain apparently is a corruption of *nuluhen*, which means hill (any hill). The Malaysian Directorate of National Mapping sheet 6/116/15 (Kinabalu quadrangle) has Nonohan in the wrong place, for a 4,386 ft hill, rather than the 10,034 ft, conspicuous, sharp-pointed mountain described by Corner (1964, p. 21) as "... the jagged north ridge runs to Gunong Nonohan and walls in the unbelievably steep and precipitous upper reaches of the Kinapasan and Nalumad rivers."

The names are listed in alphabetical order. For purposes of this paper they are located to nearest minute of latitude and longitude. They will be precisely shown to the extent possible on the location map now in preparation. In the case of long rivers, ridges, etc., the coordinates are given to a place where that feature is labeled on the map. Some place names have been used more than once, for example, Kinasepian River, Libang River, Silau-silau River, Kinateki River, and thus are indicated with more than one set of coordinates.

LIST OF PLACE NAMES

Bahab (river), 5°58'N, 116°42'E. *Mangifera* sp.

Bambangan (river), 6°00'N, 116°38'E. *Mangifera pajang*.

Bayaen (river), 5°58'N, 116°33'E. From the name of a traditional jar/urn.

Bengu (river), 6°07'N, 116°43'E.

Bidau-bidau (falls), 6°06'N, 116°32'E. Large grass.

Binembun (river), 6°06'N, 116°27'E.

Bongol [Bengel] (kampung), 6°06'N, 116°25'E. Otter.

Buluntungen (river), 6°02'N, 116°42'E. Place normally where a rainbow occurs (rainbow is *buluntung*).

Bundu-bundu (river), 6°03'N, 116°26'E. From *bundu*, *Mangifera caesia*. The word is repeated either to mean the occurrence of many *bundu*, or else to mean a tree resembling a *bundu*.

Bundu Paka (kampung), 6°08'N, 116°27'E. From *bundu* meaning *Mangifera caesia* and *paka* meaning *Imperata cylindrica*.

Bundu Tuhan (kampung), 5°59'N, 116°32'E. *Mangifera caesia* tree lost in a landslide.

Chiput (river). [Not certainly located, but in the Kaung area; might be Kuruput River; we have seen the name Chiput recorded only once, on a collection by Sabah Forest Department collector Muroh.]

Dachang (locality), approximately 6°04'N, 116°35'E. [Not precisely located; Clemens collection locality at high elevation in the Mesilau Basin; our informant suggested that it possibly was named for one of the Clemenses' guide-collectors.]

Dalas (river), 6°05'N, 116°26'E.

Dallas [Dalas] (kampung), 6°02'N, 116°28'E.

Dallas (river), 6°02'N, 116°28'E.

Dangkarai (river), 5°59'N, 116°31'E.

Dapatau (locality), 6°03'N, 116°31'E. Plateau. [Misspelled 'Dapatan' by Gibbs (1914).]

Deip (hill), 6°04'N, 116°43'E. A wild durian that occurs on the hill.

Delung (river), 6°09'N, 116°27'E. Possibly from *delungan*, the confluence of two rivers.

Denanangsat (river), 6°03'N, 116°42'E.

Denggiranuk (ridge), 6°07'N, 116°30'E.

Dili (trail), 6°02'N, 116°42'E.

Ediba Titiu (river), 6°04'N, 116°32'E. Short torch.

Gelengeng (river). [Not precisely located.]

Genipis (ridge), 6°02'N, 116°33'E. Narrow, referring to the narrow ridge.

Gigipanen (river), 5°56'N, 116°40'E. From *gipan* (shrimp/prawn); the abundant occurrence of freshwater shrimp.

Gigisen (river), 6°04'N, 116°32'E. Where frog eggs are found.

Guab (river), 6°11'N, 116°34'E.

Gurulau (spur), 6°03'N, 116°32'E. A kind of tree with edible fruits.

Haye-haye (river), 6°03'N, 116°31'E. Name of a plant.

Hempuen (hill), 6°00'N, 116°40'E.

Heur (river), 6°04'N, 116°30'E. Water darkened from organic matter.

Himbaan (kampung), 5°58'N, 116°33'E. Secondary or disturbed forest.

Kabu (river), 5°58'N, 116°32'E. Name of the first person who lived there.

Kadamaian (falls) [Kedamayan], 6°02'N, 116°32'E.

Kadamaian (river), 6°03'N, 116°28'E.

Kandaai (river), 6°11'N, 116°33'E.

Kapadadan (river), 6°12'N, 116°33'E.

Kapur (river), 6°04'N, 116°27'E. *Parashorea* spp.

Karanaan (river), 6°04'N, 116°31'E. Having a lot of mud.

Kategepan (river), 6°05'N, 116°28'E. Area where *Artocarpus* sp. is abundant.

Kaung [Keung] (kampung), 6°05'N, 116°27'E.

Kebayau (kampung), 6°10'N, 116°27'E.

Kebayau (rivers), 6°09'N, 116°27'E. Twins, referring to the two rivers close together.

Kebibi (river). [Not precisely located, but on Map 6/116/15 as what we have recorded as the Tawaras River.] Stumbling sideways.

Kebu (river). [Not certainly located; tributary of the Tinekuk from the south, between the Kinapasaen and Watu.] Place where *Donax* occurs.

Kegepen (river), 5°58'N, 116°32'E. *Castanopsis* sp.

Kegiitan Agaye (river), 6°02'N, 116°31'E. Fig with large leaves used to wrap rice.

Kegiitan Ekere [a small tributary of the Kegiitan Agaye].

Kegumpayan (river), 6°06'N, 116°27'E. From *gumpai*, a type of water-lily; the occurrence of many gumpai.

Keheben (river), 6°04'N, 116°27'E.

Kekeb (kampung), 5°59'N, 116°41'E.

Kekehitan (hill), 6°06'N, 116°26'E. From *kahit*, slightly scratching with one finger. Legend has it that after death, the spirit of the dead would scratch the hill before ascending Kinabalu.

Kelipesu (river), 6°05'N, 116°28'E. From *lipesu*, an edible, sour fruit of *Baccaurea lanceolata* (cf. Lipesu).

Kelumpisahen (river), 6°08'N, 116°28'E. Being colonized by swallows.

Kelumpisau (cave), 6°08'N, 116°42'E. Swallows.

Kemburongoh [Kemburengeh] (locality), 6°02'N, 116°33'E. "The spirit place" (Gibbs, 1914). Apparently named after the Kemburongoh 'grass' (K. Mat Salleh, pers. comm.), from which the universal Dusun charm Kemburengeh is made. The foul smell of the charm is believed to scare away evil spirits.

Kementis (river), 6°11'N, 116°33'E.

Kenipir (river), 5°56'N, 116°33'E. *Passiflora foetida*.

Kenunukan (river), 6°12'N, 116°34'E. Having numerous figs.

Kepaladan (river), 6°06'N, 116°27'E. The occurrence of many plants of *Licuala* spp.

Kepangian (river), 6°07'N, 116°27'E. From *pangi (Pangium edulis)*; the occurrence of many *pangi*.

Kepuakan (river), 6°13'N, 116°42'E. Having many owls.

Kepungitan (river), 6°14'N, 116°33'E. The occurrence of numerous bats.

Ketugungan (river), 6°11'N, 116°35'E. The occurrence of numerous, half-burned sticks of firewood.

Ketumanggung (river), 6°02'N, 116°26'E.

Ketumbalang (river), 6°13'N, 116°35'E. From *tumbalang*, a smooth-stemmed bamboo.

Keuluan (kampung), 5°59'N, 116°36'E. Having a lot of a small bamboo.

Keuluan (river), 5°59'N, 116°35'E.

Kiahuan (river), 6°09'N, 116°31'E.

Kiau 1 [Kiau Nulu] (kampung), 6°03'N, 116°30'E. A stream there does not dry up during droughts, and thus is a place for quenching thirst (Rutter, 1929, p. 247). *Nulu* means a hill.

Kiau 2 [Kiau Teburi] (kampung), 6°02'N, 116°30'E. *Teburi* is an instrument made from bamboo used for warning before fighting in wars.

Kibambang (river). [A river recorded by the Clemenses in the Kilembun basin, but not located in the field.]

Kibawing-bawing (ridge), 6°08'N, 116°43'E. Place of occurrence of many *Adinandra dumosa*.

Kibbas (kampung), 5°57'N, 116°38'E. Formerly known as Kimendeu, meaning the occurrence of a ghostly spirit. The name Kibbas is the combination of three names, i.e., Kimendeu, Batu Empat, and Sumaang.

Kibundu (river), 5°57'N, 116°42'E. Place of occurrence of *Mangifera caesia*.

Kieburi (river), 5°57'N, 116°40'E. The occurrence of a small bamboo from which a flute used for war warning is made.

Kiegiung (river), 5°58'N, 116°34'E. From *tegiung*, a graminoid plant; the occurrence of many *tegiung*.

Kigeuten (river), 6°04'N, 116°28'E. The occurrence of bushes.

Kihang (river), 6°05'N, 116°27'E.

Kihunut (river), 5°56'N, 116°38'E.

Kikulat (river), 6°12'N, 116°43'E. Occurrence of mushrooms.

Kilembun (falls), 6°05'N, 116°32'E.

Kilembun (river), 6°06'N, 116°30'E.

Kilimu (kampung), 5°59'N, 116°41'E.

Kimangaweng (river), 6°04'N, 116°41'E.

Kimanuk (river), 6°02'N, 116°30'E. Occurrence of (wild) chicken.

Kimerugi (river), 6°04'N, 116°29'E. Spiny river bank (from rattans).

Kinabalu (mountain). The highest point is Low's Peak, 4101 m, 6°05'N, 116°33'E. Chinese widow or solitary father according to Harrisson (1978) and various earlier authors. Rutter (1929, pp. 42–43) includes a fascinating discussion of the meaning of the word, concluding that the Dusun name of the mountain is Nabalu, derived from the word bahu [nonsense!, there is no such word], meaning resting-place of the dead, since the mountain is believed to be the home of departed spirits. We offer a more reasonable explanation. *Nabalu* in classical Dusun means a large rock, usually believed to be inhabited by a spirit. A small stone is called *watu*, a larger one (rock or boulder) is called *pampang*, and a huge rock usually associated with a spirit inhabitant is called *nabalu*. *Ki* simply means 'having', or 'the occurrence of', as in the case of numerous place names. Kinabalu thus means a place having a huge rock, presumably associated with a spirit or spirits. The word *nabalu* for any large rock faded from modern usage as it became overshadowed by the more dominant usage for the great mountain. Accordingly, for the modern Dusun, *Nabalu* may only be referred to the mountain.

Kinapasaan (river). [One of the major rivers on the NE side in the Mekedeu River basin, but not yet specifically located.] A place where something has rotted.

Kinapasaen (river). [Not certainly located; a tributary of the Tinekuk from the S; W of the Kebu.] Place where a rotten animal was once found.

Kinasepian (river), 6°00'N, 116°34'E. Steep place where a deer chased by a dog has its leg broken.

Kinasepian (river), 6°01'N, 116°31'E.

Kinasaraban (kampung), 5°59'N, 116°34'E. Burned area or object.

Kinateki (river), 6°02'N, 116°31'E.

Kinateki (river), 6°05'N, 116°30'E.

Kinateki (river), 6°07'N, 116°29'E.

Kine'Etungan (river), 5°57'N, 116°34'E.

Kinegitem (river), 6°09'N, 116°26'E.

Kinunut (river). [A river spelled this way by C. E. Carr for some of his plant collections made in 1933; probably it is the Kihunut River.]

Kipelupu (river), 5°56'N, 116°41'E. From a legume liana.

Kipungit (hill), 6°03'N, 116°42'E. The occurrence of bats.

Kipungit (river), 6°00'N, 116°32'E.

Kipungit River 1, 6°03'N, 116°42'E.

Kipungit River 2, 6°03'N, 116°42'E.

Kiruyeu (river), 6°01'N, 116°35'E. Place where a dead tree occurs.

Kisagut (river), 6°08'N, 116°42'E. The occurrence of a (water) spring.

Kituntul (kampung), 5°56'N, 116°41'E. The occurrence of an edible black snail near the river.

Kituntul (river), 5°57'N, 116°40'E.

Kiulan (river), 6°03'N, 116°29'E.

Kiululu (river), 6°09'N, 116°31'E. The occurrence of sparse, small bamboos.

Kolopis [Kelepis] (river), 6°01'N, 116°31'E. A large citrus fruit.

Kulampung (river), 6°02'N, 116°27'E.

Kulung (hill), 5°59'N, 116°41'E. From the shape of the leaf of *keruing kubis* (*Dipterocarpus confertus*).

Kumawanan (river), 6°01'N, 116°35'E. Going toward the right.

Kundasang (kampung), 5°59'N, 116°34'E. From the Kundasang tree, *Coelostegia griffithii*, a relative of the durian (Meijer, 1966).

Kuriau (river), 6°00'N, 116°29'E.

Kuruput (river), 6°06'N, 116°27'E. Sound of the stream.

Labi (river), 6°08'N, 116°28'E. Soft-shelled fresh-water turtle.

Lahanas (river), 5°59'N, 116°35'E.

Lakang (locality), 6°06'N, 116°43'E. Ripe betel nut; sharp, loud sound.

Langanan (falls), 6°04N, 116°41'E. Name of a man who was washed down the (Langanan) river in a flood and never seen again (Poring version); (in Paranchangen, legend has it that he was found and hung on the fork of a tree).

Langanan (river), 6°04'N, 116°41'E.

Langkuag (river), 5°56'N, 116°41'E. Probably from *lengkug*, a small nocturnal eagle.

Layang-layang (locality), 6°03'N, 116°33'E. Swallow.

Lebeng-lebeng [Lubang-lubang] (kampung), 6°04'N, 116°27'E. Numerous graves or something resembling graves.

Ledeng (river), 6°07'N, 116°43'E. Name of a tree.

Leletingan (river), 6°07'N, 116°42'E. Repeatedly positioning a guide for a straight line.

Lempuka (river), 6°10'N, 116°26'E.

Lenau (mountain). [Between Tenompok and Kemburongoh, not certainly located.] Smooth, wet soil. It might also have originated from *linau (Xylosma sumatrana)* or *lunau (Gymnacranthera contracta)*.

Lengugen (river), 5°56'N, 116°40'E. *Saurauia* sp.

Leteng (river), 6°00'N, 116°33'E. Loud sound made by a falling object.

Letingan (river), 6°06'N, 116°37'E. Positioning a guide for a straight line.

Leut-leut (river), 6°04'N, 116°26'E. From *leut*, pale yellowish or partial albinism.

Li'idan (river), 5°57'N, 116°34'E. Place where a rolling object stops.

Libang (kampung), 5°57'N, 116°41'E. Derived from a kampung in Tambunan from which the founders of this kampung came.

Libang (river), 5°58'N, 116°41'E.

Libang (river), 6°09'N, 116°30'E.

Lingkubang (kampung), 6°09'N, 116°26'E. From *kubeng*, meaning crater or concave. Evans (1990, p. 311) gave a similar derivation, indicating that *kubeng* is a pass between hills.

Linisihan (river), 6°06'N, 116°27'E. From *lisiu*, gathering. There was a house here where passersby would gather together and spend the night.

Lipesu (kampung), 5°58'N, 116°38'E. *Baccaurea lanceolata*, with edible fruit (Meijer, 1961), cf. Kelipesu.

Liwagu (river), 5°59'N, 116°36'E. Common name for any river without a name.

Lohan [Luhan] (kampung), 6°00'N, 116°43'E.

Lohan (river), 6°00'N, 116°41'E.

Luag (river), 6°05'N, 116°30'E?

Luang di Kilau (locality), 6°02'N, 116°32'E. *Lubang* of the Kadamaian; local legend has it that the luang near Kampung Kiau was used by a man, Kilau, to meditate, sometimes for months, to attain magical powers. In the end, he never returned.

Lubang (locality), 6°02'N, 116°32'E. Malay word for hole, i.e., shelter formed by overhanging boulder; frequently spelled Lobang; *luang* in Dusun. The Clemenses had several localities they referred to as 'lobangs', but the one most generally referred to by other early explorers is at the location indicated above.

Lugas (hill), 5°56'N, 116°34'E. Bald.

Lumaang (river), 6°07'N, 116°25'E. From *laang*, meaning step; stepping.

Lumetek (river), 6°10'N, 116°34'E. Extremely turbid water.

Luminedut (river), 6°00'N, 116°28'E. From *ledut*, meaning the moaning of a sick person.

Lumu-lumu (locality), 6°01'N, 116°32'E. This commonly used place name of earlier collectors and explorers on Kinabalu is virtually forgotten at the present time, and the locality is now referred to as Kiau View Gap. The word may be a corruption of *lumununu*, meaning peeling, and Dusun for *Tristaniopsis*. Griswold (1939) stated that 'Lumu Lumu' in Dusun means 'Mossy Mossy', and suggested that no more appropriate name could have been chosen, owing to the predominance of moss [on the trees and ground]. According to the Dusun-speaking authors of this paper, however, Lumu-lumu means nothing in Dusun. *Lumut* means moss (or algae) in Malay. It is possible that the place name could have had a Malay origin since the locality was used as a camp site during expeditions to the summit. Another example of a Malay place name related to expedition camps is *lubang (lobang)*.

Madaleng (mountain). The majority of people questioned in Kampung Manggis, Kampung Serinsim, Kampung Marak Parak, and Kampung Lahanas refer to what is labeled Tambuyukon (Tembuyuken) on most maps as Madaleng.

Mahandei (ridge), 6°04'N, 116°31'E.

Mahandei (river), 6°04'N, 116°31'E.

Maliu-paliu (pronounced maliw-paliw) (river), 6°03'N, 116°28'E. From *paliu*, poison in blowpipe dart, taken from *Antiaris toxicaria*.

Mamut (river), 6°02'N, 116°39'E. Derived from setting hen, *memut*.

Manggis [Menggis] (kampung), 6°12'N, 116°46'E. Mangosteen, *Garcinia mangostana*.

Mantaranau (river), 6°03'N, 116°26'E.

Marai Parai (locality), 6°05'N, 116°31'E. From the resemblance of the very common sedge, *Costularia pilisepala*, to hill padi. Hill padi is called *parai* while *marai parai* means something resembling padi refering to *C. pilisepala*, after its resemblance to padi plant especially of its movements in the wind.

Marakau (kampung), 5°57'N, 116°41'E. Habit of people travelling around bartering.

Marakau (river), 5°57'N, 116°42'E.

Marak Parak (kampung), 6°19'N, 116°44'E.

Mayabau (peak), 6°05'N, 116°36'E. [The 'Matterhorn' of the Royal Society 1961 expedition (Corner, 1964). A large boulder.

Mayampak (river), 5°59'N, 116°32'E.

Mayamut (river), 6°02'N, 116°28'E.

Mebeu-lebeu (river), 6°01'N, 116°31'E. Always turbid.

Mebeu-lebeu (river), 6°02'N, 116°32'E.

Mege-sege (river), 6°09'N, 116°27'E. From *sege*, *Calamus caesius*.

Mekedeu (river), 6°07'N, 116°40'E. Derived from the word *kedeu* meaning hard.

Melangkap (kampung), 6°10'N, 116°29'E. Named after a particular small stream.

Melangkap Kapa (kampung), 6°09'N, 116°30'E. From the words *kinapa kapa*, meaning a very simple hut.

Melangkap Tomis [Melangkap Temis] (kampung), 6°09'N, 116°29'E. From *Temis*; the first people to live here were from Tomis.

Mensahaban (river), 5°59'N, 116°40'E.

Menteki (river), 5°59'N, 116°37'E.

Mentekungen (river), 6°02'N, 116°42'E.

Mesegit (river), 5°59'N, 116°33'E. From *segit*, cold.

Mesilau (river), 5°59'N, 116°36'E. Soil in the bottom of the river is yellowish.

Mesulit (river), 6°11'N, 116°34'E.

Minalun (river), 5°58'N, 116°33'E. Passage way, appearing like a road.

Minentuhan (river), 6°10'N, 116°34'E. Having previously had a landslide.

Minenul (river), 6°07'N, 116°42'E.

Mini'irad (river), 6°00'N, 116°31'E. Alike, same (derived from the size of the river, i.e., same size as the Li'idan River.

Minirinteg (locality), 6°03'N, 116°36'E. [Apparently = Mesilau Cave.]

Miniserinam (locality), 6°02'N, 116°36'E. [Dusun name for the Pinosuk Plateau (Corner, 1963, p. 30.] Overlapping, one under the other; in a sense quite related to 'Pinosuk'.

Minitinduk (gorge), 6°02'N, 116°31'E. Confluence of two rivers.

Minteleb (hill), 6°00'N, 116°41'E. Derived from the word *tenteleb*, meaning sacred round rocks.

Mumungen (river). [Not precisely located; a Clemens locality in the Marai Parai area.]

Mureb-sureb (river), 6°09'N, 116°26'E.

Muru-turu (ridge). [Not precisely located; a Clemens locality in the Kilembun basin.] Dripping.

Nababak (river), 5°59'N, 116°33'E. Something shattered.

Nabalu [or *Pekan Nabalu*] (kampung), 6°02'N, 116°28'E. See discussion under Kinabalu.

Nalumad [Nelumad] (kampung), 6°06'N, 116°44'E. Name of a man who had an epileptic fit in the (Nalumad) river.

Nalumad (river), 6°05'N, 116°40'E.

Namadan (river), 5°58'N, 116°34'E. From *hamad*, sideways; the flow of the river went sideways.

Nasapad (hill). [Not precisely located; on the Poring-Nalumad path.] Divided by a barrier.

Nasureng (river), 5°56'N, 116°41'E. Blinded by bright light.

Negures (river). [In the area of Hempuen Hill, but not precisely located.] Scratched.

Nembuyukung (mountain). An alternate name in general use by some of the local population for Tembuyuken; it is the peak nearest, and only visible major prominence from Kampung Serinsim.

Nepungguk (mountain), 6°10'N, 116°31'E. Cut off at the top.

Neteki (river), 5°57'N, 116°34'E.

Nonohan (mountain), 6°08'N, 116°35'E. A nonsense word, apparently a corruption of *nuluhen*, Dusun for hill. However, this was called Mt. Nohan by Haviland (in Stapf, 1894, p. 75), so the word may have undergone change over the past 100 years.

Numeruk (river). [Not precisely located; a Clemens locality in the Kilembun basin. The word might correctly be *tumuruk*, which means falling water.]

Nungkek (mountain), 6°06'N, 116°29'E. [On many maps as Saduk-saduk.] The obstructed flow of a river, usually by breeding animals.

Pahu (kampung), 6°09'N, 116°46'E. *Mangifera* sp.

Paka (kampung), 5°58'N, 116°38'E. Lalang *(Imperata cylindrica)*.

Paka-paka (cave), 6°03'N, 116°34'E. Plant that looks like lalang *(Imperata cylindrica)*.

Pakeu Paliw (river), 6°08'N, 116°43'E. *Pakeu* means bottom; *paliw* is *Antiaris toxicaria*, the source of a dart poison. The place is probably named after the stump of *A. toxicaria*.

Paluan (river), 6°08'N, 116°27'E. From *paluw*, meaning small stream.

Paluw Agaye (river), 6°11'N, 116°34'E. Big stream.

Pampang (river), 6°02'N, 116°27'E. Large boulder.

Panahuan (river), 6°06'N, 116°27'E. Fish breeding area (the Dusun words for the fishes *Crossocheilus* sp. and *Paracrossocheilus* sp. are *manahu* or *betuan*).

Panaitan (river), 6°12'N, 116°33'E. A place to hang something.

Panar Laban [Pennalaban] (locality), 6°04'N, 116°34'E. Place where ritual is performed to prevent the spirit from going up Kinabalu (i.e., to prevent the person from dying).

Pangasahan (river), 6°01'N, 116°26'E. Sharpening stone.

Pemarian (river), 6°01'N, 116°26'E. From *tapari (Smilax)* sp. The place where fish poisoning took place using *tapari*, a traditional fish poison.

Penataran (river), 6°08'N, 116°30'E.

Pennalaban (locality), 6°01'N, 116°29'E.

Pendiruen (river), 6°10'N, 116°43'E. Word derived from *turuen*, which means leaky hut.

Pengakatan (river), 6°02'N, 116°43'E. Removing a bamboo fish trap from the water.

Penibukan [Pennebukan] (ridge), 6°04'N, 116°30'E. Place where fish and game are gutted.

Peniguppan (ridge), 6°04'N, 116°30'E. Rest and smoking stop; according to the informant this is the correct name for the ridge that generally in the literature and on specimens has been called Penibukan.

Pinampang (river), 6°04'N, 116°32'E. Rock face.

Pinawantai (kampung), 6°10'N, 116°47'E. Lifting an object from a lower to a higher place.

Pinintagadan (river), 6°01'N, 116°35'E. Place where trees have been chopped down.

Pinosuk [Pineusuk] (kampung), 5°58'N, 116°36E. Hidden below.

Pinosuk (plateau), 6°01'N, 116°36'E. According to Corner (1964, p. 11) the Dusun meaning is "the forest retreat from mankind;" the Geological Survey Department (Collenette, 1958) apparently originated the name Pinosuk Plateau, from Kampung Pinosuk on its lower slopes (see Miniserinam).

Poring [Pering] (kampung), 6°03'N, 116°42'E. *Gigantochloa levis* (giant bamboo).

Poring (hot springs), 6°03'N, 116°42'E.

Purak Agis (hill), 6°11'N, 116°38'E. White sands.

Radap (river), 5°58'N, 116°42'E. *Erythrina variegata*.

Ragang Tana (locality), 5°59'N, 116°41'E. Red soil.

Ranau (town), 5°57'N, 116°40'E. From *rinanau* or *ranahen* (some abbreviate it to just *ranau*) means wet padi field in Dusun. The town started as a collection of wet padi field scattered in the Ranau plain in the old days. Due to its central locality, its grew as the centre of trading to the surrounding villages, as well as becoming the administrative centre for the district as it is now. An alternative explanation is the highly improbable account by St. John (1986, vol. 1, p. 319), in reference to the 'great lake' thought at the time of his 1858 trip to be associated with Mount Kinabalu, "... they all call the lake Ranau, a corruption of the Malay Danau." According to Anthea Phillipps (pers. comm.) there is geological evidence that a lake may have existed in the Ranau plain when the Kinabalu ice-caps and glaciers were melting.

Ruhuken (kampung), 5°57'N, 116°38'E. From *ruhuk* meaning downhill; place you go downhill.

Rumuyu (river), 6°02'N, 116°30'E. The landslide-prone condition of soil, usually on riverbanks.

Samun-samun (river), 5°58'N, 116°32'E.

Sansaraben (river), 6°01'N, 116°31'E. A species of rattan.

Sapil (river), 6°04'N, 116°27'E.

Sasapan (river), 6°09'N, 116°43'E. River on which a young man with this name was sucked to death by leeches.

Sayap (kampung), 6°12'N, 116°33'E. Originating from the word *saap*, meaning fallen leaves.

Sayat-sayat (locality), 6°04'N, 116°34'E. From sayat, meaning seeds. The *sayat-sayat* plant *(Leptospermum recurvum)*, growing abundantly in this area, has leaves that look like numerous seeds.

Sediken (river). [Not precisely located; according to Clemens specimen data, in the Marai Parai area, but according to our informant a tributary to the Tahubang from the N, between the Heur and the Mahandei.] Place for trapping small animals.

Sege (river). [Not precisely located; a tributary to the Sumaang or Liwagu S of Ranau.] *Calamus caesius*.

Serinsim (kampung), 6°18'N, 116°42'E.

Serinsim (river), 6°13'N, 116°40'E.

Sesediken (river), 6°01'N, 116°35'E. Place for trapping small animals.

Silau-silau [Sileu-sileu] (river), 6°01'N, 116°32'E. Stones in the river have a yellowish colour.

Silau-silau (river), 6°05'N, 116°27'E.

Silau-silau (river), 6°05'N, 116°42'E.

Simbulen (river), 5°58'N, 116°31'E. From *simbul* meaning jump; place or object to be jumped over.

Sinanggakan (river), 6°05'N, 116°42'E.

Sinapukan (river), 6°08'N, 116°29'E. Game secured with a blowpipe.

Singgaren (former kampung), 6°02'N, 116°28'E. [This name was formerly applied to the area where Dallas and Nabalu are located.]

Sinugara (river), 6°09'N, 116°26'E.

Sosopodon [Sesepeden] (locality), 5°59'N, 116°34'E. Home of *Paragasu*, the spirit dog.

Sumaang (river), 5°56'N, 116°40'E. Act of supporting something (with an object).

Sungei (river), 5°59'N, 116°32'E. *Sungei* in Dusun has a different meaning from *sungai* (river) in Malay. In Dusun it is a name commonly given to any stream/river that does not have a specific name.

Suruban (river), 6°04'N, 116°27'E. From *surub*, meaning burning with a flame.

Taapadan (river), 6°09'N, 116°26'E. From *taapad*, meaning (in Kampung Kiau) the place in the house used as both the dining area and lavatory.

Tabawen (river), 6°11'N, 116°34'E.

Tahubang (river), 6°04'N, 116°31'E. [In the older literature and on many specimens this name is generally spelled Dahobang.]

Takutan [Tekutan] (kampung), 6°05'N, 116°46'E. From the word *pinemelingkutan*, meaning mass grave made of tree bark.

Tamalang (kampung), 5°58'N, 116°38'E. A type of bamboo, the stem glossy.

Tamur (river). [The Geological Map of the Gunong Kinabalu Area, 1:50,000 has a river labeled S. Tamara in the position we have identified as the Leteng. Possibly Tamara and Tamur are the same. The next major tributary to the Liwagu upstream is unnamed on either map.]

Place Names in Dusun

Tandahaen (river), 5°57N, 116°27E. From *tandaha*, meaning cock or rooster.

Tapapasa (river), 6°01'N, 116°35'E. River of carrion.

Taparak (river), 6°04'N, 116°30'E. *Taparak* means coin change, but this may not be related to the name of this river. It can also mean the sound produced by a group of small, hard objects hitting each other.

Taradaat (river), 5°59'N, 116°33'E. Tangled or difficult.

Tarasan (river), 6°04'N, 116°42'E. Possibly from *tarasen*, a small clearing for planting, e.g., vegetables (not amounting to an orchard or *ladang* plantation).

Tawaras (river), 5°59'N, 116°38'E.

Tawaras Teki (river), 5°59'N, 116°38'E.

Tawei Raan (river), 6°11'N, 116°33'E. Long branch.

Tebeben (river), 5°59'N, 116°31'E. A deeper part of a stream where people normally get water for domestic use.

Tehukad (river), 5°56'N, 116°35'E.

Teindik (river), 6°01'N, 116°26'E.

Tekurik (river), 5°58'N, 116°40'E.

Tembetuen (kampung), 6°08'N, 116°27'E. A type of very small bamboo.

Tembuyuken (mountain), 6°12'N, 116°39'E. This name appears on many maps, but villagers on the east side of the Kinabalu massif have never heard of it; see Madaleng and Nembuyukung.

Tengabil (river), 6°06'N, 116°28'E.

Tengeluden (river), 5°56'N, 116°34'E.

Tenompok [*Tenempek*] (locality), 6°00'N, 116°32'E. Made blunt (plateau) or tombstone. Antonissen (1958) defines *tinompok* as a long parang, and the local Bundu Tuhan also call the parang a *tenompok*. *Tenompok* can also mean a particular stone at a place where the Dusunic traditional ritual is performed. In this context, it is the latter that brought about the name Tenompok. The story goes that in the old days, people travelling from Ranau to Tamparuli (or vice versa) spent the night around this stone and performed rituals asking whether or not to proceed on the journey. The answer was by way of dreams. We were also informed that the local warriors used this stone to sharpen their parang before going to war.

Terarasak (river), 6°04'N, 116°31'E. River dries easily.

Tereben (river), 6°04'N, 116°31'E. A place in a river where a simple bath is taken.

Terili (river), 6°04'N, 116°31'E. Probably the river flows around something, for example a ridge.

Terintiden (kampung), 6°14'N, 116°32'E.

Terintiden (river), 6°13'N, 116°33'E.

Tetueng (river), 6°03'N, 116°43'E. Dark, probably because the river is deep and dark; or dark because it is shadowed by vegetation.

Tibabar (falls), 6°02'N, 116°33'E. Perpendicular.

Tibabar (mountain), 6°02'N, 116°33'E.

Timpehen (locality), 6°02'N, 116°33'E. A leveled area where an object is placed (Power Station area), in this context, the starting point of a climb.

Tinekuk (river), 6°03'N, 116°29'E. [On many specimen labels this has been spelled Pinokok.] A part of the river believed to have been dammed by a crocodile for egg laying.

Tinekuk (river), 5°58'N, 116°31'E.

Tinggenguken (hill), 6°09'N, 116°43'E.

Tinibasan (river), 6°07'N, 116°27'E. From *tibas*, meaning slashing with a parang; a place or object slashed with a parang.

Tinuman (river), 6°13'N, 116°33'E. Drinking place.

Tinuman Saraye (river), 5°56'N, 116°33'E. Drinking place upriver.

Tinuman Sawa' (river), 5°56'N, 116°33'E. Drinking place downriver.

Tipud (river), 6°07'N, 116°28'E. Container made by splitting a bamboo stem in half.

Tomis [Temis] (kampung), 6°01'N, 116°29'E. Cold.

Tudan (river), 6°01'N, 116°28'E. Source, i.e., catchment, of river.

Tudangan (kampung), 5°58'N, 116°42'E.

Tuhan (river), 5°58'N, 116°31'E. Landslide.

Tulep (river), 6°00'N, 116°31'E.

Tulid (river), 6°02'N, 116°27'E. Straight (normally, straightened after being unstraight or dented).

Tul'lung (river), 6°01'N, 116°29'E. A deep hole in the ground. Local legend has it that the *tul'lung* near Kampung Kiau was used by a man, Kilau, to meditate, sometimes for months, to attain magical powers. In the end, he never returned.

Tul'lung (river), 6°04'N, 116°27'E.

Tumbalun (river), 6°08'N, 116°27'E.

Turuntungen (kampung), 6°11'N, 116°46'E.

Waig Winatai (river), 6°09'N, 116°28'E. *Waig* means water and *winatai* is from *patai*, meaning dead, i.e., stagnant water.

Wariu (river), 6°09'N, 116°34'E.

Wasai (river), 5°57'N, 116°42'E. Waterfall.

Watu (river). [Not precisely located; tributary of the Tinekuk or Haye-haye from the S, between the Kebu and Haye-haye.] Rocky river (derived from *watu*, meaning stone).

Winekek (river), 5°58'N, 116°31'E. Having erected a river dam.

REFERENCES

Antonissen, A. 1958. Kadazan-English and English-Kadazan Dictionary. Government Printing Office, Canberra.

Beaman, J. H. & Regalado, J. C. Jr. 1989. Development and management of a microcomputer specimen-oriented database for the flora of Mount Kinabalu. *Taxon* 38: 27–42.

Collenette, P. 1958. The geology and mineral resources of the Jesselton-Kinabalu area, North Borneo. Memoir 6, Geological Survey Dept., British Territories in Borneo.

Corner, E. J. H. 1964. Royal Society Expedition to North Borneo 1961: Reports. *Proceedings of the Linnean Society, London* 175: 9–56, 21 pl.

Dyen, I. 1965. Lexicostatistical Classification of the Austronesian Languages. Waverly Press, Baltimore.

Evans, I. H. N. 1990. Among Primitive Peoples in Borneo. Oxford Univ. Press. [Reprint of work first published by Seeley Service & Co. Ltd., London, 1922.]

Gibbs, L. S. 1914. A contribution to the flora and plant formations of Mount Kinabalu and the highlands of British North Borneo. *Journal of the Linnean Society, Botany* 42: 1–240, 8 pl.

Gossens, A. L. 1924. A grammar and vocabulary of the Dusun language. *Journal of the Malayan Branch, Royal Asiatic Society* 2(2): 87–220.

Griswold, J. A., Jr. 1939. Up Mount Kinabalu. I. White man and natives begin ascent. *Scientific Monthly* 48: 401–414.

Harrisson, T. 1978. Kinabalu, The Wonderful Mountain of Change. In: Luping, M., Chin, W. & Dingley, E.R. (eds.), Kinabalu—Summit of Borneo: 23–44. Sabah Society Monograph 1978. The Sabah Society, Kota Kinabalu, Sabah, Malaysia.

Harrisson, T. & Harrisson, B. 1971. The prehistory of Sabah. *Sabah Society Journal* (1969–70, Monograph) 4: i–xxi, 1–272.

Meijer, W. 1961. Forest Botanist diary report, July 1961, including a report on a trip to Mt. Tambuyokon, 1–12th of July [unpublished].

Meijer, W. 1966. A preliminary note on the flora of Sosopodon Forest Reserve. [Report of the Forest Botanist, Sabah, unpublished].

Rutter, O. 1929. The Pagans of North Borneo. Hutchinson & Co. Ltd., London.

Stapf, O. 1894. On the flora of Mount Kinabalu, in North Borneo. *Transactions of the Linnean Society, London, Botany* 4: 69–263, pl. 11–20.

St. John, S. 1986. Life in the Forests of the Far East. 2 Vols. Oxford Univ. Press, Singapore, Oxford, New York. [Reprint of work first published in 1862 by Smith, Elder and Co., London.]

NOTES ON CONTRIBUTORS

ALIM BIUN is a Technical Assistant at the Research and Education Division of Sabah Parks, stationed at Kinabalu Park. A native of Ranau, he started with the Park in 1976 and in the early years helped in the demarcation of Kinabalu Park's boundary. He has a wide-ranging interest and involvement in research, such as the birds of Sabah, the herpetofauna of Mt. Kinabalu and also the high-altitude flora of Mt. Kinabalu.

SUSYN ANDREWS M.I. Hort., studied amenity horticulture at the National Botanic Gardens, Glasnevin in Dublin, Ireland, before leaving for Kew in 1976 to join the herbarium staff. Since 1987, she has been the horticultural taxonomist at Kew. Her interest in *Ilex* (hollies) began in 1975 and since then she has travelled extensively looking at *Ilex* both in the wild and in cultivation. In 1986 and 1988 she visited Sabah to work on *Ilex* in preparation for a floristic account of the hollies of Borneo.

GEORGE ARGENT Ph.D., is a Principal Scientific Officer at the Royal Botanic Gardens, Edinburgh. He has worked on the collection of banana cultivars in New Guinea and the ecology of Brazilian forests. He is presently working on the taxonomy of the Malesian Ericaceae (Rhododendron and Blueberry family) for which he has made several visits to Sabah. He is also a member of the Royal Society's South-east Asian Rainforest Committee and lead author of the "Rhododendrons of Sabah" (1988).

JOHN H. BEAMAN Ph.D., trained at Harvard University. He joined the Michigan State University, U.S.A., in 1956 as Assistant Professor and Curator of the Herbarium and was promoted to Professor in 1968. From 1983 to 1984 he was a Fullbright Fellow at the Universiti Kebangsaan Malaysia, where he was based at their Sabah campus. He has travelled extensively to make collections for the Beal-Darlington Herbarium, Michigan, and to conduct research in many herbaria. He is presently working on a Checklist of the Mt. Kinabalu flora.

C.L. CHAN F.L.S., F.R.E.S., is an amateur botanist and a skilled scientific illustrator, with an absorbing interest in Borneo's wild orchids. He is particularly interested in the orchid genus *Coelogyne* and related genera. He is a coordinator of the "Orchids of Borneo" series, and a co-author of Volume 1, which was published in 1994. He is also knowledgeable of the stick and leaf insects and has collected these amazing insects widely in Sabah for more than 10 years, building up what is probably the best collection of these in the region. An active member of the Sabah Society, he is also currently Vice President.

CHIN PHUI KONG A.S.D.K., P.G.D.K., B.Sc., was formerly the Director of Fisheries in Sabah and is a past President of the Sabah Society. He is co-author of the "Fresh-water Fishes of North Borneo" (1962, 1990), with R.F. Inger, as well as being the author of several other scientific papers on fishes and prawns. He was among those who went on the Royal Society Expeditions to Mt. Kinabalu in 1961 and 1964. After his retirement in 1978, he became an aquaculture consultant, and he is now actively involved in the ichthyological study of the Danum Valley Conservation Area, Lahad Datu district, Sabah.

E.J.H. CORNER C.B.E., M.A., D.Sc., F.R.S., F.L.S., is Professor Emeritus of Tropical Botany, University of Cambridge. He was the Assistant Director of the Gardens Department, Singapore, 1929 to 1946 and UNESCO Science Co-operation Officer, Latin America, 1947 to 1948. He led the Royal Society Expeditions to Mt. Kinabalu in 1961 and 1964 and to the Solomon Islands in 1965. He is the author of "Wayside Trees of Malaya (1940, 1952, 1988), "The Life of Plants" (1964, 1966), "Monograph of *Clavaria* and Allied Genera" (1950), and "*Boletus* in Malaysia" (1972). He specialises in the Moraceae, particularly *Ficus,* in the systematy of tropical trees and in higher fungi.

G.S. DE SILVA was Park Warden, Turtle Islands Park, Sandakan, Sabah from 1976 to 1986. Prior to joining the Parks service he was Assistant Chief Game Warden, Sabah and in 1964 he set up the Wildlife Branch of the Forestry Department and he was also involved in the 1964 Royal Society Expedition to Mt. Kinabalu. Among his major contributions to the conservation of endangered species is his outstanding work with the Orang-utan rehabilitation project at Sepilok which he started in 1964 and continued until 1975. In 1987 he emigrated to Canada.

JOHN DRANSFIELD Ph.D., trained at Cambridge University and is the Principal Scientific Officer responsible for Palms at the Herbarium, Royal Botanic Gardens, Kew, U.K. He has a wide field experience in South-east Asia and elsewhere in the tropics. One of his main interests has been rattan palms and their development as a plantation crop. He is the author of "The Rattans of Sabah" published by the Sabah Forestry Department in 1984, as well as several other books on palms, including the definitive "Genera Palmarum" (with Natalie Uhl) in 1987.

SOEJATMI DRANSFIELD Ph.D., trained at Bogor and Reading and was for many years a staff member of the Herbarium Bogoriense, Indonesia. She is now an honorary research fellow at the Royal Botanic Gardens, Kew, U.K., engaged in bamboo research. She is particularly interested in the generic delimitation of Old World tropical bamboos. She is the author of "The Bamboos of Sabah" published by the Sabah Forestry Department in 1992.

FATIMAH HAJI ABANG M.Sc., Ph.D., was an entomologist attached to the Biology Department, Universiti Kebangsaan Malaysia, Sabah campus (UKMS). Her main research interest in Sabah was the taxonomy of the fleas of Mt. Kinabalu and the Crocker Range. She was responsible for the curation, identification and development of a wide-ranging entomological collection housed in the Entomology Museum of the UKMS. She is currently attached to the University of Malaysia, Sarawak, in Kota Samarahan.

GABRIEL SINIT is an Assistant Park Warden in Kinabalu Park and has been trained in horticulture at the Royal Botanic Gardens, Edinburgh. One of the few remaining park personnel who helped in the first developments of the Kinabalu Park Headquarters, he was born and raised in Ranau, near Kinabalu.

GHAZALLY ISMAIL Ph.D., received his training as a medical immunologist at the Indiana University School of Medicine, USA. Since his posting to Sabah in 1981, his interest in natural history has led him to support research on varied aspects of the conservation of threatened habitats and endangered species in the State. He was an Associate Professor at the Faculty of Science and Natural Resources, Universiti Kebangsaan Malaysia in the field of microbiology and immunology, and since 1994 is the Deputy Vice Chancellor of the University of Malaysia, Sarawak.

TOM HARRISSON D.S.O., was Government Ethnologist and Curator of the Sarawak Museum for 20 years from 1945 to 1966, when he retired. He not only made the Sarawak Museum world-famous but also provided a model for museum programmes in Brunei and Sabah, and laid the foundations of organised archaeological research in the Borneo region. On retirement he became Visiting Professor and Senior Research Associate in the Department of Anthropology and Asian Studies at Cornell University, U.S.A. In 1975 he was appointed Professor at the University of Sussex. Together with his wife, Barbara Harrisson, he wrote the "Prehistory of Sabah", published by the Sabah Society in 1971. Tom Harrisson was tragically killed in a road accident in Thailand in 1976.

JEREMY D. HOLLOWAY Ph.D., visited Sabah in 1965 with Henry Barlow and Jonathan Banks, members of a Cambridge expedition to Mt. Kinabalu, which collected lepidoptera systematically on the mountain. In 1978 he visited Mt. Mulu in Sarawak and since then he has been employed as a specialist on macrolepidoptera with the International Institute of Entomology (an institute of CAB International). He has published books and papers on a wide range of topics. He has also conducted moth surveys in Indonesia (Sulawesi, Seram), New Caledonia and Norfolk Island.

R.E. HOLTTUM M.A., D.Sc., F.L.S., was Director, Botanic Gardens, Singapore, from 1925 to 1949, and Professor of Botany, University of Malaya in Singapore from 1949 to 1954. He visited Mt. Kinabalu in 1951, collecting ferns and subsequently collaborated with Carl Christensen in preparing an annotated list of all ferns then known from Mt. Kinabalu (417 species) published in the Gardens' Bulletin, Singapore in 1934. He also wrote Vol. 2 of the "Flora of Malaya—Ferns" (1954, 1968), and after retirement devoted most of his time to the study of ferns for the Flora Malesiana, publishing many papers in botanical journals. Holttum's work on orchids and bamboos also represented significant milestones in botany. He revisited Mt. Kinabalu in 1972. Professor Holttum died in September 1990, while this revision was in preparation.

ROBERT F. INGER Ph.D., has collected amphibians, reptiles and fishes in Sabah and Sarawak since 1950, carrying out research on the ecology and evolution of communities of amphibians and reptiles in the forests of South-east Asia. His major publications include "The Systematics and the Zoogeography of the Amphibia of Borneo" (1966, 1990) and the "Fresh-water Fishes of North Borneo" (1962, 1990) with Datuk Chin Phui Kong. His book "Frogs of Sabah" with Robert Stuebing was published in 1990. Dr. Inger is now the Emeritus Curator of Amphibians and Reptiles at the Field Museum of Natural History, Chicago and Honorary Curator of Reptiles and Amphibians at the Sarawak Museum, Kuching.

JAMILI NAIS B.Sc. (Hons.), a graduate of UKM (Bangi) is currently the Research Officer heading the Interpretative, Education and Exhibits Unit of Sabah Parks. Born and raised in Ranau, he is stationed at the Kinabalu Park and has research interests in the ecology, dispersal and reproductive biology of *Rafflesia* and the flora of Mt. Tambuyukon.

DAVID V. JENKINS B.Sc., was born in West Wales. He obtained his degree in forestry at the University of Edinburgh. He came to Sabah in 1969 where he held the position of Assistant Conservator of Forests and was assigned to the Kinabalu Park as Park Warden. Later he became Park Warden, Sabah in the Chief Minister's Department and was assigned to the Sabah Parks Trustees as the Assistant Director of Parks. He left Sabah in 1978, retiring to the U.K. where he became the Administrative Officer on the Island of Sark.

KAMARUDIN MAT SALLEH B.Sc., Ph.D., is a lecturer in Botany and Plant Systematics at the Universiti Kebangsaan Malaysia, specializing in the Annonaceae and Rafflesiaceae. He was Chairman of the Research Committee in the State Committee for the Conservation of *Rafflesia* in Sabah and is known for his discovery of a third species of *Rafflesia* in Sabah in 1988. His interest in Sabah *Rafflesia* resulted in his book "*Rafflesia*—Magnificent Flower of Sabah", published in 1991.

ANTHONY LAMB M.A., Dip. Ag., D.T.A., arrived in Sabah in 1962 and started work on developing agricultural settlement schemes around Tawau. In 1967 he moved to the Ulu Dusun Agricultural Research Station on the east coast to work on oil palm and in 1977 he moved again to the Tenom Agricultural Research Station in the interior where he is currently working on fruit trees and orchids. In 1981 he set up the Tenom Orchid Centre as a State Government Conservation project. He is a co-author of the "Rhododendrons of Sabah" (1988), and a coordinator and a co-author of the "Orchids of Borneo" series.

LAMRI ALI P.G.D.K., B.A. (Hons.), graduated from the University of Malaya specialising in Anthropology in 1973. Upon graduation he returned to Sabah to hold some key administrative positions, including the directorship of Sabah Parks in which he has served since 1978. He has been instrumental in the establishment of existing conservation strategies that ensure effective management of Sabah's parks.

DAVID LEE TAIN CHOI M.Sc., is the former Director of the Geological Survey of Malaysia in Sabah. He joined the Department in 1958 as a Technical Assistant. From 1960 to 1966 he studied geology at the University of New Brunswick, Canada, rejoining the department in 1967 upon his return. As a member of the technical staff he has travelled widely throughout Sabah, and along the Indonesian border. He has written two major geological reports, one of the Sandakan Peninsula and the other on Mt. Pock on the Semporna Peninsula in Sabah. He is currently Technical Advisor in the Chief Minister's Department.

FRANCIS S.P. LIEW B.Sc., is the Deputy Director of Sabah Parks. He received his degree in Resource Management from the University of New Brunswick, Canada, in 1972. After four years with the Sabah Forestry Department, he joined the Sabah Parks service in

1973. He was instrumental in developing the education programmes, as well as the overall policy of the Sabah Parks and is responsible for many of the conservation policies carried out to date.

WILLEM MEIJER Ph.D., joined the Sabah Forestry Department in 1959 after several years in Indonesia. As Forest Botanist he assisted in the Royal Society's scientific expedition to Mt. Kinabalu in 1961. He moved in 1968 to the University of Kentucky, U.S.A. He visited Sabah most recently in 1992 and 1994 to collect plants for the National Cancer Institute of the U.S.A. Dr. Meijer has revised the *Rafflesia* family for the Flora Malesiana.

ROBERT NEW B.Sc., F.R.I.C.S., F.I.S.M., is a keen mountaineer and amateur photographer who has climbed with his camera in Norway, the European Alps, East Africa and, since 1975, on Mt. Kinabalu. During two years' residence in Uganda he designed and built a 30-man hut at 13,500 ft beside Lake Kitandara in the Ruwenzori. Having lived in Kota Kinabalu for twelve years, he has climbed Mt. Kinabalu a great many times and explored areas of the mountain unknown to the average visitor. He designed and built the West Gurkha Hut which he now uses as his main base on the mountain. He is a member of the Alpine Club, an honorary member of the Mountain Club of Uganda and a Licenciate of the Royal Photographic Society.

BARBARA S. PARRIS Ph.D., has undertaken research on the taxonomy and ecology of South-east Asian ferns since 1971. From 1981 to 1988 she was head of the Fern section at the Herbarium, Royal Botanic Gardens, Kew, U.K. and has thereafter moved to New Zealand. She visited Mt. Kinabalu in 1980, 1985 and 1988 and has prepared an updated list of all the ferns known from the mountain in collaboration with Reed Beaman and Professor John Beaman.

JUNAIDI PAYNE Ph.D., has worked in Sabah for the World Wide Fund for Nature (WWF) Malaysia since 1979 on a variety of conservation projects in conjunction with the Forestry and Wildlife Departments and the Ministry of Tourism and Environmental Development. His speciality is the forest mammal fauna and in 1988 he completed an 18-month-long study of the Orang-utan in Sabah. He is co-author of "A Field Guide to the Mammals of Borneo" (1985) with Charles Francis and Karen Phillipps, and author of "Wild Malaysia" (1990) with photographer Gerald Cubitt.

ANTHEA PHILLIPPS B.Sc., was brought up in Sabah as a child. After receiving her Botany degree from the University of Durham, U.K., she worked for a year at the Sabah Museum, before joining the Sabah Parks service in 1981 as Park Ecologist, where she studied rhododendrons and pitcher-plants. She left the Parks service in 1987. She is author of "A Guide to the Parks of Sabah" (1988) and a co-author of "Rhododendrons of Sabah" (1988).

W.M. POON, photographer extraordinaire, lives in Sabah and continues to pursue his self-taught hobby of nature photography. A specialist on outdoor subjects, his passion includes photographing insects and plants, although his pictures of these and sceneries, as well as those of cultural interest have appeared in postcards, posters and books. His photographs have won acclaim and prizes in competitions held locally and abroad. He spends many weekends and holidays, with any of his several cameras, going after subjects in nature worthy of capturing on film. His portrayal of Sabah, including Kinabalu and its plant and animal life, provides a special record of the many wonders.

RAJIBI HAJI AMAN B.A., is a graduate of the Universiti Kebangsaan Malaysia. The son of a prominent Dusun native chief of Ranau, he is Assistant Director of the Sabah Parks in charge of law enforcement, and research and education. His background in social science has appropriately supported his career with the Civil Service and he has been, among others, the District Officer for Kinabatangan and Administration Officer in the Sabah Museum. He takes a keen interest in the welfare of people living around parks and in promoting a conservation buffer-zone concept for parks.

PATRICIA REGIS B.A. (Hons.), M.A., completed her undergraduate studies in social anthropology and postgraduate museum studies in the United Kingdom. She was a journalist for several years, and worked as curator of Ethnography for the Sabah Museum, and as Senior Press Officer for the Chief Minister's Department before becoming Director of the Sabah Museum from 1988 to 1994. She has travelled extensively throughout Sabah, documenting and recording local traditions, and has written several articles on local culture and people.

J.C. ROBINSON A.R.I.B.A., M.I.C.E, came to Sabah in 1950 after some years in India and Burma where jungle living had heightened his interest in natural history. In 1968 he started a collection of local butterflies which was probably the most extensive in Sabah, containing most of the recorded species from Mt. Kinabalu. He designed the Kundasang National Memorial in 1961 but died in 1989 while this revision was in preparation. He was also a founder member of the Sabah Society.

ROSEMARY M. SMITH has been a member of the scientific staff of the Royal Botanic Gardens, Edinburgh. During the past 25 years much of her research has been devoted to the Zingiberaceae of South-east Asia, with particular reference to the family as it occurs in Borneo. She has published extensively on this topic. She is also a botanical artist, specialising in line drawings, and illustrates her own papers. In order to study the Zingiberaceae in the wild, Ms. Smith visited Kinabalu Park in 1986.

B.E. SMYTHIES B.A., F.L.S., F.R.G.S., worked in the Forest Department in Burma from 1934 to 1948 and in the equivalent department in Sarawak from 1949 to 1964. He visited Mt. Kinabalu three times to study birds and plants, on the last occasion to join the first Royal Society Expedition for two weeks at the invitation of Professor E.J.H. Corner. He is the author of "The Birds of Burma" (1953), "The Birds of Borneo" (1960, 1968, 1981), "Common Sarawak Trees" (1965), and co-author of "Flowers of South-west Europe" (1973), with Oleg Polunin.

ROBERT B. STUEBING lectured in the Biology Department, Universiti Kebangsaan Malaysia, Sabah campus (UKMS). He was also Curator of the UKMS Museum of Zoology. His interests are mainly in herpetology, including the ecology of frogs, crocodiles and sea-snakes and he has also worked on the ecology of small mammals in Sabah. He is a co-author of the "Frogs of Sabah" (1990) with Robert Inger.

TAN FUI LIAN was with the Sabah Parks as a Park Naturalist attached to the Ecology Section at the Kinabalu Park Headquarters from 1980 to 1992. She has been involved in several research and education programmes but has specialised in the taxonomy and ecology of the frogs of Mt. Kinabalu and the Crocker Range. In 1989 she trained at the Chicago Field Museum of Natural History.

AKIRA UEDA M.Sc., graduated with an agricultural degree from Kyoto Prefecture University in 1984 and received his Masters degree in 1986. From 1986 to 1989 he was a lecturer in the Department of Biology at the Universiti Kebangsaan Malaysia, Sabah campus, as a member of the Japan Overseas Co-operation Volunteers and made a special study of the passalid beetles and their altitudinal distribution.

J.J. VERMEULEN M.Sc., Ph.D., is an authority on the orchid genus *Bulbophyllum* and the land snails of Borneo. He has spent more than a year carrying out field research in Sabah and is author of Volume 2 of Orchids of Borneo, devoted to *Bulbophyllum*. He regards land snails as a special hobby, on which he spends much time.

DAVID R. WELLS Ph.D., has taught zoology at the University of Malaya since 1967. His main interests are in ornithology with a special regional involvement in South-east Asia. He co-ordinates the University of Malaya bird-ringing programme, and is co-author with Lord Medway (now the Earl of Cranbrook) of Volume 5 of "Birds of the Malay Peninsula" (1976). He is also Chairman of the Asian Wetland Bureau in the Institute of Advanced Studies of the University of Malaya and is both a Trustee and member of the Scientific Committee of WWF Malaysia.

K.M. WONG Ph.D., heads the Botany section and Herbarium at the Sabah Forestry Department's Forest Research Centre, Sepilok, Sandakan. He continues his studies of tropical bamboos since completing a revision of the Malayan arborescent representatives of the taxonomically difficult Rubiaceae. He has been a Forest Botanist first with the Forest Research Institute at Kepong, Malaysia, and then in Brunei, and is also interested in plant architecture and successional ecology. He is the author of several books on Malaysian and Bornean plants and editor of the Sabah Forestry Department's botanical series "Sandakania" and the Sabah Society Journal. At present, he helps coordinate research on the tree flora of Sabah and Sarawak, and specialises in the Goodeniaceae, Hyperiaceae, Loganiaceae and Rubiaceae of Borneo.

INDEX TO SCIENTIFIC NAMES
(compiled by J.T. Pereira and K.M. Wong)

Pages with illustrations are indicated in bold

A

Abroscopus superciliaris 389, 425
Acanthephippium 235
Acanthephippium javanicum 235
Acanthizidae 423
Accipiter gularis 401
Accipiter soloensis 400
Accipiter trivirgatus 401
Accipiter virgatus 401
Accipiter spp. 380
Accipitridae 400
Acer laurinum 140
Acer niveum 176
Aceraceae 140
Aceraius 319
Aceraius kinabaluensis 319, **321**
Achasma 255
Acianthinae 227
Acianthus 227
Acolutha altipunctata 311
Acontiinae 313
Acriopsidinae 237
Acriopsis 237
Actenoides concretus 409
Actinodaphne sp. 172
Actitis hypoleucos 403
Adinandra 131, 132, 178
Adinandra anisobasis 132
Adinandra caudatifolia 132
Adinandra clemensiae 132, 175
Adinandra collina 132
Adinandra colombonensis 132
Adinandra cordifolia 132
Adinandra dumosa 132, 496
Adinandra excelsa 132
Adinandra impressa 132
Adinandra magniflora 132
Adinandra nunkokensis 132
Adinandra quinquepartita 132
Adinandra sarcosanthera 132

Adinandra verrucosa 132
Adrapsa thermesia 313
Aegithina tiphia 416
Aegithinidae 416
Aerides 222, 241
Aerides odorata 241
Aeridinae 240
Aerodramus fugiphagus 408
Aeromys tephromelas phaeomelas 450
Aeromys thomasi 450
Aethalops alecto aequalis 451
Aethalura 307
Aethopyga mystacalis 392, 430
Aethopyga siparaja 430
Agalmyla tuberculata 115
Aganainae **297, 300**
Agaristinae **304**
Agathia succedanea **304**
Agathis 138, 140, 167, 168, 175, 176
Agathis dammara 172
Agathis lenticula 139, **171**
Agathis sp. 175
Aglaia 177
Aglaia ignea 175
Aglaomorpha heraclea 159
Agrostophyllum 221, 236
Agrotis kinabaluensis 312
Agylla bisecta 307
Agylla divisa 307
Alcedinidae 409
Alcedo euryzona 409
Alcippe brunneicauda 423
Alpinia 245, 247
Alpinia havilandii **244**
Alpinia latilabris 247
Alpinia galanga 249
Alpinia glabra 247, **249**
Alpinia havilandii 247
Alpinia latilabris 247
Alpinia ligulata 247
Alpinia nieuwenhuizii 247

Alseodaphne oblanceolata 172
Amata kinensis 312
Amata megista 312
Amata pseudextensa 312
Amata teinopera 312
Amata trifascia 312
Amathusiinae 294, 295
Amaurornis phoenicurus 403
Amolops 358
Amolops whiteheadi 353
Amomum 245, 246, 251, 253, 254
Amomum anomalum 254, **254**
Amomum compactum 254, **254**
Amomum kinabaluense 253, **254**
Amomum longipedunculatum 254
Amomum oliganthum 253, **254**
Amorphophallus 169
Amphidromus martensi **283,** 286, 287
Amphidromus pictus 287
Amphipyrinae 312
Anabantidae 334, 349
Anabas testudineus 335, 349
Anacardiaceae 171
Anemone 106
Angiopteris 156
Anguilla 335
Anguilla borneensis **335,** 344
Anguillidae 334
Anisodes flavissima **303**
Anisodes melantroches 311
Annonaceae 172, **174**, 177, 514
Anoectochilus longicalcaratus 226
Anorrhinus galeritus 410
Ansonia 358, 361
Ansonia albomaculata 362, 364, 366, 367
Ansonia fuliginea 362, 366
Ansonia guibei 362, 366
Ansonia hanitschi 355, **356**, 362, 364, 366, 367
Ansonia leptopus 358
Ansonia longidigita 362, 364, 366, 367
Ansonia platysoma 362, 364, 367
Ansonia spinulifer 355, 362, 364, 367
Antheraea celebensis **306**
Anthracoceros 410
Anthracoceros albirostris 410

Anthracoceros coronatus 410
Anthracoceros malayanus 410
Anthreptes malacensis 429
Anthreptes rhodolaema 429
Anthreptes simplex 429
Anthreptes singalensis 429
Antiaris toxicaria 501, 503
Antrophyum 163
Apameini 312
Aphanamixis borneensis 172
Aphyllorchis 220, 230
Aphyllorchis montana 231
Aphyllorchis pallida 230
Aplonis panayensis 431
Apocynaceae 205
Apodidae 408
Apodytes 142
Apodytes dimidiata 142
Apophyga altapona 311
Apostasia nuda 224
Apostasia odorata 224
Apostasia wallichii 222, **223**
Apostasioideae 222
Appendicula 239
Appendicula anceps 239
Appendicula foliosa 239
Appendicula pendula 239
Appias 298
Aquifoliaceae 130
Arachnis 222, 240
Arachnis flos-aeris 240
Arachnothera affinis 430
Arachnothera chrysogenys 430
Arachnothera flavigaster 430
Arachnothera juliae 376, 430
Arachnothera longirostra 430
Arachnothera robusta 430
Araiostegia 161
Araliaceae 144, 168
Araucariaceae **171**
Arborophila hyperythra 372, 402
Arborophila hyperythra erythrophrys 402
Arctictis binturong penicillata 450
Arctiidae **293**, 312
Arctogalidia trivirgata stigmatica 450
Ardeidae 400

Ardisia 130, 178
Ardisia copelandii 177
Areca 272
Areca catechu 272
Areca kinabaluensis 272, **272**
Arenga brevipes 270
Arenga undulatifolia 269, 270
Arethuseae 219, 234
Argostemma 111
Argostemma hameliifolium **111**
Argusianus argus 402
Arichanna maculata **302**
Ariophantidae 281, 285
Aristolochiaceae 205
Aroa biformis 312
Aroa cinerea 312
Aroa transflava 312
Aromadendron elegans 168
Artamidae 416
Artamus leucorhynchus 416
Artocarpus 169, 177, 330
Artocarpus nitidus 172
Artocarpus rigidus 172
Artocarpus tamaran 172
Artocarpus sp. 494
Arundina 211, 234
Arundina graminifolia 220, 234
Arundinae 234
Ascarina 167
Ascarina philippinensis 141, 175
Ascidieria 238
Ascidieria longifolia 238
Asota kinabaluensis **297**
Asplenium 156, 157, 158, 159, 161
Asplenium nidus 161, 211
Astilbe rivularis 111
Atacira waterstradti 313
Athyrium 158
Austrozephyrus borneanus 14, 295

B

Baccaurea 169, 177
Baccaurea lanceolata 495, 499
Baccaurea macrocarpa 169
Bactocera 330

Bactocera parryi 330
Bactocera rubus 330
Bactocera thomsoni 330
Bactocera victoriana **314**
Badiza rufosa 313
Bagridae 334, 335, 348
Balanophora 121, 122, 178
Balanophora elongata 123
Balanophora lowii **122**, 123
Balanophora papuana 123
Balanophora reflexa **122**, 123
Balanophoraceae 122
Balsaminaceae 113
Batrachostomus javensis 407
Batrachostomus mixtus 407
Batrachostomus poliolophus 407
Batrachostomus sp. **371**
Belvisia 159
Bhesa paniculata **173**, 177
Bignoniaceae 169, **174**
Blechnum 154, 158, 159
Blechnum fluviatile 159
Blechnum fraseri **153**
Blechnum orientale 154
Blechnum vestitum 158
Bletiinae 234, 235
Blumeodendron 175
Blumeodendron tokbrai 168
Blythipicus rubiginosus 382, 413
Boletus 512
Bombycidae 310
Bombycoidea 310
Boraginaceae 108, 172, **173**
Borbacha altipardaria **302**
Borneodendron 172
Borneodendron aenigmaticum 140, 170, **174**
Brachinidae 318
Brachinus biguitticeps **316**
Brachypteryx montana 11, 385, 418
Bradybaena similaris 280, **283**, 286, 287
Bradybaenidae 286
Bradypterus accentor 11, 370, 398, 424
Bromheadia 234, 237
Bromheadia brevifolia 237
Bromheadia finlaysoniana 237

Bromheadia scirpioidea 237
Bromheadiinae 237
Bruchinus bigutticeps 318
Bubo sumatranus 407
Buceros rhinoceros 382, 410
Bucerotidae 410
Buchanania 172
Bufo divergens 357, 358, 361, 362, 364, 367
Bufo juxtasper 355, 362, 364, 366, 367
Bufonidae 362
Bulbophyllinae 239
Bulbophyllum 96, 216, 221, 239, 517
Bulbophyllum section *Aphanobulbon* 239
Bulbophyllum section *Cirrhopetalum* 239
Bulbophyllum section *Epicrianthes* 240
Bulbophyllum section *Globiceps* 239
Bulbophyllum section *Monilibulbus* 240
Bulbophyllum section *Sestochilus* 240
Bulbophyllum biflorum 240
Bulbophyllum coriaceum 239
Bulbophyllum flavescens 239
Bulbophyllum foetidolens 240
Bulbophyllum lobbii 221, 240
Bulbophyllum macranthum 240
Bulbophyllum microglossum 240
Bulbophyllum montense 240
Bulbophyllum salaccense 239
Bulbophyllum teres 240
Bulbophyllum undecifilum 240
Bulbophyllum vaginatum 221
Buprestidae 315
Burbidgea 245, 249
Burbidgea pubescens 249
Burbidgea schizocheila 249, **250**
Burotidae 410
Burseraceae 171
Butastur indicus 401
Butorides striatus 400
Butorides striatus amurensis 400
Butorides striatus javanicus 400
Buxaceae 140
Buxus 171
Buxus rolfei 140, 171

C

Cacodaemon 328
Cacodaemon spinicollis **316**, 328
Cacodaemon spinosus **316**, 328
Cacomantis merulinus 405
Cacomantis sepulchralis 405
Cacomantis sonneratii 405
Cacomantis variolosus 405
Caeneressa lutosa 312
Caeneressa robusta 312
Calamaria pendleburyi 353
Calamus 270
Calamus acuminatus 270
Calamus amplijugus 170
Calamus caesius 501, 505
Calamus gibbsianus 269, 274, **274**, 275
Calamus gonospermus 170
Calamus javensis 270
Calamus laevigatus var. mucronatus 170
Calamus marginatus 270
Calamus mesilauensis 269, 270
Calamus ornatus 270
Calamus tenompokensis 270
Calamus zonatus 170
Calamus sp. 270
Calanthe 219
Callidula jucunda **301**
Callidulidae **301**
Callopistria montana 312
Callosciurus adamsi 449
Callosciurus baluensis baluensis 451
Callosciurus nigrovittatus 445
Callosciurus notatus dilutus 449
Callosciurus orestes venetus 451
Callosciurus prevostii pluto 449
Calophyllum aureum 175
Calorhamphus fuliginosus 377, 411
Calyptomena hosei 413
Calyptomena viridis 373, **375**, 413
Calyptomena whiteheadi 373, 413
Camaenidae 286
Campanulaceae **110**
Campephagidae 415
Canarium pseudodecumanum 171
Cantharsius molossus 324

Capitonidae 411
Caprimulgidae 407
Caprimulgus indicus 407
Caprimulgus macrurus 382, 407
Carabidae 317
Cardamine 111
Cardamine hirsuta 113
Carea albimargo 313
Carea argentipurpurea 313
Carea ferrinigra 313
Caryota no 269, 270
Castanopsis 127, 172, 178
Castanopsis acuminatissima 125, 172
Castanopsis costata 172
Castanopsis microphylla 172
Castanopsis sp. 494
Casuarina equisetifolia 141
Casuarina terminale 141
Casuarinaceae 140
Catephia susanae 313
Catocalinae **304**, 313
Catopsilia sp. 296
Catoria proicyrta 311
Celastraceae **102**, 143, 144, **173**, 177
Celeus brachyurus 412
Centropus bengalensis 406
Centropus sinensis 406
Cerambycidae 315, 328
Ceratochilus jiewhoei **229**
Ceratostylis 221, 238
Ceratostylis ampullacea 238
Cervus unicolor brookei 450
Cetoniinae 315, 324
Cettia fortipes 424
Cettia fortipes banksi 424
Cettia fortipes oreophila 424
Cettia montanus 424
Cettia vulcania 370, 424
Cettia whiteheadi 424
Ceuthostoma terminale 140
Ceyx erithacus 409
Chalcophaps indica 404
Chalcosiinae **301**, **304**, 310
Chalcosoma 323
Chalcosoma atlas 323
Chalcosoma mollenkampi **320**, **322**, 323

Chamaeanthus 241
Chaperina fusca 362, 364
Cheiropleuria bicuspis **155**, 158
Cheirostylis 227
Chelonistele 235
Chelonistele amplissima **214**, 235
Chimarrogale himalayica phaeura 451
Chiropodomys gliroides pusillus 450
Chiropodomys major 450
Chiropodomys muroides 450
Chlamydochaera jefferyi 373, 420
Chloephorinae 313
Chloranthaceae 141
Chloritis dulcissima 287
Chloritis kinabaluensis **285**, 287
Chlorocharis emiliae 11, 48, 371, 431
Chloroclystis 306
Chloroclystis coelica 311
Chloroclystis discisuffusa 311
Chloroclystis eurystalides 311
Chloroclystis layanga 311
Chloroclystis luteata 311
Chloroclystis oribates 306
Chloroclystis oribates sayata **305**
Chloroclystis punctinervis 311
Chloroclystis turgidata 311
Chloropsis cochinchinensis 384, 416
Chloropsis cyanopogon 416
Chloropsis sonnerati 416
Chlumetia kinabalua 313
Chroniochilus 241
Chrysococcyx malayanus 405
Chrysococcyx minutillus 405
Chrysococcyx russatus 405
Chrysococcyx russatus subsp. *aheneus* 405
Chrysococcyx xanthorhynchus 405
Chrysocolaptes validus 413
Chrysomelidae 315, **326**, 330
Chrysomya 205
Cibotium arachnoideum 154
Cichlidae 334, 349
Cicindela 317
Cicindela aurulenta 317
Cicindela sp. 317
Cicindelidae 317

Cinchona 172
Cinnamomum burmanii 168
Cinnamomum parthenoxylon 168
Cissa chinensis 393, 433
Cissa thalassina 393, 433
Citronella suaveolens 142
Claderia viridiflora 221, 237
Clamator coromandus 405
Clarias 334
Clavaria 512
Clematis 106
Clematis smilacifolia 106
Clethra 141
Clethra canescens 141
Clethra canescens var. *clementis* 141
Clethra longispicata 141
Clethra pachyphylla **100**, 141
Clethraceae **100**, 141, 168
Clysters 323
Cobitidae 334, 348
Coccinellidae 315
Cocconeuron 140
Coelogyne 216, 221, 235, 511
Coelogyne section *Tomentosae* 235
Coelogyne foerstermannii 221
Coelogyne hirtella 221
Coelogyne moultonii 213, 235
Coelogyne pandurata 221
Coelogyne radioferens **223**
Coelogyne rhabdobulbon **218**, 235
Coelogyne rochusseni 221
Coelogyninae 235, 236
Coelostegia griffithii 177, 498
Coleoptera 315
Collocalia esculenta 408
Collocalia fuciphaga 408
Collyris 317
Collyris sarawakensis 317
Colombobalanus 127
Columbidae 403
Compositae 109
Condylodera tricondyloides 317
Coprosma 178
Copsychus malabaricus 419
Copsychus saularis 399, 419
Copsychus saularis adamsi 419

Coraciidae 410
Coracina fimbriata 415
Coracina larvata 383, 415
Coracina striata 415
Corgatha griseicosta 313
Corgatha nabalua 313
Cornaceae 168
Corvidae 433
Corvus enca 433
Corvus macrorhynchos 433
Corybas 227
Corybas carinatus 227
Corybas kinabaluensis 227
Corybas pictus 227
Corydon sumatranus 414
Corymborkis 219
Corymborkis veratrifolia 225
Coryphopteris 158
Cosmorhoe moroessa 311
Cossidae **301**
Cossus kinabaluensis **301**
Costaceae 256
Costera 194
Costoideae 257
Costularia pilisepala 501
Costus 256, 257
Costus speciosus **256**, 257
Coturnix chinensis 402
Coturnix chinensis lineata 402
Cranichideae 225
Cratoxylon arborescens 167
Criniger bres 418
Criniger ochraceus 385, 418
Criniger phaeocephalus 418
Crocidua baluensis 451
Crocidura fuliginosa foetida 448
Crocidura monticola 451
Crossocheilus sp. 503
Cruciferae 113
Cryptocarya crassinervia 172
Cryptostylidinae 225
Cryptostylis 219, 225
Cryptostylis acutata 225
Cryptostylis arachnites 226
Cryptostylis clemensii 226
Cryptostylis tridentata 226

Cuculidae 404
Cuculus canorus 381
Cuculus fugax 404
Cuculus fugax fugax 404
Cuculus fugax nisicolor 404
Cuculus micropterus 404
Cuculus saturatus 381, 405
Cuculus saturatus horsfieldii 405
Cuculus saturatus insulindae 405
Cuculus saturatus saturatus 405
Cuculus sparverioides 380, 404
Cuculus vagans 404
Culicicapa ceylonensis 390, 425
Cunoniaceae 129
Curcuma longa 245
Cyanoptila cyanomelana 391, 426
Cyathea 154, **160**
Cyathea contaminans 154
Cyathea havilandii 158
Cyathea tripinnata 154
Cyclommatus 319
Cyclommatus giraffa **322**
Cyclommatus montellelus **325**
Cyclophoridae 282
Cyclophorus kinabaluensis 282, **283**
Cymbidieae 222, 236, 237
Cymbidium 221, 237
Cymbidium atropurpureum 237
Cymbidium bicolor 221
Cymbidium borneense 221
Cymbidium dayanum 237
Cymbidium ensifolium 221
Cymbidium finlaysonianum 237
Cymbirhynchus macrorhynchos 413
Cynocephalus variegatus natunae 449
Cynopterus brachyotis brachyotis 449
Cynopterus horsfieldi persimilis 449
Cyornis banyumas 427
Cyornis concreta 426
Cyornis concreta everetti 426
Cyornis superba 427
Cyornis turcosa 427
Cyprinidae 334, 335
Cypripedioideae 224
Cypsiurus balasiensis 408
Cyrestis maenalis 296

Cyrestis nivea 296
Cyrtopodiinae 237
Cyrtosia 220
Cyrtosia javanica 231
Cystorchis 219
Cystorchis aphylla 226
Cystorchis variegata 226

D

Dacrycarpus 139, 175
Dacrycarpus imbricatus 139, **175**
Dacrycarpus kinabaluensis 139, 168
Dacrydium 124, 138, 139, 167, 227
Dacrydium beccarii 139
Dacrydium cf. *beccarii* 172
Dacrydium gibbsiae 139, 178
Dacrydium gracilis 139
Dacrydium kinabaluensis 139
Dacrydium pectinatum 139
Dacrydium xanthandrum 139
Dacryodes macrocarpa 175
Daemonorops longistipes 270
Daemonorops sabut 170
Danainae 295
Danaus chrysippus 296
Daphniphyllum 178
Daphniphyllum borneense 141
Daphnusa ocellaris **300**
Dasyboarmia isorrhopha 311
Datiscaceae 169
Davallia 159, 161
Davallodes 161
Davallodes borneense 161
Dehaasia caesia 168
Delias 294
Delichon dasypus 414
Dendrobiinae 239
Dendrobium 216, 221, 238, 239
Dendrobium olivaceum 239
Dendrobium parthenium 239
Dendrobium singkawangense 239
Dendrobium spectatissimum 239
Dendrochilum 221, 236
Dendrochilum alpinum 236
Dendrochilum grandiflorum 236

Dendrochilum haslamii 53
Dendrochilum kamborangense 236
Dendrochilum stachyodes 236
Dendrocitta occipitalis 11, 394, **394**, 433
Dendrocnide 141
Dendrocnide elliptica 141
Dendrocnide oblanceolata 141
Dendrocnide stimulans 141
Dendrogale melanura baluensis 451
Dendronanthus indicus 415
Dendrophthoe longituba 121
Dennstaedtia 155
Dermoptera 442
Diamesus 318
Diamesus osculans 318, **318**, **320**
Diarsia 299
Diarsia banksi 312
Diarsia barlowi **305**, 312
Diarsia serrata 312
Dicaeidae 429
Dicaeum celebicum 429
Dicaeum chrysorrheum 429
Dicaeum concolor 429
Dicaeum cruentatum 429
Dicaeum monticolum 392, 429
Dicaeum trigonostigma 429
Dicerorhinus sumatrensis 450
Dichodontus 323
Dichroa febrifuga **110**
Dicksonia 154
Dicruridae 432
Dicrurus aeneus 432
Dicrurus annectans 432
Dicrurus hottentottus 393, 432
Dicrurus leucophaeus 393, 432
Dicrurus paradiseus 432
Dideopsis aegrota 224
Didymoplexiella 220, 233
Didymoplexiella kinabaluensis 233
Dilochia 234
Dilochia cantleyi 234
Dilochia parvifolia 234
Dilochia rigida 234
Dilochia wallichii 234
Dimorphorchis 240
Dimorphorchis lowii 240

Dimorphorchis rossii 240
Dinochloa 263
Dinochloa sublaevigata 263, 266
Dinochloa trichogona 263
Dinopium rafflesii 413
Diplazium 156
Diplommatina 282, 284
Diplommatina electa 280, **283**, 284
Diplommatina plecta 284
Diplommatina recta 284
Diplommatina rubra 280, 284
Diplommatina whiteheadi 285
Diplommatinidae 284
Diplopterygium 155
Diplopterygium bullatum 155
Diplurodes refrenata 311
Diplycosia **183**, 183, 186, **187**, **188**, **189**, 200
Diplycosia abscondita **187**, 190
Diplycosia acuminata 191
Diplycosia aurea **188**, 190
Diplycosia carrii **187**, 190, 191, 193
Diplycosia caudatifolia **187**, 191, 200
Diplycosia chrysothrix **187**, 190, 191, 193
Diplycosia ciliolata **187**, 191, 192
Diplycosia cinnamomifolia **187**, 191
Diplycosia clementium **189**, **190**, 191, 192, 193
Diplycosia commutata **187**, 191, 193, 194
Diplycosia crenulata **187**, 191
Diplycosia elliptica 191
Diplycosia ensifolia **188**, 191
Diplycosia heterophylla **188**, 191, 193
Diplycosia heterophylla var. *latifolia* 192
Diplycosia hirtiflora **189**, 192
Diplycosia kinabaluensis **189**, 192
Diplycosia memecyloides **188**, **190**, 192
Diplycosia myrtillus **187**, 192
Diplycosia penduliflora **188**, 192
Diplycosia pinifolia **187**, 192, 193
Diplycosia pittosporifolia 193
Diplycosia pittosporifolia var. *elliptifolia* 193
Diplycosia pittosporifolia var. *punctiloba* **189**, 193
Diplycosia pseudorufescens **187**, 193

Diplycosia punctulata **187**, 191, 193
Diplycosia rosmarinifolia **187**, 192, 193
Diplycosia rufa **188**, 193
Diplycosia sanguinolenta **189**, 193
Diplycosia sphenophylla **187**, 193
Diplycosia urceolata **189**, 193
Diplycosia viridiflora **189**, 194
Dipodium 222, 237
Dipodium pictum 237
Dipodium scandens 237
Dipteris 157, 158
Dipteris conjugata **162**
Dipterocarpaceae 169
Dipterocarpus confertus 498
Dipterocarpus ochraceus 171
Dirades rufinervis 311
Distyliopsis dunnii 144
Diurideae 227
Donax 494
Dracaena sp. 224
Drapetes 178
Drapetes ericoides 125
Dremomys everetti 451
Drepanidae **300**
Drimys 127, 128, 167, 178
Drimys piperita 127, 128, **128**, 168, 172
Drosera 113
Drosera burmannii 113
Drosera spathulata 113, **114**, 115
Droseraceae 113, **114**
Drynariopsis heraclea 159
Dryopteris 158, 161
Dryopteris burbidgei 161
Duabanga 169
Duabanga grandiflora 141
Duabanga moluccana 141, 142, 169
Duabanga sonneratioides 141
Ducula aenea 403
Ducula badia 380, 403
Duliticola 327
Duliticola paradoxa 327
Duliticola sp. **321, 327**
Dynastes hercules 319
Dynastidae **322**
Dynastinae 319

E

Ecliptopera furvoides 311
Ecliptopera zaes 311
Ectropis geniculata 311
Ectropis ischnadelpha 298
Ectropis longiscapia 298
Elaeocarpus 142, 176, 178
Elaeocarpus congestifolius 142
Elaeocarpus mastersii 175
Elaphoglossum 161
Elettaria cardamomum 245
Elmerillia 169
Elmerillia mollis 169
Elmerrillia 128
Emballonura alecto rivalis 449
Embelia 178
Endomychidae 328
Engelhardia 142, 172
Engelhardia apoensis 142
Engelhardia kinabaluensis 142
Engelhardia rigida 142
Engelhardia roxburghiana 142
Engelhardia serrata 142
Engelhardia spicata 142
Enicurus leschenaulti 419
Enicurus leschenaulti borneensis 419
Enicurus ruficapillus 419
Ennominae **293**, 295, **299**, **302**, **303**, **304**, 311
Entomophobia 236
Entomophobia kinabaluensis 236
Epacridaceae 125, 181
Epidendroideae 221, 230
Epigeneium 239
Epigeneium kinabaluense 239
Epigeneium longirepens 221, 239
Epigeneium tricallosum 239
Epiplema caerulimargo 311
Epiplema transgrisea 311
Epiplemidae 311
Epipogiinae 233
Epipogium 233
Epipogium roseum 233
Epipogum 220
Episteme conspicua **304**

Epizeuxis ocellata 313
Eria 212, 216, 221, 238
Eria biflora 238
Eria floribunda 239
Eria javanica 238
Eria leiophylla 239
Eria nutans 239
Eria obliqua 238
Eria ornata 221, 238
Eria pannea 239
Eria rigida 238
Eria robusta 239
Ericaceae 124, 167, 168, 178, 181, 186, 511
Eriinae 238
Erithacus cyane 418
Erotylidae 327
Erythrina variegata 504
Erythrodes 227
Erythrodes triloba 227
Erythrorchis altissima 231
Erythrura hyperythra 392, 431
Erythrura prasina 431
Estrildidae 431
Etlingera 246, 255
Etlingera brevilabris 255, **255**
Etlingera elatior 255
Etlingera fimbriobracteata 255
Etlingera littoralis 255
Etlingera muluensis 255
Etlingera punicea 255, **256**
Euconulidae 281, 287
Eudynamis scolopacea 405
Eudynamis scolopacea chinensis 405
Eudynamis scolopacea malayana 405
Eugenia 123, 168, 176, 178
Eulophia 220, 237
Eulophia graminea 237
Eulophia spectabilis 237
Eulophia zollingeri 237
Eulophiinae 237
Eumorphus 328
Eumorphus felix **321**, 328
Eumorphus fryanus **328**
Eumorphus marginatus 328
Eumyias indigo 390, 426

Eumyias thalassina 426
Euonymus glandulosus **102**
Eupetes macrocerus 420
Euphorbiaceae 123, 140, 141, 169, **174**, 177
Euphrasia 107
Euphrasia borneensis 107, **107**
Euproctis 298
Euproctis altilodra 312
Euproctis anna 312
Euproctis biflava 312
Euproctis cina 312
Euproctis kamburonga **305**
Euproctis rufibasis 312
Euproctis sabahensis 312
Euproctis tuhana 312
Euproctis vespertilionis 312
Euproctis viridoculata 312
Eupterotidae **290**
Eurema 298
Eurema hecabe 296
Eurema nicevillei 296, 298
Eurema tominia 296
Eurostopodus temminckii 381, 407
Eurya 130, 131
Eurya nitida 131
Eurya obovata 131
Eurya obovata var. *reticulata* 131
Eurya reticulata 131
Eurya trichocarpa 131
Eurylaimidae 413
Eurylaimus javanicus 414
Eurylaimus ochromalus 413
Eurystomus orientalis 410
Eurystomus orientalis calonyx 410
Eurystomus orientalis cyanicollis 410
Eurystomus orientalis deignani 410
Eurytrachellelus reichei **320**, **321**
Euteliinae 313
Euthalia 298
Everettia corrugata 285
Everettia subconsul **283**, 285
Excoecaria philippinensis 171
Exilisciurus exilis 449
Exilisciurus whiteheadi 451

F

Fagaceae 125, **126**, 168, 172, 175, 176, **177**, 178
Fagraea fragrans 168
Fagus 125
Falcatifolium falciforme 139, 172
Falco peregrinus 402
Falco peregrinus japonensis 402
Falco severus 402
Falco tinnunculus 402
Falconidae 402
Fascellina albicordis **304**
Feliniopsis kinabalua 312
Felis badia 450
Felis bengalensis **446**
Felis bengalensis borneoensis 450
Ficedula dumetoria 427
Ficedula hyperythra 390, 427
Ficedula mugimaki 391, 427
Ficedula narcissina 427
Ficedula westermanni 391, 427
Ficus 96, 97, 133, 138, 177, 330, 478, 512
Ficus subgenus *Ficus* 97
Ficus carrii 135
Ficus cereicarpa 136, 138
Ficus deltoidea 133, 135
Ficus deltoidea var. *kinabaluensis* 133
Ficus dens-echini 135
Ficus disticha 135
Ficus endospermifolia 136
Ficus cf. *endospermifolia* 136
Ficus francisci 138
Ficus megaleia 138
Ficus montana 136
Ficus oleaefolia 133, 135
Ficus oleaefolia var. *memecylifolia* 133
Ficus oleaefolia var. *myrsinoides* 133
Ficus palaquiifolia 135
Ficus setiflora 136
Ficus stupenda 135, 138
Ficus subsidens 136
Ficus sumatrana 135
Ficus treubii 138
Ficus uncinata 138
Ficus uncinata var. *strigosa* **135**
Ficus virescens 138
Ficus sp. **134**
Flacourtiaceae 144, 172
Flickingeria 239
Flickingeria fimbriata 221
Flickingeria sp. 239
Formanodendron 127
Fragaria 124

G

Galeola 222
Galeola nudiflora 231
Galeolinae 231
Galium 112, 113
Galium rotundifolium 111
Gallinago stenura 403
Ganoderma **328**
Garaeus altapicata 311
Garcinia 176, 178
Garcinia bancana 168
Garcinia mangostana 501
Garcinia "*ramiflora*" 175
Garra borneensis **338**, 346
Garrulax lugubris 387, 423
Garrulax mitratus 11, 388, 423
Garrulax mitratus treacheri 423
Garrulax palliatus **386**, 387, 423
Gastrochilus 241
Gastrodia 220, 233
Gastrodia grandilabris 233
Gastrodieae 233
Gastromyzon 334
Gastromyzon borneensis 333, **338**, 346
Gastromyzon fasciatus 334, **339**, 346
Gastromyzon lepidogaster **339**, 346
Gastromyzon monticola 334, **339**, 346
Gastromyzontidae 334, 346, 477
Gathynia mesilauensis 311
Gaultheria **181**, 183, **183**
Gaultheria borneensis 183
Geanthus 255
Gentiana 107
Gentiana borneensis 108
Gentiana lycopodioides 108
Gentiana quadrifaria 107

Geodorum 237
Geodorum densiflorum 237
Geometridae **293**, 295, **299**, **301**, **302**, 303, **304**, **305**, 311
Geometrinae 311, **301**, **304**
Geometroidea 311
Geotrochus 281
Geotrochus kinabaluensis **283**, 288, 289
Geotrochus whiteheadi 288
Geotrochus sp. 288
Gerygone sulphurea 423
Gesneriaceae 115
Gigantochloa levis **258**, 263, 267, 504
Glaniopsis 334
Glaniopsis denudata 334, **340**, 347
Glaniopsis hanitschi **339**, 346
Glaucidium brodiei 381, 407
Gleichenia 152, 154, 155
Gleichenia dicarpa **156**
Globba 245, 247
Globba atrosanguinea 247
Globba franciscii 247
Globba pendula 247
Globba propinqua 247
Globba tricolor var. *gibbsiae* 247
Glomerinae 236
Gluta wallichii 171
Glyphotes simus 451
Glyptothorax major **342**, 348
Glyptothorax platypogon 348
Gomphandra cumingiana 142
Goodeniaceae 143, **143**, 517
Goodyera 219, 221
Goodyera kinabaluensis 226
Goodyera procera 226
Goodyera reticulata 226
Goodyera rostellata 226
Goodyera rubicunda 226
Goodyera ustulata 226
Goodyerinae 226
Grammatophyllum 237
Grammatophyllum kinabaluensis 237
Grammatophyllum speciosum 237
Grammitis 159, 164
Graphium 298
Griseothosea kinabaluensis 310

Guioa 172
Gunnera 102, 113
Gunnera macrophylla 113
Gunongia dendrobates 287, 288
Gunongia gregaria 288
Guttiferae 175
Gymnacranthera contracta 171, 499
Gymnacranthera farquhariana 172
Gymnopleurus marus **316**, 324
Gymnoscelis transapicalis 311
Gymnostoma sumatranum 140, 141, 172

H

Habenaria 219, 228, 230
Habenaria damaiensis 228
Habenaria setifolia 228
Habenariinae 228
Hadennia subapicibrunnea 313
Haematortyx sanguiniceps 372, 402
Haeromys margarettae 450
Halcyon chloris 409
Halcyon concreta 409
Halcyon pileata 409
Haliastur indus 400
Haloragaceae 113
Haloragis 113
Haloragis micrantha 108, 113
Hampala macrolepidota bimaculata 334, **337**, 345
Harpactes diardii 408
Harpactes duvaucelii 409
Harpactes kasumba 408
Harpactes oreskios 409
Harpactes orrhophaeus 409
Harpactes whiteheadi 373, 408
Harpalinae 317
Havilandia 108
Hedychium 245, 246
Hedychium coronarium 246
Hedychium cylindricum 245, 246, **246**
Hedyotis 112
Hedyotis macrostegia 112
Helarctos malayanus euryspilus 450
Helicarionidae 281, 288
Hemicircus concretus 413

Hemigalus derbyanus boiei 450
Hemigalus hosei 451
Hemiplecta cf. *egeria* **283**, 285
Hemiprocne comata 408
Hemiprocne longipennis 408
Hemiprocnidae 408
Hemipus hirundinaceus 415
Hemipus picatus 383, 415, 416
Hesperiidae 294, 295
Hetaeria 227
Hetaeria angustifolia 227
Hetaeria grandiflora 227
Hibiscus macrophyllus 168
Hieraaetus kienerii 401
Hirundapus giganteus 408
Hirundinidae 414
Hirundo rustica 414
Hirundo tahitica 414
Histia nivosa **304**, 310
Histiopteris stipulacea 155
Homalium panayanum 172
Hopea 171
Hopea argentea 171
Hopea beccariana 171
Hopea dryobalanoides 171
Hopea ferruginea 171
Hopea pedicellata 171
Hopea vesquei 171
Hoplocerambyx spinicornis 330
Horisme labeculata 306
Horisme maerens 311
Horithyatira decorata **302**
Hornstedtia 246, 251
Hornstedtia gracile 251, **252**
Hornstedtia havilandii 251
Hornstedtia incana 251, **252**, **253**
Hornstedtia scyphifera 251
Horsfieldia glabra 175
Horsfieldia punctatifolia 172
Huia cavitympanum 354, 363, 364, 367
Humata 161
Humata subvestita **155**
Hydnocarpus woodii 172
Hydrangeaceae **110**
Hydrocotyle 111
Hydrocotyle javanica 108

Hylobates muelleri **443**
Hylobates muelleri funereus 449
Hylomys 12
Hylomys suillus 12
Hylomys suillus dorsalis 451
Hylopetes lepidus platyurus 450
Hylopetes spadiceus everetti 450
Hylophila kinabaluensis 226
Hymenolepis 159
Hymenophyllum 163
Hypena tristigma 313
Hypericaceae 517
Hypochrosis herois **303**
Hypocometa 306
Hypocometa bathylima 311
Hypocometa leptomita 307
Hypocometa titanis **305**, 306, 307, 311
Hypogramma hypogrammicum 430
Hypolepis brooksiae 155
Hypothymis azurea **396**, 428
Hypsipetes criniger **372**, 418
Hypsipetes flavala 385, 418
Hypsipetes malaccensis 418
Hystrix brachyura 450

I

Ibycus sp. 286
Icacinaceae 142
Ictinaetus malayensis 401
Idiochlora berwicki 311
Ilex 130, 143, 178, 511
Ilex cissoidea 177
Ilex clemensiae 130
Ilex havilandii 130
Ilex oppositifolia 130
Ilex revoluta 130
Ilex spicata 130
Ilex zygophylla 130
Impatiens 113
Imperata cylindrica 493, 503
Indicator archipelagicus 411
Indicatoridae 411
Ingerana baluensis 363, 367
Iodes philippinensis 142
Iomys horfieldi thomsoni 450

Irena puella 416
Ixonanthes reticulata 177
Ixora 111

J

Juglandaceae 142, 168

K

Kalamantania whiteheadi **283**, 286
Kalophrynus baluensis 353, 362, 364, 366
Kalophrynus pleurostigma 362, 364, 367
Kaloula pulchra 362, 366, 367
Kenopia striata 421
Kerivoula papillosa malayana 449
Kerivoula pellucida 449
Kinabaluchloa nebulosa 260, **262**, 263, 265, 266
Kinabaluchloa wrayi 263
Kionghutania humilis 288
Kionghutania kinabaluensis 288
Kionghutania nephelophila 288
Knema kinabaluensis 175
Koompasia excelsa 171
Korthalsia 270
Korthalsia jala 270
Kuhlhasseltia javanica 226
Kuhlhasseltia kinabaluensis 226

L

Lacedo pulchella 409
Lagocheilus alticola 282
Lagocheilus conicus 282, **282**
Lagocheilus kinabaluensis 282
Laminae 330
Lampides boeticus 296
Lamproptera 298
Laniidae 416
Lanius cristatus 416
Lanius tigrinus 416
Larentiinae **303**, **305**, 307, 311
Lariscus hosei 449
Lasiocampidae 311
Lassaba acribomena **299**

Lauraceae 168, 169, 172, 175, 176, 178
Lecanorchidineae 231
Lecanorchis 220, 231
Lecanorchis multiflora 231
Leiocassis micropogon **342**, 348
Lenothrix canus malaisia 450
Leopoldamys sabanus 450
Lepidella sabaensis 121
Lepidogyne longifolia 226
Leptobrachella baluensis 354, 358, 361, 362, 366
Leptobrachium abbotti 362, 364, 367
Leptobrachium gracilis 354
Leptobrachium montanum 354, **354**, 355, 357, 358, 362, 364, 366, 367
Leptolalax dringi 362, 364, 367
Leptolalax gracilis 354, 357, 358, 362, 364, 366
Leptolalax pictus 353, 362, 364, 367
Leptophryne borbonica 361, 362, 364, 367
Leptopoma sericatum 284, **287**
Leptopoma undatum 280, **282**, 284
Leptopoma whiteheadi 284
Leptospermum 96, 132, 221, 227, 306, 371
Leptospermum flavescens 133, 168, 178
Leptospermum javanicum 133
Leptospermum recurvum **132**, 133, **170**, 178, 505
Lethe 298
Leucopholis sp. **321**, **324**
Licuala 495
Limacodidae 310
Limodorinae 230
Lindera bibracteata 172
Lindsaea 156, 157
Liparis 221, 236
Liparis atrosanguinea 236
Lithacodia potens 313
Lithocarpus 125, 127, 172
Lithocarpus bennettii 172
Lithocarpus bullatus 178
Lithocarpus cantleyanus 172
Lithocarpus caudatifolius 172
Lithocarpus elegans 172

Lithocarpus encleisocarpa 172
Lithocarpus ferrugineus 172
Lithocarpus havilandii 102, 127, 141, 178
Lithocarpus luteus 172
Lithocarpus nieuwenhuisii 172
Lithocarpus porcatus 172
Lithocarpus revolutus **177**
Lithocarpus sericobalanus 172
Lithocarpus turbinatus 178
Lithosiinae **293**
Litsea 172
Litsea garciae 169
Litsea sebifera 169
Lobelia borneensis **110**
Lobocheilus bo 334, **338**, 345
Locustella ochotensis 424
Loganiaceae 517
Lonchura fuscans 431
Lonchura malacca 399, 432
Loriculus galgulus 404
Lucanidae 315
Lucilia 205
Luisia 241
Lycaenidae 294, 295
Lycidae 315
Lymantria sexspinae 312
Lymantriidae **305**, 310, 312

M

Macaca fascicularis fascicularis 449
Macaca nemestrina 449
Macaranga 177
Macaranga rostrata 123
Macheiramphus alcinus 400
Macodes 178
Macodes lowii 226
Macodes petola 226
Macrobarasa xantholopha **303**
Macrocili maia **300**
Macroglossus minimus lagochilus 449
Macronous gularis 422
Macronous ptilosus 422
Macropygia emilian 380, 403
Macropygia phasianella 404
Macropygia ruficeps 380, 404

Macrosolen 121
Maesa ramentacea 143
Magnolia 128, 167, 176, 178
Magnolia candollii 129
Magnolia carsonii 175, 176
Magnolia persuaveolens subsp. *rigida* 129
Magnolia sarawakensis 172
Magnoliaceae 105, 128, 129, 167, 168, 169, 172, 175, 176, 217
Malacopteron affine 421
Malacopteron cinereum 421
Malacopteron magnirostre 421
Malacopteron magnum 421
Malaxideae 236
Malaxis 221, 236
Malaxis calophylla 236
Malaxis lowii 236
Malaxis metallica 236
Malleola 241
Malleola witteana 242
Malleola sp. 241
Malvaceae 168
Mangifera caesia 492, 493, 496
Mangifera pajang 492
Mangifera sp. 492, 503
Manglietia 128
Manis javanica **444**, 449
Marantaceae 169
Martes flavigula saba 450
Mastacembelidae 334, 343
Mastacembelus 335
Mastacembelus maculatus 343
Matonia 157
Maxomys alticola 451
Maxomys baeodon 450
Maxomys ochraceiventer 450
Maxomys surifer bandahara 450
Maxomys whiteheadi whiteheadi 450
Medama spatulidorsum 312
Medinilla speciosa **104**
Megaderma spasma kinabalu 449
Megaerops ecaudatus 449
Megalaima australis 379, 412
Megalaima chrysopogon 377, 411
Megalaima eximia 379, 411
Megalaima eximia cyanea 412

Megalaima henricii 378, 411
Megalaima monticola 378, 411
Megalaima mystacophanos 378, 411
Megalaima pulcherrima 378, 411
Megalaima rafflesii 377, 411
Meghimatium striatum 289
Meghimatium uniforme 289
Megophryidae 362
Megophrys baluensis 355, 362, 364, 366
Megophrys edwardinae 362, 364, 367
Megophrys nasuta 357, 358, 362, 364, **365**, 366, 367
Meiglyptes tristis 412
Meiglyptes tukki 412
Melanitis 298
Melanitis leda 296
Melanochyla fulvinervis 171
Melastomataceae **104**, 115, 167
Meliaceae 172
Meliosma 177
Melogale personata 12, **440**
Melogale personata everetti 451
Melolonthinae **324**
Meristogenys 358
Meristogenys amoropalamus 353, 363, 364, 366, 367
Meristogenys kinabaluensis 355, 363, 364, 367
Meristogenys orphnocnemis 353, 355, 363, 364, 367
Meristogenys whiteheadi 355, 363, 364, 367
Meropidae 410
Merops viridis 410
Metaphrynella sundana 362, 365, 367
Mezzetia leptopoda 168
Michelia 105, 128
Michelia alba 128
Michelia champaca 129
Michelia montana 129, 172
Micrixalus baluensis 354, 366
Microcos 177
Microhierax latifrons 402
Microhyla borneensis 355, 357, 362, 365, 367
Microhyla petrigena 362, 365, 367

Microhylidae 362
Micromia latistriga **303**
Microparmarion pollonerai 286
Microparmarion simrothi 286
Microparmarion sp. 286
Micropterus brachyurus 412
Microsaccus 240
Microtatorchis 241, 242
Milionia pendleburyi **304**, 311
Milletia 177
Miniopterus magnater macrodens 449
Miquelia caudata 142
Mitrastemon 121, 122, 206
Mitrastemon yamamotoi 122
Mitrastemonaceae 122, 206
Monarchidae 426
Monocarpia marginalis 172
Monosyntaxis trimaculata **293**
Monticola solitarius 419
Moraceae 96, 133, **134**, **135**, **136**, 172, 512
Mormolyce 317
Mormolyce phyllodes **316**, 317
Mormolyce quadraticollis 317
Mormolyce tridens 317
Motacilla cinerea 414
Motacillidae 414
Muntiacus muntjak pleiharicus 450
Murina rozendaali 449
Muscicapa daurica 426
Muscicapa ferruginea 426
Muscicapa indigo 426
Muscicapa latirostris 426
Muscicapa sibirica 426
Muscicapa thalassina 426
Muscicapella ferruginea 391
Muscicapella hodgsoni 391, 427
Muscicapella latirostris 391
Muscicapella sibirica 391
Muscicapidae 425, 426
Mussaenda frondosa **111**
Mussaendopsis beccariana 172, **174**
Mustela nudipes 450
Mycalesis 298
Myiophoneus glaucinus 11, 420
Myophonus glaucinus 385

Myosotis 108
Myotis ater nugax 449
Myotis muricola muricola 449
Myriactis cabrerae 109
Myrica 142, 178
Myrica esculenta 142
Myrica javanica 142, 130
Myricaceae 142
Myrioblephara 307
Myrioblephara flexilinea 307
Myrioblephara simplaria 307
Myristicaceae 171
Myrmechis kinabaluensis 226
Myrsinaceae 130
Myrsine 130
Myrtaceae 96, **126**, **132**, 168, **170**, 175
Mystus baramensis **341**, 348
Mystus nemurus **341**, 348

N

Nabaluia 216, 221, 236
Nabaluia angustifolia **232**, 236
Nabaluia clemensii 236
Nagodopsis parvimargo 310
Namachilus olivaceus **341**
Napothera crassa 374, 422
Napothera epilepidota 422
Naravelia 106
Necrophorus 318
Nectarinia jugularis 430
Nectarinia sperata 430
Nectarinidae 429
Nemachilus 334
Nemachilus olivaceus 348
Nematabramis alestes 344
Nematabramis everetti **335**, 344
Nematabramis steindachneri 344
Neocerambyx paris 330
Neochera marmorea **300**
Neoclemensia 216, 220, 233
Neoclemensia spathulata 233
Neofelis nebulosa diardi 450
Neottieae 230
Nepenthaceae **116**, **117**, **118**, **120**

Nepenthes 44, 102, 115, 117, 118, 178, 475, 478, 479
Nepenthes alata 117
Nepenthes boshiana 117
Nepenthes burbidgeae 117, **118**, 119, 478
Nepenthes edwardsiana 118, 119, 121
Nepenthes ephippiata 119
Nepenthes fusca **118**, 119
Nepenthes gracilis 118
Nepenthes kinabaluensis 478
Nepenthes lowii 41, 43, **116**, 118, 119
Nepenthes macfarlanei 117
Nepenthes maxima 119
Nepenthes pilosa 119
Nepenthes rajah 44, 117, **117**, 119, 478
Nepenthes stenophylla 121
Nepenthes tentaculata **120**, 121
Nepenthes villosa 117, 118, 119, 121, 461, 478
Nephelaphyllum pulchrum var. *latilabre* **210**
Nephelium 169
Neptis 298
Nertera granadensis **112**, 113
Nervilia 233
Nervilia punctata 233
Nerviliae 233
Nesobia mjobergi 354
Neuwiedia 224
Neuwiedia borneensis 224
Neuwiedia zollingeri var. *javanica* 224
Nicolaia 255
Ninox scutulata 407
Ninox scutulata borneensis 407
Ninox scutulata burmanica 407
Niviventer cremoriventer kina 450
Niviventer rapit 451
Noctuidae **297**, **300**, **303**, **304**, **305**, 312
Noctuoidea 312
Nola harthani 313
Nolinae 313
Nothofagus 127, 142
Notodontidae 312
Nyctemera kiauensis 312
Nyctemera kinabaluensis 312

Nyctemera montana 312
Nyctemera tenompoka 312
Nycticebus coucang **438**
Nycticebus coucang borneanus 449
Nyctixalus pictus 357, **357**, 363, 365, 367
Nyctyornis amictus 410
Nymphalidae 294, 295
Nyssa javanica 142, 177
Nyssaceae 142

O

Oberonia 236
Occidozyga baluensis 354, 363, 365, 366, 367
Octarrhena 239
Octomeles 169
Octomeles sumatrana 169
Oculocincta squamifrons 376, 431
Odontolabis femoralis **318**, 319, **321**
Oeceoclades 237
Oeceoclades pulchra 237
Oenochrominae **302**
Olea decussata 143
Oleaceae 143
Ophiderinae 313
Opiliaceae 172
Opisoplatia grandis 310
Opisthoporus boxalli **283**, 284
Orchidaceae 96, 213, 216
Orchideae 227
Orchidoideae 227
Oreocalamus hanitschi 12
Oreomyrrhis 109
Oreomyrrhis borneensis 109
Oriolidae 432
Oriolus chinensis 432
Oriolus cruentus 393, 432
Oriolus xanthonotus 432
Oroxylum indicum 169, **174**
Orthotomus cinereus 425
Orthotomus cuculatus 389, 425
Orthotomus ruficeps 425
Orthotomus sepium 425
Orthotomus sericeus 425
Osmelia philippina 172
Osteochilus spilurus 345
Osteochilus vittatus 345
Othreis kinabaluensis **304**
Otus bakkamoena 406
Otus brookei 407
Otus rufescens 406
Otus spilocephalus 381, 406
Ozola prouti 311
Ozola submontana 311

P

Pachycephala hypoxantha 376, 428
Pachycephalidae 428
Pacyodes rubroviridata **301**
Paguma larvata ogilbyi 450
Palaquium beccarianum 171
Palaquium gutta 175, 176
Pangium edulis 495
Pantlingia 227
Paphiopedilum 219, 224, 478, 479
Paphiopedilum subgenus *Brachypetalum* 224
Paphiopedilum subgenus *Paphiopedilum* 224
Paphiopedilum barbatum 224
Paphiopedilum burbidgei 225
Paphiopedilum dayanum 225
Paphiopedilum hookerae 225
Paphiopedilum hookerae var. *volonteanum* 225
Paphiopedilum javanicum 225
Paphiopedilum javanicum var. *virens* 225
Paphiopedilum lawrenceanum 224, 225
Paphiopedilum lowii 225, **238**
Paphiopedilum nigritum 224
Paphiopedilum petri 225
Paphiopedilum rothschildianum 213, **220**, 224, 225, 461, 478, 480
Paphiopedilum virens 225
Paphiopedilum volonteanum 225
Paphiopedilum sp. 480
Papilionidae 295
Paracrossocheilus sp. 503
Paracrossochilus acerus **338**, 346
Paradoxopla cardinalis 311

Paragasu 506
Parallelia flavipurpurea 313
Paraphalaenopsis 241
Paraphalaenopsis amabilis 241
Paraphalaenopsis labukensis **228**, 241
Parashorea spp. 494
Parhomaloptera microstoma **340**, 347
Parishia maingayi 171
Parkia roxburghii 177
Passalidae 319
Passiflora foetida 495
Pedostibes everetti 353, 361, 362, 366
Pedostibes maculatus 361, 362, 366
Pellorneum capistratum 420
Pellucens kinabaluensis 312
Pelophryne misera 362, 365, 366
Penicillifera purpurascens 310
Pennilabium 241, 242
Pentace discolor 172
Pentace laxiflora 172
Penthetor lucasii 449
Pericrocotus flammeus 416
Pericrocotus igneus 415
Pericrocotus solaris 384, 415, 416
Peristylus 219, 230
Peristylus brevicalcar 230
Peristylus candidus 230
Peristylus ciliatus 230
Peristylus goodyeroides 230
Peristylus grandis 230
Peristylus hallieri 230
Peristylus kinabaluensis 230
Pernis ptilorhyncus 400
Pernis ptilorhyncus orientalis 400
Pernis ptilorhyncus torquatus 400
Perrottetia 143
Perrottetia alpestris 143
Perrottetia alpestris subsp. *philippinensis* 143
Petaurista elegans banksi 451
Petaurista petaurista rajah 450
Petinomys setosus setosus 450
Phaeanthus ophthalmicus 177
Phaenicophaeus chlorophaeus 405
Phaenicophaeus curvirostris 406
Phaenicophaeus diardii 406
Phaenicophaeus javanicus 406
Phaenicophaeus sumatranus 406
Phaius 235
Phaius acuminata 235
Phaius lowii 235
Phaius tankervilleae 235
Phalaenopsis 222, 241
Phasianidae 402
Philautus 353, 357, 361
Philautus amoenus 363, 366
Philautus aurifasciatus 353
Philautus bimaculatus 354
Philautus bunitus 353, 363, 365
Philautus hosei 363, 366, 367
Philautus longicrus 363, 365, 366
Philautus mjöbergi 355, **360**, 363, 365, 366
Philautus petersi 355, 363, 365, 366
Philautus sp. **358**
Philentoma pyrhopterum **375**, 428
Philentoma velatum 428
Philomycidae 281, 289
Phlogophora kinabalua 312
Phlogophora lignosa 312
Phlogophora styx 312
Phlogophora triangula 312
Phlogophora viridivena 312
Pholidota 221, 236, 444
Pholidota gibbosa 236
Pholidota imbricata 221
Pholidota ventricosa 221, 236
Photinia 129, 178
Photinia davidiana 129
Phreatia 221, 239
Phthonoloba 306
Phthonoloba bracteola 311
Phthonoloba caliginosa 311
Phthonoloba stigmalephora 311
Phyllocladus 139, 140, 167, 178, 217
Phyllocladus hypophyllus **139**, 140, 168, 175, **175**
Phyllocrater 112
Phyllocrater gibbsiae 112
Phyllophaga sp. **321**, **324**, 325
Phylloscopidae 426
Phylloscopus borealis 424

Phylloscopus trivirgatus 389, 424
Phytocrene macrophylla var. *caudigera* 142
Picidae 412
Picoides canicapillus 412
Picus mentalis 382, 412
Picus miniaceus 412
Picus puniceus 382, 412
Pieridae 294, 295
Pinanga 269, 272
Pinanga aristata 269, 272, **273**
Pinanga capitata 269, 272, **272**, **273**, 274, 275
Pinanga dallasensis 272
Pinanga gibbsiana 272
Pinanga keahii 269, 272
Pinanga lepidota 269
Pinanga lumuensis 272
Pinanga pilosa 170, **268**, 269, 272
Pinanga variegata 269
Pipistrellus javanicus javanicus 449
Pipistrellus stenopterus 449
Pipistrellus tenuis nitidus 449
Pithecellobium havilandii 177
Pitta arquata 383, 414
Pitta baudi 414
Pitta guajana 383, 414
Pitta moluccensis 399, 414
Pittidae 414
Plagiogyria 158
Plagiostachys 245, 251, **251**
Plagiostachys strobilifera 251
Planchonella maingayi 177
Planchonella obovata 171
Platanthera 227, 228
Platanthera angustata 228
Platanthera kinabaluensis 227, 228
Platanthera saprophytica 220, 228
Platanthera stapfii 228
Platea excelsa 142
Platea excelsa var. *kinabaluensis* 142
Platea sclerophylla 142
Platycerium 211
Platycerium coronarium **150**
Platyja crenulata 313
Platylophus galericulatus 433

Platysmurus leucopterus 433
Plectocomia elongata 270, **271**
Plocoglottis 235
Plusiinae **303**
Plutodes flavescens **299**
Poaephyllum 239
Poaephyllum pauciflorum 239
Podargidae 407
Podocarpaceae **139**, 168, **175**
Podocarpus 138, 139, 167
Podocarpus brevifolius 139
Podocarpus confertus 139
Podocarpus gibbsii 139
Podocarpus globosus 139
Podocarpus imbricatus 175
Podocarpus laubenfelsii 139
Podocarpus neriifolius 139, 172
Podochilinae 239
Podochilus 239
Poecilasthena nubivaga **305**, 306
Polyalthia cauliflora 172
Polyalthia rumphii 172, **174**
Polyalthia sumatrana 172
Polyosma 178
Polyosma hookeri 130
Polypedates colletti 363, 365, 367
Polypedates leucomystax 363, 366, 367
Polypedates macrotis 363, 365, 367
Polypedates otilophus 355, 357, **359**, 363, 365, 367
Polypodium 159, 164
Polystachya concreta 236
Polystachyinae 236
Polystichum 158
Pomatorhinus montanus 387, 421
Pongo pygmaeus pygmaeus 449
Porpax 238
Porrorhachis 241
Potentilla 106, 124
Potentilla borneensis 106, 107
Potentilla leuconotis 106
Potentilla mooniana 106
Potentilla parvula 106, 107
Potentilla polyphylla 106, 107
Potentilla polyphylla var. *kinabaluensis* 107

Pouteria malaccensis 171
Presbytis hosei hosei 449
Presbytis rubicunda 449
Prinia flaviventris 424
Prioninae 330
Prionochilus maculatus 429
Prionochilus xanthopygius 429
Prionodon linsang gracili 450
Pristiglottis 226
Pristiglottis hasseltii 226
Prosobranchia 282
Protomyzon 334
Protomyzon aphelocheilus **340**, 347
Protomyzon borneensis 348
Protomyzon griswoldi **340**, 347
Protomyzon whiteheadi **341**, 347
Prumnopitys amara 139
Prunus 129, 178
Prunus javanica 129
Prunus mirabilis 129
Psaphis camadeva **301**
Psarisomus dalhousiae 413
Pseudochalcothea spathifera **323**
Pseudochalcothea spatulifera **321**, 325
Pseudognaphalium luteoalbum 109
Psittacidae 404
Pteleocarpa lamponga 172, **173**
Pteridium 154
Pterocyclos amabilis 284
Pterocyclos boxalli 284
Pterocyclos sp. 284
Pteromyscus pulverulentus borneanus 450
Pteropus vampyrus 449
Pteruthius flaviscapis 388, 423
Pterygota horsfieldii 168
Ptilidae 315
Ptilinopus jambu 403
Ptilocercus lowii lowii 448
Ptychandra talboti 295
Pulmonata 285
Puntius binotatus **336**, 344
Puntius collingwoodi **337**, 345
Puntius gonionotus 335, 345
Puntius sealei **337**, 345
Pycnonotidae 417
Pycnonotus atriceps 417
Pycnonotus brunneus 417
Pycnonotus erythrophthalmos 418
Pycnonotus flavescens 11, 384, 417
Pycnonotus goiavier 384, 417
Pycnonotus melanicterus 384, 417
Pycnonotus melanoleucos 417
Pycnonotus plumosus 417
Pycnonotus simplex 417
Pycnonotus squamatus 417
Pycnonotus zeylanicus **368**, 417
Pyrenaria tawauensis 132
Pyrus granulosa 129

Q

Quadricalcarifera trioculata 312
Quercus 125, 127, 172
Quercus pseudoverticillata *127*
Quercus subsericea 122, 175

R

Racemobambos 259, 260, 265
Racemobambos gibbsiae 260, **264**, 265, 266
Racemobambos hepburnii 259, 260, **261**, 265, 266
Racemobambos hirsuta 260, 265, 266
Racemobambos rigidifolia 260, 265, 266
Rafflesia 101, 121, 122, 169, 203, 204, 205, **205**, 206, 207, 208, 461, 479, 480, 514, 515
Rafflesia arnoldii 119, 122, 203, 204, 205, 207
Rafflesia borneensis 203
Rafflesia ciliata 203
Rafflesia keithii **202**, 203, 206, 207, 208, 461
Rafflesia pricei 203, 204, **204**, 206, 207, **207**, 208, **208**, 461
Rafflesia schadenbergiana 206
Rafflesia tengku-adlinii 203, 204, 208
Rafflesia tuan-mudae 203, 206
Rafflesia witkampii 203
Rafflesiaceae 122, 206, 514
Rallidae 402

Rallina fasciata 402
Rana 361
Rana blythi 358, 363, 364, 367
Rana chalconota 355, 358, 363, 365, 367
Rana finchi 363, 365, 367
Rana hosei 355, 357
Rana hosii 363, 364, 366, 367
Rana kuhli **356**, 358, 363, 364, 366, 367
Rana luctuosa 363, 365, 366, 367
Rana nicobariensis 363, 366
Rana palavanensis 363, 365, 367
Rana palawanensis 366
Rana signata 357, 358, 363, 364, 367
Ranidae 363
Ranunculaceae **105**, 106
Ranunculus 102, 105, 106
Ranunculus lowii 41, 105, **105**, 106
Rapanea 130, 178
Rapanea affinis 130
Rapanea aralioides 130
Rapanea avenis 130
Rapanea cruciata 130
Rapanea dasyphylla 130
Rapanea forbesii 130
Rapanea hasseltii 130
Rapanea penibukana 130
Rapanea salicina 130
Rasbora argyrotaenia **336**, 344
Rasbora hubbsi **336**, 344
Rasbora myersi 344
Rasbora sumatrana 335, 336, 344
Rattus 440
Rattus argentiventer 450
Rattus baluensis 14
Rattus baluensis baluensis 451
Rattus exulans ephippium 450
Rattus rattus diardii 450
Rattus tiomanicus 450
Ratufa affinis sandakanensis 449
Redoa sp. 312
Reinwardtipicus 383
Reinwardtipicus validus 413
Renanthera 222, 240
Renanthera bella **214**, 240
Renanthera matutina 240
Rhacophoridae 363
Rhacophorus 355, 358, 361
Rhacophorus acutirostris **352**, 366
Rhacophorus angulirostris 355, 363, 365, 367
Rhacophorus appendiculatus 363, 365, 367
Rhacophorus baluensis 357, 363, 366
Rhacophorus bimaculatus 354, 364, 365, 366
Rhacophorus dulitensis 364, 365, 367
Rhacophorus everetti 355, 364, 366, 367
Rhacophorus gauni 364, 367
Rhacophorus harrissoni 364, 365, 367
Rhacophorus pardalis 355, 364, 365, 367
Rhagastis castor **302**
Rhamnaceae 143
Rhamnus borneensis 143
Rhaphidura leucopygialis 408
Rheithrosciurus macrotis 449
Rhinocochlis nasuta **278**, 280, **283**, 286
Rhinolophus borneensis borneensis 449
Rhinolophus luctus foetidus 449
Rhinolopus acuminatus sumatranus 449
Rhinomyias gularis 391, 428
Rhinomyias olivacea 427
Rhinomyias ruficauda 428
Rhinomyias umbratilis 428
Rhinoplax vigil 411
Rhipidura albicollis 390, 425
Rhipidura javanica 425
Rhipidura perlata 390, 425
Rhizanthes 121, 122, 206, 208
Rhizanthes lowi 208
Rhizanthes zippelii 122, 208
Rhododendron 124, 125 **181**, 181, 183, 194, 475, 511, 514, 515
Rhododendron section *Vireya* 181
Rhododendron abietifolium 125
Rhododendron brookeanum **184**
Rhododendron buxifolium 124, 125
Rhododendron crassifolium **182**
Rhododendron ericoides 124, 130, **185**, 192
Rhododendron fallacinum 125
Rhododendron himantodes 125

Rhododendron javanicum subsp.
    brookeanum var. *kinabaluensis*
    124, **184**
Rhododendron lowii 124
Rhododendron meijeri 178
Rhododendron orbiculatum 125
Rhododendron rugosum **186**
Rhododendron xsheilae 125
Rhododendron stapfianum 125
Rhododendron stenophyllum 125, 192
Rhododendron suaveolens **180**
Rhyticeros undulatus 382, 410
Risoba avola magna **303**
Robiquetia 241
Rohana paristatis 298
Rollulus rouloul 402
Rosaceae 106, 123, 129
Rubia 102, 112
Rubia cordifolia 112
Rubiaceae 111, **111**, **112**, 172, **174**, 517
Rubus 124, 123
Rubus alpestris 124
Rubus benguetensis 124
Rubus elongatus 124
Rubus fraxinifolius 123, 124
Rubus lineatus 123
Rubus lowii 123
Rubus moluccanus 124
Rubus rosifolius 124
Ruttellerona lithina **293**

S

Sabalimax cyanantyx 288
Sabalimax pantherina 288
Sabaria cf. *incitata* **302**
Salacca 270
Salacca dolicholepis 269, 270
Sandoricum 177
Sanicula 111, 113
Sanicula elata 109
Sanicula europa 108
Sanicula europea 109
Sapotaceae 171
Sarawakodendron 144
Sarcandra glabra 141

Sarcinodes cf. *aequilinearia* **302**
Sarrothripinae **303**
Sasia abnormis 412
Saturnidae **306**
Satyrinae 295
Saurauia sp. 499
Sauris quassa 311
Saxifragaceae 111
Scaevola 143
Scaevola chanii **143**, 144
Scaevola frutescens 143
Scaevola micrantha 143
Scaevola sericea 143
Scaevola verticillata 144, 178
Scarabaeidae 315, 319, **322**
Scarabaeinae 323
Schefflera 144, 178
Schefflera rachyphlebia 144
Schima 131, 178
Schima brevifolia 168
Schima wallichii subsp. *brevifolia* **131**
Schizaea 158
Schizaea fistulosa 158
Schizostachyum 263
Schizostachyum brachycladum 263, 267
Schizostachyum lima 263, 267
Schoenorchis 240, 241
Schoenorchis juncifolia 241
Scleroglossum 164
Scolopacidae 403
Scopula brookesae 311
Scorodocarpus borneensis 171
Scrophulariaceae 107, **107**
Scyphostegia borneensis 144
Seicercus montis 389, 425
Semecarpus cuneiformis 171
Shorea monticola 171, 175, 177
Shorea parvistipulata ssp. *nebulosa* 171
Shorea platyclados 169, 171
Shorea venulosa 171
Silphidae 318, **318**
Sisoridae 334, 335, 348
Sisyphus 324
Sitta frontalis 416, 428
Sittidae 428
Smilax sp. 504

Sonerila 115
Sonerila crassiuscula 115
Sonerila tenuifolia 115
Sonneratiaceae 141, 169
Spathoglottis 211, 235
Spathoglottis aurea 235
Spathoglottis microchilina 235
Sphingidae **300, 302**
Spilornis cheela 379, 401
Spilornis kinabaluensis 376, 401
Spiranthes 219, 227
Spiranthes lancea 225
Spiranthes sinensis 225
Spiranthinae 225
Spiranthoideae 225, 227
Spizaetus alboniger 401
Spizaetus cirrhatus 401
Stachyris erythroptera 422
Stachyris maculata 422
Stachyris nigriceps 387, 422
Stachyris nigricollis 422
Stachyris poliocephala 422
Stachyris rufifrons 422
Staurois latopalmatus 355, 363, 364, 367
Staurois natator 363, 364, 367
Staurois tuberilinguis 355, 363, 364, 367
Stemonurus umbellatus 142
Sterculia parvifolia 177
Sterculiaceae 168
Stereosandra 220, 233
Stereosandra javanica 233
Sterrhinae 311, **303**
Stransvaesia davidiana 129
Stransvaesia integrifolia 129
Streptopelia chinensis 404
Streptophlebia obliquistria 312
Strigidae 406
Sturnidae 431
Styphelia malayana 125
Styphelia suaveolens 125
Subulina octona 280, **283**, 289
Subulinidae 289
Suncus ater 451
Sundamys infraluteus infraluteus 451
Sundamys muelleri 14
Sundamys muelleri borneanus 450

Sundasciurus brookei 451
Sundasciurus hippurus pryeri 449
Sundasciurus jentinki jentinki 451
Sundasciurus lowii lowii 449
Sundasciurus tenuis 445
Sundasciurus tenuis parvus 449
Surniculus lugubris 405
Sus barbatus barbatus 450
Swertia 108
Sycopsis dunnii 176
Sylviidae 424
Symbrenthia anna 296, 298
Symbrenthia lilaea 296
Symplocaceae 144, 168, 175
Symplocos 144, 178
Symplocos buxifolia 144
Symplocos cochinchinensis 144
Symplocos colombonensis 144
Symplocos laeteviridis 144
Symplocos trichomarginalis 144
Symplocos zizyphoides 144
Synegia potenza 311
Synegia punctinervis 311
Syntominae 312
Syzygium 96, 132, 176, 178
Syzygium alcinae 172
Syzygium brachirachis 172
Syzygium cf. *bankense* 172
Syzygium fastigiatum 172
Syzygium sandakanensis 172
Syzygium cf. *tenuicaudatum* 172

T

Taenia 235
Taenia purpureifolia 235
Taeniophyllum 222, 240, 242
Tagora asclepiades **290**
Takakia 12
Tanaecia 298
Tarsius bancanus bancanus 449
Tectaria 156
Tenaris horsfieldii 294
Tephrodornis gularis 415
Tephrodornis virgatus 415
Teratophyllum 157

Ternstroemia lowii 132
Terpsiphone paradisi 428
Tetrastigma 204, 480
Tettigoniidae 317
Thalictrum 106
Theaceae 131, **131**, 167, 168, 175
Thecopus maingayi 237
Thecostele alata 237
Thecostelinae 237
Thelasiinae 239
Thelasis 221, 239
Thelasis carnosa 239
Thelypteris 156, 158, 161
Theodosia westwoodi 325
Thrixspermum 241
Thrixspermum triangulare 241
Thyatiridae **302**
Thymelaeaceae 125, 169
Thysanoplusia bipartita **303**
Tilapia mossambica 335, 349
Tiliaceae 172, 177
Timaliidae 420
Tor douronensis 334, **337**, 345
Tortriciforma tamsi 313
Trabala rotundapex 311
Trachymene 109, 178
Trachymene saniculifolia **108**, 109
Tragulus javanicus klossi 450
Tragulus napu borneanus 450
Treron curvirostra 403
Treron olax 403
Treron vernans 403
Trichastoma bicolor 421
Trichastoma malaccense 421
Trichastoma pyrrhogenys 386, 421
Trichastoma rostratum 421
Trichastoma sepiarium 421
Trichogaster trichopterus 335, **342**, 349
Trichoglottis 222, 241
Trichogomphus 323
Trichomanes 163
Trichotosia 238
Trichotosia ferox 238
Trichys fasciculata 450
Tricondyla cyanipes **316**

Tridrepana flava **300**
Trigoniastrum hypoleucum 172
Trigonobalanus 97, 127, 129, 135, 172, 176
Trigonobalanus verticillata 125, **126**
Trigonotis 108
Trigonotis borneensis 108
Trimeresaurus chaseni 353
Tristaniopsis 132, 172, 176, 178, 500
Tristaniopsis bilocularis **126**, 133, 168, 175, 176
Tristaniopsis elliptica 133
Tristaniopsis whiteana 168
Trochocarpa celebica 125
Trochomorpha rhysa 281, 289
Trochomorphidae 281, 289
Trogonidae 408
Trogonoptera brookiana 298
Tropidia 219, 225
Tropidia curculigoides 225
Tropidia pedunculata 225
Tropidia saprophytica 225
Tropidieae 225
Trycondyla 317
Trycondyla cyanea 317
Tuberolabium 241
Tupaia glis longipes 448
Tupaia gracilis gracilis 448
Tupaia minor minor 449
Tupaia montana baluensis 451
Tupaia tana paitana 449
Turdidae 418
Turdus ericetorum 371
Turdus obscurus 419
Turdus poliocephalus 12, 48, 370, 419
Tylonycteris robustula 266, **443**, 449

U

Umbelliferae 108, **108**
Upupa epops 381
Urobotrya parviflora 172
Urosphena whiteheadi 374, **374**, 424
Urticaceae 141

V

Vaccinium 183, **185**, 194, **196**, **199**, 200
Vaccinium section *Bracteata* **181**, 194
Vaccinium section *Rigiolepis* 181, 194, 200, 201
Vaccinium bancanum 197, 198, **199**
Vaccinium bancanum var. *kemulense* 197
Vaccinium bancanum var. *tenuinervium* 197
Vaccinium claoxylon **195**, 197
Vaccinium clementis **195**, 197, **197**, 198
Vaccinium cordifolium 194, **195**, **198**, 198
Vaccinium coriaceum 183, **195**, 198, 201
Vaccinium elliptifolium **195**, 198
Vaccinium laurifolium **199**, 200
Vaccinium laurifolium var. *sarawakense* 200
Vaccinium moultonii 194, **196**, 200, 201
Vaccinium pachydermum **195**, 200, 201
Vaccinium phillyreoides **199**, 200
Vaccinium retivenium **196**, 200
Vaccinium simulens **199**, 200
Vaccinium simulens var. *leptopodium* 201
Vaccinium stapfianum 183, **195**, 198, 201
Vaccinium stapfianum var. *minus* 201
Vaccinium tenerellum 201
Vaccinium uroglossum 194, **199**, 201
Vaginularia 163
Vagrans 298
Vanda 222, 241
Vanda hastifera var. *gibbsiae* 241
Vanda helvola 241
Vandeae 222, 240
Vanilla 222, 230, 231
Vanilla kinabaluensis 231
Vanilla pilifera 231
Vanilla sumatrana 231
Vanilleae 231
Vernonia arborea 109
Viola 109, 111, 113
Viola curvistylis 109
Viola serpens 109
Viola sumatrana 109
Violaceae 109

Viscum 121
Vittaria 163, 164
Viverra tangalunga **442**
Viverra tangalunga tangalunga 450
Vrydagzynea 227
Vrydagzynea argentistriata 227
Vrydagzynea bicostata 227
Vrydagzynea grandis 227

W

Weinmannia 129
Weinmannia aphanoneura 130
Weinmannia blumei 130
Weinmannia borneensis 130
Weinmannia clemensiae 130
Wikstroemia tenuiramis 169
Wintera 128
Winteraceae 127, 128, **128**, 217

X

Xanthomyrtus 178
Xanthophyllum affine 168
Xanthophyllum palembanicum 168
Xanthorhoe mesilauensis 311
Xestia 306
Xestia c-nigrum 306
Xestia isolata 312
Xixuthrus microcerus **320**, 330
Xixuthrus sp. 315
Xylosma luzonense 172
Xylosma sumatrana 499
Xylotrupes gideon 319, **321**, **322**, 325

Y

Ypthima 298
Yuhina everetti 388, 423
Yuhina zantholeuca 388, 423
Yushania niitakayamensis 259
Yushania tessellata 259, 260, **262**, 264, 265, 267

Z

Zeuxine 227
Zeuxine gracilis 227
Zeuxine papillosa 227
Zeuxine strateumatica 227
Zingiber 245, 246, 253
Zingiber cassumunar 253
Zingiber coloratum 253
Zingiber officinale 245, 253
Zingiber pseudopungens 253
Zingiber pupureum 253
Zingiber zerumbet 253
Zingiber sp. **248**
Zingiberaceae 245, 249, 257
Zizina otis 296
Zoothera citrina 373, 419
Zoothera everetti 373, 420
Zoothera interpres 420
Zosteropidae 431
Zosterops atricapillus 392, 431
Zosterops everetti 392, 431
Zygaenidae **301**, **304**, 310
Zygaenoidea 310

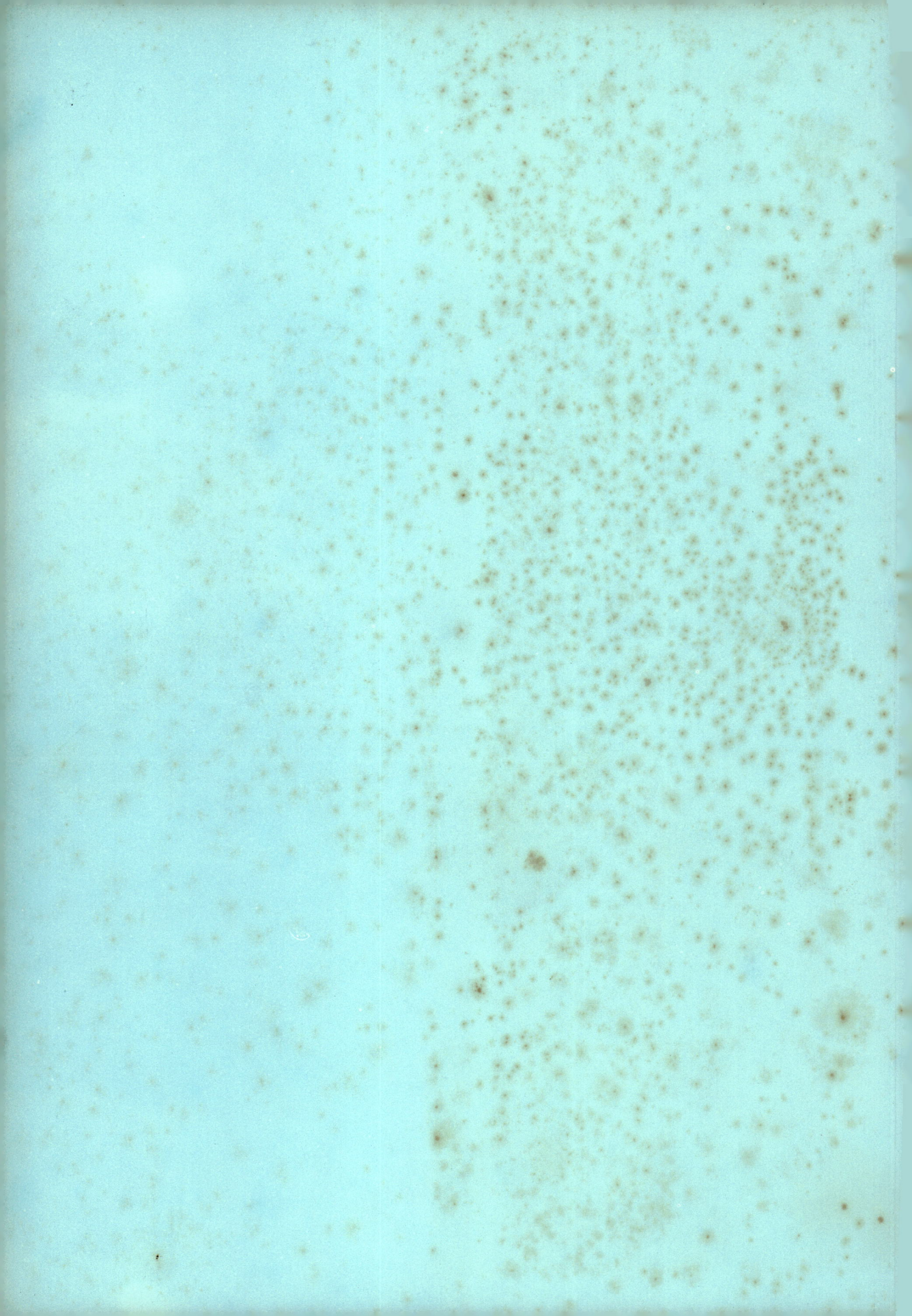